AF754659

HYBRID JUSTICE

More than thirty years after the fall of the Pol Pot regime, a UN-backed tribunal, fusing Cambodian and international law, procedure, and personnel, was established to try key Khmer Rouge officials for atrocities committed in the late 1970s. In this definitive scholarly treatment of the "Extraordinary Chambers in the Courts of Cambodia" (ECCC) from legal and political perspectives, John D. Ciorciari and Anne Heindel examine the ECCC's institutional features, compare it to other hybrid and international criminal courts, evaluate its operations, and draw lessons for the future.

Ciorciari and Heindel begin by discussing the political factors and historical contingencies that led the United Nations and Cambodian Government to create a hybrid tribunal with a number of unique features. Next, they examine the tribunal's operations to date, focusing on how its institutional form has affected its various intended functions. They argue that many aspects of the ECCC's judicial proceedings have been broadly consistent with international standards and that the Court's in-country location has provided important benefits in terms of public outreach and victim participation. Nevertheless, the authors demonstrate that the ECCC's complex, divided institutional structure and wrangling between national and international actors have slowed the proceedings, contributed to administrative irregularities, led to due process concerns, and jeopardized the Court's public legitimacy and ability to leave a legacy of credible justice. Ciorciari and Heindel argue that the ECCC's experiences reveal many of the challenges of managing a mass crimes process, especially in the context of a hybrid court. They conclude with recommendations on measures that can be taken to meet some of those challenges going forward.

John D. Ciorciari is an assistant professor at the Gerald R. Ford School of Public Policy at the University of Michigan.

Anne Heindel is legal advisor to the Documentation Center of Cambodia.

Law, Meaning, and Violence

The scope of Law, Meaning, and Violence is defined by the wide-ranging scholarly debates signaled by each of the words in the title. Those debates have taken place among and between lawyers, anthropologists, political theorists, sociologists, and historians, as well as literary and cultural critics. This series is intended to recognize the importance of such ongoing conversations about law, meaning, and violence as well as to encourage and further them.

Series Editors: Martha Minow, Harvard Law School
Austin Sarat, Amherst College

RECENT TITLES IN THE SERIES

Hybrid Justice: The Extraordinary Chambers in the Courts of Cambodia, by John D. Ciorciari and Anne Heindel

The Justice of Mercy, by Linda Ross Meyer

Dying Inside: The HIV/AIDS Ward at Limestone Prison, by Benjamin Fleury-Steiner with Carla Crowder

Sacred Violence: Torture, Terror, and Sovereignty, by Paul W. Kahn

Punishment and Political Order, by Keally McBride

Lives of Lawyers Revisited: Transformation and Resilience in the Organizations of Practice, by Michael J. Kelly

Among the Lowest of the Dead: The Culture of Capital Punishment, by David Von Drehle

Punishing Schools: Fear and Citizenship in American Public Education, by William Lyons and Julie Drew

Suing the Gun Industry: A Battle at the Crossroads of Gun Control and Mass Torts, edited by Timothy D. Lytton

Transformative Justice: Israeli Identity on Trial, by Leora Bilsky

Jurors' Stories of Death: How America's Death Penalty Invests in Inequality, by Benjamin Fleury-Steiner

The Jurisprudence of Emergency: Colonialism and the Rule of Law, by Nasser Hussain

Communities and Law: Politics and Cultures of Legal Identities, by Gad Barzilai

From Noose to Needle: Capital Punishment and the Late Liberal State, by Timothy V. Kaufman-Osborn

The Limits to Union: Same-Sex Marriage and the Politics of Civil Rights, by Jonathan Goldberg-Hiller

Pain, Death, and the Law, edited by Austin Sarat

Bad Boys: Public Schools in the Making of Black Masculinity, by Ann Arnett Ferguson

Whispered Consolations: Law and Narrative in African American Life, by Jon-Christian Suggs

Laws of the Postcolonial, edited by Eve Darian-Smith and Peter Fitzpatrick

Hybrid Justice

THE EXTRAORDINARY CHAMBERS IN THE COURTS OF CAMBODIA

John D. Ciorciari
and Anne Heindel

The University of Michigan Press
Ann Arbor

Copyright © by the University of Michigan 2014
All rights reserved

This book may not be reproduced, in whole or in part, including illustrations, in any form (beyond that copying permitted by Sections 107 and 108 of the U.S. Copyright Law and except by reviewers for the public press), without written permission from the publisher.

Published in the United States of America by
The University of Michigan Press
Manufactured in the United States of America
♾ Printed on acid-free paper

2017 2016 2015 2014 4 3 2 1

A CIP catalog record for this book is available from the British Library.

Library of Congress Cataloging-in-Publication Data

Ciorciari, John D. (John David), author.
Hybrid justice : the extraordinary chambers in the courts of Cambodia / John D. Ciorciari and Anne Heindel.
pages cm. — (Law, meaning, and violence)
Includes bibliographical references and index
ISBN 978-0-472-11930-1 (cloth : alk. paper) — ISBN 978-0-472-12021-5 (e-book)
1. Courts—Cambodia. 2. Courts—Cambodia—Cases. 3. Justice, Administration of—Cambodia. I. Heindel, Anne, author. II. Title.
KNM1580.C56 2014
347.861'01—dc23

2013040221

CONTENTS

Acronyms vii

Acknowledgments ix

Introduction 1

CHAPTER 1 Forging a Hybrid Court: "A Mountain Never Has Two Tigers" 14

CHAPTER 2 Pairing the Court's National and International Features 41

CHAPTER 3 Serving Two Masters: Dual Administration, Oversight, and Funding 70

CHAPTER 4 Case 001—Convicting an Infamous Khmer Rouge Torture Chief: "You Cannot Cover an Elephant with a Rice Basket" 104

CHAPTER 5 Case 002—The Centerpiece Case against Senior Leaders: "Cutting the Head to Fit the Hat" 134

CHAPTER 6 Cases 003 & 004—The Politics of Personal Jurisdiction: "No Gain in Keeping, No Loss in Weeding Out" 167

CHAPTER 7 A Historic First: Recognizing Victims as Case Parties 202

CHAPTER 8 Connecting to Cambodians:
Outreach and Legacy 231

Conclusion 261

Notes 279

Selected References 403

Index 417

Illustrations following page 166

ACRONYMS

ASEAN	Association of Southeast Asian Nations
BAKC	Bar Association of the Kingdom of Cambodia
CGDK	Coalition Government of Democratic Kampuchea (1980s)
CIJ	Co-Investigating Judges (ECCC)
CPC	Criminal Procedure Code (Cambodia)
CPK	Communist Party of Kampuchea
CPP	Cambodian People's Party
CSD	Center for Social Development
DC-Cam	Documentation Center of Cambodia
DESA	United Nations Department of Economic and Social Affairs
DK	Democratic Kampuchea
DSS	Defence Support Section (ECCC)
ECCC	Extraordinary Chambers in the Courts of Cambodia
ICC	International Criminal Court
ICCPR	International Covenant on Civil and Political Rights
ICTR	International Criminal Tribunal for Rwanda
ICTY	International Criminal Tribunal for the former Yugoslavia
JAC	Judicial Administration Committee (ECCC)
OA	Office of Administration (ECCC)
OCIJ	Office of the Co-Investigating Judges (ECCC)
OCP	Office of the Co-Prosecutors (ECCC)
OLA	Office of Legal Affairs (United Nations)
OSJI	Open Society Justice Initiative
PAS	Public Affairs Section (ECCC)
PRK	People's Republic of Kampuchea (Cambodia, 1979–89)
PTC	Pre-Trial Chamber (ECCC)

RGC	Royal Government of Cambodia
SCC	Supreme Court Chamber (ECCC)
SCM	Supreme Council of Magistracy (Cambodia)
SCSL	Special Court for Sierra Leone
SCU	Serious Crimes Unit (East Timor)
SPSC	Special Panels for Serious Crimes (East Timor)
STL	Special Tribunal for Lebanon
TPO	Transcultural Psychosocial Organization
UNAKRT	UN Assistance to the Khmer Rouge Trials
UNDP	UN Development Program
UNTAC	UN Transitional Authority in Cambodia (1991–93)
VU	Victims Unit (ECCC)
VSS	Victims Support Section (ECCC)
WCC	War Crimes Chamber (Bosnia and Herzegovina)

ACKNOWLEDGMENTS

Justice is notoriously elusive in the aftermath of mass atrocities. In Cambodia, more than three decades after the demise of the Pol Pot regime, many survivors still seek some form of legal accountability. Almost all seek a better understanding of the tragedy that befell them and the healing that may come from a process that acknowledges, dignifies, and in some measure responds to their suffering. Many international actors, too, have engaged in the quest for justice, cognizant of the lingering stain of Khmer Rouge impunity on efforts to strengthen global accountability norms and promote the rule of law. This book emerges from our own efforts to advance law and meaning in the shadow of Khmer Rouge violence.

We focus on the most prominent official undertaking to address the Khmer Rouge legacy—the Extraordinary Chambers in the Courts of Cambodia (ECCC)—a hybrid judicial institution managed by the Cambodian Government and United Nations and tasked with putting former Khmer Rouge officials on trial. We endeavor to shed light on specific institutional features and practices that boost or inhibit a tribunal's capacity to meet its many, and sometimes conflicting, mandates. As in other societies coping with violent pasts, trials are not the only ways to meet survivors' needs or strengthen the law, but the ECCC is an integral part of Cambodia's engagement with its troubled past. It also holds important lessons for other societies that prosecute mass crimes as part of broader transitional justice processes.

Conducting a detailed analysis of the ECCC would not have been possible without many helping hands. A number of current and former officials from the ECCC, United Nations, Cambodian Government, and other key states and non-governmental groups took time out of busy schedules to help us navigate this complex hybrid institution and the politics surrounding it. These include Anees Ahmed, Kris Baleva, Mychelle Balthazard, Andrew Cayley, Hans Corell,

Rowan Downing, Clair Duffy, Diana Ellis, Craig Etcheson, Elisabeth Simonneau Fort, Peter Foster, Anta Guissé, Steve Heder, Huy Vannak, Andrew Iannuzzi, Larry Johnson, Michael G. Karnavas, Karim Khan, Marcel Lemonde, Agnieszka Klonowiecka-Milart, Zach Lampell, Panhavuth Long, Jasper Pauw, Michiel Pestman, Caitlin Rieger, Richard Rogers, Nushin Sarkarati, David Scheffer, Rupert Skilbeck, William Smith, Christoph Sperfeldt, Jeanne Sulzer, David Tolbert, Clint Williamson, and You Bunleng. Sometimes their assistance took the form of an interview, and on other occasions they helped us by responding to specific questions or providing us with useful background information. We also thank a number of current and former Cambodian officials at the ECCC who completed confidential questionnaires or otherwise helped us to understand the workings of the Court.

This research project has grown out of our work with the Documentation Center of Cambodia (DC-Cam), an independent organization dedicated to memory and justice in Cambodia. We have both had the privilege of serving as legal advisors to DC-Cam for a number of years, and our dedicated colleagues at the Center have been sources of both inspiration and expertise. Executive Director Youk Chhang, Chy Terith, Dy Khamboly, Kok-Thay Eng, Samphors Huy, Kim Sovanndany, Sokvisal Kimsroy, Ly Sok-kheang, Ros Sampeou, Savina Sirik, Dara P. Vanthan, and many others have helped advance our research by sharing their knowledge of the ECCC and Cambodia's broader efforts to account for the past. Much of our knowledge also comes from years working with our fellow international advisors to DC-Cam—including Randle DeFalco, Alex Hinton, Jaya Ramji-Nogales, Ron Slye, Sarah Thomas, and Beth Van Schaack.

We are indebted to a number of talented researchers who helped inform our analysis on specific aspects of international criminal law and the workings of hybrid and international criminal tribunals. Many have been legal associates at DC-Cam, including Kimberly Ang, Tessa Bialek, Adam Coady, Chad Spencer Cryder, Andy Diamond, Joanna Geneve, Charles Jackson, Lise Reuss Muff, Anna Mumford, Elizabeth Nielsen, Richard Kilpatrick, Tatiana Sainati, Della Sentilles, Valerie Stranieri, and Charline Yim. Ben Goldman also assisted us, and a pair of University of Michigan students—David Sukenik and George Tam—helped us examine features of other hybrid courts as part of the university's Undergraduate Research Opportunity Program.

We are grateful to Martha Minow and Austin Sarat, the editors of the series "Law, Meaning, and Violence" in which this book appears, and our anonymous reviewers for their support of the project and the useful feedback they provided. We also thank Melody Herr, Susan Cronin, Kevin Rennells, and others at the University of Michigan Press for their careful and timely work in bringing this book to fruition.

Last but certainly not least, we thank our spouses, who have provided love and encouragement even during the many odd hours when we huddled over our respective copies of an evolving manuscript. We dedicate this book to them.

INTRODUCTION

Every year, the monsoon rains come to Cambodia. The Mekong floods, and the country's lowland plains become glassy lakes punctuated by palm trees and stilted wooden homes. The tranquil water washes the earth and furnishes new life. When the floods recede, however, the land reveals that it still bears the scars of the country's brutal past. Thousands of large pits are scattered across the landscape—reminders of bombardment during years of war and innumerable mass graves dug during the Pol Pot years. Scores of *stupas* and memorials serve as bandages that Cambodians have used to dress their wounds. Beside them, survivors can often be seen praying and leaving offerings for the departed. Like others who have suffered mass human rights abuses, Cambodians remain engaged in a complex process to deal with past atrocities and make sense of their country's troubled modern history.

No part of Cambodia's past involved greater suffering than the Pol Pot era, when Cambodia descended from being a "sideshow" to the Vietnam War to the neglected site of some of history's most appalling atrocities. That period began in April 1975, when communist Khmer Rouge guerrillas emerged victorious in a five-year civil war against the U.S.-backed military regime of General Lon Nol. On April 17, Khmer Rouge fighters streamed into Phnom Penh. Most were young peasants, carrying AK-47s on their shoulders and dressed in simple black cotton uniforms, traditional checkered headscarves known as *krama*, and black rubber sandals made from old tires. A beleaguered city, swollen with refugees, greeted their arrival with a sigh of relief and hope that their triumph would bring peace.[1] Those hopes faded quickly. Within hours, the young guerrillas began rounding up and executing Lon Nol officials and other suspected enemies of the revolution. They also began evacuating the city, forcing people of all ages onto dusty roads with little knowledge of their destinations.[2]

Khmer Rouge leaders thus began a radical and ruthless program for social transformation. Their ideological impetus, which one scholar has described as "hyperMaoism,"[3] was to create a self-sufficient agrarian state immune to unwanted foreign influence. The Khmers Rouges emptied the cities so that "new people"—such as urban merchants and bourgeois intellectuals—would be dispersed among the "base people" already working in rural cooperatives.[4] Monks and other religious leaders were defrocked, currency was abolished, and families were forcibly separated to weaken traditional social bonds and replace them with loyalty to *Angkar,* the faceless revolutionary "Organization" only later revealed to comprise the top leadership of the Communist Party of Kampuchea (CPK).

The Standing Committee of the CPK's Central Committee, the "highest leading body" of the renamed state of Democratic Kampuchea,[5] built a nationwide bureaucratic and security apparatus on foundations of party allegiance and fear. One of its chief aims was to "sweep clean" the state by "smashing" and "screening out" the "enemies" of the revolution and other "no-good elements."[6] *Angkar* was said to have "eyes like a pineapple" on constant vigil, as Khmer Rouge cadres—often victims themselves, with guns rather than pencils thrust into their hands as children—detained, tortured, and killed suspected "enemies," sometimes in public view to set an example and often for offenses as minor as stealing small portions of food to feed their families.[7] Schools and other buildings were converted into makeshift prisons, where many suspects were subjected to primitive torture devices before being dispatched to their deaths, often by bludgeoning to save precious bullets.[8]

When radical Khmer Rouge economic and social policies failed to deliver a "Super Great Leap Forward,"[9] countless others died of hunger or disease. Between April 1975 and January 1979, an estimated 1.5 to 2 million people—roughly a quarter of the country's population—perished under CPK rule.[10] For survivors, Democratic Kampuchea lingers in their memories as "hell on earth," a "prison without walls"[11] in which people of all ages toiled endlessly in poorly managed factories or fields, parroted lifeless revolutionary slogans, and hoped that they and their families would not be the next to be summoned before juvenile cadres to face charges that so often swiftly turned to death. Personal accounts provide windows into survivors' immense individual suffering as they mourn the loss of loved ones, search for understanding, and grasp for justice and a sense of healing.[12]

Dealing with atrocities like those committed in Democratic Kampuchea raises difficult questions. What exactly happened? Who is most to blame? How can victims achieve some form of redress? How can a society heal social divisions, build a rule of law, and lessen the likelihood of future abuses? All of these questions have been asked in Cambodia, and none has been easy to answer. The opacity of the Pol Pot regime has left survivors scouring for information about why the Khmers Rouges killed and what became of many victims whose families still do not know their fate. Apportioning blame has been difficult in a state where Khmer Rouge veterans—and the foreign powers that contributed to the rise and rule of the CPK—remain influential. The sheer scale of the violence has been a daunting impediment to redressing victims for their losses. Promoting social reconciliation and the rule of law have been generational challenges.

Societies emerging from mass terror have implemented a variety of transitional justice mechanisms to pursue truth, accountability, reconciliation, and other aims. These include truth commissions, lustration schemes, amnesty programs, and criminal trials. None is a silver bullet. The legal and institutional arrangements conducive to promoting some desired ends do not always advance other objectives, and choices need to be made. Addressing mass atrocities thus presents both moral imperatives and confounding policy challenges. To make good on the former requires wrestling with the difficulties of the latter.

Cambodia's path to historical truth, justice, and reconciliation has been marred by inadequate and inconsistent official efforts to deal with the Khmer Rouge legacy. A spate of hasty domestic criminal trials followed the overthrow of the Pol Pot regime by Vietnam-backed forces but had little effect on Khmer Rouge leaders, who retreated to the jungle and led a protracted insurgency with foreign support. Selected amnesty programs coaxed some Khmers Rouges away from the insurgency but were not accompanied by an official truth commission process. While ordinary Cambodians and non-governmental groups worked to promote grassroots-level reconciliation, that process was frustrated by the lingering impunity of top Khmer Rouge leaders and lack of a credible official accounting of the atrocities of the Pol Pot era.[13]

Roughly two decades after the demise of Democratic Kampuchea, the Cambodian Government, United Nations, and key UN member states began to focus more seriously on the issue of Khmer Rouge accountability. Although they could have pursued a number of institutional mechanisms, they chose to make a criminal tribunal the centerpiece of transitional justice efforts in the country. To that end, they created a novel judicial body, the Extraordinary Chambers in the

Courts of Cambodia (ECCC), which opened its doors on the western outskirts of Phnom Penh in 2006. The ECCC is a "hybrid" tribunal that fuses local and international laws, procedures, and personnel.

Like other mass crimes courts, the ECCC was created primarily to deliver justice and secondarily to advance other aspects of social healing and development. Its principal mandate is to try "senior leaders" of the Pol Pot regime and others deemed "most responsible" for crimes committed under CPK rule.[14] More than three decades after the Khmer Rouge tragedy, only a few senior Khmer Rouge figures survive. The ECCC will likely be the last officially sanctioned opportunity to seek a measure of justice and pronouncement of legal truth on the inner workings of the Pol Pot regime. It also provides an opportunity to empower survivors through speech acts, facilitate discussion of a subject that has often been taboo in Cambodian society, and promote more far-reaching objectives such as reconciliation and the rule of law.

Satisfying such lofty goals is difficult for any court of law. Criminal trials are not designed to carry out all—or even most—of the functions needed to address past atrocities. Yet tribunals are often part of the societal response, and when they function well, they can play crucial roles within broader transitional justice processes. When they fail, they can dash hopes and consume resources that would better have been expended on other measures. This book examines how the ECCC's unique structural features and the agency of key official actors have affected its capacity to deliver credible jurisprudence, administer complex proceedings, provide meaningful engagement for survivors, and leave a positive societal legacy.

We argue that the ECCC's experience shows some advantages of incorporating local legal principles and personnel but reveals even more strikingly the risks of operating a mixed court. Our title—*Hybrid Justice*—evokes the awkwardness of an accountability process based on fusing national and international laws, procedures, personnel, and political interests. The ECCC shows how susceptible mass crimes courts are to legal confusion, procedural delay, and financial and administrative impasses when authority and responsibility are divided. It also shows the danger of creating a court with inadequate institutional safeguards against administrative malfeasance and political interference, especially when the host government has a weak track record of judicial integrity and independence. Agency clearly matters, but a court's structural design can make its functional success much more or less likely.

The goals of our analysis are twofold. First, we aim to contribute to a better understanding of the transitional justice process in Cambodia by providing a detailed account of why the ECCC was endowed with unique institutional features and how the Court has advanced, or sometimes failed to advance, its stated objectives. Second, by examining the Cambodian case in comparative perspective, we seek to shed light on the types of institutional features and personnel choices that help tribunals meet their mandates or impair their functional effectiveness—lessons that can help guide the reform of existing courts and design of new ones.

A UNIQUE HYBRID COURT

The ECCC and other hybrid courts exist along a wider spectrum of criminal tribunals ranging from ordinary domestic courts to the three purely international bodies now in operation—the *ad hoc* International Criminal Tribunals for the former Yugoslavia and Rwanda (ICTY and ICTR) and the International Criminal Court (ICC). Hybrid courts emerged in the late 1990s, largely in response to perceived problems with fully international tribunals. In 1993 and 1994, the UN Security Council established the ICTY in The Hague and the ICTR in Arusha, Tanzania. Their creation was a watershed for international criminal accountability, but it quickly became apparent that both tribunals would consume much more time and money than originally foreseen, and "tribunal fatigue" spread among key UN donor states.[15]

Sovereignty was another major concern. To many critics—including the governments of powerful developing countries such as China and Brazil—the ICTY and ICTR were projections of Western power and set dangerous precedents for justice meted out by the strong against the weak.[16] The out-of-country locations of the *ad hoc* courts also made investigations more cumbersome, arguably weakened deterrence, and reduced the tribunals' contact with the government and survivor population, which limited opportunities for capacity-building and outreach and education programs.[17] To critics, distant trials run by foreign powers lacked not only local ownership but also political legitimacy.[18]

Domestic proceedings were one possible alternative, but some national court systems lacked the capacity or credibility to manage complex criminal trials. For example, a generation of conflict and foreign rule left East Timor with fewer than 10 trained lawyers by the end of Indonesian occupation in 1999.[19] In Cambodia, UN-appointed experts and officials deemed national courts unappealing, both due to capacity constraints and because they were riddled with corruption and political interference.[20]

In theory, hybrid courts would deliver justice meeting international standards but at a lower cost, easing sovereignty concerns by operating with host government consent and enjoying the functional advantages of proximity to the *locus delicti* and aggrieved population.[21] The greater ease of transporting investigators, evidence, and witnesses within the host country would save money, as would the lower cost of local operations and personnel.[22] Local judges and lawyers would contribute linguistic skills and country knowledge to complement the legal expertise of their international counterparts.[23] The late Antonio Cassese, who served first as ICTY president and later as president of the hybrid Special Tribunal for Lebanon, emphasized hybrid courts' potential "spill-over effect" of training local legal personnel and ability to promote a "cathartic process" by connecting with and educating the nearby survivor population.[24]

Hybrid courts also carry risks, however. Too much international control exposes them to charges of imperialism, but too little subjects them to the vicissitudes of local judicial systems and the risk that local actors would use the court to convict their enemies and defend their domestic allies.[25] As scholar Suzannah Linton argues, the hybrid model was "a radical move away from the earlier prevailing wisdom that the non-inclusion of nationals of the country most affected would preserve impartiality, objectivity and neutrality."[26] The danger of political interference from local executive authorities is clear.[27] Where national authorities engage in obstructive or dilatory tactics, hybrid tribunals generally lack the legal authority to compel state cooperation, precisely because they are created consensually rather than by binding resolutions of the UN Security Council—as in the case of the ICTY and ICTR.[28] The mixed composition of courts also increases their complexity and poses administrative and operational challenges quite apart from political haggling.[29]

Funding and political commitment are further potential challenges. Unlike the ICTY and ICTR, which receive funds from the general UN budget, hybrid courts generally have relied on voluntary funding, leaving them vulnerable to financial gaps. To a significant degree, they took shape precisely because key donor states were unwilling to invest the financial and political capital needed to set up fully international courts.[30] These risks explain why many human rights advocates have been skeptical of mixed courts, and even some international lawyers and officials instrumental in designing hybrid courts have not presented them as models that should be followed in the future.[31]

Cambodia was not the first site for a hybrid court. From 1996 to 2003, pursuant to the Dayton Peace Agreement, a hybrid Human Rights Chamber operated in Bosnia and Herzegovina, staffed with judges from the national system and elsewhere in Europe.[32] In East Timor, UN transitional administrators created hybrid "Special Panels for Serious Crimes" in the Dili District Court to deal with violence by Indonesian Special Forces and allied militias after the Timorese referendum for independence in 1999.[33] They also created a Special Crimes Unit funded and staffed by the United Nations to investigate offenses.[34] In Kosovo, a proposal to establish a hybrid war crimes court was shelved due to cost considerations,[35] but UN administrators did establish hybrid panels to hear cases involving interethnic strife and possible judicial bias.[36]

In both East Timor and Kosovo, hybrid courts were part of the domestic judicial system but had international majorities on the bench—a feature UN officials adopted in Kosovo after early judgments by majority-domestic courts suggested that only international majorities would ensure impartiality.[37] In 2002, the United Nations and Sierra Leonean government signed an agreement establishing the Special Court for Sierra Leone—which is based in Freetown and likewise featured a majority of foreign judges and key personnel—to hear criminal cases related to that country's civil war.[38] The ECCC was established the following year by a 2003 agreement between the United Nations and Cambodia and subsequent 2004 domestic implementing law.

The ECCC identifies itself as part of the family of hybrid courts and asserts that hybridity has several advantages:

> The hybrid tribunal model is seen as a way to provide full national involvement in the trials while at the same time ensuring that international standards are met. Unlike tribunals for Rwanda or the former Yugoslavia, these trials are not removed from the place where the crimes occurred. They are held in Cambodia, conducted mainly in Khmer, open to participation by Cambodian people and reported via local television, radio and newspapers.[39]

It is important not to treat all hybrid courts as products of the same template, however. Hybrid courts differ in crucial ways, and the ECCC is *sui generis* in many respects. It has a strong domestic legal basis and civil law character and is the first mixed court with a majority of domestic judges. It is the only mass crimes court with national and international co-prosecutors and co-investigating judges, who share responsibility for the investigation. Judicial, defense, and administrative roles are also divided between Cambodian and UN appointees, splitting the Court into two distinct "sides." It is also the first to include victims in the proceedings as civil parties. These unique aspects of the ECCC proceedings have had profound effects on its function.

IMPORTANCE OF THE CAMBODIAN CASE

Understanding the ECCC's institutional features and functions is important both for Cambodia scholars and for analysts of international criminal law and transitional justice. The Court represents the apex of Cambodia's tormented accountability process. Human rights activist Kek Galabru spoke for many when she said that the start of Khmer Rouge trials finally gave "hope for justice to victims, who have been waiting thirty years"[40] to take a stand against Khmer Rouge impunity. The tribunal also has importance well beyond Cambodia's borders. It represents what human rights lawyer James Goldston has called "an extraordinary experiment in transitional justice"[41]—the first hybrid tribunal in which the United Nations effectively took a back seat to a national judicial system. Assessing the results of this and other novel, experimental aspects of the Court is imperative as lawyers and diplomats seek to reform the ICC, advise national governments on best practices for mass crimes trials, or create or modify hybrid tribunals.

A few hybrid courts have taken shape since the ECCC was established. In 2005, the government of Bosnia and Herzegovina agreed with the international Office of the High Representative to create a mixed War Crimes Chamber as part of the national court system with authority to try cases for lower- to mid-level perpetrators referred to it by the ICTY.[42] In 2009, the United Nations and Lebanese government established a majority-international Special Tribunal for Lebanon to address the murder of Prime Minister Rafiq Hariri in 2005 and related crimes. In 2012, Senegal and the African Union agreed to create "Extraordinary African Chambers"[43] to try former Chadian dictator Hissène Habré. Like the ECCC, Senegal's extraordinary chambers exist "within the existing Senegalese court system"[44] and feature a majority of domestic judges. Variants on the Cambodian model of a domestically led hybrid court may appeal to governments eager to retain political control while reaping some of the financial, technical, and reputational benefits of international involvement. This book evaluates the extent to which that model has worked in Cambodia.

The ECCC has had some important successes. It conducted its first trial largely in line with international standards and issued the first credible conviction of a Khmer Rouge official for crimes of the Pol Pot era against Kaing Guek Eav *alias* "Duch," former head of the infamous CPK prison at Tuol Sleng, where thousands of prisoners were tortured and sent to their untimely deaths. The Court has featured a zealous prosecution and defense, extensive investigations of its first two cases, and numerous credible judicial rulings. It has also developed an innovative victim participation program, conducted local outreach programs, and maintained high public favorability ratings. Cambodia's Deputy Prime Minister Sok An has trumpeted the ECCC experiment as a success, saying in a 2010 speech before UN Secretary-General Ban Ki-moon that "[t]he ECCC is now internationally recognized as a good model not only for Cambodia, but also for internationally assisted courts that may be established in the future."[45]

Many observers disagree, as the Court's significant failings have been apparent. It has become mired in controversies over corruption allegations, administrative mismanagement, and a nearly debilitating feud between key Cambodian and international personnel on the scope of prosecution. As scholar Duncan McCargo argues, these feuds have been "inextricably bound up in politics," undermining the credibility and integrity of the process.[46] The ECCC has also proven slower and more costly than anticipated, leading to frequent funding shortfalls and a decision to truncate its most important case against a group of surviving senior Khmer Rouge leaders.

Brad Adams of Human Rights Watch, a strident critic of the tribunal, reports widespread agreement in UN circles that the ECCC is "a mistake that should never be repeated elsewhere."[47] Scholar Peter Maguire argues that the United Nations entered a "Faustian" arrangement and should "relegate the 'mixed tribunal' model to the dust bin of history."[48] Former UN Legal Counsel Hans Corell, who resisted Cambodian preponderance during the tribunal negotiations, said in 2012:

> I am sure that, today, even people without courtroom experience realize that the solution chosen for the ECCC should not be used as a model for any future effort of this nature. The UN hallmark should not be given to institutions over which the Organization does not have full administrative control.[49]

Many analysts have argued that operating as the junior partner to the Cambodian Government exposes the United Nations to serious reputational risk.[50] Former ECCC official Craig Etcheson asserts that difficulties in the Khmer Rouge trials have made the Cambodian model "radioactive" to most of the relevant officials in the UN Secretariat.[51] To its many detractors, the ECCC is a black sheep within the family of UN-backed tribunals. We evaluate the extent to which that reputation is warranted.

AN OUTLINE OF OUR ARGUMENT

We argue that the ECCC is not a model to be followed and that the Court's design flaws have added considerably to the challenge of delivering a credible and efficient accountability process, often undermining the best efforts of many of its staff. The Court's key structural flaws lie more in its uniqueness than in its status as a hybrid institution. Given the state of Cambodia's judiciary, the ECCC's greatest built-in weakness is that the United Nations has too much involvement to escape responsibility for the Court but too little authority to run it. That has contributed to halfhearted UN ownership and relatively weak international responses to serious problems that have originated on the Cambodian side. Weak oversight mechanisms also leave the UN side subject to inadequate scrutiny, while bifurcation between its national and international "sides" prevents decisive leadership, contributes to inefficiency, and facilitates politicization of contentious issues. An awkward mix of civil and common law features only add to the confusion and challenge of running a fair and efficient process.

As we discuss in chapter 1, these flaws were readily apparent during the lengthy negotiations between UN and Cambodian officials. Most would have been difficult to avoid, however, due to Cambodia's acute sovereignty concerns and the absence of international will or capacity to impose a different structure. The same political tensions and distrust that led to the ECCC's divided structure have continued to stress the institution at its weak points throughout the process. The ECCC's challenges raise the obvious question of whether and when the United Nations should ever participate in hybrid arrangements with difficult domestic partners.

To help answer that question, we conduct a detailed analysis to identify which of the ECCC's functional shortcomings result from idiosyncratic institutional features, which reflect more general problems with hybrid or international courts, and which have little to do with institutional structure at all. Of course, a tribunal's performance depends on which of many possible criteria are invoked to judge it. It is too early to discern the ECCC's long-term effects on Cambodian reconciliation and the rule of law—and even what its ultimate judicial findings will be—but the first seven years of the tribunal's operations enable us to evaluate several core functions that are part of the Court's expressed mandate. In chapter 2, we discuss efforts to pair the two sides of the ECCC—managing complex investigations efficiently, filling lacunae in the 2003 UN-Cambodian agreement and 2004 domestic implementing law, and applying a mix of vastly different national and international laws and procedures.

Chapter 3 examines how the Court's divided administration, funding, and oversight have affected its management of people and money. Critics of the ECCC's structure feared that heavy Cambodian participation would be a recipe for bureaucratic ineptness and corruption. Both issues have surfaced, nearly knocking the Court off the rails before its first trial began, exposing serious flaws in its split structure and frail oversight mechanisms, and contributing to inefficiency and frequent funding shortfalls.

The ECCC's legal proceedings also bear the imprint of the Court's problematic structure. Chapter 4 discusses "Case 001," the trial of Duch. Case 001 was a relative success and ended in a conviction but was the ECCC's easiest functional test, as it was based on abundant evidence and was relatively uncontroversial from a political standpoint. Chapter 5 turns to a tougher test—the Court's more complex second trial involving four former Khmer Rouge leaders—Deputy Secretary of the Communist Party of Kampuchea Nuon Chea, Deputy Prime Minister Ieng Sary, Social Affairs Minister Ieng Thirith, and President of the State Presidium Khieu Samphan. The greater scope of alleged offenses and higher political stakes of "Case 002" strained the Court's judicial and administrative capacity, delayed the proceedings, and resulted in an unprecedented split indictment. Ieng Thirith was severed from the case due to dementia, and Ieng Sary passed away in early 2013, leaving only two frail and elderly defendants on trial. Even if Nuon Chea and Khieu Samphan are convicted of some offenses, most of the alleged crimes of surviving Khmer Rouge leaders will go unpunished, and the trial will deliver only a modest revelation of official truth.

An even more difficult institutional test for the ECCC has been to deal with further potential prosecutions—the subject of chapter 6. Since 2008, the Cambodian Government and Cambodian judges and staff have stonewalled attempts by the international co-prosecutor to try an additional five to six suspects. The highly politicized dispute has rocked the institution to its core, drained the tribunal of donor enthusiasm and public legitimacy, and shown the Achilles' heel of the ECCC's institutional structure—its acute vulnerability to political interference and paralysis.

The remaining chapters concentrate on some purported strengths of in-country hybrid courts: victim participation, outreach, and legacy. Chapter 7 examines the ECCC's ambitious victim participation scheme allowing certain victims to join the trials as civil parties. Like the inclusion of investigating judges, the ECCC's pathbreaking civil party scheme is drawn from the French civil law tradition, which has played a more prominent part in the Khmer Rouge trials than any other internationalized mass crimes proceedings.[52] The civil party scheme had some success in the *Duch* trial but proved difficult to implement in Case 002 given the vast number of Cambodian victims of the various crimes alleged.

Chapter 8 turns to outreach, which should be a relative strong suit of the ECCC due to the Court's in-country location and access to relatively robust local media and civil society organizations. It also discusses legacy initiatives, including capacity-building and setting a positive example. Like victim participation, legacy efforts have faced challenges common across mass crimes courts—relative neglect, weak funding, and a lack of clear ownership.

Throughout the book, we show how the ECCC's unique structural features have affected its function, sometimes helping it achieve successes but more often rendering it vulnerable to inefficiency and political interference. We also show that the mere novelty of the Court's design has compromised its efficiency and fairness, as appointees from various national backgrounds have spent much of their time and energy learning new principles of law, crafting new procedures, and resolving myriad judicial and administrative questions for which no clear precedent existed. The Cambodian experience thus suggests that even a new court without some of the ECCC's particular design flaws would have had difficulty delivering efficient due process, outreach, and capacity-building on a limited budget and in a limited period of time.

Any tribunal that confronts mass atrocities faces the challenge of optimizing between interests such as efficiency, due process, and social impact. Budgetary pressures and political constraints only add to the difficulty. Some trade-offs are inevitable, but tracing the effects of the ECCC's institutional features can help identify which have functional promise and which should be studiously avoided at the ICC, national mass crimes proceedings, and any future hybrid tribunals. Learning from the ECCC can also help other courts reduce the start-up costs of developing, testing, and modifying new rules and practices.

Of course, not all of the ECCC's successes or shortcomings are attributable to its institutional design. International Deputy Co-Prosecutor William Smith emphasizes that the Court operates within a structure that results from political compromise, but within that frame, "everything comes down to people."[53] As we discuss throughout the book, judges, lawyers, and staff have sometimes made important positive contributions to the Court, while at other times they have contributed to functional shortcomings. Moreover, the Court does not exist in a vacuum. Regular interventions by interested officials—such as Prime Minister Hun Sen and donor and UN officials—clearly have affected outcomes. Any institution's effectiveness is a function of both structure and agency, and although we focus primarily on the former, our analysis provides regular reminders that experienced, principled, independent, and proactive appointees are crucial to maximizing the potential of any judicial institution and overcoming its inevitable structural imperfections.

Chapter 1

FORGING A HYBRID COURT

"A Mountain Never Has Two Tigers"

Transitional justice could have taken many forms in Cambodia. A truth commission, lustration policies, amnesty programs, and domestic or international trials were all considered or attempted in the years following the Khmer Rouge reign of terror, but it was the ECCC that became the centerpiece of accountability efforts. Both the decision to focus on selected criminal trials and the features of the tribunal created to hold the trials were products of political compromise. Officials from the UN Secretariat and Cambodian Government forged the Court through difficult negotiations that boiled down, in the words of one journalist, to "bitter mutual distrust and an ensuing battle for control."[1]

U.S. officials brokered key compromises, and key UN member states—particularly Japan, Australia, France, and the United States—pressed the UN Secretariat to conclude a deal. Partly for that reason, Cambodia won the battle for control, leading to an unprecedented hybrid court with majority domestic control and a bifurcated institutional structure. This chapter shows how a legacy of distrust and competing contemporary political interests translated into a hybrid tribunal with unique—and in many respects problematic—structural features.

A FOUNDATION OF POLITICAL DISTRUST

The emergence of a hybrid tribunal in Cambodia owes much to distrust. By the late 1990s, when official talks on a Khmer Rouge tribunal began, neither the Cambodian Government nor the UN Secretariat trusted the other side to run the process. Both sides had ample historical reasons to be suspicious of one another.

Battle Lines Drawn during the Cold War

A brief history of the Khmer Rouge movement is essential to understanding the challenges of accountability in Cambodia and the positions key actors would later take in negotiating the ECCC. The Khmer Rouge ("Red Khmer") movement was deeply embedded in the domestic and international political conflict that has engulfed Cambodia for most of its modern history. The Khmers Rouges emerged in the early 1960s as a radical offshoot of the broader Indochinese communist movement,[2] rebelling against the royalist regime of Prince Norodom Sihanouk during a period when Cambodia was slowly drawn into the vortex of the Vietnam War.[3]

In 1970, Marshal Lon Nol led a right-wing military coup against Sihanouk, who formed a government-in-exile in Beijing. With U.S. support, the corrupt and draconian Lon Nol government intensified repression of left-wing fighters and alienated much of the rural peasantry as the country descended into a brutal civil war. The United States, still at war in Vietnam, launched a massive aerial bombing campaign against Vietnamese sanctuaries and Khmer Rouge targets in Cambodia,[4] causing widespread civilian casualties and driving more peasants into the arms of an increasingly radical and uncompromising communist insurgency.[5] China and Vietnam funneled guns and grain to the Cambodian revolutionaries, who overran government defenses and captured Phnom Penh soon after a war-weary U.S. Congress withdrew financial support for Lon Nol in early 1975.

After the Khmer Rouge victory, darkness descended over the country. U.S. President Gerald Ford and Secretary of State Henry Kissinger asserted in May that a "bloodbath" and "atrocity of major proportions" was unfolding.[6] Some accounts from refugees escaping to Thailand provided corroborating evidence, but those reports largely fell on deaf ears or were discounted as attempts to justify the Vietnam War after the fact.[7] Some prominent Western intellectuals even offered sympathetic accounts of Khmer Rouge rule in the newly renamed state of "Democratic Kampuchea" (DK).[8] The United Nations and Western powers did little in response to mounting evidence of atrocities, as the Vietnam Syndrome took hold in Washington and other key capitals.

China did worse, emerging as the Pol Pot regime's main external sponsor, furnishing aid and weapons to the Khmers Rouges to balance against Vietnamese influence in Indochina at a time of intense rivalry between Beijing and Vietnam's principal patron—the USSR.[9] In addition to material support, China provided an ideological model for the Khmers Rouges, who designed their agrarian society roughly on a Maoist model and pledged to achieve a "super great leap forward."[10] Pol Pot pointedly chose to unveil himself as leader and announce the existence of the Communist Party of Kampuchea (CPK) during a 1977 visit to China—a favor to his comrades in Beijing.[11]

With most of the international community disengaged and China providing aid uncritically, the Pol Pot regime survived in power for nearly four years and exacted an immeasurable cost in human life and suffering. In addition to the countless losses and injuries sustained during the Pol Pot era, Khmer Rouge rule left deep scars in the country's social and political fabric that remain relevant today and affect the course of the country's accountability efforts. One was an utter devastation of the country's educated population. The CPK launched a merciless campaign to purge foreign and bourgeois influence from the country. Merchants, intellectuals, military officers, and bureaucrats were suspect; those wearing glasses or speaking a foreign language were sometimes set aside to be purged.[12] The Khmer Rouge regime left behind a country with very few trained doctors, lawyers, counselors, teachers, bureaucrats, and other professionals to lead effective efforts at justice, truth-telling, reconciliation, and personal healing.

Another core feature of Khmer Rouge rule was a relentless assault on traditional social structures, including family units and ethnic and religious groups. Family members were often split; marriages were frequently somber, forced affairs designed to break apart the urban "new people";[13] and family members were taught to report one another for the slightest infractions or face harsh punishment themselves. The Khmers Rouges banned all "reactionary religions detrimental to Democratic Kampuchea," sent out explicit orders to "defrock the monks," razed the Catholic cathedral, and forced Cham Muslims to eat the same pork-laden food as others to survive.[14] Ethnic minorities and hill tribes, viewed as politically suspect and possible fifth columns for foreign intelligence agencies, were also targeted for dispersion and sometimes destruction.[15] Large-scale forced migration has left many survivors searching for loved ones, and the Khmer Rouge assault on faith and families has meant that the social structures most needed to help survivors heal have had to be rebuilt. Indeed, the Khmer word for reconciliation, *phsas phsa*, literally means "putting the broken pieces back together."

The opacity of Khmer Rouge rule has also contributed to a lack of public understanding of what happened and why. The regime's rhetoric spoke of broad revolutionary goals and the faceless "Organization," *Angkar*. Victims of purges were sometimes killed in public to set an example, but often they simply disappeared into CPK prisons or were sent away to be killed on the false pretense of redeployment. Years later, many Cambodians still ask who or what *Angkar* was. Many report that they still do not know with certainty whether some of their closest family members are dead or alive.[16] One of the most common refrains is an inability to understand how such shocking violence could be possible, or what it could hope to achieve. In sum, CPK rule left Cambodians asking many painful questions but meager social resources with which to answer them—a major justification for international involvement later in the process.

Regime Change and False Starts toward Transitional Justice

The Pol Pot regime came to an end in January 1979, when the Vietnamese army and allied Cambodian resistance fighters invaded Cambodia and ousted the CPK. Leading the Cambodian resistance were former Khmers Rouges who had defected into southern Vietnam during the Pol Pot era. Importantly, these included the current President of the Senate Chea Sim, chairman of the National Assembly Heng Samrin,[17] and Prime Minister Hun Sen, who defected to Vietnam in 1977 after serving as a relatively junior CPK military commander.[18] Although no compelling evidence has implicated these senior officials in atrocities,[19] links between the current Cambodian administration and the CPK raise the possibility of charges against sitting officials, which almost certainly adds to the government's resolve to control the Khmer Rouge trials.[20]

By early 1979, the Vietnamese army and Cambodian resistance secured most of the country and established the new People's Republic of Kampuchea (PRK) as Khmer Rouge leaders took refuge in the hills and jungles.[21] The PRK's top priorities were to defeat the large Khmer Rouge insurgency and pacify a country where impulses for revenge were strong. Some Khmers Rouges were tried and convicted in local courts, and others fell prey to revenge killings, but violent reprisals threatened to exacerbate Cambodia's civil war and push more former Khmer Rouge rank and file into the jungles. The PRK thus instituted a kind of reconciliation plan. It coaxed Khmer Rouge cadres to join reeducation programs by issuing leaflets and transmitting radio broadcasts promising leniency to those who apologized and rejoined the fold.[22] Alongside that carrot, it wielded the formidable stick of counterinsurgency warfare.[23]

In the summer of 1979, with help from Vietnamese officials,[24] the PRK government established a "People's Revolutionary Tribunal" to address the crimes of the Khmers Rouges. The PRK Ministry of Justice conducted trials *in absentia* of former DK Prime Minister Pol Pot and Deputy Prime Minister Ieng Sary. The trial sought to win support for the PRK domestically and advance its claim for Cambodia's seat at the United Nations—an important mark of international legitimacy. Shortly before the trial, the presiding judge said publicly:

> Trying the Pol Pot–Ieng Sary clique for the crime of genocide will on the one hand expose all the criminal acts that they have committed and mobilize the Kampuchean people more actively to defend and build up the people's power, and on the other hand show the peoples of the whole world the true face of the criminals who are posing as the representatives of the people of Kampuchea.[25]

After an abrupt five-day trial, Pol Pot and Ieng Sary were found guilty of genocide and sentenced to death—history's first genocide conviction.[26]

Although few observers doubted that the defendants were guilty of grave crimes, procedural flaws and politicization deeply undermined the trial's credibility. The tribunal's title nearly announced the defendants' guilt: "The People's Revolutionary Tribunal Held in Phnom Penh for the Trial of the Genocide Crime of the Pol Pot–Ieng Sary Clique."[27] Pol Pot and Ieng Sary had no communication with their appointed lawyers, who were not permitted to cross-examine witnesses. Their counsel's feeble defense was to seek mitigation by asserting that their clients were mere accomplices to a Chinese master plan of genocide—an accusation that only confirmed the tribunal's nakedly political nature. Most outsiders disregarded the proceedings as a show trial to justify Vietnam's occupation of Cambodia. The 1979 tribunal did have elements of a hybrid nature, with an American communist defense lawyer working beside his Cambodian peer and an East German prosecutor advising the court,[28] but the trial's main legacy was to highlight the risk that a domestically led judicial process could lead to a crudely stage-managed affair.

The 1979 verdicts had little practical effect. Pol Pot and Ieng Sary were beyond the PRK's reach, surrounded by Khmer Rouge insurgents who gained support from governments opposed to Vietnam and its principal ally, the Soviet Union. The Thai military provided sanctuaries and channels for aid, while China gave an estimated $100 million per year to the Khmers Rouges in military assistance and other aid.[29] Western powers and other members of the Association of Southeast Asian Nations (ASEAN) helped organize a "Coalition Government of Democratic Kampuchea" (CGDK) composed of royalists, right-wing republican factions, and the Khmers Rouges to occupy Cambodia's UN General Assembly seat. Although Prince Sihanouk was the nominal head of the CGDK and republican leader Son Sann was Prime Minister, former DK head of state Khieu Samphan was vice president, and the Khmers Rouges were the coalition's dominant fighting force.

Western and ASEAN governments successfully framed the Vietnamese invasion as a violation of state sovereignty rather than a case of liberation. In 1982, by a large majority vote, the CGDK kept Cambodia's seat at the UN General Assembly.[30] Like the *mujahidin* in Afghanistan or paramilitaries in Central America, the Khmers Rouges became useful proxies in a geopolitical game. Private human rights advocates based in the United States promoted accountability, twice attempting to bring cases against the CGDK in the International Court of Justice.[31] However, those efforts had little effect without high-level political interest in putting the Khmers Rouges on trial.

Official efforts at transitional justice were limited during the 1980s and closely connected to the geopolitical struggle. In 1982 and 1983, a PRK organization called the *Renakse* (Salvation Front) organized a nationwide review and condemnation of Khmer Rouge atrocities comprising community meetings, site investigations, and thousands of survivor petitions bearing more than one million signatures or thumbprints.[32] Yet the findings were not broadly disseminated, Khmers Rouges did not participate, and PRK officials revealed a nakedly political purpose: to wrest control from the CGDK in the UN General Assembly.[33] The PRK also established a national "Day of Anger" to recall Khmer Rouge abuses. Perhaps more helpfully, the PRK erected Buddhist *stupas* and other memorials at former terror sites across the country and helped dig up remains from mass burial pits. Private efforts at reconciliation also arose, such as ceremonies during the annual *pchum ben* festival, a traditional Khmer day of remembrance of the dead.[34] These practices helped Cambodians begin to heal, but they did little to address the scar of continuing Khmer Rouge impunity.

A Slow Crawl toward Accountability

In the late 1980s, the thawing of the Cold War led to UN-sponsored talks in Paris for a peace settlement in Indochina, but the United Nations and key member states continued to downplay Khmer Rouge accountability as part of a peace-before-justice approach. China insisted on Khmer Rouge representation, and other Security Council members agreed, believing Khmer Rouge participation provided useful leverage in securing a Vietnamese withdrawal and reduced Khmer Rouge incentives to spoil the peace.[35] The talks led to the 1991 Paris Peace Agreement, which established a UN Transitional Authority for Cambodia (UNTAC) with mandates for various peacekeeping activities, civil administration, and organizing elections to produce a new Royal Government of Cambodia (RGC). UNTAC's mandate did not call for Khmer Rouge accountability. Politically, UNTAC helped marginalize the Khmers Rouges, which boycotted the UNTAC-sponsored 1993 elections, but from a military standpoint UN peacekeepers did little to defang the insurgency.[36] That task would fall to the newly elected RGC.

The royalist party Funcinpec finished first in the 1993 elections. It was led by Sihanouk's son, Norodom Ranariddh, and enjoyed support from many Western governments. The Cambodian People's Party (CPP)—the successor to the PRK's governing party—finished second, and its leader was a young Hun Sen, who had served as Prime Minister in the pre-UNTAC period. Ranariddh lacked an outright majority, however, and Hun Sen maintained strong authority within the bureaucracy and security services. After some negotiation, Ranariddh agreed to share power with Hun Sen as Co-Prime Ministers in a newly refashioned constitutional monarchy, with Sihanouk as King and head of state.[37]

Although the Khmers Rouges remained a significant fighting force, their foreign support dwindled, and the movement weakened. International interest in trying the Khmers Rouges rose in 1993–94, as the International Criminal Tribunals for the former Yugoslavia (ICTY) and Rwanda (ICTR) inaugurated a new phase in international criminal law. In 1994, the U.S. Congress passed the Cambodian Genocide Justice Act and established a special Office of Cambodian Genocide Investigation at the State Department.[38] That office funded Yale University's Cambodian Genocide Program to establish the Documentation Center of Cambodia (DC-Cam), which helped lay groundwork for trials by accumulating information about DK atrocities.[39]

In 1994, the Cambodian National Assembly formally outlawed the Khmer Rouge organization.[40] The Government's main focus was to defeat the insurgency by attracting defections and emphasizing "national reconciliation"—a policy shared by the CPP and the royalist leaders.[41] The CPP did call for trials on occasion, however, focusing on senior Khmer Rouge officials.[42] In a January

1995 conversation with U.S. officials, senior Cambodian diplomat Hor Namhong voiced his government's support for Khmer Rouge trials, which would be "Cambodia's responsibility to instigate."[43]

Efforts to secure defections continued, and in August 1996 Hun Sen brokered a deal under which Ieng Sary defected to the Government with roughly 3,000 of the estimated 7,500 active Khmer Rouge guerrillas.[44] In exchange, Sihanouk formally pardoned Ieng Sary for the death sentence handed down during the 1979 tribunal and granted him amnesty from prosecution under the 1994 law barring Khmer Rouge membership. Ranariddh approved the deal. It was unpopular among many members of both the CPP and Funcinpec and would later produce tension in the tribunal negotiations, but it did help cripple the insurgency and prompt Khmer Rouge infighting. In 1997, after former DK Defense Minister Son Sen began talking to Cambodian officials, he and his family were murdered. Khmer Rouge cadres arrested and convicted Pol Pot and three others for the killing in July 1997 at a "People's Tribunal," sentencing him to life in a makeshift prison.[45]

Fragmentation of the Khmer Rouge movement enabled talks about accountability to proceed but did not determine what form accountability would take. In January 1997, UN Special Representative for Human Rights in Cambodia Thomas Hammarberg called for a truth commission,[46] but the proposal won little support, and conversations quickly shifted toward criminal trials. Some scholars have argued that officials dispensed with the idea of a truth commission too quickly in Cambodia,[47] and indeed there appears to have been little serious discussion on the topic. A truth commission would consume resources and would not deliver the form of justice that many UN and Western officials sought. Moreover, a broad fact-finding inquiry would draw attention to the numerous dirty hands in Cambodia's recent history.[48] These factors likely explain why the main political protagonists agreed on a prosecutorial approach. Despite that point of agreement, building an institution to conduct the trials would not be easy. After years of conflict, the key actors had clear stakes in the process and reasons to be wary of one another.

COMPROMISING ON A HYBRID COURT

In June 1997, with encouragement from the UN Commission on Human Rights,[49] Hun Sen and Ranariddh sent a joint letter to UN Secretary-General

Kofi Annan requesting help in bringing the Khmers Rouges to justice and adding:

> Cambodia does not have the resources or expertise to conduct this very important procedure. Thus, we believe it is necessary to ask for the assistance of the United Nations. We are aware of similar efforts to respond to the genocide and crimes against humanity in Rwanda and the former Yugoslavia, and ask that similar assistance be given to Cambodia.[50]

That week, reports of Pol Pot's whereabouts intensified efforts to set up a tribunal. The U.S. government advocated passing a UN Security Council resolution to create an ad hoc international court like the ICTY or ICTR, which appeared consistent with the Cambodian Co-Prime Ministers' request. U.S. officials also developed plans to capture Pol Pot and other Khmer Rouge leaders for trials outside of Cambodia.[51]

At the same time, both Hun Sen and Ranariddh continued to seek Khmer Rouge defections on terms that would benefit their respective political camps.[52] That competition for defections helped splinter the Khmer Rouge movement,[53] but it also contributed to a domestic crisis. In July 1997, shortly after Khmer Rouge leaders reportedly pledged to ally with Funcinpec,[54] Hun Sen carried out what most analysts characterized as a coup.[55] Troops loyal to him defeated their royalist opponents, solidified control over most areas of the country, and executed an uncertain number of Funcinpec officials. Ranariddh fled the country.[56] Hun Sen's takeover led to widespread criticism abroad and exacerbated an already sour relationship between CPP leaders and some of the foreign governments most actively promoting Khmer Rouge trials—particularly the United States. The Clinton administration suspended bilateral aid to condemn Hun Sen's forces for the violence.[57]

Nevertheless, movement toward the trials continued, and both the CPP and Funcinpec leaders in exile continued to voice their support.[58] Hammarberg took the case to the UN headquarters but avoided the Security Council due to China's expressed opposition to the trials. China expressed its opposition as a defense of sovereignty but was also loath to draw attention to its role as the ideological inspiration and principal patron of the Pol Pot regime.[59] In December 1997, Hammarberg thus raised the issue at the UN General Assembly, which passed a resolution recommending that the Secretary-General dispatch experts to Cambodia to evaluate the possibility of putting surviving Khmer Rouge officials on trial.[60]

In April 1998, the top target for prosecution, Pol Pot, was pronounced dead in Thailand days after a *New York Times* article revealed secret U.S. plans to capture and hold him for trial.[61] The cause of his death remains shrouded, as his body was soon cremated without an autopsy, raising speculation that he was murdered by fellow Khmers Rouges or others keen to forestall a trial.[62] Another senior Khmer Rouge suspect, Mok—the infamous one-legged CPK Central Committee member known by many as "the Butcher" for his brutality—said: "The world community should stop talking about this now that Pol Pot is dead. It was all Pol Pot."[63]

If Pol Pot was killed to derail the American push for a trial, the plan failed. The U.S. government continued to press the Security Council to create a fully international tribunal under its Chapter VII authority. In late April, U.S. officials circulated a draft Security Council resolution that would create an "International Criminal Tribunal for Cambodia" in The Netherlands sharing many components of the ICTY, including its registry and appeals chambers.[64] The U.S. proposal generated little interest in the Security Council. China argued that Khmer Rouge accountability was an internal Cambodian affair and that invoking Chapter VII authority would require a threat to international peace and security that was no longer present in Cambodia.[65] Russia and France emphasized the importance of Cambodian consent,[66] and many Latin American governments saw the *ad hoc* tribunals as illegitimate.[67] In addition, some European officials disfavored U.S. efforts to build another *ad hoc* tribunal as they lobbied states to sign the Rome Statute to create the International Criminal Court (ICC). Facing stiff headwinds, the U.S. draft resolution was never formally introduced.

Meanwhile, Hun Sen began to solidify domestic control and regain international legitimacy. In July 1998, the CPP won national elections funded largely by Japan and the European Union, and the new CPP-led government was widely recognized despite concerns that the elections were not free and fair.[68] As his position in power became more secure, Hun Sen's position toward the trials shifted. U.S. Ambassador for War Crimes David Scheffer met him in August 1998 and concluded:

> Hun Sen's first preference was to have the senior Khmer Rouge leaders fade away as long as their troops were neutralized. His second choice seemed to be a

> trial that he controlled. Obviously, if this were to happen, given his track record, it would be seen as lacking credibility and would taint everyone associated with it.[69]

The U.S. government continued to challenge Hun Sen's legitimacy. The most strident attack came in October 1998, when U.S. Congressman Dana Rohrabacher (R-CA) introduced a successful House resolution accusing Hun Sen of serious crimes during the DK era, PRK period, and thereafter and advocating an international criminal trial against him, not just "a handful of geriatric Khmer Rouge leaders"[70]—a resolution that CPP leaders deeply resented.[71]

In December of that year, Thailand helped arrange the defection of former DK leaders Khieu Samphan and Nuon Chea.[72] Although the U.S. government and others pressed for justice, Hun Sen emphasized the need for "national reconciliation." He said that Khieu Samphan and Nuon Chea should be welcomed "with bouquets of flowers, not with prisons and handcuffs" and that Cambodia "should dig a hole and bury the past and look ahead to the 21st century with a clean slate."[73]

Opposition parties and international critics attacked Hun Sen's remarks and accused the CPP of negotiating with the United Nations in bad faith. King Sihanouk refused to countenance an amnesty and said that an international tribunal "would have the perfect right to take up the case of genocide in Cambodia" because it concerned "all the world's people."[74] Hun Sen said that he considered the possibility for trials but emphasized that they should be done "in the context of war and peace [and] in the context of national reconciliation, which is all one package."[75] To many critics, Hun Sen simply sought to bolster his own domestic control, which was more a cause of than a solution to Cambodia's contemporary problems and certainly did not justify an amnesty for some of history's most heinous mass crimes.[76]

The debate magnified with the completion of the UN Group of Experts' report, which recommended that the UN Security Council establish an *ad hoc* international tribunal. The Group advised the UN not to support domestic trials due to corruption and political interference in the Cambodian judicial system and rejected a "mixed Cambodian-foreign court."[77] As Group member Steven Ratner later explained, the experts believed a mixed tribunal "would depend too much on the cooperation of the Cambodian government."[78] Hun Sen fired back, appealing to sovereignty norms and asserting that any international tribunal would also need to investigate foreign countries' roles in supporting the Khmers Rouges after 1979.[79] He also wrote to Kofi Annan, stressing the dangers of an international trial:

> If improperly and heedlessly conducted, the trials of Khmer Rouge leaders would panic other former Khmer Rouge officers and rank and file, who have already surrendered, into turning back to the jungle and renewing the guerrilla war in Cambodia.[80]

He added that Cambodia was considering a truth and reconciliation commission along South African lines as an alternative—a suggestion that U.S. Secretary of State Madeleine Albright promptly and publicly rejected. Albright asserted that "we want these top leaders to be brought to justice" and insisted that a truth commission was "not a substitute for an international tribunal" focused on top Khmer Rouge suspects.[81]

Just days after Hun Sen's letter arrived, the last pillar of the Khmer Rouge leadership fell when government forces near the Thai border arrested Mok. Hun Sen announced that he intended to try Mok in a domestic court[82] and informed Hammarberg that outside legal experts would be allowed only as observers after being invited by the Cambodian court.[83] Foreign Minister Hor Namhong put the government's case bluntly:

> The international community talks about finding justice for the Cambodian people . . . But what has the international community been doing vis-à-vis the Khmer Rouge lately? Once the genocidal Khmer Rouge regime was toppled, the so-called international community continued to support the Khmer Rouge. The so-called international community forced Cambodia to accept the Khmer Rouge as partners in the Paris Peace talks. . . . It said nothing about responsibility of the Khmer Rouge, let alone prosecution of them. But now that Cambodia has achieved peace and reconciliation, they call for an international tribunal. Can we trust them?[84]

Hun Sen launched a similarly stinging critique:

> It took me 20 years to destroy the political and military organization of the Khmer Rouge and to bring the leaders of this organization to a court of law. . . .

> [W]hen we were fighting against them, when we were demanding that the leaders of the Khmer Rouge be brought to trial, there were some people in some countries, including America, who were against us. . . . If foreigners have the right to lack confidence in Cambodian courts of law, we Cambodians also have the right to lack confidence in an international court of law. Why? Because those who would mandate an international court used to support the Khmer Rouge . . . [85]

Hun Sen exclaimed that the only jobs the UN Secretary-General would give Cambodians would be to "go into the jungle to capture the tiger."[86]

Cambodian officials may have noted the experience of Rwanda, which requested an international tribunal after the 1994 genocide but later became the only country to vote against the Security Council resolution establishing the ICTR. Like its Cambodian counterparts, the Rwandan government highlighted UN abandonment during the conflict and emphasized that its forces "had to fight alone . . . in order to stop the carnage."[87] It resented the failure to situate the court within Rwanda where the crimes occurred and where there would be an opportunity "to promote the harmonization of international and national jurisprudence."[88] And as in Cambodia, Rwandan authorities sought some control over the process for political reasons; perhaps the primary unstated reason for Rwanda's objection to the ICTR was the Security Council's decision to include jurisdiction over crimes committed by the Rwandan Patriotic Front—the new government's armed forces.[89]

Cambodian leaders distrusted a UN-led process that their domestic and foreign foes could use to undermine the CPP's standing, either by pressing charges against sitting officials or taking credit for justice that the CPP had failed to deliver. Nevertheless, Cambodia's leaders faced pressure to cooperate with the United Nations from a number of sources, including Cambodian opposition leader Sam Rainsy, the UN Commission on Human Rights, Western donors, international media, and civil society actors.[90] Critics argued that Cambodian courts could not deliver credible trials due to endemic corruption, mismanagement, and a questionable commitment to justice. Yet a purely international tribunal was unlikely. The International Criminal Court would not be an option due to its non-retroactive temporal jurisdiction, which limits that court to crimes committed after July 2002. China, Russia, and others opposed creating an *ad hoc* international tribunal for Cambodia, and China would likely veto any such proposal at the UN Security Council.[91]

To break the impasse, U.S. and UN officials began to consider a "mixed" tribunal. In April 1999, U.S. Senator John Kerry met Hun Sen to discuss including both Cambodian and international judges and personnel.[92] UN leaders took no immediate official position on the proposal, but in a step toward compromise, Hun Sen informed Kofi Annan in late April that he planned to try Mok and others in domestic courts but that "foreign judges and prosecutors would be allowed to take part fully," rather than merely observing the process, to ensure that the trials met "international standards of due process."[93] Meetings between Hun Sen and Hammarberg explored the mixed tribunal option more fully in the months that followed.

Meanwhile, conditions on the ground continued to evolve. In May, government forces arrested Duch, the infamous former chief of the CPK's central internal security office. Custody of Duch and Mok—as well as the Cambodian Government's close watch over Ieng Sary, Khieu Samphan, and Nuon Chea—gave it added bargaining leverage. Moreover, by 1999 the CPP was in a strong domestic position and had managed to restore largely positive relations with China, which had become the country's second-largest donor (after Japan) and offered much-needed financial support with relatively few political conditions attached.[94] This reduced the Cambodian Government's reliance on the West and made it unlikely that the CPP would hand over the suspects to an international body. Without UN participation, however, the CPP would lose financial resources and a stamp of international legitimacy. The hybrid court option had appeal, provided that Cambodians would have control.

UN officials could also countenance a hybrid court if they had sufficient control. The ICTY and ICTR had provided valuable legal judgments and precedents, but donors were weary of their high costs and lengthy proceedings. Out-of-country locations had compromised their ability to connect with survivor populations and to transfer skills and legal principles to ailing domestic systems. To many critics, these courts also presented sovereignty problems and were essentially instruments of Western power. A hybrid court could thus have both functional advantages and a better chance of winning political support. In June 1999, Hun Sen wrote to Kofi Annan requesting UN assistance to draft legislation for "a special national Cambodian court to try Khmer Rouge leaders [which] would provide for foreign judges and prosecutors to participate in its proceedings."[95] The UN Office of Legal Affairs accepted that starting point for negotiations, and both the UN and RGC convened teams to represent their respective sides.

A BATTLE FOR CONTROL

Despite convergence toward a hybrid arrangement, Cambodian and UN officials had very different views on how to organize the tribunal. As Tom Fawthrop and Helen Jarvis note:

> Who would be in control of the Khmer Rouge trials was the key issue over which the Cambodian government and the United Nations constantly locked horns. This underlay all the points of controversy and compromise in the three rounds of negotiations, numerous exchanges of letters and interventions by third parties from 1999 to 2003.[96]

As talks began in August 1999, UN officials insisted that the tribunal should be a *sui generis* court, and a majority of judges and key personnel should be international appointees.[97] The Cambodian side rejected that proposal,[98] and in September Hun Sen met with Kofi Annan and offered three options—the United Nations could participate in a tribunal within Cambodia's existing courts, provide legal advice without direct participation, or withdraw.[99] Hun Sen explained to Hammarberg in October:

> Cambodia wants to be given opportunity to be masters of its own situation. You can participate, but do not try to be masters of the issue. . . . I do not wish a foreign woman to come to Cambodia and dress up in a Khmer dress. I want a Khmer woman to dress in a Khmer dress and for foreigners to come and help put on the make-up.[100]

To overcome the deadlock, the United States again intervened—initially by approaching the Cambodian Government without consulting the UN team.[101] U.S. Ambassador to Cambodia Kent Wiedemann and U.S. Ambassador for War Crimes David Scheffer floated the idea of establishing a "special chamber" (later "extraordinary chambers") within the Cambodian court system.[102] Scheffer also introduced the idea of a supermajority vote. If the court were to have a Cambodian majority, the vote of at least one international judge would be required for any judicial decision. Scheffer advanced the measure to "manage a Cambodian majority on the bench (if that proved to be the endgame)" and to establish "the minimum threshold of international oversight in the decision-making process of the judges."[103] The Cambodian Government welcomed the U.S. proposals, which they regarded as a viable path to a Cambodian-majority court. U.S. diplomats pressured Annan and his legal staff and encouraged them to "play ball," but UN officials pushed back. UN Legal Counsel Hans Corell argued that the supermajority idea was a "recipe for paralysis" and insisted on an international majority on the bench.[104]

UN officials also insisted that the Secretary-General should appoint all judges and prosecutors to ensure international standards and reduce the risk of political interference. The Cambodian Government instead proposed allowing the Secretary-General to nominate only international judges, who would then be appointed formally by the Supreme Council of Magistracy, the body responsible for judicial appointments under Cambodian law.[105]

The question of control was linked to the Court's jurisdiction, because neither side wanted to entrust the other with the power to determine the scope of prosecution. Both the UN Secretariat and RGC agreed to focus on alleged Khmer Rouge crimes committed between April 17, 1975, and January 6, 1979.[106] Hun Sen periodically threatened to pursue a "package deal" including U.S. abuses in the preceding civil war period,[107] but he too had ample reasons to avoid a broader temporal frame that would draw attention to crimes committed in the 1980s.[108]

Personal jurisdiction was more contentious. UN officials argued that both senior Khmer Rouge leaders and others deemed most responsible for the atrocities should be eligible for prosecution, in line with the UN Group of Experts' recommendation.[109] Corell also asserts that he "never discussed who should be prosecuted," reasoning that international law requires an independent prosecutor to decide.[110] Hun Sen publicly agreed that it would be the "unique jurisdiction of the court to make charges" and said that he had "no rights whatsoever to charge this or that person, or to pre-determine how many people will stand trial."[111]

The discussion of numbers and particular defendants was never far beneath the surface, however. U.S. and UN officials generally favored more expansive prosecution, sometimes pointing to the UN experts' recommendation of roughly 20 to 30 defendants. Hun Sen announced in late 1999 that he intended to try only "four or five of the people responsible."[112] He later admitted that he "should not comment on or say anything that is within the bounds of the judiciary,"[113] but a number of other statements indicated his preference for a small universe of defendants, whom he sometimes identified by name.[114]

Casting too wide a net, he argued, would invite instability and jeopardize the government's reconciliation plan. Critics argued that Hun Sen also sought to limit the number of potential defendants out of self-interest, as he and other high-ranking CPP members had been part of the Khmer Rouge organization before defecting to Vietnam to lead the resistance.[115] Hun Sen pointedly said that trials should exclude those who (like himself) had "helped to overthrow the genocide."[116] A broad prosecutorial net also could draw attention to defection deals between the CPP and notorious former Khmer Rouge fighters. The most prominent case, that of Ieng Sary, remained a bone of contention between the UN and Cambodian sides, as the latter resisted UN demands to invalidate Ieng Sary's 1996 amnesty and pardon.

Despite disagreement on the basic issues of control and the scope of the Court's jurisdiction, the Cambodian Government pressed ahead, drafting a domestic law to create a tribunal and submitting it to the National Assembly without UN approval. The draft law foresaw a court with a Cambodian court president, Cambodian majorities in each of the chambers, a Cambodian Co-Prosecutor, and a Cambodian head of administration—all to be drawn from the ranks of the Cambodian judiciary and civil service. Moreover, both the national and international Co-Prosecutors would have to sign indictments, which UN officials feared would leave the CPP with a veto over prosecutions. To the UN side, all of these features made the structure unacceptably vulnerable to political influence. Annan responded quickly, demanding an international majority of judges and an internationally appointed prosecutor.

The draft law also provided for Cambodian and UN-appointed Co-Investigating Judges. Investigating judges, who share investigatory duties with the prosecutors, are derived from the French civil law tradition and exist in the Cambodian judicial system. According to Corell, the Cambodian side regarded the inclusion of investigating judges as "a natural thing to do," and the UN team elected not to oppose the concept, which would have frustrated negotiations.[117] Hammarberg was concerned that investigating judges would unnecessarily complicate the process and serve as another possible barrier to prosecution.[118] Corell was more focused on the complication introduced by having twin pairs of prosecutors and investigating judges.[119] Both concerns would prove to be warranted.

To manage the risk of disagreement and deadlock between the Co-Prosecutors and Co-Investigating Judges, U.S. officials pushed for the establishment of a special judicial panel for that purpose. UN and Cambodian officials soon agreed to create a Pre-Trial Chamber composed of three Cambodian and two international judges, empowered to block investigations or indictments only by supermajority vote. Although the new chamber would add a layer to the judicial process, Corell and his team regarded it as a necessary safeguard for the integrity of the proceedings.[120] Cambodia's agreement was a significant concession, as it would enable an international Co-Prosecutor to forge ahead in the absence of a countervailing supermajority.[121]

The UN team remained highly skeptical of a majority-Cambodian court but agreed in July 2000 that the tribunal would be "a Cambodian court with the participation of international judges and prosecutors."[122] Corell also unveiled a draft UN-Cambodian "Framework Agreement" to govern UN-Cambodian cooperation on the tribunal. It proposed giving the United Nations authority to appoint international judges, the international Co-Prosecutor, and two new officials: a deputy international prosecutor and Deputy Director of Administration. The Cambodian side gave little ground, and in January 2001 the Cambodian National Assembly approved a draft law (the "2001 Law").[123] It retained the Cambodian majorities in each chamber and gave Cambodia control over all appointments, subject to UN nomination of international appointees. Opposition leader Sam Rainsy argued that the 2001 Law would merely produce CPP-led show trials,[124] but King Sihanouk signed it in August.

The UN team warned that international funds and political support would come only if the Cambodian Government amended the 2001 Law to correspond more closely to the draft Framework Agreement. The two sides also struggled over which would have legal primacy: the Framework Agreement or the Cambodian law. Deputy Prime Minister Sok An asserted that the Framework Agreement would establish "modalities of cooperation . . . concerning foreign technical and financial support" but would not have the power to modify or prevail over a domestic law.[125] Annan argued that the Framework Agreement must have the status of a binding treaty, because reducing the agreement to a technical memorandum of understanding would "deprive it of its substantive role of ensuring [ ] international standards of justice."[126]

This and other sticking points—including the scheme for appointments, the validity of Ieng Sary's 1996 amnesty and pardon, and the rights of the accused, victims, and witnesses—led a frustrated Kofi Annan to withdraw his UN team from negotiations in February 2002. Corell explained:

> [T]he UN should not be part of a court that would fail to provide victims of the Khmer Rouge with the credible justice they deserve . . . UN affiliation to such a court could set a precedent for lowering international standards . . . [and] the UN's name would [be] attached to a judicial process over which it had little or no control.[127]

He later recalled that the UN team had "lost confidence." To Corell, "the lodestar was that if the UN was going to engage in any project of this nature, it had to rise to the standards required by international agreements," such as the International Covenant on Civil and Political Rights. When Corell saw those standards as unmet, he "put [his] foot down."[128] Many human rights advocates supported the pullout. Kek Galabru, head of the human rights group LICADHO, argued that the UN would "lose all credibility" if it partook in a trial that fell short of international standards.[129] Dinah PoKempner of Human Rights Watch called the decision "sad but courageous" and praised the UN team for refusing to support trials vulnerable to procedural irregularity and political interference.[130]

UN demands were consistent with how hybrid courts had been designed elsewhere. While negotiations dragged on in Cambodia, hybrid courts or panels with international majorities of judges began work in East Timor, Kosovo, and Sierra Leone. The mixed panels in Kosovo and East Timor were created by UN transitional administrations in those territories and thus had fundamentally different origins than the ECCC, but the Special Court for Sierra Leone (SCSL)[131] was a directly relevant comparison for the Cambodian tribunal talks. The SCSL was a tribunal established by agreement between the national government and United Nations, given limited personal jurisdiction over those who bore "the greatest responsibility for serious violations" during Sierra Leone's civil war, and endowed with substantial funding, bureaucracy, and a brick-and-mortar facility in Freetown. Most key personnel at the SCSL were international, including an international prosecutor and registrar and majorities of judges in the trial and appeals chambers.[132]

Corell, who worked on the SCSL negotiations as well as the ECCC talks, asserts that he "made the comparison all the time between a state really committed to a credible and effective process and Cambodia, which was different."[133]

While the Sierra Leonean government deferred to UN leadership at the SCSL and did not even fill all of its allocated slots with national personnel,[134] the Cambodian Government refused to cede control over the process. Sok An said the UN withdrawal was "[n]o problem at all"—Cambodia would hold domestic trials if necessary but would "keep the door open" to further talks.[135] The RGC waited and faced only modest local political pressure when 14 members of the opposition Sam Rainsy Party demanded an explanation for the apparent failure of the tribunal talks.[136]

Internationally, most pressure was directed at the UN side. The United States, Japan, and Australia were particularly active, and all were keen to see trials in Cambodia.[137] These and other states, as well as the European Union, pressed Annan to reconsider.[138] In April, Indian Prime Minister Atal Bihari Vajpayee visited Phnom Penh and offered to send an Indian judge to the court if the United Nations backed out, as Hun Sen warned that the RGC's "patience was limited" and threatened to initiate domestic trials[139]—though he took no evident steps to do so. The UN Human Rights Commission also passed a resolution urging the parties to restart talks,[140] and the Secretary-General's Special Representative for Human Rights in Cambodia, Peter Leuprecht, urged the UN team to reengage.[141] In July, ASEAN Foreign Ministers—who generally took a hands-off approach to the tribunal in line with the ASEAN norm of non-interference[142]—issued a gently worded request for UN reengagement at Cambodia's request.[143] After Hun Sen indicated his willingness to modify the 2001 Law to accommodate UN concerns, Japan began convening interested UN member states to press Annan to resume negotiations.[144]

PRESSURE, COMPROMISE, AND THE CREATION OF THE ECCC

In December 2002, France and Japan sponsored a UN General Assembly Resolution requesting that Annan "resume negotiations, without delay, to conclude an agreement" with Cambodia "so that the Extraordinary Chambers may begin to function promptly."[145] The resolution emphasized the importance of ensuring "international standards of justice, fairness, and due process of law" but also welcomed the passage of the 2001 law and its "provision for the role of the United Nations," suggesting acceptance of a subordinate UN role.[146] Thirty nations, including many European states, abstained from the vote out of concern that it left the Secretary-General in a weak bargaining position. Nevertheless, the resolution passed.

Corell has since expressed resentment that "the UN was forced back to the negotiating table" and that "[i]n some respects, our hands were tied."[147] In January 2003, the UN team reengaged, again demanding a majority of international judges and a single international prosecutor. The Cambodian Government refused, and after further pressure from key member states,[148] the UN team returned to Phnom Penh in March. In a report to the General Assembly, Kofi Annan lamented:

> [C]ertain Member States . . . made it clear to me that they expected me not to seek any changes to the structure and organization of the Extraordinary Chambers . . . The Government of Cambodia was obviously aware that this position had been communicated to me and acted accordingly.[149]

The UN team did win some concessions—such as a Cambodian pledge not to request amnesties or pardons for crimes under the ECCC's jurisdiction—but the revised Framework Agreement was largely a victory for the Cambodian Government. It followed the 2001 Law in most respects, retaining a number of the same unique institutional features. The ECCC would be a Cambodian-majority court "within the existing court structure of Cambodia,"[150] the first hybrid court with national control of most key positions. It would also be the first tribunal split into national and international "sides" with separate hiring and reporting structures, including Co-Prosecutors, Co-Investigating Judges, and a divided administrative apparatus. It would be empowered to try "senior leaders" and others "most responsible" for the crimes of Democratic Kampuchea—language that resulted from extensive negotiations between the two sides but failed to produce a meeting of the minds and would lead to further impasses—a topic discussed at length in chapter 6.[151]

Annan expressed serious concerns about the "structure and organization of the Extraordinary Chambers" and reported that he "would very much have preferred . . . a majority of international judges."[152] He argued that Cambodian courts showed "little respect . . . for the most elementary features of the right to a fair trial" and warned of a record of "interference by the executive with the independence of the judiciary."[153]

By contrast, the Cambodian Government welcomed the result. In an address to the National Assembly, Sok An characterized the "Cambodian model" as an institutional form that could "stand as an example to others in the future."[154] He said that the ECCC satisfied the government's three "guiding principles"—justice for the victims, maintenance of "peace, political stability and national unification," and "respect for national sovereignty."[155] He added proudly:

> [T]he history of international tribunals shows that they were organized by foreign judges and initiated and imposed from without. But our mechanism . . . is organized within the structure of the Cambodian courts. We have invited the international community to join with us.[156]

Some observers considered the ECCC's structure the best outcome possible under trying circumstances and better than the likely alternatives. The counterfactual question loomed large: What would happen if the UN were to withdraw from the tribunal? Few outside observers expected a credible domestic process, and many anticipated that trials would not occur at all. If so, as scholar Craig Etcheson argued, "[t]he Khmer Rouge leadership would die quiet, peaceful deaths in their beds, having successfully defended their impunity for their entire lives."[157] Scholar Gregory Stanton warned that "perfection is the enemy of justice,"[158] and Leuprecht agreed—"rather this tribunal than no tribunal."[159]

Supporters believed that the Framework Agreement gave the UN enough leverage to keep the Court on track.[160] Behind this cautious optimism was the expectation that the UN would actively ensure the Court's adherence to international standards.[161] Indeed, Annan asserted that it would be "essential" for the UN to "remain engaged in the process of overseeing the implementation of the draft agreement" and threatened that "any deviation by the Government from its obligations could lead to the United Nations withdrawing its cooperation and assistance from the process."[162]

Critics were skeptical that the UN could police a Cambodian-led court effectively.[163] Mike Jendrzejczyk of Human Rights Watch argued that it embodied "the lowest standards yet for a tribunal with U.N. participation" and that "with Cambodia's judiciary at the center of the tribunal, the agreement ensures that it will be politics and not law that dominate the tribunal's work."[164] An important subtext of such critiques was that Hun Sen's government could exploit a trial for political gain—a prospect that many human rights advocates regarded as a step backward for Cambodia. Amnesty International argued that the ECCC's agreed structure would "not only threaten the integrity of the legal process for [Cambodia but also] would set a dangerous precedent that could compromise fair trial standards for any future international or mixed tribunals . . ."[165] Even if a majority-domestic court was the best available option in Cambodia, it could set an unhelpful example of local control—an issue of particular concern to UN officials and human rights groups who anticipated engaging in negotiations with other states in the future.

Despite UN misgivings and critiques from human rights groups, the two sides signed the revised Framework Agreement in June 2003, and after a domestic political impasse in Cambodia following the 2003 national elections, the National Assembly passed an amended domestic law (the "ECCC Law") creating the ECCC in 2004.[166] It also ratified the Framework Agreement, agreeing that it would "apply as law within the Kingdom of Cambodia"[167]—an important concession to the UN insistence that the Agreement carry the legal force of a treaty, not just a technical memorandum of understanding.[168]

The Framework Agreement and ECCC Law undoubtedly created a tribunal that is structurally vulnerable to strong national influence. Its Pre-Trial and Trial Chambers have three national and two international judges, while the appellate Supreme Court Chamber has four Cambodian and three international judges. Decisions require an affirmative supermajority vote, meaning that at least one international judge must join in every decision[169]—a provision that limits the scope for Cambodian judicial dominance but also prevents international judges from driving outcomes by convincing a single Cambodian "swing judge."

The Cambodian Government also controls several key administrative posts. Unlike other mixed tribunals, which have had an international registrar to manage administrative operations, the ECCC has an Office of Administration (OA) responsible for general administrative functions.[170] The OA has a Cambodian Director and international Deputy Director. The Chief of Public Affairs and head of the Victims Support Section are also Cambodian appointees, enabling the Government to exert strong influence over public communication. The ECCC's Defence Support Section and a few administrative units are led by international appointees.

The ECCC's appointment mechanism gives the Cambodian Government further influence. Although key UN personnel and judges are nominated by the Secretary-General, they are appointed by the Cambodian Supreme Council of Magistracy, giving the RGC a mechanism to challenge or resist UN appointments.[171] If foreign court staffers "fail or refuse to participate" in ECCC proceedings or the UN withdraws its support from the Court and no foreign candidates are identified to fill vacant positions, the RGC may select Cambodian replacements.[172] The ECCC Law thus foresees the possibility that, under certain conditions, the ECCC could function as a fully national court without international staffing.

The RGC's influence over the Court is not simply a question of numbers. It also relates to the general lack of judicial independence in Cambodia and the dearth of qualified judicial personnel in a country that is still recovering from the relentless Khmer Rouge attack on intellectuals and the lean years that followed. Partly for that reason, personal connections have commonly driven senior judicial appointments and continue to do so, including at the ECCC. The close nexus between senior personnel and the executive branch makes the ECCC vulnerable to political interference. Indeed, all high-level Cambodian personnel at the ECCC continue to hold important jobs either in the national judicial system or in the Government itself.[173]

The Framework Agreement and ECCC Law left many aspects of the Court undecided, including the precise rules and legal principles to be applied, the mechanisms for engaging victims, how the Court would be funded, and what oversight mechanisms would be put in place—an issue closely linked to concerns about corruption and executive interference, which would later prove to be prescient. All of these issues are discussed in subsequent chapters and help to illustrate how the Court's unique (and in some respects ambiguous) institutional form has affected its function.

EXPLAINING THE OUTCOME

The Cambodian Government won significant control over the ECCC due to several factors that gave the RGC bargaining leverage. First, discord on the UN Security Council blocked the possibility of a fully international court based on a Chapter VII Security Council resolution that would override Cambodian objections. China's likely veto was the most obvious constraint, but many other states also regarded the ICTY/ICTR model as problematic and favored a consensual arrangement with strong national participation to uphold sovereignty, save costs, and connect the process more closely to the surviving local population. The fact that the RGC obtained custody of key suspects also made it highly unlikely that any international process would be viable without Cambodian consent.

Second, the state of politics in and around Cambodia helped the RGC resist UN pressure to consent to a majority-international hybrid court. Domestically, the Cambodian Government had achieved a commanding domestic political position by the time the tribunal's features were negotiated. A victory in the 1998 national elections and series of successful measures to co-opt or repress their domestic political foes left the CPP firmly in charge and enabled its leaders to withstand occasional pressure from opposition parties to consent to UN leadership.

Internationally, although Cambodia received considerable amounts of international aid, the RGC was less dependent on the United Nations or Western powers for security or political legitimacy than the leaders of East Timor, Kosovo, or Sierra Leone when tribunals were established in those postconflict settings. A great deal of international pressure would have been required to convince Cambodian leaders to cede primary control of the trials. The United States led efforts to establish a tribunal but had limited leverage without custody of the defendants. Moreover, U.S. officials had little aid with which to bargain, because after Hun Sen seized power in 1997, U.S. appropriations legislation barred most forms of direct assistance to the RGC throughout the negotiation process.[174]

Other key donors, such as France and Japan, supported the trials but did not condition their aid on RGC agreement to an international-majority court. Such donors had multiple strategic and humanitarian interests in Cambodia and were loath to spend much political capital trying to force an unlikely change in the RGC's position. For example, France maintained significant investments in transportation, hotels, and energy, close ties to the royal family, a range of development projects, and an enduring interest in promoting French language and culture in its former colony.[175] All of these interests militated against a coercive approach toward the tribunal talks.

For Japan, aid and a low-key diplomatic approach were means to develop influence in Southeast Asia and access the region's markets and resources—often in competition with China.[176] Japan resisted U.S. demands to suspend aid to

Cambodia after the July 1997 coup[177] and was Cambodia's largest development aid donor between 1998 and 2004, providing roughly half a billion dollars over that period[178] and supporting the RGC even during periods of deadlocked tribunal talks.[179] Other donors generally followed suit. Cambodia obtained large and consistent annual aid packages throughout the process, despite frequent criticism from donors on human rights issues—including a pledge of $635 million in 2002, when the dispute over the Khmer Rouge tribunal was near its zenith.[180]

A further reason for Cambodia's negotiating success was that the United States and other key governments were adamant about pursuing prosecutions. Although the RGC expressed a strong interest in trials as well, Hun Sen's shifting positions cast doubt on the strength of that commitment. The RGC's lack of urgency in arranging for trials after the UN pullout in early 2002 and its decision not to submit the revised ECCC Law to the National Assembly in June 2003, which led to a lengthy delay, raise doubts as well. At a minimum, the RGC was willing to wait.

It is a basic principle of bargaining that the side more prepared to accept an alternative to a negotiated agreement enjoys superior leverage in the talks.[181] From a Cambodian standpoint, a breakdown in talks would likely have led to one of two acceptable (if not ideal) outcomes: domestic trials without a stamp of UN legitimacy or no trials at all. For key states involved in the talks, those outcomes would have been much less acceptable. As long as the Cambodian Government was willing to wait, an international thirst to see justice done—and the absence of easy ways to force Hun Sen's hand—made it likely that key states would pressure the UN side to compromise and undercut the Secretariat's bargaining leverage. That is precisely what happened. Corell argues that there were "many involved behind the scenes," including several interested states, which explains why "the UN Secretariat was obliged to accept features that have led to the difficulties that now exist."[182]

CONCLUSION

The ECCC's first international Co-Prosecutor, Robert Petit, has said: "In the end, the victims of the Khmer Rouge got the tribunal that Hun Sen and his allies, including other former Khmer Rouge throughout the regime, wanted."[183]

Critics have argued from the outset that the CPP enjoys too much control over the tribunal, allowing it to interfere with and corrupt the process for pecuniary or political gain, putting the UN's reputation at risk, and setting a troublesome precedent for future mass crimes courts. Given the Cambodian Government's strong bargaining position, however, a UN-led process along the Sierra Leone model was highly unlikely. Etcheson argues that from the standpoint of the tribunal's key international sponsors, "to a pretty large extent, this deal was about as good as could be had under the circumstances."[184]

The resulting ECCC is undeniably a cumbersome and fragile institution, depending heavily on a government with a weak record of judicial integrity and independence and requiring the cooperation of two sides with a long record of mutual distrust. Political compromises also left the ECCC with a complex structure—including a bifurcated administration, pairs of Co-Prosecutors and Co-Investigating Judges, and a Pre-Trial Chamber—that raises serious efficiency challenges.

As the remainder of this book will show, the Court has struggled to carry out its functions efficiently given its institutional complexity, and it has often been on the verge of falling off of its tracks as political interference, corruption allegations, and other integrity concerns test its basic viability. The behavior and initiative of individual actors have sometimes helped the Court achieve important successes, but the ECCC's structure has presented even its most talented and committed personnel and supporters with an uphill battle for functional effectiveness.

Chapter 2

PAIRING THE COURT'S NATIONAL AND INTERNATIONAL FEATURES

All new mass crimes courts involve considerable establishment challenges, from the mundane to the extraordinary. Funds must be raised, staff must be hired, suitable premises must be equipped, basic administrative procedures and support must be developed. The court's procedures and the scope of its jurisdiction and authority must be determined. Because foundational documents are political compromises inevitably riddled with lacunae, much of the character of a new court is created over time through practice instilled by those entrusted with decision-making power, such as administrative heads, prosecutors, and judges. Appealable rulings may take years to reach finality on key issues—time a court with a limited lifespan can ill afford.

The ECCC has faced all these difficulties and more. As the first civil-law-based mass crimes tribunal, the ECCC has been required to forge a new legal path. Compounding this challenge, its unique hybrid features raised many hurdles as Court officials worked to translate the 2003 Framework Agreement and 2004 ECCC Law into a functioning judicial institution. In particular, ECCC officials have had to manage the difficult task of "pairing" the international and domestic aspects of the Court. Although that theme pervades all of the Court's operations, this chapter focuses on three distinct sets of challenges that the ECCC faced almost immediately after it opened its doors in the summer of 2006. First, the Court has struggled to run an efficient and transparent judicial process in an institution staffed by two pairs of officials with investigatory powers and comprising two chambers of appeal. Second, it has endeavored to pair national and international substantive laws, both of which present interpretive challenges due to the Court's temporal jurisdiction in the late 1970s. Third, the ECCC has had to determine what blend of national and international procedural rules to apply. The difficulty of fusing the tribunal's various domestic and international elements has arguably resulted in the most complex, cumbersome, and challenging mass crimes process to date.

THE ECCC'S AMBIGUOUS INSTITUTIONAL IDENTITY

Many of the ECCC's challenges are rooted in the fact that it was born with an ambiguous legal identity, neither fully domestic nor fully international in nature. Although the Framework Agreement set many of the terms for the ECCC, the Court was created by the ECCC Law within the national judicial system, making the ECCC the only hybrid court featuring UN involvement to be established by an act by a domestic legislature.[1] Cambodian Deputy Prime Minister Sok An has called it "a national court with international characteristics," noting that it is "firmly located in the national courts but involv[es] both national and international law; national and international judges, prosecutors, staff; and national and international financing."[2] UN Secretary-General Ban Ki-moon has described it similarly.[3] The ECCC's Pre-Trial Chamber (PTC) has called the Court "a special internationalized tribunal" because "[f]or all practical and legal purposes . . . [it] is, and operates as, an independent entity within the Cambodian court structure."[4] Likewise, the Trial Chamber has found that the ECCC "is a separately constituted, independent and internationalized court."[5] "Internationalized," an ambiguous term denoting courts with both national and international legal features, obscures rather than elucidates the Court's legal status, however, as none of the Court's chambers has explained precisely what this appellation means.

Neither the Framework Agreement nor the ECCC Law addresses the relationship between the ECCC and other Cambodian courts. The ECCC has an independent structure and specialized jurisdiction, and it incorporates foreign staff. It is functionally autonomous, but unlike the Special Court for Sierra Leone (SCSL) and Special Tribunal for Lebanon (STL), it does not have concurrent jurisdiction with domestic courts or primacy over them.[6] Although in practice it is unlikely that any ordinary Cambodian court would concurrently seek to indict persons for crimes of the Khmer Rouge era, there is no legal prohibition on one doing so, nor is there provision for a jurisdictional conflict. The ECCC has neither the power to take a case away from, nor the ability to review the decisions of, other Cambodian courts. As found by the ECCC Trial Chamber, "There is no line of authority between the ECCC and other courts in the Cambodian Judicial system."[7]

The ECCC's legal basis and unclear legal status distinguish it from the SCSL and STL. Although the SCSL is also a hybrid court,[8] its Appeals Chamber ruled that it is "an autonomous and independent institution" outside of Sierra Leone's domestic judiciary and a "new jurisdiction operating in the sphere of international law" that was "vested with juridical capacity" by a treaty between the UN and Sierra Leone.[9] The STL—set up to address the assassination of former Lebanese Prime Minister Rafiq Hariri in 2005 and related offenses—has been characterized as primarily international in nature for similar reasons.[10] The ECCC's legal status is somewhat closer to the models followed in Kosovo and Bosnia and Herzegovina, which are primarily domestic but include international participation.

The ECCC's legal identity is potentially relevant to many issues faced by the Court, such as the choice of procedural rules to apply, the scope of its jurisdiction, and the applicability of Cambodia's penal code to sentencing. Nevertheless, it is likely to remain ambiguous. Unlike the SCSL, no final verdict on its legal character seems possible, because of both the extreme hybridity of the Court and the intensely political nature of the question. Instead, the impact of the Court's hybrid status on which legal principles to apply has been determined on a case-by-case basis, exposing the Court to allegations of cherry-picking laws and rules to achieve desired results.

PAIRING CAMBODIAN AND UN INVESTIGATORS: CHALLENGES TO EFFICIENCY

Although the ECCC is described as a mixed tribunal, it could just as accurately be described as a "divided" one. The ECCC is the only court to be split into national and international "sides" with separate hiring and reporting structures. These unique structural features were intended to accommodate Cambodian ownership of the process while insulating the Court from Cambodian political interference and safeguarding its compliance with international standards. However, they have created a Rube Goldberg–like apparatus that at times seems designed to ensure that few of the aging accused will live until judgment. During tribunal negotiations in 2003, the UN Secretary-General argued that the ECCC was "structured and organized in a way that was highly complex and which afforded ample scope for obstruction and delay in the conduct of their proceedings."[11] Former Ieng Sary defense lawyer Michael G. Karnavas wonders:

> Did the people negotiating from New York actually know what they were doing? Because I think the locals did. They wanted a process in place that had all sorts of safety valves that would allow it to stall or to be controlled at the local level. And that's a major flaw.[12]

The ECCC is unique in having national and international Co-Prosecutors and in having national and international Co-Investigating Judges (CIJs).[13] The ECCC's structure grants investigatory powers to both pairs of individuals and the offices they co-lead: the Office of the Co-Prosecutors (OCP) and Office of the Co-Investigating Judges (OCIJ). Together, the Co-Prosecutors conduct preliminary investigations into crimes within the jurisdiction of the Court.[14] Unique among hybrid courts, the ECCC retains the French-based civil law preference for giving investigative judges the primary investigatory role. The Co-Prosecutors open a judicial investigation by sending the CIJs an introductory submission outlining the facts and naming persons to be investigated.[15] The CIJs can only investigate the facts set forth in the introductory submission unless they receive permission from the Co-Prosecutors in the form of a supplementary submission.[16] They may also charge persons not named in a submission after "seeking the advice" of the Co-Prosecutors.[17] The Co-Prosecutors thus control which crime sites are investigated, while the CIJs make the final decision about which persons to send to trial and for what alleged offenses.[18]

The Framework Agreement requires the "cos" in each office to "cooperate with a view to arriving at a common approach,"[19] but it also anticipates disagreements. If the national and international heads of the same office cannot agree, they may register the dispute and take it before the Pre-Trial Chamber (PTC). Former international CIJ Marcel Lemonde has described this as "probably the worst structure that you can imagine."[20] The Court also has two distinct appellate bodies—the PTC and Supreme Court Chamber (SCC)—whose decisions cannot be appealed. Yet PTC decisions are final only with regard to "co" disputes; SCC decisions are final on all other matters. This duplication of authority allows challenges to be brought four or more times before resolution. PTC Judge Rowan Downing has called this remarkably complex system "a waste of time which has caused years of delay[.]"[21]

Two Pairs of Two Investigators

The political decision to endow the Court with two co-equal prosecutors and investigating judges presents a serious structural challenge to judicial efficiency.[22] Although the Co-Prosecutors' investigation is intended to be "preliminary," and in the civil law system may be brief, in practice the Co-Prosecutors had over one year to investigate due to the judges' inability to finalize the Court's rules of procedure until mid-2007.[23] This delay is thus not attributable to conflicts within the OCP, and it appears that the national and international sides generally have had a productive relationship despite an ongoing disagreement over whether or not to charge additional suspects (discussed in chapter 6). Early difficulties in the working relations between the predominantly common law–trained staff of the OCP and the civil law–trained staff of the OCIJ have often been attributed to their different legal orientations.[24]

Due to the secrecy of the judicial investigation, it is difficult to determine if delays in indicting the first five charged persons were the consequence of the different viewpoints or work styles of the national and international CIJs or other factors. The international CIJ at that time has noted that because there are "co" heads of the office, "[E]very decision is like negotiating a treaty. In France or elsewhere, taking a decision takes half an hour, here we need 8 days."[25] After receiving the Co-Prosecutors' first introductory submission, the Co-Investigating Judges split accused Kaing Guek Eav *alias* Duch's role in the S-21 detention center (Case 001) from the case against the other four charged persons (Case 002), citing the need for "expedited resolution."[26] The judicial investigation of Duch then took an additional 10 months to close[27]—resulting in nearly two years of investigation of an accused who admitted to most of the facts against him. The judicial investigation against the other four charged persons, who contested their guilt, took an additional two and a half years[28]—an investigation almost as long as the original life expectancy of the Court.

Investigating Judges and Mass Crimes Trials: Efficiency vs. Transparency

The inclusion of CIJs in the ECCC's structure has posed challenges to the Court's transparency and efficiency. In adversarial legal systems, the parties investigate the facts and present their versions of events orally at trial in the light most beneficial to their legal interests. In inquisitorial systems, all evidence is gathered confidentially by a public official, such as an investigating judge, and placed in an evidentiary case file for review by the trial court.[29] Although all previous international and hybrid courts have been predominantly common-law oriented, in theory, the inquisitorial system could have two advantages over the adversarial system in mass crimes trials: efficiency and objectivity. An independent and neutral official "seeks the truth" by gathering both inculpatory and exculpatory evidence in a written dossier[30] and presenting all information necessary for the trial judges to reach judgment. An impartial collection of facts in a case file could result in a more efficient process and greater historical accuracy than the partial view of events offered by adversarial parties.

However, there are conceptual and practical problems with following the civil law approach in mass crimes trials. Significantly, the judicial investigation—which at least according to the French model is "by far the longest part of the case"—is confidential, with the public trial intended only to verify rather than fully air the detailed findings.[31] Although criminal prosecutions of individuals must be focused on particular crime sites and charges and cannot be confused with a truth commission process addressing an entire historical period, such proceedings inevitably address and establish facts within the context of larger, often politicized events. The logic of trying a few top leaders for serious crimes so that the public can witness accountability and learn why and how events occurred is undermined if the public cannot see justice in action. Clint Williamson, former UN Special Expert to advise on the UN Assistance to the Khmer Rouge Trials, argues:

> The idea that having a judicial investigation process behind closed doors would speed the process was deeply flawed, because there is so much appetite from the public to hear the story . . . a lengthy trial phase is bound to happen.[32]

The voluminous materials at issue in large-scale atrocity trials also diminish the benefits of a judge-led investigation. At the ECCC, the burden of becoming familiar with the structure, workings, and policies of the Communist Party of Kampuchea, sifting through the plethora of existing documentary evidence, and speaking to the substantial number of potential witnesses of crimes occurring over 30 years ago is enormous. In these circumstances, placing all investigative responsibility on the shoulders of two co-judges may have offered no advantage in the goal of seeking "truth," as the CIJs' capacity and time was limited, and their findings inevitably selective. They simply could not be expected to conduct as exhaustive an investigation as would four separate defense teams and a prosecutor's office, each actively seeking and contesting evidence.[33] Moreover, because the CIJs were required to assemble a complete case to put before the Trial Chamber, their lengthy investigation created a bottleneck preventing the entire process from moving toward public trial proceedings.[34]

Some ECCC officials expected that the Court would combine the best of civil law and common law: an efficient judge-led investigation followed by a short, somewhat adversarial trial with a few key witnesses.[35] The first international CIJ initially estimated six months for investigation and three months for trial.[36] However, due to his decision to not allow defense teams to confront witnesses during the investigation,[37] the Trial Chamber's inability to become familiar with all the information in the massive case file or apply hybrid rules consistently, and the public interest in observing the process, the Court's trial proceedings incorporate a jumbled assortment of inquisitorial and adversarial practices undercutting the anticipated expediency of a civil law trial. Former CIJ Marcel Lemonde says the idea was to adopt a system to ensure more efficiency due to the age of the suspects. However, "the dish was not exactly what we ordered." The ECCC has not held the first civil law mass crimes trial, he suggests, because a genuine civil law process didn't happen.[38]

Numerous witnesses have been heard—to all appearances both to edify the public and to familiarize the Trial Chamber with the nuances of these complex cases. Although civil law judges normally direct the questioning of parties and selected witnesses, in Case 002 the judges reduced their burden to become experts with the case file by tasking the parties with primary responsibility for questioning judicially selected witnesses.[39] Moreover, responding to challenges to the fairness of the judicial investigation, the Trial Chamber decided that it would place greater weight on evidence supported by oral testimony. In civil law jurisdictions, and at many mass crimes courts, trial judges often rely on written witness statements in lieu of oral testimony when the statements do not speak to the acts or conduct of the accused.[40] However, the ECCC Trial Chamber has found that, though witness statements taken by the CIJs are "entitled to a presumption of relevance and reliability[,]"[41] they may be entitled "to little, if any probative value or weight" if the witness does not testify at trial due to the lack of prior opportunity for confrontation.[42] These incongruous results highlight the ongoing tension between the desire for trial efficiency and the obligation to provide a fair, highly visible, public trial.

The ECCC's procedure—two separate investigations, preparation of a dossier containing all the evidence, followed by an oral hearing of the evidence in court—is both slow and repetitive.[43] International Deputy Co-Prosecutor William Smith contends that "[a] party-driven system is better for mass crimes as it is the fastest way to get to the truth," but nevertheless believes, "[I]t is important to use the local legal system so the process is relevant."[44] Cambodian CIJ You Bunleng argues that although the investigation procedures have been time-consuming, the procedures used during trial are more efficient than those of the common law system.[45] Yet to most observers, the ECCC's hybrid structure has produced the "worst possible outcome."[46] Most ECCC actors agree.[47] As Trial Chamber Judge Silvia Cartwright has noted, it is indeed "anomalous" that the ECCC model necessitates a "full-length judicial investigation and a full-length trial."[48]

The Pre-Trial Chamber: A Duplicate Appeals Chamber

The ECCC's inefficiency is due not only to the novel challenge of incorporating a judicial investigation into a mass crimes context. It also results from the incorporation of a pretrial chamber. Under the ECCC Law, the PTC's only responsibility is to decide disagreements between pairs of national and international Co-Prosecutors or CIJs.[49] However, the Internal Rules adopted by the ECCC in 2007 expanded the PTC's jurisdiction to include appeals against orders of the CIJs. PTC decisions are not appealable, but the Internal Rules do not address the extent to which its appellate decisions bind the Trial Chamber. The Trial Chamber has held that it has "no competence to review decisions of the Pre-Trial Chamber."[50] As a consequence, before being finally resolved, core questions can be raised at least four times before different judicial bodies: the CIJs, the PTC, the Trial Chamber, and the Supreme Court Chamber.[51]

For example, before Ieng Sary's death, the effect of his pardon and amnesty was addressed by the CIJs twice, reviewed by the PTC twice on appeal, then reviewed *de novo* by the Trial Chamber before it was appealed to the SCC for final resolution.[52] His defense counsel Michael Karnavas called this a waste of both money and effort. "Now I have to jump through four different hoops in order to be due diligent so I can say I preserved my record for appeal."[53]

The PTC recognized the potential overlap and in general exercised its jurisdiction narrowly. It emphasized that questions raised on appeal that are also explicitly within the jurisdiction of the Trial Chamber can "be raised and addressed fully at later stages of the proceedings[.]"[54] For example, in response to Duch's request for a remedy for illegal detention by the Cambodian Military Court, the PTC determined, "It would not be appropriate for the Pre-Trial Chamber to make the statements requested when another judicial body may well become seized of this case for trial and will have to make its own decisions on the basis of the evidence and the submissions made before it."[55] Similarly, it reportedly did not want to "pre-empt" the Trial Chamber's ruling on the application of "Joint Criminal Enterprise" liability to ECCC proceedings.[56]

This approach has not forestalled repeated rulings on fundamental issues, however. In assessing the impact of Ieng Sary's 1996 pardon and amnesty on the appropriateness of his detention, the Pre-Trial Chamber focused narrowly on the Court's ability to hold him in provisional custody and did not reach the underlying jurisdictional issue.[57] However, when Ieng Sary again raised the question on appeal from the Closing Order, the PTC was obligated to address the heart of the matter.[58]

The defense argued, "Such a fundamental issue as whether the ECCC has jurisdiction to try Mr. IENG Sary may not be left for resolution at a later date [by the Trial Chamber] when it can be decided now."[59] The PTC agreed, emphasizing that by sending Ieng Sary to trial the CIJs had implicitly confirmed the Court's jurisdiction over him.[60] "Concluding otherwise would deprive Ieng Sary from exercising his right of appeal on a jurisdictional issue that was properly raised before the Co-Investigating Judges but upon which the later failed to make a judicial determination."[61] As a consequence, it issued a ruling on this matter in the same decision in which it sent Ieng Sary before the Trial Chamber, which was immediately requested to review the issue *de novo*.

In this and many other instances, the ECCC's complex hybrid structure has compromised the Court's efficiency.[62] As discussed in subsequent chapters, this has not prevented the Court from making decisions on sound judicial bases and in a manner consistent with international standards. It has, however, elongated a process that has far outlived its original three-year mandate and contributed to further delays in trials that are already well overdue.

PAIRING INTERNATIONAL AND CAMBODIAN SUBSTANTIVE LAW: JURISDICTIONAL CHALLENGES

In addition to pairing two hybrid investigatory offices and managing a pair of appeals chambers, the ECCC has had to couple elements of domestic and international criminal law. Hybrid substantive jurisdiction is a hallmark of a mixed court like the ECCC. The ECCC has authority to try suspects for the domestic crimes of homicide, torture, and religious persecution under the 1956 Cambodian Penal Code and the well-known international offenses of genocide, crimes against humanity, and war crimes.[63] The Court is also mandated to try the novel crimes of destruction of cultural property and attacks against diplomatic personnel; however, these have not been charged, likely because the elements of both offenses are unclear.[64]

Applying both national and international criminal law always introduces complexity, but the ECCC faced particular challenges due to the scope of its temporal jurisdiction. It is the only hybrid court to prosecute international crimes committed in the 1970s, after the Nuremberg trials laid the foundation for modern international criminal jurisprudence but well before the International Criminal Tribunals for the former Yugoslavia and Rwanda (ICTY and ICTR) developed international criminal law rapidly in the 1990s. As a result, the ECCC has had to do more than simply apply two bodies of law: it has had to determine the scope of criminal liability for international crimes during the 1970s and the effect of a domestic statute of limitations. The ECCC Chambers did not accept defense arguments mooting the applicability of international crimes, but disagreement between national and international judges regarding the applicability of the domestic statute of limitations has prevented conviction on the basis of national crimes.

Jurisdiction to Apply International Crimes

The ECCC's ambiguous hybrid form has led to challenges to its authority, as defense teams have highlighted the Court's national character and argued that it lacks jurisdiction to prosecute international crimes and modes of liability. In indicting the accused in Case 002, the Co-Investigating Judges found that "[t]he question whether the ECCC are Cambodian or international 'in nature' has no bearing on the ECCC's jurisdiction to prosecute [international] crimes, provided that the principle of *nullum crimen sine lege* [no crime without law] is respected."[65] To the contrary, the defense said the issue was "fundamental" to the applicability of international crimes and forms of liability in ECCC proceedings.[66]

Nullum crimen sine lege prohibits the retroactive application of criminal laws. The Framework Agreement, ECCC Law, and Internal Rules do not include an explicit *nullum crimen* prohibition, but the Agreement references Article 15(1) of the International Covenant on Civil and Political Rights (ICCPR), which states in part: "No one shall be held guilty of any criminal offence on account of any act or omission which did not constitute a criminal offence, under national or international law, at the time when it was committed." In the *Duch* appeal judgment, the SCC explicitly recognized this provision's applicability to the ECCC.[67]

The ICTY has held that for international courts to conform to this principle of legality, acts that are not criminalized under either domestic or international law at the time they are committed may not be prosecuted. Moreover, the proscribed mode of responsibility or offense must have been sufficiently foreseeable and accessible to the accused. This requires that a charged person "be able to appreciate that [his or her] conduct is criminal in the sense generally understood, without reference to any specific provision."[68] The prohibited act may have been proscribed under either conventional or customary law, and need not have been criminalized in precisely the same terms in which it is prosecuted as long as the underlying conduct is the same.[69] The appalling character of the act may undercut any claim by the accused that they were unaware that their acts were criminal.[70]

Because the ECCC is the first internationalized court with a temporal jurisdiction falling between World War II and the rapid development of international criminal law after the Cold War, it is the first to authoritatively define the existence and scope of international crimes during that period. The Chambers cannot merely assume that each substantive crime and mode of liability placed within the Court's jurisdiction by the ECCC Law complies with the *nullum crimen* principle, but must consider this principle with regard to each substantive crime and mode and define its elements accordingly.[71]

Modes of liability refer to the various ways by which an individual can participate in the commission of a crime, either directly or indirectly. This is a crucial concept—particularly in mass-atrocity trials targeting leadership figures who may never have personally killed or tortured anyone. At the ECCC, accused persons may be charged with either direct responsibility or their failure to exercise responsibility as a superior. Article 29 of the ECCC Law provides that direct responsibility attaches whenever an accused person "planned, instigated, ordered, aided and abetted, or committed" a crime over which the Court has jurisdiction.

In the Court's second case the defense teams argued that, because the ECCC is a national court, in accordance with Cambodian law's narrow definition of *nullum crimen sine lege*,[72] it could only prosecute acts criminalized under Cambodian domestic law during the 1975–79 period.[73] In their view, because no international crimes or modes of liability were criminalized in Cambodia's 1956 Criminal Code, and international law is not directly applicable in Cambodia's dualist system, the ECCC has no power to try them.[74]

The SCC has not yet considered this Case 002 challenge, but in its Case 001 judgment it found the international *nullum crimen* principle applicable to the proceedings due to the ECCC Law's reference to ICCPR article 15, and without elaboration followed international jurisprudence in determining that chargeable offenses may have existed under either national law or international law including treaties, custom, or general principles.[75] However, the ICTY authority cited by the SCC specifically states that the "accessibility" requirement does not exclude reliance on customary international law "in the case of an international tribunal[.]"[76] It therefore remains unclear on what doctrinal basis the SCC has found this approach likewise appropriate for a hybrid national court.

Addressing the defense challenge directly, the Pre-Trial Chamber found that by giving the ECCC the authority to apply international law in accordance with the ICCPR's formulation of *nullum crimen sine lege*, Cambodia created an exception to the rule of legality under national law.[77] It ruled: "Even if the ECCC were considered to be a simply domestic court, jurisdiction is not in question as long as a law that grants it exists and related requirements are met."[78] Following this reasoning, international crimes and modes of liability in existence during the temporal jurisdiction of the Court need not have been implemented by domestic Cambodian law at that time to be applied by the ECCC.[79] The PTC thus determined that the nature of the court as national or "internationalized" has no bearing on the Court's ability to apply international law.[80] The issue is currently before the Trial Chamber, which has chosen not to issue its ruling until judgment.

The defense also raised concerns with regard to the legality of prosecuting specific international crimes. Two of their arguments touch on areas of long-standing uncertainty in international law. Because of disagreement among the ECCC Chambers on the appropriate interpretation of sketchy past precedent, even when there is finality for the parties, the legal questions are likely to linger for consideration by other courts as well as legal scholars.

Because the Nuremberg Charter required a nexus between crimes against humanity and another crime within its jurisdiction (crimes against peace or war crimes), there has long been a dispute as to whether this nexus was required by international law, and if so, at what point in time the nexus was no longer a required legal element. In the *Duch* case, the Trial Chamber charted new territory in finding that the customary definition of crimes against humanity from 1975 to 1979 did not require the existence of a nexus with an armed conflict.[81] However, in considering an appeal from the Closing Order in Case 002, the Pre-Trial Chamber reviewed the precedent at length and found that, due to a lack of clarity in the law, a nexus was required.[82] Reviewing the same historical precedent, but with different emphasis, the Trial Chamber once again affirmed that no nexus was required.[83] This issue will be finally determined by the SCC, but due to the restrictive right of interlocutory appeal, not until its review of the first Case 002 judgment.[84]

Because the crime of rape was an enumerated crime against humanity in the statutes of post–World War II courts, the ECCC Trial Chamber found that it existed as a crime under international law during the temporal jurisdiction of the Court.[85] Nevertheless, in Case 001 it characterized the one proved instance of rape as the crime against humanity of torture. On appeal, the SCC overturned the Trial Chamber's finding that rape existed as a distinct crime against humanity in the 1970s, finding that "[a]lthough rape had . . . been well established as a war crime by 1975, its status as a crime against humanity under international law had not yet crystallized" until the 1990s.[86] Nevertheless, it upheld the Trial Chamber's finding that the rape could, and in this circumstance did, amount to the crime against humanity of torture.[87]

In Case 002, the Pre-Trial Chamber likewise found that rape did not exist as an enumerated crime against humanity during the temporal jurisdiction of the Court and struck the charge from the indictment, instead characterizing the act as falling within the residual category of crimes against humanity of "other inhumane acts."[88] Because the first Case 002 trial does not include rape charges, there will be no judgment on this characterization unless a second trial is held.

Differences between the Chambers on these questions do not appear to be the product of the Court's hybrid nature but instead of the challenges inherent in assessing trends in customary international criminal law prior to its exponential development in the 1990s. Such challenges suggest that, to the extent possible, hybrid courts with a limited lifespan and tenuous funding should not be tasked with applying novel crimes—as was the ECCC with regard to crimes of destruction of cultural property and attacks against diplomatic personnel. It is incongruous to expect such courts to both act swiftly and drive the development of new law.

JURISDICTION TO APPLY INTERNATIONAL MODES OF LIABILITY

The primary controversy that the ECCC has addressed with regard to modes of liability is the appropriateness of charging the accused with "committing" crimes through their active participation in a common criminal plan, also known as a "joint criminal enterprise" or JCE. JCE is a theory of liability first articulated in ICTY jurisprudence and, though not listed in the ICTY/R or SCSL Statutes, has been found to be contained therein as a form of "commission." It is used to connect high-level accused—the planners, organizers, and ideologues who may not be physically connected to criminal acts but were catalysts for them—to the lower-level offenders who executed the crimes at their behest. It is particularly useful in a situation such as that faced by the ECCC, where those who carried out crimes (for example, Duch in Case 001) claim they were acting under duress, and those at the top of the organizational hierarchy (the senior leaders in Case 002) claim the crimes were committed by errant or overenthusiastic lower-level cadres.

There are three JCE categories.[89] All three involve "a plurality of persons" acting with a common purpose to commit crimes within the jurisdiction of the Court. The accused must contribute to this common plan. Each JCE category has a different mental or *mens rea* requirement. Participants in a JCE-1 or "basic" JCE must share the intent to commit a crime within the jurisdiction of the court. JCE-2, also known as "systemic" JCE, is a variant of the basic form and is characterized by the existence of an organized system of ill-treatment.

Thus far, it has only been found in cases involving prison camps, including the S-21 detention center. To be held liable for JCE-2, participants must have had personal knowledge of the system of ill-treatment and intended to further that system. An accused who participates in a basic or systemic JCE can also be held responsible for JCE-3, known as "extended" JCE, for crimes falling outside the scope of the plan if it was foreseeable that those crimes would be committed in furtherance of the plan and the accused knowingly took that risk. JCE-3 is the most contentious due to the fact that the accused need not intend or play a role in the "extended" crime with which he or she is charged.

The status of JCE liability as of 1975 has never been addressed squarely in legal proceedings. In the *Tadic* case, the ICTY determined that JCE has existed under customary international law as of 1992. In so doing, it relied primarily on post–World War II, pre-1975 international and domestic precedent. However, its reasoning remains highly controversial.

When the issue of JCE arose in the ECCC's first case, Ieng Sary sought to offer submissions on its applicability, even though he was not an accused in the proceedings. His defense argued, "The application of JCE liability at the ECCC fundamentally affects Mr. IENG Sary because he is alleged [in the indictment] to be part of the same 'common criminal plan' as Duch. In these circumstances, Mr. IENG Sary has a clear interest in the outcome of the appeal[.]"[90] The PTC noted that Ieng was not a party to the case, and that neither the Internal Rules nor the Cambodian Code of Criminal Procedure provides a right for third-party intervention. Moreover, the decision would "not be directly applicable to Ieng Sary, who will still have the possibility to challenge the application of the theory of joint criminal enterprise in [the case] to which he is a party."[91] A joint intervention by co-accused Ieng Thirith, Nuon Chea, and Khieu Samphan was similarly rebuffed. The Pre-Trial Chamber reasoned:

> [I]t is inherent to courts where several proceedings are pending that a decision in one case on a legal issue will guide the court in future similar cases where no new circumstances or arguments are raised. It does not result from that situation that charged persons have the right to intervene in a case file to which they are not parties to submit their views on an issue.[92]

This ruling was later confirmed by the Trial Chamber, which found no violation of "equality of arms," as this principle "cannot be applied to parties in separate and distinct trials."[93]

Although these decisions are based on sound precedent, they disregard the fact that the ECCC, unlike other domestic and some international courts, will try only a handful of defendants for related crimes. Moreover, Duch, who essentially pled guilty, had little motivation to argue vigorously against the applicability of JCE, yet the final ruling was likely to be followed in Case 002, in which it would have a major impact. Indeed, the Trial Chamber found that JCE-1 and JCE-2 fall within the jurisdiction of the Court both in the *Duch* case[94] and also subsequently in Case 002.[95]

The Trial Chamber did not, however, make any findings about JCE-3 in Case 001. When the applicability of JCE-3 arose in the Court's second case, the Trial Chamber agreed with the Pre-Trial Chamber that the precedent cited by the *Tadic* court was unclear and its legal reasoning was unconvincing.[96] As a consequence, it ruled that JCE-3 "did not form part of customary international law and was not a general principle of law at the time relevant[.]"[97] Although the Trial Chamber's decision is limited to the ECCC's temporal jurisdiction, it is a direct challenge to *Tadic*'s finding that JCE-3 existed in customary international law at the time that decision was handed down, and thus one of the Court's most notable jurisprudential legacies.

In addition to direct responsibility, Article 29 of the ECCC Law allows accused persons to be held responsible as superiors for the crimes of their subordinates if they "had effective command and control or authority and control over the subordinate . . . knew or had reason to know that the subordinate was about to commit such acts or had done so, and . . . failed to take the necessary and reasonable measures to prevent such acts or punish the perpetrators." All international and hybrid courts provide for liability for superior responsibility. However, the application of this doctrine to civilian (as opposed to military) hierarchies as of 1975 has not been litigated previously.

In the *Duch* judgment, the ECCC Trial Chamber found the accused, a civilian prison chief, responsible as a superior for international crimes committed by his subordinates.[98] In Case 002, the accused have argued that superior responsibility did not exist in customary international law during the temporal jurisdiction of the Court, and if it did, it was applicable only to military commanders and war crimes. Although finding the post–World War II jurisprudence articulation of the doctrine to be "not always clear or complete" and the application of its elements "at times inconsistent and incomplete," the Pre-Trial Chamber has ruled that this mode of liability existed under customary law by 1975[99] and extended to nonmilitary superiors.[100] As the Trial Chamber has already accepted the applicability of this mode in Case 001, it is likely to uphold this ruling.

Jurisdiction to Apply National Crimes

The ECCC's ability to try national crimes has been questioned on the basis of the domestic statute of limitations. Article 3 of the ECCC Law gives the Court the jurisdiction to hear cases involving the crimes of homicide, torture, and religious persecution in the 1956 Cambodian Penal Code. The inclusion of domestic offenses in a court's jurisdiction is often highlighted as one of the key indicators of a hybrid tribunal. For example, the SCSL Statute provides for jurisdiction over domestic offenses relating to the abuse of girls under the Prevention of Cruelty to Children Act of 1926 and to the wanton destruction of property under the Malicious Damage Act of 1861. According to the Secretary-General, this authority was provided "in cases where a specific situation or an aspect of it was considered to be either unregulated or inadequately regulated under international law."[101]

As both the national and international crimes within the ECCC's jurisdiction are likely to cover the same underlying acts, this was probably not the reason for which both are provided. The inclusion of national law offers a practical benefit: it allows the prosecution to charge an accused person with both international and domestic offenses with different elements, making it more likely that they will be able to secure a conviction.[102] For example, even if the Co-Prosecutors were unable to establish that an accused was responsible for murder committed as part of an attack against the civilian population (a crime against humanity of murder), they might still be able to prove that he or she was responsible for simple murder under the domestic code.[103]

Domestic law charges may also provide symbolic benefits. Prosecution of domestic charges demonstrates that Khmer Rouge leaders violated not only international law but also Cambodian law, possibly making the proceedings less "foreign" and therefore more meaningful to Cambodians. As noted by the Co-Prosecutors in their appeal of the *Duch* Closing Order, some commentators "have argued that charging national crimes will foster a sense of 'ownership' of the judicial proceedings for the Cambodian judiciary and the population as a whole."[104]

At the SCSL, no charges were ever brought for crimes under national law.[105] Comparatively, the ECCC Co-Prosecutors charged all accused in Cases 001 and 002 with national offenses but were thwarted from pursuing them due to a split between the national and international judges on the applicability of the domestic criminal code's 10-year statute of limitations.

Statute of Limitations for National Crimes

The 1956 Cambodian Criminal Code includes a ten-year statute of limitations (SOL) for indicting criminalized acts. The ECCC Law extended the SOL by thirty years,[106] raising *nullum crimen sine lege* questions. If the 1956 Law's SOL began running in 1979, the time available for prosecution would have lapsed in 1989 unless it was "tolled"—suspended because of the Khmers Rouges' complete destruction of the Cambodian justice system. The prosecution argued that the Cambodian judiciary was incapable of prosecuting Khmer Rouge leaders from 1979 until at least 1993. If the SOL expired in 2003, its extension in 2001 would be valid, and the accused could be prosecuted for crimes under the 1956 Code without violating fair trial standards.

In Case 001, there was a strict divide between the national and international judges of the Trial Chamber on the issue, with the national judges opining that the Cambodian judiciary continued to be dysfunctional until the establishment of the Kingdom of Cambodia in 1993, and the international judges finding that the prosecution had not proved that investigation and prosecution of Khmer Rouge crimes before that time would have been impossible, not merely challenging.[107] Politically this was a remarkable development, as the Government has in the past referenced with pride the 1979 *in absentia* trial of Pol Pot and Ieng Sary. Of greater legal significance, the national judges found they had no competence to review the correctness of a 2001 decision by the Cambodian Constitutional Council that "in substance" found the limitations period to be compatible with the constitution.[108]

In contrast, the international judges considered the Council's decision ambiguous and thus found it necessary to construe national law in light of international standards.[109] Considering jurisprudence of the European Court of Human Rights and other national jurisdictions, as well as the recent approach of the Cambodian legislature toward statutory limitations in the domestic code, they found that the ECCC Law provided an "insufficient basis" to prosecute national crimes before the ECCC.[110] In the absence of a supermajority of judges, the Chamber found itself unable to consider the accused person's responsibility for national crimes.[111]

As a consequence of the Trial Chamber's split decision, the Co-Investigating Judges were unable to reach a consensus on how to proceed with national crimes in the Case 002 Closing Order. In order to avoid slowing down the proceedings, they did not file a dispute but instead by mutual agreement left the matter for the Trial Chamber to decide.[112] However, the Trial Chamber noted that the Closing Order provided neither a description of the material facts on which the charges could be based nor the applicable modes of liability.[113] For that reason it found that the Closing Order failed to inform the accused of the scope of the national charges, and they could not form the basis for trial proceedings.[114] It was therefore unnecessary for them to rule again on the substance of the statute of limitations argument. As a consequence, the most national of all hybrid courts will not be prosecuting any national crimes.

The ECCC's efforts to pair Cambodian and international criminal law reinforce the difficulty of operating an unprecedented hybrid court. Considerable time and judicial attention had to be devoted to determining the Court's substantive jurisdiction before trials could be held. The Chambers have issued sound jurisprudence on complex issues of first impression, most notably charting their own path on the contentious topic of JCE-3. However, the Trial Chamber's split decision on the Court's jurisdiction over national crimes illustrates the propensity of national and international judges at the ECCC to fall into distinct camps on politically sensitive issues. Although international judges have disagreed with each other numerous times, there appears to have been only one public instance of Cambodian judges on the same bench disagreeing with each other.[115] This tendency and its detrimental impact on the Court's jurisprudence is related to the important issue of judicial independence, discussed in detail in chapter 6.

PAIRING LOCAL AND INTERNATIONAL RULES OF PROCEDURE

The ECCC faced an even greater challenge in blending domestic and international rules of procedure. The Framework Agreement and ECCC Law dictate that the ECCC's procedure must be "in accordance with Cambodian Law,"[116] with guidance from international procedural rules only where there is a lacuna, uncertainty in interpretation, or a question of consistency with international standards.[117] This provision emphasizes the national institutional character of the ECCC and differentiates the Court from international tribunals such as the SCSL, which was mandated to apply the rules in force at the ICTR and to amend those rules or adopt new ones as necessary.[118] However, the significance of this distinction diminished after the ECCC adopted its own Internal Rules—necessitated by the lack of existing Cambodian procedures. Like other hybrid tribunals, the ECCC generally has interpreted and applied its procedures in conformity with international precedent.

More than almost any other feature of the Court, the decision to have the Court apply Cambodian procedures—despite the lack of an authoritative code, the difficulties of adapting domestic criminal law rules to mass crimes practice, and the lack of precedent for using civil law rules in mass crimes cases—engenders the greatest criticism from Court actors. Although the ECCC is formally part of the Cambodian judicial system, as it grew and evolved through practice, it acted more and more like an international court applying a mixture of both civil and common law procedures, as well as procedures specific to mass crimes courts. In the absence of statutory guidance for many of the novel topics faced by this special court, the only available precedent was the practice of the heavily common law–oriented international tribunals, at which numerous international ECCC staff had previously worked.[119] Nevertheless, Cambodian procedures have remained a source of reference and, especially for the SCC, often a point of departure. Inconsistent practice in pairing these two sources of law by the Chambers led to uncertainty and perceptions of arbitrary or ends-driven decision-making. Michael Karnavas says, "Whenever it suits them they just create new rules" instead of first looking at what is in place in the Cambodian Code: "By judicial fiat they make these decisions. Today we're going to apply this; tomorrow we're going to apply that. Just tell me what the rules are so I know what to expect and how to proceed."[120]

Ieng Thirith Co-Lawyer Diana Ellis says that a hybrid approach to procedures is "generally not a good idea" because meshing together two different culturally based approaches into a coherent system is challenging and time consuming.[121] Michael Karnavas believes that, in hindsight, it would have been better to have modeled the Court's procedure on the simpler ICTY rules than to tinker with the existing system by adding adversarial features, which has created more problems than it has solved.[122] Civil Party Lead Co-Lawyer Elisabeth Simonneau Fort says detailed rules such as those applied by the International Criminal Court, but specifically tailored to the ECCC context, would have been most appropriate for a civil law court, and made it easier to apply international mass crimes jurisprudence.[123] Most interviewees emphasize that domestic procedures are inappropriate for mass crimes trials and should never have been made the basis for the Court's work.[124]

Legal Status and Legitimacy of the ECCC Internal Rules

Unlike the core documents of the ICTY, ICTR, and SCSL, the ECCC Law does not authorize the judges to adopt or amend the Court's rules of evidence and procedure. As originally conceived, the ECCC was intended to directly apply domestic Cambodian rules of criminal procedure and to draw on international rules only as needed.[125] Article 12(1) of the Framework Agreement provides:

> The Procedure shall be in accordance with Cambodian law. Where Cambodian law does not deal with a particular matter, or where there is uncertainty regarding the interpretation or application of a relevant rule of Cambodian law, or where there is a question regarding the consistency of such a rule with international standards, guidance may also be sought in procedural rules established at the international level.

Until the Cambodian Criminal Procedure Code (CPC) was adopted in August 2007, Cambodia lacked a comprehensive criminal procedural code for the Extraordinary Chambers to consult. The ECCC negotiators had blindly deferred to national procedures that did not yet exist and were unlikely to meet the needs of a specialized mass crimes court. For that reason, the ECCC judges almost immediately began drafting rules of procedure and evidence specifically tailored to ECCC proceedings.

According to the former Co-Chairman of the Inter-Governmental Support Group for the Extraordinary Chambers, the Cambodian Government took the position that Article 12(1) could be interpreted to grant the ECCC "rule-making authority as 'effectuated guidance' sought in internationally established procedural rules."[126] In the preamble to the Internal Rules, the judges state that the rules were drafted in order "to consolidate applicable Cambodian procedure for proceedings before the ECCC, and . . . to adopt additional rules where these existing procedures do not deal with a particular matter, or if there is uncertainty regarding their interpretation or application, or if there is a question regarding their consistency with international standards."

Since the adoption of the Internal Rules, there have been challenges to their legality. Both the civil parties and defense teams have argued that their adoption amounts to an act of legislation in violation of the Cambodian Constitution's separation of powers.[127] The *Nuon Chea* team has emphasized that the ECCC is a domestic court that must apply national legislation, with variance from Cambodian procedural rules allowed only on a case-by-case basis.[128] Nuon Chea's lawyers have argued that the Court's Internal Rules go far beyond their expressed aim to "consolidate applicable Cambodian procedure" and are thus *ultra vires* and without legal force.[129]

Considering the language of the Framework Agreement and ECCC Law and the Court's status as a Cambodian court, these arguments are compelling. Unsurprisingly, however, the Trial Chamber judges (who participated in the plenary adopting the Internal Rules) have found that:

> While [the Court's] procedure is in accordance with Cambodian law, the ECCC is entitled to adopt its own Internal Rules in compliance with international standards, which take into account the specific mechanisms necessary to adjudicate mass crimes.[130]

The judges did not address the allegation that they lack statutory authority to convene a rule-making plenary, except to note that "[o]ther international courts" have also adopted rules targeted to complex criminal proceedings.[131] Moreover, they found that the rules of such courts "represent prevailing international standards in relation to cases adjudicating international crimes" and are consistent with the ECCC's obligation to conduct proceedings in accordance with international standards.[132]

The defense also challenged specific provisions of the Internal Rules for departing too drastically from the CPC. For example, when the Rules were amended in 2008 to narrow the scope of appeal, the Defence Support Section (DSS) said, "This means that, at the ECCC, an accused now has a more limited right of appeal than at any other trial court in Cambodia."[133] Although the DSS accepted that the ECCC Law provided the judges authority to "supplement" Cambodian procedural law in "expressly limited circumstances," in its view the judges lacked legal authority "to depart from the Cambodian procedural law to the extent required to adopt the amendment."[134] To this the judges responded by again highlighting the distinct and unique nature of the ECCC's jurisdiction as the basis for their decision to more closely follow international practice.[135]

The CPC is a detailed code drafted by French legal experts and only recently adopted after years of confusion about the applicable procedures in force.[136] Moreover, it is well documented that Cambodian criminal hearings are often abbreviated and fail to comply with basic standards of fairness.[137] Thus, in practice, the procedures that comprise the CPC are to a great extent just as novel for many Cambodian lawyers and judges as they are for the international staff. It has been notable during trial hearings that the Cambodian Trial Chamber Judges often appear more deferential to the views of New Zealand Judge Cartwright on procedural questions, including on the appropriate role of civil parties, than to those of her French counterpart Judge Lavergne.[138] For this reason, the *Nuon Chea* team's argument that the CPC "embodies the legal system [their client] is most familiar with"[139] is not precisely true. Arguably, the decision to provide national "ownership" through the application of incipient domestic procedural law was always a matter of form over substance.

Problematically, the CPC is not even a contemporary representation of French law, which has been modified to address European Court of Human Rights criticisms and perceived weaknesses in the system—including to minimize the role of the investigating judge.[140] Judge Lemonde says, "I regret that the French experts gave Cambodia a tool that was obsolete before it was even used."[141] Therefore, it bears considering that existing domestic procedure may not be the best practice or even one that domestic lawyers support.[142] For example, in 2000, Sok Sam Oeun, Director of the Cambodia Defender's Project, expressed concern about the incorporation of investigative judges into the ECCC structure:

> [W]hat worries me most is what will happen if the tribunal law is passed and implemented before the function of the investigating judge is abolished from the justice system in general. A KR tribunal with an investigating judge will create a strong precedent and make the function of investigating judge much more difficult to remove in the future.[143]

As highlighted by this statement, putting aside the added legal complications of applying domestic criminal procedures in the context of a mass crimes court, in practice there will be multifaceted and unanticipated interactions between a weak national legal system developing after a period of upheaval and an internationalized court. Giving precedence to fledgling national law as an end in itself is questionable, as it may mask more nuanced domestic legal controversies.

Rule-Drafting Controversies

Although both international and national judges accepted the practical need for the Court to adopt its own rules, during the drafting process there were sharp divisions on topics including the relationship between Cambodian and international law[144] and how the ECCC would operate within the Cambodian court structure.[145] The international judges believed that international law standards would need to be applied in many cases; however, the national judges argued that Cambodian law must have primacy because the ECCC is part of the Cambodian judicial system.[146]

Some foreign observers believed that the Cambodian judges unified around a pro-Cambodian law position because they were ill prepared to argue the substance of the legal questions involved.[147] Others suggested that the primary stumbling block was the reluctance of Cambodian judges "to allow international barristers to conduct a robust scrutiny of the case against the accused" due a lack of experience with vigorous defense:[148] "After 28 years everyone thinks they know who the guilty men are. Just put them in prison."[149] Some, however, claimed that the Government was deliberately holding things up. For example, in the view of former Khmer Rouge soldier Lath Nhoung, "The court's process is to show internationals that they are working to try [the Khmer Rouge leaders], but actually they will delay the process until they all die."[150] Most incisively, many noted that "[t]he government only wants to be part of a process it can control[.]"[151]

This view may be borne out by the national judges' apparent efforts to scuttle the power-sharing arrangement painstakingly negotiated in the Agreement and gain control over who would be tried. One of their proposals was that if a disagreement arose between the nationals and internationals about whether or not to issue an indictment, the person under investigation could appeal to the Pre-Trial Chamber for a decision and, if there were no supermajority decision, the case would not proceed.[152] This procedure would not only have directly contradicted the Agreement and Law, but as noted by the American Embassy, would have also given the Cambodians "total veto power" over indictments.[153]

The major issue of public contention was over the scope of defense rights, both with regard to the creation of an ECCC defense office and the ability of foreign defense counsel to appear in court,[154] and to many it appeared that the Court would collapse over the impasse. At one point the international Co-Investigating Judge stated, "If next month the new rules are not adopted . . . [t]hen we would have to examine the possibility of the international judges asking the UN to withdraw and drop the whole process."[155]

President of the Bar Association of the Kingdom of Cambodia (BAKC) Ky Tech, who was widely seen to be acting on behalf of the Government, took the lead in attacking the draft rules. He argued that "only [BAKC] can approve the list of defense attorneys for Khmer Rouge suspects, oversee lawyers' training and discipline them for misconduct."[156] BAKC also demanded that the ECCC Defense Unit be renamed the Office of Defense Support and Cooperation and instituted under Cambodian leadership.[157] At one point the national judges argued that the rules should not provide for a defense office at all and the BAKC should administer all ECCC defense matters.[158]

The issue was picked up by Deputy Prime Minister Sok An, who argued that "the administration, role, and functions" of the ECCC defense office and its relationship with the BAKC were not addressed in the Agreement, and the appointment of its international head was "insufficiently attuned to the specifics of the ECCC and its position 'within the courts of Cambodia.'"[159] He apparently sought "to reopen negotiations on the role of that office"—a request rejected by the UN.[160] After months of strained discussions between the judges and political interlocutors,[161] it was eventually agreed that the newly named "Defence Support Section" would consult with BAKC on procedures for assignment of lawyers and legal trainings, and that all foreign lawyers would be required to register with BAKC.[162]

The final stumbling block was BAKC's demand that foreign lawyers pay a $500 membership application fee whether or not they were selected as counsel, plus a $2,000 one-time fee and a $200 per-month fee if they were selected. Although this issue was technically outside the purview of the judges, the international judges threatened to boycott the plenary at which the rules were to be finalized if the fees were not lowered. They argued that the high fees would reduce the number of foreign counsel interested in applying and lead to defense arguments that the accused had been denied the right to counsel of their choice.[163] Ky Tech called the threat childish and said it was proof that the foreign judges, not the Cambodian Government or the Bar Association, were "hindering the tribunal."[164]

When the international judges threatened to exclude the BAKC entirely from the process of organizing foreign lawyers' participation unless the fees were lowered, the national judges said they would not participate in the Court under those circumstances.[165] National Co-Investigating Judge You Bunleng argued, "This tribunal is not the UN's tribunal so how can [the Bar] be cut out? . . . When foreign lawyers come to work in a foreign country, there is international law that they must respect the laws of their host country."[166] However, many observers viewed the BAKC demand as a form of extortion, especially as the Bar was unspecific about how the fees would be used.[167] The BAKC eventually agreed that foreign lawyers could pay a flat $500 fee.[168] At the final May 2007 plenary, it seemed to some present that the national judges were acting under new, more flexible instructions, and for the first time there were "noticeable points of disagreement among [them]—not on key issues, where all the Cambodian judges held firm—but on less contentious matters[.]"[169] With the final hurdles overcome, the Rules were adopted in June 2007.

Debate over the Hierarchy of Rules

Although the judges acted without explicit statutory authority in adopting the Internal Rules, the Trial Chamber has affirmed that the Rules have primacy over the Cambodian Code of Criminal Procedure:

> The Internal Rules . . . form a self-contained regime of procedural law related to the unique circumstances of the ECCC, made and agreed upon by the plenary of the ECCC. They do not stand in opposition to the Cambodian Criminal Procedure Code . . . but the focus of the ECCC differs substantially enough from the normal operations of Cambodian criminal courts to warrant a specialized system. Therefore, the Internal Rules constitute the primary instrument to which reference should be made in determining procedures before the ECCC where there is a difference between the procedures in the Internal Rules and the CPC.[170]

Nevertheless, uncertainty remains regarding when it is appropriate to supplement the Internal Rules by reference to the CPC. Elisabeth Simonneau Fort says that, from a civil law perspective, the Internal Rules are not well written and lack sufficient detail to be precise. Moreover it is unclear what to do to fill the gaps, as the Court refers sometimes to civil law, sometimes common law, sometimes international law, and sometimes Cambodian law.[171]

The SCC has stated that the civil law rules of interpretation require consideration of a provision's language, its place in the system including "its relation to the main underlying principles," and its objective.[172] However, in a *sui generis* system such as the ECCC, this approach necessarily leads to confusion as to how related provisions of the Internal Rules and the CPC should be reconciled, as every question is a matter of first impression.[173] Indeed in the same decision the SCC found that one CPC provision provided no guidance for a similarly worded Internal Rules provision, and that a second CPC provision provided essential guidance for a differently worded Internal Rules provision.

Internal Rule 68 and CPC Article 249 both establish a four-month limit for pretrial detention upon issuance of a closing order indicting an accused. The SCC found that, despite their similar time frame, Internal Rule 68 has no equivalent in the national code with regard to when this time limit commences if there is an appeal against the closing order. Thus, even though the CPC clock starts running when the closing order is issued, the Internal Rules should be interpreted to start the clock when the appeal is actually filed, as each set of rules "must be evaluated against their systematic background."[174] In the case of the Internal Rules this background includes "the gravity of crimes and complexity of investigations, the need for greater pre-trial scrutiny over the charges and the need to broaden recourse [to appeal] by the defence" to include, for example, jurisdictional grounds.[175] Consequently, "the [CPC] does not provide guidance for the matter at hand, as its provisions in the related area are not adequate for appeals designed for indictments in international crimes."[176]

In the same decision, a supermajority of the SCC determined that provisions of the Internal Rules and the CPC should be considered together with regard to when a defendant should be detained, as they both must be read "in the light of the presumption of liberty."[177] It found that Internal Rule 82(2), which provides the ECCC Trial Chamber general authority to release or detain an accused, must be interpreted in light of CPC article 306, which explicitly requires trial courts to make this decision on the basis of the statutory criteria for pretrial detention. Thus, although there is no such requirement in the Internal Rules, the SCC found that, because of the wording of CPC article 306, the

ECCC's pretrial detention statutory criteria are incorporated into Internal Rule 82(2).[178] Judge Noguchi dissented on this point:

> Due to the special mandate, jurisdiction, and structure of the ECCC, there are many provisions in the Internal Rules which do not exist or differ from the procedures for ordinary domestic cases to be tried before ordinary domestic courts. Therefore, the context within which to interpret the Internal Rules is first and foremost the Internal Rules themselves. Otherwise, it will be difficult for readers of the Internal Rules to know precisely what the procedural rules are before the ECCC. . . . When the meaning of a particular provision of the Internal Rules is sufficiently clear in its own context, recourse to the Code of Criminal Procedure is not necessary.[179]

This practical approach had been followed for five years by the lower chambers and relied on by the parties.[180] The SCC's favored interpretive process is arguably one more unnecessary complication for a very complicated tribunal. Nevertheless, in undertaking this cumbersome approach, the SCC is showing national procedures the deference they are intended to be shown under the ECCC Law and providing a potentially valuable legacy for the national judiciary.

For example, in the Case 001 appeals judgment, the SCC began discussing the criteria for civil parties by emphasizing that under the Framework Agreement and ECCC Law, "Cambodian law remains the controlling procedural law for proceedings before the ECCC, save where that law is inadequate according to the criteria specified in these provisions."[181] Any other approach arguably undermines respect for Cambodian law by merely assuming its inadequacy. In a country like Cambodia where compliance with the law is low, this undermines not only local confidence in national law but also faith in the rule of law generally.

Next, the Chamber considered the applicable national procedures in accordance with international standards—such as "the presumption of liberty" as discussed above—thereby demonstrating to domestic lawyers the process of applying national law in a manner that promotes fair trial rights. The SCC noted: "the ECCC, its hybrid nature notwithstanding, acts as an emanation of the State of Cambodia and is duty bound to respect international standards of justice and generally recognized human rights precepts."

The Cambodian legal system can derive no benefit from the facial primacy of the CPC if this hierarchy is disregarded in practice. The need to grapple with both Cambodian procedures and international procedures promotes inconsistencies in application between Chambers and uncertainty among the parties. Nevertheless, this is the hybrid system that the ECCC framers bequeathed. At its worst, this structure promotes arbitrary and seemingly ends-driven decisions. At its best, the Court's unwieldy efforts may contribute to the future domestic application of Cambodian procedures in conformity with international fair trial principles.[182]

CONCLUSION

From the start, the Court's civil law orientation and complex structure, its responsibility to interpret and apply two sets of laws to events in the 1970s, and its lack of clear procedures targeted to mass-crimes cases presented significant barriers to its efficacy. The challenges of having "two of everything"—including prosecutors, investigating judges, appeals chambers, and sets of rules—continue to affect its functioning.

This chapter has illustrated some of the particular technical challenges the ECCC faced as it began operations and prepared for trial. The ECCC's struggle to pair the two sides of the Court has affected its operations in other important ways as well, including a number that have received considerably more civil society and media attention. These include the challenge of administering a mixed court effectively and transparently, stewarding its resources efficiently, providing for the rights of victims and defendants, and dealing with the shadow of political interference. Those are the principal subjects of the chapters that follow.

Chapter 3

SERVING TWO MASTERS

Dual Administration, Oversight, and Funding

International and hybrid tribunals need much more than agreed legal provisions and procedural rules to operate effectively. They also require significant funding support and functioning bureaucratic institutions subject to sound oversight. Every public judicial hearing or decision is akin to the tip of an iceberg; beneath the surface are scores of administrative tasks. These are particularly important given the complexity and high profile of many of the cases. Teams of staff investigators must travel to the field, documents must move securely around the building, records must be kept, numerous visitors must be led safely in and out of the premises, and court personnel must be paid, just to name a few necessary functions. These routine-sounding processes pose significant challenges for newly created tribunals that do not have the luxury of relying on preexisting administrative practices. Donors and court officials have to act quickly—raising money, hiring manpower, and establishing bureaucratic procedures to meet the myriad demands of administering transitional justice.

Hybrid tribunals have some potential administrative advantages. Most have been located in the country where atrocities occurred. They are thus closer to crime sites and potential witnesses, reducing the logistical difficulty and cost of mounting field investigations. They also tend to be less expensive, because national staffers generally draw lower salaries, and the cost of operations are usually lower in postconflict countries than they are in The Hague. The ECCC's proximity to the *locus delicti* and involvement of Cambodian personnel offer these possible benefits.

Hybrid courts also face serious administrative challenges, however. Each is largely *sui generis*, blending different organizational ingredients from the host country and the United Nations and opening space for jockeying between and among national and international officials about personnel, resource allocation, and procedures. The ECCC's institutional design contains particularly serious shortcomings that would be difficult for appointed court officials to overcome. These include a split administrative structure, weak international oversight system, and shaky financial foundation. Those institutional features have adversely affected the ECCC's function in areas including human resources, financial management, and translation.[1]

THE ECCC'S MANAGERIAL AND FINANCIAL STRUCTURES

Like many of the ECCC's institutional features, its administrative setup, oversight mechanisms, and funding structures are unique. Its administrative apparatus is divided between national and international "sides," each funded through a separate stream and each reporting to different political masters. David Tolbert, former UN Special Expert to advise on the UN Assistance to the Khmer Rouge Trials, argues that this represents the "worst possible design" for an effective Court.[2]

Two-Headed Administration

At the top of the ECCC's administrative structure is an Office of Administration (OA) responsible for providing administrative support to the various organs of the ECCC. The OA wields considerable power due to its role in allocating resources and responsibility for providing an array of non-judicial services essential for the ECCC's work. Authority is segregated within the office. The Cambodian-appointed OA Director is the tribunal's top administrator but does not have ultimate authority over "matters that are subject to United Nations rules and procedures."[3] That authority belongs to an international Deputy Director, who is charged with the "recruitment and administration of all foreign staff."[4] The Framework Agreement is silent on how to resolve any conflicts between the Director and Deputy Director,[5] merely asserting that they "shall cooperate in order to ensure an effective and efficient functioning of the administration."[6] The ECCC Law also offers no guidance. In practice, Cambodian staff members have generally reported to the Director, and international staffers have treated the Deputy Director as their superior.[7] This possibility was clearly foreseen by the drafters of the Framework Agreement and reduces the likelihood of unity and coherence in the office.[8]

Beneath the OA are seven distinct administrative sections, each composed of a mix of national and international personnel. Cambodian appointees head Public Affairs, which manages communication, and the Court Management section responsible for records and archives, translation, witness and expert support, and related functions. UN appointees lead the units for information technology, safety and security, and "general services," which refers to facilities management, transportation, mail, procurement, and related issues. The two remaining units—Personnel and Budget & Finance—have two heads each to manage their respective sides of the court.[9] The ECCC also has two special stand-alone administrative units: the Cambodian-led Victims Support Section, which manages victim complaints and supports civil parties, and the UN-led Defence Support Section, which aids the various defense teams. Thus, at almost all levels of administration, the two sides of the Court have been kept separate to a significant degree.

The ECCC's split administrative structure cuts against the established norm in international and hybrid courts. Most have followed the example of the International Criminal Tribunals for the former Yugoslavia and Rwanda (ICTY and ICTR) by establishing registries to provide administrative support for the judicial organs of the court. That model centralizes authority under a single registrar who makes decisions on personnel and budgetary matters and other administrative policies. The International Criminal Court (ICC) has a registry, as do the Special Tribunal for Lebanon (STL) and Special Court for Sierra Leone (SCSL), which both entrust administrative authority to a UN appointee.[10] The advantages of a registry headed by a UN appointee include the efficiency gains from having a single lead administrator and added confidence that administrative practices will conform to international standards. In 2006, former ICTY deputy prosecutor David Tolbert recommended that the ECCC establish a registry atop the ECCC's administration.[11] The absence of a single responsible registrar has made it unclear which side of the OA has the authority to lead a particular task and who should be held accountable for it.[12] Former UN Legal Counsel Hans Corell argues that divided administrative leadership is not a "happy solution" for Court administration, because "you have to have somebody who makes decisions."[13]

The division of the ECCC's administration accommodated Cambodian sovereignty concerns—indeed, a pair of UN-appointed experts concluded in a 2007 review of the ECCC's administration that they perceived no good reason for the division of the Court into separate administrative sides except possibly "to protect the 'sovereignty' of the National Staff side."[14] Even before the tribunal began operations, however, critics charged that the structure made the United Nations the junior partner to a debased, opaque national judicial system and stressed the need for stronger UN oversight to safeguard the Court from corruption and political interference.[15] In fact, U.S. officials cited this as a reason for their initial reluctance to fund the tribunal. In 2005, U.S. Ambassador-at-Large for War Crimes Issues Pierre-Richard Prosper said:

> The U.S. wants to be in the position where we will be able to support this politically and financially. . . . What we want to avoid is some of the problems that exist in the ordinary judiciary being transferred to the Khmer Rouge tribunal. . . . It must be free from corruption. It must be free from political manipulation or influences and must be transparent.[16]

Those concerns later would prove prescient.

The lack of strong UN leadership within the tribunal was accentuated by the appointment of Chinese diplomat Michelle Lee as the first OA Deputy Director. Lee lacked experience in court administration, and according to numerous sources, she took a hands-off, deferential approach to affairs within the ECCC and on the Cambodian side in particular.[17] Soon after the Court began operations, concerned UN and donor officials began to press for her removal,[18] which did not occur until late 2007.[19]

Lee's replacement, Knut Rosandhaug, has been more involved and has forged a more cooperative partnership with acting OA Director Tony Kranh,[20] but Rosandhaug has also been criticized for being too deferential to his Cambodian counterparts.[21] According to many staffers, Rosandhaug could have sought to play a role more akin to a registrar but has instead emphasized the limits of his power.[22] The ECCC's split structure has made it difficult for UN officials at the ECCC to lead, but the agency of individual appointees has also had a major impact both in the OA and throughout the Court.

A Split Financing Model

The ECCC's funding scheme also divides its national and international sides. The ECCC Law requires that the salaries and expenses of the Cambodian judges, prosecutor, administrative officials, and staff be "borne by the Cambodian national budget,"[23] and the Cambodian Government has provided some direct financial support. The ECCC may also receive additional voluntary contributions from foreign governments, international institutions, NGOs, or others,[24] and in practice the Cambodian Government has relied primarily on such contributions for its share of the ECCC's costs.

The United Nations bears the expenses and salaries of international judicial and administrative personnel[25] as well as the remuneration of defense counsel.[26] In addition, the United Nations agreed to fund utilities and services, witness travel, safety and security provisions, and "such other limited assistance as may be necessary to ensure the smooth functioning of the investigation, the prosecution and the Extraordinary Chambers."[27] The United Nations has met its financial obligations by soliciting earmarked donations from selected UN member states.[28]

The ECCC's structure differs considerably from the models of the *ad hoc* international courts and the ICC, which have been able to rely more heavily on assessed contributions. The ICTY and ICTR are both funded through assessed contributions from UN member states as part of the UN General Budget, and the General Assembly's budget committee reviews their budgets every two years.[29] Both may also receive additional voluntary contributions. The ICC, which was created outside of the United Nations umbrella, derives most of its funding through assessed contributions by State Parties to the Rome Statute but may also receive voluntary contributions from the United Nations and donor states.[30] These funding schemes remain subject to shifts in donor preferences, but much less so than the ECCC model.

The funding structures for other hybrid courts have varied widely. The Kosovo Regulation 64 Panels and Special Panels for Serious Crimes in East Timor both received funds from the UN peacekeeping authorities that created them. The STL is funded 51% through voluntary contributions by UN member states and 49% by the government of Lebanon.[31] The budget of the SCSL depends primarily on voluntary contributions from donor states. The Security Council imposed that mechanism to reduce the costs of the proceedings, despite the objections of UN Secretary-General Kofi Annan, who warned that "[a] special court based on voluntary contributions would be neither viable nor sustainable."[32]

By comparison to its peers, the ECCC's funding structure is most similar to that of the SCSL and has a few distinct characteristics. Like the SCSL, it relies heavily on voluntary donor contributions. The risk of that arrangement was foreseen when the tribunal was created. In 2003, before the conclusion of the Framework Agreement, Annan requested that the UN General Assembly fund the ECCC out of assessed UN member state contributions, arguing that the Court needed an "assured and continuous source of funding" to meet its mandate and that its operation "should not be left to the vagaries of voluntary contributions."[33] The General Assembly refused.[34]

Corell contends reliance on voluntary contributions was a mistake. In addition to the danger of financial uncertainty and instability, "it's hard to have a credible institution with voluntary contributions," Corell argues. "Who is financing the court? Why?"[35] A senior Court official adds that reliance on voluntary replenishments increases the Court's vulnerability to pressure from donors, giving a small number of states the power to exercise undue influence.[36] Some examples are discussed later in this chapter.

More uniquely, the ECCC's funding structure reinforces the separation between the national and international sides of the court. International personnel are funded through UN channels, while Cambodian personnel are paid by the Cambodian Government. In theory, that distinction encourages national ownership and burden-sharing, but in practice the Cambodian Government has relied almost exclusively on foreign grants. This funding structure makes it easy for donors to target assistance to the international side of the court. That provides a source of leverage against the Cambodian Government but has also caused delays and undermined confidence in the Court's staying power.

Weak and Separate Oversight Mechanisms

The ECCC was created without a clear internal or external institutional mechanism to oversee its administrative and financial operations. In most international and hybrid tribunals, a registrar works under the court's president—its head judicial officer. At the SCSL, the president links the tribunal's internal oversight to external oversight mechanisms by submitting annual reports to the UN Secretary-General and the government of Sierra Leone.[37]

The ECCC has neither a president nor a registrar. As a partial alternative, the Internal Rules established a "Judicial Administration Committee" in 2007 composed of three Cambodian and two international judges. Under the Internal Rules:

> The Committee shall advise and guide the Office of Administration concerning all activities relating to the administrative and judicial support provided to, the Office of the Co-Prosecutors, the Office of the Co-Investigating Judges and the Chambers, including the preparation and implementation of the budget.[38]

The OA Director and Deputy Director participate in a "consultative capacity."[39] The Committee's authority to "advise and guide" the OA does not, however, institutionalize its authority or grant it express supervision over the OA's activities.[40] Thus, the ECCC's internal oversight structure remains weak relative to other institutionalized courts—reflecting the unwillingness of either side of the Court to submit to unified authority led by the other.

The United Nations: More Support than Oversight

To a large extent, the United Nations has taken what one senior ECCC official calls a "hands-off" approach,[41] accepting a supportive role rather than pushing for strong external oversight. The design of the tribunal clearly and deliberately limited the scope for UN oversight. Former UN Assistant Secretary-General Larry Johnson asserts that the Cambodians' insistence on "strict equality" left the United Nations with "virtually no remit over the Cambodian half" of the Court, and that the split hybrid design erected "a big brick wall that the Cambodians worked to keep up at all times."[42]

From the outset, the United Nations put oversight of its side of the tribunal in the hands of the UN Controller rather than the Office of Legal Affairs (OLA), which had negotiated the Framework Agreement.[43] The apparent rationale was to focus on cost reduction—one of the purported advantages of a mixed court over *ad hoc* tribunals,[44] but in the early years the OLA appears to have acquiesced in the Controller's oversight partly to "wash its hands" of a court that it feared would encounter serious problems as a result of its majority-Cambodian structure.[45]

For more quotidian matters, such as recruitment, the Controller relied on the Department of Economic and Social Affairs (DESA). Neither the Controller nor DESA had experience running a mass crimes court, however. Rather than concentrating on judicial management, initial UN oversight treated the ECCC much like an ordinary technical assistance project—a narrow and conservative reading of the UN's mandate. Although the OLA became more closely involved over time, the lines of oversight remained unclear.

In 2005, the United Nations established a project called the UN Assistance to the Khmer Rouge Trials (UNAKRT) to provide technical assistance to the Cambodian Government in conducting the trials.[46] In 2006, the Cambodian Government signed a project document with the UN Development Program (UNDP), which administers international funds to the Cambodian side of the court. Among other things, that document established a "Project Board" chaired by the ECCC's OA Director and including representatives from UNDP, DESA, and the European Community. The Project Board was ill equipped to provide strong oversight, however. It was charged with holding only one meeting per year and had no formal legal authority over the ECCC. The fact that its chair was the lead administrator at the ECCC also posed a possible conflict of interest.[47] In 2007, when serious questions arose about the effects of the hybrid structure on the OA's functionality, the UNAKRT spokesperson emphasized that "the UN is here to help, not to lead," and that its mandate to provide mere assistance did not allow for a stronger leadership role, which would "require high-level political re-negotiation of the court's founding tenets."[48]

Senior UN officials became more directly involved in early 2008, following allegations of mismanagement and corruption (discussed below) and with the Court's first trial approaching. Donors and civil society actors also applied pressure for stronger oversight mechanisms. A representative of the Japanese government, the Court's top funder, reportedly said that the UN needed to "exercise more appropriate stewardship of the process" and that while UN staff was "hardworking and conscientious, they are not adequately supported by UN headquarters."[49] Civil society observers suggested creating a special international advisory position and a committee similar to the SCSL's Management Committee to monitor the Court's administrative and budgetary operations.[50]

The Cambodian side did not want "a new party to be above the court" and insisted that any such post would entitle it to a similar Cambodian position.[51] Clint Williamson, then U.S. Ambassador-at-Large for War Crimes Issues, recalls that donors generally supported a "more proactive UN role" but were concerned about "Cambodian receptivity to it."[52] Some—particularly the French,

Japanese, and Australians—argued that the UN and key donors could not "shove it down the Cambodians' throats."[53] The UN nevertheless went forward in March 2008, unilaterally appointing former ICTY deputy prosecutor David Tolbert as a Special Expert to UNAKRT for a period of approximately six months.[54]

The post's title—the "Special Expert to advise on the United Nations Assistance to the Khmer Rouge Trials"—reinforces UN caution in overstepping its bounds. Despite that initial caution, the Special Expert has become a key actor raising funds and negotiating with the Cambodian Government on sensitive issues. Craig Etcheson, a former investigator in the Office of the Co-Prosecutors, argues that it "quickly became apparent that something like [the Special Expert post] was needed" at the ECCC.[55] Williamson adds that donors and UN officials soon came to see Tolbert's role as a "positive factor" and concluded that "the Court was suffering by not having that role," leading the UN to restart the post shortly after Tolbert's temporary post expired.[56] The post has been filled since 2010 by a pair of former U.S. war crimes ambassadors—Williamson and David Scheffer.[57]

Inside the Court, an informal mechanism temporarily evolved on the UN side. In November 2011, it became public that for six months prior, Trial Chamber Judge Silvia Cartwright, then international Co-Prosecutor Andrew Cayley, and OA Deputy Director Knut Rosandhaug held "regular meetings" without the presence of the defense. According to Rosandhaug, the meetings concerned only administrative and organizational matters,[58] and the idea for such meetings came from UN Under Secretary for Legal Affairs Patricia O'Brien. He added:

> The aim was to add focus to communication between the UN component of the ECCC and UN Headquarters. Such meetings would replicate, in an informal way, the coordination committees that are standard in the other UN and UN-assisted tribunals.[59]

Andrew Cayley reportedly said, "Administrative management meetings such as these take place in the ICC, ICTY, and the ICTR. They are normal. If they did not take place, these institutions, including the ECCC, would be paralyzed."[60] The Internal Rules do not provide for such meetings, however, instead creating the hybrid Judicial Administration Committee.

Defense lawyers objected, contending that meetings between Cartwright and Cayley raised concerns of judicial bias.[61] In seeking Cartwright's disqualification for the appearance of bias, the *Nuon Chea* team noted that coordination councils at other courts are made up of the president, head prosecutor, and registrar and "meet pursuant to clearly defined and publicly available terms of reference" and are not "ad hoc" bodies.[62] The *Ieng Sary* team likewise contended that comparisons with the practice of international courts were inappropriate, as the ECCC is a national court with a unique structure, including national and international personnel, no president, no registrar, and a prosecutor who, unlike at the *ad hoc* courts, is directly involved in ongoing proceedings.[63]

The Trial Chamber rejected the defense arguments and found that the meetings resembled other mass crimes tribunals' coordination councils, which "are integral to address the unique administrative challenges faced by international tribunals." It held that "[t]he ECCC confronts certain administrative matters which pertain exclusively to the United Nations component of the court," and while the ECCC lacks a presidency, Judge Cartwright fills a similar position as Vice-President of the plenary. Moreover, the OA Deputy Director has functions "akin" to those of a registrar. Although such meetings are not explicitly provided for by the Internal Rules, "nor does the ECCC legal framework debar coordination by the United Nations component of the ECCC, where required."[64] On appeal, the SCC found that to address the "appearance of asymmetrical access enjoyed by the prosecutor to the trial judge," defense representatives should be included, but it did not ban the meetings.[65] Nevertheless, by all accounts, at that point the meetings ceased. Thus, if only for a short time, in the absence of formal internal management structures, a less transparent and authoritative institutional mechanism emerged to fulfill this function.

Monitoring by Donors

Since the ECCC depends on voluntary contributions, donors have had regular opportunities to exert influence on the proceedings. If used wisely, that engagement can strengthen a court's operations, but at the ECCC donors have generally acquiesced in a weak structure for donor coordination and oversight. The Framework Agreement did not provide a structure for donor monitoring and oversight, and most key donors accepted a relatively hands-off role. In 2005, the U.S. government proposed establishing a donor management committee akin to the one established in the statute creating the SCSL,[66] which sets forth that:

> . . . interested States will establish a management committee to assist the Secretary-General in obtaining adequate funding, and provide advice and policy direction on all non-judicial aspects of the operation of the Court, including questions of efficiency, and to perform other functions as agreed by interested States.[67]

The SCSL Management Committee includes representatives from the UN Secretary-General's office, state donors, and Sierra Leone. Its mandate gives the committee an opportunity to play a significant oversight role in the SCSL's management. The STL has a similar Management Committee.[68]

Other key ECCC donors were not enthusiastic about the U.S. proposal. The Australian government responded that the Framework Agreement did not create such a mechanism and that donors had "missed their chance" to do so:

> The current structure of the KRT [Khmer Rouge Tribunal] simply did not allow for a Management Committee. . . . The Australians would prefer to monitor the KRT through their embassies in relevant countries abroad and through the UN. . . . Cambodian political will was key to the KRT's success . . . and donors might send the wrong signal if [they] pushed to take over too much control of the process. . . . For Australia, as for the UN, the Agreement—and in particular the provision allowing the UN to withdraw—alone provides sufficient international oversight by making international assistance "contingent on the KRT continuing to meet international standards."[69]

Instead of a management committee, a group of key donors responded to a May 2006 request from Deputy Prime Minister Sok An to create an informal group of donors to provide advice and support to the ECCC.[70] The following month, with Cambodian officials in attendance, the French and Japanese Ambassadors chaired the inaugural meeting of the "Friends of the ECCC" group and laid out several proposals for the Friends group. These included holding meetings every other month, limiting the group to a nonjudicial advisory role, avoiding a formal institutional structure, keeping discussions confidential, limiting participation to governments, and respecting the independence of the ECCC and prerogative of the OA.[71] According to a Japanese participant, the Friends group was "non-coercive and non-interventional . . . mindful of the sovereign inviolability of the local State from which the local component of the Office of Administration derives" and based on the idea that "friendly advice could be more effective than excessive pressure and inquisitorial consultations."[72]

A U.S. Embassy cable reveals that the Cambodian Government sought to exploit differences among donors to prevent an oversight mechanism that would favor the UN side of the court:

> The Japanese were to have taken on the role as sole chair of the Friends of the ECCC; the idea of co-chairing the Friends was Sok An's. According to the Japanese, Sok An is unhappy with Japanese unwillingness to side with the RGC against Michelle Lee and the UN side of OA, and is hoping that the French will be more supportive.[73]

In a March 2007 cable, U.S. Ambassador Joseph Mussomeli expanded on the notion that divergent donor priorities weakened the Friends group's potential as a serious monitoring body. Mussomeli argued that the French and Japanese Embassies "have shown no willingness to discuss contentious issues" related to the ECCC's administration.[74] He added:

> The French and Japanese positions are fairly consistent: the Friends should not play an activist role; individual missions—if they are so inclined—can intervene with the ECCC or the government, but the Friends should not act in any collective diplomatic way.[75]

Mussomeli also asserted that national political interests were at the heart of the hands-off approach to court monitoring. He expressed concern that France and Japan were "focusing exclusively on the preservation of their bilateral relationship with the RGC in their discussions about the ECCC" and that Japan was especially loath to press the government:

> The Japanese position is particularly sensitive due to the balancing act the [Government of Japan] plays with China in Cambodia. The Chinese, Sean [Visoth] believes, are placing pressure on the government with respect to moving forward with the Tribunal. The Japanese want the Tribunal to succeed at virtually any cost, and therefore will be loathe to put any pressure on the government that might make the RGC accord more sympathy to Chinese views.[76]

Thus, the donors approached the Friends group as an information-sharing device, rarely raising sensitive topics with the ECCC officials present and avoiding collective action despite the fact that "ECCC judges and staff have noted that the donors and interested states would be most effective if they could speak with a single voice."[77] Donors instead worked through bilateral channels with relatively rare exercise of coercive pressure.[78] Williamson argues that although the Friends group has provided a "very useful" information-sharing function, it was invested with too little formal structure and authority and thus does not offer a good institutional model for hybrid courts.[79]

An additional thin layer of donor oversight has operated in New York, where a relatively informal "steering group" of representatives of interested states, including Cambodia, have met periodically to share information about the ECCC, as well as a smaller "principal donors group." The lines of responsibility between the New York–based group, typically including the legal officers of countries' UN missions, and the Phnom Penh–based Friends group have not been clear, and at times wires have crossed.[80] More important, neither has had authority approaching that of the SCSL Management Committee.

Donors also removed a layer of oversight by shifting toward a model of direct financing of the Cambodian side of the Court. Until late 2009, UNDP's representative office in Cambodia administered most international grants to the Cambodian side of the Court. By then, however, donors had increasingly moved to provide funds to the Cambodian Government directly.[81]

The extent to which donors have contributed to the ECCC has clearly affected the nature of donor oversight. During its formative years between 2006 and 2009, Japan provided nearly 50% of all contributions to the Court, followed by Australia at 8% and France at 6%. The United States and United Kingdom combined for just 6%. Although the U.S. share rose slightly to 8% by mid-2013, Japan remained the dominant donor at 41%. Perhaps more importantly, Japan has accounted for more than 60% of all bilateral donations to the Cambodian side of the Court, whereas European states have contributed much less, and the United States has not contributed any funds to the national side.[82] This is in stark contrast to the SCSL, which between 2002 and 2009 depended heavily on funds from the United States (29%), United Kingdom (16%), Netherlands (12%), and Canada (9%).[83] Japan's relatively hands-off diplomatic approach at the ECCC contrasted with the more assertive Anglo-American engagement with the SCSL.

Cambodian Government Oversight

The Cambodian Government also has an oversight mechanism in place for its side of the court, headed by Sok An, who has chaired the Royal Government Task Force on the Khmer Rouge Trials since negotiations for the ECCC began in the late 1990s. In addition to his formal position as chair, Sok An has had a close working relationship with key ECCC administrative personnel, such as his longtime advisor Helen Jarvis, who headed the Public Affairs Section and Victims Unit, former OA Director Sean Visoth, and the omnipresent Rong Chhorn, who has filled a number of administrative roles at the Court. Sok An has also served as the key interlocutor for senior UN and donor officials on sensitive issues facing the Court.[84] He and other senior Cambodian officials, including Prime Minister Hun Sen, have been much more closely focused on the ECCC than anyone at the highest levels at UN headquarters. On the Cambodian side, oversight problems have not occurred due to a lack of engagement—they have come from too much political interference.

Structural Handicaps

All new tribunals face challenges when building a new bureaucracy, but the process of administering the ECCC has been particularly contentious and problematic. In a private June 2007 report, two UN-appointed experts—former SCSL Registrar Robin Vincent and former ICTY Chief of Administration Kevin St. Louis—argued that the ECCC's hybrid administrative structure was "divisive and unhelpful" and "serve[d] only to constantly hinder, frequently confuse, and certainly frustrate the efforts of a number of staff on both sides of the operations."[85] They cited divided administrative authority as a serious hindrance to core functions such as witness protection, public communications, and document translation.

Tolbert notes that the administration was "totally bifurcated" with "little communication" between national and international staffers sitting on opposite sides of the hall—an arrangement inimical to the goals of a hybrid court.[86] That bifurcation has caused inefficiency and contributed to frequent misunderstandings. Within the first year of its operations, the Court came under fire for human resources mismanagement and corruption. Each problem arose partly from the decisions of individual agents, but the Court's structural design played a key enabling role.

FUNCTIONAL CHALLENGES: HUMAN RESOURCES

One of the ECCC's first major administrative problems pertained to human resources. Any hybrid court has the difficult task of fusing national and international personnel with very different skill sets, experience, work styles, and expectations. International personnel often have stronger formal technical training and more experience pertaining to transitional justice, whereas national officials generally have superior knowledge of local language, culture, and administrative practices. How those skills are prioritized in terms of hiring, pay, and seniority is a sensitive matter. It affects the court's efficiency, the relative standing of national and international staffers, and staff morale. Control over personnel decisions is thus one of the most powerful levers for influence on the court.

The fact that each side of the ECCC hired its staff separately meant that hiring standards and procedures were bound to differ. The UN side used its normal formal recruitment process, while OA Director Sean Visoth approved a draft summary recruitment manual in June 2006 for the Cambodian side.[87] Both got off to a quick start, leading court monitors from the Open Society Justice Initiative (OSJI) to conclude that the ECCC was "coming together faster than any other past international tribunal.[88] Yet OSJI soon expressed concerns to donors about the opacity of Cambodian hiring practices.[89] UNDP responded by requesting an audit focusing on the Cambodian side of the OA.[90]

Problems on the Cambodian Side

Completed in June 2007, the audit was scathing. It argued that the ECCC's divided structure inhibited effective management, as international section heads were deliberately kept away from recruiting, evaluating, and even keeping track of Cambodian staffers' time in the office.[91] It found that out of 29 Cambodian personnel files reviewed, 18 staff "did not meet the minimum requirements specified in the vacancy announcements in terms of either academic qualifications or working experience" and that "recruitment was not performed in a transparent, competitive and objective manner."[92]

The auditors criticized Cambodian staff salaries as well. In 2004, UN and Cambodian negotiators had agreed that professional Cambodian staffers would be paid at 50% of the UN salary scale used by UNDP, but in 2006 Deputy Prime Minister Sok An approved a tax exemption for all Cambodian ECCC staffers, which effectively raised their salaries above anticipated levels.[93] The audit recommended that the UN lower Cambodian salaries accordingly and consider withdrawing from the tribunal if the Cambodian Government resisted measures the UNDP deemed necessary to maintain the integrity of the Court. Most dramatically, it suggested nullifying all past recruitments and launching a new hiring process under "close supervision of UNDP."[94]

Cambodian officials issued a response acknowledging "weaknesses" as the ECCC began its work but objecting to the "unbalanced" critiques of ECCC hiring practices, the auditors' decision to cancel key exit interviews, and the audit's recommendation for closer UNDP oversight.[95] They viewed control over the hiring and management of national staff as part of the RGC's sovereign authority over its side of the OA—authority recognized in the Framework Agreement.[96] The Cambodian reply said the UNDP recommendations were:

> completely out of proportion to the issues raised in the report [and] unacceptable and non-negotiable to the Cambodian side as to implement them would essentially mean a re-negotiation of the entire basis and character of the ECCC, as a national court with international participation and assistance already agreed in an international treaty.[97]

The Cambodian Government did not perceive authority for hiring as a narrow technical matter. It was a fundamental part of the political deal surrounding the Court.

UN officials acknowledged that fact and avoided pursuing structural reforms that could arrest the entire process.[98] UNAKRT spokesman Peter Foster noted that agreement on the tribunal had taken many years and that "we certainly don't want to reopen that."[99] He said that the UN could take a stronger "leadership role" but "[that] doesn't necessarily mean that we have to renegotiate part of the contract or part of the agreement or change the basic fundamentals of how we're structured." Instead, he advocated changes "within the existing structure" providing "greater assistance and greater advice to our Cambodian colleagues."[100]

Criticism of local staff pay and qualifications were also sensitive. As in many postconflict environments, there were relatively few national applicants with relevant judicial experience. Nevertheless, some Cambodians resented the implication that they were less qualified to work at the ECCC or deserved lesser pay. In April 2007, Secretary-General of the Cambodian Bar Association Ly Tayseng demanded that Cambodian lawyers at the ECCC should receive the same pay as international lawyers. "Cambodian lawyers are more qualified than foreign lawyers who don't speak Khmer and don't understand the working culture of Cambodia," Ly said. "It's unfair. It's discrimination."[101] Trial Chamber judge Thou Mony added that the wage differential demeaned Cambodian staffers.[102] The ratio did not change, but it revealed a challenge that all hybrid tribunals face—adopting pay scales that balance the needs of attracting talent, managing costs, and showing respect for local competencies.[103]

Oversight Failures

The UNDP audit argued that flawed hiring practices were related to the ECCC's split administration and weak oversight, especially on the Cambodian side. It noted that the ECCC's 2007 budget included 80 more staff positions than the ECCC and donor representatives planned in June 2006. Although ECCC officials "could not provide any justifications for the significant increase in the staffing," UNDP officials were "not aware of the additional posts," and the additional positions had "not given rise to comments or questions by the members of the project board."[104] The audit noted the potential "conflict of interest" of having the OA Director chair a Project Board intended to oversee and monitor its activities, and recommended that someone else chair the board.[105] The Cambodian Government objected by arguing that no chair could be "considered neutral"—a concession that the OA Director was not—and noting that "the Project Board operates on a consensus basis," preventing the Chair from acting unilaterally.[106] While correct, that consensus requirement also meant the OA Director could block actions by other members of the board.

Oversight by the Friends of the ECCC donor group was also weak, partly due to similar structural flaws. In late 2006 and early 2007, the group did not even discuss the concerns about the possible mismanagement of human resources "due to the presence of ECCC staff throughout the meetings."[107] The structure of the Friends group—comprised only of bilateral donors and the ECCC staff, but lacking engagement from other UN agencies or civil society—militated against consideration of that serious issue.

Reforms in Human Resource Procedures

While the UNDP audit was ongoing, the ECCC and Project Board took remedial steps. In March 2007, the ECCC's Personnel Section produced a Personnel

Handbook for the Cambodian side of the Court including guidelines on recruitment, pay, promotion, and performance evaluation. The Personnel Section revised it in August after the release of the UNDP audit.[108] The Project Board did not point fingers but noted in September that it was "taking measures to boost the ECCC's capacity."[109] In early 2008, the Project Board commissioned a review from the international auditing firm of Deloitte and Touche to assess the ECCC's reforms. Deloitte's report, issued in April, found major improvements. It noted that some "handholding" and "capacity building" would be needed to help the ECCC meet international standards, particularly on the national side, but praised the "willingness and commitment amongst ECCC staff to meet the expectations of the international community" and found that "robust" human resources systems had been implemented that would "address previous shortcomings" and "minimize the risk of questionable [human resources] practices occurring in the future."[110] It also found that the pay scale for Cambodian staff was "at the top of the market" but not unreasonable.[111]

UNDP and the Project Board issued a press release indicating that they were "quite satisfied" and commended the ECCC on its reforms.[112] European Commission chargé d'affaires Rafael Dochao Moreno, a key member of the Project Board, said, "we [now] have a system that can work."[113] Since that time, at least two key Cambodian appointees have gotten their jobs without competitive recruitment in violation of the new rules established.[114] However, international staff has helped select many Cambodian staff members,[115] and the Cambodian side of the ECCC has dealt with human resource management more transparently and effectively.

Thus, the split administrative structure delayed but did not prevent the development of reasonably sound human resource practices. Although oversight was weak at the outset and civil society had to take the lead in calling attention to problems, UNDP, the Project Board, and the ECCC all responded relatively quickly. This qualified success story contrasts with the Court's handling of the more contentious dispute surrounding reports of corruption.

CORRUPTION AND KICKBACK ALLEGATIONS

Concerns about corruption had been present since the introduction of the concept of a hybrid court in Cambodia. They came to the fore in early 2007, when the most salient corruption allegations to face any internationalized court arose at the ECCC. Media reports and an Open Society Justice Initiative press release included allegations that Cambodian staffers had to kick back a sizable share of their salaries in exchange for their jobs.[116] Again, OSJI called for an investigation.[117] Cambodian officials denied the allegations and accused OSJI of "bad faith and bias."[118] Sok An accused OSJI of trying to smear the Cambodian Government's reputation,[119] and the Cambodian Government considered closing OSJI's local office.[120]

Considerable evidence supported the allegations. In addition to a video of a Cambodian ECCC official describing the kickback scheme, a U.S. Embassy cable noted in March 2007 that "some ECCC international staff members are well aware that the practice exists because their Cambodian colleagues have told them so."[121] Donors were displeased with the public revelation of the allegations. In a meeting with former U.S. Ambassador for War Crimes Issues David Scheffer in mid-March, key donors "expressed disappointment over how OSJI has conducted itself and precipitated its current problems with the RGC."[122] French and Japanese officials did not comment or offer "signs of support for joint action" in the form of a demarche regarding OSJI's possible expulsion, and Scheffer sought assurance from OSJI that future disclosures of information potentially harmful to the ECCC would be given to the Court before the press. While donors focused on managing OSJI's fate and the drafting of the Internal Rules, "the allegations over corruption and kickbacks [were] nearly forgotten."[123]

The UNDP audit also skirted the corruption issue in the face of Cambodian Government resistance to an investigation. UNDP later issued a statement indicating that "[t]he audit did not find evidence [of kickbacks] . . . primarily because the allegations pertained to personnel beyond UNDP's jurisdiction. UNDP would have had to obtain irrefutable evidence to address the specific allegations."[124] Thus, UNDP did not consider itself entirely barred from addressing the corruption issue but chose not to pursue the matter. International judges at the ECCC were also aware of the allegations but believed it was not within their purview to intervene[125]—again drawing attention to the hybrid structure that set Cambodian administrative matters apart. More reports of the kickback scheme surfaced in the media in late 2007 and early 2008.[126]

In July 2008, the UN set up a new anticorruption scheme for the international side of the Court featuring appointment of an international ethics officer and a process for receiving and reviewing complaints.[127] Although designed for the international side of the Court, a number of disgruntled Cambodian staffers confidentially complained to UN officials about ongoing kickback demands on employees. UNDP froze the funds it administered to the Cambodian side of the tribunal.[128] In August, at Special Expert David Tolbert's request, the UN's Office of Internal Oversight Services began a confidential "review." Although a formal investigation of the Cambodian side would likely have exceeded the UN's legal purview, the "review" was a means to pressure the Cambodian Government to respond to corruption allegations.[129] Tolbert found the allegations credible and sent a confidential report to the Cambodian Government in September, recommending an RGC investigation.[130]

Cambodian Government spokesman Phay Siphan denied any corruption on the national side and argued that allegations were merely efforts to discredit the Government or the tribunal.[131] The RGC insisted that it alone had the jurisdictional authority to investigate allegations against its officials. It did, however, issue public assurances, create a new anticorruption committee,[132] and name two Cambodian "Ethics Monitors" to receive complaints of corruption and report directly to Sok An.

Office of Administration Director Sean Visoth was at the center of the controversy. Multiple reports named him as the recipient of kickbacks within the office. Tolbert privately recommended Sean Visoth's removal, and the UN Office of Legal Affairs in New York supported him in this.[133] Tolbert communicated that recommendation to Sok An in a private meeting.[134] Sok An did not agree initially but said after some discussion that Sean Visoth would depart from the tribunal "on my timetable, not yours."[135] In November, Sean Visoth went on extended medical leave and did not return to the tribunal[136]—a significant diplomatic victory for the United Nations.

The Cambodian Government did not acquiesce to an independent UN investigation or UN-led reporting process. In February 2009, UN Assistant Secretary-General Peter Taksoe-Jensen visited Phnom Penh to meet with Sok An, and the two issued a Joint Statement revealing the "essential elements of a structure" to prevent corruption, including "parallel national and international mechanisms to receive complaints."[137] Their interpretation of that language differed, however. Taksoe-Jensen argued that Cambodian staffers should be able to complain either to national Ethics Monitors or a new UN-appointed international Ethics Monitor. Sok An insisted otherwise, emphasizing Cambodian sovereignty and the plain text of the statement.[138]

Donors pushed for a swift resolution to the dispute, eager to avoid delays in the first trial as funds dwindled on the Cambodian side of the Court. Some key donors favored the Cambodian Government's position on the anticorruption system. The French ambassador said privately that "Cambodia has real arguments," and his Australian counterpart said, "Cambodia is in the right."[139] Japan's Deputy Chief of Mission argued that donors should provide funds to keep the Cambodian side from depletion and that withholding funds had gotten Cambodia's attention but increasingly looked like "international blackmail." The French and Australian governments agreed, and the U.S. ambassador added "moral support."[140] Japan thus injected $200,000 to pay the salaries of 251 Cambodian staff members,[141] and Australia requested that UNDP release $456,000 of its frozen funds.[142]

Sok An continued to insist on separate anticorruption reporting structures, despite a call from the U.S. ambassador urging him to "take the deal." U.S. Embassy officials concluded that the Cambodian proposal was inadequate and that "[i]t may fall to the donors to push the Cambodians to take that next step."[143] Instead, donors eased off on the pressure. In April, Japan authorized a release of a further $4.17 million to the Cambodian side of the tribunal. Late that month, key donor states met and converged on taking an "even-handed approach to the negotiations" between the UN and Cambodian Government and pressing for a prompt resolution involving mutual compromise.[144] U.S. Ambassador Carol Rodley encouraged donors to "send a message to the UN and Cambodia that, as a group, the donors want the two sides to engage seriously and get past the one last sticking point in the negotiations"—namely, the mechanism whereby Cambodian staffers could issue confidential complaints of misconduct.[145]

The Friends group issued a public statement in May praising the ECCC's progress on anticorruption measures. Shortly afterward, U.S. Ambassador-at-Large for War Crimes Issues Clint Williamson traveled to Phnom Penh to broker a deal. After consulting with Japanese officials,[146] he proposed a model to Sok An featuring a single counselor who would receive all complaints. Sok An initially objected, assuming that the proposed position would be international, but warmed to the idea when Williamson raised the possibility of a Cambodian appointee.[147] The core donors embraced the proposal the following day.[148]

During the ensuing weeks, donors and the Cambodian Government discussed who the appointee would be and the importance of independence.[149] In August, the Cambodian Government and United Nations issued a press release announcing that Uth Chhorn, the Auditor General of Cambodia, would fill the role.[150] Uth's appointment reflected a relatively weak, face-saving UN response to Cambodian obstruction and donor ambivalence. One expressed aim of an official reporting mechanism was to provide "full protection of staff on both sides of the ECCC against any possible retaliation for good faith reporting or wrongdoing."[151] Uth's status as a senior Cambodian official undermined the likelihood that Cambodian staffers would feel safe reporting malfeasance. Moreover, Uth had shown little transparency as auditor-general of a domestic system riddled with corruption.[152]

Since the appointment of the Independent Counsellor in August 2009, no new public allegations of administrative corruption have surfaced at the ECCC. At the time of Uth's appointment, a confidential U.S. diplomatic cable asserted, "[T]he ECCC is now likely Cambodia's first corruption-free court."[153] In 2010, Secretary of State Hillary Clinton noted in a confidential cable that:

> [the ECCC had] made considerable progress on strengthening management systems and eliminating corruption. Notably, there have been no allegations of corruption within the court administration since the removal of Cambodian Chief of Administration Sean Visoth in December 2008.[154]

Thus, international pressure curbed public allegations of kickbacks at the ECCC—though anecdotal reports of other types of financial corruption continue.[155] In the best light, the Court's hybrid composition gave Cambodian staffers a channel through which to complain. Such complaints would have been much less likely in a purely domestic court. To some extent, UN and domestic responses to the corruption allegations helped infuse international standards into a Cambodian judicial entity—an explicit aim of the hybrid model.

Nevertheless, the corruption issue showed more problems than strengths of the ECCC's hybrid structure. Corruption at the ECCC was not predetermined by the Court's hybrid form—misconduct required human agency, as did official responses to the allegations—but the tribunal's structure facilitated corruption by segregating the two sides of the Court and providing for weak independent oversight. The Court's structure also hampered UN efforts to deal with corruption allegations swiftly and effectively.

Despite substantial evidence of the kickback scheme, no serious investigation was mounted. Faced with the possibility that the Khmer Rouge trials would grind to a halt, key donors—above all Japan and Australia—relieved pressure on the Cambodian Government in spring 2009 by releasing funds to the Cambodian side and voicing support for the tribunal's anticorruption efforts. Those decisions helped keep the ECCC functioning, but it also sapped the UN side of negotiating leverage and made a serious investigation much less likely.[156] Donors clearly contemplated that fact. A confidential U.S. cable reported from a Friends group meeting in May 2009:

> [A]s the French co-chair underscored, it is time for the ECCC to put an end to looking backward at past acts of corruption and instead look ahead to the real challenges facing the court in order to maintain the international standards expected of it.[157]

The situation was in some respects reminiscent of the negotiations to establish the tribunal. With the UN and Cambodian Government deadlocked, donors prioritized the continuation of the accountability process.[158] Donor interest in proceeding toward justice was legitimate, both from an efficiency standpoint and to pursue long-overdue justice, but the RGC was able to use that interest to avoid bargaining concessions to the United Nations. Although new anticorruption measures were put in place, past acts were largely swept under the rug. Moreover, the anticorruption mechanism established has been secretive. In March 2010, Uth announced that he would publish a report of his work, but he reversed course in October 2010, when he indicated that UN officials had instructed him to keep his report confidential.[159] Not until October 2012 did Uth Chhorn establish office hours at the ECCC during which staffers can raise concerns.[160] It is unclear whether corruption complaints have ceased or whether new allegations simply have not come to light.

FUNCTIONAL CHALLENGES: FUNDING AND FINANCIAL MANAGEMENT

From a financial standpoint, a tribunal's success depends both on its efficient use of funds and its ability to access sufficient funding to meet its legitimate needs. One possible advantage of a hybrid court is that proximity to crime sites and survivors and reliance on lower-paid national personnel could trim the cost of proceedings. Indeed, donor fatigue from the costly ICTY and ICTR contributed to the emergence of hybrid courts. Yet pursuing lower-cost justice also carries risks, as underfunded tribunals cannot meet their stated functions effectively. Indeed, the tribunals that are not endowed with predictable funding streams are likely to be the very ones donors are least committed to financing voluntarily.

The ECCC's unique hybrid structure has contributed to both challenges. As discussed in chapter 2, its complex structure has made the Court much less efficient than it might have been. On the other hand, the ECCC's heavy reliance on voluntary donor contributions, split funding model, and structural vulnerability to problems such as corruption and political interference have undermined its stability and contributed to frequent budgetary crises.

Cost (In)efficiency

Hybrid tribunals have been created with the expectation that they will be less expensive than fully international courts for the reasons noted above. Like most international and hybrid courts, the ECCC has been much more expensive than originally foreseen. The annual cost of its operations has risen over time, amounting to $173.3 million expended by the end of 2012 (see Figure 1). In a country where the annual budget for the entire national judicial system was a mere $3.3 million in 2007,[161] the cost of the trials has brought criticism. This was foreseen early in the process.[162] Court officials expect costs to trend downward after 2013, but projecting cost savings in future years is a routine—and often unfulfilled—part of bureaucratic budget planning.

In 2012, Brad Adams of Human Rights Watch stressed that "[a]fter five years and more than $150 million, the court has tried just one defendant."[163] Helen Jarvis, a key advisor to the Cambodian Government, countered that the funds spent were "not a great amount of money." She added, "It's about the cost of a bridge. Is one bridge worth more than justice for so many? I don't think so."[164]

The ECCC has been considerably less expensive than fully international courts in terms of total cost but much less of a bargain when one considers the number of persons indicted or the number of cases completed by each court against charged individuals (see Table 1). Crude cost comparisons between tribunals inevitably gloss over variables that provide legitimate bases for variation. Some tribunals perform more complex functions than others, require more extensive investigations, or operate in more expensive areas due to costs of living

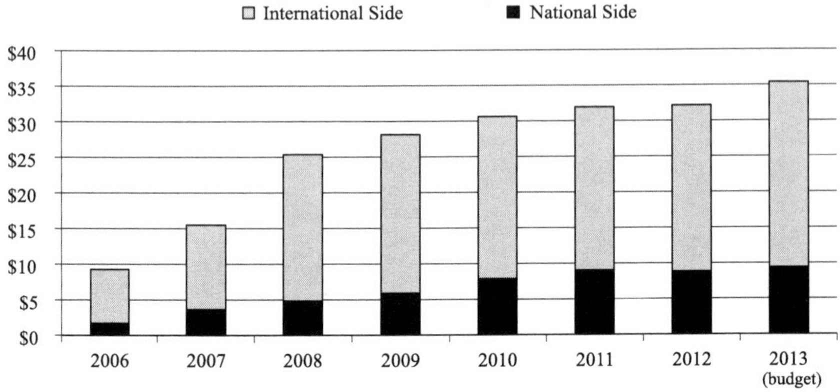

Fig. 1. Annual expenditures at the ECCC. (Spending in U.S. dollars, unadjusted for inflation. Data from the *ECCC Financial Outlook*, July 31, 2013.)

TABLE 1. Comparing the Cost of Selected Tribunals

Tribunal	Estimated Cost (at end of 2013)	Years of Operation	Avg. Cost/ Year	Persons Convicted or Acquitted	Cost/Person Convicted or Acquitted
ICTY	$2,330 m	20	$116 m	87	$27 m
ICTR	$1,860 m	19	$98 m	63	$30 m
ICC	$1,270 m	12	$106 m	2	$635 m
ECCC	$173 m	8	$22 m	1	$173 m
SCSL	$280 m	12	$23 m	9	$31 m

Source: Data from the ICTY, ICTR, ICC, ECCC, SCSL, and UN websites.
Note: Costs in U.S. dollars (unadjusted for inflation).

or security costs. Start-up costs for a new judicial institution also can be considerable. Still, it is clear that unless its number of completed cases rises unexpectedly, the ECCC will not be considered a cost-saving institution.

The ECCC is an expensive hybrid court, even relative to Sierra Leone—the most costly mixed tribunal to come before it. This is a lesser problem than pursuing justice too cheaply, as shown by the experience of the Special Panels for Serious Crimes in East Timor. As David Cohen argues, their trials were "[h]andicapped from the beginning by a debilitating lack of resources."[165] Their 2001 budget was a mere $6.3 million, of which $6 million went to the prosecution, and only $300,000 was provided to the rest of the court.[166] The average annual budget for the Special Panels between 2003 and 2005 was just $4.8 million.[167] The Special Panels even lacked an appeals court for nearly two years due to a lack of funds.[168] Their Serious Crimes Unit was also grossly underfunded. Some of its investigators had caseloads including more than 300 murders. For months, the Unit had no forensic pathologist despite collecting 30 sets of human remains for examination.[169] A shortage of skilled translators hampered efforts at all judicial levels.[170] In May 2005, the Security Council abruptly cut all funds for the Special Panels, which shut their doors soon afterward.[171] The East Timor model was cheap, but it was hardly a model for effective financing.

A more promising example of cost-efficient justice comes from Bosnia-Herzegovina. The War Crimes Chamber (WCC) in Bosnia and Herzegovina is a tribunal rooted more decisively in the local court system, but with support from a minority of international judges, prosecutors, and staff. The WCC has had a budget of roughly $20 million per year, similar to the SCSL and ECCC, but has eight trial chambers and more than 50 judges processing several hundred cases per year.[172] The WCC's example shows that efficiency gains are indeed possible when the host government has the will and capacity to handle cases reasonably effectively. In Cambodia, UN officials wisely rejected the possibility of playing an even more junior part, and higher costs were a predictable result of heavier international engagement.

A greater concern than the ECCC's total price tag is the inefficient use of funds that the Court has received, which could usefully have been redeployed to other ends—particularly outreach and victim participation. Some of the Court's inefficiency is built into its structure—such as the duplicative investigations and appeals discussed in chapter 2 and its cumbersome administrative structure. One senior staff member notes that roughly 30% of the ECCC's budget goes to administration—a much higher total than other mass crimes courts.[173] In other instances, the lack of clear responsibility for tasks has driven up costs.

For example, the Court's construction of a physical facility was delayed by ambiguities in its split authority structure. Under the Framework Agreement, the Cambodian Government is to "provide at its expense the premises . . . [and provide] utilities, facilities, and other services necessary for their operation."[174] The United Nations bears the costs for "utilities and services,"[175] however, making it unclear precisely how to divide responsibilities. Moreover, UN-appointed officials believed that their role as guarantors of international standards entitled them to intervene in the planning and construction of certain aspects of the facilities—such as the detention center and sites for defense and witness support services.[176] As a consequence, after a full year of operations, the ECCC had not finished its courtrooms, installed audio/video equipment, or established an effective translation system.[177]

A Tower of Babel

Translation has also presented a serious challenge for the ECCC. In most mass crimes courts, staffers, participants to the proceedings, and observers converge from diverse national or ethnic backgrounds. English and French have been the dominant currencies of communication. They are the official languages of the ICTY and ICTR and the working languages of the ICC. With the exception of the SCSL, which adopted English as its official language, hybrid courts have had to deal with multiple languages to accommodate strong national participation. The East Timor Special Panels Court had the greatest burden of four official languages: English, Portuguese, Bahasa Indonesia, and Tetum.[178] The STL uses English, French, and Arabic. The ECCC also has three official languages: English, French, and Khmer.

Language issues have bedeviled the Court from its inception. In addition to the communication divide that tends to result between many national and international officials, the Court's international side is also somewhat split between Francophone and Anglophone personnel, not all of whom are mutually conversant. At initial training sessions in 2006, French judicial officials complained that sessions were conducted in English and Khmer.[179] Years after its inception, the ECCC still lacks the capacity to undertake the prodigious task of translating all of the documents generated by the parties or referred to in their submissions into three languages.[180] In May 2009, ECCC administrators reported that the Court was still short-staffed by one-third, particularly lacking French interpreters. Most Cambodian students now elect to study English as a foreign language, making French-speaking translators a scarce commodity. The ECCC thus had to resort to a cumbersome "relay system"—Khmer to English to French or vice versa—to facilitate discussion with French lawyers on the defense teams.[181]

One Cambodian staffer laments that translation "has generally been consuming more than double" the time that would be required to proceed in a single language.[182] Craig Etcheson, who served on the staff of the Office of the

Co-Prosecutors, agrees that translation has been "one of the greatest challenges in the entire exercise" and has been "immensely time-consuming."[183] Translation issues have arisen on numerous occasions in the courtroom and prompted repeated challenges from the defense, especially the Khieu Samphan team, which has demanded complete translations of documents into French and has faulted inaccuracies in official translations.[184] The Court rejected Khieu Samphan's request for a complete translation of materials, reasoning that doing so would take too much time,[185] but his request that the Court review transcript translations is compelling, since French is both an official language of the Court and the language of his international Co-Lawyers. Khieu Samphan's Co-Lawyer Anta Guissé asserts that some translations have included important mistakes, and argues that defense teams should not have to read documents in all three languages to be sure of their meaning.[186] As with many other aspects of the Court's operations, efficiency concerns and scarce resources are in tension with the demands of a fair trial.

The inclusion of three official languages may have complicated the Court's work unnecessarily. Etcheson, like many others, notes that "from an operational perspective, it's hard to think of anyone at the Court who was [or is] solely Francophone."[187] One official adds that some ECCC personnel refer to French as "the third superfluous language."[188] The decision to include French may have been politically expedient for the ECCC, but given the paucity of French-language documents and English proficiency of most French lawyers involved, in retrospect its inclusion appears to be one of the more avoidable sources of inefficiency at the ECCC.

Difficulties in Financial Management

The ECCC's funding structure has introduced challenges in financial planning and management as well. Budgets have to be prepared by the Cambodian and international sides separately and shuttled from one side to another for comments and modification as they are reconciled.[189] In addition, finances have come from a number of different channels. The international side has received funds from more than 20 UN member states and a handful of private donors. The national side has been funded through contributions from the Cambodian Government, direct bilateral aid from more than 10 different donor states, foreign aid channeled through UNDP and the Cambodian Government, and disbursement of multilateral funds managed by the United Nations. Donors have differing requirements for their grants to the ECCC, including auditing and reporting requirements and grant periods.

The ECCC's financial management challenges are compounded by the lack of a centralized international oversight mechanism. At the SCSL, the Management Committee monitors all court finances and reports to the UN Secretary-General.[190] At fully international courts, reports go to the United Nations. The diversity of the ECCC's funding sources places a heavy burden on the OA's Budget and Finance Unit. Financial management is considerably easier at domestic courts—which receive funds exclusively from the government—or fully international tribunals that have their funds channeled through the United Nations.[191] The OA must report separately to the Cambodian Government, UN entities, and individual foreign donors—consuming resources that could be better spent on legal or outreach functions.

Unpredictable Funding Streams

The ECCC has also faced the challenge of unpredictable and sometimes inadequate funds arising from its reliance on voluntary donor contributions. Its initial budget was determined only after the passage of the ECCC Law. UN and Cambodian officials agreed that the two sides would split a budget of $56.3 million spread over the tribunal's three-year expected lifetime. International donors would pay roughly $43 million, and the Cambodian Government would fund the remaining $13.3 million. That agreement quickly came under strain, however. After an intergovernmental pledging conference in New York in March 2005, roughly 90% of the required donations on the international side were in place. Japan was the largest initial donor, contributing $21 million.[192] Other major bilateral donors included Australia, France, Germany, and the United Kingdom.[193] The Cambodian Government announced that it could contribute only $1.5 million, however.[194] Cambodian officials argued that their most important contributions would be in-kind donations, such as providing a physical site for the tribunal. Foreign donors provided the rest, and this precedent set the stage for a series of episodes in which funds for the Cambodian side would nearly expire before an international rescue—a game reminiscent of the negotiations to create the tribunal.

Just months after the tribunal began operating, it became clear that the ECCC would far exceed the rosy initial cost estimates.[195] That was not a surprise, both because such institutions are habitually sold to donors with overly optimistic projections and because initial budget plans were based on unrealistic estimates by planners with little or no experience managing civil law or mass crimes trials.[196] Since then, the ECCC has lurched from funding crisis to funding crisis. In January 2008, ECCC officials sent a revised budget to donors requesting $114 million more to fund the tribunal's work through March 2011. As discussed above, most international donors were unenthusiastic amid allegations of mismanagement and corruption. Many demanded justification for the increased costs, and some withheld funds to press for reforms to the ECCC's administration, but Australian and French infusions helped keep the court functioning.[197]

The ECCC later shaved its budget request, requesting an additional $46 million through 2009—$36 million for the international side and $10 million for the Cambodian side.[198] Pledges from Germany ($4.3 million) and the United States ($1.8 million) on the international side and from Japan ($2.9 million) and Cambodia ($1 million) on the domestic side and other key donors met some of that request, but the tribunal continued to require urgent fundraising to avoid depleting its resources.[199]

Another funding impasse occurred in early 2009 amid the debate over an anticorruption mechanism. A Japanese grant of $21 million helped fill the shortfall on the international side, and as described above, funds on the Cambodian side dwindled before Australia and Japan infused more resources. Further crunches occurred in late 2010, when Cambodian staffers had to go without salaries pending donor replenishments,[200] and similar crises occurred again in late 2011, 2012, and 2013.[201]

In facing funding uncertainties and impasses, the ECCC is certainly not alone. The SCSL also was not created under Chapter VII authority and thus lacked access to assessed contributions from UN member states.[202] Yet the existence of a donor-led Management Committee and a stronger UN role in the Sierra Leone tribunal helped the SCSL access international funds. The UN General Assembly's budget committee took $16 million from its "subvention fund" of unused assessed contributions to help the SCSL through a budget crisis in 2004[203] and again used subvention funds to help the SCSL overcome serious funding shortfalls in 2011 and 2012 amid its final trial against Charles Taylor.[204] No such subvention funds have been forthcoming for the ECCC.

ECCC officials and staff present varying views on how funding uncertainties have affected the Court's functional efficacy. Cambodian Co-Investigating Judge You Bunleng asserts that the funding crises "affect, to some degree, the motivation and budget plans of staff and their families," but staff in the Office of Co-Investigating Judges still exhibit "high commitment in fulfilling their duty" and "do not stop working . . . regardless of getting their salary on time."[205] Etcheson asserts that in the Office of the Co-Prosecutors, "with one exception, our national colleagues bit the bullet and did the work when they weren't being paid" but that "it never did them any good in morale," especially as months passed.[206] One Cambodian staffer believes that "the international community would not let the Court's work collapse," so funding rescues are expected.[207] By contrast, other staff say that funding impasses "really affect the Court's work,"[208] because staff lose motivation,[209] depart, and need to be replaced—which causes delays—and because "without clear funding," the Court's offices have "unclear work plan[s]."[210]

Both inefficiency and funding crunches have contributed to the underfunding of some important ECCC functions. By the end of 2012, the ECCC employed 176 international personnel and 292 Cambodians and had spent $173.3 million since its inception—$131.2 million funded through the UN side, and $42.1 million through the Cambodian side.[211] By that point, the ECCC had spent approximately $135 million for total staff salaries, other staff costs, and nonstaff compensation; roughly $25 million for supplies, furniture and equipment, facilities alteration, general operating costs, and various contractor services; but much smaller amounts for training, legacy, outreach trips, defense and victims support, and experts and witnesses.[212]

Funding shortfalls have also affected the Court's core judicial operations. The UN has cut many positions to reduce costs but has lost key staff members as a result. In October 2012, the Trial Chamber announced that staff cuts required it to hear courtroom proceedings only three days each week—a measure it acknowledged would further delay Case 002, its most important trial.[213] UN Special Expert David Scheffer warned of further impending layoffs, and Secretary-General Ban Ki-moon said that if donors did not fill a funding shortfall of several million dollars in the Court's 2012–13 budget, the crisis "could jeopardize the judicial proceedings."[214] Indeed, it has. In December 2012, international Co-Prosecutor Andrew Cayley had to tour Europe to help the Court raise funds to avoid bankruptcy.[215] This is hardly the function one would wish for a prosecutor to undertake in the midst of the Court's headline trial. In March 2013, approximately 20 Cambodian translators and interpreters went briefly on strike after going three months without pay, delaying the proceedings in Case 002 by more than a month.[216] In July, the Court let 10% of Cambodian staff go to save money,[217] but new threats of strikes came the following month after still another suspension of pay due to gaps in funding for the Cambodian side of the Court.[218] In September, 134 Cambodian staff went on strike for three weeks until a UN loan to Cambodia covered their summer back pay. In October, the Cambodian Government pledged to fill the $1.8 million shortfall on the national side until the end of the year, but further funding gaps are almost certain in 2014.

Throughout the process, the Cambodian Government has funded less than 20% of the budget for the national side, relying on foreign donors to pay Cambodian personnel at the Court. The hybrid nature of the Court enables the Cambodian Government to force donors' hands, because as Council of Ministers spokesman Ek Tha stressed during one recent pay freeze, "the international side will not be able to work without assistance from the Cambodian side."[219] Some believe the Cambodian Government wants the Court to close. In early 2013, after national judges and staff had gone nearly three months without pay, one Cambodian staffer said: "The government won't pay these salaries. They just want the court to shut down . . . By creating this situation, they just want to embarrass the U.N."[220] At a minimum, Cambodian officials have been willing to take the risk that the Court will close—or that the proceedings will drag out until all of the defendants die—while donors continue to blink first, providing just enough funds to keep the national side afloat.

Funding problems relate closely to broader political disputes at the Court. In 2011, the ECCC's administration faced pressure to wind down the work of the Office of the Co-Investigating Judges (OCIJ) in order to pour all available funds into Case 002. The Defence Support Section was initially refused funds for suspects in Cases 003 and 004,[221] and more than one donor has reportedly sought to earmark funds for Case 002. In October 2012, Scheffer noted that a donor had withdrawn its pledge to fill the Court's 2012 shortfall. According to rumors in Court circles, Japan was that donor and withdrew its pledge when the UN rejected Tokyo's request to earmark funds for Case 002 only.[222] Earmarking for an international court can easily verge into political interference, especially when it limits or withholds resources for particular cases. Some human rights advocates warned donors against imposing such limits in the lead-up to the 2012 Session of the Assembly of States Parties to the ICC.[223] A court relying on voluntary contributions is particularly vulnerable.

Should the ECCC decide to proceed with Cases 003 and 004, the cost of the process will rise again. Indeed, the Court revised its 2012–13 budget to add or reinstate 18 positions in the OCIJ after the new international CIJ Mark Harmon arrived in October 2012 and indicated his intention to press forward with further investigation of Cases 003 and 004—investigations often stymied during the politicized deadlock over those cases since 2009.[224] Donor demands for earmarks will likely escalate over time, further eroding what little remains of the Court's independent prosecutorial discretion.

CONCLUSION

The structure of the ECCC has posed serious challenges to effective administration and financial management. The United Nations agreed unenthusiastically to a partnership with a government fixated on maintaining a strong measure of political control. The ECCC's split administrative and managerial structures have made it difficult for UN officials to deal decisively with problems arising on the Cambodian side of the court. Administrative inefficiencies and impasses have also lengthened the process, made it more expensive, and sapped donor interest.

The United Nations has sometimes been passive in dealing with administrative and financial problems at the ECCC, ambivalent about the Court as a whole, and unwilling to take strong ownership of a process it does not control. This is reminiscent of the situation in East Timor. Former Chief Justice of the Special Panels Phillip Rapoza suggests that:

> [T]he question of ownership overlapped with the issue of control and neither the U.N. nor East Timor wished to take responsibility for what they did not consider wholly their own. In that sense, the hybrid process was too much a bastard child for either to claim paternity.[225]

Deputy Director Knut Rosandhaug, the most senior UN administrative official, has reiterated the UN's position that gives considerable deference to the Cambodian side of the Court, differentiating the ECCC as "a national court with UN backing, whereas other war crimes courts are run by the UN[.]"[226] The division of authority between DESA, OLA, and UN officials in Phnom Penh has also been ambiguous, contributing to the lack of clear international ownership of difficult administrative decisions.[227] Despite the creation of a Special Expert position, donors generally have taken a hands-off managerial approach as well, seldom using the Friends group to exert strong managerial guidance, even when such guidance is sorely needed. Without tougher, more concerted donor engagement, the United Nations is in a difficult structural position indeed.[228]

While it is true that changes to the structure of the Court would require renegotiation, the UN does have considerable capacity to fulfill its partnership obligations as outlined in the Agreement.[229] The international responses to human resources mismanagement and the kickback scandal at the ECCC show that pressure from the United Nations and donors can drive reforms even within a difficult structural environment and in the face of domestic stonewalling. In administration and finance, as in other aspects of the Court's operations, the United Nations and key donors have been eager to trumpet successes but too ready to distance themselves from the ECCC when adverse developments occur. The structure of the tribunal certainly provides incentives and opportunities to do so, but it does not predetermine that outcome.

Chapter 4

CASE 001—CONVICTING AN INFAMOUS KHMER ROUGE TORTURE CHIEF

"You Cannot Cover an Elephant with a Rice Basket"

The ECCC's early challenges—including struggles over procedural rules, administrative delays, corruption allegations, and funding shortfalls—tended to confirm fears that the Court's complex hybrid structure would compromise its operational effectiveness. Given the ongoing political tension between the national and international sides in their awkward institutional marriage, it was unclear that the ECCC would be able to carry out its most important function of delivering credible criminal trials.

The ECCC's first test was its easiest: the trial against Kaing Guek Eav, better known by his alias "Duch." Duch was the former head of the notorious S-21 security center in Phnom Penh, and this chapter's subtitle—a courtroom quote from Duch's Cambodian co-counsel, Kar Savuth—conveys the widespread knowledge of horrific crimes that took place there.[1] The ECCC ultimately found that at least 12,273 prisoners,[2] many of them Khmer Rouge cadres caught up in internal political purges, were tortured and executed at S-21 from 1975 to 1979.[3]

It was not coincidental that Duch's trial came first. Donors and Court officials believed that trying Duch would be the best start for the Court, as his case is the "one with the greatest amount of documentation, witnesses, the suspect has already confessed, and it would be easy to bring to trial."[4] Signed orders by Duch to torture and execute prisoners, the available testimony of former S-21 prison guards and prisoners, and Duch's own previous admissions all reduced the legal and administrative complexity of the case.[5] Duch also had not been tried or granted any form of amnesty or pardon in the past. It was thus very likely that the ECCC could produce a credible conviction.

Just as important, Duch's trial was not deemed politically sensitive. Unlike other key Khmer Rouge suspects, he had few previous dealings with the Cambodian Government or foreign powers. His offenses were concentrated around events at S-21, making it less likely that his trial would feature discussion of foreign powers and time periods outside of Democratic Kampuchea (DK). The key stakeholders agreed that he should stand trial, making political feuds over the case unlikely. The *Duch* trial was therefore the best-case scenario for testing the effect of the ECCC's unique hybrid form upon its function. If the ECCC were unable to try Duch effectively, its ability to manage more difficult cases would be doubtful. As it turns out, the trial was largely successful, but not without challenges that raised doubts about the Court's ability to manage tougher, more politically contested cases.

OVERVIEW OF THE *DUCH* CASE

Although Duch was not one of the most senior Khmer Rouge leaders, he had long been identified as one of the individuals most likely to stand trial at the ECCC under the rubric of those "most responsible" for crimes of the Pol Pot era. He was born in 1942 and became interested in communism while a student, spending two years in prison for pro–Khmer Rouge activities. He was freed in 1970 in a general amnesty of political prisoners after Prime Minister Lon Nol overthrew Prince Sihanouk's government, and rejoined the communist insurgency. Within a few years he had set up and was running two Khmer Rouge prisons in Kampong Speu—M13 and M99—and had begun perfecting the torture interrogation techniques he later implemented at the S-21 (Tuol Sleng) security center.

The S-21 security center was established in Phnom Penh in 1975 after the Khmers Rouges overthrew Lon Nol. In 1976, Duch took over as chief, a position he held until the Vietnamese army and allied Cambodian resistance fighters captured Phnom Penh in 1979. In its judgment, the Trial Chamber found that as chief of S-21, Duch was also in charge of the S-24 (Prey Sar) work camp and had established the Choeung Ek killing fields, where most of the S-21 prisoners were executed.[6] Duch also implemented and refined S-21's interrogation/torture techniques, authorized executions, and personally oversaw the interrogation of the most important prisoners.

The first prisoners to arrive at S-21 were officials and soldiers connected to the overthrown Lon Nol regime, but later they comprised primarily Khmer Rouge cadres and their families, some foreigners including Vietnamese prisoners of war, and S-21 staff. Nearly all prisoners were tortured until they confessed to antirevolutionary crimes and named their "accomplices," who would then be arrested and tortured until they confessed their crimes and named additional traitors in turn.[7]

After the fall of the DK regime, Duch lived among the senior Khmer Rouge leaders in Thai border refugee camps until 1984 when he was sent to China to teach and changed his name to Hang Pin. When he returned to Cambodia, he taught in Banteay Meanchey province until 1995 when his house was attacked, either as part of a robbery or a revenge attack, and his wife was killed. At that time he moved to Battambang province, where he converted to Christianity and joined a local church. During this period he continued to teach and also worked in camps along the Thai border with non-governmental organizations.[8] In 1999 he was identified and arrested, and he was thereafter held by the Cambodian Military Court for over eight years without trial. In 2007, he was indicted by and transferred to the custody of the ECCC.

Although limited to one detention site where primarily Khmer Rouge cadres and their families were executed, the *Duch* trial was of major significance in providing the first opportunity for Cambodians to hear public discussion and debate on policies of the DK period that resulted in the deaths of nearly two million people in only three years, eight months, and twenty days. Duch's confession of his crimes and the Court's judgment of his actions had potential significance even for survivors unconnected to S-21, as they spoke to the responsibility of the many Khmer Rouge cadres who will never be held accountable for other atrocities.

Partly due to the limited points at issue, the *Duch* proceedings were a successful first effort. In general, the Court produced reasonable jurisprudence, and it took significant steps to connect the *Duch* trial to the surrounding survivor population. These included an unprecedented civil party scheme, which engaged nearly 100 survivors of the DK period in the case against Duch, and extensive outreach activities made possible by its in-country location.[9] It also issued a credible verdict. On July 26, 2010, the ECCC pronounced the first internationally recognized conviction of a key Khmer Rouge official for crimes of the Pol Pot era, finding Duch guilty of crimes against humanity and war crimes.[10]

The Court did encounter difficulties related to its institutional structure, however. The *Duch* trial suffered from delays and confusion as the testing ground for the ECCC's complex hybrid structure, the first-time application of its mixed civil law and common law rules, and the experimental inclusion of civil parties. The case also featured a dramatic split between Duch's national and international lawyers that undermined his defense and a struggle to resolve perhaps the most politically sensitive issue at the trial—how to account in sentencing for Duch's lengthy and illegal pretrial detention by the Cambodian Military Court. Each of these issues is examined below.

DUCH'S HYBRID DEFENSE

Given the overwhelming evidence against Duch, much of the intrigue at trial pertained to the strategies his co-lawyers would mount in his defense. From the start, Duch agreed to most of the factual allegations against him;[11] the only unknown was what sentence he would receive.[12] Throughout the trial, Duch's co-lawyers appeared to pursue a joint strategy of pleading guilty to most charges, repeatedly expressing remorse, and cooperating with the prosecution in the hope of receiving a reduced sentence. Duch's international and national lawyers took somewhat different approaches, however, leading to one of the most dramatic events at the mixed Court at that time: an eleventh-hour split between the co-lawyers resulting in two fundamentally different pleas for their client.

International Counsel's Strategy—Critiquing the Court's Mixed Rules

Duch's French international counsel François Roux emphasized Duch's admission of most allegations in his continued efforts to seek a pseudo "guilty plea" and reduce the scope of evidence introduced against his client at trial. Roux also raised concerns regarding efficiency and equality of arms due to the first-time inclusion of civil parties in a mass crimes trial, seeking to reduce victims' impact on sentencing. The Trial Chamber struggled to find the right balance between fully airing the facts and minimizing the length of proceedings. Debates over the applicable rules provided an early indication of the difficulties of applying domestic civil law procedures in a field of law dominated by common law precedent.

Minimizing the Scope of Evidence Presented

The French civil law system does not recognize "guilty pleas" that lead to truncated proceedings; however, during the investigation phase a judge collects all evidence and narrows down the issues in dispute. He or she examines witnesses, and very few are recalled to testify at trial. This procedure keeps trials short and focused. Because of the large amount of evidence at issue at the ECCC, "[m]aterial on the Case File is considered evidence and relied on by the Chamber in decision making only where it is *put before* the Chamber and subjected to examination.[13] Evidence is considered "put before" the Chamber "if its content has been summarised, read out, or appropriately identified in court."[14] Although this common law–like innovation arguably makes trial proceedings fairer because everything is debated in public, it has the potential to negate much of the time savings of having a case file, as all evidence must be presented a second time at trial.

In an apparent effort to reduce the scope of evidence admitted, Duch's French co-lawyer François Roux often argued that the Internal Rules should be interpreted in light of international practice, and Duch's admissions of responsibility and remorse should be accepted as a type of guilty plea.[15] But after 30 years of impunity for Khmer Rouge crimes, the public arguably had the right—and the need—to hear all the facts discussed. This was especially true because Duch's admissions were undercut by their selectivity. He often had perfect recollection of people and events, but he denied all facts that were not proved by documentation[16] and became vague and forgetful when the evidence pointed to his active and willing involvement in the crimes, such as through personally committing torture,[17] or going beyond what was required to fulfill his orders.

Although there were doubts about the sincerity of Duch's public apology on the second day of trial, it provoked much-needed discussion and debate among Cambodians. Significantly, it was the first ever offered by a senior Khmer Rouge official:

> Now, I would like [survivors and the families of the dead] to know that I wish to apologize, and I would like you to consider my intentions. I do not ask that

> you forgive me here and now. I know that the crimes I committed against the lives of those people, including women and children, are intolerably and unforgivably serious crimes. My plea is that you leave the door open for me to seek forgiveness.[18]

Some people believed his remorse was genuine.[19] Others were more suspicious. Survivor Chheav Hourlay said, "We cannot infer from the confession whether he is honest . . . [h]e might have talked to have his sentence reduced or the charges dropped[.]"[20]

The prosecution never recognized Duch's statements as either a guilty plea or as an expression of unqualified remorse. Duch never said, "I plead guilty as charged," but instead fought the charges, arguing, for example, that there had been no armed conflict before 1977 and he therefore could not be charged with war crimes before that date. As discussed below, he also denied that he acted voluntarily—an argument that goes to the heart of his criminality. Due to the historic nature of the case, his limited expressions of responsibility, and public expectations of hearing all the evidence, the prosecution—and the judges—believed it was necessary to have a full trial.

Unsuccessful in limiting the scope of crime evidence put before the Chamber, Roux then sought to limit the prosecution's character evidence:

> And when an accused pleads guilty before an international criminal court—please listen carefully—an agreement is struck with the prosecutors, enabling the accused to bring forward character witnesses and the prosecutor does not challenge them. The prosecutor refrains when someone pleads guilty in common law—refrains from questioning or challenging character witnesses. That is the solution. That is the solution.[21]

The Trial Chamber did not accept this argument, but as discussed below, Roux was able to persuade it that as auxiliary prosecutors the civil parties should not have an equal opportunity to challenge Duch on the key issues of character and sentencing.

Managing Civil Party Participation

With four civil party teams and at least one national and one international lawyer per team in Case 001, the defense faced a minimum of eight additional lawyers supporting the prosecution in court. The teams began cooperating among themselves to a greater extent over time, but they for the most part worked independently, resulting in questioning repetitive not only with the prosecution but also with each other.[22] While some lawyers spoke to individual clients' interests, and thus asked questions perceived as irrelevant, others honed closely to the prosecution's case, contributing to a perception that they were acting as a second prosecutorial team.[23] Judge Silvia Cartwright called the process of involving victims "cumbersome" and said that "it has frequently had the unlooked-for effect of slowing the trial while not providing for victims' needs which includes achieving timely justice for their suffering."[24]

Although many of the complications arising from civil party participation in Case 001 have been laid at the feet of the civil party lawyers, the Court itself was unprepared to manage their participation and addressed problems only as they arose rather than planning in advance. Little forethought was put into how the civil party scheme would work in practice; instead, it developed over time through trial and error. As one Court monitor has noted: "Many of the problems that would emerge during the trial seemed to be the result of inadequate planning and preparation on the Court's behalf with regard to the civil party process as a whole."[25] Instead of managing civil party representation from the outset, the Court blamed the civil party lawyers for not organizing themselves.

Civil party lawyer Alain Werner did not believe the civil parties' participation in Case 001 unacceptably lengthened the *Duch* trial. In his view, considering that the ECCC is the first international court to apply mainly civil law and to include civil party participation, "this trial has shown that the system can certainly work in theory, maybe with some adaptations" depending on the number of accused and civil parties.[26] Journalist Thierry Cruvellier opined:

> At the end of the day, even though it was messy and the representation was often poor, it seems that it did bring to the [*Duch*] trial a dimension considered missing at the other tribunals . . . Anyone who says that this is not an interesting experiment here at the ECCC forgets how frustrated the victims were in the [International Criminal Tribunal for the former Yugoslavia (ICTY)].[27]

A more worrisome problem than duplication and delay was the four civil party teams' impact on equality of arms. Duch's lawyer argued that although in civil law systems there is no question that civil parties are entitled to question all witnesses and experts, it was inappropriate when there are numerous civil parties acting as auxiliary prosecutors:

> And so, yes, indeed you have civil law on your side. That's true. Looking at the letter of the law, the law is on your side. But the law is a living organism and, more specifically, we all know here that we are in a tribunal that creates law.[28]

As part of François Roux's efforts to have Duch's cooperation and apology accepted as a *de facto* guilty plea, from the early stages of trial proceedings he challenged the right of the civil parties to make submissions on sentencing. The civil parties argued that facts relating to guilt or innocence cannot be separated from facts relevant to sentencing and noted that at the ECCC there is no separate sentencing hearing.[29] Moreover, they emphasized that neither the ECCC Internal Rules nor the Cambodian Code of Criminal Procedure nor other civil law jurisdictions preclude civil parties from being heard on sentencing, and that as full parties, they have a general right to be heard on any topic.[30] They wished to draw on the testimony of individual civil parties and discuss topics such as the impact of the crimes and Duch's admissions and expression of remorse on the civil parties and their families.[31]

However, the Trial Chamber said that the ECCC civil party model is based on "but is not identical to" Cambodian procedure, because it has been adapted to take into account the unique context of complex mass crimes trials with numerous victims, which requires "a restrictive interpretation of rights of civil parties" in proceedings before the ECCC.[32] It highlighted the fair trial rights of the accused, including to face only one prosecuting authority.[33] Ultimately, it found that civil parties could not make submissions on or recommendations concerning sentencing, because their right to assist the prosecution is limited to establishing the guilt of the accused in order to secure their claim for reparations.[34]

Finding that civil parties could not opine on sentencing, the Chamber tacked onto this decision the determination that they also could not question witnesses and experts about Duch's character. In their view, questions relating to character relate solely to aggravating and mitigating circumstances, and therefore are relevant solely to sentencing, in which the civil parties had no interest.[35]

These decisions appeared to be a belated effort to manage civil party interventions by limiting their right to participate as a party. The *Duch* trial was never about proving Duch's guilt, which he freely admitted. It was from the start only about sentencing. Bearing this in mind, it is arguable that the Chamber excluded the civil parties from the most important part of the trial—the heart of the matter. It made this decision against civil law practice and the Court's own rules. It seems likely that the judges' daily experience of watching four civil party legal teams repeat prosecution arguments over and over convinced them to accept François Roux's appeal to leave domestic civil law rules behind:

> When one is in a national civil law trial where there is an accused who has committed one murder and when you have one, perhaps two, civil parties applying, well, if the civil party lets his or her suffering overflow, that might happen but it won't go any further than that. However, in proceedings such as this one dealing with mass crimes, if you have one, two, three, five, 10 or 20 or more civil parties who come and let out their legitimate suffering then we find ourselves in a situation that is unimaginable from the point of view of a fair trial because the accused is no longer facing one prosecutor but 20, 30, 50 prosecutors.[36]

Blending Civil and Common Law Procedures

After the *Duch* trial, major actors offered different perspectives on the results of the blending of legal systems. Australian Acting international Co-Prosecutor William Smith said, "[T]he conflict between the civil law and common law systems was 'more myth than reality' and that the greater challenge was managing the copious evidence."[37] However both the French Co-Investigating Judge and the French international Co-Lawyer criticized the Co-Prosecutors for not following civil law procedures.

Former CIJ Marcel Lemonde has repeatedly argued that the prosecutors failed to use the judicial investigation in the Case 001 trial sufficiently. In his view, as common law lawyers, they "have sometimes given the impression that they did not know how to use the investigation file . . . ; if there had been no [judicial] investigation, the trial would probably not have been fundamentally different."[38] As his key example, he points to the "reenactment" he staged at the Choeung Ek killing fields and S-21, where Duch was confronted with witnesses including former guards and some victims. Lemonde says that at this meeting, Duch provided useful information, such as explaining that the S-21 site had not changed since 1979, which was important because a number of people said that the crime site may have been manipulated by the Vietnamese.[39] However, other civil law lawyers say that the CIJ investigation was underutilized at trial because Duch admitted most of the charges. Indeed, there is a widespread consensus that the reenactment had little evidentiary significance, but was primarily—in Judge Lemonde's own words—"a great moment."[40]

Comparably, François Roux said that the need for evidence to be heard publicly at trial caused ECCC procedure to evolve as "a combination of both civil and common law, which has sometimes led to confusion and dispute."[41] In his view, the worst of both systems was sometimes implemented when the parties employed common law procedures due to a "lack of understanding" of the civil law system.[42] Nevertheless, in seeking a *de facto* guilty plea for his client and reduced civil party participation, he likewise advocated a common law approach on more than one occasion, albeit in the guise of adapting procedures to mass crimes proceedings. He asked the Chamber to be "pragmatic," "take account of the particular context of the Duch case," and "hand down a specific decision; specific to the Duch case."[43] Despite Roux's frustrations, he appears in accord with Trial Judge Silvia Cartwright's view that the blending of law is part of "a move towards 'a homogenous system' at the international level" involving the adaptation of procedures from both traditions "to ensure they fit the realities on the ground."[44]

However, in tasking the Court with applying Cambodian procedures, the drafters of the Framework Agreement and ECCC Law did not give the Court authority to apply hybrid procedures adapted to mass crimes, nor did they give it authority to look to the practice of international courts except where there is a lacuna, uncertainty, or inconsistency with international standards. From the start, the Court has grappled with the reality that, even when such problems do not exist, domestic procedures are often inappropriate in a mass crimes context—where, for example, there is a greater need to publicly demonstrate justice being done. At the same time, because international procedures are not based in civil law, they do not offer a clear way forward. Although the Internal Rules foresee some hybrid solutions, they fail to address many of the problems that have arisen, and have created others. As seen in chapters 5 and 7, the appropriate "blending" of systems has been viewed differently by different judges and applied differently by each chamber, sometimes resulting in confusion and inconsistency.

National Counsel's Strategy: Mounting Legal Defenses

Some public reluctance to accept Duch's cooperation and expressions of remorse as a guilty plea stemmed from his parallel efforts to diminish his responsibility by arguing that he had no choice but to act as ordered by his superiors in the CPK hierarchy. Although Duch's counsel never formally argued the applicability of the legal defenses of duress or superior orders during trial, his Cambodian lawyer Kar Savuth raised them during closing arguments, and they are thus addressed by the Trial Chamber in its findings. Both of his counsel also questioned if Duch was being used as a scapegoat for the crimes of the regime. Although they never made a legal case for selective prosecution, Kar Savuth made a compelling plea for "fairness" that resonated with many Cambodian survivors. During closing arguments he went further and broke with his international Co-Counsel to argue that these factors excluded Duch from the Court's jurisdiction over "senior leaders" and "persons most responsible" for the crimes of the DK era. This turn of events paralleled efforts to close Cases 003 and 004 on the same grounds, generating concern that political opposition to more trials might taint the Case 001 verdict.

Superior Orders and Duress: "A Cog in an Unstoppable Machine"

While admitting to gruesome facts and apologizing for his role at S-21, Duch also denied that he acted voluntarily, arguing that he was coerced to carry out his superiors' orders and had no leeway in executing them. On the second day of trial, Roux noted that the Chamber would determine "what was the degree of autonomy or lack thereon of in Duch in his duties as the head of S-21?"[45] This is likely one reason why Duch adamantly denied that anyone had ever been released from S-21.[46]

Duch portrayed himself as a prisoner of the regime. He said he had been "reluctant" to become an S-21 deputy and that his request to instead work at the Ministry of Industry had been denied.[47] "[M]y acceptance of duties in the security centres, starting with M-13, was something that I was not able to avoid."[48] "I found myself serving a criminal organization which smashed a large number of its own people and from which I could not withdraw. I was a cog in an unstoppable machine."[49] He said he acted out of fear for his own life and the lives of his family.[50]

International courts do not accept duress as a complete defense to charges of crimes against humanity and serious war crimes. For example, in the ICTY *Erdemovic* case in which a Bosnian Serb soldier was found to have taken part in a massacre or be killed himself, duress was only taken into account in the mitigation of his sentence.[51] The International Criminal Court's Rome Statute, which provides the most detailed definitions of defenses among international court documents, does not exclude a duress defense to serious crimes, but defines it as resulting from a threat of imminent death or of continuing or imminent serious bodily harm against someone or another person, where he or she acts necessarily and reasonably to avoid this threat, and does not intend to cause a greater harm than the one sought to be avoided.[52] Thus, consistent with ICTY jurisprudence, under this definition the need to protect oneself and one's family would never be a complete defense to participation in the murder of thousands of people.

The ECCC Trial Chamber ruled consistent with this international precedent in finding that "[d]uress cannot . . . be invoked when the perceived threat results from the implementation of a policy of terror in which [Duch] himself has willingly and actively participated."[53] "The Chamber accordingly finds that the Accused did not act under duress as Deputy and later Chairman of S-21. Duress as such is therefore irrelevant both in relation to the Accused's criminal responsibility and in mitigation of sentence."[54] Nevertheless, it did consider the "coercive climate" during the DK period as a mitigating factor.[55]

Duch also said he was only acting in accordance with superior orders. For example, when asked how he could have viewed mothers with babies as enemies he said, "It was not me . . . there was an order[.]"[56] Superior orders, which is related to duress, is the only defense mentioned in the core ECCC documents; however, it is explicitly excluded.[57] It has been disallowed as a defense at least since the Nuremberg trials but may be accepted as a mitigating factor in sentencing.

Despite the clarity of the law on this point, during closing arguments and on appeal Kar Savuth argued that Duch could not be found to be most responsible under Cambodian law[58] as he was merely acting under superior orders.[59] However, even if Cambodian substantive law were applicable before the ECCC, it, like international law, does not recognize an exception for someone who acted pursuant to superior orders he knew were unlawful, which the Trial Chamber found to have been the case.[60] The Chamber also refused to consider superior orders as a mitigating factor due to the long span of time over which the crimes were committed, the large number of victims, and Duch's dedication to improving S-21 operations.[61]

Scapegoat: Selective Prosecution

For foreigners who have visited Cambodia, S-21 is synonymous with the crimes of the DK era. The Tuol Sleng Genocide Museum housed at the S-21 prison complex and the Choeung Ek killing fields are among the most visited tourist attractions in Phnom Penh. Most Cambodians, however, have never visited either one. That began to change only after the ECCC was established, and outreach programs brought tens of thousands of students and visitors from the provinces to learn about what had transpired. The large cache of documents found at S-21, including forced confessions, has contributed to the site's notoriety and made it the subject of numerous scholarly studies. It is also the primary reason why the crimes that took place at S-21 and Duch's role in them have always been a focus of accountability efforts, and why he was tried first: his guilt is inescapable.

As the subjects of the first trial for Khmer Rouge crimes committed during the DK period, S-21 and Duch inevitably became emblematic of the harms suffered at that time. Although many of those killed at S-21 were Khmer Rouge cadres, many Cambodians lost family members at other Khmer Rouge prisons that shared distressing features with S-21, including routine torture. In this way S-21 "symbolically represents the larger suffering that people experienced; in some sense, it stands in for and embodies their own suffering."[62]

Unsurprisingly, the idea that Duch was a "scapegoat" for all DK crimes arose at the start of trial. François Roux used the term in its allegorical sense: "No, Duch does not have to bear on his head all the horrors of the Cambodian tragedy."[63] In contrast, Kar Savuth attempted to argue that Duch was the subject of selective prosecution. Throughout the proceedings, Kar Savuth made occasional references to the other 195 chiefs of other Khmer Rouge security centers, and especially the fact that more people died at some of those prisons than at S-21.[64] "[I]s it fair? Because each person receives that same orders from the same Angkar, and each person also conducted torture, executions, and why only Duch is brought for trial? And only Duch is the only scapegoat on behalf of those 195 chiefs of prisons."[65]

In response, the prosecution emphasized that while all persons must be treated equally before the law, this does not mean that no one can be prosecuted if all others who commit the same crimes are not prosecuted.[66] Moreover, they argued that the special nature of S-21 as a central CPK organ made it distinct and more important than the other detention centers, even if more people died at other prisons.[67]

Although legally Kar Savuth's argument was a dead end, to many Cambodians whose families suffered at the hands of other prison chiefs and mid-level cadres, it was compelling. One woman whose father had been taken away for reeducation was quoted as saying, "[t]o me, [Duch] represents all the Khmer Rouge[.]"[68] Kar Savuth appealed to survivors' desire to know the truth about what happened when he said that if the prosecution could not provide a list of everyone who was most responsible and explain why, there would be no justice.[69] And he spoke to their fears when he emphasized that if only a "small fish" like Duch—someone who had "only" killed 12,380 people—was prosecuted but not those responsible for many more deaths, then what would be the lesson for Cambodia? A similar regime could return to power.[70] However, he went too far when he asked for Duch's acquittal instead of following Roux's efforts to seek a sentence reduction.

Defense Strategy Split and Implosion

The *Duch* trial strategy, a fine balance of admission and evasion, was upended during closing arguments when Duch's national counsel, Kar Savuth, challenged the Court's jurisdiction over Duch and said that he should be found not guilty. In retrospect, there were clear signs from the beginning that Kar Savuth and François Roux were not pursuing the same defense.

On the second day of trial, Kar Savuth's opening statement immediately attacked the Court's jurisdiction over Duch, arguing that there were 14 senior leaders and persons most responsible, and Duch was not one of them.[71] Instead, Duch was merely one of many former heads of security centers who filled the same roles and responsibilities, and if he were the only one to be prosecuted it would be a violation of the Cambodian Constitution's protection of equal treatment and therefore a violation of Cambodia's sovereignty.[72] Moreover, if all senior leaders and all persons most responsible were not identified and tried, it would be unjust to prosecute anyone at all, and would fuel the suspicion of former Khmer Rouge cadres that they might be tried next.[73] At the Co-Prosecutors' prompting, the judges asked his intent in raising these arguments. Kar Savuth responded:

> [W]hen the Co-Prosecutors asked whether I challenge the jurisdiction, I am not intending to challenge it because I am quite aware already and I could have raised it in the initial hearing already if I wished to do so.[74]

Sometime before closing arguments Kar Savuth—and apparently Duch—reversed this position. In offering his final words, Duch gave no hint that he had changed his mind, but instead typically offered a history of CPK policies that he apparently believed proved he was merely a cog in its machine. Kar Savuth picked up this theme, and following the logic of his opening statement, insisted that there were 14 people who were senior leaders or most responsible for the crimes of the DK period, and Duch was not among them.[75] Moreover, if he was among them, so are the other 195 prison chiefs and if he is alone prosecuted it would be a violation of the Constitution as well as the 1956 Cambodian Criminal Code, which (he claimed) established a defense of superior orders.[76] In conclusion, he requested that Duch be freed from prosecution.[77]

When Roux spoke the next morning, he made it immediately clear that he was taken by surprise by this new tack. "For reasons that will be clear to legal practitioners, we have had to review the entire plan of our pleadings after Mr. Kar Savuth's pleadings yesterday afternoon."[78] He also distanced himself from the legal arguments:

> You have clearly understood that our team has not laboured without disagreements; there have been disagreements. . . . As I can appreciate what my esteemed colleague said last night, national laws are not applicable and, therefore, international law must prevail. This is a given. In this trial, international law has made its introduction into Cambodian national law through our national prosecutor and through my esteemed colleague, Mr. Kar Savuth.[79]

Roux gamely tried to stay on message, arguing that the breach might not have happened if he had been allowed to enter a guilty plea on Duch's behalf, with a sentencing recommendation acknowledging his cooperation, recognition of responsibility, and genuine remorse.[80] He then asked to have these facts, as well as the fact that Duch was working within a repressive criminal dictatorship, recognized as mitigating factors. Responding to suggestions that the split defense position was caused by the defense's failure to develop a comprehensive strategy, Roux denied that the defense had ever had a "strategy," as this was not a civil law concept. Instead, the defense "attempted to convert into a legal framework" Duch's acceptance of responsibility and desire for forgiveness.[81]

In an apparent attempt to bridge the rupture, Roux called for Duch to receive a 10-year sentence: time served. When the prosecution requested clarification as to whether they were seeking acquittal, Roux said:

> Acquittal was not used this morning—this word was not used. Both defence lawyers asked that the accused's sentence, were he to be found guilty, should be

> reduced and that he should be freed as soon as possible. . . . He should be freed after being imprisoned for ten years and after fully recognizing his responsibility for the crimes in S-21.[82]

Asked what he wanted, Duch said, "I would ask the Chamber to release me."[83] Pressed as to whether this meant acquittal on all charges or a sentence reduction, he referred the question to Kar Savuth, who clarified: "release means acquittal."[84]

Shortly before the judgment was pronounced, Duch fired Roux,[85] the architect of his trial strategy, and after reportedly seeking the services of a Chinese lawyer "who better understands the communist mindset of the Khmer Rouge,"[86] eventually replaced him with a second Cambodian lawyer, Kong Ritheary.[87] "[B]esides the Chinese, there can only be Khmer," Kar Savuth was quoted as saying.[88] The new co-counsel team appealed the Trial Chamber verdict on the basis of a lack of personal jurisdiction.[89]

Much speculation has arisen about why the breach occurred. When Roux was first appointed, expectations were high. The Defence Support Section Deputy said, "I think it's going to be a great team[.] We've got one of the most experienced Cambodian lawyers . . . working alongside one of the most experienced international lawyers[.] . . . It's good for the ECCC[.]"[90] After the breach, Roux said, "it was surely a mistake to have two co-lawyers and a lead counsel system would have been far better."[91] "A detainee is always in his lawyers' hands. It is an impossible situation for him when he has two lawyers who say two different things."[92]

This raises the question of whether Roux sufficiently consulted with Kar Savuth about a common strategy—in particular after their divergence became apparent at the start of trial. Former Ieng Sary Co-Lawyer Michael Karnavas has described the "co" lawyer relationship as "like a marriage." In his view, all members of the legal team must feel they have ownership in a collective approach or it will be a forced marriage and unlikely to succeed.[93] As Duch preferred Kar Savuth's approach, it also raises the question of whether Roux sufficiently apprised Duch in advance about the defense he sought to pursue and its potential sentencing consequences. Kar Savuth likely had better understanding of Duch's views and wishes, linguistically, culturally, and as his legal representative since the Military Court first detained him in 1999.

The most popular conspiracy theory was that Kar Savuth, who is also a lawyer for the family of Prime Minister Hun Sen, had intentionally betrayed

Duch at the Prime Minister's behest. It was obvious that Kar Savuth's principal arguments directly supported the publicly expressed desire of the Prime Minister to limit the number of persons brought to trial. Although Roux originally denied that political interference had been the cause, he later appeared willing to countenance the possibility:

> In substance [Kar Savuth] says, 'I ask you to render a decision in which you will say you are taking care of the three persons you have, not one more[.]' . . . It is exactly the same as the remarks that Hun Sen made some time ago. . . . The message [Mr. Savuth] is addressing to the three Cambodian judges is far from being neutral. . . . To have such a collapse at the end of the Duch trial, it is after all sending a very strong signal: 'your tribunal is not ours.'[94]

However, reading the transcripts in hindsight, it is notable that Kar Savuth several times mentions Meas Muth and Sou Met as among those most responsible for crimes at S-21 and argues that the trial judges failed to take this into account or to call them as witnesses.[95] As both are reportedly unnamed suspects in the Court's contentious Case 003, it is possible Kar Savuth instead thought—and convinced Duch—that he might be able to leverage the Case 003/004 controversy to put pressure on the judges to acquit. This would have fit perfectly with Duch's view that he was merely a cog in the machine and was being unfairly singled out for prosecution.

For his part, Kar Savuth said the rupture "was due to a divergence between the defense lawyers on whether to follow domestic or international law[.]"[96] He wanted to argue Cambodian law, under which (in his view) Duch could not be prosecuted for following orders; however, Roux argued international law, which does not recognize this defense.[97] He also said that Duch fired Roux because Roux didn't understand communist law. From Duch's perspective, "China is a communist country and the Pol Pot regime was communist [and] [c]ommunist law is contradictory to free law."[98]

Some lawyers have suggested one more possibility: that there was a genuine misunderstanding. Roux and Kar Savuth took consistent positions throughout the trial, with the difference in their approach assuming significance only when the Court asked for a consequential remedy. In the view of then DSS Head Richard Rogers, as Cambodia has an undeveloped legal system, it is possible that Kar Savuth did not appreciate the legal difference between asking for a sentence of time served and asking for acquittal, as both would result in immediate release. Pushed into a corner, rather than backtrack and lose face, he might have felt the need to press forward with his demand for acquittal.[99] Nuon Chea's former Co-Lawyer Michiel Pestman says that because Cambodian lawyers' approach to strategy is different, "What happened to Roux could happen to anyone."[100]

The best and perhaps only way to prevent it appears to be Karnavas's intensive team approach: spending time together, reviewing drafts together, and analyzing daily trial developments together, so that everyone has a stake in the same strategy. It is an immensely time-consuming process, but Karnavas says it's "magic" when team members come to embrace and advocate as their own a strategy that emerges from a deliberative process.[101]

VERDICT AND APPEAL

The verdict and appeal in the *Duch* case raised important issues regarding the relationship between the ECCC and the Cambodian court system, as well as the relationship between Cambodian and international sentencing rules and other legal principles. The Trial Chamber judgment showed that a hybrid court can satisfy international legal standards when it is able to exercise its authority independently. It found Duch guilty, via direct and superior responsibility, of crimes against humanity and war crimes (grave breaches of the Geneva Conventions of 1949) and sentenced him to 35 years imprisonment, minus 5 years for the human rights violation he suffered when detained illegally by the Cambodian Military Court prior to his transfer to the ECCC. Due to the negligible amount of evidence of Duch's personal involvement, and inconsistent witness testimony, the Trial Chamber found that Duch was not responsible for personally participating in the commission of crimes.[102] After subtracting the 11 years Duch had already spent in detention, he was sentenced to serve less than 19 years in prison.

The judgment was generally well reasoned and well received—except with regard to the length of sentence, which most Cambodians thought was far too short. Cambodian Foreign Minister Hor Namhong expressed his personal view that the sentence was too light, but said, "[B]ecause this is the work of the Khmer Rouge tribunal the government has no position."[103] In stark contrast to his statements regarding Cases 003 and 004, after the announcement Prime

Minister Hun Sen said, "I respect the verdict handed down by the court. The government has no right to interfere or put any pressure on the court."[104]

During the proceedings, Duch had said that he would not run away from the crimes he had committed and that Cambodians could punish him however they liked.[105] Further, he would accept any sentence handed down by the Court and would not appeal the judgment.[106] Nevertheless, before the Trial Chamber had announced the judgment, Kar Savuth vowed to appeal if Duch was sentenced to even one day in jail.[107] On appeal, the prosecution asked for a life sentence for Duch, to be reduced to 45 years after taking into account the human rights violation he suffered by being held in unlawful detention by the Cambodian Military Court before his transfer to the ECCC. The defense asked for acquittal and immediate release, and for Duch's time in detention since 1999 to be considered a form of witness protection.[108] Duch explicitly supported the arguments of his defense counsel denying the Court's jurisdiction.

Impact of National Law on Sentencing

Debate over the relationship between Cambodian and international law in ECCC proceedings arose again in the context of sentencing. The prosecution of international crimes is unprecedented in Cambodia; there are no national sentencing principles or guidelines.[109] However, Article 95 of the 2009 Cambodian Penal Code provides, "If the penalty incurred for an offence is life imprisonment, the judge granting the benefit of mitigating circumstances may impose a sentence of between fifteen and thirty years."[110] The Trial Chamber did not find Article 95 to be applicable, noting that it "was doubtful whether . . . the Chamber could follow a subsequent national legislative provision in preference to provisions of the Agreement. Such an interpretation could mean that future acts of the national legislature concerning sentence might frustrate the agreement."[111]

Judge Lavergne dissented on this point in light of the Penal Code provision and the International Criminal Court's similar provision providing for a maximum term of 30 years when life imprisonment is not warranted.[112] Although Judge Lavergne did not think the Code was directly applicable to the ECCC, he found it particularly relevant for statutory interpretation of the ECCC instruments in light of the hybrid nature of the Court and the absence of specific sentencing guidelines.[113] He noted that although the ECCC regime "may be deemed *sui generis*, it is difficult to imagine that it is entirely extraneous to domestic law."[114]

At the appeal hearing, Judge Klonowiecka-Milart emphasized this same point. Under Cambodian Penal Code Article 10 and the principle of *lex mitior*, a criminal law applies as soon as it comes into force if it is more favorable to the accused. If the Cambodian Penal Code were to be found applicable to the ECCC in this instance and mitigating circumstances were found, the ECCC would be prevented from imposing a sentence of more than 30 years.

The Co-Prosecutors argued that because the ECCC is *sui generis*, domestic law should not be applicable "because 'the focus of the ECCC differs substantially enough from the normal operation of Cambodian criminal courts to warrant a specialized system.'"[115] Moreover, the ECCC Law drafters did not ask the Court to consider national sentencing standards, whereas that is explicitly required by the statutes of courts such as the ICTY, International Criminal Tribunal for Rwanda (ICTR), and Special Court for Sierra Leone. Instead, the Internal Rules require the sentence to be "in accordance with the Agreement, the ECCC Law, and the[] IRs."[116] Additionally, they pointed out that the Penal Code is not applicable to special criminal legislation, which in their view must be interpreted to include the ECCC Law.[117]

Judge Klonowiecka-Milart said that she found the Co-Prosecutors' arguments unconvincing, as the ECCC is part of the national system and there is no direct conflict between Cambodian Criminal Code article 95 and ECCC Law article 39, pursuant to which the ECCC is authorized to issue a sentence of between five years and life imprisonment.[118] She noted,

> The ECCC Law copiously references the penal code of Cambodia, which by the way was the legal basis on which prosecution sought convictions in case 1. Moreover, ECCC Law treats national Cambodian procedure as a plane of reference on procedural matters. This would indicate that ECCC Law is not a stand alone piece of legislation, but has to be seen in the context of the legal system.[119]

In the Supreme Court judgment, a supermajority of the Chamber—including all four Cambodian judges and Japanese judge Motoo Noguchi—agreed with the prosecutors. The supermajority ruled that the Cambodian Code did not apply because it is a law of general application applicable to all Cambodian courts, whereas the ECCC Law was created specifically for ECCC proceedings. In accordance with the principle of *lex specialis*, the ECCC Law's sentencing provisions therefore control.[120] In support of this, it found that

ECCC Law fell within the category of "special criminal legislation" explicitly exempt from the applicability of this provision.[121]

Two international judges disagreed, saying the principle of *lex specialis* is relevant only where two rules sanction similar crimes. Instead, they found the 2009 Code inapplicable for another reason: because it defines criminal conduct under domestic law, and the ECCC established special jurisdiction over international crimes.[122] Nevertheless, they found that the Court should give "substantial weight" to domestic sentencing practices as the ECCC Law provides little guidance, and international guidelines are limited.[123] Finally, they argued that as the ECCC is part of the Cambodian court system, in the absence of an established international standard, "the ECCC should deviate from the Cambodia sentencing regime only where there is a good reason under the circumstances."[124] However, this plea for hybridity fell on deaf ears.

Mitigation

Lacking guidance from Cambodian law, the Trial Chamber followed international precedent in considering both aggravating and mitigating factors in determining what sentence to impose.[125] As aggravating factors, the Court highlighted the shocking and heinous character of the crimes and the way they were carried out, the defenselessness of the victims (including children), Duch's abuse of power, and his superior responsibility for the crimes of his subordinates. As mitigating factors, the Court considered Duch's general cooperation with the Court, admission of responsibility, expressions of remorse, and the potential impact of these factors on national reconciliation, as well as his potential for rehabilitation and the coercive environment of Democratic Kampuchea.

In considering the weight of these factors, the Chamber emphasized that, because of Duch's last-minute request for acquittal, his many expressions of remorse had to be considered "limited":

> The Accused repeatedly made public apologies and expressed remorse for his crimes when given the opportunity. The Chamber finds, however, that the mitigating impact of his remorse is undermined by his failure to offer a full and unequivocal admission of his responsibility. In particular, the Accused's request during the closing statements for acquittal, despite earlier apparent admissions of responsibility, diminishes the extent to which his remorse would otherwise mitigate his sentence.[126]

Nevertheless, in determining the sentence the Trial Chamber concluded that there were "significant mitigating factors" mandating the imposition of a term of years rather than a life sentence.[127] Although the 35-year sentence it issued falls within the wide range of sentences meted out by international tribunals—which range from the comparatively short sentences of the ICTY to the frequent life sentences of the ICTR[128]—on appeal the Supreme Court found it to be incapable of being reconciled "with the principles governing sentencing" due to the gravity of the crimes and particular aggravating factors.[129]

In making this determination, the Supreme Court Chamber ruled that the Trial Chamber's finding of "significant mitigating factors" was an error of law.[130] It agreed with the prosecution that Duch's cooperation was limited, as he had made efforts to minimize his personal role in the crimes, sought to blame others, and made statements inconsistent with the evidence.[131] Moreover, it observed that in his last statement to the Court denying the Court's jurisdiction over him, "he effectively gave up his final opportunity to demonstrate the sincerity of his prior statements on remorse and apology."[132] Emphasizing that the high number of deaths and the extended period of time over which Duch committed his crimes "undoubtedly place this case among the gravest before international criminal tribunals," the Supreme Court Chamber sentenced Duch to life in prison.[133] The Supreme Court sentence is also in accord with international precedent, despite the existence of limited mitigating factors[134] and the fact that life sentences are rarely handed down except by the ICTR.[135] As discussed above, however, it is not in accord with current Cambodian sentencing law.

Illegality of Duch's Military Court Detention

To many, the topic of greatest legal significance in the *Duch* case, and the decision most likely to leave an immediate jurisprudential legacy for Cambodian courts, was the Trial Chamber's provision of a remedy for the over eight years Duch was detained without trial by the Cambodian Military Court before being handed over to the ECCC for investigation.

The Trial Chamber, like the Pre-Trial Chamber before it, had determined that because of the ECCC's formal and functional independence from domestic Cambodian courts and lack of connection to the Military Court proceedings, the ECCC could not be attributed with prior violations of Duch's rights.[136] Nevertheless, the Trial Chamber found:

> The ECCC Law not only authorizes the ECCC to apply domestic criminal procedure, but also obligates it to interpret these rules and determine their conformity with international standards prescribed by human rights conventions and followed by international courts.[137]

It therefore ruled that the Court has "both the authority and the obligation to consider the legality of his prior detention"[138] in determining his sentence. Finding that Duch's prior detention was a violation of applicable Cambodian and international law, the Chamber decided that he was entitled to a remedy for this human rights violation, the nature and extent of which would be determined at sentencing.[139] Implementing this decision in its final judgment, the Trial Chamber subtracted five years from Duch's sentence as a remedy.[140]

Due to the existence of routine and legally excessive pretrial detention in Cambodian courts, this decision was of major political importance. The Cambodian judges joined in a unanimous recognition of Duch's human rights violation, and the implicit censure of ECCC Pre-Trial Chamber Judge Ney Thol, who also serves as the president of the Military Court. One commentator noted, "This sort of challenge is unprecedented in modern Cambodian history and a great victory for the rule of law."[141]

Distressingly, the potential impact of the Trial Chamber's decision was substantially muted when a supermajority of the Supreme Court ruled *sua sponte* that the decision to grant Duch a remedy for the violation was an error of law.[142] This outcome was unexpected, as the prosecution had not challenged the reduction and it was not discussed on appeal. Then international Co-Prosecutor Andrew Cayley was quoted as saying that the prosecution received more than it asked for.[143] International monitors viewed the outcome as a political decision calculated to please the Cambodian public. Rupert Abbott of Amnesty International said, "The decision to overturn the legal remedy for Duch's unlawful detention and to provide no alternative may be perceived as a case of public opinion trumping human rights."[144] To former DSS head Richard Rogers, it also suggested the weakness of the ECCC's hybrid structure, which allowed a bloc of domestic judges and a single international judge to determine a politically sensitive outcome.[145]

In the *Barayagwiza* case, the ICTR Appeals Chamber found that where it shares "constructive custody" over an accused detained by a national jurisdiction, it is required to consider whether the length of his prior detention violated norms of international human rights and, if it has, provide an appropriate remedy.[146] The *Barayagwiza* court determined the existence of constructive custody by considering "the relationship between [the national state] and the Tribunal with respect to the detention of the Appellant."[147] As pointed out by the *Duch* defense, "In February 2002, the charges against Mr KANG and the orders placing and holding him in detention were based explicitly on the [ECCC Law]" and the crimes over which it has jurisdiction.[148] Moreover, the ECCC is not an international tribunal like the ICTR, but an internationalized court situated within the Cambodian judicial system. Nevertheless, the Supreme Court supermajority considered the *Barayagwiza* standard narrowly and ruled that because the ECCC is an independent entity, absent evidence of its "concerted action" with the Military Court, no remedy was warranted.[149] Compared to the judgment's otherwise exacting analysis, this decision is supported by surprisingly superficial legal reasoning.

The two dissenting international Supreme Court judges drew attention to the fact that the ECCC is not an international tribunal, but a hybrid court, and found as a consequence that it was not appropriate to apply the standard of "concerted action" but, instead, a "larger principle of shared responsibility."[150] In applying this standard, they considered among other factors that the ECCC is part of the domestic Cambodian system, established by a Cambodian law, and intended to apply Cambodian procedures; the "intimate connection" between the period of Duch's illegal detention and the ECCC proceedings; and the extreme violation of his rights.[151]

Moreover, they considered the unique position of the ECCC to offer "an effective remedy that will not frustrate the mandate of the Court."[152] The ECCC Law provides:

> The Extraordinary Chambers of the trial court shall exercise their jurisdiction in accordance with international standards of justice, fairness and due process of law, as set out in Articles 14 and 15 of the 1966 International Covenant on Civil and Political Rights [ICCPR].[153]

As a State Party to the ICCPR,[154] the Cambodian Government, including all of its branches, is obligated to "respect and ensure to all individuals within its territory and subject to its jurisdiction the rights recognized in the . . . Covenant[,]"[155] including the right to be tried "without undue delay."[156] The dissenting judges noted, "[A] state which unlawfully limits an individual's physical liberty is obligated to provide an adequate remedy."[157] In their view, this required that the ECCC both acknowledge his illegal confinement and reduce his life sentence to a term of 30 years:[158]

> Our remedy ensures that KAING Guek Eav's crimes are strongly condemned and forcefully punished. It also ensures, however, that his sentence is consistent with internationally recognized standards of fairness and that this Court continues to serve as a model for fair trials conducted with due respect for the rights of the accused.[159]

It was anticipated that the ECCC would play an important role in bringing justice to Cambodia. This includes not only its core mandate of trying the most responsible Khmer Rouge leaders, but also in setting an example for the Cambodian judiciary. After the Trial Chamber decision recognizing the violation of Duch's rights, a Cambodian NGO noted, "The approach of the ECCC sets a strong precedent to the Cambodian justice system for the universal recognition of fair trial rights and how violations of such rights should be acknowledged in sentencing."[160] And Judge Nil Nonn, the Trial Chamber's president, "highlighted the problem of lengthy detention without charge [in Cambodia]. . . . He noted the solution used in Duch's case, to reduce his ultimate sentence of imprisonment further for a breach of his fair trial rights, and that he would seek to implement this when he returned to his national practice."[161]

For eight years, Duch was held in detention without any apparent attempt to bring him to trial. He is not the only detainee in Cambodia who has been held for an extended period without process. The Trial Chamber decision promoted a rule-of-law culture within the national judiciary that would extend far beyond the ECCC's limited mandate and the short period of time during which it will be in operation. The Supreme Court Chamber supermajority reversal of that decision, while comforting to many outraged Khmer Rouge victims, was deleterious to the Court's legacy for domestic judicial reform.

Civil Party Reparations

At the ECCC, civil party participants are entitled to pursue "collective and moral reparations against the Accused." At the time of the *Duch* trial, the Internal Rules provided that reparations "shall be awarded against, and be borne by convicted persons."[162] Although the Rules provided as an example of reparations "An order to fund any non-profit activity or service that is intended for the benefit of Victims,"[163] because the Trial Chamber found that Duch was indigent, it rejected most civil party requests as either falling outside the Court's jurisdiction or lacking sufficient specificity.[164] It therefore awarded only the inclusion of the names of civil parties and the immediate victims in the final judgment, and the compilation and publication of all statements of apology made by Duch during the trial.[165]

The civil party teams argued that if the Court read the Rules to limit reparations awards only to those that could be paid for by Duch, "the promise of providing justice through reparations to the victims of S-21 would be meaningless."[166] Instead, they asked that the Court follow international standards and practices and encourage the Cambodian Government to fulfill its state responsibility to remedy victims' harm by setting up a reparations fund or to itself set up a voluntary trust fund through the Victims Unit.[167]

Moreover, they requested that Duch be ordered to write the Government letters requesting a state apology and that part of the entrance fees for S-21 and the Choeung Ek killing fields be used to fund reparations awards, the installation of memorials at S-21 and Choeung Ek and the transformation of Prey Sar work camp into a memorial site, paid visits by civil parties to those sites, provision of medical treatment and psychological services to civil parties, dissemination of audio and video material about the trial, and the dedication of 17 public buildings to named victims.[168] They emphasized that supposed indigence should have no effect on the reparations order, as Duch may be found to have undiscovered assets or may acquire assets in the future. Moreover, nonpecuniary and administrative requests to the Government to remedy human rights violations should not be considered punishment but a state responsibility.

The Chamber found that it has no jurisdiction over Cambodian or other authorities, cannot issue orders that are incapable of enforcement due to a lack of specificity, and "at most . . . can merely encourage" outside actors to provide victims financial support.[169] Although recognizing international principles obligating states to redress victims of gross human rights violations, the Chamber found itself "constrained in its task by the requests before it and the type of reparation permitted under its Internal Rules. Limitations of this nature cannot be circumvented through jurisprudence but instead require Rule amendments."[170]

Legally, this is unassailable. However, it comes across as disingenuous. First, as discussed above, the Trial Chamber had constricted the participation of civil parties at sentencing based in part on the premise that they were primarily seeking to avail themselves of reparations.[171] Second, the judges were the ones who drafted the Rules and (as discussed in chapter 7) had amended them six months earlier to provide expanded opportunities for reparations implementation in future cases. Michael Karnavas, like many others, thinks the civil parties got nothing and calls the reparations regime "a mockery."[172]

The Supreme Court Chamber upheld the Trial Chamber's reparations judgment, noting that the ECCC has a unique reparations regime specifically tailored to its "mechanism and mandate[,]" which limits both the relevance of Cambodian law and the application of international principles.[173] ECCC reparations are "intended to be essentially symbolic rather than compensatory"[174] and to be borne by convicted persons, not the Cambodian Government.[175]

However, unlike the Trial Chamber, the Supreme Court Chamber began with the premise that, notwithstanding the ECCC's hybrid character, it "acts as an emanation of the State of Cambodia."[176] As a Cambodian court, the ECCC is "duty bound to respect international standards of justice and generally recognized human rights precepts"—including Cambodia's international obligations to provide an effective remedy for human rights violations.[177] Nevertheless, as a criminal tribunal, the ECCC has no authority to evaluate Cambodia's human rights compliance.[178]

Although the Supreme Court reached the same result as the Trial Chamber, its reasoning is both more empowering for victims and more consistent with the aims of the hybrid model. By assessing the reparations regime from the perspective of a national court, it provides an example for the domestic judiciary of how to apply Cambodian law in conformity with international standards. Moreover, although finding that it lacks competence to assess Cambodian authorities' compliance with its international obligations to provide an effective remedy, it strongly affirms that those obligations must be respected. While the Chamber's narrow holding is lamentable, its reasoning demonstrates the subtle yet potentially powerful jurisprudential legacy a hybrid court can provide.

National and International Reactions to the Verdict

The reaction of international observers to the trial proceedings and the Trial Chamber's judgment was largely positive. Although the civil party reparations award was disappointing, trial observers triumphed the sentence's compatibility with international standards,[179] and human rights advocates lauded the Chamber for reducing Duch's sentence as a remedy for the time he spent in illegal detention at the Military Court—a noteworthy precedent in a country with exceedingly weak protection for defendants.[180]

Although many members of Cambodian civil society shared this view, anecdotal evidence suggests that across the country, a large proportion of the general Cambodian public was outraged.[181] Many people expressed deference to the Court's decision but clarified that they personally believed the sentence was far too lenient. A civil party said,

> The final decision rests with the Court. But if I were the Court, Duch would receive at least 40 years. Today, if you kill one person, you could be imprisoned for life and here we are talking about tens of thousands of lives. This Court was established to seek justice for millions of lives lost, millions of tear drops shed and, if Duch is released, the whole thing is just meaningless.[182]

One member of the Cambodian Diaspora offered: "In Buddhism, we believe that killing is a gravely sinful act. People should go to hell for killing people. Although Duch was sentenced to 19 years in prison in the human world, he will have to face hell for years before he's reborn as a human." In his view, the ECCC was like the 1993 election assisted by UNTAC: although the international community has spent many millions of dollars to run it, it has not been very beneficial for the Cambodian people.[183]

Many Cambodians were nevertheless philosophical about the outcome, typically noting Duch's advanced age and the likelihood that even if the sentence was too low, it would be sufficiently long if he died in prison. Others felt that his age was irrelevant: "The focus should not be on his age, it should be on the crimes committed. He should have been sentenced to life."[184] A minority said that only a sentence of death fit his crimes, and among those a few wanted him to suffer tortures similar to those he inflicted on prisoners during the DK period.

When asked, a few former cadres said that the sentence was too long.[185] However, Soam Met, a former S-21 guard, and Him Huy, a deputy chief of guards at S-21 in charge of transporting prisoners to the Choeung Ek killing fields, both emphasized that Duch's judgment of guilt had made their neighbors understand that they were not in charge of the prison and that they had also lived in fear during that time.[186]

After the appeal verdict increased Duch's sentence to life, several local and international NGOs had grave concern about the failure of the Supreme Court Chamber to remedy the violation of Duch's rights while he was held illegally by the Military Court.[187] The Cambodian Center for Human Rights called it "a dangerous precedent for the Cambodian judiciary."[188] In contrast, the Friends group of donors expressed strong support for the fairness of the verdict.[189] Many Cambodians, and civil parties in particular, were also pleased by the life sentence, having never truly accepted that a torturer could be compensated for having his own rights violated. One said, "Seeing Duch being sentenced to life term imprisonment, I feel so delighted and satisfied with this final judgment. . . . I don't think I am angry with Duch anymore because he is now in and will die in prison. He will suffer the way my husband did."[190] Another said:

> I am satisfied that Duch has been sentenced to life imprisonment. However, I cannot forgive him, given that he killed thousands and thousands of people. And my brother was one of those killed there. . . . I feel relieved and, to some high degree, get a sense of closure after decades of having been traumatized with the legacy of the Khmer Rouge. Duch's final verdict makes people get a sense of closure, and it is a historical lesson for our nation.[191]

A third civil party offered, "When comparing the reparation and the sentence, I think the sentence was more important. Reparation cannot replace what I lost during the [Khmer Rouge] regime, nor can it compare with justice. This is what I believe."[192]

CONCLUSION

Overall, the *Duch* trial suggests that the Cambodian model can function reasonably well when there is political agreement to prosecute a case and overwhelming evidence exists. It was a relatively easy test, however, and also evinced some of the Court's structural frailties. In addition to the obvious risk of divergence between Cambodian and international co-decisionmakers—as evident in the defense split—it showed the difficulty of merging local and international rules and procedures and the cumbersomeness of having individual victims participate as civil parties.

The *Duch* trial also portended one of the most politicized issues that the ECCC has faced—the question of the scope of the mixed Court's jurisdiction. Kar Savuth's efforts to shield Duch from liability failed, but they did raise a question that has never been adequately resolved: Who should stand trial for Khmer Rouge atrocities? Neither national nor international law provides a definitive answer. Instead, 30 years of contentious politics separate Cambodian and international approaches toward that question. Kar Savuth was defending the wrong case, as there were no political objections on either the national or international side to the conviction of his client on solid legal grounds. With other suspects in Cases 003 and 004, where political agreement is lacking, the same jurisdictional arguments have been redeployed with very different results.

Chapter 5

CASE 002—THE CENTERPIECE CASE AGAINST SENIOR LEADERS

"Cutting the Head to Fit the Hat"

Case 002 is likely to feature the Court's last trial and is viewed by many as its centerpiece. It is considered the most important Khmer Rouge case because it involves the four most senior leaders who were alive when the Court was created: Nuon Chea, Ieng Sary (now deceased), Khieu Samphan, and Ieng Thirith. Many questions about Democratic Kampuchea's (DK) three-year, eight-month, and twenty-day rule have not been answered. Unlike Duch, the defendant in the Court's first case, these leaders have never admitted any responsibility for the crimes of that period but instead have blamed the lower cadre and rogue elements. Their trial offered the first and likely only opportunity to show how decisions made by those at the center of power during the DK caused the deaths of an estimated two million Cambodians.

With four accused and thousands of documents in the case file, the proceedings were often called the most complex since Nuremberg.[1] The evidence connecting individual defendants to atrocities is less overwhelming than in Case 001, and while Duch essentially pled guilty, in Case 002 the defense teams mounted vigorous defenses. The case is also more politically sensitive than Case 001, because unlike Duch, the Case 002 defendants had extensive dealings with foreign powers and with the Cambodian Government after the fall of the DK regime. All of these factors made Case 002 a much tougher functional test for the ECCC judges and prosecutors, who are charged with delivering a fair trial and credible justice expeditiously and at an acceptable cost.

One of the Court's first hurdles was determining if it had the power to try Ieng Sary, who was convicted *in absentia* in 1979 and granted amnesty and pardon in 1996. His challenges to the Court's jurisdiction tested the hybrid Court's ability to navigate tensions between international accountability norms and Cambodian law. All judicial chambers addressed the issue at least once, but without final resolution due to the ECCC's convoluted structure and extraordinarily narrow provision for immediate appeal. The Court's unique civil law approach to investigations has contributed to other problems, leading to legitimate defense concerns. In particular, the Court's heavy reliance on Co-Investigating Judges (CIJs), who are endowed with immense responsibility and discretion, rendered that office—and the entire investigation—vulnerable to charges of incompetence and bias. Decisions by national judges that suggest a lack of independence from the Cambodian Government prompted accusations of political interference, particularly in connection with the Court's efforts to summon government witnesses.

The ECCC's inefficiency in getting the case to trial also generated problems. It resulted in the suspects' lengthy preindictment detention and prompted the Trial Chamber to seek to expedite judgment by severing the indictment into a series of "mini trials." Although "Case 002/01" involved senior leaders at the pinnacle of the Democratic Kampuchea hierarchy, the crimes it addressed are not representative of the harms suffered by most victims during the Pol Pot era. Further challenges arose as trial judges who lack experience managing mass crimes trials inconsistently developed and applied hybrid rules, leading to procedural confusion and delay. One of the octogenarian accused was severed from the case before trial hearings began due to dementia, and another died a few months before the end of trial. With additional Case 002 trials unlikely due to the advanced age of the two remaining accused and donors' eagerness to conclude the tribunal's work as soon as possible, the ECCC's centerpiece case is greatly reduced in scope and, regrettably, in its likely significance to many survivors.

BACKGROUND

The Co-Prosecutors elected to try the four surviving senior leaders together, both in the hopes of increasing efficiency and to facilitate trying them under the theory of Joint Criminal Enterprise[2]—among other modes of liability. The accused were charged with responsibility for genocide, war crimes, and crimes against humanity committed pursuant to a joint criminal plan to implement "rapid socialist revolution in Cambodia through a 'great leap forward' and defend the Party against internal and external enemies, by whatever means necessary."[3] The Closing Order found that they did so, *inter alia*, by forcing population movement; establishing and operating work cooperatives; reeducating "bad elements" and killing "enemies" inside and outside of the party; targeting "specific groups, in particular the Cham, Vietnamese, Buddhists, and former officials of the Khmer Republic, including both civil servants and former military personnel and their families"; and regulating marriage.[4] Their positions as cabinet-level DK officials and participants in the key decision-making committees of the Communist Party of Kampuchea (CPK) gave them the apparent capacity to develop and influence those high-level policies.

Nuon Chea is often referred to as "Brother Number Two," though he has denied that he was called this and that he was second in command after Pol Pot. He was born in 1926 in Battambang Province, and went to high school and took law classes in Bangkok, where he became politically active and joined the Communist Party of Thailand. When he returned to Cambodia in 1950, he joined the local communist party and became a senior member by 1960. During the DK period, he was Deputy Secretary of the CPK and a member of the CPK Central and Standing Committees—the key decision-making bodies in Democratic Kampuchea.[5] He was allegedly responsible for military and security affairs, including control over S-21, with Duch reporting directly to him during the last years of the regime. After Pol Pot's death in 1998, Nuon Chea defected from the Khmers Rouges. According to his lawyers, "Nuon Chea disputes the charges against him and, notwithstanding his position in the government of Democratic Kampuchea, he argues that he had no direct contact with the bases and was not aware of what was happening there."[6]

Ieng Sary was born in 1925 in Vietnam. He became politically active at Collège Sisowath in Phnom Penh and then studied in France, where he became a member of the French Communist Party. He returned to Cambodia and became a history professor in 1957, allegedly joining the Khmers Rouges in 1963. During the DK period, he was Deputy Prime Minister and Minister for Foreign Affairs and a member of the CPK Central and Standing Committees. He is alleged to have either encouraged or failed to prevent the transfer of large numbers of Foreign Ministry personnel to the S-21 detention center. As discussed in chapter 1, he and Pol Pot were convicted of "genocide" *in absentia* by the 1979 People's Revolutionary Tribunal, a special court established by the Vietnamese-backed government, and sentenced to death and confiscation of all their property. In 1996, to entice Ieng to defect from the Khmer Rouge movement with thousands of his followers, at Hun Sen's behest King Sihanouk issued a royal decree pardoning him from the 1979 tribunal's sentence and providing him amnesty from potential prosecution under the 1994 law banning Khmer Rouge membership. Ieng moved to Phnom Penh with his wife, Ieng Thirith, and argued that the pardon and amnesty prevented the ECCC from exercising jurisdiction over him.[7] Ieng Sary died on March 14, 2013, shortly before the end of the Case 002/01 trial hearings.

Khieu Samphan was born in Svay Rieng province in 1931. He went to France to study in 1955, where he was active in the French Communist Party before returning to Cambodia to become a professor. In 1962, he was appointed Secretary of State for Commerce in then Prince Sihanouk's government. Threatened with arrest, he went into hiding in 1967 and by the early 1970s had joined the Khmers Rouges. From 1976, Khieu Samphan served as head of state (President of the State Presidium), taking over this title from Sihanouk. He alleges that, like the former King, in this role he was merely a figurehead. He was a member of the Central Committee and participated in many Standing Committee meetings, and had duties in the Ministry of Commerce. He disputes allegations that he was Chairman of the Party's Political Office. In 1987, he replaced a retiring Pol Pot as the official head of the Khmers Rouges and representative at the 1989 Paris Peace Conference. After Pol Pot's death in 1998, Khieu Samphan left the Khmer Rouge movement and defected to the Government.

Ieng Thirith was born in Phnom Penh in 1932. She studied at the Lycée Sisowath in Phnom Penh and then obtained a degree in English Literature in France. She married Ieng Sary in 1951; her sister later married Pol Pot. Ieng Thirith returned to Cambodia in 1957 to work as an English professor. During the DK period, she was Minister of Social Affairs and Action and a candidate member of the CPK Central Committee. She was sent to investigate and report on health issues in the Northwest Zone and therefore may have known that many Cambodians were starving under the DK regime. She is also alleged to have either encouraged or failed to prevent the arrest and execution of ministry staff. She denied this during a pretrial hearing and placed all blame on Nuon

Chea.[8] Along with her husband, she defected from the Khmer Rouge movement in 1996. The charges against Ieng Thirith were severed from the rest of Case 002 immediately before the start of trial hearings after she was found to suffer from dementia.

TRYING IENG SARY: TENSION BETWEEN INTERNATIONAL LAW AND PAST DOMESTIC PRACTICE

Long before Case 002 began, analysts foresaw that the prosecution of Ieng Sary would pose special challenges for the ECCC. As discussed in chapter 1, Ieng Sary and Pol Pot were convicted of genocide *in absentia* in 1979 by the People's Revolutionary Tribunal—a special court established by the Vietnam-backed government that ousted the Khmers Rouges. The 1979 tribunal sentenced them to death and confiscation of all of their property.[9] Years later, as part of a 1996 deal with the Cambodian Government to facilitate Ieng Sary's defection from the Khmers Rouges with his followers, King Sihanouk issued a Royal Decree pardoning Ieng from his 1979 sentence and providing him an amnesty from prosecution under the 1994 Law to Outlaw the Democratic Kampuchea Group. He is the only Khmer Rouge leader to have received an amnesty, raising obvious tensions with international norms against granting amnesty for crimes such as genocide.[10]

As the ECCC is an "internationalized" court, its obligation to recognize the validity of the Ieng Sary amnesty has been debated since negotiations began. The ECCC framers failed to address the effect of the Royal Decree on the Court's jurisdiction, but instead gave the ECCC Chambers explicit authority to determine the scope of any preexisting amnesty or pardon.[11]

After Ieng was taken into custody, he argued that as a consequence of the Royal Decree, the ECCC did not have jurisdiction to try him. In brief, he argued that his amnesty from the effects of the 1994 Law was intended to prevent his prosecution for all criminal acts committed by the Khmers Rouges from 1975 to 1979—the temporal jurisdiction of the ECCC. Similarly, he argued that he could not serve any sentence for the underlying acts for which he was found culpable by the 1979 tribunal. Moreover, he argued that international law does not prohibit domestic amnesties for *jus cogens* crimes[12]—those crimes with a higher legal status implicating, among other state obligations, the duty to prosecute or extradite offenders. To the contrary, the Co-Prosecutors argued that the pardon only prohibited execution of the 1979 sentence of death and property confiscation, and the amnesty applied only to future violations of the 1994 Law, which merely criminalized membership in the Khmer Rouge organization. In the alternative, they argued that amnesty for *jus cogens* crimes is not recognized under international law.[13]

There is wide, though not universal, agreement that domestic amnesties for serious international crimes are invalid under international law. Acceptance of their invalidity is broadest with regard to crimes for which a state has a treaty obligation to prosecute or extradite. For example, the Special Court for Sierra Leone (SCSL) Appeals Chamber has said:

> [G]iven the existence of a treaty obligation to prosecute or extradite an offender, the grant of an amnesty in respect of [the international crimes set forth in the SCSL Statute] is not only incompatible with, but is in breach of an obligation of a State towards the international community as a whole.[14]

Cambodia has treaty obligations to prosecute or extradite persons who commit grave breaches under the 1949 Geneva Conventions and genocide under the 1948 Genocide Convention,[15] both of which were charged in Case 002. As a consequence of these obligations, the ECCC Trial Chamber found that the 1996 Decree could not "relieve it of the duty to prosecute these crimes or constitute an obstacle thereto."[16]

There is also growing support for the view that domestic amnesties for other serious crimes, such as crimes against humanity, are invalid under customary international law. For example, discussing the effect on the jurisdiction of the SCSL of the amnesty clause in the Lomé Peace Agreement between the warring factions, the UN Secretary-General said:

> While recognizing that amnesty is an accepted legal concept and a gesture of peace and reconciliation at the end of a civil war or an internal armed conflict, the United Nations has consistently maintained the position that amnesty cannot be granted in respect of international crimes, such as genocide, crimes against humanity or other serious violations of international humanitarian law.[17]

The SCSL Appeals Chamber then found that there is a "crystallizing international norm that a government cannot grant amnesty for serious violations under international law[.]"[18]

The ECCC Trial Chamber examined the views of international, regional, and state courts, as well as human rights bodies, and agreed that there is an emerging consensus that blanket amnesties violate states' duty to investigate serious international crimes and punish the perpetrators. Notably, it found the creation of the ECCC and other hybrid courts to evince the determination of states that serious crimes should not go unpunished.[19] It therefore concluded, "[S]tate practice demonstrates at a minimum a retroactive right for third States, internationalized and domestic courts to evaluate amnesties and set them aside or limit their scope should they be deemed incompatible with international norms."[20] Having previously found that the Royal Decree may have been intended to grant Ieng Sary general immunity for *any* criminal acts committed before 1996,[21] the Trial Chamber ruled that, because this is at odds with Cambodia's treaty obligations and the trend in customary international law, it had the discretion to find that the scope of the amnesty excludes the serious international crimes with which Ieng is charged.[22]

The Trial Chamber did not make this finding on the basis of the ECCC's hybrid character, but ruled solely on the basis of Cambodia's state obligations. The decision thus strongly affirms fully domestic Cambodian courts' obligation to prosecute and punish all persons responsible for serious international crimes, and concomitantly the accountability of all those who perpetrate them. As Documentation Center of Cambodia (DC-Cam) Director Youk Chhang emphasized after Ieng Sary was taken into detention in 2007, "The arrests of the most politically untouchable of the Khmer Rouge leaders is a powerful message to the people of Cambodia[.]"[23] The Ieng Sary defense appealed the Chamber's decision in part on the basis that the Chamber acted *ultra vires* by evaluating not only the scope but also the validity of the Decree.[24] However, there will be no final determination of this question, because a Supreme Court Chamber supermajority found that the issue falls outside the narrow scope of its interlocutory review authority.[25]

The ECCC avoided a politicized showdown over the Ieng Sary pardon and amnesty—which some observers feared while the Court was taking shape. Though it is troubling that the Supreme Court found it had to wait till judgment to determine whether the Court had the competence to try him in the first place, the lower Chambers' decisions on this topic were based on reasonable jurisprudence and were consistent with the trend in international practice. On other issues, however, the Court has run into significant obstacles in managing Case 002.

CHALLENGES TO THE INVESTIGATION

Given the nationwide scope of the alleged offenses, investigating Case 002 was bound to be a monumental task for the ECCC's Office of the Co-Investigating Judges (OCIJ). There are many potential advantages to a judicial investigation. In mass crimes cases, defense counsel have difficulties gathering evidence due to a lack of resources and cooperation. In theory, it would be fairer for an impartial judge to question witnesses on behalf of all parties and take statements under oath that could be used as evidence at trial. A judge-led investigation should also be more professional, thorough, and balanced, preventing interviews riddled with leading questions and hearsay statements, and ensuring that all inculpatory and exculpatory evidence is brought to the fore. Finally, it should be more efficient, testing and narrowing the scope of evidence presented at trial.

However, when asked to identify the ECCC's principal structural flaw, many Court officials interviewed for this book immediately named the OCIJ. As discussed in chapter 2, having two investigations followed by a full-length trial is inefficient. Former CIJ Lemonde believes this duplication resulted "because the lawyers who were recruited [to implement the system] were mostly from countries of common law, in any case it was practitioners who were familiar with the operation of other international courts and saw no reason to change their practice."[26] To an extent this may be true; however, there are also more fundamental concerns. Khieu Samphan Co-Lawyer Anta Guissé says that in France, where there are questions about a witness's story, the parties can ask for confrontation during the investigative stage.[27] Although this appears to be true in all modern domestic civil law systems, Cambodian procedures, which (as discussed in chapter 2) are based on obsolete French law, do not provide for it. At the ECCC, the failure to include the parties in witness interviews has necessitated the reexamination of core evidence at trial. To many Court officials and analysts, this duplication is the main reason the judicial investigation was a wasted effort.

Investigating judges have enormous discretionary power, which has led France and other national judicial systems to limit or eliminate their role.[28] The Case 002 defense teams have attacked the investigatory process, alleging bias, methodological failures, procedural irregularities, and a lack of transparency. Their criticisms are directed largely toward the attitudes and professionalism of specific judges but have also helped reveal intrinsic weaknesses in the ECCC's institutional capacity to meet the needs of a mass crimes process.[29]

Concerns about Impartiality

According to the ECCC Internal Rules, the CIJs "may take any investigative action conducive to ascertaining the truth. In all cases they shall conduct their investigation impartially, whether the evidence is inculpatory or exculpatory."[30] The power to investigate is exclusive to the CIJs. Concomitantly, the parties are prohibited from undertaking their own investigations, though they "are entirely free to review any document from any public source in their search for evidence" and to request that the CIJs place it in the case file.[31] They may also request the CIJs to undertake an investigative action they consider "useful for the conduct of the investigation."[32] The CIJs have said:

> Before this Court, the power to conduct judicial investigations is assigned solely to the two independent Co-Investigating Judges and not to the parties. . . . The capacity of the parties is thus limited to such preliminary inquiries as are strictly necessary for the effective exercise of their right to request investigative action.[33]

Because the CIJs act independently, they have broad discretion to decide whether or not an investigative act is useful.[34] In making this evaluation, they have no explicit duty to consult with a party requesting an investigative action before rejecting it, nor have they done so. The Pre-Trial Chamber (PTC) found in one case that it would have been "sensible" for the CIJs to consult the requesting party, but it did not reach the question of whether this amounted to an obligation.[35] Some investigative requests were rejected without adequate reasoning, and others were never addressed, obligating the PTC to itself review the merits.[36] Fewer than 20% of the *Nuon Chea* team's investigative requests were carried out.[37] "You tie our hands, and then you don't go out and do what you are supposed to do," laments Ieng Sary's former Co-Lawyer Michael Karnavas.[38]

At other internationalized tribunals, investigators are not expected to be neutral, so there is no presumption that their witness statements will be disinterested, it is difficult to challenge their integrity, and a successful challenge is unlikely to infect the entire case. In contrast, at the ECCC the CIJs have near-total investigative discretion,[39] and thus the fairness of the entire process is dependent on their independence and impartiality.[40] The CIJs and some investigators provided easy targets for multiple personal bias challenges. A former CIJ investigator alleged that during a weekend meeting at his home Judge Lemonde said, "I would prefer that we find more inculpatory evidence than exculpatory evidence."[41] Lemonde responded that if he indeed said that, it would have been in jest.[42] The defense sought his disqualification, arguing that this statement expressed actual bias,[43] but the PTC found that Lemonde's remark did not amount to an instruction to the investigators.[44]

Co-Investigating Judge You Bunleng was also challenged for appearance of bias due to his refusal to summon requested government witnesses, discussed below. Moreover, two key CIJ staff members provided fodder for repeated bias claims because they had written books that indicated prejudgment, and one had also worked in the Office of the Co-Prosecutors for several months during the drafting of the initial submission.[45] However, the PTC rejected this concern, emphasizing that because the CIJs have sole authority to conduct the investigation, their independence and impartiality safeguard the entire process.[46] Finally, the defense argued that national CIJ staff members' presumed participation in the kickback scheme discussed in chapter 3 could impact judicial integrity. The PTC likewise rejected this allegation, finding that "the allegations that staff members possibly have paid money to a superior cannot lead to the conclusion that these staff members can influence the Judges to manipulate the outcome of proceedings[.]"[47] Although none of these challenges succeeded, they raised questions about the OCIJ's impartiality and contributed to doubts about the integrity of the ECCC as a whole.

Investigative Capacity and Fairness Concerns

Although the ECCC's in-country hybrid form has clear investigative advantages—such as proximity to crime sites, and witnesses and investigators fluent in the local language—the Court struggled to conduct a full investigation in Case 002. This is due both to its reliance on CIJs to perform that function and to the sheer enormity of potential evidence, which includes forensic remains, witness testimony, and nearly one million pages of documents collected by DC-Cam since 1995.

For example, after filing their introductory submission for Case 002, the

Co-Prosecutors placed an additional 18,000 documents they had not cited on a shared materials drive, because they could not exclude the possibility that the documents might include exculpatory evidence. When defense teams asked the CIJs to search the drive for exculpatory information, the CIJs emphasized that, while they could not arbitrarily exclude evidence they knew to exist, they were not "required to conduct an exhaustive search for all evidence; an impossible task."[48]

A structure that relies on investigating judges arguably carries an inherent bias toward the prosecution's case—at least when it involves complex mass crimes—because the prosecutors furnish vast amounts of information in the initial submission. Guissé says, "In the domestic [French] system, as soon as an investigative judge is assigned, the prosecution is no longer in charge of the investigators. Here the prosecutors had a long time to shape the case; everyone is already biased."[49] The CIJs essentially acknowledged this when they said: "The logic underpinning a criminal investigation is that the principle of sufficiency of evidence outweighs that of exhaustiveness: an investigating judge may close a judicial investigation once he has determined that there is sufficient evidence to indict a Charged Person."[50] The Pre-Trial Chamber disagreed, finding that the judges have a duty to examine all documents in which there is a *prima facie* reason to believe exculpatory evidence may exist before assessing the sufficiency of the evidence for trial.[51]

Yet investigating judges have limited capacity to digest a vast introductory submission and pursue extensive further investigation. Former Defence Support Section (DSS) head Richard Rogers says that due to the complexity of Case 002, the CIJs were unable to examine carefully all the documents referenced in the Prosecutors' introductory submission, let alone develop exculpatory evidence. Rogers contends that, as a practical matter, a mass crimes court dependent on investigative judges requires defendants to provide guidance on where to seek exculpatory evidence and is therefore incompatible with the right to remain silent.[52] Michael Karnavas says, "[The CIJs] never did an investigation; they only did a validation. The investigation was done for them by the prosecution." When the CIJs began, they had nothing but the prosecution's submission, and "natural instinct says, let me rely on what has already been done."[53] Employing investigators from diverse legal traditions may exacerbate this tendency. Arguably, "It's not in the DNA of investigators from the Anglo-Saxon system to look for exculpatory evidence in the sense of the French system."[54]

Anta Guissé notes that, unlike the practice in France, the CIJs delegated their power to investigators without a standardized methodology or code of conduct. "The [CIJs] need to take more control over investigators." She suggests that the ideal system may be to let the parties investigate first and then have an investigating judge sift through the evidence they have collected.[55]

Internal Rule 56(1) provides: "In order to preserve the rights and interests of the parties, judicial investigations shall not be conducted in public. All persons participating in the judicial investigation shall maintain confidentiality." The confidentiality of the investigation makes it difficult for the public—and even the parties—to assess its quality. Former co-counsel for Nuon Chea Michiel Pestman argues that confidentiality did not require secrecy from the parties.[56] Repeated refusals by the CIJs to share information raised suspicions that they invoked the "fig leaf" of confidentiality to hide their incompetence as domestic law judges unaccustomed to managing an enormously complex investigation.[57]

The *Ieng Sary* defense unsuccessfully sought to learn if an overall strategy existed and if investigative work was being carried out according to a consistent methodology.[58] Among its complaints was that the "[c]ollection of witness interviews are arbitrarily placed on the Case File, often months after the interviews were conducted, with little or no explanation of how these interviews fit into the judicial investigation."[59] Moreover, interviews were riddled with leading questions, were not consistently recorded, and some interviewees were questioned on multiple occasions, suggesting no line of questioning had been developed in advance.[60]

Karnavas says that because the defense is not allowed to do its own investigation, the case file must be a primary source for determining which lines of investigation to request. "But over here, with a case of this magnitude, it's virtually impossible. Especially when you don't know what is their process, how they are going about doing it."[61] This impeded the parties' ability to participate fully in the investigation. As discussed in the next chapter, concerns that the veil of secrecy around the OCIJ was shrouding incompetence and bias grew substantially with the arrival of a new international investigating judge.

Allegations of Government Interference

During the investigative phase of Case 002, another important functional constraint on the ECCC became apparent—its inability or unwillingness to call certain senior Cambodian officials to testify at the Court. The defense repeatedly sought to have the CIJs interview King-Father Norodom Sihanouk and high-level Cambodian officials, including Prime Minister Hun Sen. The Cambodian Government resisted, and national judges supported the RGC. The controversy again spotlighted the preponderance of domestic judges at the ECCC and their susceptibility to political pressure.

The ECCC Internal Rules give the CIJs the explicit authority to issue orders "necessary to conduct the investigation, including summonses," and "take statements from any person whom they consider *conducive to ascertaining the truth*[,]" subject only to the right against self-incrimination of witnesses.[62] The Trial and Supreme Court Chambers have similar authority, which they may exercise at their discretion.[63] International CIJ Marcel Lemonde, acting alone, found it would be "conducive to ascertaining the truth" to request an interview with King-Father Sihanouk. He also summoned several high-level officials to appear in closed session on a date when they were available: Senate and CPP President Chea Sim, National Assembly President Heng Samrin, Minister of Economy and Finance Keat Chhon, Senator Ouk Bunchhoeun, Senator Sim Ka, and Minister of Foreign Affairs Hor Namhong.[64] None responded.

Caution at International Courts

The ECCC Internal Rules define "summons" as "an order to any person to appear before the ECCC."[65] Once summoned, witnesses *must* appear. "In the case of refusal to appear, the Co-Investigating Judges may issue an order requesting the Judicial Police to compel the witness to appear."[66] The Internal Rules provide blanket authority to summon witnesses with no exception. The International Criminal Tribunal for the former Yugoslavia (ICTY) Rules provide similar authority; nevertheless, the ICTY has said with regard to subpoenas that they "should not be issued lightly, for they involve the use of coercive powers and may lead to the imposition of a criminal sanction."[67] Therefore,

> While a Trial Chamber should not hesitate to resort to this instrument where it is necessary to elicit information of importance to the case and to ensure that the defendant has sufficient means to collect information necessary for the presentation of an effective defence, it should guard against the subpoena becoming a mechanism used routinely as part of trial tactics.[68]

The SCSL agreed that subpoenas should be used "sparingly" and therefore evaluated whether officials' testimony was both helpful and necessary.[69] Referencing

ICTY jurisprudence, the SCSL said that "convenience is not a sufficient justification for the issuance of a subpoena, and that when the evidence sought to be proffered can be obtained through other means, it would be inappropriate to grant such an order."[70]

In the *Norman* case at the SCSL, defendants from the Civil Defense Force (CDF) sought to call President Ahmad Tejan Kabbah, alleging that Kabbah was "commanding, materially supporting, and communicating with various members of the alleged CDF leadership" during the war.[71] The SCSL Trial Chamber found that the accused had failed to identify "with sufficient specificity" how his testimony would relate to a charge in the indictment or materially assist their case.[72] By contrast, in the later *Sesay et al.* decision, the Trial Chamber found that testimony from Kabbah, who by then was former President, could materially assist the accused in specified ways.[73] The concurring opinion of Judge Itoe suggested that the result differed because the testimony sought in the *Sesay* case was more directly relevant to the determination of guilt or innocence,[74] and the court viewed the *Norman* request as one made solely to embarrass Kabbah and expose his involvement in the conflict.[75]

In his dissent to the *Norman* decision, Judge Thompson argued that the SCSL should adopt a more flexible standard for compelling testimony to uphold fairness norms and "ensure that no relevant evidence vital to the discovery of the truth is foreclosed by reasons of legal technicalities."[76] His preferred approach appears close to the civil law standard in the ECCC Internal Rules requiring the CIJs to consider only whether it would be "conducive to ascertaining the truth" to issue a summons. In Judge Thompson's view, it is inappropriate to consider in advance whether the evidence a witness may provide is favorable or adverse to the applicant as it amounts to "a predetermination of the probative value of such evidence."[77] Instead, he believed only *prima facie* evidence should be required to show that the information sought is necessary for the investigation or trial.[78] Similarly, the *Ieng Sary* team has argued that a "best evidence" rule is inapplicable in a civil law investigation.[79]

Calling Senior Cambodian Officials

As in Sierra Leone, at the ECCC, calling senior officials is a politically charged process given the links that many have to the Khmer Rouge period—including Prime Minister Hun Sen, who was a lower-level CPK official early in the DK period, and King-Father Sihanouk, who served for a year as the regime's head of state and was effectively under house arrest in Phnom Penh for most of the DK period. In rejecting the request to summon Prime Minister Hun Sen, the CIJs determined that he was not likely to have useful information on the topics highlighted, and moreover many other witnesses who have personal knowledge of the events have been interviewed. Thus his testimony would not be useful.[80] It therefore appears that the international CIJ took factors similar to those highlighted by the SCSL into consideration and determined that the persons he did summon *could* provide information conducive to seeking the truth.

In addition to statutory standards, privileges and immunities may limit a Court's ability to issue summons. As Philippe Sands noted in the context of an arrest warrant issued against a head of state, lawfulness of process "depends on the Court's powers and attributes and the legal basis upon which it was established."[81] The ECCC's hybrid character makes this analysis more complex than it would be for a clearly national or international court.

The request to interview the late King-Father Sihanouk, who passed away on October 15, 2012, was particularly controversial. After Cambodia first requested UN assistance to try the Khmers Rouges, Sihanouk said on multiple occasions that he would testify to share his experiences.[82] In recent years, however, he expressed a negative view of the Court and unwillingness to participate, especially after Court officials declined his 2007 invitation to the Royal Palace, which he described as "the only chance for the court to get his input."[83]

The Cambodian Constitution provides, "The King of Cambodia shall reign but shall not govern. The King shall be the Head of State for Life. The King shall be inviolable."[84] Sihanouk retired in 2004 and his son, Sihamoni, assumed the throne. That October, the Cambodian National Assembly passed a law granting various privileges to Sihanouk and bestowing on him the title "Great Valorous King" or "Hero King."[85] Persons close to the royal family argued that the 2004 law entitled Sihanouk to "the same immunity he had as a reigning King"[86] and that calling him to the ECCC would violate the constitution and the 2004 law.[87] National Assembly Deputy President Nguon Nhel similarly asserted that Sihanouk "cannot rightfully be summoned to testify at the tribunal."[88] In contrast, the Asian Human Rights Commission argued that the Cambodian Constitution confers immunity on "the reigning monarch and not upon anybody else. No act of parliament can confer the same inviolability upon former King Sihanouk."[89]

To remove any doubt within domestic law, Cambodia's Constitutional Council would need to issue a pronouncement on the legal effect of Article 7 of the Constitution and the 2004 law.[90] If the ECCC were an ordinary domestic Cambodian court, a Constitutional Council decision would bind it. However, because the ECCC is "a special internationalized tribunal," it might also have been necessary to consider whether international law entitled him to immunity from testifying at the ECCC. Realities on the ground made this a moot question; absent immense diplomatic pressure, the ECCC lacked the power to compel Sihanouk to testify before it. This may explain why the PTC declared without analysis that Cambodian law on this question was settled—"[T]he King Father cannot be subpoenaed, nor can coercive measures be used against him[,]"[91]—and assumed without question that national law bound the ECCC.

Unlike the King, high-level Cambodian officials are not "inviolable," but enjoy waivable procedural immunity from arrest and detention.[92] It appears that neither the Constitution nor any other Cambodian law offers officials immunity from testifying at a domestic or international court. Nevertheless, it remains possible that Cambodian courts would decide that Prime Minister Hun Sen, and possibly other high-level officials, are exempt from process due to the offices they hold. Judge Itoe of the SCSL has cited a French case in which the Cour de Cassation found that President Chirac was not under any obligation to appear as a witness at the pretrial stage of a trial because "the obligation is accompanied by a measure of a constraint . . . and is punished by a criminal penalty."[93] Similarly, the Supreme Court of Sierra Leone has found that "A serving Head of State is entitled to absolute immunity from process brought before national courts[.]"[94] By contrast, international tribunals have rejected such immunities. The ICTY and International Criminal Tribunal for Rwanda (ICTR) Trial Chambers have found that government officials have no immunity from being subpoenaed to testify before them[95] and may be compelled to attend pretestimony interviews.[96] However, they have never found it necessary to subpoena incumbent officials after evaluating the statutory requirements discussed above.

There is no indication in the public record that, at least initially, the CIJs considered domestic immunities an impediment to summoning the named officials. According to information released by the *Ieng Sary* team, national CIJ You Bunleng instead objected to the request due to the need to close the investigation in a reasonable time[97]—a common refrain of the judges when dismissing defense motions. International CIJ Lemonde, acting alone, issued summons to the government officials, suggesting that he believed he had authority to do so. Court spokesperson Lars Olsen reportedly said:

> I don't want to get into any speculation about any immunity because we would expect that any law-abiding citizens would comply with a summons issued by a court of law[.] . . . I would assume that this would particularly apply to people representing the very law-making organs that have created this court.[98]

Nevertheless, Lemonde did not request enforcement after the recipients did not respond, apparently raising the issue of their immunity only after the fact.[99]

Lemonde, following the lead of Judge You, justified his failure to seek enforcement on the basis that "coercive measures is [*sic*] fraught with significant practical difficulties, and, in the best-case scenario, would unduly delay the conclusion of the judicial investigation, contrary to the need for expeditiousness," leaving it to the Trial Chamber to decide if coercive measures were warranted.[100] He may have decided that coercive action was politically impossible without the agreement of the Cambodian Government, as the Cambodian judicial police are tasked with enforcement under the ECCC Law and Internal Rules.[101] However, upon review, the Pre-Trial Chamber said that the biggest hurdle was the summoned officials' likely invocation of parliamentary immunity, which would at the very least "significantly delay" the proceedings. They therefore agreed that the question should be deferred to the Trial Chamber, preserving the right of the accused to seek exculpatory evidence at a later date.[102]

Nevertheless, due to a number of government statements reported in the press, the PTC directed the CIJ to assess "whether or not a nexus exists between RGC discouragement and the actual failure of the summoned witnesses to provide statements."[103] For example, Hun Sen reportedly claimed to have personally vetoed the testimony of "some people,"[104] and government spokesperson Khieu Kanharith was reported to say:

> [T]hough the individuals could appear in the court voluntarily, the government's position was that they should not give testimony. He said that foreign officials involved in the court could "pack their bags and return home" if they were not satisfied with the decision.[105]

In response, the CIJs merely noted that Hor Namhong, Cambodia's Foreign Minister, claimed to have disregarded his summons because Judge Lemonde acted alone in issuing it, which Hor believed did not meet the necessary formal requirements.[106] Without mentioning any of the other witnesses or providing any additional reasoning, the CIJs said they did not believe an investigation into government interference was warranted.[107]

On appeal, the PTC was unable to reach a supermajority decision. The national judges found, in part, that the statements of a government spokesperson could not prevent higher-level officials from testifying.[108] The international PTC judges determined that after considering all of the allegations and their sequence, no reasonable trier of fact could fail to find that "one or more members of the RGC may have knowingly and willfully interfered with witnesses who may give evidence before the CIJs."[109] However, due to the lack of supermajority agreement, by default the CIJ decision not to investigate remained in effect.

The defense teams have since highlighted government opposition to the testimony of these officials multiple times before the Trial and Supreme Court Chambers, with the *Nuon Chea* team in particular seeking to link these events to the Government's well-documented disapproval of obstructed Cases 003 and 004,[110] discussed in the next chapter. Michiel Pestman's prediction that the requested government witnesses would not be called has proven true.[111] The *Nuon Chea* team continues to contend that the summoned officials are important to his client's case.[112] After leaving office, Judge Lemonde said these witnesses "clearly had something to say, because they were aware of events and facts for which their testimony was important."[113]

With little hope that the requested officials would be summoned, the *Nuon Chea* defense team sought to prove government interference by persistently interjecting the officials' names into the proceedings, and being castigated for doing so—including having their microphone regularly shut off. For example, the team sought to question a witness about a 2004 statement he provided an NGO claiming to have seen Hun Sen meet Nuon Chea and other high-level DK officials in the 1970s.[114] The Trial Chamber, not for the first time, warned two international members of the *Nuon Chea* team against further "misconduct," including their continual "irrelevant" references to government officials.[115] This strategy severely tested the bounds of advocacy in a country unaccustomed to witnessing the exercise of vigorous defense rights and challenges to senior officials. Although the team's escalating antics achieved diminishing returns for its client, the effort exposed the vulnerability of the majority-domestic hybrid tribunal to charges that it lacked the independence to deliver credible justice.

MORE EFFICIENCY AND FAIRNESS PROBLEMS: LENGTHY PRETRIAL DETENTION AND EFFORTS TO EXPEDITE TRIAL

Efficiency has also been a serious challenge to the Case 002 proceedings. Despite the ECCC's in-country location and heavy reliance on domestic personnel, it has been hard-pressed to deliver justice swiftly and at a low cost—two of the anticipated benefits of the hybrid model. As discussed in previous chapters, the ECCC faced long delays establishing itself as an institution, developing rules, conducting investigations, and preparing for trial. Those delays raised problems for the Court related to lengthy pretrial detention. More recently, cost concerns, frustration with embarrassing political disputes, and the fragile health of the Case 002 defendants led to increasing donor pressure on the Court to complete Case 002 quickly. In an effort to speed the trial, the Trial Chamber split the indictment, likely reducing the impact of the verdict, and held trial in the physical absence of the accused, raising fairness concerns.

Pretrial Detention

Some of the early legal challenges before the ECCC related to the charged persons' lengthy pretrial detention. As a hybrid court, the ECCC has an opportunity to directly influence the Cambodian judiciary's habitual failure to respect detention limits.[116] Its jurisprudence generally has followed precedents from international courts but leaves mixed lessons for Cambodian domestic courts.

Under the Internal Rules, the ECCC may only provisionally detain a Charged Person if there exist both a "well founded reason to believe" that he or she has committed the charged crimes and evidence that detention is "necessary" to prevent him or her from pressuring witnesses or victims, colluding with accomplices, destroying evidence, or fleeing; or to protect the Charged Person's security or preserve public order.[117]

The various grounds for finding detention necessary are disjunctive, meaning that the existence of any one alone provides a sufficient basis for retaining a charged person in custody. Provisional detention is allowed for one year and may be extended only twice.[118] The Court found that provisional detention was appropriate for all five charged persons in 2007, and extended their detention by one year in 2008 and again in 2009. Despite the advanced age of the accused in Case 002 and the length of time that had passed since their alleged crimes, the Court refused to release them on bail or allow for home detention. As the three-year limit approached, the CIJs made it clear that they would issue the Closing Order in time to ensure their detention for trial. Although the Court's jurisprudence has been facially consistent with international standards, it is questionable whether it has adhered in spirit, as to all appearances no Chamber ever genuinely contemplated the possibility of release. This is troubling due to the widespread abuse of pretrial detention in the domestic courts and the potential for a negative precedent.

Human rights bodies such as the European Court of Human Rights, Inter-American Commission and Court of Human Rights, and UN Human Rights Committee have determined that pretrial detention should be allowed only on an exceptional basis.[119] The ICTY, ICTR, and SCSL have justified more restrictive pretrial detention policies by highlighting the gravity of the crimes charged and their inability to ensure the return of an accused released to his or her home jurisdiction.[120] However, once the ICTY began having a more cooperative relationship with the states of the former Yugoslavia, it increasingly released accused on bail pending trial. The International Criminal Court (ICC) has also granted accused provisional release.[121] Neither the ICTR nor the SCSL granted provisional release to any accused.

Although the ECCC is located in Phnom Penh, and the Cambodian Government appears well equipped to ensure the return of the charged persons, the ECCC has taken a restrictive approach to release. For example, the Pre-Trial Chamber held that Ieng Sary and Ieng Thirith must be detained to ensure their presence, despite their age, ill health, and failure to flee during the many years the tribunal was being established.[122] The PTC acknowledged that human rights law requires "specific evidence" of a threat to public order but cited only an analyst's view that the proceedings could "lead to the resurfacing of anxieties" in Cambodia in determining that Ieng Sary's release "would actually disturb the public order"[123]—a concern the Government has similarly invoked to resist charging additional suspects (see chapter 6).

The ECCC also denied Ieng Sary's repeated requests for hospital or house arrest due to his ill health, concluding that it would not satisfy the objectives of provisional detention and could jeopardize his safety.[124] Neither the Internal Rules nor the rules of other international criminal tribunals explicitly allow provisional release on the basis of health concerns, but in practice other tribunals have allowed temporary release to a confined medical area in three circumstances: when treatment is unavailable at the detention unit or in the host country, on humanitarian grounds when an accused's condition is so grave that it is incompatible with any form of detention, and when an accused is found unfit to stand trial.[125] Accused have been released home only in a few cases involving inoperable and incurable cancer with a prognosis of at most a few months to live.[126]

With regard to Ieng Sary, the Pre-Trial Chamber held, "There is no evidence of an immediate need for long-term hospitalisation and the ECCC Detention Facility is properly equipped to provide medical assistance as required."[127] As Ieng Sary's heart condition was neither untreatable nor imminently terminal, there was no obligation under international precedent to grant him house arrest. Nevertheless, no international tribunal has tried accused of such advanced age, and absent a greater risk of flight or public disorder, it might have behooved the Court to create new precedent in this area[128]—if for no other reason than to ensure the accused persons' continuing fitness to stand trial.

The gradual decline of Ieng Thirith, first noted in 2008,[129] may have been exacerbated by her four years of pretrial detention.[130] The ECCC, like international courts, applies the ICTY's *Strugar* fitness test, which requires the defense to show that the accused's mental incapacity prevents her from exercising her rights effectively at trial.[131] Once it became inescapable that Ieng Thirith was unable to participate in her own defense,[132] the Trial Chamber appropriately decided that it must release her.[133] The Chamber could not reach a supermajority, and absent guidance from the Internal Rules on how to proceed, it looked to "general provisions of international criminal and human rights law" and found that it must follow the interpretation of the law most favorable to the accused.[134]

On appeal, the Supreme Court Chamber determined that not all possible medical steps had been taken to improve her condition and ruled that she should remain in detention in an appropriate medical facility for an initial six months of treatment.[135] When the Trial Chamber decision was announced, there were public expressions of distress,[136] and the Supreme Court decision was seen by many as an effort to appease Cambodian opinion despite the fact that her chances of improvement were slight to none.[137] She was not sent to a suitable mental health facility, as there are none in Cambodia—a legacy of destruction of the medical system under the Khmer Rouge regime. As a result, she remained in the general ECCC detention facility until September 2012, when the SCC finally released her after three medical experts reassessed her condition and found that despite additional treatment her mental health had worsened.[138]

A final example of the Court's propensity to maintain the Charged Persons in detention was the CIJs' last-minute push to ensure the Closing Order would be issued before the expiration of the three-year maximum provisional detention period. A 2009 U.S. Embassy cable reported Deputy Director of Administration Knut Rosandhaug's concern about "massive political consequences" if the suspects had to be released.[139] The Closing Order was issued on September 15, 2010, four days before Nuon Chea's release would have been mandatory.[140] The Court made clear its awareness of the impending deadline in a press release explaining the consequences of the issuance of a Closing Order on continued detention.[141] If the Charged Persons had been released, under the Internal Rules there would have been no basis for their redetention during trial unless they failed to appear.[142]

Upon issuing the Closing Order, the CIJs had the authority to extend their detention four more months until the accused were brought before the Trial Chamber.[143] Saved by the bell, the Court soon faced another impending deadline. Unclear wording in the Internal Rules regarding the impact of an appeal of the Closing Order on the four-month limit[144] convinced the Pre-Trial Chamber that it must issue its decision within the same four months. Practically unable to make the deadline, it issued its disposition without providing reasons. The Trial Chamber found this to be a violation of the rights of the accused, but not severe enough to warrant release.[145] The Supreme Court Chamber overturned that finding, ruling that the filing of the appeal started a new four-month detention period, and thus the PTC had issued its fully reasoned decision within the required period.[146] The accused remained safely in detention awaiting trial, with no violation of their rights.

The factors considered in determining the need for provisional detention are highly speculative and subjective in their application, and the ECCC has not clearly violated international standards in finding the accuseds' continuing detention "necessary."[147] Yet the reasons the Court has provided likely obscure its underlying rationale: a reluctance to release the accused due to the horrific nature of their alleged crimes, the many years that they have lived in impunity, and the adverse public reaction that would accompany their release. Michael Karnavas believes the international judges were "intellectually dishonest" in their detention rulings:

> My client should have been provisionally released. End of story. By any stretch of the imagination. But he wasn't. . . . [The international judges] have gone along to get along, with what might have appeared as smaller battles early on, as opposed to taking principled positions. . . . They are always finding creative ways to get around [the rules].[148]

The ECCC's legacy for the Cambodian judiciary, which routinely disregards excessive pretrial detention, is therefore mixed. The Court has strictly complied with mandatory detention limits, but it has consistently interpreted the Court's rules to avoid releasing unpopular accused, perhaps demonstrating how judges can both facially observe the letter of the law and achieve an ends-driven result. The predilection of judges to find prolonged pretrial detention necessary is likely greater in the context of an *in situ* hybrid court than a court physically removed from the crimes and their societal impact.[149] It is an open secret that if, as has now come to pass, one or more of the accused die of old age before reaching judgment, their preverdict detention may be the only "justice" victims receive after 30 long years.

Efforts to Expedite Trial

The slow pace of the proceedings did more than raise pretrial detention issues; it put the completion of Case 002 in jeopardy. Using its authority under Internal Rules, the Trial Chamber decided in September 2011 to separate the proceedings and hold sequential trials related to different parts of the indictment.[150] The ECCC is the first mass crimes court to contemplate consecutive trials based on one indictment.

The Trial Chamber made this decision to reach a timely verdict given the advanced age of the accused and many of the victims. Paradoxically, it has also greatly limited the relevance of the first trial for Cambodians, as it no longer includes many types of harm suffered during the DK regime. Although the decision to divide the proceedings may allow a judgment to be reached before the death of more accused, the first mini-trial did not proceed swiftly, partly due to many novel procedural questions raised. The age and maladies of the accused, which led to problematic efforts to try Case 002/01 without their physical attendance, make a second trial extremely unlikely. If the Court reaches judgment in Case 002 only with regard to limited charges, the potential meaningfulness of this "centerpiece" case will be substantially diminished.

Presence and Fitness

Given the age and fragile health of the octogenarian accused, it has long been feared that they would not live to see judgment. That concern was realized in late 2011, when Ieng Thirith was separated from Case 002 due to a lack of mental fitness, and again in March 2013 with the death of Ieng Sary. Both Ieng Sary and Nuon Chea had physical ailments and difficulty concentrating for long periods, which prevented them from sitting through a full day of trial, leading Ieng Sary to request early in the process for trials to be conducted in half-day increments.[151] After trial began, all three accused spent time in the hospital, leading to delays in the proceedings.[152] Accused Khieu Samphan required hospitalization most recently in late 2012, but otherwise has been the most robust of the defendants, and the only one to consistently attend full days of trial. Accused Nuon Chea was hospitalized twice in 2013 and participated in the last several months of hearings from outside the courtroom.

The ECCC, like all internationalized courts, guarantees the right of an accused to "be tried in his or her presence,"[153] though that right may be waived or forfeited where there are "substantial trial disruptions."[154] In order to mitigate the day-to-day effects of the accused's ill health, the ECCC set up a special room where the accused may watch the trial and instruct their counsel through a two-way audio-video link.[155] Internal Rule 81(5) provides that the Accused may be ordered to participate by video when "the Accused's absence reaches a level that causes substantial delay and[] where the interests of justice so require." Defense counsel have argued that "video-link technology must not be equated with physical presence at trial"[156] and that if an accused "falls asleep in the holding cell, that is not active participation. . . . That would be nothing but a charade to suggest that he is following the proceedings."[157] Nevertheless, in an effort to mitigate the effects of Ieng Sary's declining health, in late 2012 the Trial Chamber ordered him to participate by video-link from the holding cell despite his refusal to waive his right to be physically present.[158] The age and ill health of the Khmer Rouge defendants thus posed a serious and ongoing handicap not only to an efficient trial but also to fair proceedings. Ieng Sary's lawyers challenged the ruling and sought a reevaluation of his fitness for trial;[159] however, these motions unfortunately became moot when the proceedings against him were terminated.

When an accused dies prior to verdict, international courts have uniformly terminated the proceedings,[160] depriving victims of a judgment of guilt or innocence, as well as an explanation of the factual basis for the judgment. According to an ECCC judge, in theory the Closing Order would have been very beneficial as "mini judgment" operating on probability instead of certainty. But because the CIJs did not include particulars related to charges it is impossible to tell on what facts the charges are based.[161]

The Split Indictment: Conviction or Truth Telling?

In severing the Case 002 indictment, the Trial Chamber noted that in cases of similar complexity at international courts, trial chambers have required as long as ten years to reach judgment.[162] Its aim was therefore "to limit the number of witnesses, experts and civil parties called," enabling it "to issue a verdict following a shortened trial, safeguarding the fundamental interest of victims in achieving meaningful and timely justice, and the right of all Accused in Case 002 to an expeditious trial."[163] Other mass crimes courts have likewise reduced the scope of large indictments; however, in accordance with their adversarial approach the prosecution has played the primary role in determining which charges are cut. At the ECCC, none of the parties' lawyers was asked for his or her views in advance, despite their many years of mass crimes case experience, as the Trial Chamber believed a consultative procedure would itself result in unacceptable delays.[164]

The first trial, Case 002/01, addresses only the evacuation of Phnom Penh and other major cities after April 17, 1975, killings of soldiers and civil servants of the defeated Khmer Republic government at the Tuol Po Chrey execution site in Pursat Province contemporaneous with the evacuation, the forced migration of Cambodians to the DK North and North West Zones from 1975 to 1977, and related crimes against humanity.

> No co-operative, worksites, security centers, [other] execution sites or facts relevant to the third phase of population movements will be examined during the first trial. Further, all allegations of, *inter alia*, genocide, persecution on religious grounds as a crime against humanity and Grave Breaches of the Geneva Conventions of 1949 have also been deferred to later phases of the proceedings in Case 002.[165]

In a press release announcing its decision to sever, the Trial Chamber justified the narrow topic selected for the first trial in part by noting, "The forced movement of population also affected a very broad cross-section of the Cambodian population at the time, including a large percentage of civil parties in Case 002."[166] Although supporting the purpose behind the severance order, the Co-Prosecutors objected to the form:

> [T]he charges selected for the first and likely only trial of the Accused would not be representative of their alleged criminal conduct, in contrast to international practice; it would not promote an accurate historical record; and would diminish the legacy of ECCC proceedings in advancing national reconciliation.[167]

Rather than sever the indictment into policy segments, the Co-Prosecutors argued the first trial should include representative crimes: the evacuation of Phnom Penh as well as crimes at a few security centers, work sites, and cooperatives.[168]

The *Ieng Sary* team argued that in effect the prosecution was asking the Trial Chamber to amend the Closing Order, which is outside the scope of its authority.[169] This is because, unlike in an adversarial system where the prosecution has the authority to make deals with the defense and drop charges from an indictment, the civil law focus is on finding the "material truth." Therefore, once a formal determination has been made that a crime has been committed, discretion cannot be exercised to dismiss it:[170] crimes can only be severed in a way that preserves the totality of the Closing Order.[171]

In the view of some persons interviewed, the Co-Prosecutors should have filed a shorter, tighter introductory submission in the first place.[172] This criticism has been leveled at most mass crimes courts, where the prosecution, due to the massive quantity of information available, "throws a net hoping something will stick."[173] Considering the extremely limited mandate of the ECCC, it was arguably important to establish a comprehensive record of major crimes in Case 002, even if some charges are never adjudicated. Moreover, according to one civil law–trained lawyer, there is no legal reason why the judges could not have severed the facts of the indictment in a more creative and representative manner as requested by the prosecution.[174] It is also unclear whether the Court had the authority to sever the charges and exclude genocide and religious persecution from the first case. If the facts of the forced transfer prove religious persecution, the ECCC should be able to issue convictions on that basis. Deciding otherwise limits the effect of the indictment and amounts to prejudgment.[175]

Michael Karnavas says:

> Now it's a race to finish, to convict them before somebody dies. That's the madness of this [severance order]. [Is the Court] more interested in getting a conviction, or in getting a cohesive narrative that deals with the issues in a contextual manner that allows the Cambodian people to see what exactly happened—why, when, and how?[176]

The severance order reminds Panhavuth Long of a saying by senior Khmer Rouge figure Ta Mok during the DK period: "Cut the head to fit the hat."[177] Victims have expressed concern that the Court will never address some key topics, such as the crime of genocide.[178] Fourteen months into trial the Supreme Court Chamber overturned the Trial Chamber severance order and upbraided the Trial Chamber for, among other things, failing to consider the representativeness of the charges.[179] Although the Trial Chamber reconsidered its terms of severance from scratch, due to acute awareness of the substantial time already spent hearing evidence tailored to the original severance decision and the need to reach an expeditious end to proceedings, the narrow scope of charges to be addressed in Case 002 remained the same, a *fait accompli*.[180]

MIXED RULES AND TRIAL MANAGEMENT PROBLEMS

The trial in Case 002/1 lasted two years.[181] In its press release announcing the severance of Case 002, the Trial Chamber speculated: "The advantage of separation of proceedings into segments is that each trial will take an abbreviated time for the Chamber to complete."[182] The Co-Prosecutors disagreed that the severance order would promote efficiency, and they appear to have been proven correct.[183] The novelty of the severance procedure, as well as the unconsidered application of mixed national and international rules rooted in both civil and common law traditions, caused significant confusion and delay.[184]

Due to Case 002's procedural complexity—including the large number of documents and witnesses involved—the parties sought to have management meetings before the start of trial.[185] These requests were rebuffed in an effort to start trial as quickly as possible.[186] Although none of the Trial Chamber judges has mass crimes trial management experience, they have a propensity to make immediate oral decisions without consulting each other, the parties, or their legal officers. Moreover they demonstrated what some called a face-saving reluctance to revisit their rulings even when they proved unworkable. As a consequence, procedural debates riddled the trial, and there was widespread criticism that the adoption and application of rules was arbitrary and inconsistent. This resulted in confusion among the parties and prevented the trial from offering an engaging narrative for Cambodians. Just one of the procedural debates that consumed trial proceedings is discussed below.[187]

Questioning of Witnesses

In civil law practice, the judges first question the witnesses and then ask the parties if they have additional questions.[188] Unlike in Case 001, during which the judges each took responsibility for developing expertise on a topic and led the questioning of related witnesses, in Case 002 the Trial Chamber decided to delegate its responsibility to one of the parties.[189] Both defense and civil party lawyers believe the judges' abdication of their responsibility to direct questioning resulted in procedural confusion.[190]

The responsibility to question fell primarily on the prosecution. In the common law and at the ICTY and ICTR, the prosecution presents its evidence by selecting the witnesses it wishes to call, determining the order of their appearance, and preparing witnesses by, for example, comparing prior witness statements and highlighting potential inconsistencies.[191] By contrast, in civil law the judges control these matters and parties are not allowed to vet witnesses beforehand.[192] As a result of the mixture of these practices, the ECCC Co-Prosecutors had to determine solely on the basis of prior statements and evidence in the case file what questions to ask of a witness selected by the Trial Chamber. They had no ability to proof witnesses in advance to determine the extent of their knowledge on the topic at hand or the consistency of their current memories with statements made years prior.

For example, two witnesses were on the civil parties' list to discuss internal purges, a subject not included in Case 002/01. Unexpectedly, the Trial Chamber called them to provide historical background, and tasked the prosecution with primary responsibility for extracting relevant information from them. Michiel Pestman believes that after the indictment was split, the Trial Chamber used footnotes in relevant paragraphs of the Closing Order to determine whom to call rather than asking the parties. Thus, the prosecution was confronted with questioning witnesses they did not want to hear. Pestman and others argue that the trial should have started with experts who could establish the overall context of the proceedings.[193]

While putting parties in charge of questioning, the Court forbade them from using leading questions to more efficiently draw out information, even when a witness was uncooperative. Leading questions are generally disallowed in civil law trials because all witnesses are court witnesses—they are not considered adverse to any party—and the court does most of the questioning, unlike the process in Case 002. However, once the Chamber delegated this role to the parties, no justification remained for a blanket prohibition.

The Trial Chamber's hybrid practice maintained its control over who testified when and on what topic, yet relied on adversarial questioning (without the opportunity for proofing or leading questions) to elicit information. The prosecution had the burden of proof, but no control over where the case was going.[194] The consequence was a lack of coherence: Neither the parties nor the Cambodian public understood precisely why some witnesses were called, nor what they were expected to contribute to the process. Andrew Ianuzzi, former lawyer for Nuon Chea, says, "It's as if Case 002 was designed to be the most boring trial possible."[195]

A further problem—resulting more from delays and the severance decision than the Trial Chamber's hybrid rules—has been establishing appropriate limits on what evidence witnesses may present. The Co-Prosecutors argued that witnesses scheduled for Case 002/01 who have information relevant to other parts of the indictment should be allowed to present it, partly because many are elderly and may not be available later.[196] The Trial Chamber held that questions to witnesses should be "limited to facts relevant to the first trial" but allowed the prosecution to make oral requests for further testimony,[197] and in practice some witnesses were allowed to testify to a broader scope of issues.[198] In May 2012, the Trial Chamber agreed to a prosecution request to hear elderly witnesses on the full scope of Case 002.[199] Some expert witnesses were also heard on all subjects.[200] As a consequence, the Chamber heard some of the same evidence as if the trial had never been split, while the defense only challenged issues related to population movement and the Tuol Po Chrey execution site, and the judgment should be limited to those facts. Michael Karnavas contended during trial that due to procedural controversies and understandable efforts by the prosecution to take advantage of unclear rules to place as much evidence as possible on the record in the first case, "Had they not severed, [the hearings] would probably be further ahead."[201]

Of greater fair trial concern, shortly before the end of hearings, in response to prosecution arguments that severance had jeopardized its ability to meet its burden of proof, the Trial Chamber suddenly declared, "From the outset, the Chamber has ruled that all parties may lead evidence in relation to the roles and responsibilities of all Accused in relation to all policies of the DK era"—citing only a decision on expert witness testimony.[202] The Khieu Samphan lawyers called this development "shocking," arguing that they were "never given the opportunity to refute allegations relating to the elaboration and implementation" of policies other than forced evacuation, and that the result would be prejudgment of legal issues which are theoretically the subject of forthcoming "mini-trials."[203] The repercussions are as of yet unclear, but this development highlights the disorder resulting from novel and equivocal procedures.

Barriers to Further Case 002 Trials

Procedural complexities are also likely to prevent the expeditious start to a possible second trial. The Trial Chamber asserted that it selected the subject matter "to ensure that the issues examined in the first trial provide a basis to consider the role and responsibility of all accused, and to provide a foundation for the remaining charges in later trials."[204] As the Co-Prosecutors have noted, the only way for the Trial Chamber to adopt facts established in the first trial into a subsequent trial would be through judicial notice of adjudicated facts or *res judicata*.[205] However, it is unclear whether the Trial Chamber has the ability to take judicial notice of adjudicated facts, as it has previously found "no legal basis in the Law on the Establishment of the ECCC or in the Internal Rules for the Chamber to take judicial notice of adjudicated facts . . . before the ECCC."[206]

Moreover, neither mechanism would likely be available in Case 002/02 until the Supreme Court Chamber issued its final judgment on Case 002/01, as some rulings of the Trial Chamber may be overturned. In the *Duch* case, eighteen months elapsed between the issuance of the trial and appeals judgments. The Trial Chamber has held that there is no impediment to using a trial verdict as a legal and factual foundation for a second trial without waiting for the Supreme Court judgment.[207] Even if this were possible, it is questionable how the Trial Chamber could draft a complex foundational judgment while overseeing a new trial.[208] In the *Duch* case, the Trial Chamber took over eight months to draft the judgment. With limited charges being addressed, and the very real potential that another accused could die before judgment is handed down, there is little likelihood that much of the Khmer Rouge era will ever be addressed by the ECCC.

CONCLUSION

In its most important case, the ECCC faced dilemmas common to international and hybrid tribunals as they carry out their judicial functions: how to deliver justice efficiently while observing fair trial norms and attempting to develop a factual narrative that addresses the needs and demands of survivors. These challenges were accentuated by its hybrid form, which has rendered the Court susceptible to accusations of bias and political interference and contributed to procedural delays and confusion. Both the common law and the civil law systems have mechanisms refined over the years to promote both fairness and efficiency. When civil and common law features are haphazardly combined, however, a schizophrenic process results and jeopardizes both objectives. The fact that the ECCC's investigatory and trial judges lack prior experience managing complex criminal trials has only exacerbated the problem.

Pestman argued that the blending of legal systems and inconsistent rule application has produced troubling unpredictability.[209] Elisabeth Simonneau Fort added that personalities play an important role as the Court swerves between "some civil law, some common law, and then some civil law again."[210] Guissé said the reason the rules were constantly changing had less to do with the civil law/common law mix and more to do with the judges, who lack experience working in other international jurisdictions.[211] Karnavas called the trial process "chaotic" and contended, "They are trying to have it every which way: It's the French system, it's not the French system, it's the national system, it's the ICTY. Whenever it suits them they are constantly changing the rules as the game is being played."[212] Although these concerns have not irreparably tainted the Case 002 proceedings, they do pose serious risks to the case. The ECCC's experience shows the folly of creating special rules for a hybrid court with such a narrow mandate and limited lifespan. For trials to proceed smoothly and expediently, specific, clear, established rules tailored to a mass crimes process must be in place at the start of any future hybrid court process.

In addition to concerns about fairness, the ECCC's functional challenges led to questions about its capacity to deliver meaningful justice for the myriad Cambodians who have suffered from the atrocities of the Pol Pot era. Neither international nor hybrid courts can function as truth commissions and address all historical harm. Of necessity, they must focus on particularly serious crimes and the responsibility of a limited number of persons. As discussed in chapter 1, the ECCC's jurisdiction was intended to be narrow, focusing on senior Khmer Rouge leaders and others "most responsible" and on crimes committed in Cambodia between April 17, 1975, and January 6, 1979.

The Case 002 defense teams sought to broaden the historical discussion. Son Arun, Cambodian Co-Lawyer for Nuon Chea, argued that "[o]ne needs a full picture of these facts in order to properly assess the acts and intentions of the DK leaders when they came to power."[213] Pestman argued that Nuon Chea had essentially admitted ordering the evacuation of Phnom Penh, and the trial should focus on evaluating his legal justifications.[214] The Court resisted efforts to focus on topics such as the U.S. bombardment of the civil war era, Vietnamese intervention, and abuses by various Cambodian factions outside of the DK era. Trial Chamber President Nil Nonn issued a directive informing all parties that:

> Background contextual issues and events outside the temporal jurisdiction of the ECCC will be considered by the Chamber only when demonstrably relevant to matters within the ECCC's jurisdiction and the scope of the trial as determined by the Chamber.[215]

The reluctance to discuss those topics owes partly to politics, but it also obviously represents the pressure of time. It has taken over 30 years to bring the accused to trial, and the pressure has been intense to reach a verdict quickly. The severance order further limited the scope of the historical discussion, leaving doubt about whether it offered Cambodians a meaningful slice of "truth."

All mass crimes courts struggle with the need to balance the obligation to prevent undue delay in the proceedings with the need to provide a comprehensive, coherent narrative of events. There is little purpose in holding a small number of exemplary trials if a judgment is never reached, or if a judgment is so narrow that it fails to resonate with the affected population. Slobodan Milosevic's death before verdict on a massive indictment created an impetus toward narrower indictments and shorter trials. However, this approach, as exemplified by the ICC's *Lubanga* single-charge indictment, risks being nonrepresentative of the victims' primary concerns.[216] The ECCC's Case 001 addressed one detention center at which primarily Khmer Rouge cadres and their families were killed. The Case 002 indictment has been split in an effort to reach judgment quickly primarily on one narrow topic—mass population movements. As of October 2013, with Case 002/01 closing arguments underway, it appears doubtful that most of the story of the senior leaders of Democratic Kampuchea will ever be told in a judicial forum, and an enormous gap will remain in the official legal record. This is of particular concern because, as discussed in the next chapter, it is unlikely any other persons will be tried by the ECCC.

Workers unearthing remains at a mass grave at Tram Kak district, Takeo province, circa 1979. (Courtesy of the Documentation Center of Cambodia.)

One of many village meetings organized throughout Cambodia in 1982–83 by the People's Republic of Kampuchea to shed light on the crimes of the Pol Pot regime. (Courtesy of the Documentation Center of Cambodia.)

The People's Revolutionary Tribunal, which issued history's first genocide convictions against Pol Pot and Ieng Sary *in absentia,* held in the Chaktomuk Theatre, Phnom Penh, July–August 1979. (Courtesy of the Documentation Center of Cambodia.)

UN Legal Counsel Hans Corell and Cambodian Deputy Prime Minister Sok An return to the Chaktomuk Theatre for the signing ceremony of the ECCC's Framework Agreement, June 6, 2003. (Photo by Heng Sinith, courtesy of the Documentation Center of Cambodia.)

Head of the UN Transitional Authority in Cambodia Yasushi Akashi (*left*) and King Norodom Sihanouk (*right*) during the UN's interregnum in Cambodia in 1992–93. (Photo by Benny Widyono, courtesy of the Documentation Center of Cambodia.)

Khmer Rouge soldiers in the mountainous northwestern province of Anlong Veng turning over their weapons to defect to the government with Ieng Sary in 1996. (Photo by Khun Ly, courtesy of the Documentation Center of Cambodia.)

Prime Minister Hun Sen (*front left*) and Prince Norodom Ranariddh (*front right*) at the National Assembly in October 2004, when the ECCC Law was passed. Deputy Prime Minister Sok An (*far right, head bowed*) and current Acting Director of the ECCC Office of Administration Tony Kranh (*top center*) are among those in the background. (Photo by Heng Sinith, courtesy of the Documentation Center of Cambodia.)

UN Secretary-General Ban Ki-moon (*left*) addresses the ECCC judges and staff in the courtroom gallery during an October 2010 visit to the tribunal. (Courtesy of the Extraordinary Chambers in the Courts of Cambodia.)

The ECCC complex, including the courtroom (*top*) and administration building (*bottom*) on the site of a former military base on the western outskirts of Phnom Penh. (Photos by Socheat Nhean, courtesy of the Documentation Center of Cambodia.)

Duch on the day of the appeal judgment. (Courtesy of the Extraordinary Chambers in the Courts of Cambodia.)

Villagers watching Duch's trial on screen at an outreach event in a pagoda at the former Khmer Rouge stronghold of Pailin in northwestern Cambodia. (Photo by Keo Dacil, courtesy of the Documentation Center of Cambodia.)

Civil party Chum Mey, one of few survivors of the infamous Tuol Sleng prison, explaining how he was tortured to the Court (*top*) and later holding a copy of the *Duch* verdict with fellow Tuol Sleng survivor Vann Nath outside the ECCC (*bottom*). (Courtesy of the Extraordinary Chambers in the Courts of Cambodia.)

Co-Prosecutors Andrew Cayley and Chea Leang on the first day of opening statements in Case 002, November 2011. (Courtesy of the Extraordinary Chambers in the Courts of Cambodia.)

Nuon Chea (*back, with cap*) and his Co-Lawyers Michiel Pestman (*left*) and Son Arun (*right*) at the initial Case 002 hearing, June 27, 2011. (Courtesy of the Extraordinary Chambers in the Courts of Cambodia.)

Nuon Chea, former Deputy Chairman of the Communist Party of Kampuchea, addressing Chinese visitors to Democratic Kampuchea (*top*) and addressing the ECCC Trial Chamber on December 14, 2011 (*bottom*). (Courtesy of the Documentation Center of Cambodia and the Extraordinary Chambers in the Courts of Cambodia.)

Khieu Samphan (*left*) and Ieng Sary (*right*) with Lao Prince Souphanouvong (*center*) during his visit to Democratic Kampuchea. (Courtesy of the Documentation Center of Cambodia.)

Khieu Samphan during the proceedings against him at the ECCC. (Courtesy of the Extraordinary Chambers in the Courts of Cambodia.)

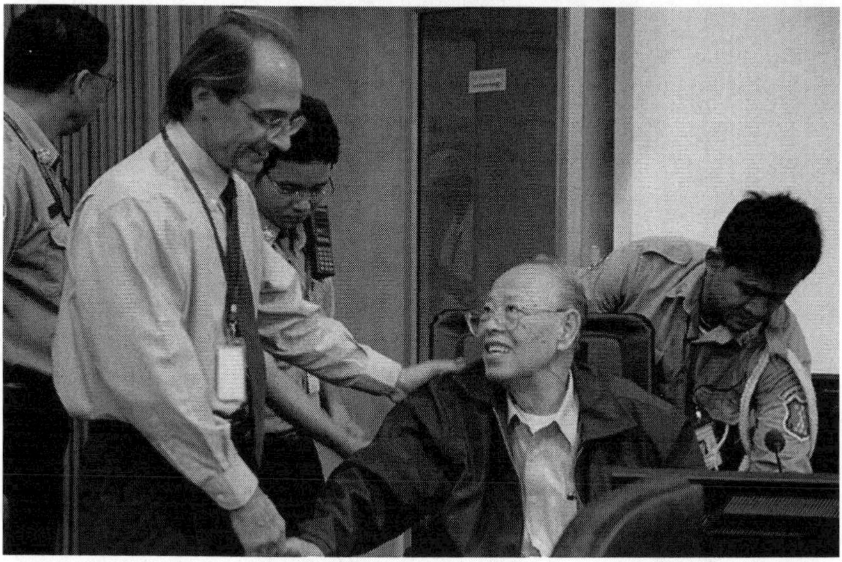

Ieng Sary toasting the Chinese ambassador as foreign minister of Democratic Kampuchea (*top*) and greeting his international defense lawyer Michael Karnavas in the ECCC courtroom on November 23, 2011. (Courtesy of the Documentation Center of Cambodia and the Extraordinary Chambers in the Courts of Cambodia.)

Former DK Minister of Social Affairs Ieng Thirith, wife of Ieng Sary, in 1999 in Pailin (*top*, photo by Youk Chhang) and at a hearing in Case 002 on August 30, 2011 (*bottom*) before she was severed from the case due to dementia and lack of fitness to stand trial. (Courtesy of the Documentation Center of Cambodia and the Extraordinary Chambers in the Courts of Cambodia.)

Public visitors to the ECCC on the third day of Case 002 opening statements, November 23, 2011. (Courtesy of the Documentation Center of Cambodia.)

Visitors being briefed in the public courtroom gallery before a Case 002 trial hearing as prosecutors and civil parties (*left*) and defense teams (*right*) take their seats. (Courtesy of the Extraordinary Chambers in the Courts of Cambodia.)

Case 004 suspect Im Chaem (*far left*) in 1979 and at her home in Anlong Veng in 2011 (*bottom*, photo by Dara Vanthan). (Courtesy of the Documentation Center of Cambodia.)

Case 004 suspect Ta An in Battambang, Cambodia, on August 1, 2011. (Photo by Dara P. Vanthan, courtesy of the Documentation Center of Cambodia.)

Deputy Director of the Office of Administration Knut Rosandhaug and acting OA Director Tony Kranh (*left*) in 2011 with Cambodian Co-Investigating Judge You Bunleng and his then international counterpart, Siegfried Blunk (*right*). (Courtesy of the Extraordinary Chambers in the Courts of Cambodia.)

ECCC Press Officer Neth Pheaktra and Public Affairs Officer Huy Vannak leading an outreach event at Pon Teuk secondary school in October 2011. (Courtesy of the Extraordinary Chambers in the Courts of Cambodia.)

An outreach event on Khmer Rouge history and the ECCC in a Cham Muslim community, led by the Documentation Center of Cambodia. (Photo by So Farina, courtesy of the Documentation Center of Cambodia.)

Chapter 6

CASES 003 & 004—THE POLITICS OF PERSONAL JURISDICTION

"No Gain in Keeping, No Loss in Weeding Out"

The presumptive lack of independence and experience of Cambodia's judges, and the contentious politics between the Cambodian Government and United Nations, led many to write off the ECCC from the beginning. However, when not directly addressing topics that challenge the wishes of the Cambodian Government, the hybrid Court's decisions for the most part have been made on sound judicial bases consistent with international standards.[1] In stark contrast, efforts to pursue several more suspects in Cases 003 and 004—which the Cambodian Government deems politically unacceptable—have engendered untenable decisions, procedural improprieties, and credible allegations of obstruction of justice. Defense lawyers in Case 002 have pointed to this debacle, arguing that all of the Court's work, including the investigation of the Khmer Rouge senior leaders, is tainted by political interference,[2] while the United Nations and donors have largely shirked the problem in their determination to make Case 002 a "success." The dispute procedures and supermajority rule were put into place precisely to address the potential impact of government interference at the Cambodian-majority court. However, in practice these rules have proven an inadequate substitute for an independent and impartial judiciary.

The dispute in Cases 003 and 004 revolves around personal jurisdiction. Since the first five ECCC suspects were arrested, there has been pressure from human rights advocates, both Cambodian and international, to charge more people. In 2008, UN Special Representative Yash Ghai speculated:

> [A]lthough the jurisdiction of the ECCC was restricted to 'senior leaders of the Democratic Kampuchea and those who were most responsible for the crimes committed,' if only the persons currently in the custody of the ECCC are accused, the people may not feel that this is adequate. The real test will be if a suspect in or close to the government is brought before the ECCC.[3]

The Open Society Justice Initiative (OSJI), the most active international court monitor, took the lead in pressing for more indictments:

> Given the sheer scale of the atrocities that occurred during the Khmer Rouge period, limiting prosecutions to five individuals would surely seem inadequate to those who survived Khmer Rouge era atrocities and would risk creating the perception that five individuals were in effect scapegoats for the crimes of others[.][4]

After the Co-Prosecutors made public their dispute over whether to investigate more people, OSJI emphasized that additional investigations would "test[] the ability of the court to operate free of political interference,"[5] and the Cambodian Human Rights Action Committee argued that failing to act independently and exercise its mandate to investigate more persons would "undermine the impact and legacy of the court."[6]

In this way, some observers have framed Cases 003 and 004 as a key test of the Court's overall legitimacy. The Cambodian Government appears to see the cases as a different kind of test—a challenge to its resolve and primary political control over the process. The dispute highlights fundamental questions for those seeking lessons from the ECCC model: Is a hybrid court that is subject to political interference better than a purely domestic process or no trials at all? As Judge Geoffrey Robertson wrote at the Special Court for Sierra Leone (SCSL):

> If the structure of any body purporting to exercise judicial power is so fundamentally flawed that its judges may realistically be perceived as puppets moved by purse strings or the politics of their progenitors or paymasters, then it cannot be acknowledged as a "court" at all.[7]

All mass crimes tribunals involve political decisions to some degree. At what point do politically imposed constraints rob a tribunal of credibility? And when should the United Nations participate in an institution vulnerable to domestic executive influence?

Those who see the exercise of judicial independence as a key barometer of the Court's success or failure will judge it largely by how it functions at its most vulnerable in Cases 003 and 004. Others, including people who have spent years seeking justice for victims, regret that the effort to prosecute more than five has overtly politicized the entire process, put the centerpiece Case 002 in jeopardy, and threatens to eclipse the Court's potentially positive legacy for Cambodia.[8]

WHO SHOULD BE TRIED?

Deciding whom to try has been a recurrent challenge for mass crimes courts. Evidence generally permits far more prosecutions than tribunal architects deem politically and financially desirable, but limiting the scope of prosecution risks creating a false narrative in which a handful of individuals are held responsible for collective wrongs while others go free.[9] The ECCC, like the SCSL, was designed to focus on a relatively narrow field of suspects.[10] As discussed in chapter 1, both the United Nations and Cambodian Government were loath to expand beyond a modest number of former Khmer Rouge officials. They did not seek agreement on a specific number, however, which might have resulted in a further negotiating impasse and certainly would have curbed the independence of the Co-Prosecutors and Co-Investigating Judges (CIJs).

The Framework Agreement and ECCC Law limit the Court's mandate to officials who were either senior leaders of Democratic Kampuchea (DK) or persons most responsible for the crimes committed from 1975 to 1979.[11] At the SCSL, a "greatest responsibility" requirement has been interpreted as a guideline for the exercise of prosecutorial discretion and not a threshold jurisdictional requirement.[12] Similarly the ECCC Supreme Court Chamber has ruled that the criteria of "senior leaders" or others "most responsible" are not jurisdictional. Instead:

> [They] operate exclusively as investigatorial and prosecutorial policy to guide the independent discretion of the CIJs and Co-Prosecutors as to how best to target their finite resources in order to achieve the purpose behind the establishment of the ECCC.[13]

Although this statement might suggest that the Office of the Co-Prosecutors (OCP) and Office of the Co-Investigating Judges (OCIJ) have equal discretion in determining whom to prosecute, the functional relationship between these offices suggests otherwise.

Discretion to Charge

In the French civil law system, as in the common law system, the prosecutor has discretion to decide whether or not to initiate a prosecution after considering not only "the legal basis of the case" but also "the appropriateness of prosecution."[14] "At any point in the investigation, the prosecutor may decide to drop the case, either because the prosecution is time-barred by statute, or by exercise of the discretion to prosecute[.]"[15] At the ECCC and other international and hybrid courts designed to prosecute a limited number of offenders for widespread crimes, prosecutorial discretion is even broader.[16] There are no explicit limits on prosecutors' exercise of discretion beyond each court's jurisdictional mandate, the professional obligations of prosecutorial independence, and the (usually quite limited) opportunities for judicial review of their decisions. Importantly, the ECCC Internal Rules state: "Co-Prosecutors shall be independent in the performance of their functions and shall not accept or seek instructions from any government or any other source."[17]

The scope of CIJ discretion is less clear. It is not described in the core ECCC documents; but it is circumscribed by the rules governing the investigation, in particular those defining the relationship between the functions of the Co-Prosecutors and the CIJs. Importantly, although the Co-Prosecutors may investigate any crimes they believe to be within the jurisdiction of the Court, the CIJs can only investigate the facts set out in prosecutorial submissions.[18] Indeed, they *must* investigate those facts.[19] The international Pre-Trial Chamber judges have said:

> [T]he applicable Rules . . . imposes [*sic*] upon [the CIJs] a legal obligation to conduct a judicial investigation into "the *crimes* under the jurisdiction of the ECCC," which means that the obligation to investigate is directed toward the criminal acts set out in the . . . Submissions.[20]

However, after completing the investigation, they do not have to follow the Prosecutors' submissions in deciding *whom* to charge.[21] They have the authority to charge anyone named in the introductory submission *or*, with the permission of the Prosecutors, anyone else against whom there is sufficient evidence of responsibility.[22] They also do not have to follow the Prosecutors' submissions in deciding to indict or dismiss a case.[23] Nevertheless, their discretion is not unlimited: they may dismiss a case only in three circumstances:

> a) The acts in question do not amount to crimes within the jurisdiction of the ECCC;
> b) The perpetrators of the acts have not been identified; or
> c) There is not sufficient evidence against the Charged Person or persons of the charges.[24]

The Pre-Trial Chamber has found that "this decision does not involve the exercise of any discretionary power; when circumstances as prescribed [in this rule] are present, the Charged Person should be indicted in relation to these acts."[25] Thus it is arguable that unless, after investigating, the CIJs find that the *criminal acts* do not fall within the jurisdiction of the Court, they cannot dismiss an active case solely because they disagree with the Prosecutors' selection of who is most responsible for the crimes. The CIJs' function is precisely to determine who should be charged, and then to do so.[26]

"Senior Leaders and Those Most Responsible"

The jurisdictional dispute hinges partly on the narrow interpretive question of who qualifies as "senior leaders" and others "most responsible" for DK atrocities. Cambodian CIJ You Bunleng, former international CIJ Siegfried Blunk, and national Co-Prosecutor Chea Leang have all expressed public doubt about the Court's jurisdiction over the Cases 003 and 004 suspects due to their "comparably lower rank."[27] To the contrary, Blunk's successor, Laurent Kasper-Ansermet, issued a decision finding that that the suspects in Case 003 squarely meet the Court's personal jurisdictional requirements.[28]

International courts emphasize two primary considerations when determining whether persons fall within criteria similar to the ECCC's "senior leaders and those most responsible" standard: the "leadership or authority position of the accused, and [the] sense of the gravity, seriousness or massive scale of the crime."[29] These factors are not considered in isolation, but holistically. For example, the International Criminal Tribunal for the former Yugoslavia (ICTY) has allowed referral of an accused to local courts when his crimes were "limited in scope both geographically and temporally, and in terms of the number of victims affected," and he did not have "any rank of military significance" or a political role.[30]

"Senior leaders" is not a fixed term referring only to those in the highest echelons of power. The ECCC Supreme Court Chamber has found the term to be "sufficiently flexible that it may not necessarily be limited to former members of the CPK and/or Standing Committees."[31] Likewise, in construing the term "most senior leaders"—a narrower category than the one applicable before the ECCC—the ICTY has found that is not restricted to the "architects" of an "overall policy" forming the basis of the crimes: "Were it true that only cases against military commanders, who were at the highest policy-making levels of an army . . . [met this criteria], this would diminish the true level of responsibility of many commanders in the field and those at the staff level."[32]

The term "most responsible" further broadens the scope of who may be prosecuted to include persons who were in less senior positions yet played a significant role in grave crimes. The UN Group of Experts noted:

> The list of top governmental and party officials may not correspond with the list of persons most responsible for serious violations of human rights in that certain top governmental leaders may have been removed from knowledge and decision-making; and others not in the chart of senior leaders may have played a significant role in the atrocities. *This seems especially true with respect to certain leaders at the zonal level, as well as officials of torture and interrogation centres such as Tuol Sleng.*[33]

Likewise, in designing the SCSL, UN Secretary-General Kofi Annan defined the term "most responsible" to include, in addition to the political or military leadership, "others in command authority down the chain of command . . . judging by the severity of the crime or its massive scale."[34] The Appeals Chamber of the International Criminal Court (ICC) has emphasized that "individuals who are not at the very top of an organization may still carry considerable influence and commit, or generate the widespread commission of, very serious crimes."[35] A former ICTY prosecutor has said similarly:

> [S]ome individuals who have no particularly important functional role may have distinguished themselves in committing numerous crimes in the most

> overt, systematic or widespread manner . . . [s]uch individuals often play a great role in *setting the example* and encourage . . . the commission of other gruesome crimes.[36]

Thus, international legal precedents do not compel the ECCC to construe the terms "senior leaders" and "most responsible" narrowly; they give the ECCC prosecutors and judges considerable discretion to investigate suspects at a "comparably" lower level than the most senior leaders.

Maintaining Peace?

Due to the large number of suspects who potentially fall within the personal jurisdiction of mass crimes courts, international prosecutors also consider subjective factors in determining whom it is most appropriate to charge—factors including the possible societal effects of prosecutions. At the ICC, the prosecutor is explicitly mandated to consider "the interests of justice" once she has established that jurisdictional requirements have been met.[37] In the case of the ECCC, the UN Group of Experts advised that the future Khmer Rouge prosecutor should "as a matter of prosecutorial policy . . . exercise his or her discretion regarding investigations, indictments and trials so as to fully take into account the twin goals of individual accountability and national reconciliation in Cambodia."[38]

French civil law does not appear to provide investigating judges with discretion to consider nonobjective factors in determining whether to indict or dismiss a case. Notably, the ICC Pre-Trial Chamber—a body with quasi–civil law power to review prosecutorial decisions—has the authority to evaluate the interests of justice only when the prosecutor decides *not* to continue with an investigation or prosecution solely on this basis.[39] Conversely, it is *not* authorized to consider subjective factors for the purpose of second-guessing the prosecutor's decision to proceed.[40]

As the ECCC Law contains a similar statutory presumption that investigations and prosecutions shall move forward, it is arguable that even if the CIJs have some measure of discretion allowing them to dismiss a case in the interest of justice, its scope should be viewed quite narrowly. Because the ECCC is the first mass crimes court to include an investigating judge, this question has never been addressed. Due to the politically charged context in which it has arisen, the answer is highly vulnerable to the political interests of those seeking to drop Cases 003 and 004.

The primary Cambodian Government justification for limiting the number of suspects has been consistent: prosecuting too many suspects could lead to renewed civil war.[41] National Co-Prosecutor Chea Leang, echoing these objections, has said additional investigations are inappropriate in part due to "Cambodia's past instability and the continued need for national reconciliation[.]"[42] She argued that although no violent reactions had yet occurred due to ECCC proceedings, "If prosecutions of lower-ranking officials were to be initiated . . . 'ex-members [of the Khmers Rouges] and those who have allegiance to the Khmer Rouge Leaders may commit violent acts.'"[43]

However real such worries may have been in the past, there currently appears to be little if any basis for concern.[44] The arrest and indictment of the first five accused provoked no significant disturbances or threats, nor did the public leak of the names of suspects in Cases 003 and 004. ECCC officials have traveled to Khmer Rouge strongholds and held outreach events to assure former guerrillas that the scope of prosecution will remain narrow. Moreover, the Khmer Rouge organization is defunct, and there is no evidence that the Case 003 or 004 suspects have the capacity or desire to organize resistance.[45] In a 2009 survey, more than half of Cambodians interviewed expressed no concern about potential public disorder if more suspects were investigated, as they have confidence in the Government's ability to control any disturbances.[46]

Chea Leang may be correct that, "[i]f investigations could be extended to all such low-ranking suspects, there 'would be many more suspects of this level to be prosecuted,' which could 'adversely affect the stability of Cambodia' and cause a 'frightening situation of unrest in Cambodian society,' particularly among those holding equivalent ranks."[47] However, no Court official has suggested pursuing investigations beyond Cases 003 and 004. Moreover, it is notable that in the one case where a question of accountability vs. peace has squarely arisen—the 1996 amnesty of Ieng Sary—the full Trial Chamber apparently found the issue to be of such minimal concern that it did not bother to address it. It merely noted that the amnesty "may have been a useful tool in ending the conflict," as Ieng's defection resulted in the reintegration of a large number of Khmer Rouge combatants, promoting the restoration of peace.[48] However, in finding the Decree inapplicable to ECCC proceedings, the Chamber did not feel compelled to consider the effect of its decision on the potential for a re-eruption of violence. Instead, as discussed in chapter 5, it focused solely on Cambodia's obligation to prevent impunity. Former Co-Investigating Judge Marcel Lemonde says,

> [T]he Government tended to play the card of reconciliation when it felt that the process was getting out of its control and could have undesirable side effects politically for it.... One therefore had the impression that the alibi of peace was a convenient way to prevent the Tribunal from going into areas where it should not go.[49]

MORE THAN FIVE?

Debates at the ECCC over peace and justice and who qualifies as "senior leaders" or persons "most responsible" have sharpened to a focus on numbers: Should the Court try five or ten former Khmer Rouge suspects? Panhavuth Long of the Cambodian Justice Initiative sees the numbers debate as differing perspectives on the meaning of accountability. He says, "For internationals, justice must be seen to be done. For nationals, it is enough if justice is done. Internationals would say there is justice if there are more cases. Nationals say what's the difference between one or two or three cases. One and two are enough symbols of justice."[50] Although both the United Nations and Cambodian Government intended only a small number of prosecutions, the criteria they established do not limit the appropriate number of suspects to five.

A strong argument can be made that additional prosecutions would contribute to the fulfillment of the ECCC's mandate.[51] As Margaret deGuzman argues, selecting whom to prosecute at mass crimes courts involves "expressive" choices about the norms and types of victimization that trials emphasize.[52] Any limited number of Khmer Rouge trials will imply primary responsibility for those charged, result in impunity for all others, and omit important facts from the official judicially sanctioned narrative. However, a modest number of additional trials could expand meaningfully on the facts revealed in Cases 001 and 002—which focus on Tuol Sleng, forced movement, and the Phnom Penh policy leadership. Additional trials could examine crimes that took place at cooperatives and work sites, such as forced marriage; how the Communist Party of Kampuchea (CPK) operated at the regional level and in the military; and how the overall machinery of the DK regime worked. Such trials would also serve to stress—albeit in a limited way—the crucial norm that superior orders are not excuses for grave human rights abuses.[53]

Unlike other internationalized courts, the ECCC is not coupled with domestic trials or a truth commission,[54] and national courts will not pursue DK-era crimes once the ECCC closes. Many Cambodians have expressed their interest in the larger historical narrative, and while the Court cannot pretend to be a truth commission, the cases it decides to hear offer an opportunity to tell a slightly broader story than what is popularly known.[55] With all that has been invested in the ECCC process, and with no further chances for justice, four or five further prosecutions hardly seem excessive. The struggle over additional suspects has once again highlighted tensions between national and international officials and challenged the viability of the hybrid enterprise.

"Too Many Names": The Co-Prosecutors' Disagreement and First Test of the Dispute Settlement Rules

In 2008, former international Co-Prosecutor Robert Petit decided to initiate two new judicial investigations and named six additional suspects.[56] Although the targets of these investigations are still officially confidential, their names have been widely reported in the media, and they are alleged to be "among the most brutal implementers of the policies set up by the Khmer Rouge leadership[.]"[57]

In Case 003, they are Sou Met, former commander of the air force and a member of the Assisting Committee of the Central Committee of the CPK; and Meas Muth, former commander of the navy, who was allegedly either a member of the Central Committee or a member of the Assisting Committee of the Central Committee, and is said to have controlled the port town of Kampong Som (present day Sihanoukville) and its coastal islands.[58] Both are alleged to have had responsibility for internal purges resulting in the deaths of possibly tens of thousands of persons, among other crimes. Sou Met died in June 2013. Van Rith, the last DK Minister of Commerce, was also a suspect in Case 003, but he died in 2008 and was removed from the case.

In Case 004, there are three suspects. Ta An, former Deputy Secretary of the Central Zone among other positions, is alleged to have led a group of cadres from the Southwest Zone to purge and replace cadres in the Central Zone, and to have had responsibility for forced labor worksites and prison centers, as well as for committing genocide against the Cham Muslim population. Ta Tith, former Acting Secretary of the Northwest Zone among other positions, is alleged to have purged and replaced the existing Northwest Zone cadre acting together with the deceased Ta Mok *aka* the Butcher. He is also allegedly responsible for prison and execution sites, as well as forced labor sites. His crimes overlap with that of Im Chaem, former Secretary of Preah Net Preah District among other positions, who is allegedly responsible for purging the area under her control. She faces charges of overseeing prison and execution sites, and forced labor at the notorious Trapeang Thma Dam. Together these suspects may be responsible for over 100,000 deaths and other crimes.[59]

Unable to reach an agreement with national Co-Prosecutor Chea Leang to forward the initial submissions in these cases, Petit filed a notice of disagreement between the Co-Prosecutors and asked the Pre-Trial Chamber to resolve the dispute.[60] The ECCC Internal Rules provide that in the event of a disagreement between the Co-Prosecutors, either one may record the disagreement, and bring it before the Pre-Trial Chamber. The Pre-Trial Chamber must settle the dispute by an affirmative vote of at least four judges. If there is no supermajority decision, "the prosecution shall proceed."[61]

The Pre-Trial Chamber took nearly a year to decide the dispute; however, an affirmative vote by four of the Pre-Trial Judges could not be reached: the three Cambodian judges voted against the investigations and the two international judges voted in favor.[62] This was the first of many Case 003/004 PTC decisions, all divided on national/international lines.[63] Due to the failure to reach a supermajority, the international Co-Prosecutor's request for judicial investigation was allowed to proceed by default. Acting international Co-Prosecutor Bill Smith forwarded the two new introductory submissions to the CIJs, emphasizing that he had "no plans to conduct further preliminary investigations into suspects at the ECCC."[64]

There was a widespread perception that both Chea Leang and the national PTC judges did not act impartially in rejecting the additional cases, but instead followed the lead of the Government, which has consistently opposed charging new suspects.[65] Prime Minister Hun Sen expressly told visiting UN Secretary-General Ban Ki-moon that Case 002 would be the last trial as "case three is not allowed."[66] Information Minister Khieu Kanharith said international staff seeking to investigate Cases 003 and 004 should "pack their bags and return home."[67] Government spokesperson Phay Siphan said: "We will stand our ground regarding the ECCC. There will be no case 003 or 004. The government doesn't want failure; that's why it only allows Case 002 to take place."[68] Foreign Minister Hor Namhong told French diplomats, "[O]nly Cambodia can decide how many additional suspects the Khmer Rouge tribunal will prosecute."[69]

This was not the first time Co-Prosecutor Chea Leang had opposed investigating more than five. In its first submission, the OCP originally planned to charge six suspects, including Van Rith; however, the day before they filed, Chea Leang suddenly claimed there was not enough evidence against him.[70] The international side found this argument unconvincing because she had already read—or should have read—the introductory submission numerous times over the previous weeks.[71]

Nevertheless, in this instance the "co" dispute mechanism worked as intended,[72] the investigation moved forward, and by all accounts the disagreement did not damage the relationship between the Co-Prosecutors or impact their ongoing work.[73] In retrospect, it is notable that the national and international Co-Prosecutors issued joint press releases about their dispute[74] and have never criticized each other in public.[75] Debate became increasingly acrimonious as the matter reached the Office of the Co-Investigating Judges.

Co-Investigating Judges' Dispute Round 1: Agree to Disagree

Cases 003/004 were transferred to the OCIJ in September 2009; however, that office took little action until the summer of 2010. On June 2, 2010, international Co-Investigating Judge Marcel Lemonde wrote to national Co-Investigating Judge You Bunleng:

> On several occasions in the last months, we discussed the way we were planning on conducting the investigation in case file 003 and case file 004 (. . .) I thought we agreed on the immediate signing of a Rogatory Letter, to allow the investigators to start "crime base" investigations in several crime sites (. . .) for three weeks now, this Rogatory Letter has been ready for signature. I was therefore surprised to hear you say, on 28 May 2010, that you needed more time to sign it, since the content is extremely simple (. . .) if this Rogatory Letter has not been signed on Friday 4 June at noon, I will be compelled to officially acknowledge our disagreement, with all of the negative consequences this might lead to.[76]

Although both judges then proceeded to sign the Rogatory Letter on June 4, You Bunleng crossed off his signature on June 7, telling Judge Lemonde that he would reconsider moving forward with these cases only after the completion of the Case 002 Closing Order in September, as that should be the priority, but also referencing the potential effects on "the current context of Cambodian society as a whole."[77]

The timing of Judge You's decision to withdraw, as well as his reasoning, led to speculation that he had done so because of political pressure from the Government. This is because also on June 7, after an ECCC UN spokesperson publicly announced that both judges had signed the Rogatory Letter, an Interior Ministry spokesperson responded by saying that the Court could try only five persons. "Not six. Just five. The court must secure the stability and the peace of the nation."[78] A few days later Judge Lemonde issued a new Rogatory Letter, and acting alone gathered some witness statements before his departure from the Court in December 2010.[79]

Co-Investigating Judges' Dispute Round 2: Agree to Dismiss

Judge Lemonde was replaced by reserve Judge Siegfried Blunk. In February 2011, the CIJs jointly issued a joint press release in response to media speculation that Case 003 was being actively investigated. They said that they were not conducting field investigations but instead focusing only on documents available in the Case 001 and 002 case files.[80] Then in April, the CIJs summarily closed the Case 003 investigation, issuing a one-sentence press release that provided no information for potential civil parties who now had just 15 days to join the case and request final investigative actions before the judges ruled on whether to indict or dismiss.[81]

In response to this glaring lack of information, new international Co-Prosecutor Andrew Cayley released a statement providing basic facts about the charges and crime sites at issue, the criteria to join as a civil party, and notification of the impending deadline for civil party applications—which he sought to have extended six weeks due to the lack of notice.[82] The CIJs ultimately extended the deadline; however, they made that announcement public *one day* before the expiration of the new deadline.[83] When asked if he thought victims had been unfairly prevented from joining Case 003 due to a lack of information, Judge Blunk reportedly said they had "ample" opportunity to receive information about the case from the Victim Support Section[84]—although the CIJs had provided that office with no information to distribute. Seized with an appeal by a rejected civil party applicant, the international Pre-Trial Chamber judges highlighted:

> [N]o civil party applicant has been in a position to effectively exercise the right to participate in the judicial investigation expressly provided for under the Internal Rules and . . . this situation appears to result, to a significant extent, from a lack of information surrounding the investigation in Case 003. . . . Refusing them the possibility to participate in the investigation may deprive the Co-Investigating Judges of important information in their search for the truth, leading to an incomplete investigation and raising doubts about its impartiality.[85]

Cayley, who had access to the case file, publicly stated his view "that the crimes alleged . . . have not been fully investigated."[86] Blunk had interviewed only around 20 witnesses, including Duch, who had confirmed that the suspects in Case 003 were assistants to the Central Committee and members of the standing committee of the General Staff, and said that one was his equal in rank and had been responsible for sending people to S-21.[87] The CIJs had not even spoken to the suspects or examined all crime scenes.[88]

In closing the case, the CIJs had emphasized that the case file contained "more than 2.000 pieces of evidence, comprising more than 48.000 pages." However, it was later revealed that OCIJ's national staff had stuffed it with documents from the Case 002 case file on the eve of dismissal to make it appear that more work had been done.[89] The international PTC judges slammed the CIJs for inconsistencies in the way they handled the investigation and enumerated procedural irregularities in the filing of documents.[90] They also noted "significant unexplained delays in processing documents and placing these in the case file[.]"[91] Other sources have revealed that rogatory letters authorizing the collection of statements were issued only after potential witnesses were interviewed, "perhaps offering the judges the chance to pick and choose which testimony to enter into the record and which to ignore."[92]

"Case File 003 was closed against the unanimous oral and written advice given to the Co-Investigating Judges from the international side of the Office."[93] Blunk reportedly threatened his staff with disciplinary action for disloyalty when they raised their concerns with the UN Secretary-General.[94] When the UN took no action, all six UN legal officers in the OCIJ quit.[95] Investigator Steve Heder, a respected expert on Democratic Kampuchea, released portions of his resignation letter:

> In view of the judges' decision to close the investigation into Case File 003 effectively without investigating it, which I, like others, believe is unreasonable;

> in view of the UN staff's evident growing lack of confidence in your leadership, which I share; and in view of the toxic atmosphere of mutual distrust generated by your management of what is now a professionally dysfunctional office, I have concluded that no good use can or will be made of my consultancy services[.][96]

Likely due to the enormous amount of negative publicity over events in Case 003, the CIJs did not close Case 004. In June 2011, Andrew Cayley announced that he had requested additional investigative actions in that case and filed a supplementary submission based on civil party claims.[97] In October, Judge Blunk shocked everyone by abruptly resigning, claiming that perceived government interference in Cases 003 and 004 may lead people to question his independence and the integrity of the proceedings.[98] Council of Ministers spokesman Phay Siphan said, "He failed to understand the wisdom of setting up the ECCC, which is the partnership between the government and the UN . . . We still stand on our ground regarding the ECCC. There will be no case 003 or 004."[99] Months later, Judge You Bunleng recalled that he and Blunk had "a common judicial approach with almost 100 percent agreement."[100]

Co-Investigating Judges Dispute Round 3: "A Breach of the Agreement"

According to the terms of the Agreement and Law, Judge Blunk should have been automatically replaced by the reserve international Co-Investigating Judge, Laurent Kasper-Ansermet. ECCC Law Art. 27 new provides, "In the event of the absence of the foreign Co-Investigating Judge, he or she shall be replaced by the reserve foreign Co-Investigating Judge."[101] Nevertheless, Kasper-Ansermet was hindered from taking office. Although the Secretary-General selects the international judges, the power of appointment resides with the Cambodian Supreme Council of Magistracy (SCM),[102] which first refused to convene and then upon meeting failed to confirm his appointment.[103]

The Government denied that Cambodia had any obligation under the Framework Agreement to make the appointment, ironically claiming that to force the SCM to do so would amount to judicial interference. A Council of Ministers official said:

> The word 'must' is not properly used. The word is 'should'. . . . Must means to force. We cannot force our independent and highest institution. When the word 'must' has been used, it seems that we interfere into the jurisdiction of the independent Supreme Council of the Magistracy.[104]

Kasper-Ansermet had already been appointed and sworn in as a reserve judge by the SCM in February 2011, however.[105] The Framework Agreement does not require him to be appointed again to assume his functions, and in fact the purpose of having reserve judges is to assume the responsibilities of an absent colleague.[106]

The Cambodian Government nevertheless sought to prevent Judge Kasper-Ansermet from taking office, citing concerns about his active "tweeting" during the Blunk uproar, including reposting articles critical of the way Cases 003 and 004 had been handled by his predecessor. When the SCM finally met, it decided against his appointment, echoing the Government's concerns:

> [T]he meeting reached the view that Judge Laurent Kasper-Ansermet's posting of a considerable number of documents on his Twitter account . . . specifically concerning Cases 003 and 004 . . . would appear to violate the Code of Judicial Ethics, the Internal Rules and legal principles . . . [by] compromising the confidentiality and integrity of investigations by the public circulation of five names connected [to these cases] . . . and criticizing both of his own colleagues . . . [which] could have an adverse impact and cause confusion or doubts regarding [his] impartiality[.][107]

The United Nations argued that the ethical concerns about Kasper-Ansermet were unfounded, called the SCM decision a breach of the Framework Agreement,[108] and insisted that Kasper-Ansermet was entitled to immediately carry out the responsibilities of his office.[109] However, UN officials did not reach a political agreement with the Cambodian Government allowing him to conduct his work unimpeded.

The national side of the Court, following the lead of Judge You Bunleng, never recognized Judge Kasper-Ansermet's authority to act and continually interfered with his efforts to investigate Cases 003 and 004.[110] You Bunleng took the position that Kasper-Ansermet "does not have legal accreditation to undertake any procedural action or measure with respect to the Case Files[.]"[111] From nearly the moment Judge Kasper-Ansermet arrived in Phnom Penh, he and You Bunleng issued vitriolic dueling press releases,[112] and Judge Kasper-Ansermet claimed to be impeded by the national side at every turn.[113] For example, the Acting Director of Administration told a national staff person not to accept a summons from the judge during an internal investigation, and the president of the PTC refused to accept the filing of a dispute with Judge You. On instructions from Judge You, the case file officer refused to place Judge Kasper-Ansermet's orders in the case file and ignored his orders to grant access to the Case 003 case file to the lawyers of civil party applicants. Moreover, Kasper-Ansermet was denied access to the seal of office—the symbol of his authority to file decisions; as well as drivers, transcribers, and interpreters.[114] Frustrated by the obstruction and a complacent UN administration, he resigned in May 2012.[115]

A Lack of Resolution

The SCM swiftly appointed a fourth international CIJ, Mark Harmon, who inherited an unenviable set of challenges,[116] and—no doubt conscious of his predecessors' contentious tenures—has taken pains to stay out of the public eye. In his first year of office, he unilaterally reaffirmed Kasper-Ansermet's authority to act (including his re-opening of the Case 003 investigation and notification to all suspects of their right to counsel), unilaterally informed potential witnesses and civil parties of new crime sites he is investigating in Case 004, and unilaterally granted Case 003 and 004 case file access to recognized civil party lawyers.[117] However, these actions were taken without the support of his Cambodian counterpart, the national side of the Office is not assisting his investigative efforts, and the Pre-Trial Chamber judges remain split down national/international lines.[118] As of October 2013, Cases 003 and 004 have languished in the OCIJ for more than four years, and there has been no indication that they are proceeding to trial. As the deadlock continues, the Case 003 and 004 suspects have expressed little fear of going to trial.[119]

With Cases 003 and 004 in the hands of the OCIJ, the ECCC no longer has the luxury to debate whether or not the prosecution of more suspects is necessary for the Court to fulfill its mandate, or is a necessary test of the Court's legitimacy. Because these cases exist, the rules must be followed in determining whether they go to trial or are dismissed, or it will taint the rest of the Court's efforts. Former international Co-Prosecutor Andrew Cayley has emphasized, "[C]ases 003, 004, need to come to some kind of legitimate conclusion. There needs to be due process. The law needs to be followed. The rules need to be followed. Otherwise it's going to create a huge mess in the court."[120] Former Ieng Sary Co-Lawyer Michael Karnavas says, "It would be terrible if at the end of the day everything is discredited because the process is flawed—because a lot of good things are happening, a lot of good rulings are being issued."[121] However, in Cases 003 and 004, procedures continue to be bent and broken, and delays and obstruction have prevented them from proceeding normally, despite the existence of rules intended to address exactly this type of political impasse.

PROCEDURES INTENDED TO SAFEGUARD AGAINST POLITICAL INFLUENCE

As discussed in chapter 1, international officials anticipated that Cambodian personnel at the ECCC would be vulnerable to government pressure on politically sensitive topics. They therefore insisted on the adoption of rules to insulate the Court from the possible consequences. In particular, the Framework Agreement and ECCC Law allow one Co-Prosecutor or Co-Investigating Judge to act alone to push an investigation forward, and no Chamber can make a decision without the support of at least one international judge.

These rules have featured prominently in the proceedings. The national and international Co-Prosecutors have registered two disputes, and the national and international CIJs have sought to register several. The PTC has had numerous split decisions pitting three Cambodian judges against two internationals—all on topics on which the Cambodian Government expressed strong public contemporaneous opinions, leading to enduring allegations of political interference.[122] However, rather than resolving the problem of interference, the dispute and supermajority rules have diminished incentives for international actors to criticize and confront it. The hybrid Court was designed in expectation of government meddling, and its coping mechanisms have had the unforeseen effect of entrenching political interference as a tolerable feature of the institution. Moreover, in their application, the rules have themselves been manipulated for political ends, demonstrating their inadequacy as a substitute for independent and impartial judges.

Effect on the Ability of "Co" to Act Alone

The United Nations wanted the ECCC, like other internationalized courts, to have only one international prosecutor to ensure that government interference would not inhibit investigations. When the Cambodian Government refused, UN negotiators fell back on a mechanism to allow one Co-Prosecutor or CIJ to act alone when political disputes arose.[123] However, as described in the Internal

Rules, the dispute procedures are complex, creating opportunities for disparate interpretations of their effect. Prior to the CIJ's closure of Case 003, no one had seriously questioned the ability of a "co" to act alone; however, when the international Co-Prosecutor publicly challenged the validity of the decision, those who sought to bury the case reinterpreted the rules to frustrate the intent of the drafters and prevent any forward action.

The ECCC Internal Rules state that both "cos" share joint responsibility in carrying out their duties and are expected to work by consensus.[124] The ECCC core documents provide authority for one to act alone under certain circumstances; but the scope of that authority in practice is not always clear. According to the Internal Rules, "Except for action that must be taken jointly under the ECCC Law and these [Internal Rules]," the Co-Prosecutors/CIJs "may delegate power to one of them, by a joint written decision, to accomplish such action individually."[125] The only provisions that mandate joint action govern the Co-Prosecutors' and CIJs' ability to release public information about otherwise confidential actions.[126] Thus every other action may potentially be delegated to one Co-Prosecutor or one CIJ acting alone.

When delegation is not possible because of a disagreement between the "cos," Internal Rules 71 and 72 govern the authority to act alone. The "cos" may record the nature of the disagreement and within 30 days may bring it to the Pre-Trial Chamber for resolution. Even when a disagreement is recorded, one "co" normally may act alone without going to the PTC, or while waiting for the PTC to rule on a recorded dispute.[127] For example, the CIJs recorded a disagreement related to the timing of the Case 003/004 investigations on June 9, 2010.[128] Although this disagreement was never brought before the PTC, a Rogatory Letter to investigate in Case 003 was signed only by Judge Lemonde, who proceeded with the investigation on his own authority.[129] In specified exceptional cases, the PTC must decide *before* unilateral action may commence, but even in such cases one "co" may proceed 30 days after a disagreement is recorded if the opposing "co" did not put the dispute before the PTC.[130]

Although "either or both of [the "cos"] may record the exact nature of the disagreement,"[131] the PTC has found that, because of the presumption to move forward with the subject of a disagreement, the obligation to record it logically falls on the disagreeing party.[132] This fact, together with the use of the word "may," suggests that a decision to record is discretionary. If no disagreement is filed, the party seeking to investigate or prosecute may act alone toward that goal. Indeed, the entire PTC has found that "the Co-Investigating Judges are under no obligation to seize the Pre-Trial Chamber when they do not agree on an issue before them, the default position being that the 'investigation shall proceed'[.]"[133]

Despite this unanimous jurisprudence, in politically charged Case 003, the ability of a prosecutor or investigative judge to act alone was flatly rejected for the first time by Judges Blunk and You and all the national PTC Judges. In May 2011, international Co-Prosecutor Andrew Cayley, acting on his own, filed a request for additional investigative actions in Case 003 in an effort to ensure the case would not be dismissed without a proper investigation.[134] The CIJs rejected Cayley's request, finding that the Internal Rules "leave no room for . . . solitary action" except by delegation of power or after the registration of a disagreement.[135] On appeal, the international PTC Judges reaffirmed the Court's previous rulings in a split decision:

> The Internal Rules indicate that the use of the procedure provided to settle disagreement is not mandatory but rather optional. In other words, it is a matter of discretion as to whether the disagreement procedure is utilized by either or both Co-Prosecutors and to what extent a matter is taken.[136]

However, the national Pre-Trial Chamber judges agreed with the CIJs without acknowledging or providing any reasoning for their departure from the Chamber's prior decisions.[137] Because there is no presumption to move forward with an investigation when there is no disagreement between the CIJs, the CIJ order dismissing the request remained in effect.

Likewise, in the dispute between Judges You and Kasper-Ansermet, Judge You argued that neither judge had the authority to put documents in the Case 003 case file because the two "cos" must agree to file documents.[138] To the contrary, Judge Kasper-Ansermet and the international PTC judges have emphasized that his actions are "fully enforceable."[139] Although this view is legally correct, because the national side refused to acknowledge Judge Kasper-Ansermet's judicial authority, it appears that none of Judge Kasper-Ansermet's efforts will be officially recognized unless they are adopted by Judge Harmon. As Judge Kasper-Ansermet learned the hard way, the formal capacity to act alone does not ensure that national staff in the OCP or OCIJ will cooperate or assist in the work of their international colleagues.[140] Former UN Legal Counsel Hans Corell argues, "The [Court's main structural] problem isn't the investigating judge or prosecutor; it's the 'cos.'"[141]

Supermajority Rule

The supermajority rule, intended to serve as a bulwark against government interference, was a prerequisite for UN willingness to participate in a Cambodian-majority court. When a judicial investigation was opened in Cases 003/004, the U.S. Embassy called it a "vindication" of the supermajority rule.[142] However, in subsequent disputes the rule has been insufficient to protect the Court from political interference. The rule does not address all politically driven scenarios that have arisen. As foreseen by OSJI, the rule suffers from two potential problems that have since become realized: "the potential for delay and judicial deadlock" and "ineffectiveness in critical circumstances."[143] Hans Corell recalls, "The supermajority scheme was mind-boggling to someone with courtroom experience. . . . The idea of introducing such a cumbersome procedure . . . as a judge I had concerns."[144] More problematically, it appears to have had the antithetical effect of shielding political decision making from accountability.

When the two Co-Prosecutors or two CIJs file a disagreement about whether or not to move forward with a prosecution or investigation, if there is no supermajority agreement by the PTC in deciding the dispute, there is a presumption that the prosecution or investigation shall proceed.[145] However, even in its first "successful" application in the Co-Prosecutor dispute, PTC disagreement reportedly led to a four-month postponement in announcing the split national/international decision,[146] resulting in a one-year delay in sending it to the OCIJ.

Efforts by the international Co-Prosecutor to seek investigative action and by civil party applicants to participate during Judge Blunk's tenure were blocked by the CIJs and a divided PTC. This made political interference appear both conspicuous and intractable, because a joint decision by the CIJs will stand if there is no supermajority agreement by the PTC. Consequently, when Judge Blunk joined together with his counterpart Judge You to bury Case 003,[147] a divided PTC was incapable of overturning their eccentric and politically suspect opinions. Negotiators did not foresee the possibility that both CIJs would act together to derail an investigation "due to political or other influence."[148] With similar effect, when there were serious concerns about interference with the summoning of government officials in Case 002, the international PTC judges had no power to initiate an investigation in the face of joint CIJ inaction and the opposition of their Cambodian colleagues.[149]

Thus one flawed premise of the supermajority rule is that "UN judges will behave perfectly."[150] As an example of the inherent problem with this presumption, former head of the Defence Support Section Richard Rogers highlights the Supreme Court Chamber supermajority decision overturning Duch's pretrial detention remedy. He says that this action should have required agreement by a majority of unbiased judges; instead it was (theoretically) decided only by one. This gives too much power to the one international who joins with the nationals. More than one impartial judge is needed for important decisions because sometimes he or she can be wrong.[151] Although the dissenting opinions of the international PTC judges have served an important role in highlighting serious problems in the way politically sensitive issues have been handled by the OCIJ, they were powerless to overturn the deplorable legal reasoning.

Of potentially greater concern, when Blunk's successor Judge Kasper-Ansermet sought to revive Case 003, the Cambodian PTC president prevented the PTC from hearing the issue in an apparent effort to avoid the effect of the supermajority rule. When Kasper-Ansermet submitted two disputes in Case 003 to the PTC, Judge Prak Kimsan, the President of the Chamber, returned the Records of Disagreement to the Acting Director of Administration without providing an opportunity for the full Chamber to hear the issue, stating that the "'PTC judges' had met . . . and that they had not 'reached their consent to take into account their consideration of the substance of those documents,'" based on Judge Kasper-Ansermet's lack of legal authority.[152] The two international PTC judges issued a joint opinion in which they disclosed that, following deliberations on the disagreement, the President had returned the documents without their knowledge or consent, and had refused their request to withdraw his memorandum.[153] Judge Prak said that the national judges thought the matter was "only administrative" and outside the jurisdiction of the PTC.[154] He blamed Kasper-Ansermet's "invalid" efforts to bring the dispute for creating "unprecedented confusing procedures before the Pre-Trial Chamber, leading to settlement irregularity[.]"[155] However, the international judges believed it was their judicial duty to issue a reasoned decision. Unlike their national colleagues, they found the disagreement admissible, found that Judge Kasper-Ansermet had the authority to bring it before the Chamber, and ruled that because the

PTC could not reach a supermajority decision he had the authority to proceed with his investigative actions.[156] Then, when Kasper-Ansermet sought to have Judge Prak disqualified from the case due to his obstruction, Judge Prak again refused to pass this request on to the rest of the Chamber,[157] leading to stalemate and acrimony in the PTC.

If incumbent international CIJ Mark Harmon should decide to send Cases 003 and 004 forward to the Trial Chamber, there could again be obstruction. Decisions to convict must be made by supermajority.[158] As noted by negotiator David Scheffer, this ensures that "[w]ith respect to due process rights, no defendant will be convicted without the vote of at least one international judge."[159] However, while the supermajority rule may prevent the conviction of an accused against whom there is inadequate evidence, it cannot stop a Cambodian block from acquitting a culpable accused. Moreover, as demonstrated by the Trial Chamber's original impasse on the consequences of Ieng Thirith's mental fitness (discussed in chapter 5), there is no guidance as to how a split Trial Chamber should proceed on any issue *except* conviction. Based on past experience, where such a split occurs on a politically sensitive topic, there will be no will to iron out a compromise, as was possible on that occasion.

Potential for delay, deadlock, and obstruction aren't the only concerns that parties have with the supermajority rule. Many say it makes political interference more difficult to address, co-opting the international judges in the process. Michael Karnavas argues that the rule put pressure on the international judges to "go along to get along," with what appeared to be smaller battles early on, making it harder for them to take principled positions when larger battles arose over Cases 003 and 004:[160] "The sad truth is that through inaction, or in the spirit of being diplomatic, the international judges have been . . . complicit in[] re-enforcing certain systemic weaknesses embedded in Cambodian courts."[161] Likewise, Panhavuth Long says that international staff have a principle of "don't rock the boat" instead of ensuring that the proceedings meet international standards. "Maybe instead they are just legitimizing the [flawed] process."[162] Former Nuon Chea Co-Lawyer Michiel Pestman contends that everyone working at the ECCC knows about political interference and accepts it, tainting every aspect of the Court's work. "The Trial Chamber international judges have never dissented on any ruling. They must be afraid everything will collapse if they point out problems."[163] Former CIJ Lemonde emphasizes:

> Cambodian judges are in the majority and at any time they can remind us that we are in Cambodia, we cannot do what we want, they are at home, and believe me, they care to remind you if you forget it. So this is a permanent structural difficulty.[164]

Richard Rogers asserts that although the supermajority rule was intended to protect against the lack of independence of the national judges, it in fact entrenches it. Because it is seen as a systemic "safeguard," the international judges avoid addressing independence issues head on. He notes that UN Legal Counsel Patricia O'Brien has said that judges have "different approaches," suggesting that some act more independently than others. However, this is a clear violation of the right to be tried by independent and impartial judges.[165]

Thus Far, a Failed Test

The national/international split over whether more persons should be charged has, as predicted, been the major test of the Court's hybrid character. The dispute resolution rules worked as intended in solving the Co-Prosecutors' disagreement. However, when the cases moved to the OCIJ, which is tasked with conducting the bulk of the investigation and deciding if the cases should go to trial, the Cambodian judges, with the apparent collusion of an international judge, sought to avoid the presumption to move forward with the investigation through inaction, irregular practices, and untenable decisions, debasing the rights of all of the parties[166] and the reputation of the entire Court in the process. According to reports, "the rapidly deteriorating situation . . . has embroiled almost all offices, splitting staff down national and international lines in respect to cases 003 and 004."[167] The experience of the ECCC demonstrates that future hybrid courts should not use work-around rules to address a lack of judicial independence and impartiality. Instead, all judges selected, whether national or international, must be presumptively unbiased.

JUDICIAL INDEPENDENCE AND IMPARTIALITY

The potential for hybrid courts to become politicized makes the need for professional, independent, and impartial judges all the more critical. The supermajority rule appears discredited as a mechanism for avoiding the fundamental obligation to select judges who are independent and impartial. Hans Corell says that, due to the Court's structural flaws, "We had to hope that appointees to key positions would comport with the standards and ethics required."[168] However, the actions of Judge Blunk have raised concerns about the vetting process for international judges participating in hybrid courts and highlighted the importance of selection and election procedures for all serving judges, whether national or international.

Process of Selection, Election of Judges

International ECCC judges are selected by the United Nations Secretary-General, but all ECCC judges are appointed by the Cambodian Supreme Council of Magistracy (SCM)[169]—a constitutionally independent judicial body[170] that makes all judicial appointments for Cambodian courts. However, the SCM is not independent of the Government.[171] Moreover, SCM members include four ECCC personnel, including Co-Prosecutor Chea Leang and Co-Investigating Judge You Bunleng. You Bunleng was himself promoted to President of the national Court of Appeal extraconstitutionally—not by the SCM, but at the request of the executive branch.[172]

The United Nations released a list of candidates short-listed for judicial positions in November 2005. This encouraged civil society calls for a transparent Cambodian process.[173] Nevertheless, the national selection process went ahead "in a closed manner with no input from civil society."[174] There is evidence that all the national ECCC judges and prosecutors were preapproved by the Cambodian Prime Minister Hun Sen, rather than selected by SCM.[175] As noted by Mark Ellis, "In effect, the incorporation of Cambodian selection procedures into the ECCC is tantamount to similarly incorporating the system of patronage that cripples the domestic judiciary."[176]

Although the selection of international judges is more transparent, there have long been calls for reform of the process for appointment. Cherie Booth and Philippe Sands note that selection "is often a highly politicized affair, with some of the most independent and qualified candidates being passed over by the electing bodies, usually comprised of states. Once elected, there is the potential problem that some judges may find it difficult not to be loyal to their own states."[177] As part of UN efforts to improve the transparency and quality of selections, the ECCC was the first court for which it accepted nominations not only from States, but also from anyone else (including self-nominations), which were entered into a database by OSJI.[178] Also for the first time, candidates were interviewed by a panel of experts,[179] including two ICTY judges and UN Office of Legal Affairs staff. This new procedure "is said to provide a better guarantee than previous mechanisms of the selection of impartial and professional officials."[180] Nevertheless, it did not lead to the selection of many judges with mass crimes experience, nor did it prevent the selection of Judge Blunk, who, when asked his motivation for coming to the ECCC, said it was to share the experience he gained working at the hybrid tribunal in East Timor.[181] However, serious concerns have been raised about the quality of some of the international judges who served in East Timor, as well as the quality of their decision making.[182] It can be hoped that the track records of international judges are more thoroughly vetted in the future.

Judicial Qualifications and Disqualification

The potential lack of independence of the Cambodian judges was a key concern during negotiations to establish the Court due to entrenched and pervasive corruption in the national judiciary, where verdicts are commonly decided on the basis of political influence and bribery.[183] In a 2010 interview, Trial Chamber President Nil Nonn reportedly said: "We also have problems because judges aren't independent in Cambodia—[government officials] threaten and put pressure on judges, the judges accept money, so all this is not very good."[184]

The ECCC Law states:

> The judges of the Extraordinary Chambers shall be appointed from among the currently practicing judges or are additionally appointed in accordance with the existing procedures for appointment of judges; all of whom shall have high moral character, a spirit of impartiality and integrity, and experience, particularly in criminal law or international law, including humanitarian law and human rights law. Judges shall be independent in the performance of their functions, and shall not accept or seek any instructions from any government or other source.[185]

The appointed Cambodian judges were criticized for a lack of judicial independence, competency, and qualifications.[186] Several had rendered politically suspect verdicts, one reportedly lacked a degree in law, and one lacked any judicial experience. All of the national ECCC judges concurrently serve in the national judicial system, and some have been high-level members of the ruling party.[187]

While serving at the ECCC, nearly all of them have been the subject of unsuccessful defense disqualification challenges. The Internal Rules provide:

> Any party may file an application for disqualification of a judge in any case in which the Judge has a personal or financial interest or concerning which the Judge has, or has had, any association which objectively might affect his or her impartiality, *or objectively gives rise to the appearance of bias.*[188]

As pointed out by Richard Rogers, the supermajority rule, which presumes that the national judges are not independent, renders meaningless the entire concept of "appearance of bias" for the ECCC.[189]

For example, Judge Ney Thol was challenged on the basis of, *inter alia,* his membership in the ruling party and his participation in cases with suspect progovernment outcomes. The Pre-Trial Chamber applied the test established by the ICTY Appeals Chamber for appearance of bias: "The circumstances would lead a reasonable observer, properly informed, to reasonably apprehend bias."[190] It found that merely because a judge is a member of a political party doesn't create an inference that his decisions are politically motivated. The Chamber also highlighted that the ECCC has no institutional connection to the Cambodian judicial system, and the judges take an oath of office. Moreover, the defense had not provided authority "for the proposition that a judge's analysis in a different case could suggest bias in the case currently being heard" or evidence that he had acted on instructions from the ruling party.[191]

Trial President Nil Nonn was challenged on the basis of a 2002 interview in which he admitted taking money from parties to disputes over which he presided.[192] The Trial Chamber also denied this application, stating, "[D]isqualification pertains to bias against a particular accused in relation to a particular case, and cannot be used to lodge a general complaint about the fitness of an individual to serve as a judge."[193] It noted that overall fitness for judges could only be determined by the SCM under Cambodian law, as "[n]o relevant mechanisms are provided in the ECCC Law and Agreement" for either discipline or removal.[194] As a consequence, the Court lacks competence to address "general questions of judicial independence and integrity" or "alleged deficiencies in national mechanisms designed to uphold the independence of the judiciary"[195]—an apparent oblique reference to the SCM's well-known lack of independence, discussed above.

In all of these challenges, the ECCC, like fully or preponderantly international courts, has emphasized the presumption of objectivity arising from the "internationally agreed" selection criteria and the judicial oath.[196] However, as discussed above, it is not clear that at the ECCC these criteria were met in spirit, let alone in fact. Moreover, as emphasized by SCSL Judge Robertson, factors such as "the content of the judicial oath or the application of statutes containing proper international standards . . . cannot, even collectively, legitimize an arrangement which produces undue pressure."[197] He advocates that "reasonable observers" be credited with "a fairly hard-nosed appreciation of how institutional pressures and 'old boy networks' can operate" and says, "The standpoint of an experienced journalist or human rights researcher may not be inappropriate" in assessing appearance of bias.[198]

The likelihood of the Court disciplining itself became even more hollow when, as discussed above, Pre-Trial Chamber Judge Prak Kimsan returned Judge Kasper-Ansermet's order seeking his disqualification, "without deliberation or consultation" with the international judges of the PTC.[199] A letter from the two international PTC judges to the Judicial Administration Committee (JAC), announcing that they were recusing themselves from the (nonexistent) proceedings due to their prior critical comments, and requesting that it appoint two judges to sit in their place, was then rejected by the JAC, which failed to convene a panel to hear Kasper-Ansermet's allegations.[200]

Although the participation of international judges was expected to compensate for national judges' lack of experience and impartiality, all parties to Case 002 have expressed frustration that most of the international judges—and all of the Trial Chamber judges—do not have the necessary mass crimes trial experience to efficiently and fairly direct the proceedings.[201] The lack of requisite experience of many international judges is a common cause of concern at mass crimes courts[202] but is arguably indispensable at a hybrid tribunal where the international judges are by definition serving in order to ensure procedural fairness. Hans Corell emphasizes, "It's absolutely necessary that [appointees] have courtroom experience," adding that he is very critical of how ICC judges are appointed, as that court's proceedings are too long and costly due in part to a lack of good courtroom management.[203]

Notably, the required qualifications for ECCC judges—persons who are judges or who are appointed in accordance with "existing procedures"[204]—are extraordinarily low compared to other internationalized courts, which customarily require qualification for one's home country's "highest judicial office" and competence in either national or international criminal law.[205] At the hybrid Kosovo tribunal, the standard for placement on the judicial roster is even higher: an advanced university degree, a minimum of ten years criminal law experience including five as a judge, and familiarity with human rights standards.[206] Although all of the international ECCC judges are more qualified than required by the listed criteria, greater emphasis on mass crimes trial experience when selecting qualified candidates would be the best practice for future hybrid courts.

POLITICAL INTERESTS AND HYBRID COURTS

Cambodia is unique compared to other postconflict states where hybrid courts are likely to be established due to the length of time that has passed since the end of the Khmer Rouge regime, the end of the fighting, and the establishment of a new government. UN Special Representative Yash Ghai has noted: "[P]ost-conflict development, with which the international community has been closely associated, has led to the formation of a strong state[.] . . . Its monopoly of force has endowed it with enormous capacity for coercion, balanced by neither legislature nor judiciary."[207] As a consequence, the government of Cambodia is well entrenched.

Nevertheless, executive control over the judiciary, including the *de facto* power to appoint and remove judges,[208] is a problem endemic to most post-conflict states, and one that makes hybrid courts vulnerable to domestic political influences. In Cambodia, as in many other countries, as a consequence "[p]rosecutorial and judicial functions are subordinated to the executive in political cases or cases involving powerful interests, and judges' rulings are too often influenced by money."[209]

However, the Cambodian Government is not the only stakeholder with a political interest in the outcome of ECCC proceedings. At the ECCC, as at other mass crimes courts, the United Nations and donors both have interests that they can leverage to influence proceedings, albeit in a more subtle fashion. Politicization of international and hybrid courts is not unusual; in fact it is the norm.[210] Journalist Thierry Cruvellier notes, "Tribunals are always a reflection of the power of those who support it."[211]

Control by the Conflict State

It is not entirely clear why the Cambodian Government has opposed Cases 003 and 004. Analysts have speculated that senior officials of the Cambodian People's Party (CPP) are either concerned about former Khmer Rouge colleagues being implicated, believe the issue could be exploited by rival domestic political factions, are thumbing their noses at the United Nations, or are concerned about the Court's potential to continue in perpetuity, much as the foreign NGO community that arrived with the UN Transitional Authority in Cambodia in 1992 has justified its bloated presence for more than 20 years.

However, there is a general consensus that, for a variety of reasons, CPP leaders want to control the process and the narrative that the trials create. As noted by the UN Group of Experts in 1999:

> To the extent that fair trials may reveal a different historical picture from that asserted by the Cambodian People's Party, with the involvement of additional people, the Government may have concerns about a tribunal over which it does not exercise control.[212]

UN negotiator Hans Corell reportedly handed the Secretary-General a note during the negotiations stating:

> The Cambodian Government does not intend to allow a free, fair, and non-selective trial process of all Khmer Rouge leaders living in its territory, but rather a carefully monitored process under its full political control.[213]

Indeed, in 2000 Hun Sen said explicitly: "The ones who committed crimes, genocide, and cooperated with crimes and genocide should be punished, not the ones who overthrew the genocide."[214]

At international tribunals, conflict states have also sought to influence the proceedings. For example, the government of Uganda referred the "situation concerning the Lord's Resistance Army" to the ICC, apparently seeking to exclude the culpability of government forces from review. The prosecutor informed the government that his office would instead be "analyzing crimes within the situation of Uganda by whomever committed."[215] Nevertheless, his decision to announce the referral jointly with the Ugandan president has been heavily criticized as undermining the population's perception of the court's independence.[216] No doubt suspicions of bias have been buttressed by the lack of public information suggesting that government forces were ever investigated for their crimes.[217] Rwanda has been notorious for using the threat of noncooperation to get its way with the International Criminal Tribunal for Rwanda (ICTR), including in its successful effort to prevent the tribunal from issuing indictments against members of the government's Rwandan Patriotic Front forces accused of committing crimes against humanity as they drove the genocidal Hutu regime out of power.[218]

Because international tribunals are structurally independent, they have had greater ability to resist or redirect such pressures, in particular where the United Nations or donor states have supported their efforts. Even where conflicting state agendas have impacted decisions of whom to charge, the process of judging those who are ultimately taken into custody has been less obviously impacted.[219]

Interests of the United Nations and Donor States

Foreign states, in particular donors, also have interests in mass crimes proceedings.[220] For example, China has not been in favor of the ECCC from the start due to its close ties with the DK regime.[221] However, even states that support and fund the ECCC have bilateral and financial interests that they prioritize over positions of principle, leading to action—or inaction—that has appeared to condone Cambodian Government interference. As discussed in chapter 3, the Australians have twice announced donations to the national side of the Court during credibility crises, in effect supporting the Government's refrain that there is "no problem."[222] With similar effect, Japan and France, originally the two largest Court funders, reportedly "gave their blessing" to government plans to kick OSJI out of the country when it revealed the kickback scheme, even though David Scheffer and others believed that this would be a breach of the Agreement.[223]

Judge Blunk's willingness to close Case 003 without a genuine investigation led to speculation that the United Nations and/or donors had either explicitly or implicitly given him directions to get rid of it.[224] The Cambodian Center for Human Rights said, "[Blunk's] actions raise the question of whether the United Nations has conceded to the demands of the RGC and is now acting to prevent any further cases from going to trial and to ensure the closure of the ECCC with the conclusion of Case 002."[225] This perception has been fed by reports (and long-standing rumors) that donors attempted to "intervene directly with Blunk and Cayley multiple times—by phone and in person" on Cases 003 and 004.[226] Clearly donors have a financial motivation to get rid of these cases, as acknowledged by U.S. War Crimes Ambassador Stephen Rapp, who also reportedly spoke to Blunk. He has said, "We expect people . . . to be making decisions that you can't pursue every case. We want them to make them on a proper basis with an understanding that resources are limited and they need to prioritize."[227]

The potential to influence judicial decisions is greatest when there are voluntary and thus irregular contributions. One commentator has said, "[P]erhaps the most pernicious form of influence is control over the budget of the court by the organ that constitutes it."[228] Hans Corell has noted that a prosecutor's discretionary powers are "very much related to circumstances, not least a willingness at the political level to support the institutions, including the provision of adequate funding."[229] Thus, when Cases 003 and 004 were forwarded to the CIJs, Court sources assumed that the judges, already busy with Case 002, would "await decisions by UN donors on additional resources for Case 003" before spending their existing "precious" resources on the investigation.[230] Moreover, the Deputy Administrator "desiring to cut costs where possible" spoke to the "Friends" group about "transferring case 003 to the domestic court to further reduce the total amount required for the tribunal"[231]—after the cases were already in the hands of the CIJs and thus subject to a judicial process outside the scope of his authority. It would have been obvious to anyone in Cambodia that this step would be the equivalent of dismissing the case for political reasons[232]—exactly what the supermajority rule was intended to prevent.

At the SCSL, an accused challenged the independence of the Court, arguing that its voluntary funding structure and the involvement of state donors in a Management Committee that provided assistance to the Secretary-General on nonjudicial matters could result in political pressure on the Chambers. The Appeals Chamber said the appropriate test was "whether such funding arrangements leads [*sic*] to a real likelihood that the court will be influenced by such arrangements to give decision, not on the merits of the case, but to please the funding body or agency."[233] In particular, the Chamber emphasized the importance of the fact that at the SCSL judicial remuneration is not contingent on voluntary payments but instead protected from funding inadequacies.[234] In his separate opinion, Judge Robertson suggested:

> Courts which are so starved of funds that they cannot do justice should close themselves down rather than continue under the expectation that sufficient funding will be forthcoming only if they render verdicts acceptable to the funding body.[235]

Such tainted verdicts should be seen to include the dismissal of existing cases not on their legal merit but based on budgetary concerns.[236]

This highlights a related method of donor pressure: the imposition of a completion strategy that "gives a clear directive to Prosecutors that limits their prosecutorial discretion"[237] or to Chambers to speed up proceedings. One commentator has reported that donors "constantly" tell ECCC officials that they want to see a completion strategy.[238] At the ICTY, one judge has made an explicit link between that court's completion strategy and decisions by the Appeals Chamber to depart from existing jurisprudence protecting the fair trial rights of accused:

> [The Majority] Decision unfortunately follows the trend of other recent decisions of the Appeals Chamber which reverse or ignore its previously carefully considered interpretations of the law or of the procedural rules, with a consequential destruction of the rights of the accused . . . The only reasonable explanation for these decisions appears to be a desire to assist the prosecution to bring the Completion Strategy to a speedy conclusion.[239]

Assuming that the United Nations and donors did not give Blunk license to shut down the cases, their failure to publicly address the serious dysfunction in the OCIJ—voiced by numerous staff, judges, and observers over a period of months—and investigate the serious and well-documented allegations[240] had the effect of sanctioning the conduct of that office and continued RGC obstruction.[241] For example, when Judge Blunk resigned after months of public allegations of improprieties, the UN merely thanked him for his service;[242] and when Judge Kasper-Ansermet resigned after being stymied by the Cambodian side for six months—in what the UN itself had called a breach of the Agreement—

the United Nations issued a brief statement expressing "serious concern."[243] As noted by Amnesty International:

> What is at stake here is the UN as the key driver of international justice. If it keeps using strong words but never takes any action . . . it demonstrates that interference by the [RGC] will win . . . and impunity overrules accountability.[244]

Former OSJI monitor Clair Duffy has said that it is "partly because of these general statements about the importance of the court's independence [instead of real engagement] that the crisis facing the court has worsened."[245]

For example, when UN Legal Counsel Patricia O'Brien visited Phnom Penh during the scandal over the premature closure of Case 003, she "strongly urged" the Government to stop making statements opposing Cases 003 and 004, but did not mention interference as such.[246] Ou Virak, president of the Cambodian Center for Human Rights, said that "the tone of his meeting [with her] indicated that the UN did not want an investigation into the OCIJ, with UN staff seemingly focused on the fallout such a probe might have on the pending trial of the senior leaders of the Khmer Rouge."[247] She reportedly told Ou, "'Look: We do take this issue very seriously, we are considering all options very carefully[.]'" Nevertheless, because an investigation into interference could open the door to defense challenges in Case 002, the UN had made a preliminary decision not to undertake an investigation.[248] She repeated this position at an American Bar Association meeting in Washington, DC.[249] The message is: "The Court [i.e. Case 002] has to succeed"[250] at whatever cost. The impact of O'Brien's mixed messages may be seen in the government response to her visit. A spokesperson alleged that when she met with the Deputy Prime Minister, she had merely complimented the tribunal on its "good work."[251]

CONCLUSION

David Scheffer has noted that the ECCC operates at "greater risk of institutionally collapsing than any other international or hybrid court."[252] In 2003, UN Secretary-General Kofi Annan emphasized that under the terms of the Agreement, "any deviation by the Government from its obligations could lead to the United Nations withdrawing its cooperation and assistance from the process."[253] Some local and international human rights advocates have called on the United Nations to consider withdrawing due to Cambodian Government interference.[254] That possibility appears to have given the United Nations little leverage because the Cambodian Government knows that a UN pullout is highly unlikely. Donors are keen to see their investment in Case 002 pay off. Moreover, a UN withdrawal would not necessarily disadvantage the ruling CPP, which would likely cite the move as another example of international perfidy requiring the CPP to shoulder alone the Khmer Rouge legacy.[255]

UN participation was intended to ensure that the ECCC would meet international standards, but where the United Nations is unable or unwilling to fight for those standards, a hybrid court is left to the mercy of national interests.[256] The split authority between national and international leadership at the ECCC makes the Court particularly vulnerable to RGC interference and makes the problem difficult for the UN to address. Indeed, the tribunal was designed precisely to limit the scope for UN action. However, this structural barrier is compounded by the fact that UN officials, unhappy with the institutional arrangement since the outset, have been loath to take strong ownership of what has become a sinking hybrid vessel. The United Nations has interpreted its mandate narrowly, acting too much like a technical assistance provider and not enough like a founding partner.

One interviewee notes that, although the UN administration says it is just here to "assist," that is merely an excuse. In his view, "the UN needs to assist by leading. [Internationals] were brought in because theoretically they know what to do."[257] UN ambivalence has translated into relative passivity and allowed the process either to stagnate, or—when political interests are at stake—to be controlled by the Cambodian side. As Judge Rapoza noted in the context of the East Timor Special Panels, "if you don't buy it, you don't own it."[258] The ECCC features enough UN involvement to pose the UN serious reputational risk, but not enough to ensure it will act to uphold its reputation.

Chapter 7

A HISTORIC FIRST

Recognizing Victims as Case Parties

One of the main arguments in favor of in-country hybrid tribunals is that they facilitate robust victim participation. Victims can more easily observe or participate in the proceedings, which offer them an opportunity to engage in truth-telling, contribute to the search for justice, and otherwise seek empowerment and a degree of personal and collective reconciliation. Addressing the rights and needs of victims—including the right to accountability for atrocities and the right to the truth—has been one of the core stated objectives of all mass crimes courts. Locating a hybrid tribunal beside the survivor population gives it a potentially formidable functional advantage in that regard.

The ECCC has developed an unprecedented scheme for victim participation. In addition to involving victims as witnesses and complainants, the ECCC is the first internationalized mass crimes court to follow the civil law practice of including victims as parties in the proceedings. For that reason, there is no direct precedent for it to follow, requiring it to forge its own path and establish new law that will in turn guide the decisions of future courts. Acting Director of Administration Tony Kranh has said that "[v]ictims' participation is one of the areas in which the ECCC is breaking new ground and setting new standards for courts with international support and involvement."[1]

Notwithstanding frequent self-laudatory rhetoric, the ECCC has struggled to manage its expansive victim participation scheme. The Court's under-resourced Victims Support Section (VSS) has been hard-pressed to respond to thousands of victim complaints and provide other services. The novel civil party scheme has been even more difficult for the Court to administer. Unlike some aspects of the Court's work, victim participation has not been hobbled by political feuds between its national and international sides. Rather, the ECCC's challenges in this area reflect relative UN neglect, a tepid Cambodian commitment, and the inherent difficulty of involving myriad survivors in the process. The Court's example suggests that an in-country mixed tribunal cannot fulfill its potential for victim participation without ample resources and advance planning. The ECCC also shows that however meaningful individual civil party participation may be, it is unlikely to be practicable in mass crimes proceedings.

GENESIS OF CIVIL PARTY PARTICIPATION AT THE ECCC

The ECCC's civil party scheme is one of its most notable innovations. The mandates of previous mass crimes tribunals, including the International Criminal Tribunals for the former Yugoslavia and Rwanda (ICTY and ICTR) and the hybrid Special Court for Sierra Leone (SCSL), provided a role for victims only as simple witnesses. Critics argued that these courts missed an opportunity to provide victims a more central role in the proceedings.[2] ICTY Prosecutor Carla Del Ponte told the Security Council:

> The voices of survivors and relatives of those killed are not sufficiently heard. Victims have almost no rights to participate in the trial process, despite the widespread acceptance nowadays that victims should be allowed to do so. . . . It is regrettable that the Tribunal's statute makes no provision for victim participation during the trial, and makes only a minimum of provision for compensation and restitution to people whose lives have been destroyed. . . . We should therefore give victims the right to express themselves, and allow their voice to be heard during the proceedings.[3]

In response to such critiques, the Rome Statute was drafted to include a role for victims to participate directly at the International Criminal Court (ICC).[4] In formulating these provisions, the drafters looked back to the UN Declaration of Basic Principles of Justice for Victims of Crime and Abuse of Power of 1985,[5] a watershed document for the victims movement.[6] Although the Declaration is not legally binding, it is the first international instrument to establish minimum standards for crime victims. It affirms that victims should have both "access to the mechanisms of justice" and the ability to receive redress for their harms.[7] At the ICC, victims do not have the full rights of a party but are considered "victim participants." The Special Tribunal for Lebanon (STL) offers victims a similar participatory role, while the Extraordinary African Chambers, much like the ECCC, will include civil parties based on a domestic law model.[8]

Neither the 2003 UN-Cambodian Framework Agreement nor the 2004 law establishing the ECCC set forth any participatory role for victims in the proceedings. There is only one offhand reference in the ECCC Law, which requires the Supreme Court Chamber to decide on appeals by victims from decisions of the Trial Chamber.[9] However, as a former French colony, Cambodia's modern legal system has its roots in the French civil law tradition. Unlike in common law countries, where civil actions are brought separately from criminal actions, civil law countries based on the French model often provide a role for victims as a party to the public proceeding. Because the ECCC was mandated to apply Cambodian procedures, NGOs and other observers expected that the Court would include civil party participation.

According to former U.S. Ambassador-at-Large for War Crimes Issues David Scheffer, who helped negotiate the Framework Agreement:

> [The ECCC] was never conceived by those who negotiated its creation as an instrument of direct relief for the victims[.] . . . The victims' numbers are simply too colossal and the mandate and resources of the ECCC far too limited to address the individual needs, including the award of reparations, for so many victims.[10]

Reportedly, most of the ECCC's international judges agreed that it would be unwise to follow the French model on this question. Their major concern was the Court's ability to provide reparations. The accused likely would be found indigent, and the ECCC would have no power or funding to provide redress. Some found it problematic that due to the large number of victims in Cambodia, in theory almost everyone might qualify to be a civil party. Why privilege only victims with the knowledge or affluence to file a civil claim? Instead, most international judges favored recognizing the needs of victims by including them as "injured parties" or "subsidiary prosecutors," a mode of participation in some civil law countries that is separate from any compensation claim.[11]

Nevertheless, the first international Co-Investigating Judge, Marcel Lemonde, and one of his legal advisors pressed for the adoption of a civil party scheme modeling French law.[12] Japan, the largest ECCC funder, was worried about the added financial burden a civil party scheme would impose,[13] but France—also a major donor to the Court—supported the scheme. Cambodian judges, although initially hesitant about the extra work involved, became amenable because the scheme would apply Cambodian law.[14]

The Internal Rules, adopted in 2007, provide victims the opportunity both to submit complaints to the Co-Prosecutors[15] and to participate in the proceedings as civil parties with the right to "symbolic and moral" reparations. The ECCC thus became the first mass crimes process to include victims as full parties.[16] Because the ECCC's unprecedented victim participation scheme was not anticipated in the Court's framework documents but instead designed from scratch by independently acting judges, this ambitious experiment was vulnerable from the outset to resource constraints. There was no money in the budget for civil parties, no vision of how the scheme would work in practice, and relatively few people at the Court—or in the United Nations or Cambodian Government—interested in prioritizing the effort to ensure its success.

VICTIM ADMINISTRATION

In public relations efforts, the ECCC Office of Administration (OA) has often emphasized the historic importance of the Court's victim participation scheme—in particular when countering bad publicity or seeking funds. For example, as corruption allegations mounted in 2008, OA Deputy Director Knut Rosandhaug asserted to donors in New York "that the Tribunal will be remembered for its novel approach to victim participation[.]"[17] In practice, however, the United Nations and international administrators at the ECCC offered limited support for victim participation due to concern about the financial and administrative burden it entailed. Without strong UN interest and engagement, the Court's support for victims became increasingly nationalized[18] with little international involvement or oversight.

Weak Institutional Support

Reportedly, the original budget for the ECCC had an attached note explaining that UN planners, fearing that victim participation would cost too much, explicitly rejected funding a victims unit.[19] Nevertheless, the 2007 Internal Rules instructed the OA to establish an autonomous Victims Unit (VU) and provide it administrative support. The mandate of the VU—later renamed the Victim Support Section (VSS)—encompasses maintaining a list of eligible lawyers who wish to represent victims, facilitating victims' representation, conducting outreach to victims, and helping victims submit complaints and civil party applications.[20]

In October 2007, the ECCC issued a Practice Direction on Victim Participation outlining relevant procedures and establishing an application form.[21] As a consequence of its late creation, the VU had neither a budget nor a chief until 2008. By the time it started functioning, it faced a large backlog of complainant and civil party applications but lacked the personnel and procedures to respond in a timely fashion.[22] With little funding or staff, the mundane task of processing thousands of application forms overwhelmed the VU and limited its capacity to provide victims a broader range of services. The VU had few resources to conduct outreach to potential victim participants or to support their legal representation in proceedings.[23] From the beginning, the VU was perceived by many—in particular the OA—as little more than an administrative processing unit,[24] and it was actively discouraged from conducting outreach.

In the absence of a well-resourced Victims Unit, a few Cambodian NGOs conducted victim participation tasks,[25] and were also discouraged from reaching out to large numbers of victims. OA international Deputy Director Knut Rosandhaug expressed concern about the capacity of the VU to process large numbers of applications and suggested that NGOs seek quality and not quantity. This approach both recognized serious practical limitations on involving large numbers of victims and demonstrated a clear policy preference for supporting perceived "core" legal functions of the court. One report on the early phases of the Court's work confirms:

> A number of interviewees felt that the unit was never properly supported by the ECCC's administration, one of whom suggested that this may have been because of a fear of escalating costs and difficulties in securing sufficient funding for the structure of the court as it then stood without the added complication of a fully-staffed and fully-operational Victims' Unit[.][26]

As a consequence of resource constraints, of the millions of victims who might have chosen to participate in ECCC proceedings, only a small fraction were informed of their right to take part. A large majority of those learned their rights through NGOs, which served as their primary connections to the Court.[27]

Of the ECCC's 479 staff members in 2011, only 28 (including a single international staffer) served in the Victims Support Section, and 3 served in the newly created Civil Party Lead Co-Lawyer Section.[28] Aside from associated staff salaries and overhead, the Court had only spent $300,000 on victims support since its inception and only about $1.5 million on total travel—an essential cost for conducting nationwide outreach to victims.[29] The Court's 2010 funding shortfall had led to cuts to the Victims Unit and no backfilling of some vacant jobs.[30]

After November 2008, the VSS was primarily supported by earmarked contributions to the Cambodian side from the German Ministry of Foreign Affairs through the German Society for Technical Cooperation (GTZ), now reconstituted as the German Agency for International Cooperation (GIZ). As of February 2012, Germany had contributed 1.9 million Euros to the VSS, but in 2010, OSJI noted the OA's failure to dispense German funds:

> The Office of Administration has been reluctant to authorize planned expenditures by the VSS because of the court's overall budget concerns. The need for improved VSS leadership is dramatically illustrated by the fact that the court was required to return over $340,000 in December 2009 to the German Technical Cooperation (GTZ), because it had not been programmed or spent in accordance with the grant under which it was given.[31]

That impasse supports a conclusion that the OA has had other spending priorities and has been loath to spend resources on victim participation. Dedicating less than 10% of its overall personnel and expenditures to those functions has compromised one of the chief potential advantages of Cambodia's in-country hybrid court.

Nationalization of Victim Participation

Although unstated in the Internal Rules, it was agreed that the Head of the VU would be a Cambodian and the Deputy a UN appointee. However, over time the unit has been increasingly nationalized. As of August 2013, despite being almost entirely funded by German earmarked contributions, the VSS had one international consultant funded by GIZ pursuant to an agreement with the national side, but no UN expert on victim participation and reparations.[32]

The first national and UN staff to head the unit were criticized for neglecting the timely processing of victim participation applications. Nevertheless, they were widely considered to be knowledgeable about victims' issues and dedicated to supporting a strong role for victims. Both left after little more than a year. Former civil party Theary Seng alleges that Rosandhaug "drove away" unit head Keat Bophal.[33] According to a leaked U.S. diplomatic cable and anecdotal accounts, Keat also faced resistance from the Cambodian judges, who "[did] not favor victims coming forward as civil parties."[34]

When the UN deputy left, the OA was slow to post the opening and recruit her replacement, and the position was vacant for nearly a year. Her successor lasted less than a year and was never replaced. This position was eliminated entirely in the 2010–11 budget, which found that a UN deputy was "no longer warranted," because "the Victims Unit is staffed predominantly under the National Component, and has adequate human resources to support its programme of work."[35] Since that time, with the exception of a few international consultants, the office has been fully staffed by Cambodians.[36]

The second person to head the office was Helen Jarvis, the former OA Chief of Public Affairs. She is a key advisor to Deputy Prime Minister Sok An, which raised concerns about her independence.[37] Her lack of experience working with victims,[38] avowed Marxist-Leninist views, and Australian origins prompted complaints from survivors.[39] One civil society leader said, "I myself—and I am a victim—I would want a Cambodian person to represent me."[40] Indeed, it was awkward for a hybrid tribunal not to entrust the leadership of a victims unit to a Cambodian survivor. Nevertheless, Jarvis worked hard to prove herself, and due to her government connections she was more successful in fighting for resources.[41]

Jarvis's replacement, Rong Chhorng, also lacked experience working with victims. He was transferred while remaining head of the Personnel Unit.[42] He has since occupied other ECCC jobs concurrently, as well as holding down his position as secretary-general of the Cambodian Council of Ministers' National Committee for Population and Development.[43] Rong's multiple roles again raised concerns about the political independence of the VSS. Nevertheless, when the Office of Lead Co-Lawyers was created in 2010 to represent civil party interests, Rosandhaug immediately delegated all UN administrative power over that office to Rong for two years.[44] This made the Office dependent on the VSS, contrary to its establishment as a functionally independent unit in the amended Internal Rules.[45]

Lack of institutional support for robust victim participation can be explained largely by the additional time, money, and effort required, but the Government also has incentives to control victims' input into the ECCC. Some prominent victims affiliated with the political opposition have vilified the Government and its role in the ECCC process.[46] Such victims could undermine the Cambodian People's Party's self-portrayal as the party responsible for ridding Cambodia of the Khmers Rouges, either by painting the Government as an obstacle to UN-led justice or by naming perpetrators who are now members of the Government. One observer recorded speculation that the Cambodian judges' initial opposition to including a role for civil parties was a reflection of the Government's "fear of encouraging people to submit new evidence."[47]

This fear can be noted in the reaction to Prince Sisowath Thomico's declaration of intention to file a complaint against a government official for the death of his parents. A news account speculated:

> Following the prince's example, countless relatives of Khmer Rouge victims could follow suit and launch their own individual complaints, disrupting the UN and government's carefully-scripted plans to try only a handful of top ex-leaders[.][48]

That possibility reportedly made those with past Khmer Rouge associations "uneasy."[49] Although the ECCC Law and Internal Rules do not allow complaints to trigger ECCC investigations automatically, it was anticipated "that much finger-pointing could be expected from other victims' families."[50] The realization that victims' voices could propel the process forward in unforeseen and politically unfavorable directions may be one reason why the national side has eagerly filled the void left by the UN's abdication of responsibility.

Whatever the cause, the consequence is a lack of international input, including the expertise the hybrid model was intended to offer. Panhavuth Long of the Cambodia Justice Initiative believes it is positive that the VSS has become nationalized because it empowers national staff to be the ones taking care of victims. He says, "They understand the issues of victims, they know their audience." At the same time, he notes that the nationals have no independent capacity—planning, skills, or will—to deal with the enormous number of victims.[51] There is no UN presence contributing capacity, ensuring the work meets international standards, or providing checks and balances on decision making, and the office is widely viewed as nontransparent and nonconsultative.[52] One court monitor found a few years ago that "the section as a whole has suffered from inadequate strategic planning and leadership and has not been fully effective in carrying out the expanded mandate given to it with the revised internal rules in February 2010."[53] As discussed below, this assessment remains valid.

An Office for Civil Party Support

As originally conceived, the VU "facilitated" victim representation but had no resources to develop a legal aid scheme comparable to the one established for the accused.[54] As a consequence, victims participating as civil parties were immediately at a disadvantage in finding qualified lawyers to protect their interests in the proceedings. In the Court's first case, legal representation was arranged through partnerships between those NGOs who had assisted victims in filing civil party applications and attorneys who either acted pro bono or received funding from sources outside of the Court.[55] National civil party lawyers in Case 001 highlighted "serious problems of funding, lack of office space and resources, and limited opportunities to see all their clients who may live in far-flung provinces all around Cambodia."[56] Everyone on civil party co-lawyer Karim Khan's team worked *pro bono* except for his Cambodian counterpart, who received a small grant from the British Embassy. He says, "A Court can't operate on charity; it must operate on the basis of professionalism."[57]

Due to perceived problems in the civil party scheme in Case 001, in particular the large number of legal teams and the repetitive nature of argumentation, in February 2010 the Internal Rules were amended to make the trial process more efficient for Case 002. Among the changes was the establishment of a court-funded Civil Party Lead Co-Lawyers Section,[58] headed by one national and one international.[59] The Co-Lawyers have "[u]ltimate responsibility to the court for the overall advocacy, strategy[,] and in-court presentation of the interests of the consolidated group of Civil Parties during the trial stage and beyond."[60] In doing so, they are required to ensure effective organization of the civil parties "whilst balancing the rights of all civil parties and the need for an expeditious trial within the unique ECCC context."[61] Whereas the original Internal Rules gave civil parties the right to legal representation but did not mandate it,[62] since this rule change civil parties may only participate as individuals at the pretrial stage and at trial *must* be represented by the Lead Co-Lawyers as part of a single, consolidated group.[63] This change was made due to concerns about the efficiency of the process and the fairness to the accused in Case 002, to which thousands of applicants sought to be joined.[64]

WHO SHOULD QUALIFY AS A CIVIL PARTY?

The question of which civil parties to admit to the ECCC's cases points to a crucial dilemma for any hybrid court—how to promote robust victim participation without compromising undue efficiency or prejudicing the proceedings against the accused. The ECCC's proximity to the crimes facilitates the involvement of survivors. However, in a country with millions of victims, the breadth of the criteria adopted for civil party participation impacts not only which of many victims may participate but also the Court's practical capacity to administer justice—a major concern for a hybrid tribunal funded through voluntary contributions and expected to deliver a swifter, less costly form of justice than its purely international peers.

ECCC jurisprudence on admissibility has suffered from the lack of initial vision of the appropriate role civil parties should play in the proceedings. To a certain extent this is understandable due to the novelty of the endeavor. As at all new courts, innovations must be perfected in practice, not only on paper. Nevertheless, the ICC experience should have provided an early indication of some of the inherent challenges of mass victim participation. Documentation Center of Cambodia (DC-Cam) Director and survivor Youk Chhang has called the lack of planning "a legal experiment at victims' expense."[65]

Although apparently not clear to all parties in advance, the admissibility standards applied in Case 001 are sound and in conformity with the Internal Rules and Cambodian procedures. In Case 002, the Court applied these standards arguably too inclusively together with a broad definition of victimization that allowed most applicants to participate. Paradoxically, this development occurred contemporaneously with decisions in Case 003 that disregard the Internal Rules and the Court's own jurisprudence in an apparent effort to prevent victims from meaningfully contributing to a politically controversial investigation.

Determining Who Is a Victim of the Crime

At the time the Internal Rules were adopted, the only explicit requirements for civil party status were a "physical, material or psychological" injury received as a "direct consequence of the offence" that was "personal and [had] actually come into being."[66] Language in the Practice Direction on Victim Participation soon clarified that "[a]ny victim of a crime coming within the jurisdiction of the ECCC may join the proceedings as a civil party in a case concerning *that crime*[,]"[67] suggesting that a causal link must be shown between a crime charged and the harm suffered.[68] Some argued this was an additional requirement unduly restricting the definition, but a subsequent revision of the Internal Rules clarified:

> Civil Parties must demonstrate *as a direct consequence of at least one of the crimes alleged against the Charged Person,* that he or she has in fact suffered physical, material, or psychological injury upon which a claim of collective and moral reparation might be based.[69]

The Supreme Court Chamber has since found that "[t]his clarification does not entail a change in the substance of the definition of civil party"[70] and is consistent with both Cambodian law and international standards.[71]

When the *Duch* verdict was announced, the Trial Chamber also ruled on whether the admitted civil parties had proved that they were victims of harm as a consequence of Duch's actions at specific crime sites.[72] Of the 92 civil parties who participated throughout the *Duch* proceedings, 24 had this status revoked when the Trial Chamber found that they had not sufficiently proved that they or their family members were victims of security centers under Duch's control, or that they had "any special bonds of affection or dependency" with direct S-21 victims.[73] According to research conducted by the Transcultural Psychosocial Organization, the day after the verdict reading, those rejected "reacted with intense emotional distress" and viewed it as shameful and a personal failure "as they could not fulfill the felt obligation to seek justice for the spirits of their relatives."[74] The Supreme Court Chamber upheld this criterion but disagreed with its application in specific cases by the Trial Chamber and admitted 10 more persons as civil parties.[75]

An Over-Broad Approach to Case 002

In Case 002, nearly 4,000 victims applied to be civil parties, and nearly half were rejected. On appeal, a supermajority of the Pre-Trial Chamber took a broadly inclusive approach, joining an additional 1,728 applicants to the case.[76]

First, they noted that the Internal Rules do not require a link between the injury and the facts investigated, but instead between the injury and "one of the crimes alleged."[77]

> While the facts investigated are limited to certain areas or crime sites, the legal characterizations of such facts . . . include crimes which represent mass atrocities allegedly committed by the Charged Persons by acting in a joint criminal enterprise together and with others against the population and *throughout* the country.[78]

As a consequence, it was not necessary for applicants to link their injuries to crime sites in the Closing Order, which "serve only as examples in order to demonstrate how all these centres and sites functioned *throughout* Cambodia."[79] The Pre-Trial Chamber accepted the applications of victims who suffered from the implementation of the criminal policies charged in the Closing Order, including in areas of the country where specific crime sites were not investigated.[80] The effect of its decision was to allow nearly 4,000 civil parties to join Case 002.

Judge Marchi-Uhel dissented in part from this decision, arguing that the Chamber's acceptance of victims who were not alleging harms related to the specific crime sites named in the indictment was legally inappropriate and would undermine the role of the consolidated group, delay the process, frustrate civil parties who met the specific admissibility requirements, and disappoint wrongly admitted civil parties who would not have the harms they suffered discussed at trial.[81] She found that the broader interests of victims could instead be addressed through the new scheme for nonjudicial measures, discussed later in this chapter.

The full Pre-Trial Chamber also adopted a broad perspective of the nature of victimization from international crimes and the resulting psychological impact on victims. The PTC held that victims who witnessed mass atrocities 30 years ago could still experience a high level of fear and that "psychological injury should be considered within the specific context of the Cambodian society in general and especially of its nature and organization during the period of the [Communist Party of Kampuchea] regime."[82] The Chamber found that because fear was instilled collectively, indirect injury could occur even if the direct victim was not a family member but was a member of the same persecuted group or community.[83] Further, the Chamber adopted a presumption that members of the same targeted group or community will have suffered psychological harm as a result of the injury to the direct victim.[84] A supermajority found that under the new scheme for civil party representation (discussed below), admitting a large number of victims participating as a consolidated group would not affect the rights of the accused.[85]

French Co-Lead Lawyer Elisabeth Simonneau Fort agrees with Judge Marchi-Uhel that the PTC took an overly permissive approach to Case 002 civil parties, who must be subjected to reasonable admissions criteria to distinguish them from the general victim population.[86] Jeanne Sulzer, a former Legal Officer in the Lead Co-Lawyers Section, asserts that the Court's inconsistent approaches to admission created inefficiency: had her office known the PTC would apply admissions criteria so loosely, it could have spent its resources gathering testimony rather than parsing thousands of applications.[87]

After the PTC's admissibility decision, the Trial Chamber severed the Case 002 indictment in anticipation of holding more than one trial on the crimes charged. As discussed in chapter 5, the case is limited to "population movement phases 1 and 2," including the forced evacuation of Phnom Penh and the Tuol Po Chrey execution site. As a consequence, alleged criminal policies related to genocide, forced marriage, cooperatives, worksites, security centers, and forced movement from the Eastern Zone have been excluded from the first Case 002 trial. In making the decision to sever, the Trial Chamber stated that because (as discussed in the next section) civil parties no longer participate as individuals at trial but instead as a consolidated group with collective interests, "limiting the scope of the facts to be tried during the first trial . . . has no impact on the nature of civil party participation at trial[.]"[88]

Civil party lawyers disagreed. Because Case 002/01 would only address a limited range of offenses—rather than the policies "throughout Cambodia" referenced by the Pre-Trial Chamber—numerous civil parties could have been excluded from the consolidated group.[89] Out of the 3,864 civil parties, only about 750 were admitted due to harm related to the forced movement at issue in Case 002/01.[90] However, the new Internal Rules make the PTC's admissibility decisions final, and the Trial Chamber has let all victims participate by default.[91] If they have not suffered harm from one of the crimes charged in the case, however, their inclusion as civil parties devalues the significance of that standing. Judge Marchi-Uhel's admonition that overadmission would undermine the role of the consolidated group therefore appears prescient.[92] Nevertheless, Simonneau Fort believes that civil party participation in Case 002/01 could still be meaningful if civil parties were clearly informed that they may not hear their specific harms discussed, may not be able to speak in Court, and may not have their names listed in the judgment. For some civil parties, being in Court and experiencing participation is more important than legal nuances.[93]

Restricting Civil Party Access to Case 003

While the Chambers were loosening the criteria for participation in Case 002, the CIJs constricted it in Case 003 to such an extent that all but direct victims would be rejected. With regard to an applicant whom the OCIJ had already accepted in both Cases 001 and 002, and whose harm was unquestionably factually linked to the crimes alleged in Case 003, CIJs You Bunleng and Siegfried Blunk found against all precedent and logic that the murder of his brother at Tuol Sleng was not the direct cause of his psychological injury. Instead there was an intermediate causal link: "the death of his brother."[94] Acknowledging the fact that they had already accepted him as a civil party in previous cases, the CIJs said that the prior decision had been made under great time pressure, and that at the time the judges had failed to consider causation in depth.[95]

Soon afterward, Judges You and Blunk rejected a woman who had been forced to marry during the Democratic Kampuchea period, and whose husband had then been forced to labor at Kampong Chhnang Airport (a crime site in Case 003) before being tortured and executed at S-21 prison. Although she likewise had been previously admitted in Cases 001 and 002, they reasoned again that she was not harmed by the crime committed against her husband, but instead by an intervening cause: his forced labor.[96] Adding insult to injury, they found it "highly unlikely" that she experienced psychological harm from her husband's forced labor 34 years ago and surmised that she had claimed this "based on unsound advice by a third person."[97] Finally, they said that she should not be admitted because she was already a civil party in Cases 001 and 002.[98]

These findings directly contradict the Court's own jurisprudence and all international and national standards relating to victim participation.[99] In Case 002 *dicta*, the full Pre-Trial Chamber has rejected the standard applied,[100] and on appeal, the international PTC judges eviscerated the OCIJ's reasoning.[101] Although these decisions are discredited, they have nevertheless contributed to the lack of consistency between Chambers, and a concern that civil parties are not taken seriously. Yet the CIJs' approach to victim participation in Case 003 was consistent with other evidence of their efforts to quickly bury the investigation and eliminate costs arising from Cases 003 and 004.

The ECCC's struggles to apply admissibility criteria doubtlessly derive in part from the judges' recognition that most Cambodians are victims, and a legal decision to charge one crime site over another is an unsatisfactory basis for excluding those who wish to participate in seeking justice after more than 30 years. The judges are also aware that the time required for making individual determinations and hearing appeals for thousands of victims can easily overwhelm the resources of a court.[102] One judge estimated that defense challenges to even 1,000 civil party claims would last at least eight months.[103] Donor demands and the age of the Case 002 defendants—and many victims—both militated strongly toward reducing the amount of judicial time devoted to the civil party scheme. In the face of these pressures, rather than regulate the number of admitted civil parties, the judges redrafted the rules to limit the scope of their participation.

LIMITING CIVIL PARTY ROLES AND REPRESENTATION

In the midst of the Court's first case, efficiency concerns and worries about equality of arms led the ECCC to reduce the scope of individual civil party participation, for example, eliminating their right to speak and removing their freedom to select legal representation for trial proceedings. Changes were necessary to allow even a fraction of the 4,000 civil party applicants to participate in Case 002, but the changes reduced the robustness of the mechanism, making the victims' role look less like that of a full party and more like a participant. In that sense, the ECCC has been forced to adapt its ambitious initial model in a direction that converges toward the practice of the ICC. Although this outcome was a necessary move toward efficiency, there is a general consensus that too much was promised too early and then taken away. Former OCP investigator Craig Etcheson argues that for a mass crimes court, "one of the greatest challenges is the problem of managing expectations," and the ECCC has been "more or less a complete failure" on that score—mainly due to its management of civil party participation.[104]

Reducing the Scope of Civil Party Participation

Victims may participate as civil parties in ECCC proceedings by "supporting the prosecution" for the purpose of seeking "collective and moral reparations."[105] Under the Internal Rules, civil parties have many enumerated participation rights, including to request investigative actions, to lodge appeals and participate as a party therein, to call witnesses, to have access to the case file, to respond to preliminary objections, to question accused, to exercise the right of audience, to make written submissions, and to make closing arguments.[106] Their participation has made important contributions to the proceedings, most notably the addition of forced marriage charges to the Case 002 indictment,[107] and the decision of the international prosecutor to request the investigation of crimes against the Kampuchea Krom minority in Case 004.[108]

Nevertheless, the right of victims to participate must be balanced against the right of the accused to a fair trial, including the right to be presumed innocent and the right to be tried without undue delay.[109] As noted by one commentator:

> If the victims were able to exercise [participation] rights freely without any control by a judge, the proceedings could last indefinitely, infringing the rights of the accused. The number of victims in cases of war crimes and crimes against humanity often runs into the thousands or even tens of thousands. Furthermore, the nature of the damage they have suffered adds to the emotive power of their intervention in the proceedings. If not controlled, their participation could therefore interfere with the smooth conduct of trials and the rights of the accused, as well as the search for truth.[110]

The European Court of Human Rights has recognized that the scope of civil parties' right of access to court proceedings may be limited "[h]aving regard to the role accorded to civil actions within criminal trials and to the complementary interests of civil parties and the prosecution . . . , their roles and objectives being clearly different."[111] However, "these limitations must not restrict or reduce a person's access in such a way or to such an extent that the very essence of the right is impaired[.]"[112] Moreover, any limitations must pursue a legitimate aim and have "a reasonable relationship of proportionality between the means employed and the aim sought to be achieved."[113]

The first request to limit civil party participation at the ECCC arose when the defense objected to four civil parties participating in a hearing on Nuon Chea's appeal against the CIJ's provisional detention order. The *Nuon Chea* team, citing ICC jurisprudence, argued that civil parties should only be allowed to participate in the trial, and not during pretrial proceedings, because they did not have a personal interest in the outcome.[114]

At the ICC, victims are not considered "true" parties but are limited to presenting their "views and concerns . . . at stages of the proceedings determined to be appropriate by the Court" where their "personal interests are affected."[115] Therefore, "participation is not a once-and-for-all event but rather [is] decided on the basis of the evidence or issue under consideration at any particular point in time."[116] In contrast, at the ECCC, once a victim is found to meet the Internal Rules' criteria to join a case as a civil party, he or she is a full party to the proceedings with rights similar to those of the accused, including extensive rights to participate during the investigative process.[117] As emphasized by an ICC Appeals Judge:

> The right of victims to participate enunciated by article 68(3) [of the Rome Statute] has no immediate parallel or association with the participation of victims in criminal proceedings in . . . the Romano-Germanic system of justice, where victims in the role of civil parties or auxiliary prosecutors have a wide-ranging right to participate in criminal proceedings.[118]

In ruling on the *Nuon Chea* challenge, the ECCC Pre-Trial Chamber found that the text of the Internal Rules, read in light of the Cambodian Code of Criminal Procedure, was clear that, unlike victim participants at the ICC, "Civil Parties can participate in all criminal proceedings, which includes the procedure related to appeals against provisional detention before the Pre-Trial Chamber."[119] Nevertheless, the scope of civil parties' right to participate equally in proceedings has been reduced over time to limit the right of individual victims to speak in court, make opening statements, or make submissions on sentencing and character.

Right to Speak in Person

Under the original version of the Internal Rules, there were no specific limitations on civil parties speaking for themselves at any time during proceedings, except for closing statements.[120] However, early in the proceedings, the Pre-Trial Chamber restricted civil parties' right to speak in person.[121] During a

Nuon Chea detention appeal hearing, a civil party made remarks that "largely amounted to a victim statement" and were consequently disregarded by the Pre-Trial Chamber in making its ruling.[122] At the subsequent Ieng Sary detention hearing, when the PTC prohibited her from speaking personally, she summarily dismissed her lawyer but was still not allowed to speak. Judge Downing dissented, noting a conflict between Internal Rule 23, granting a general right of appearance, and Rule 77(10), providing that only lawyers for the parties may make observations. Because the civil party was now unrepresented, he found it unfair not to permit her to address the Court.[123] A group of unrepresented civil parties submitted that they must be able to exercise all of their rights under the Internal Rules, even if unrepresented.[124] Recognizing that unrepresented civil parties "may be unrepresented not through choice, but for financial reasons," the Chamber said "legitimately" unrepresented civil parties could personally address the Court when their interests and those of the prosecution were different and advance notice was provided.[125]

No situations arose again where unrepresented civil parties sought to speak before either the Pre-Trial or Trial Chambers. With the changes to the legal representation regime discussed below, representation by the Lead Co-Lawyers at trial is now mandatory. Although the Cambodian Code of Criminal Procedure allows oral submission by civil parties during trial, whether represented or not,[126] a blanket prohibition was codified in the Internal Rules: "When the Civil Party is represented by a lawyer, his or her rights are exercised through the lawyer."[127] This limitation is necessary in light of the large number of victims who participate in proceedings. Nevertheless, it prevents the active participation of victims unless they are called to provide evidence.

In the *Duch* trial, 22 of the initial 93 civil parties were called by the Court to share their experiences.[128] A common refrain was the momentousness of victims' opportunity to express themselves directly to Duch—often to reject his pleas for forgiveness. For example, Ou Kamela, the daughter of an S-21 victim, said in a letter read in Court, "On behalf of my father, I refuse to express the slightest amount of pity. On behalf of my father, I request that justice be handed down."[129] When asked how his clients had felt after providing testimony to the Court, civil party lawyer Alain Werner said, "About 20 Civil Parties recounted their experiences in Court, and it is difficult after just these hearings to make a global assessment of their experiences. I know that some of my own clients were very relieved immediately after their testimony and some even felt empowered."[130]

Indeed, the testimonies of civil parties—including accounts of Tuol Sleng by well-known survivors such as Bou Meng and Chum Mey—provided some of the most powerful moments in the *Duch* trial. Their ability to confront the accused in court helped forge a connection between the hybrid court and the community of survivors in which it operates. In the Case 002 trial, only 32 of 3,864 civil parties had the opportunity to share their experiences in their own words.

Right to Make Opening Statements

In both Case 001 and Case 002, civil party representatives sought the opportunity to make opening statements and had their requests denied.[131] The ECCC Internal Rules limit this right to the Co-Prosecutors and the accused.[132] The Chamber has highlighted that Cambodian law also does not provide this right to civil parties.[133] However, civil law practice, including Cambodian procedure, does not provide *any* party an opportunity to make opening statements, as the proceedings are not adversarial. The civil parties thus argued that a fair application of the Cambodian Criminal Procedure Code would exclude *all* parties from making opening statements, and that it was discriminatory to limit the right to two of three parties.[134] To respect the parties' equality of arms and the symbolic significance for the nearly 4,000 civil parties, they asked the Trial Chamber to exercise its discretion to give them 30 minutes to make preliminary remarks.[135] However, this was summarily rejected by the Trial Chamber, which ruled with evident irritation: "The Chamber reiterates that there is no legal basis in the ECCC legal framework for granting the Co-Lawyers' request."[136] Even the defense teams have expressed dismay at this unequal treatment.[137]

At the ICC, representatives of victim participants have the potential right to make opening statements, and have in practice.[138] It is unclear why the ECCC does not also grant that right, as time limitations could be imposed to encourage expediency. The judges drafted the rules, so their finding that they have no choice because "that's what the rules say" is not compelling. Because civil parties are entitled to equal rights as parties, the failure to issue a reasoned decision explaining why they are not entitled to participate equally on this symbolically important occasion makes the ruling appear arbitrary and perhaps discriminatory.

Right to Make Submissions on Sentencing and Question Witnesses about Character

In the *Duch* case, the Trial Chamber emphasized the defense's right to equality of arms when it departed from civil law practice and precluded the civil parties from making submissions on sentencing or questioning witnesses and experts about Duch's character. Judge Lavergne dissented on both rulings, finding them to be "inconsistent with the law currently applied before the Chambers" and to "misrepresent, for no valid reason, both the role and the meaning of Civil Party participation."[139] Although recognizing the need to adapt Cambodian procedures to the challenges of prosecuting mass crimes, he asked:

> How far can one go without breaching the spirit of the law, or fundamentally distorting the meaning of the involvement of the Civil Parties before the ECCC and the purpose of the trial as a whole[.][140]

In his view, civil parties, as equal parties to the proceedings, are entitled to participate at all stages, except where expressly limited.[141] Due to their "personal knowledge" of the accused, they may be in the best position to provide the Court relevant character information, and in fact during the Case 001 trial they had on a number of occasions asked witnesses and the accused questions related to character.[142]

Judge Lavergne also looked to ICC jurisprudence to assess international practice. Although he found it to be generally supportive of his views, at the time the ICC had not completed any cases and the evidence was fragmentary. Subsequently the ICC Trial Chamber issued its first verdict of conviction and invited the prosecution and the legal representatives of victims "to file written submissions on the procedure to be adopted for sentencing . . . and the principles to be applied by the Chamber when it is considering the appropriate sentence to be imposed[.]"[143] Likewise, at the Special Tribunal for Lebanon, victims may, with the authorization of the Trial Chamber, make impact statements at the sentencing stage of proceedings.[144]

The Role of Civil Party Lawyers

As noted earlier in this chapter, the ECCC amended its rules governing civil party representation, requiring that they be part of a single consolidated group represented by the Lead Co-Lawyers at trial. International Civil Party Lead Co-Lawyer Elisabeth Simonneau Fort has said the change "can permit a kind of coherent and strategical defence, avoiding opposite positions or repetitive pleadings."[145] Overloaded by the number of victims seeking to participate in its cases, the ICC appears to be moving toward a similar model due to its perceived potential for improving efficiency, reducing costs, and improving the quality of representation.[146]

Nevertheless, obligatory representation eliminates the right of a party to select his or her own lawyer. Moreover, it no longer takes the individual needs of the civil parties into consideration. Under the prior Internal Rules, "the distinct interests" of each victim as well as the potential for conflicts of interests had to be considered before the Court could decide to designate a common lawyer.[147] Now, though civil parties still retain individual counsel, their primary in-court representation is predetermined with no such assessment.

Under the revised rules, civil party lawyers' control over the representation of their clients is substantially diminished once trial proceedings begin. Although the Lead Co-Lawyers are expected to "seek the views of the civil party lawyers and endeavor to reach consensus in order to coordinate representation[,]"[148] there are no mechanisms in the Rules governing disputes or procedures by which a dissenting civil party lawyer can make his or her views known to the Court or secure a remedy for a conflict of interest between civil party groups.[149] Instead of directing the representation of their clients, they are expected to provide support to the consolidated group that is "mutually agreed" and "coordinated by" the Lead Co-Lawyers, including "oral and written submissions, examination of their clients and witnesses and other procedural actions."[150]

The system was first tested when a civil party lawyer sought to submit a proposed witness and civil party list directly to the Trial Chamber. She argued that the document was "not the common interest" of the consolidated group, and therefore fell outside of the Lead Co-Lawyer's mandate; however, the Trial Chamber rejected it because it was not signed and sent by the Lead Co-Lawyers.[151] In requesting the Chamber to accept the documents as a belated filing, the Lead Co-Lawyers noted, "[S]ome of [the Civil Party lawyers] still believed that with the power of attorney they have the rights to submit motions as individuals."[152]

The rule change also severs the civil party attorney-client relationship. The civil party Lead Co-Lawyers derive their powers only from the Internal Rules,[153] and civil party lawyers are now unable to represent their clients' interests in court, such as by making oral or written submissions, without agreement from the civil party Lead Co-Lawyers. Concomitantly, civil parties are unable to hire or fire the Lead Co-Lawyers, to determine the overall objectives of their legal representation, or to participate in deciding the means of carrying out those objectives. Instead: "Ultimate responsibility to the court for the overall advocacy, strategy and in-court presentation" falls to the Lead Co-Lawyers,[154] who represent the interests of the consolidated group, not individual civil parties.[155] As noted by an ICC Judge with regard to victim participation at that court:

> Even if these common legal representatives organize themselves to take instructions from a great number of victims, it will be very difficult if not impossible to relay these instructions to the court. In those circumstances, can legal representation be anything more than symbolic? And if it is only symbolic, how meaningful can it be?[156]

With such a broad scope of authority, the Lead Co-Lawyers have the authority to shut some or all civil party lawyers out of the trial process. One civil party lawyer expressed frustration at the Lead Co-Lawyers' "seemly arbitrary" rejections of submissions she sought to file on behalf of her clients:[157] "We have NO body to complain to about whatever decision they take. We are fully in their hands. They do not have only a coordinating role, they decide which content is submitted and which is excluded. They have uncontrolled power."[158] Despite such complaints, which are likely inevitable given the balance of authority in the new scheme and the strong views of legal representatives advocating on behalf of their clients, it appears that the Lead Co-Lawyers selected have made every effort to follow the intent of the rules and work collaboratively in recognition of the enormous workload involved.[159]

The Trial Chamber has occasionally appeared dissatisfied with this inclusive approach and has made decisions limiting the participation of civil party lawyers. For example, the Chamber classified medical reports regarding accused Ieng Thirith and Nuon Chea as strictly confidential and limited distribution specifically to the Lead Co-Lawyers, with authorization for them to share the documents only with civil party lawyers specifically tasked with providing support to the consolidated group.[160] The Lead Co-Lawyers argued that all civil party lawyers should be granted access, as under the new regime decisions regarding strategy and drafting of submissions is a collective and joint decision of the group.[161] The Lead Co-Lawyers "can not discharge their primary duty of consultation and seeking a consensus in order to consolidate representation . . . if the civil party lawyers do not have access to procedural materials."[162] Moreover, without access, civil party lawyers cannot defend the interest of their clients.[163]

A supermajority of the Trial Chamber rejected the request, finding that the Lead Co-Lawyers were not required to obtain the consensus of civil party lawyers in all circumstances.[164] Judge Laverne dissented, saying that restricting access from some party counsel is at odds with Cambodian law.[165] Moreover, he argued that merely because at the trial stage the civil parties act as a consolidated group, this does not alter the civil party lawyers' responsibilities to their clients.[166] He rejected the view that representation at the trial stage was not a shared responsibility, and called the measure "discriminatory" and "undeniably prejudicial to the adequate representation of the Civil Parties' interests[.]"[167]

The Trial Chamber also pressed the Lead Co-Lawyers to be the only civil party voices in Court. One way it made this apparent is by seeking to limit the number of lawyers who could speak for each team on particular issues, which though intended to improve efficiency, also directly impacts the opportunity of individual civil party lawyers—and their clients—to participate.[168] The Trial Chamber has also expressed displeasure when lawyers other than the Lead Co-Lawyers speak in Court.[169]

Moreover, the Trial Chamber has at times appeared irritated that the civil parties intervene separately from the prosecution. Although the civil party teams "assist the prosecution," they do not collaborate, and their interests are different.[170] In one instance, the international Lead Co-Lawyer made a brief interjection, and when the prosecution also sought to make a small point, the President took more time than their statements to admonish him:

> What is on your mind, Mr. Co-Prosecutor? Do you have anything else to add? Can you organize yourself amongst the parties to express your objections or comments in order? And, as you know, the Lead Co-Lawyer is on the support side of the Prosecution, and on the other side is the Defence, and if you keep taking turn, this morning session would not be efficient. I believe you need to organize yourself so that your objection shall be done once and together to make it more efficient, as we shall adhere to the principle of proceedings—a fair trial proceeding.[171]

International Lead Co-Lawyer Elisabeth Simonneau Fort has said, "Sometimes it is clear that the [Trial] Chamber considers that civil parties have not such an important role as a party[.]"[172]

Changes to the civil party scheme were necessary for efficiency and arguably to avoid breaching the equality of arms. Etcheson argues that the civil party scheme in Case 001 was "absolutely untenable and did a lot to discredit the whole idea of civil party participation." Case 002 was "much closer to the mark" in striking the right balance between active victim participation and the need for fair and efficient proceedings, and the idea of lead colawyers "makes perfect sense," but the Court may have overcompensated for the flaws of Case 001 and cut back too dramatically on civil parties' time in court.[173] The result is that civil parties no longer participate as individual parties in the trial proceedings.[174] They instead form part of a collective group of victim participants with no direct connection to the lead lawyers who represent them.

REPARATIONS AND NONJUDICIAL MEASURES

Reparations

The effort to provide reparative justice has presented the ECCC with further challenges. Like other international and hybrid courts, the ECCC is designed with a primary institutional focus on criminal trials rather than reparative measures.[175] The limits of hybrid courts are compounded by expectations of cost efficiency. Pursuant to the Internal Rules, the ECCC, in contrast to the ICC, has no authority to grant individual reparations, only "collective and moral."[176] The Trial Chamber has noted:

> [T]he ECCC lacks the competence to award individual monetary compensation to Civil Parties. . . . Such departures from national law were considered necessary in view of the large number of Civil Parties expected before the ECCC and the inevitable difficulties of quantifying the full extent of the losses suffered by an indeterminate class of victims. Reparations before the ECCC were therefore intended to be essentially symbolic . . . rather than compensatory.[177]

As discussed in chapter 4, at the time the Case 001 verdict was issued, the ECCC Internal Rules only authorized reparations "awarded against, and . . . borne by convicted persons."[178] The Trial Chamber found that it had no jurisdiction to order Cambodian authorities to provide reparations to civil parties, and that at most it could "encourage" the Government and other entities to offer financial and other forms of support. The Chamber also said that no legal mechanism existed "allowing the ECCC to substitute or supplement awards made against [accused] with funds provided by national authorities or other third parties."[179]

The accused was found indigent, and the Trial Chamber awarded civil parties only the inclusion of their names and those of the immediate victims in the final judgment, and the compilation and publication of statements of apology made by the accused during the trial.[180]

In anticipation of the ECCC's second trial, the judges expanded the Court's authority to provide reparations, giving the Trial Chamber the authority to recognize a specific project designed in cooperation with the VSS that has secured sufficient external funding.[181] When the Trial Chamber provided initial observations about the types of requests that may be entertained, it notably excluded the possibility of a trust fund being established to financially compensate civil parties.[182]

At the behest of the Trial Chamber, the Lead Co-Lawyers have identified a prioritized list of reparations projects, which have been accepted by the Chamber "in principle" if sufficient funding is secured in advance: (1) Government recognition of a new remembrance day for Khmer Rouge victims; (2) the creation of three to six public memorials acknowledging the harms of Case 002 civil parties; the funding of mental health services for Case 002 civil parties including (3) testimonial therapy and (4) self-help groups; (5) a mobile exhibition with short films and live testimonials by civil parties; (6) a permanent exhibition space with documents, multimedia testimonials and artistic displays to preserve civil party accounts of the harms they suffered; and (7) a booklet explaining the ECCC judicial process, civil party participation, and the crimes encompassed in Case 002.[183]

In addition to proof of sufficient outside funding, before final endorsement the Trial Chamber requires, when relevant, proof of the Government's willingness to support the projects, and additional specificity (such as who will be responsible for project implementation, the projects' duration, and whether the participation of non-governmental organizations listed as partners is dependent on available funding).[184]

According to Simonneau Fort, shortly before closing arguments there were only "a very small number of [financial] sponsors" for the requested projects. An unnamed advisor to a mental health NGO collaborating with the VSS on a reparations project says the problem lies "in part" with VSS: "There are no staff [there] who are actually experienced enough to deal with project management . . . proposal writing, dealing with donors and all that. . . . Also, [there is] probably a lack of motivation to really go forward and systematically and effectively address it with potential donors."[185] Any failure to sufficiently develop and fund reparations programs in accordance with the Internal Rules thus also stems from the UN side's unwillingness to dedicate international expertise to the running of this office.

Civil party lawyer Nushin Sarkarati notes that, under the revised rules, everything proposed for reparations must be essentially completed before judgment and the ECCC will merely rubber-stamp the completed project. She argues that this sets a horrible legal precedent, as reparations should be paid for either by the convicted person or by the state, not by NGOs through third-party funding. Most concerning, the Court is putting the burden on victims to design and fund reparations themselves. She says, "The Court is essentially allowing concerns over the implementation of an award to belie an appropriate judgment on reparations. I hope no [other] court adopts this system."[186]

The splitting of the indictment in Case 002 has also changed the import of reparations, which are intended to "acknowledge the harm suffered by civil parties as a result of the commission of the crimes for which an Accused is convicted" and "provide benefits to the Civil Parties which address this harm."[187] However, if only civil parties with harms related to crimes in the severed indictment are entitled to reparations, many in the consolidated group would be excluded. At the urging of the civil party lawyers, the Trial Chamber has therefore decided that reparations requests that do not result in enforceable claims against a convicted person, but are instead funded externally under the new rule, may benefit all civil parties in the consolidated group.[188] As a result, the implementation of this aspect of the civil party scheme has also moved the ECCC toward a collective victim participation model, and away from the recognition of individual victims as "parties" to the proceedings.

Nonjudicial Measures

In discussions with NGOs before the civil party role was revised, the Senior Judicial Coordinator and the reserve international Trial Chamber judge emphasized that restrictions on the role of civil parties would be balanced by expanding the mandate of the VSS to reach out more broadly to the general victim population.[189] A new Internal Rule was therefore adopted, which provides:

> The Victim Support Section shall be entrusted with the development and implementation of non-judicial programs and measures addressing the broader

> interests of victims. Such progress may, where appropriate, be developed and implemented in collaboration with governmental and non-governmental organisations external to the ECCC.[190]

Judge Silvia Cartwright said the judges believed that nonjudicial measures "will be a major legacy of this Tribunal."[191] The Open Society Justice Initiative, a key Court monitor, explained:

> This development is important because, as stated previously, large numbers of Cambodians who do not become formal civil parties are victims of the Khmer Rouge and have an interest in the same kinds of information and services offered by the court to civil parties. . . . Examples of additional activities planned by the Victims Support Unit pursuant to its expanded mandate include presenting public forums with court officials, providing the opportunity to view proceedings, and disseminating information about the nature of the cases before the court.[192]

However, these ambitions have not been realized. Over two years later, the VSS "ha[d] not yet even identified what non-judicial projects it will pursue or clearly differentiated these measures from court-ordered reparations."[193] The nonjudicial program manager told a local paper, "We have a mandate on this, but we are not really implementing, so we need to facilitate and then work with NGO partners to implement these non-judicial measures[.]"[194] The VSS Chief responded to criticisms by noting that the unit had since late 2011 been implementing a two-year joint project with local NGOs on "Promoting Gender Equality and Improving Access to Justice for Female Survivors and Victims of Gender Based Violence under the Khmer Rouge Regime."[195] Moreover, "[s]imilar projects" had already been implemented by a number of NGOs, "which could be seen as [Non-Judicial Measures] projects."[196] It thus appears that in most cases, the VSS will merely put its stamp of approval on projects planned and executed by NGOs.[197]

Although the Trial Chamber has noted that VSS projects developed during the life of the Court may eventually turn into a form of Court-sanctioned reparations upon conviction,[198] they are two separate, if potentially overlapping, Court mandates. Nevertheless, with the creation of a "Reparation and

Non-Judicial Measures" team, and efforts to create a foundation to fund the implementation of both, they have been welded together, and are stagnating as a result. The Open Society Justice Initiative has said that to effectively implement this broader mandate, international input and expertise is required, but as discussed above, there is currently no UN reparations expert within the VSS. Initial hopes that with its expanded mandate the VSS would undertake basic outreach to the general victim population during the trial proceedings appear guaranteed to remain unrealized.[199]

CONCLUSION

Victim participation was bound to be difficult for the ECCC, especially after the judicial creation of an unprecedented civil party scheme that neither the national nor international side of the Court fully embraced. Some questioned the feasibility of transposing this domestic civil law practice to a mass crimes court. Others questioned the additional effort and funding required for what they viewed as a peripheral endeavor. The scheme was disadvantaged from the start due to general neglect, and the haphazard manner in which it was implemented in the Court's first case caused delays, confusion, and sometimes dashed victim expectations.[200] In Case 001, many of the relatively small number of civil parties involved were able to participate directly in the proceedings, which appears to have been meaningful and even cathartic for most of the civil parties involved.[201]

Since that time, the participation rights of civil parties—and their lawyers—have been reduced in anticipation of the practical realities of accommodating thousands of victims into the Case 002 proceedings. Now participating indirectly and represented as a group, the system is functioning more efficiently, but it is questionable if civil parties in Case 002 are still accorded the rights of "parties" or will have the same quality of experience as those who joined Case 001.[202] Indeed, the primary ECCC lesson for future internationalized courts may be the impracticability of individual civil party participation in mass crimes proceedings.[203]

Sulzer suggests that instead of individuals, perhaps organizations and associations with common interests should be accorded party status in future proceedings—a model building off mass claims processes in both the common and civil law and the expanding role of victims' organizations in postconflict societies.[204] Ieng Sary's former international lawyer, Michael Karnavas, suggests a two-phase trial: upon conviction, a restitution hearing could be held during which victims are given a genuine opportunity to be heard.[205] Both proposals take into account the need to design future hybrid tribunals with realistic expectations of the forms of victim participation that a tribunal can manage effectively and that donors are willing to fund.

Chapter 8

CONNECTING TO CAMBODIANS

Outreach and Legacy

A strong link to the society most affected by atrocities is arguably central to achieving many of the expressed objectives of hybrid and international tribunals—such as deterring future crimes, developing legal norms and institutions, ministering to victims' needs, and providing an official account of past atrocities.[1] In addition to cost considerations and sovereignty concerns, the hybrid model is premised in significant part on the notion that *in situ* proceedings with strong national participation help connect survivors to the criminal process and build institutional ties that promote local judicial reform.[2]

In a 2004 report to the Security Council, UN Secretary-General Kofi Annan laid out that argument clearly, writing that hybrid *in situ* tribunals have important benefits, "including easier interaction with the local population, closer proximity to the evidence and witnesses and being more accessible to victims."[3]

> Such accessibility allows victims and their families to witness the processes in which their former tormentors are brought to account. National location also enhances the national capacity-building contribution of the [ ] tribunals, allowing them to bequeath their physical infrastructure (including buildings, equipment and furniture) to national justice systems, and to build the skills of national justice personnel. In the nationally located tribunals, international personnel work side by side with their national counterparts and on-the-job training can be provided to national lawyers, officials and staff. Such benefits, where combined with specially tailored measures for keeping the public informed and

> effective techniques for capacity-building, can help ensure a lasting legacy in the countries concerned.[4]

The ECCC touts those advantages, emphasizing that unlike the International Criminal Tribunals for the former Yugoslavia and Rwanda (ICTY and ICTR), the Khmer Rouge trials provide for "full national involvement in the trials" and are "held in Cambodia, conducted mainly in Khmer, open to participation by Cambodian people and reported via local television, radio and newspapers."[5] The ECCC also asserts that its proceedings present "an excellent opportunity to bolster the understanding of the criminal trial process within Cambodia."[6] This chapter examines the extent to which the ECCC's hybrid institutional structure, high level of national participation, and in-country location have in fact contributed to effective outreach to survivors, capacity-building, and judicial reform.

THE RELATED FUNCTIONS OF OUTREACH AND LEGACY

Mass crimes courts tend to cluster activities that promote social engagement and impact under the overlapping umbrellas of "outreach" and "legacy." Neither term has a single standard definition, but outreach normally refers to a bundle of communication activities that inform and engage the affected population. Outreach functions are closely linked to public affairs and media relations but are not synonymous. Outreach implies at a minimum dissemination of basic information about court processes, but preferably goes further to promote dialogue with victims and their communities in terms they can understand.[7] For example, the International Criminal Court (ICC)'s public information strategy defines outreach as:

> [A] process of establishing sustainable, two-way communication between the Court and communities affected by situations that are the subject of investigations or proceedings. It aims to provide information, promote understanding and support for the Court's work, and to provide access to judicial proceedings.[8]

Effective outreach can enhance a tribunal's legacy by demonstrating best judicial practices and building public trust in the rule of law. For example, Ou Virak,

President of the Cambodian Center for Human Rights, has noted that outreach, including media coverage and public attendance at hearings, "can play a role in demonstrating and developing an understanding of core fair trial rights and the processes and procedures of a court operating based on international standards of justice."[9]

The Office of the UN High Commissioner for Human Rights (OHCHR) defines legacy as a court's "lasting impact on bolstering the rule of law in a particular society, by conducting effective trials to contribute to ending impunity, while also strengthening domestic judicial capacity."[10] This definition encompasses professional development, the provision of physical infrastructure, catalysis of domestic legal reform, and development of local confidence in the rule of law. A positive legacy thus depends both on a court's "demonstration effects" and capacity-building measures.

OUTREACH

It is often said that justice needs to be seen to be done.[11] However, outreach has been a weakness of international tribunals and is not an automatic strength of hybrid courts. Outreach in postconflict states inevitably faces serious obstacles, although they vary from case to case. Low levels of literacy and poor information infrastructure have been consistent hurdles for international and hybrid courts. Political resistance to these courts in certain communities has been a challenge in most instances as well[12]—a concern in Cambodia with respect to former Khmer Rouge strongholds in the northwestern parts of the country.

Mixed institutional design presents the same risks of political discord and ownership struggles over outreach initiatives as are evident in other aspects of hybrid courts' functions. Moreover, as with international courts, hybrid courts' budget and staffing allocations, and perceived institutional priorities, have consistently favored core judicial functions, giving short shrift to programs that share their work with the public.[13] The ECCC is no exception, and thus the natural advantages that its location and composition afford have been tempered by shortcomings in its institutional design, endowment, and political will.

Positive and Negative Precedents

By the time of the ECCC's creation, a number of lessons could be drawn from the courts that preceded it. Outreach proved to be a major deficiency at the

ICTY and ICTR. Neither tribunal launched an outreach program until 1998, several years after they were created. By that time, both had suffered reputational damage partly due to criticism from local government authorities suspicious of their activities.[14] In Rwanda, a 2002 survey showed that eight years after the ICTR's establishment, 87% of respondents indicated that they were not well informed about the tribunal or knew nothing at all about it.[15] The ICC also got a slow start. It provided few funds for outreach, tried to adopt a low-profile presence in countries in which it conducted investigations, and relied on brief "fly-in-fly-out" visits to provide public information.[16]

The Special Court for Sierra Leone (SCSL) demonstrated that in-country hybrid courts can have significant advantages in terms of outreach.[17] SCSL officials began connecting with the public almost immediately, setting the ambitious goal of visiting all of the major towns in each of Sierra Leone's 12 districts in the first four months after the Court's creation. There was virtually no mass media in Sierra Leone, so outreach teams had to travel around the country to keep the population informed.[18] Led by Prosecutor David Crane and Registrar Robin Vincent, they achieved this by holding town-hall meetings—day-long affairs preceded by meetings between court outreach officials and local elders or chiefs.[19] The SCSL also deployed outreach officers to each of the country's districts and added outreach officers in Liberia and Guinea for the *Charles Taylor* trial.[20] The fact that the prosecutor's office began the outreach process at the SCSL led to some public conflation between the court and the prosecution.[21] Once an outreach team was assembled, however, it took responsibility, and by 2004 the entire outreach staff was Sierra Leonean. By 2009, it had a dedicated Outreach Office with 17 officers and was reportedly conducting 272 outreach programs per month in Sierra Leone and 16 per month in Liberia.[22] It created a booklet entitled *Special Court at a Glance* to explain the tribunal in simple illustrated terms, as well as weekly radio programs with updates on the court proceedings, and screenings of short video trial segments.

The SCSL nevertheless faced funding challenges that limited its ability to do much more than disseminate basic information about the court, especially outside of the capital.[23] The SCSL's management committee decided not to fund the outreach program at all, and indeed outreach never appeared in the court's budget, forcing staff to find finances elsewhere.[24]

Not all in-country hybrid courts have been as effective at disseminating information. In East Timor, the underfunded and understaffed Special Panels for

Serious Crimes (SPSC) never created either a general public affairs or outreach office for the court. The Serious Crimes Unit (SCU) made only modest efforts to reach out to victims, some of whom became highly critical of the process.[25] A single staff person was assigned, among other duties, to serve as the public affairs officer for both the SPSC and SCU.[26] The United Nations considered outreach primarily a Timorese responsibility, but Timorese officials showed little interest or initiative.[27] The SPSC's most substantial outreach effort occurred in 2005 when the deputy Prosecutor General for Serious Crimes visited 11 communities to explain why the United Nations had decided to end the trials.[28] The Timorese experience shows that effective outreach is not an automatic function of proximity or hybridity—it requires financial and political support.

The Institutional Structure for Outreach at the ECCC

Despite the relatively clear lessons provided by preceding tribunals, the ECCC was designed without explicit institutional provision for outreach. The Framework Agreement and ECCC Law say nothing about the Court's outreach to victims and the general population. Before the Court began operations in 2006, UN and Cambodian officials agreed to create a small public affairs office. A Cambodian appointee would head the office, reflecting the logic that national ownership can help connect survivors to the process as well as the Government's desire to control public information. To head the office, the RGC selected Australian-born Helen Jarvis, an advisor to Deputy Prime Minister Sok An with close ties to the government. She worked alongside UN-appointed Public Affairs Officer Peter Foster and Cambodian-appointed Press Officer Reach Sambath.

The history of public feuds between the United Nations and Cambodian Government and the inherent sensitivity of public information functions—especially in a postcommunist state such as Cambodia—made outreach an obvious potential battleground at the Court and an area in which the hybrid institution would likely be strained. Foster notes that "the UN's expectations for the mixed [public information] and communication office were low,"[29] as UN officials anticipated struggles over how the ECCC's work would be portrayed.

It was also unclear how the Court would prioritize goals such as information provision, support for victims, survivor participation, and critical engagement. NGO outreach advocates urged the ECCC to move beyond a "transparency model" focused on information provision toward an "engagement model" premised on social dialogue,[30] but doing so would entail resource commitments and openness to possible public critiques. Craig Etcheson, a former investigator in the Office of the Co-Prosecutors (OCP), recalls that different ideas on what forms of outreach to prioritize "manifested themselves all along at the ECCC" and became sources of "constant struggle."[31]

Institutionally, the Court divided outreach functions and assigned responsibilities to two distinct offices, though neither was invested with the express mandate or resources to prioritize extensive two-way public dialogue. In 2007, the ECCC judges formalized the public affairs office with the passage of the Internal Rules, which provided that the OA "shall establish a Public Affairs Section which shall have the duty of disseminating information to the public regarding the ECCC."[32] As discussed in chapter 7, the Internal Rules also established a Victims Unit (VU) headed by a Cambodian with an international deputy, responsible for "[assisting] the Public Affairs Section in outreach activities related to victims," such as planning public forums with Court officials, sharing information with victims, and arranging for survivors to visit the proceedings.[33] These offices are formally independent of each other.

Although the Public Affairs Section (PAS) and the Victims Unit—later renamed the Victim Support Section (VSS)[34]—both undertake outreach functions, neither is a dedicated outreach office per se. Their mandates overlap to a certain extent, but in practice, the PAS has concentrated on what it calls the "macro" approach to outreach—focusing on public information and a broad audience of donors, NGOs, and the general population.[35] The VU/VSS has primarily taken a "micro" approach of facilitating participation by civil parties and complainants in the Court proceedings.[36]

The Court's Outreach Functions[37]

The ECCC's mixed composition and in-country location have offered significant advantages for outreach and led to important successes, but the Court never reached its full potential. The early decision not to compete with NGOs for funding was the most important initial constraint on effective Court outreach, but over time the key concern for NGOs and activists became a lack of institutional will to engage in two-way communications with the broader victim population, especially at times when the ECCC was wracked by political divisions. The Court's mixed structure also presented a significant impediment to institutional accountability, as both UN and Cambodian officials have been loath to speak for the entire Court on sensitive issues.

Scarce Funding and Reliance on Civil Society

Like other mass crimes courts, the ECCC's initial budget provided scant funding for public affairs and little funding for travel to conduct outreach activities. Helen Jarvis and Peter Foster presented this as a conscious decision to leave outreach to NGOs and focus PAS efforts on public relations. The decision may have been driven by a lack of willing funders. Foster asserts that the restrictions on the outreach budget "came from all sides, the UN, the donors and the Cambodian officials."[38] However, to a large degree, the budget for outreach was kept small within the ECCC due to the fact that Cambodia had a developed NGO sector with some organizations well-equipped to assist in outreach and help the Court conserve resources.[39]

Indeed, civil society was more developed in Cambodia than in Sierra Leone or East Timor, and to date at least 15 civil society groups have worked with the ECCC on outreach in a variety of areas.[40] Thus, in November 2006, OA Director Sean Visoth told the Friends group of donor states that most of the ECCC's challenges stemmed from the lack of funds to support public outreach trips and encouraged donors to fund NGO projects if outreach was to be successful.[41] However, former ICTY official David Tolbert cautioned U.S. officials that the underfunded outreach scheme would be "detrimental to any hopes for a legacy effect of the ECCC on Cambodia's judicial system."[42]

The ECCC received modest additional resources for outreach activities in 2007 when the Swiss government paid for an international Outreach Officer for one year.[43] In 2008–9, the PAS budget increased,[44] partly due to the efforts of new PAS chief Reach Sambath to secure Cambodian Government funding to bring members of the public to observe proceedings. By 2011, the Court had five Cambodian staff positions in outreach alongside two UN-appointed officials, in addition to six Cambodian staffers within the VSS assigned specifically to outreach.[45] Yet resources remained limited and dwindled after the *Duch* trial. In 2011, the budget for outreach—which had grown to approximately 500,000 dollars per year—was slashed due to fewer planned outreach sessions, and not all of the funds in the budget were actually received or spent on outreach. Outreach functions also suffered significant cuts as part of the Court's "austerity measures" in 2013.[46]

The ECCC's slim outreach budget was predicated on its ability to lean heavily on local civil society organizations throughout the process to spread word about the tribunal.[47] Early in the Court's lifetime, the Open Society Justice Initiative (OSJI) established monthly informational exchange meetings for NGOs. The Public Affairs Section was soon attending and "using their [outreach] programs as a vehicle for public outreach."[48] Christoph Sperfeldt, who worked first as an advisor to the Cambodian Human Rights Action Committee and later with the VSS, recalls: "Cambodian NGOs filled the gap and dominated the field of outreach until at least 2009, after which the Court gave further attention to its outreach program."[49]

Partnering with NGOs was a sensible strategy, as NGOs have extensive field networks and experience in local communities and are able to operate at relatively low costs. However, some experts suggest overreliance on civil society had drawbacks. Sperfeldt argues that "the lack of an outreach strategy among the ECCC and civil society created problems with developing consistent messages about the Court," as well as managing victims' expectations.[50] Moreover, some civil society groups found it difficult to engage with the ECCC on outreach due to the lack of a "focal point within the Court," such as an NGO liaison officer,[51] as well as PAS's preference for public relations over dialogue. Scholar Mychelle Balthazard notes research indicating that mass media is a more efficient means of communication than specific community outreach activities—especially at the beginning of a process—and says, "The absence of an early [ECCC] mass media campaign and the focus on community meetings was a limitation of relying too much on NGOs."[52]

NGOs started losing outreach funding after 2010, perhaps partly due to the increase in PAS activities, particularly bringing large numbers of persons to observe Court proceedings. Currently, there is little available funding for civil society to complement Court activities, reportedly in part due to the fact that state donors do not want to fund outreach related to Cases 003/004.[53]

Printed and Online Outreach Materials, Radio Program

One of the first public outreach initiatives was the creation of a booklet entitled "An Introduction to the Khmer Rouge Trials" with basic information about the Court. The booklet was designed to be accessible to ordinary Cambodians, with lean text and engaging images. In spring 2008, the ECCC launched a helpful monthly newsletter called *The Court Report* in English and Khmer including updates on various aspects of its work, later posting it online and using NGOs to help distribute it.[54] After the *Duch* verdict, the Court produced a short and simple leaflet on his verdict, and in June 2013 the Court produced a booklet on how to become a civil party in Cases 003 and 004.[55] The ECCC has also built and maintained a sophisticated website with a wealth of information and Court documents. Independent of the Court, the "Cambodia Tribunal Monitor," co-hosted by the Northwestern University School of Law and the Documentation Center of Cambodia (DC-Cam), provides live online feeds of the proceedings and relevant documents and analysis.[56]

These efforts have made information about the Court quite easy to find for Cambodians and foreigners with Internet access. They appear to have had a relatively small impact in the countryside, however, due to high rates of functional illiteracy, the limited numbers of booklets printed, and uneven distribution across the country.[57] Posters and stickers about the Court also advertise its activities with the obvious drawback of extremely limited content in the form of a single phrase or slogan.[58] In November 2011, the Court launched its first radio program, offering weekly highlights of the Court's Case 002 trial hearings and a call-in program with guest speakers.[59] Regrettably, that program had to be suspended in late 2012 for lack of funds but was relaunched for Case 002/01 closing arguments.[60]

Village Forums

Other PAS initiatives have tried to build broader public understanding through trips to provincial villages, schools, and public forums. The Court's proximity to survivors and involvement of Khmer staff indisputably raised its capacity to conduct these forms of outreach. A few outreach events have been instigated and organized by the Court. For example, in early 2008 the Co-Investigating Judges planned a town hall–style outreach meeting in the former Khmer Rouge stronghold of Pailin, largely to put potential witnesses at ease, followed by a PAS effort to distribute informational materials in the area.[61]

Most village forums related to the ECCC process have been led by civil society organizations, however. NGO enterprise has increased the remit of outreach activities to include education and dialogue beyond the Court's in-house capacity.[62] Activities that build on the ECCC's mandate to address broader themes are part of a "multiplier" effect that has enabled NGOs to use the trials as a portal through which to address other topics, including some that had long been taboo.

For example, the Center for Social Development (CSD) held a series of public forums involving various ECCC officials, including dialogue on "justice and history" and "reconciliation and healing" alongside question-and-answer sessions with selected Court officials.[63] DC-Cam also organized a series of village forums including ECCC officials to educate the public about the tribunal and encourage dialogue about the Khmer Rouge experience.[64] The Khmer Institute for Democracy, human rights group ADHOC, and others have also organized outreach sessions.[65] Although all organizations except DC-Cam cut general outreach activities in 2010 when less donor funding became available, some continued to broadcast radio shows or distribute newsletters, and others focused their scarce resources on civil party participation.

Public Access to the Proceedings

Among the most noteworthy aspects of the ECCC's outreach has been its success—often through NGO partnerships—in making the trial proceedings publicly available. The ECCC is designed to be accessible to the public. The Framework Agreement emphasizes that openness is a mechanism for ensuring fairness and "credibility of the procedure."[66] The ECCC Law therefore mandates:

> Trials shall be public and open to representatives of foreign States, of the Secretary-General of the United Nations, of the media and of national and international non-government organizations unless in exceptional circumstances the Extraordinary Chambers decide to close the proceedings for good cause in accordance with existing procedures in force where publicity would prejudice the interests of justice.[67]

The Internal Rules provide further that, with certain exceptions, "[t]he Office of Administration shall ensure a public broadcast of the trial hearings."[68] Neither international law nor Cambodian domestic law requires that criminal trials be broadcast publicly.[69] Thus, in adopting the rules, the ECCC judges took an unprecedented step toward promoting transparency.

Relative to other international and hybrid courts, the ECCC has been extremely active in arranging for public visits to the courtroom gallery and tribunal premises, arranging for free public transport to the premises or partnering with civil society groups. This became a particular focus of Reach Sambath, who replaced Helen Jarvis as head of the PAS in June 2009. The ECCC has the largest public viewing gallery among mass crimes tribunals with nearly 500 seats. The gallery was full nearly to capacity each day during the *Duch* trial[70]—a marked contrast to the experience of fully international courts—and has also had a regular stream of attendees for Case 002 hearings. This is also a striking improvement over the SCSL, which in its early years often had just 10 to 20 people in the public viewing gallery—primarily court reporters and relatives of the accused.[71]

Significant numbers of people have also participated in the Khmer Rouge Tribunal Study Tour Program, which involves a one-day village information session, followed by a one-day tour of the ECCC, Tuol Sleng Genocide Museum, and Choeung Ek Killing Fields (time permitting). More than 31,000 people observed the *Duch* trial in 2009, including approximately 4,000 who came to the Court for the reading of the verdict in the case. Scholars Kheang Un and Judy Ledgerwood argued on the eve of the *Duch* verdict:

> While Cambodians and concerned foreigners have been divided on the value of the tribunal, particularly given the hybrid nature of the tribunal and the limited number of prosecutions, the public education value of the trial of Duch has been worth the expense and difficulties faced thus far.[72]

Between the start of the *Duch* trial in 2009 and the end of 2011, an impressive 111,543 people visited the Court, either to see live proceedings or as part of a Study Tour.[73] In all, nearly 100,000 people attended the 212 days of Case 002 trial hearings held from November 21, 2011, to July 23, 2013.[74] Of these, over 83% were Cambodians who availed themselves of the ECCC's provision of free transportation for group visits.[75] Former Cambodian Public Affairs Officer Huy Vannak says, "Villagers are proud to have been to Court; to them it's like visiting Angkar Wat temple." He also notes that although many government officials would never bother to attend a domestic judicial hearing because they are not seen as important, ministers have visited the ECCC. "These things help change the attitude of [ordinary] people toward courts. It will encourage them to bring cases to court and change their perception of judges."[76]

Of course, outreach is not only a question of numbers. Its success also depends on how well informed individuals are about the process. One Cambodian ECCC staffer repeats a commonly heard criticism that the Court's outreach is "only successful [in terms of] the quantity but not the quality," arguing that the public only understands general facts about the Court but has difficulty following complex factual and legal issues "even [if] they are in the courtroom."[77] Huy acknowledges that the PAS has focused more on the quantity of visitors than the quality of their individual learning experiences.[78] Although more than

200,000 Cambodians have visited the Court, it lacks a budget to enable them to stay overnight in Phnom Penh. Villagers who live in distant provinces must as a consequence travel overnight to reach the Court early in the morning for a full day of activities, becoming tired and losing focus before returning to their homes late that night.[79] This makes it difficult for villagers from remote areas, including many minority groups, to attend. Nevertheless, Huy argues that there is value in bringing large numbers of Cambodians to witness proceedings because "they feel like they own the process."[80]

Outcomes in Public Knowledge and Understanding

The ultimate measure of success in outreach is the extent to which the public—including victims of Khmer Rouge atrocities and their families—are able to understand the process and derive meaning from it. Although it is too early to draw definitive judgments about the ECCC's impact on the Cambodian population, studies on public opinion allow interim assessments to be made. A 2008 survey conducted by the Human Rights Center at the University of California at Berkeley provided impetus for the Court to redouble its outreach efforts. Although most respondents who knew of the ECCC viewed it favorably, 39% of those surveyed were unaware of the Court, and a further 46% had little knowledge of the tribunal.[81]

A second Berkeley survey indicated increasing public knowledge. By 2010 the number of people with no awareness of the ECCC dropped to 25%, and the percentage of people reporting "moderate or higher" knowledge of the Court rose from 15% to 25%.[82] Two-thirds of respondents were able to identify the ECCC as a hybrid court in 2010, in contrast to roughly one-half in 2008.[83]

Several factors likely contributed to this improvement, including expanded NGO programs, the start of the *Duch* trial in 2009, and greater interest and coverage on the part of local media. Some credit certainly belongs to the ECCC, which coordinated media and public access to the Court. The PAS set up live video feeds to the proceedings. With PAS support, Asian International Justice Initiative and Khmer Mekong films also produced a weekly television show called "Duch on Trial," which appeared on Cambodia's leading television network. Nearly one-quarter of people responding to the 2010 Berkeley survey reported watching "Duch on Trial."[84]

On the other hand, the attention paid by the regular Khmer-language media to the ECCC has been minimal and inconsistent. Journalists tend to cover the Court on a big news day, such as the first day of trial, but then attention tapers off. Moreover, often the local media merely reproduces content from PAS press statements without adding any analysis. In this way, the PAS controls the message, and Cambodians generally have no knowledge of internal court debates unless they read the English-language *Cambodia Daily* or *Phnom Penh Post* newspapers.[85]

As mentioned above, the PAS was established primarily to conduct media and public relations—a narrower and less resource-intensive function than outreach. Due to its narrow mandate, it operates more like a press office than an outreach office. The primary consequence is that it has never prioritized engaging victims in two-way conversations. Thus, while an impressive number of people have witnessed Court proceedings and know the Court exists, there is little if any evidence that outreach efforts lead participants to understand the process in any depth. Even people who are interested in the ECCC's work often have unrealistic expectations about what it can achieve.

Some Cambodians hoped that international participation in the Court would bring "complete justice" and understanding about what happened to the country and to their families, and result in reparations and compensation. The Court has largely failed to temper these expectations by explaining why and how it makes decisions that shape the scope of what will be addressed at trial and affect the participatory rights of victims. For example, the PAS did not distribute any information about how the Case 002 indictment was split into different trial segments, why this was done, and what the impact would be on the story told at trial. Eight months after severance, some civil parties said they didn't understand how or why the case had been divided.[86] Panhavuth Long of the Cambodian Justice Initiative says, "Court officials always say, 'The role of the court is to prosecute. It's your problem you don't understand what's going on because you don't ask and don't turn on your TV.' But you can't betray your constituency."[87]

Challenges of a Split Public Affairs Section

In addition to resource constraints, ECCC outreach sometimes has faced challenges in managing a single coherent and credible message between the two sides of the Court. Its divided outreach structure, like so many of its elements, leaves it acutely vulnerable to conflict between its national and international halves. Tasks and authorities were vague from the outset, and "official lines of responsibility were very unclear."[88] The PAS was initially less divided than other aspects of the Office of Administration (OA), due both to its small size and to the fact that its members generally saw eye-to-eye on the importance of outreach and public dialogue.[89] Yet there were significant differences in Cambodian and international approaches to outreach at the Court.

According to Foster, the PAS had support from essentially all international officials at the ECCC and most of the judges. Senior Cambodian administrators and Court officials appeared to "not understand the impact of communication and outreach fully and had some reservations about the level of transparency for which we were advocating," although they "did not interfere with our work" and became appreciative in some cases.[90] The two sides also favored different styles of communication. Foster asserts that "[s]enior Cambodian officials saw it as a mostly one-way communication flow to give information, while the international side understood it as more of a two-way dialogue."[91]

Both its small budget and the abundance of "bosses" that its Cambodian personnel are required to satisfy have constrained the national side of the PAS, making it more reactive than proactive and compromising the staff's ability to assert independence and forge unified messages.[92] When controversies have arisen, the PAS has reflected the broader division between the two sides of the Court, with the national Press Officer authorized only to speak on behalf of the Cambodian side, and the UN-appointed Press Officer entitled only to speak for the international side.[93] Foster argues that the challenges faced by the PAS were closely tied to the structure of the Court:

> The split administration . . . was a nightmare. Everything was duplicated, lines of responsibility were not clear, there was a clear division between national and international staff in terms of working conditions, rights and protections, and most frustratingly, there were often strong disagreements over key issues between senior officials, leaving the [public affairs] office struggling to find a way to work with a single voice. This was most clearly evident from the corruption scandal.[94]

In such instances, the lead Cambodian and UN public affairs representatives have sometimes contradicted one another as they speak for their respective sides. For observers of the Court, and particularly for ordinary Cambodians, dueling press releases have caused confusion and reduced confidence and trust in the process.[95]

A particularly notable example occurred in June 2010, when UN Legal Communication Officer Lars Olsen announced that "the first investigative acts in Cases 003 and 004 [had been] taken [on the previous] Friday in the form of confidential rogatory letters [. . .], which were signed by *both* [Co-Investigating Judges]."[96] In response, Cambodian Interior Ministry spokesman Lt. Gen. Khieu Sopheak reiterated the government's opposition to the new prosecutions, citing Hun Sen's warnings of possible unrest. "Just only the top five leaders [are] to be tried," he said. "Not six. Just five."[97] As discussed in chapter 6, the next day, Cambodian Co-Investigating Judge (CIJ) You Bunleng struck his signature from the rogatory letters and returned them to his international counterpart, Marcel Lemonde, with a note explaining that he no longer believed it was "opportune to take action in Cases 003 and 004."[98]

That evening, ECCC Public Affairs Chief Reach Sambath issued a statement on You Bunleng's dissociation from the rogatory letters, describing the media statement based on Lars Olsen's comments as "non-basis information."[99] Although Reach Sambath originally said that his statement was issued in consultation with the UN side of the office, soon afterward, he acknowledged publicly that his media alert "was unilaterally sent on behalf of the national component of the court . . . without consultation or advance information to the international component of the ECCC."[100] That admission was an evident attempt to mend relations with his UN counterparts, but showed that on the most sensitive subjects, the PAS, like the rest of the Court, would break down into its two component sides.

Transparency Concerns

Some of the Court's most important work has been confidential, leading to diminished public transparency and limiting the information outreach officials can provide.[101] That issue is directly tied to the structure of the Court—the ECCC's adoption of a civil law model of confidential investigations necessarily shrouds some of its work in secrecy.[102] According to Panhavuth Long, this prolonged period of concealment contributed to unrealistic victim expectations about what the Court would be able to address. He says, "The moment the investigation becomes public it contributes to realistic expectations. . . . It is [the Court's] responsibility to manage expectations and if they don't it is a bad model. You can't go back and undo expectations."[103]

The parameters of confidentiality were tested by counsel and journalists who have sought to keep the public informed about procedural controversies. For example, when the CIJs closed Case 003 with a one-sentence press statement, the international Co-Prosecutor released public information about the crime sites and his additional investigative requests, and was rebuked for acting beyond his authority.[104]

The Court has occasionally threatened to sanction persons who have revealed nonpublic information, relying on a provision in the Internal Rules allowing it to discipline anyone who "interferes with the administration of justice."[105] For example, in 2009, the CIJs warned Ieng Sary's defense counsel for publicly releasing confidential documents—their own motions related to their client's health and strictly legal issues—on a public website.[106] The team had questioned the Court's selective publication of documents, suggesting that the CIJs were "suppressing Defence filings which may be embarrassing or which call into question the legitimacy and judiciousness of acts and decisions of the judges" under the "fig leaf" of confidentiality.[107] Both civil parties and the Co-Prosecutors supported the team's underlying request for greater transparency. Nevertheless, to date there is a lack of clarity and, in the view of some parties, a lack of consistent reasoning as to why some motions and decisions are made public (with redactions if necessary) and others remain confidential.[108]

Although some degree of confidentiality is legitimate, the Court has applied its coercive power inconsistently and primarily in relation to revelations associated with judicial interference.[109] For example, in 2010 the Court threatened to sanction reporters who referenced confidential documents from Pre-Trial Chamber (PTC) proceedings that alleged political bias at the Court.[110] In 2011, the PTC judges issued a press release similarly threatening journalists with sanctions amid the Case 003/004 dispute, as media reports referenced two leaked prosecutorial submissions describing the crimes of the five new suspects,[111] whose names first had been made public by an enraged civil party months previously. The release of the submissions was an egregious (though not unprecedented) breach of the Court's confidentiality rules and a potential danger to witnesses named therein. However, it also revealed the depth of internal frustration over the CIJs handling of the cases and failure to share basic information with the public about its work through the Public Affairs Section.[112]

Problems related to corruption and judicial interference have led to an extended media focus on those issues, discouraging judges and other Court officials from participating in outreach events, and consuming time and resources that could otherwise have been used to educate the public about the ECCC's activities. Moreover, scandals and crises provide strong incentives for Court officials to defend the institution and reduce transparency, which can undermine the credibility of its communications as a whole.[113] For example, when ECCC staff, Court monitors, and the media were all alleging that the CIJs had closed Case 003 without fully investigating, the PAS Court Report contained only a sanitized discussion of Court investigation procedures, neglecting to mention the existence of the raging controversy.[114] According to civil society advocates, the Court's early lack of outreach and information on Cases 003 and 004—even after the suspects' names were leaked to the press in early 2011—is a major reason why fewer victims have submitted complaints and civil party applications for those cases.[115]

These events have contributed to an impression that the ECCC seeks to prevent unflattering information from emerging about the tribunal, which risks diminishing the credibility of the Court's own informational functions.[116] Nevertheless, Huy Vannak points out that the ECCC is the first court in Cambodia to have a public affairs section, and this makes it more transparent than other Cambodian courts. He says that Cambodians "know almost everything" about what is going on, and this provides a good model for building rule of law.[117]

Overall Outreach Performance

To the extent that the ECCC faced funding challenges in outreach, it was largely able to surmount those challenges by relying on NGO initiatives. The depth of understanding that many Cambodians have of the process is shallow, but the Court and its civil society partners together have made impressive progress in terms of the number of individuals they have reached and the range of outreach mechanisms they have designed. Most ECCC officials rightly consider outreach to be one of the Court's relative successes.[118]

Yet the Court's other functional problems—the slow pace of the proceedings, corruption allegations, and political interference—put its outreach efforts in jeopardy. Chandra Lekha Sriram notes that in Sierra Leone, "outreach, and perhaps the image of the Court generally, suffered from an obstacle beyond its control—embedded biases and preconceptions. For at least some who view the Court as politicized, it is possible that no amount of outreach will change their minds."[119] That is a real risk to the ECCC as well. Although the ECCC is fortunate to have had relatively strong public support in Cambodia to date, that support could erode if the Court is not perceived to produce independent and impartial judicial results.

LEGACY

The United Nations has participated in hybrid tribunals with the explicit goal of strengthening national judicial systems. In a 2010 report to the Security Council, UN Secretary-General Ban Ki-moon noted that the purpose for creating the SCSL and ECCC "includes the strengthening of the local judicial system." In East Timor and Kosovo, "[b]uilding capacity was one of the principal aims," and at the Bosnian War Crimes Chamber, the "aim was to build the capacity of judges, prosecutors and staff."[120] Kofi Annan expressed the expectation that the ECCC should have "considerable legacy value, inasmuch as it will result in the transfer of skills and know-how to Cambodian court personnel."[121]

The potential of hybrid courts to leave a stronger positive legacy than off-site international courts is only that—a potential. Proximity to the survivor population and local judiciary can backfire and create a negative or "reverse" legacy by draining talent from the local system, diverting attention from the need for domestic reform, or producing shoddy trials that undermine public confidence in national courts.[122] There are also legitimate concerns among tribunals' staff and donors that hybrid courts are not the right institutions to lead efforts at local capacity-building, because doing so diverts scarce human and financial resources from their main task of conducting complex criminal trials.[123]

Indeed, capacity-building has been a challenge at other hybrid courts. Like its hybrid peers, the SCSL was justified partly on its capacity-building potential. Former Registrar Robin Vincent argued that the SCSL could provide three types of legacy to Sierra Leone: brick-and-mortar infrastructure, human resource development, and institutions.[124] Its constitutive documents include no mention of legacy, however. Modest legacy initiatives were late to emerge, and contact between the Special Court and ordinary courts was limited, leading a key trial monitor to conclude that the SCSL had "fallen far short of expectations in contributing to national legal development."[125] The mixed panels in Kosovo suffered from shortfalls in resources and difficulty recruiting experienced international staff that hampered capacity-building.[126] For similar reasons, the Timorese Special Panels have also been criticized for failing to exercise their full capacity-building potential.[127] Elena Baylis argues that, with respect to legacy, "hybrid courts have thus far failed to fulfill their promise."[128]

The Lack of a Legacy Mandate or Office

Perhaps in part due to concerns about limited resources, the Framework Agreement, ECCC Law, and Internal Rules include no explicit mention of the Court's legacy and do not mandate the ECCC to undertake specific activities to build local capacity or encourage domestic legal reform. The Internal Rules include only a single such provision, requiring the Defence Support Section (DSS) to "[o]rganize training for defense lawyers in consultation and cooperation with the BAKC" (the Bar Association of the Kingdom of Cambodia).[129] With the exception of the DSS, the absence of a clear legacy mandate has contributed to uncertainty among ECCC officials regarding who has the authority or responsibility to lead capacity-building activities and other legacy initiatives.[130] The lack of a specific mandate allows Court units to be entrepreneurial and capitalize on opportunities for legacy projects,[131] but in practice Court officials have tended to prioritize work associated with the criminal cases and other mandated Court functions.[132]

The ECCC's Legacy Functions

In August 2009, OSJI issued a damning interim conclusion about legacy efforts at the ECCC:

> One of the primary justifications for locating the court within the Cambodian court system was the hope that it would leave a positive legacy on rule of law reform in Cambodia. This does not appear to be happening in any material way. Capacity building, developing model practices for domestic courts, and providing an example of justice that meets international standards and defies impunity are often cited as goals of the ECCC. Yet these goals are unlikely to be met without a sustained and concerted effort from senior court officials and political will from the government. Unfortunately both appear to be lacking . . . Little has been done by the court to build the understanding or capacity of legal professionals and personnel outside of the ECCC.[133]

Despite the lack of a formal legacy mandate, in early 2010 the ECCC established within the OA a Legacy Advisory Group to discuss issues related to the Court's legacy and a Legacy Secretariat to decide upon and execute strategies.[134] In early 2010, the OHCHR also established a post for a Legacy Officer to work with the ECCC. Both the Advisory Group and Secretariat are composed of a mix of national and international officials, but neither group has been very active to date. According to one senior court official, the 30-member Advisory Group "is more or less set up to fail," having as of fall 2012 completed only a 12-page memorandum on meeting procedures.[135] Due to a lack of leadership, neither side has demonstrated the will or ability to take on responsibilities beyond the Court's narrow judicial mandate. Although some international personnel seek to engage in legacy initiatives, senior UN administrators want legacy to be the responsibility of the national side, leading to an overall lack of accountability.[136]

The potential residual benefits of hybrid courts for domestic legal systems are commonly classified into at least four types: physical infrastructure and materials, professional development, law reform, and promotion of a rule-of-law culture.[137] ECCC contributions to each are discussed briefly below.[138]

An Informational Legacy

The ECCC is contributing to two archival efforts: a physical repository for ECCC records—"The ECCC Documentation Center"—to be housed in a new building paid for by the Japanese Government, and a virtual repository of Court and NGO documents called the "Virtual Tribunal" (VT) that will be based at that location.[139] The VT project is being created as a joint project by the ECCC together with the Hoover Institution at Stanford University, the War Crimes Studies Center at the University of California at Berkeley, and the East-West Center in Honolulu.

Although other online tribunal resources exist—most notably the Court's own website and the Cambodia Tribunal Monitor—the Virtual Tribunal project would include additional multimedia interactive and educational features specifically designed for domestic capacity-building. It thus offers a potentially valuable resource for a new generation of Cambodian law students and scholars, as well as other interested survivors.[140] Although Internet penetration remains low in outlying areas of Cambodia, it is increasing steadily, especially among the university and secondary school students most apt to join the ranks of the legal profession.

Like other areas of the ECCC's work, the creation of a physical legacy entails political considerations and a meeting of the minds between national and international officials. In the case of the Virtual Tribunal, the United Nations has deferred to national leadership. In its 2012–13 budget proposal, the ECCC requested no funding for the international side of the tribunal for legacy but $905,000 for the Cambodian side over a two-year period, "particularly related to the Virtual Tribunal."[141] It also requested five new posts, all on the national side of the Court, focused on developing the Virtual Tribunal.[142] None of that budgetary request was approved, and the proposed Legacy Component has received no funding or personnel.[143] UN disengagement and denial of funds show that legacy remains a low priority at the ECCC and suggests donor disinterest in (or distrust of) the proposed Cambodian-led legacy program.

Strong national participation in legacy functions is entirely appropriate, but the absence of UN involvement will enable the Cambodian Government to control the content of the Virtual Tribunal site and other legacy programs, and to exclude information it considers controversial or unfavorable. Given the contentious politics surrounding the tribunal and current weakness of the rule of law in Cambodia, that poses a considerable risk to the endeavor. There is also concern that expensive and centralized legacy projects are highly susceptible to graft, and that some government officials seek to pursue them for that purpose.[144] This has implications both for donor interest and the willingness of those implementing these projects to see them through in a way that makes them meaningful for ordinary Cambodians.

Capacity-Building

Both international appointees and Cambodians working at the ECCC consistently emphasize that the skills development of individuals working at the ECCC will be a Court legacy. A number cite the advantages of hybrid legal teams—both in terms of efficacy and knowledge sharing. Former head of the Defence Support Section Rupert Skilbeck emphasizes the complementary nature of the skills of local and international lawyers.[145] International lawyers generally have taken the lead on written submissions—which are not a prominent part of normal Cambodian practice—and help develop their Cambodian counterparts' ability to engage in effective legal drafting and reasoning. Cambodian lawyers play more prominent roles in witness interviews and review of Khmer-language materials, providing social and historical context that helps educate their UN-appointed peers.[146] Lawyers practicing at the ECCC, such as Karim Khan who led a civil party team in Case 001, say their work has been facilitated immensely by the presence of Cambodian lawyers.[147] They speak the three languages of the Court and understand the evidence, the context, and the factual matrix (i.e., setting) best. They also best understand Cambodian procedures—the foundation of the Internal Rules.

Unsurprisingly, skill sharing and knowledge transfer have occurred most readily when nationals and internationals have worked together—which has not been the case in all ECCC offices, with some physically segregated on opposing sides of the hall. The Office of the Co-Prosecutors has been praised for making a concerted effort to have mixed local and international teams working together to share their knowledge. Etcheson notes: "From the beginning, both Robert Petit and Bill Smith emphasized the need for close cooperation. To a great extent, Chea Leang and [her deputy] Yeth Chakrya reciprocated that point of view."[148] Although OCP personnel often "spoke metaphorically about the two sides of the hall," they decided early in the process to integrate the office, with the international side hiring some Cambodian staffers and vice versa.[149] The OCP also initiated a staff "happy hour" every Friday afternoon, which one former Cambodian staff member cites as an important mechanism for generating office unity. He says, "each side had a different boss with a different agenda, but the happy hour built team spirit."[150]

Etcheson argues that while "organizational change happens on a generational scale," at the ECCC "technical transfer has been quite marked" and cites the example of the uses of precedent. At the time of the ECCC's inception, there were few if any records of judicial decisions in the country, and judges relied largely on oral traditions and their own past experience. At the ECCC, "national colleagues began to understand the need for precedents in deciding complex legal questions."[151]

OA Director Tony Kranh emphasizes regularly that Cambodians who work at the Court will be an asset to the Cambodian legal system when they return.[152] Indeed, both ECCC advocates and some Cambodians point to the possibility that norms and practices at the ECCC will "trickle down" to the domestic judicial system.[153] Cambodian defense and civil party lawyers involved in the ECCC proceedings have by all accounts improved their knowledge of relevant laws and procedures and their skills as advocates, and they continue to practice as part of the local bar association. In a legal system with limited capacity, though they are only several in number, their ability to train others could have a nonnegligible impact. For example, Judge Nil Nonn, president of the Trial Chamber, has said that he has appreciated learning from the "reasoning culture" of his international counterparts on the bench and would seek to raise capacity of Cambodian judges he trains in the future.[154] Nevertheless, it is not clear incidental job training alone can generate an ECCC capacity-building legacy.

Court monitor Heather Ryan has been more circumspect about the likelihood that capacity will "trickle down":

> [S]ome transfer of skills has already resulted from the ECCC structure of having experienced international judges, prosecutors, and defence counsel working side by side with Cambodian counterparts, who are less experienced in complex criminal cases. As the first trial progressed, there was visible improvement in the skill demonstrated by the Cambodian trial judges and counsel for the parties . . . However, it remains to be seen if, and how, they will be able to transfer these skills when they return to the domestic court setting.[155]

OA Deputy Director Knut Rosandhaug has similarly noted that the fruits of capacity-building will be seen only when the ECCC finishes its work and national staff return to the domestic system.[156]

The Court has undertaken only modest efforts to train non-ECCC personnel. Targeted education and training initiatives have primarily involved one-off workshops, conferences, and lectures, as well as a few internships, but little has been done to formalize the capacity-building process. Skilbeck argues that the ECCC's capacity-building potential will be unfulfilled absent considerably more concrete institutional focus on training activities.[157] The DSS—the only part of the ECCC with a specific mandate to that effect—has indeed been active. Its legacy program is organized around three pillars: training sessions for Cambodian defense lawyers who will practice at the ECCC, internal training seminars, and an outreach program to draw attention to defense rights in the NGO community and general public.[158] It has worked with the OHCHR to organize a months-long training for Cambodian law students about fair trial rights.[159] Many of those programs have been arranged with civil society organizations. The OCP has also offered training sessions to local prosecutors, and the ECCC offers a range of internship programs for aspiring Cambodian lawyers and judges.[160] However, prosecutors and civil party lawyers have emphasized the limits on their offices' possible investment in capacity-building given the workload associated with the main criminal cases.[161]

Demonstration Effect: A Model Court?

Another means of promoting the rule of law is by setting a positive example for local courts to emulate.[162] UN and Cambodian officials, donors, and the Trial Chamber have described the ECCC as a "model court."[163] Deputy Prime Minister Sok An has said more specifically that the ECCC can serve as a "model court" for the Cambodian domestic system.[164] The extent of its ability to serve that function is questionable given the comparatively minuscule resources of local courts,[165] the very different types of legal cases they hear, the existence of powerful incentives to engage in corruption and bow to political pressure, and the mixed example the ECCC has set in those regards.

Some observers stress that the Court is setting an important example for the domestic courts by promoting fair trial concepts—including in particular the presumption of innocence and equality of arms[166]—and the adoption of procedures that promote transparency, certainty, and accountability. In national courts, decisions do not include legal reasoning or citations to authority justifying arrest, detention, or indictment; there are no replies to motions; no active defense; no initial hearing for an accused who may spend an extended period in pretrial custody before seeing a judge. Witnessing how the ECCC handles such issues is exposing both the legal community and the public to fair trial practices and may provide an example of best practices.[167]

For example, former Ieng Sary Co-Lawyer Michael Karnavas argues that, because the ECCC is part of the national court system, its jurisprudence can serve as a model for how domestic courts should be applying international fair trial principles incorporated into Cambodian law through the Constitution.[168] One Cambodian staffer anticipates that domestic courts in Cambodia might follow the ECCC's example by holding an initial hearing before the facts are presented.[169] Panhavuth Long notes that the *Nuon Chea* defense strategy, which included pointing fingers at the Government, would be unheard of in Cambodian courts. He says, "If this defense happened in a national court the lawyers would be disbarred. The process teaches professionalism, and provides an example of how judges should behave."[170] Concomitantly, others note that President Nil Nonn is widely respected for the authoritative manner in which he leads the Trial Chamber's proceedings, and say observers' ability to hear his pronouncements in Khmer makes him a positive role model, building pride in the national judiciary.[171] Moreover, CIJ You Bunleng has already instituted some changes to practices at his second job at the Court of Appeals, including the introduction of a witness room, an audio system, and a computerized case file system to "protect the rights of victims and accused."[172] He is also promoting the creation of a judicial registry to manage administrative matters—which are currently the responsibility of individual judges and their clerks—as well as the publishing of decisions online.[173] Judge You believes the ECCC will have both direct and indirect impacts, including capacity-building and modernizing the procedures followed by Cambodian courts.[174]

There is little evidence yet of ECCC impact on the Cambodian judiciary as a whole. Many Court personnel and analysts emphasize that such change is a "multi-generational project."[175] One Cambodian staff member at the ECCC thinks that "there will be an impact, but very little," because improving the Cambodian domestic legal system has less to do with formal laws and procedures than with individual choices to participate in a culture of judicial corruption.[176] Similarly, a former staff member says that judicial reform will take many years and must begin with individuals. He asserts that some procedures Cambodians have learned working at the ECCC will carry over—but not when politics takes precedence. In his view, the fact that Sean Visoth is still technically the Director of OA is a perfect example of the tension between politics and justice and the barriers to judicial reform: the Cambodian Government does not acknowledge that Visoth is corrupt, just as corruption is unacknowledged as a problem in local courts. He argues, "It's never going to change. The Government doesn't want to look bad so they used other excuses for his departure."[177] Ou Virak has likewise emphasized that whatever role the Court plays in developing local skills and knowledge, there will be little change "without a fundamental shift in the government's commitment to the rule of law."[178]

Cambodian judicial reform cannot be accomplished simply through technical training or new laws.[179] States taking part in the Council on Legal and Judicial Reform have long seen the continued failure to adopt three fundamental laws regulating different aspects of an independent judiciary to be the major stumbling block preventing implementation of best practices throughout the country. However, Cambodia has passed 400 laws since 1993, including 16 in 2011 alone,[180] and most laws remain unenforced or unevenly enforced by the judiciary. The largest barrier to rule of law is a domestic legal culture characterized by executive dominance, patronage, and corruption.

Regrettably, the ECCC's institutional weaknesses, including inconsistent application of the rules and susceptibility to corruption and political interference, reinforce negative realities in the local judicial system. These have unquestionably been the "Achilles' heel" of the Court's efforts to date to leave a positive legacy.[181] Michael Karnavas argues that if a court wants to leave behind a rule-of-law legacy and induce people to trust the courts, it needs "uniformity, consistency, and predictability." He notes that if the parties feel uncertainty about the ECCC's rules, the public doubtless does as well. "Are we not teaching additional skills to our local counterparts on how to avoid the application of the rule of law? I think that this is going to be the darkest part of this legacy."[182] This is echoed by a former national ECCC staff member, who wonders if the Cambodian Government's increased invocation of procedural formalities will be used to mask political ends. He says: "When you give them a knife, they can use it."[183]

Numerous court observers also have questioned the impact of the Court's handling of Cases 003 and 004 on its legacy. Professor Sophal Ear has said that the Court will have a negative legacy if the UN lets political interference go unchallenged:

> If the Cambodian Courts have any sort of lesson from that experience, it would probably be that even though you involve the international judicial process, you can still undermine them and go around their will and do whatever you want and get away with it.[184]

Nevertheless, questions of accountability—why crimes are not investigated and the persons responsible brought to justice—and corruption of process, which regularly arise in ordinary Cambodian court proceedings often without raising a stir, are a topic of debate in the context of the ECCC. Although Jeanne Sulzer also worries about the potential for a negative legacy, she finds it hopeful that the Government is discussing impunity issues. She notes that even though it does not support its views with strong legal reasoning, it is being forced to justify its position.[185]

Impact on Cambodian Reality and Perceptions

Thus far, there is no evidence that the ECCC proceedings have impacted the incidence of corruption and political interference in ordinary Cambodian courts. Although the Cambodian National Assembly passed a long-dormant anticorruption law in 2010,[186] judicial corruption remains endemic. In 2012, Cambodia finished 157th in the annual Transparency International rankings on corruption—a ranking that has not changed appreciably in recent years.[187]

It is therefore surprising that there is some evidence suggesting ECCC proceedings have contributed to a modest shift in public perceptions of the rule of law. A striking 72% of Cambodians surveyed in 2010 said that they had more trust in the law than before the *Duch* trial, and the numbers reporting general trust in the court system rose from 36% to 52%. However, 68% reported that going to court involved paying bribes to judges (up from 61% in 2008), and 82% said that involving the police in disputes meant paying bribes (up from 77%).[188] If the substance of the domestic judicial system remains unchanged, it is unlikely that any bump in public trust arising from the *Duch* trial will be long-lasting.

Cambodians have been relatively sanguine about the ECCC itself—perhaps reflecting both their support for the Court's general aims and the nature of the limited information most have received. The Berkeley surveys showed that both before and after the *Duch* trial, large majorities of Cambodians expressed high opinions of the ECCC. In 2008, 67% of respondents said that they believed the Court was neutral, 67% said they believed the judges would be fair, and 87% supported having the ECCC involved in responding to what occurred during the Khmer Rouge period.[189] In 2010, 75% of respondents perceived the Court as neutral, 79% saw it as fair, and 83% wanted it involved in the response to Khmer Rouge crimes.[190] Most also believed that the ECCC would have a positive impact in terms of promoting national reconciliation (from 67% in 2008 to 81% in 2010), rebuilding trust in Cambodia (from 71% to 82%), and bringing justice to Khmer Rouge victims and their families (74% to 76%).[191]

A further survey, conducted in 2011 by the Cambodian human rights group ADHOC and Harvard Humanitarian Initiative, revealed strong support for the Court among Case 002 civil parties as well. The survey focused on 414 ADHOC-assisted civil parties, including 120 designated Civil Party Representatives who have served as "focal points" for the participation of nearly 2,000 others. Most were interviewed shortly before the initial Case 002 hearing, and the results were striking. More than 90% believed that the ECCC would bring justice to them and their families, build trust in Cambodia, and promote reconciliation; more than 70% said the Court was doing enough for victims; and nearly 90% perceived the ECCC as neutral and its judges as fair.[192] Respondents generally demonstrated considerable knowledge about the Court proceedings, getting their information from a range of sources including television and radio,

ADHOC and other NGOs, contact with their lawyers, and meetings with government and Court officials.[193] Whether the Court's subsequent challenges have affected civil party support for the process is unclear.

These public surveys provide some reason for optimism at the Court. Former UN Legal Counsel Hans Corell argues that despite the ECCC's structural flaws and functional challenges, Cambodians have welcomed the trials, and thus the Court "has had a function in Cambodia."[194] If the ECCC is successful in convincing Cambodians that Case 002 is a success, many Cambodians may judge it to have contributed to a positive legacy for the country. However, if the public survey data reflect an uninformed public's inflated expectations about what the Court will accomplish, reaching judgment in Case 002 may not be enough to overcome their disappointment.

A Catalyst for Social Change?

Like any mass crimes court, the ECCC is at best an important part of a broader social process of dealing with past atrocities. The ECCC's core functional responsibilities pertain to administering criminal justice and associated outreach and legacy functions, but its ultimate social impact will depend largely on the extent to which its limited judicial process can help catalyze, unlock, or facilitate other social activities conducive to healing.

Panhavuth Long argues that if it is agreed that the existence of a tribunal is not the end of the process, then the ECCC is a good start. Cambodians are discussing whether crimes were committed, the voices of the victims have been heard, and there is potential accountability for Democratic Kampuchea (DK) crimes. He says that after the Court is concluded, there will be ongoing debate about the regime. "Even though the hearing is not telling you everything, it will enable you to understand somehow about who is *Angkar*."[195] Youk Chhang, a leading accountability advocate who heads DC-Cam, believes that the Court exists at a fortuitous historical moment. Older Cambodian politicians are beginning to retire, and the Court is creating space for new people and new ideas to "break the circle." He says that, in the past, discussions of the Khmer Rouge era were ideological and controlled by elites; but with the creation of the ECCC, all segments of society are able to present their views as equals, contributing to decentralization and increased tolerance for freedom of expression.[196]

Thus, to date, one of the ECCC's greatest contributions is only tangentially related to its mandate—serving as a catalyst for public discussion on topics that were formerly taboo in many corners of Cambodian society. Foremost among these is the discussion of the Khmer Rouge period itself, which shockingly received only a sentence of treatment in official Cambodian history books until very recently. As former UN Special Expert Clint Williamson argues, "proceedings at the Court have brought this issue front and center" in the Cambodian media and helped legitimate it as a topic of public education and discourse.[197] Youk Chhang believes the impact of this discussion will be far-reaching: "By opening a dialogue on some of the most sensitive and controversial parts of their history, Cambodians have been forced to confront basic questions on human rights, the rule of law, and the relationship between a government and its people."[198]

NGOs have used the ECCC process as a springboard for a number of important educational initiatives. For example, DC-Cam and the Ministry of Education have launched an expansive Genocide Education Program throughout Cambodia, embedding Khmer Rouge history as a core part of public high school and college curricula.[199] This has been particularly important in a country where 70% of the population was born after the Pol Pot era. DC-Cam has also used a variety of media including films, books, magazines, photo exhibitions, and radio programs to educate Cambodians about DK history, often presenting such information in village forums while also collecting applications for participation in the ECCC legal proceedings.[200] The Transcultural Psychosocial Organization (TPO) has conducted outreach through events and radio to raise awareness about trauma, including trauma inflicted under Khmer Rouge rule, and has provided therapy to some survivors in connection with the proceedings.[201] This is also of great significance in a country where knowledge of mental health issues is lacking and the availability of professional services is woefully inadequate. Although these initiatives are not directly related to the Court, the existence of the Court has in many ways made them possible by generating interest among Cambodians in confronting the consequences of the DK period.

CONCLUSION

The potential for strong outreach and legacy functions is key to justifying the risks of in-country hybrid courts—especially one like the ECCC, in which the United Nations grudgingly accepted a role as junior partner to a government beset by corruption, judicial incapacity, and political interference. Most interviewees identify the Court's in-country location as beneficial, with one senior UN appointee at the ECCC describing it as "an overwhelming positive."[202] Yet many aspects of the ECCC's function predictably have suffered as a result of its hybrid form, and it has not been a financial bargain. Outreach and legacy are among the few aspects in which its function ought to exceed that of fully international courts or fully domestic proceedings with minor UN technical support.

With respect to outreach, ECCC efforts have been a qualified success. The Court and supporting NGOs have managed to make the proceedings accessible to the public on a scale unseen at previous tribunals. Despite confidentiality limitations, the existence of the PAS has contributed to robust media coverage of the proceedings. When compared to the outreach efforts of other international and mixed tribunals—admittedly not a high bar—the Court has performed reasonably well—but not up to its full potential.

All mass crimes courts outreach efforts suffer from a lack of adequate resources, due to the perception of some that this task falls outside of "core" functions and is an extra expense. A court created to try only five or ten persons can be judged a success only if the public understands what it is doing. Due to short life spans and narrow personal jurisdictions, a hybrid court process is inevitably symbolic and thus must achieve more than reaching judgment. Panhavuth Long says, "The trials are not only to prosecute those most responsible. There is also a moral obligation to educate people about how the regime operated, create a historical record and contribute to reconciliation."[203] Although a hybrid court's locale certainly promotes information "trickling down" to the population, a well-developed outreach program is critical to ensuring a positive court legacy and should be counted among its indispensable functions.

Despite indications of relatively strong public support and evidence that the Court has played a useful role in catalyzing discussion about the Khmer Rouge era, the ECCC's legacy remains highly uncertain. Its impact on the modest number of Cambodian ECCC personnel may well have some salutary effects, and the record the Khmer Rouge trials create will be useful for a generation of Cambodian law students, but the ECCC will not catalyze seismic legal reform in Cambodia—an unrealistic demand of any hybrid court, especially in a state with entrenched power structures such as Cambodia. Although the ECCC could prioritize legacy activities more purposefully, it must also attend to myriad other functions. The most important of these is to hold trials that will set a positive example of due process, judicial integrity, and impartiality. The Court's dysfunction in these respects puts its legacy in peril.

CONCLUSION

The ECCC has evoked a wide range of reactions from Cambodian survivors. At times, they have been strongly positive. On the day the Supreme Court Chamber handed down a life sentence to Duch, civil party Bou Meng said, "I am fully relieved and fully satisfied with the court's ruling. 100 percent . . . This court is a good model for the world."[1] Sopheap Chak, program director for Cambodian Center for Human Rights, said, "today is quite historic for Cambodia . . . It is a long-awaited resolution for the victims of Khmer Rouge."[2] Surveys continue to show that large majorities of Cambodians support the ECCC's work even though the Court has not addressed—and almost certainly will not adjudicate—the crimes that most survivors suffered individually.

Yet the ECCC has had a precarious existence, often teetering on the precipice of collapse. Inefficiency and recurrent political impasses have eroded the patience of many Cambodians, especially those most informed about the process. Amid corruption and mismanagement allegations, scholar Sophal Ear, a survivor of the Pol Pot era, expressed frustration with the "theater of the absurd" taking place at the Court and lamented that "the tribunal was essentially hijacked to advance domestic and international agendas."[3] As political interference engulfed Cases 003 and 004 and as scope for victim participation narrowed in Case 002, prominent former civil party Theary Seng withdrew from the process and called the ECCC "a political farce, and irredeemable sham"[4]—citing government obstruction and UN failure at "fulfilling its duties, and more than that [helping] enable the impunity."[5]

International observers have also rendered increasingly bleak assessments of the tribunal. In an early 2012 report, Mark Ellis of the International Bar Association, an "early supporter" of the ECCC who still supports its "overall mission," lamented that "a growing number of problems" undermine "the very legitimacy of the court."[6] Scholar Peter Maguire argues that the Court is perilously close to failing:

> Even if there is no third case, a credible trial of Khieu Samphan, Ieng Sary, Noun Chea and Ieng Thirith, would make it possible to overlook the court's many failings. If Cambodia's E.C.C.C. cannot try the surviving Khmer Rouge leaders before they die, the "mixed tribunal" should be considered an expensive farce never to be tried again.[7]

Now only two defendants remain in Case 002, and if the Court is not seen to have delivered a sound trial and reasonable verdicts, few analysts will consider the ECCC anything more than a costly failure.

From the perspective of those seeking to address impunity in Cambodia, the ECCC's highly flawed structure was arguably the best of an unappealing menu of institutional options. David Scheffer, one of the prime architects of the ECCC, argues that "there is no question that the ECCC was an experiment, but one for which there really was no viable alternative after years of negotiations."[8] He adds:

> It's a humbling exercise for the international community. You're dealing with a sovereign government. You don't necessarily get to dictate the process. You have to negotiate the process . . . In the aftermath, it's extremely easy for critics to point out all the mistakes. But let's talk pragmatically about how you achieve justice.[9]

Given the Cambodian Government's strong bargaining position, a UN-led court was unlikely to win Cambodian consent. The likely alternatives to the ECCC—crude domestic trials by a discredited court system or the absence of charges altogether—would likely have been worse, and advocates for the Court had good reasons to take risks in pursuing accountability for some of history's most heinous crimes. Whether or not the ECCC completes Case 002 effectively and pulls at least modest success from the jaws of possible failure—and whether it thus justifies consuming funds and political capital that could have been expended on other initiatives—the Court must be judged in relation to realistic counterfactuals.

Of course, addressing impunity in Cambodia is not the only impetus behind international involvement in the Khmer Rouge tribunal process. It is also part of a broader effort, led by international criminal lawyers, to entrench and enforce accountability norms. From that perspective, the ECCC has been more problematic, because its functional shortcomings damage the UN's reputation and could undermine the credibility of mass crimes processes in general. To some UN officials and human rights advocates, the Court also sets a "dangerous precedent" for international criminal justice,[10] perhaps encouraging other states to demand majority-domestic courts.

Hans Corell, who as the lead UN negotiator objected to the ECCC's structure, asserts, "I did not want . . . the U.N. emblem to be given to an entity that did not . . . represent the highest international standards,"[11] and adds, "everything I warned against has been happening."[12] Corell argues that many of the Court's problems "could have been avoided with a majority of international judges and a single prosecutor and investigating judge," which would have made the court "a different creature."[13] Looking forward, Corell would "immediately discourage anything like [the ECCC]."[14]

The Court's structural handicaps have indeed contributed to inefficiency and credibility problems, and the Cambodian case thus offers some clear lessons: the Court's divided, cumbersome structure should not be mimicked, and the United Nations should resist arrangements in which it plays junior partner to a national judicial system with dubious capacity and independence. It is important to go beyond these headline lessons, however. Many of the ECCC's problems—such inefficiency, jurisdictional debates, and barriers to effective outreach and capacity-building—reflect common challenges in mass crimes trials that are likely be present even in better-designed courts. Many are also problems of agency more than reflections of the Court's peculiar structure, and in this respect the Court's experience also bears some important (if unfortunate) parallels with proceedings at other mass crimes courts. The Khmer Rouge proceedings offer insights into a number of ways in which these challenges can be addressed.

INTERNATIONAL STANDARDS OF JUSTICE?

Officials and analysts have justified UN involvement in the Khmer Rouge trials, like UN participation in other hybrid courts, partly to ensure compliance with international standards of justice. The ECCC has issued many decisions in line with international precedents. Due to their more extensive formal legal training and experience, international judges at the Court have tended to take the lead in drafting opinions and formulating the legal rationales for decisions. On judicial matters that do not affect clear domestic political sensitivities, the ECCC has functioned much like a fully international court—open to legitimate legal challenges but demonstrating a good faith effort to follow established norms of accountability and due process.

Applying the Court's procedural rules has been a challenge, however, and the Court has breached international standards over highly politicized issues, especially the jurisdictional dispute. These flow foreseeably (though not inevitably) from the ECCC's structure and have been the Court's greatest weakness to date, undermining its judicial credibility despite its many sound decisions on less contentious issues.

The Need for Predictable and Targeted Rules

The novelty of a civil law–based approach to mass crimes cases and the awkward fusion of Cambodian and international procedures via the ECCC's Internal Rules have led to inconsistency in the application of the rules. The absence of predictable rules arguably violates the basic due process rights of defendants and exposes the ECCC to charges of cherry-picking to achieve desired outcomes.

Basing a hybrid court's rules partly on national procedures may facilitate local capacity-building by helping to illustrate sound application of local procedures,[15] but it has proven highly problematic in Cambodia. The use of national procedures as a point of departure at the ECCC was part of an overall government effort to assert ownership and control over the process—a kind of home-field advantage. Sovereignty arguments are weak in this regard, however, especially when local rules are half-formed and unfamiliar to local lawyers.

Domestic rules are also not tailored to mass crimes cases, and in states emerging from conflict, they will seldom if ever be suited to handle such cases without major modification. That is certainly the case in states like Cambodia, where domestic rules were ill-equipped to manage the complex Khmer Rouge trials. In practice, hybrid courts will inevitably look to international precedent, so the lesson for designing future mixed courts is to use existing international procedures as a base. These can be customized to fit country conditions, but the International Criminal Court (ICC) and other existing courts (including the ECCC) should be able to provide a strong template, obviating the need to reinvent the wheel with each new hybrid court—a process that created delay in addition to fairness concerns at the ECCC.

An Independent Majority on the Bench

More serious deviations from international standards of justice have occurred when the Court's judges and other key personnel have locked horns over politically sensitive topics. Corruption has been an important concern, but even more damaging has been the evident political interference in Cases 003 and 004. The Cambodian Government has offered no strong justification for its public opposition, and the United Nations has evaded its responsibility to ensure an independent process through legal fig leaves—arguing that it cannot interfere in an independent judicial process even amid widespread and credible allegations by ECCC staff that the process is not independent.

The supermajority rule adopted at the ECCC—an effort to mitigate the risks of a majority-domestic bench—has been ineffective as a stopgap measure. Indeed, the supermajority rule has arguably contributed to the problem by suggesting that political interference is an inherent part of the process, embedding that expectation in how the Court functions, and reducing incentives for international actors to confront it. These problems exemplify what many critics of the ECCC's hybrid structure asserted during its creation: the imperative of having a strong independent majority on the bench.

Independent judges need not be foreign, but in practice governments that lack the capacity to hold credible domestic proceedings are often the same governments that lack judicial independence. Mass crimes cases invariably have great local political importance, making domestic judges all the more vulnerable to political pressure. The ECCC shows how controlling that pressure can be and how badly it can damage the perceived integrity of the judicial process. Beyond the issue of sovereign control, the ECCC provides almost no evidence that having a majority of domestic judges on the bench improves the Court's function or its public legitimacy or legacy. A court does not need a national majority to communicate the active involvement and ownership of the host government. Architects of future mixed courts should therefore adopt a strong presumption in favor of international majorities on the bench. Doing so will not render a tribunal immune from political influence—international judges can also be subjected to pressure—but offers a much better model than the majority-domestic system at the ECCC.

Retaining Judges with Relevant Training and Expertise

The ECCC example also shows the importance of selecting a greater number of judges with expertise in international criminal law and, even more important, experience managing complex criminal cases. "It's absolutely necessary that they have courtroom experience," asserts Corell.[16] In postconflict states, there is unlikely to be a large number of judges with relevant training. Hybrid courts should select international judges with mass crimes experience. In some instances, as in Cambodia, many international judges also lack such experience, contributing to uncertainty in rule application and inefficiency—an issue that has plagued the ECCC and other hybrid courts and undermines much of the purpose for international involvement.[17] Although judges with international criminal experience have been difficult for hybrid courts to recruit, the proliferation of tribunals should ease that constraint somewhat.[18] Tribunals should also invest in capacity-building on the front end, immersing judges in training in The Hague or elsewhere for several months before commencing cases.[19] The up-front costs of such preparation would likely be more than offset in efficiency savings and more effective, credible jurisprudence.

The Question of Jurisdiction

The Cambodian Government insisted on a majority of Cambodian judges and other elements of control partly to guard against an overly zealous prosecution. National concerns about controlling the scope of prosecution are not necessarily illegitimate, and international actors often share those concerns, but they must be addressed more clearly in negotiations over the statute for a hybrid court. The question of jurisdictional bounds is one of the most difficult to resolve in creating any mass crimes tribunal. Judicial independence requires allowing the prosecutor some discretion to "follow the evidence," but in mass crimes courts there normally will (and must) be limits imposed by political decision-makers. The ECCC is a painful example of what happens when two passengers embark on a journey together without a sufficiently clear agreement on their destination.

The result of the failure to reach a political agreement has been overt political interference during the judicial proceedings, which has undermined the ECCC's legitimacy and caused costly, inefficient delays. The most obvious interference has occurred on the Cambodian side, but weary donors and the United Nations have exercised the power of the purse strings in a manner that could also be construed as political interference.

Some of the problem could be resolved by designing a court's structure to give the domestic government less control, but even majority-international courts have faced jurisdictional disputes, as in the cases of East Timor and Sierra Leone. The governing documents for a hybrid court cannot spell out a precise list of suspects to minimize this challenge, which would be an intolerable constraint on prosecutorial discretion. They must, however, be premised on mutual understanding about what would constitute "red lines." The United Nations should not agree to a mixed tribunal in the future—and donors should not force it to do so—without a candid assessment of the political boundaries that its partner is apt to impose.

ADVANTAGES IN EFFICIENCY?

The ECCC's experience shows that hybrid courts with substantial UN participation do not automatically deliver major cost savings. From a financial perspective, the Court has been much more "international" than "domestic." It has been vastly more expensive than a domestic proceeding would be and much less cost-efficient than the Bosnian War Crimes Chamber or even the more comparable Special Court for Sierra Leone (SCSL). On a per-defendant basis, it is even more costly than the International Criminal Tribunals for Rwanda (ICTR) or the former Yugoslavia (ICTY). Generous pay packages and benefits for personnel have contributed, and the Cambodian experience suggests that managing the merger of staff at a mixed court will more likely lead to cost inflation on the national side than savings on the UN side.

The financial situation at the ECCC is certainly an improvement on East Timor, which was crippled from birth by a lack of funds. Hybrid courts are sure to fail if they are created simply to avoid the costs of credible justice, and the ECCC's ability to marshal nearly $200 million for the accountability process is largely positive. Resource allocation and management is a bigger problem than the total price tag. The ECCC has dedicated too few resources to the vital functions of outreach and victim participation, which its location and form empower it to conduct effectively. Resources for those tasks would be much more abundant if the Court were not saddled with structural inefficiencies and plagued by delays and political impasses.

Avoiding Unnecessary Duplication

To a considerable degree, the ECCC's inefficiency stems from its messy and duplicative structure, a result of successive political compromises and a lack of foresight about the functional effects of dividing the Cambodian and international sides and fusing civil law and common law features. The ECCC's separation of national and international staff in key legal and administrative offices is one of its most glaring deficiencies, reducing efficiency and overall organizational cohesion. Hybrid teams can be advantageous in some respects, coupling staff with complementary skills, but the ECCC shows convincingly that two-headed arrangements should be avoided. A hybrid court with a single integrated investigation office and registry would be able to function much more efficiently and decisively.

The fusion of civil law and common law has also produced redundancy. In theory, the idea of investigating judges has appeal as a way to improve efficiency. Former international Co-Investigating Judge Marcel Lemonde contends that they may still "represent the future" of international criminal trials and attributes many of the ECCC's troubles with the OCIJ to common law lawyers who weren't familiar with the civil law system and in some cases "had no desire to become familiar with it."[20] Even if future mass crimes tribunals were to focus on hiring judges and prosecutors with civil law experience, the ECCC proceedings suggest that mass crimes cases will often be too large for one judicial office to investigate completely, creating an institutional logjam. In addition, mass crimes trials will almost inevitably entail an expansive courtroom process—and thus a second full vetting of the evidence—given survivors' compelling interest in observing a public proceeding. At the ECCC, the absence of a defense right to challenge the evidence in a pretrial proceeding made a lengthy trial phase imperative from a due process standpoint as well. Although this latter problem could be corrected by allowing a pretrial defense challenge, the architects of future mass crimes proceedings would be wiser to avoid investigating judges altogether. Their role has created problems due to inefficiency, fairness, and credibility—too much of the process at the ECCC has hinged on the perception of their competence and impartiality.

Lemonde describes the structure of the "cos" and the complex dispute resolution scheme as "a bit monstrous" and "a model of inefficiency,"[21] and many other Court officials agree. Even if future courts include co-prosecutors and/or investigating judges, there is little apparent utility in having a separate pretrial chamber whose decisions are neither final nor appealable. The ECCC's Pre-Trial Chamber also has had too much overlapping responsibility with other chambers, requiring multiple appeals and wasting both funds and time. If a pretrial mechanism does exist, its authority must be circumscribed to a relatively narrow range of functions, such as reviewing indictments and dealing with pretrial detention issues. The Special Tribunal for Lebanon, in which one international judge serves as a pretrial judge performing these functions, provides a more efficient model.[22] So do the ICC's pretrial chambers, which have limited authority to review the pretrial phases of the investigation, ensure the pretrial rights of the accused, and confirm charges.[23] The ECCC's problem of multiple appeals bodies also suggests that parties should have a direct right to appeal pretrial rulings to the appeals chamber, the decisions of which will be final and binding on the trial chamber. Such a mechanism, which exists at the ICC, would offer ample due process with much more efficiency.

Part of the reason why such a cumbersome system was adopted is that relatively few of the people most crucial to the negotiations for the Court were practiced courtroom lawyers with mass crimes experience. Former international Co-Prosecutor Robert Petit argues,

> [The ECCC] was a cut-rate court. It was designed by people who had insufficient knowledge of the actual court process. Then it was cut up by accountants in terms of structures, staffing, and budget . . . [I]f you had wanted to devise a court that wouldn't work, you would be hard pressed to find a better model.[24]

Corell agrees. "People involved in this kind of process should listen closely to persons with courtroom experience . . . listen to those with courtroom experience," he asserts, repeating the point for emphasis.[25]

Unifying Court Leadership

One of the most common complaints from ECCC personnel is the lack of decisive leadership under the ECCC's two-headed structure. Future hybrid courts should have a court president and registrar with the authority needed to drive through key decisions and impose administrative and budgetary discipline. The individuals chosen to occupy those and other key positions also matter. The ECCC has benefited from having a few personnel with expertise in Khmer Rouge history, as well as a number of officials and defense counsel with ample experience at other hybrid and international courts. Funds would also have been better spent, however, if officials experienced in judicial administration had occupied key administrative positions from the start. The president and registrar must be viewed, inside and outside of the building, as credible and competent in the working of a mass crimes court. They do not necessarily need to be international appointees, but given the limited number of likely candidates in states emerging from conflict, they usually should be.

Strengthening Oversight Mechanisms

Many of the ECCC's problems are related to the weak oversight structures in place for the Court. The United Nations is deeply involved in the Khmer Rouge trials but has been reluctant to exert firm ownership of the process. This is closely related to the lack of clear lines of authority. Among multiple UN entities and personnel involved—the Office of Legal Affairs, Controller's Office, Department of Economic and Social Affairs, UN Development Program, the Special Expert, and the UN-appointed Deputy Director of Administration—it has often been unclear who is in charge, confusing and weakening administration.

As the saga over Cases 003 and 004 drags on, Rupert Abbott and Stephanie Barbour of Amnesty International argue that although the United Nations has used "strong words" regarding Cambodian political interference, it has been guilty of a "lackluster response."[26] Brad Adams of Human Rights Watch has accused the United Nations of "burying its head in the sand."[27] When the UN Secretariat does not "buy into" a hybrid court fully, it is likely to have weak, indecisive management, which contributes to financial inefficiency and administrative irregularities. The United Nations and donor states need to decide in advance whether to own a process or to distance themselves from it. The ECCC shows the reputational and financial problems of going halfway.

If international actors decide to invest heavily in a hybrid court, there needs to be a formal process of donor oversight. Donor states are not stewarding their taxpayers' money well when they agree to fund a court that they cannot or do not meaningfully supervise. Supervision does not mean overreach into judicial functions—it means ensuring that money is productively and transparently spent. The ECCC example also shows that donors should fund a hybrid court as a single entity rather than setting up financial structures that reinforce divisions and add to uncertainties and delays. In general, the best model for any mass crimes court is to be funded through UN-assessed contributions but subjected to rigorous and regular questioning on costs from a dedicated UN office with expertise in the management of mass crimes cases—an office that still does not exist after two decades of UN involvement in international criminal tribunals.

A STRONGER NEXUS TO SURVIVORS?

Without major cost advantages and with the risks that the hybrid model poses to judicial standards, the justification for mixed courts must rest to a large extent on their potential connection with the survivor population and societal contribution in the state where atrocities occurred. The ECCC's performance suggests that hybrid courts can confer those functional advantages but that mixed personnel and an in-country presence by no means guarantee effective victim participation or capacity-building functions.

Outreach to the General Public

The ECCC's ability to connect with victims and the general Cambodian population has been one of the clearest functional advantages flowing from the Court's in-country setting. Although the ECCC has not met its full outreach potential or achieved the SCSL's level of success—which has been the best among mass crimes trials to date—it has exceeded the fully international courts and the Special Panels in East Timor.

The Court's divided structure and unclear lines of responsibility posed modest obstacles to outreach from the start, but the main barrier to its effectiveness has been the decision by donors and Court management not to fund outreach adequately. The Court's problems in other areas, such as the corruption scandal and evident political interference, have also affected outreach adversely by forcing Court officials to play defense and distracting attention away from positive elements of the ECCC's judicial example.

When the ECCC has had sufficient funds, it has been able to conduct effective outreach in partnership with Cambodia's well-developed NGO community. Its efforts to ensure strong public participation in the courtroom have been unparalleled, and its use of diverse media and civil society networks has allowed information to reach many of Cambodia's poorly connected communities. Crucially, the ECCC proceedings have served as a vehicle for raising awareness about issues ranging from human rights to mental health, and they have signaled that it is now acceptable to speak publicly about the Khmer Rouge period and to educate youth about it. The ECCC has not led most such efforts, but its participation has magnified their impact by offering an official imprimatur.

Even when the Court has struggled through successive crises, it has set a positive example of transparency by comparison to national courts and may increase popular expectations of transparency in domestic proceedings. While there are mixed views of the ECCC, especially among better-informed observers and members of the opposition parties, general public support for the process has been strong.[28] Yet inefficiency, corruption, and political interference have turned many international and Cambodian observers against the Court, and further problems could lead it to fail the public's expectations for a credible judicial process.

In sum, public outreach at the ECCC has been far from perfect, but it has been a relative success compared to most mass crimes courts. It shows some important advantages of in-country hybrid proceedings but also the need to fund such efforts appropriately if future hybrid courts are to provide social benefits that justify their administrative and jurisprudential risks. Moreover, the Cambodian case shows the importance of supportive NGO networks in outreach activities—a lesson vital for national courts, hybrid tribunals, and above all for the ICC, which conducts its trials far from the locus of atrocities.

Engaging Victims

The ECCC's victim participation scheme, featuring a novel system enabling some victims to join the proceedings as civil parties, has been an important experiment for mass crimes courts. The attention that the ECCC's ambitious scheme drew to victim's needs is a positive aspect of its performance and legacy and contributes to a general trend of international criminal courts to incorporate victims in accountability processes. The participation of civil parties in the *Duch* trial, while inefficient, succeeded overall in giving victims a central place in the related processes of justice-seeking, truth-telling, and empowerment. However, moving beyond that small universe of victims, the larger numbers of potential civil parties in Case 002 has taxed the Court's resources and led to inconsistent and sometimes unfair rulings. The ECCC's difficulties suggest that a system of direct civil party participation will often be untenable at a mass crimes court. Limited participatory rights—such as those existing at the STL and ICC—offer a more realistic path forward, coupled with a process that ensures victims are able to share their stories as witnesses and complainants.

Any victim participation scheme is apt to fall flat if it is not strongly supported by donors. The Court's meager capacity to issue "collective and moral reparations" undercuts public expectations regarding its ability to provide victims with relief. The efforts of the underfunded Victim Support Section to correspond with many thousands of general Khmer Rouge victims also highlights that even in a state with a large and active NGO community, a hybrid court can only engage victims meaningfully if it has the resources to do so. There will necessarily be significant constraints on what volume of funds are available, putting stress again on the need for more efficient structures for judicial administration.

Delays and inefficiency have also led to a further problem at the ECCC with regard to victim involvement: the Trial Chamber's decision to split the Case 002 indictment and proceed with a trial that is not representative of the harms endured by most Cambodian survivors. For a mass crimes court with limited personal jurisdiction and finite resources to connect meaningfully to large numbers of survivors, its trials need to present a compelling narrative relevant to their experiences.

Capacity-Building and the Rule of Law

Hybrid courts like the ECCC naturally result in some transfer of skills between national and international personnel. Current and former personnel at the Court assert that mixed legal teams worked well and provided opportunities to play to their comparative advantages and to develop skills. The fact that some Cambodians are being trained at the ECCC and remain engaged—or will later engage—with the local judicial system makes this a nonnegligible positive outcome of the Khmer Rouge trials. Of course, this function need not be limited to hybrid courts. The ICC should look for opportunities to expand the involvement of personnel from states emerging from mass crimes and to provide technical assistance to proceedings conducted by national governments with an evident commitment to fair proceedings. A capacity-building focus flows directly from the ICC's complementarity principle, which stresses its mandate to complement the exercise of sovereign judicial authority.

The ECCC's broader effect on the Cambodian judiciary or rule of law is much less apparent. Major change in the domestic legal system in the near term is unlikely, and as of yet there are few signs that the ECCC's role as a "model court" is translating into better function in Cambodia's ordinary courts. Other hybrid courts have not fared particularly well on this score, suggesting that the capacity-building potential of mixed tribunals is modest at best without dedicated resources and programs. Perhaps the ECCC's most promising example for the rule of law in Cambodia has been the demonstration—for the most part—of fair trial rights through a vigorous defense and procedural safeguards.[29] The ECCC also provides a valuable resource to Cambodian educators, students, and practitioners, many of whom are already using its voluminous documentary record and outreach materials to study various points of law. For the ICC and other mass crimes courts, a key lesson is to provide the public with clear and relevant information, even though doing so will often lead to critiques. A tribunal's functions do not all need to be successful to be useful as a catalyst for dialogue and reflection on what it means to have a rule of law.

NEGOTIATING THE TERMS OF FUTURE MASS CRIMES COURTS

The design and operation of mass crimes courts are invariably the products of complex negotiations and ongoing political and financial compromises, and the motivations of the actors vary. The capacity and will of the host government matter greatly, and the Cambodian case shows plainly how difficult it is to build and run an effective tribunal when the host government is more focused on political control than a credible and independent judicial process. When a host government rejects the types of institutional features and personnel choices that would optimize a court's function, as the Cambodian Government did, mounting effective trials is difficult indeed.

For this reason, some human rights advocates have argued that the United Nations should have avoided the Khmer Rouge trials altogether. Doing so would have protected the United Nations from involvement in troubled proceedings and might have averted a further blemish on the reputation of international criminal justice, but it would also have forfeited an importance chance to promote accountability for some of history's most egregious offenses. The UN should not easily walk away from opportunities to forge workable hybrid arrangements, even in difficult cases like Cambodia; the alternative of dubious domestic proceedings—or no trials at all—would sometimes be much worse. The Cambodian case does not justify an end to hybrid courts; rather, the most constructive lessons to draw from the ECCC are ways that some of the problems of structure and agency adversely affecting the Court could be fixed, even when working with a difficult sovereign partner. Although the ECCC will be the only mass crimes proceeding in Cambodia in the foreseeable future, the United Nations and international justice advocates will surely deal with challenging conditions again.

One lesson to draw from Cambodia is that the United Nations and key donors need to be more concerned with, and more informed about, the prospective function of a mass crimes court during the design phase. Representatives of the United Nations, major donor states, and civil society come to the table with diverse agendas and typically engage in horse-trading that leads to overly complex structures and mandates that the realized court will lack the funding and capacity to meet effectively. Thoughtful reflection on the implications of design features can reduce (if not eliminate) this problem. Including negotiators with mass crimes court experience is imperative.

The inclusion of investigating judges and three official languages have created foreseeable challenges that should have been weighed more heavily during negotiations. In some cases, design flaws have resulted partly from a failure to spell out specific provisions during the negotiations. For example, the ECCC's civil party scheme began with too many legal teams offering largely redundant contributions in court. The judicial structure enabling certain legal issues to be raised four times, including Pre-Trial Chamber review of orders by the Co-Investigating Judges, has been unnecessarily cumbersome as well. Both of these problems arose from the Internal Rules, which were drafted by judges seeking to fill lacunae in the tribunal's constitutive documents with little explicit authority and official oversight.

These technical aspects of the Court are not easily detachable from the political rivalries that ran throughout the negotiations, which largely explains why such inefficient features were adopted. At least some such problems can be avoided, however, if negotiators concentrate on their interests in an effective proceeding, not just their narrower interests in exerting influence over a particular aspect of the proceedings. Increasing efficiency would have gone a long way toward improving the ECCC's performance and public legitimacy, and those who design other courts should take heed.

Enhanced efficiency would not eliminate problems such as corruption and political interference, however, and the Cambodian case demonstrates that international negotiators should insist on stronger institutional safeguards—citing the ECCC's problems as support for such demands. The ICC was not an option for Cambodia given its temporal jurisdiction, but in the future the threat of ICC action will often be available in negotiations, which could help overcome unreasonable assertions of host government prerogative. Donor states also need to be committed to ensuring necessary safeguards, because without their backing, the UN Secretariat usually has little independent leverage. Donors have ample incentive to reflect carefully on the functional implications of the design features they endorse, as they will bear the ultimate bill for the proceedings that result.

Even if international officials and civil society leaders engage thoughtfully, there will be cases in which an acceptable hybrid arrangement is simply unavailable. Where a host government has custody of suspects and enjoys the political clout to resist a credible judicial process, the UN should be circumspect about offering its explicit imprimatur to the court, which risks diluting the already compromised standards of international criminal justice. When all measures to ensure an adequately designed hybrid court have been exhausted, the United Nations would be wiser to provide only limited technical support. That would allow UN officials to threaten to exit credibly and to disengage, if necessary, without bringing the process to an end. Donors should not force the UN Secretariat to enter into a majority-domestic hybrid arrangement, and if they disagree fundamentally with UN experts, they should participate through other channels.

When a deal is concluded for a hybrid court, however, the United Nations needs to engage actively and assertively to uphold standards of administrative integrity, judicial independence, and due process. The Cambodian case shows the danger of ambivalent and halting UN engagement, which can lead to passivity and become a form of collusion in a substandard process. Worse still, where the United Nations fails to defend core principles such as transparency and judicial independence, it risks contributing to a negative legacy, both for the country involved and for the UN system itself. If the United Nations and enough of its key members do commit themselves to defending international standards, hybrid courts can have a valuable role to play alongside the ICC and domestic proceedings in advancing the cause of justice.

NOTES

Introduction

1. William Shawcross, Sideshow: Nixon, Kissinger, and the Destruction of Cambodia 365–66 (1979).

2. *See* François Ponchaud, Cambodia Year Zero (1978); Bernard Hamel, De Sang et De Larmes: La Grande Déportation du Cambodge (1977).

3. Stephen J. Morris, Why Vietnam Invaded Cambodia: Political Culture and the Causes of War 72–73 (1999).

4. *See* Ben Kiernan, The Pol Pot Regime: Race, Power, and Genocide in Cambodia under the Khmer Rouge, 1975–79 ch. 2 (2d ed. 2002).

5. *See* Statutes of the Communist Party of Kampuchea, art. 23; Stephen Heder with Brian D. Tittemore, Seven Candidates for Prosecution 46–55 (2d ed. 2004); Craig Etcheson, After the Killing Fields: Lessons from the Cambodian Genocide 77–106 (2005).

6. *See* John D. Ciorciari with Youk Chhang, *Documenting the Crimes of Democratic Kampuchea, in* Bringing the Khmer Rouge to Justice 221, 240–86 (Jaya Ramji & Beth Van Schaack eds., 2005).

7. For some leading historical accounts of the terror, *see generally* Kiernan, *supra* note 4; Craig Etcheson, The Rise and Demise of Democratic Kampuchea (1984); David P. Chandler, The Tragedy of Cambodian History: Politics, War, and Revolution since 1945 236–72 (1993); Michael Vickery, Cambodia, 1975–1982 (1984); Elizabeth Becker, When the War Was Over: Cambodia Under the Khmer Rouge Revolution (1986).

8. The most infamous such prison was located at a former high school in Phnom Penh and is now the Tuol Sleng museum. *See generally* David P. Chandler: Voices of S-21: Terror and History at Pol Pot's Secret Prison (1999).

9. Henri Locard, Pol Pot's Little Red Book 70–72 (2004).

10. The sheer volume of survivor accounts and human remains has made the death toll difficult to estimate, but most scholarly estimates lie in this range. *See* Ben Kiernan, *The Demography of Genocide in Southeast Asia: The Death Tolls in Cambodia, 1975–1979, and East Timor, 1975–1980,* 35 Crit. Asian Stud. 586–88 (2003).

11. Alexander Laban Hinton, Why Did They Kill? Cambodia in the Shadow of Genocide 1–2 (2005).

12. *See, e.g.*, Chanrithy Him, When Broken Glass Floats (2001); Luong Ung, First They Killed My Father: A Daughter of Cambodia Remembers (2006); Children of Cambodia's Killing Fields (Dith Pran ed., 1997).

13. *See* John D. Ciorciari, *Cambodia's Trek Toward Reconciliation*, 23 Peace Rev. 438, 438–46 (2011).

14. Agreement between the United Nations and the Royal Government of Cambodia Concerning the Prosecution under Cambodian Law of Crimes Committed During the Period of Democratic Kampuchea (June 6, 2003) [hereinafter Framework Agreement], art. 1; Law on the Establishment of Extraordinary Chambers in the Courts of Cambodia for the Prosecution of Crimes Committed During the Period of Democratic Kampuchea, as amended and promulgated on Oct. 27, 2004, NS/RKM/1004/006, art. 1 [hereinafter ECCC Law].

15. Steven R. Ratner et al., Accountability for Human Rights Atrocities in International Law 246 (3d ed. 2009); David Cohen, *"Hybrid" Justice in East Timor, Sierra Leone, and Cambodia: "Lessons Learned" and Prospects for the Future*, 43 Stan. J. Int'l L. 1, 1–6 (2007).

16. Ratner et al., *supra* note 15, at 252.

17. M. Cherif Bassiouni, Introduction to International Criminal Law 578 (2003) (arguing that "probably the biggest weakness in these [ad hoc tribunals] is their failure to contribute to the enhancement of national judicial systems").

18. Laura A. Dickinson, *The Promise of Hybrid Courts*, 97 Am. J. Int'l L. 295, 302–3 (2003).

19. Bassiouni, *supra* note 17, at 559.

20. *See* Suzannah Linton, *Putting Cambodia's Extraordinary Chambers into Context*, 11 Sing. Y.B. Int'l L. 195, 204–8, 223–26 (2007).

21. Antonio Cassese, International Criminal Law 332–33 (2d ed. 2008). *See also* Bassiouni, *supra* note 17, at 580.

22. Cassese, *supra* note 21, at 333–34; Ratner et al., *supra* note 15, at 248.

23. Ratner et al., *supra* note 15, at 248.

24. Cassese, *supra* note 21, at 334; Dickinson, *supra* note 18, at 307 (arguing that "side-by-side working arrangements allow for on-the-job training" that is more effective than classroom learning); Ethel Higonnet, *Restructuring Hybrid Courts: Local Empowerment and National Criminal Justice*, Yale Law School Legal Student Scholarship Papers 6 7–24 (2005).

25. Dickinson, *supra* note 18, at 306; Cassese, *supra* note 21, at 334 n. 41; Higonnet, *supra* note 24, at 45–46.

26. Suzannah Linton, *Cambodia, East Timor, and Sierra Leone: Experiments in International Justice*, 12 Crim. L. Forum 185, 199–202 (2001).

27. RATNER ET AL., *supra* note 15, at 253.

28. The Special Tribunal for Lebanon was created by a Security Council resolution, but only after an agreement was signed between the Lebanese government and UN Secretary-General. S.C. Res. 1757, U.N. Doc. S/RES/1957 (May 30, 2007).

29. Cohen, *supra* note 15, at 36.

30. That was particularly so in East Timor, where despite local calls for an international tribunal, UN officials and potential donors were loath to bear the costs or responsibility for politically sensitive charges against Indonesians. Suzanne Katzenstein, *Hybrid Tribunals: Searching for Justice in East Timor,* 16 HARV. HUM. RTS. J. 245, 246–47.

31. *See* Dickinson, *supra* note 18, at 296 n. 4 (citing David Scheffer, who was instrumental in setting up the ECCC and SCSL, and Hansjörg Strohmeyer, who worked to establish the East Timor and Kosovo courts, rejecting them as models in comments made in 2002).

32. *See* General Framework Agreement for Peace in Bosnia and Herzegovina, *signed* Dec. 14, 1995, art. II(1) (establishing the chamber to address human rights violations); Gret Haller, *The Human Rights Regime in Bosnia and Herzegovina in the European Context, in* HUMAN RIGHTS IN BOSNIA AND HERZEGOVINA AFTER DAYTON 25, 25–27 (Wolfbang Benedek et al. eds., 1999).

33. Regulation No. 2000/15 on the Establishment of Panels with Exclusive Jurisdiction over Serious Criminal Offenses, UNTAET, U.N. Doc. UNTAET/REG/2000/15 (June 6, 2000). "Serious crimes" were defined to include genocide, war crimes, crimes against humanity, murder, and sexual abuses.

34. Regulation No. 2000/16 on the Organization of the Public Prosecution Service in East Timor, UNTAET, U.N. Doc. UNTAET/REG/2000/16 (June 6, 2000).

35. Sylvia de Bertodano, *Current Developments in Internationalized Courts,* 1 J. INT'L CRIM. JUST. 226, 238–39 (2003).

36. *See* UNMIK Resolution 2000/64 of 15 December 2000 On Assignment of International Judges/Prosecutors and/or Change of Venue.

37. Fidelma Donlon, *Hybrid Tribunals, in* ROUTLEDGE HANDBOOK OF INTERNATIONAL CRIMINAL LAW 85, 88–89 (William Schabas & Nadia Bernaz eds., 2011).

38. Agreement between the United Nations and the Government of Sierra Leone on the Establishment of a Special Court for Sierra Leone, *signed* Jan. 16, 2002.

39. Extraordinary Chambers in the Courts of Cambodia, *Why was this model chosen for the ECCC?* http://www.eccc.gov.kh/en/faq/why-was-model-chosen-eccc (last visited Jan. 7, 2013).

40. *Main Trial for Prison Chief Gets Underway,* VOA KHMER (Mar. 30, 2009), http://www.voacambodia.com/content/a-40–2009–3–30-voa1–90171097/1353228.html.

41. James Goldston, *An Extraordinary Experiment in Transitional Justice,* JUST. INITIATIVES (Spring 2006), at 1.

42. ICTY Rules of Procedure and Evidence (rev. 46), *rev'd* Oct. 11, 2011, r. 11 *bis.*

43. Human Rights Watch, *New Court to Try Chad Ex-Dictator in Senegal* (Aug. 22, 2012), http://www.hrw.org/news/2012/08/22/senegal-new-court-try-chad-ex-dictator-senegal.

44. Gouvernement du Sénégal, Conseil des ministres du 04 octobre 2012 (Oct. 4, 2012), http://www.gouv.sn/Conseil-des-ministres-du-04,1268.html.

45. Sok An, Deputy Prime Minister, Remarks during a visit to the ECCC of UN Secretary-General Ban Ki-moon, Phnom Penh, Oct. 27, 2010, available at http://agencekampucheapress.blogspot.com/2010/10/he-dr-sok-deputy-prime-minister-speaks.html.

46. Duncan McCargo, *Politics by Other Means? The virtual trials of the Khmer Rouge Tribunal*, 87 INT'L AFF. 613 (2011).

47. Luke Hunt, *War Crimes and the Price of Justice*, BANGKOK POST, Jan. 22, 2012.

48. Peter Maguire, *ECCC's Tarnished Legacy and the UN*, CAMBODIA TRIBUNAL MONITOR (Mar. 27, 2012), http://www.cambodiatribunal.org/sites/default/files/03-27-12-Maguire Commentary.pdf (calling the ECCC an "expensive, overcomplicated experiment that should never be tried again").

49. Hans Corell, *Reflections on International Criminal Law over the Past 10 Years*, Keynote address at the Robert H. Jackson Center, Chautauqua, NY, Aug. 27, 2012, at 4 (on file with the authors).

50. *See, e.g.*, M. Cherif Bassiouni, *Mixed Models of International Criminal Justice*, *in* INTERNATIONAL CRIMINAL LAW: VOL. III: INTERNATIONAL ENFORCEMENT 155, 186–87 (M. Cherif Bassiouni ed., 3d ed. 2008); Linton, *supra* note 26, at 186.

51. Interview with Craig Etcheson, former investigator in the ECCC Office of the Co-Prosecutors, via telephone (Oct. 22, 2012).

52. Kathia Martin-Chenut, *Proces International et Modeles de Justice Penale*, *in* DROIT INTERNATIONAL PENAL 847, 862 (Hervé Ascensio et al. eds., 2d ed. 2012).

53. Interview with William Smith, ECCC deputy international Co-Prosecutor, Phnom Penh (June 5, 2012).

Chapter 1

1. Tom Fawthrop, *UN Abets Khmer Rouge Impunity*, ASIA TIMES ONLINE (June 12, 2002).

2. *See generally* BEN KIERNAN, HOW POL POT CAME TO POWER: COLONIALISM, NATIONALISM, AND COMMUNISM IN CAMBODIA, 1930–1975 (2d ed. 2004); STEVE HEDER, CAMBODIAN COMMUNISM AND THE VIETNAMESE MODEL: IMITATION AND INDEPENDENCE, 1930–1975 (2004).

3. *See* DAVID P. CHANDLER, THE TRAGEDY OF CAMBODIAN HISTORY: POLITICS, WAR, AND REVOLUTION SINCE 1945 107–15, 125–30 (1993); Ben Kiernan, *The Samlaut Rebellion, 1967–70: The Origins of Cambodia's Liberation Movement* (Monash University Centre of Southeast Asian Studies Working Papers No. 4 and 5, ca. 1975).

4. *See* Taylor Owen & Ben Kiernan, *Bombs Over Cambodia*, THE WALRUS, Oct. 2006, at 66–67.

5. *See* WILLIAM SHAWCROSS, SIDESHOW: NIXON, KISSINGER AND THE DESTRUCTION OF CAMBODIA chs. 16–19 (1979); BEN KIERNAN, THE POL POT REGIME: RACE, POWER AND GENOCIDE IN CAMBODIA UNDER THE KHMER ROUGE, 1975–1979 349–93 (1996).

6. *The President's News Conference of May 6, 1975*, *in* PUBLIC PAPERS OF THE PRESIDENTS OF THE UNITED STATES: GERALD FORD 1975, at 650 (1976); *Kissinger Sees Atrocity in Events in Cambodia*, N.Y. TIMES, May 14, 1975.

7. JAMIE FREDERIC METZL, WESTERN RESPONSES TO HUMAN RIGHTS ABUSES IN CAMBODIA, 1975–80 22–30 (1996); SAMANTHA POWER, A PROBLEM FROM HELL: AMERICA AND THE AGE OF GENOCIDE 107–33 (2002).

8. *See, e.g.*, Noam Chomsky & Edward Herman, Distortions at Fourth Hand, THE NATION, June 25, 1977; GEORGE HILDEBRAND & GARETH PORTER, CAMBODIA: STARVATION AND REVOLUTION (1976).

9. ROBERT S. ROSS, THE INDOCHINA TANGLE: CHINA'S VIETNAM POLICY, 1975–1979, at 155–67 (1988); KIERNAN, *supra* note 5, at 357–85; SOPHIE RICHARDSON, CHINA, CAMBODIA, AND THE FIVE PRINCIPLES OF PEACEFUL CO-EXISTENCE (2010); John D. Ciorciari, *China and the Pol Pot Regime*,13 COLD WAR HISTORY 1 (2013).

10. POL POT PLANS THE FUTURE: CONFIDENTIAL LEADERSHIP DOCUMENTS FROM DEMOCRATIC KAMPUCHEA, 1976–1977, at 11 (David Chandler, Ben Kiernan, & Chanthou Boua eds. and trans., 1988). *See also* Karl D. Jackson, *The Ideology of Total Revolution*, *in* CAMBODIA 1975–1978: RENDEZVOUS WITH DEATH 37 (Karl D. Jackson ed., 1989).

11. NAYAN CHANDA, BROTHER ENEMY: THE WAR AFTER THE WAR 98–102 (1988).

12. DENISE AFFONÇO, TO THE END OF HELL 54 (2005); George Chigas & Dmitri Mosyakov, *Literacy and Education under the Khmer Rouge*, Yale Cambodian Genocide Program, http://www.yale.edu/cgp/literacyandeducation.html (last visited Nov. 2, 2012).

13. Kalyanee Mam, *An Oral History of Family Life Under the Khmer Rouge*, Yale Genocide Studies Working Paper No. 10 (1999); Men Kimseng, Experts See Trauma After Khmer Rouge Forced Marriage, VOA KHMER (Nov. 3, 2012), http://www.voacambodia.com/content/experts-see-trauma-after-khmer-rouge-forced-marriage--106958698/1354516.html.

14. John D. Ciorciari with Youk Chhang, *Documenting the Crimes of Democratic Kampuchea*, *in* BRINGING THE KHMER ROUGE TO JUSTICE 221, 263–69 (Jaya Ramji & Beth Van Schaack eds., 2005).

15. *Id.* at 261–64; KIERNAN, *supra* note 5, ch. 7.

16. *See, e.g.*, Documentation Center of Cambodia, *Survivors' Stories*, http://www.d.dccam.org/Survivors/Index.htm (last visited Nov. 2, 2012).

17. CHANDA, *supra* note 11, at 198 (citing an interview with Stephen Heder), 255.

18. KIERNAN, *supra* note 5, at 210 n. 115, 370–72.

19. *Id.*; STEPHEN R. HEDER, REFLECTIONS ON CAMBODIAN POLITICIAL HISTORY 11–12 (1991).

20. *See, e.g.*, Stephen R. Heder, *Dealing with Crimes Against Humanity: Progress or Illusion?*, *in* SOUTHEAST ASIAN AFFAIRS 2001, at 129–30 (2001); Kheang Un & Judy Ledgerwood, *Is the Trial of Duch a Catalyst for Change in Cambodia's Courts?* 95 ASIA PACIFIC ISSUES 8 (E.-W. Ctr., June 2010). In fact, in at least one instance, the possibility of an investigation into the activities of current CPP leaders has appeared during the proceedings. *See* Forwarding Order, Case No. 003/07-09-2009-ECCC-OCIJ (May 4, 2012) (including a request by reserve international Co-Investigating Judge Laurent Kasper-Ansermet to investigate alleged Khmer Rouge crimes in Vietnamese territory in which senior CPP leaders may have been involved, citing Steve Heder, *Reassessing the Role of Senior Leaders and Local Officials in Democratic Kampuchea Crimes: Cambodian Accountability in Comparative Perspective*, *in* BRINGING THE KHMER ROUGE TO JUSTICE 377 (Jaya Ramji & Beth Van Schaack eds., 2005)).

21. *See* Stephen P. Heder, *The Kampuchean-Vietnamese Conflict*, *in* THE THIRD INDOCHINA CONFLICT 21, 21–62 (David W.P. Elliott ed., 1981).

22. Sok-Kheang Ly, *State and Individual Efforts to Bring about Reconciliation* (Documentation Center of Cambodia, Aug. 2009).

23. EVAN GOTTESMAN, AFTER THE KHMER ROUGE: INSIDE THE POLITICS OF NATION-BUILDING 231–37 (2002).

24. CRAIG ETCHESON, AFTER THE KILLING FIELDS: LESSONS FROM THE CAMBODIAN GENOCIDE 17 (2005).

25. Keo Chanda, Minister of Information, Press, and Culture, Chair of Legal Affairs Committee, press conference of July 28, 1979, *cited in* GENOCIDE IN CAMBODIA: DOCUMENTS FROM THE TRIAL OF POL POT AND IENG SARY 47 (Howard J. DeNike et al. eds., 2000).

26. For brief accounts of the trial, *see* GOTTESMAN, *supra* note 23, at 60–66; ETCHESON, *supra* note 24, at 14–17.

27. Decree Law No. 1: Establishment of People's Revolutionary Tribunal at Phnom Penh to Try the Pol Pot-Ieng Sary Clique for the Crime of Genocide (July 15, 1979), *reprinted in* PRK RESEARCH AND PUBLICATION OFFICE, TRIBUNAL FOR THE PROSECUTION OF THE GENOCIDAL POL POT-IENG SARY CLIQUE 305 (1979).

28. Gregory L. Stanton, *The Cambodian Genocide and International Law*, in GENOCIDE AND DEMOCRACY IN CAMBODIA 141, 142 (Ben Kiernan ed., 1993); Howard J. De Nike, *East Germany's Legal Advisor to the 1979 Tribunal in Cambodia*, SEARCHING FOR THE TRUTH (July 2008).

29. Ben Kiernan, *The Cambodian Genocide and Imperial Culture*, *in* 90 YEARS OF DENIAL (Apr. 2005), *available at* www.yale.edu/cgp/KiernanCambodia30thAnniversaryEssay.doc.

30. STEPHEN P. MORRIS, WHY VIETNAM INVADED CAMBODIA 221–22 (1999).

31. *See* Gregory Stanton, *The Call*, *in* PIONEERS OF GENOCIDE STUDIES 401, 403 (Samuel Totten & Steven L. Jacobs eds., 2002); ETCHESON, *supra* note 24, at 131–32.

32. *See* William J. Schulte, *The History of the Renakse Petitions and Their Significance to the ECCC Proceedings*, SEARCHING FOR THE TRUTH (Dec. 2007).

33. CRAIG ETCHESON, RECONCILIATION IN CAMBODIA 43 (2004).

34. *See* John D. Ciorciari & Jaya Ramji-Nogales, *Lessons from the Cambodian Experience with Truth and Reconciliation*, 19 BUFF. HUM. RTS. L. REV. 193 (2012–2013); Lor Chandara, *Festival of the Dead Remembers Torture Victims of KR*, CAMBODIA DAILY, Sept. 25, 2000; John D. Ciorciari & Sok-Kheang Ly, *The ECCC's Role in Reconciliation*, *in* ON TRIAL: THE KHMER ROUGE ACCOUNTABILITY PROCESS 294, 307–12 (John D. Ciorciari & Anne Heindel eds., 2009).

35. Mats Berdal & Michael Leifer, *Cambodia*, *in* THE NEW INTERVENTIONISM, 1991–1994, 32, 33–35 (James Mayall ed., 1996).

36. Khmer Rouge forces repeatedly violated the cease-fire, but UNTAC's Japanese leader interpreted his peacekeeping mandate narrowly, emphasizing neutrality and consent and allowing force only when UNTAC units were attacked. *See* STEVEN R. RATNER, THE NEW UN PEACEKEEPING 157–86 (1996).

37. *See* Duncan McCargo, *Cambodia: Getting Away with Authoritarianism?* 16 J. OF DEMOCRACY 98, 99–100 (2005) (emphasizing the limited extent of the postelectoral transfer of power).

38. Cambodian Genocide Justice Act, 22 U.S.C. 2656, Part D, §§ 571–74.

39. DC-Cam became an independent Cambodian NGO in January 1997. ETCHESON, *supra* note 24, at 53–76. For a review of DC-Cam materials, *see* Ciorciari with Chhang, *supra* note 14, at 224–34.

40. Law on Outlawing the Group of "Democratic Kampuchea," KHM/30, July 15, 1994, *available at* http://www.unhcr.org/refworld/docid/3ae6b51f8.html.

41. King Sihanouk asked Pol Pot to retire abroad in the interests of national reconciliation. *King Sihanouk Asks Pol Pot to Retire Abroad*, CHRON. NEWS SERVICE, Jan. 24, 1995.

42. Steve Heder, *The Personal Jurisdiction of the Extraordinary Chambers in the Courts of Cambodia . . .* 8–9 (Apr. 26, 2012), *available at* http://www.cambodiatribunal.org/sites/default/files/reports/Final Revised Heder Personal Jurisdiction Review.120426.pdf.

43. Cable 95PHNOMPENH152, U.S. Embassy Phnom Penh, *Views of Hor Namhong, Cambodian Ambassador to France* ¶7 (Jan. 11, 1995), *available at* http://www.cablegatesearch.net/cable.php?id=95PHNOMPENH152 (in which Hor supports the U.S. initiative to investigate Khmer Rouge crimes and asks for U.S. "assistance").

44. Heder, *supra* note 42, at 9–12.

45. *See* ROSS MARLAY & CLARK D. NEHER, PATRIOTS AND TYRANTS 195–96 (1999).

46. Report of the Special Representative of the Secretary-General for Human Rights in Cambodia, Mr. Thomas Hammarberg . . . , U.N. Doc. E/CN.4/1997/85, 31 Jan. 1997, §D.

47. *See, e.g.*, Wendy Lambourne, *The Khmer Rouge Tribunal: Justice for Genocide in*

Cambodia? Paper for the Law and Society Association of Australia and New Zealand (Dec. 10–12, 2008), at 6–9; Jaya Ramji, *Reclaiming Cambodian History: The Case for a Truth Commission*, 24 FLETCHER F. WORLD AFF. 127 (2000).

48. *See* Ciorciari & Ramji-Nogales, *supra* note 34.

49. U.N.C.H.R. Res. 1997/49 (XVIII), E/CN.4/1997/L.80 (Apr. 11, 1997) (requesting that the Secretary-General examine seriously any Cambodian request to try the Khmers Rouges).

50. Letter dated June 21, 1997, from the First and Second Prime Ministers of Cambodia to the UN Secretary-General, *in* U.N. Doc. A/51/930-S/1997/488 (June 24, 1997).

51. *See* DAVID SCHEFFER, ALL THE MISSING SOULS 345–59 (2012).

52. *See* DAVID W. ROBERTS, POLITICAL TRANSITION IN CAMBODIA 1991–99: POWER, ELITISM AND DEMOCRACY 140–44 (2001); Heder, *supra* note 42, at 15.

53. Seth Mydans, *The Khmer Rouge Implosion*, N.Y. TIMES, June 16, 1997.

54. Nate Thayer, *Pol Pot: The End*, FAR EAST. ECON. REV., Aug. 7, 1997.

55. *See, e.g.*, PETER H. MAGUIRE, FACING DEATH IN CAMBODIA 135–38 (2005); Nicholas J. Cummins, *The 1997 Coup in Cambodia* (Monash Asia Institute, 2007).

56. For one description of events, see SORPONG PEOU, INTERVENTION & CHANGE IN CAMBODIA: TOWARDS DEMOCRACY? 290–310 (2000).

57. *See, e.g.*, Barbara Crossette, *Cambodian Leaders in Exile Seek International Monitoring of New Elections*, N.Y. TIMES, Sept. 28, 1997; *Newsmaker: Hun Sen*, PBS NEWSHOUR, Oct. 21, 1997.

58. Thomas Hammarberg, *How the Khmer Rouge Tribunal Was Agreed*, SEARCHING FOR THE TRUTH (June 2001), at 38.

59. ETCHESON, *supra* note 24, at 154–55; John D. Ciorciari, *Great-Power Posturing and the Khmer Rouge Tribunal*, SEARCHING FOR THE TRUTH (Fall 2002).

60. U.N.G.A. Res. 52/135 (Dec. 12, 1997). Kofi Annan later appointed Australian Ninian Stephen, Mauritian Rajsoomer Lallah, and American Steven Ratner to the group. The resolution used the term "group of experts" rather than "commission," which had been used for the ICTY and would suggest adherence to that model. Hammarberg, *supra* note 58, at 38–39.

61. Philip Shenon & Eric Schmitt, *Clinton Orders Arrest of Cambodia's Pol Pot*, N.Y. TIMES, Apr. 9, 1998.

62. Philip Shenon, *Death of Pol Pot: The Questions*, N.Y. TIMES, Apr. 18, 1998.

63. Nate Thayer, *Dying Breath*, FAR EAST. ECON. REV., Apr. 30, 1998.

64. David Scheffer, *The Extraordinary Chambers in the Courts of Cambodia*, *in* INTERNATIONAL CRIMINAL LAW 219, 222–23 (M. Cherif Bassiouni ed., 3d ed. 2008); Scheffer, *supra* note 51, at 364.

65. SCHEFFER, *supra* note 51, at 377–78.

66. Hammarberg, *supra* note 58, at 39.

67. SCHEFFER, *supra* note 51, at 369–70 (noting that Kenya, Portugal, and Britain supported the concept).

68. Sorpong Peou, *Diplomatic Pragmatism: ASEAN's Response to the July 1997 Coup*, ACCORD (1998), at 35.

69. SCHEFFER, *supra* note 51, at 370–71.

70. *See* House Resolution 533, 105th Congress, 2d Session (1998); *NGO Letter to Congress on Cambodia*, INDOCHINA INTERCHANGE 9:1 (Jan. 1999).

71. Sorpong Peou, *Cambodia in 1998: From Despair to Hope?* 39 ASIAN SURVEY 20, 25 (1999).

72. TOM FAWTHROP & HELEN JARVIS, GETTING AWAY WITH GENOCIDE? ELUSIVE JUSTICE AND THE KHMER ROUGE TRIBUNAL 134 (2004); Nate Thayer, *End of Story? Last Khmer Rouge Defections Don't Bring Closure—Yet*, FAR EAST. ECON. REV., Dec. 17, 1998 (noting that Thai forces initially detained Khieu Samphan, Nuon Chea, and Ta Mok at the request of the United States, who wanted them held for trial).

73. Seth Mydans, *Cambodian Leader Resists Punishing Top Khmer Rouge*, N.Y. TIMES, Dec. 29, 1998.

74. *Cambodia King Refuses to OK Khmer Rouge Amnesty Offer*, ASSOC. PRESS, Dec. 30, 1998.

75. *Cambodian Prime Minister Seeks Reconciliation Through Reconstruction*, EIR NEWS SERVICE, Feb. 12, 1999 (interviewing Hun Sen).

76. *See* Anthony Spaeth, *Apologies and Outrage*, TIME, Jan. 11, 1999; Terry McCarthy, *Where Fear Reigns*, TIME, Mar. 22, 1999.

77. *See* Report of the Group of Experts for Cambodia, established pursuant to G.A. Res. 52/135, U.N. GAOR, 53d Sess., Annex, ¶ 110, U.N. Doc. A/53/850, S/1999/231 (Mar. 16, 1999) [hereinafter Group of Experts Report]. The Group recommended considering a truth commission for lower-level offenses. *Id.* ¶¶ 200, 219.

78. STEVEN R. RATNER ET AL., ACCOUNTABILITY FOR HUMAN RIGHTS ATROCITIES IN INTERNATIONAL LAW 350 (3d ed. 2009).

79. *Hun Sen War Crimes Court Would Try U.S.*, SYDNEY MORNING HERALD, Jan. 22, 1999.

80. Letter from Prime Minister Hun Sen to UN Secretary-General Kofi Annan (Mar. 3, 1999), *available at* http://www.camnet.com.kh/ocm/government7.htm.

81. Keith B. Richburg, *U.S. Wants Tribunal for Top Khmer Rouge*, WASH. POST, Mar. 4, 1999.

82. *Premier Says Khmer Rouge Leaders Will Be Tried in the Country*, BBC SUMMARY OF WORLD BROADCASTS, Mar. 15, 1999.

83. Letter dated 24 March 1999 from the Prime Minister of Cambodia to the Secretary-General, U.N. Doc. A/53/875, S/1999/324 (Mar. 1999).

84. Thomas Hammarberg, *How the Khmer Rouge Tribunal Was Agreed*, SEARCHING FOR THE TRUTH (Aug. 2001), at 43. *See also* Elizabeth Becker, *Cambodia Spurns U.N. Plan for Khmer Rouge Tribunal*, N.Y. TIMES, Mar. 13, 1999.

85. Terry McCarthy, *Hun Sen: Cambodia's Mr. Justice?* TIME, Mar. 22, 1999 (quoting from an interview).

86. Presentation by His Excellency Sok An, to the Stockholm International Forum: Truth, Justice and Reconciliation, at 6 (Apr. 23–24, 2002).

87. Verbatim Record, U.N. Doc. S/PV.3453, at 14 (Nov. 8, 1994).

88. *Id. See also* THIERRY CRUVELLIER, COURT OF REMORSE: INSIDE THE INTERNATIONAL CRIMINAL TRIBUNAL FOR RWANDA 10 (2010) (noting that "the new Rwandan government was envisioning the establishment of a court in Kigali where Rwandans would be involved . . . [but] the UN Security Council chose to set up the tribunal outside the country and, in order to guarantee its impartiality, barred Rwandans from having any judicial responsibility.").

89. *See* Verbatim Record, *supra* note 87, at 14–15; International Federation for Human Rights, *Victims in the Balance: Challenges Ahead for the ICTR*, at 16 (2002) (noting President Paul Kagame's objections).

90. *See, e.g.*, Situation of human rights in Cambodia, Commission on Human Rights resolution 1999/76 ¶¶ 12–14 (Apr. 29, 1999); *Rejection of International Khmer Rouge Trial Frustrates Opposition*, DEUTSCHE PRESSE-AGENTUR, Mar. 15, 1999; *Cambodia Arrests Last Khmer Rouge Leader*, CNN, Mar. 6, 1999.

91. *See* Greg Torode, *Beijing May Veto Genocide Tribunal*, S. CHINA MORNING POST, Feb. 6, 1999; ETCHESON, *supra* note 24, at 154–55; RATNER ET AL., *supra* note 78, at 281.

92. Scheffer, *supra* note 64, at 226.

93. Letter from the Cambodian Prime Minister to the UN Secretary-General (Apr. 28, 1999).

94. Nayan Chanda, *China and Cambodia: In the Mirror of History*, 9 ASIA-PAC. REV. 1, 5–9 (2002).

95. *Report of the Secretary-General on Khmer Rouge Trials*, ¶ 7, U.N. Doc. A/57/769 (Mar. 31, 2003).

96. Jarvis participated in the talks as an advisor to the Cambodian Government. FAWTHROP & JARVIS, *supra* note 72, at 155.

97. Thomas Hammarberg, *How the Khmer Rouge Tribunal Was Agreed*, SEARCHING FOR THE TRUTH (Sept. 2001), at 38–39.

98. Kay Johnson, *UN-Cambodia Split on Khmer Trial*, STRAITS TIMES (Singapore), Aug. 27, 1999; Philip Shenon, *U.N. Plans Joint War Crimes Tribunal for Khmer Rouge*, N.Y. TIMES, Aug. 12, 1999.

99. Youk Chhang, *The Thief of History—Cambodia and the Special Court*, 1 INT'L J. TRANS. JUST. 157, 164 (2007).

100. Hammarberg, *supra* note 58, at 39–40. King Sihanouk argued that a UN-majority arrangement with Cambodian consent would not violate Cambodian sovereignty. *Id.*

101. *Id.*

102. SCHEFFER, *supra* note 51, at 387–89 (noting that the Cambodian Government found the label of a "mixed tribunal" offensive to its sovereignty).

103. *Id.*

104. *Id.* at 392–93; Scheffer, *supra* note 64, at 229–30.

105. Kelly Whitley, *History of the Khmer Rouge Tribunal: Origins, Negotiations, and Establishment*, *in* THE KHMER ROUGE TRIBUNAL 29, 41 (John D. Ciorciari ed., 2006).

106. John D. Ciorciari, *History and Politics Behind the Khmer Rouge Trials*, *in* ON TRIAL: THE KHMER ROUGE ACCOUNTABILITY PROCESS 33, 73 (John D. Ciorciari & Anne Heindel eds., 2009).

107. Hammarberg, *supra* note 58, at 40.

108. Opposition leader Sam Rainsy stated that a tribunal considering the period after 1979 would implicate Hun Sen. *Cambodian Opposition Leader Says Wider Tribunal Would Implicate PM*, DEUTSCHE PRESSE-AGENTUR, Jan. 19, 1999. After defecting in December 1998, Khieu Samphan and Nuon Chea warned that any trial would feature information about American abuses in the early 1970s. *Rouge Threat to 'Expose US, China,'* THE STANDARD (Hong Kong), Jan. 2, 1999.

109. David Scheffer, *The Negotiating History of the ECCC's Personal Jurisdiction*, CAMBODIA TRIBUNAL MONITOR (May 22, 2011), *available at* ki-media.blogspot.com/2011/05/negotiating-history-of-ecccs-personal.html; Heder, *supra* note 42, at 24–38.

110. Interview with Hans Corell, former UN Legal Counsel, via telephone (Nov. 15, 2012).

111. Identical letters dated 19 Mar. 1999 from the Permanent Representative of Cambodia to the United Nations Addressed to the Secretary-General and to the President of the Security Council: Annex: Declaration of Prime Minister Hun Sen of the Kingdom of Cambodia on the Issue of the Trial of Ta Mok, U.N. Doc. A/53/867, S/1999/298 (Mar. 19, 1999) at 2 (citing Mok as an exception).

112. *Only a Few Khmer Rouge to Face Trial: Hun Sen*, UN WIRE, Dec. 23, 1999.

113. *Hun Sen Regrets Stating Number of K. Rouge Leaders to Be Tried*, KYODO NEWS AGENCY, Jan. 7, 2000.

114. *See, e.g*, Heder, *supra* note 42, at 37 (citing Foreign Minister Hor Namhong's March 12, 1999, remarks at a press conference, asserting that Hun Sen would focus on Nuon Chea, Khieu Samphan, and Mok).

115. Sorpong Peou, *The Challenge for Human Rights in Cambodia*, *in* HUMAN RIGHTS IN ASIA 123, 136–38 (Thomas W.D. Davis & Brian Galligan eds., 2011).

116. Heder, *supra* note 42, at 37.

117. Corell interview, *supra* note 110.

118. Thomas Hammarberg, *How the Khmer Rouge Tribunal Was Agreed*, SEARCHING FOR THE TRUTH (Oct. 2001), at 42.

119. Corell interview, *supra* note 110.

120. *Id.*

121. SCHEFFER, *supra* note 51, at 396–99.

122. *U.N., Cambodia Agree on Court to Try Khmer Rouge Leaders*, DEUTSCHE PRESSE-AGENTUR, July 6, 2000.

123. Law on the Establishment of the Extraordinary Chambers in the Courts of Cambodia for the Prosecution of Crimes Committed during the Period of Democratic Kampuchea, promulgated Aug. 7, 2001, NS/RKM/0801/12 [hereinafter 2001 Law].

124. *See, e.g., For the Record,* WASH. POST, Mar. 15, 2001.

125. Letter from Sok An, Senior Minister in Charge of the Council of Ministers, to Hans Corell, Under Secretary-General for Legal Affairs (Nov. 23, 2001). *See also* Statement from the Royal Government of Cambodia Task Force on the Khmer Rouge Trial (Mar. 15, 2002).

126. Daily Press Briefing by the Office of the Spokesperson for the Secretary-General (Feb. 8, 2002).

127. Hans Corell, *Why the UN Backed Off: No Justice for Victims of the Khmer Rouge,* INT'L HERALD TRIBUNE, June 19, 2002.

128. Corell interview, *supra* note 110.

129. Seth Mydans, *Khmer Rouge Trials Won't Be Fair, Critics Say,* N.Y. TIMES, Feb. 10, 2002.

130. Dinah PoKempner, Letter to the Editor, *Khmer Rouge on Trial,* N.Y. TIMES, Feb. 20, 2002.

131. The U.S. government pressed for a fully international tribunal, but British and Sierra Leonean officials favored a hybrid court in Freetown featuring strong national ownership. *See* SCHEFFER, *supra* note 51, at 322–31.

132. Agreement between the United Nations and the Government of Sierra Leone on the Establishment of a Special Court for Sierra Leone, 16 Jan. 2002, arts. 1–2. The Special Tribunal for Lebanon later used a similar formula. *See* Statute of the Special Tribunal for Lebanon, art. 8, Annex, U.N. Doc. S/RES/1757 (May 30, 2007).

133. Corell interview, *supra* note 110.

134. The Sierra Leonean government did not insist on the full scope of national involvement foreseen in its agreement with the UN, partly due to a loathness to take full responsibility for the prosecutions of rebel leaders. Thierry Cruvellier, *From the Taylor Trial to a Lasting Legacy: Putting the Special Court Model to the Test,* International Center for Transitional Justice and Sierra Leone Court Monitoring Program, at 31 (2009). *See also* Sarah Kendall & Michelle Staggs, *From Mandate to Legacy: The Special Court for Sierra Leone as a Model for "Hybrid Justice,"* UC Berkeley War Crimes Study Center, at 3, n. 4 (Apr. 2005) (noting that although the government nominated one judge on each trial chamber, nominees were not required to be Sierra Leonean, and Trial Chamber II had no national judge).

135. Mydans, *supra* note 129; *Cambodia Says Keeping Door Open for UN on Khmer Rouge Trial,* REUTERS, Feb. 9, 2002.

136. Lor Chandara & Thet Sambath, *Lawmakers Seek Explanation for KR Delay,* CAMBODIA DAILY, Feb. 22, 2002.

137. Corell interview, *supra* note 110.

138. *See EU Asks U.N. to Seek Khmer Rouge Trials,* WASH. TIMES, Feb. 22, 2002; Tran-

script of press conference by Secretary-General Kofi Annan, U.N. Doc. SG/SM/8160 (Mar. 13, 2002).

139. Joint Statement, *Indian Prime Minister's Visit to Cambodia*, Apr. 11, 2002, http://www.mfaic.gov.kh/mofa/Products/595-indian-prime-ministers-visit-to-cambodia.aspx.

140. UN Commission on Human Rights, Situation of Human Rights in Cambodia, U.N. Doc. E/CN.4/2002/89 ¶ 18 (Apr. 26, 2002).

141. Bill Myers, *Cambodian Tribunal Pushed*, CHICAGO TRIBUNE, Mar. 9, 2002.

142. *See* ETCHESON, *supra* note 24, at 151–54.

143. Joint Communique of the 35th Annual ASEAN Ministerial Meeting, Bandar Seri Begawan ¶ 45 (July 29–30, 2002).

144. FAWTHROP & JARVIS, *supra* note 72, at 195. Civil society organizations including the Open Society Institute reportedly played a key convening role. Interview with David Scheffer, UN Special Expert to advise on UN Assistance to the Khmer Rouge Trials and former U.S. Ambassador-at-Large for War Crimes Issues, Phnom Penh (June 16, 2012).

145. G.A. Res. 57/228, ¶ 1, U.N. Doc. A/RES/57/228 (Dec. 18, 2002) [hereinafter Resolution 57/228].

146. *Id.* pmbl. ¶¶ 7–8, ¶¶ 1, 4–6. *See also* Elizabeth Becker, *U.N. Revives Plan to Try Remnants of Khmer Rouge in Cambodia*, N.Y. TIMES, Nov. 21, 2002 (noting that 37 states had abstained from a key committee vote for similar reasons).

147. Hans Corell, *Reflections on International Criminal Law over the Past 10 Years*, Keynote address at the Robert H. Jackson Center, Chautauqua, NY, Aug. 27, 2012, at 4 (on file with the authors).

148. Diplomats from the United States, France, Japan, Australia, India, and the Philippines reportedly met with Annan and Corell on March 13 to express their displeasure. Tom Fawthrop, *Khmer Rouge: "Last Chance" for Justice*, ASIA TIMES ONLINE (Feb. 18, 2003), http://www.atimes.com/atimes/Southeast_Asia/EB19Ae01.html.

149. *Report of the Secretary-General*, *supra* note 95, ¶ 21.

150. Agreement between the United Nations and the Royal Government of Cambodia Concerning the Prosecution under Cambodian Law of Crimes Committed During the Period of Democratic Kampuchea (June 6, 2003) [hereinafter Framework Agreement], pmbl. ¶ 4.

151. On the debates regarding the tribunal's personal jurisdiction, *see generally* Heder, *supra* note 42; Scheffer, *supra* note 109.

152. *Report of the Secretary-General*, *supra* note 95, ¶ 29.

153. *Id.* ¶¶ 28–29. Similar concerns have justified the international majority at the SCSL. *See* Erika Kinetz, *Eyes of the World Turn to ECCC for Lessons*, CAMBODIA DAILY, Nov. 12, 2007 (paraphrasing SCSL Chief Prosecutor Stephen Rapp as saying that although the SCSL's national staff members are essential, international control of hybrid courts is needed, because national courts lack "a good record of prosecuting members of a seated regime or its allies").

154. Presentation by Deputy Prime Minister Sok An to the National Assembly on

Ratification of the Agreement Between Cambodia and the United Nations, at 8 (Oct. 4–5, 2004) [hereinafter Sok An 2004 Presentation]. *See also* Erika Kinetz, *ECCC Hopes to Be New Model for Tribunals*, Cambodia Daily, Oct. 19, 2009 (quoting ECCC official and current acting Director of Administration Kranh Tony as saying the Cambodian Government wanted to create "something new" to be faster, more affordable, and more immediate to the affected population).

155. Sok An 2004 Presentation, *supra* note 154.

156. *Id.*

157. Tom Fawthrop, *Will Cambodians Ever Get Justice?* Asia Times Online (Nov. 30, 2002), http://atimes.com/atimes/Southeast_Asia/DK30Ae02.html.

158. *See, e.g.*, Gregory H. Stanton, *Perfection Is the Enemy of Justice: A Response to Amnesty International and Human Rights Watch's Criticisms of the Agreement Between the Cambodian Government and the U.N. to Establish the Khmer Rouge Tribunal*, Genocide Watch (May 19, 2003), www.genocidewatch.org/aboutgenocide/stantonperfectionjustice.htm.

159. *Id.*

160. *See* Molly Ball & Thet Sambath, *Observers React Positively to KR Tribunal Deal*, Cambodia Daily, Mar. 19, 2003.

161. *Id.*

162. *Report of the U.N. Secretary-General*, *supra* note 95, ¶¶ 30, 81.

163. *See, e.g.*, Seth Mydans, *Flawed Khmer Rouge Tribunal Better than None*, N.Y. Times, Apr. 16, 2003; Matt McKinney, *Scholars Cite Flaws in KR Trial Agreement*, Cambodia Daily, Apr. 24, 2003.

164. Human Rights Watch, *Serious Flaws: Why the U.N. General Assembly Should Require Changes to the Draft Khmer Rouge Tribunal Agreement* (Apr. 30, 2003), http://www.hrw.org/legacy/backgrounder/asia/cambodia043003-bck.pdf.

165. Amnesty International, *Kingdom of Cambodia: Amnesty International's Position and Concerns Regarding the Proposed "Khmer Rouge" Tribunal*, Document ASA 23/005/2003 (Apr. 24, 2003), http://www.amnesty.org/en/library/info/ASA23/005/2003/en.

166. Law on the Establishment of Extraordinary Chambers in the Courts of Cambodia for the Prosecution of Crimes Committed During the Period of Democratic Kampuchea, as amended and promulgated on Oct. 27, 2004, NS/RKM/1004/006 [hereinafter ECCC Law].

167. *See* 2001 Law, *supra* note 123, art. 31; ECCC Law, *supra* note 166, art. 47 *bis* new.

168. *Report of the U.N. Secretary-General*, *supra* note 95, ¶ 25 (arguing that the Agreement constituted an "international agreement" that must be "implemented in accordance with the requirements of the law of treaties"). *See also* ECCC Law, *supra* note 166, art. 2(2) (specifying that the Vienna Convention on the Law of Treaties applies to the agreement).

169. Framework Agreement, *supra* note 150, art. 4; ECCC Law, *supra* note 166, art. 14 new; Internal Rules of the ECCC, *rev'd* Aug. 3, 2011, r. 77(13) [hereinafter ECCC Internal Rules (rev. 8)].

170. *See* chapter 3 for discussion of the OA.

171. ECCC Law, *supra* note 166, art. 11 new; Framework Agreement, *supra* note 150, art. 3.

172. ECCC Law, *supra* note 166, art. 46 new. To save costs, the United Nations has indeed abolished international posts or made them national posts where "expertise is available locally and the functions can be met through national recruitment." ECCC, *ECCC Revised Budget Requirements 2010–2011*, at 7 (Jan. 24, 2011).

173. Key examples include Co-Prosecutor Chea Leang, Co-Investigating Judge You Bunleng, Director of the Office of Administration Tony Kranh, and VSS head Rong Chhorng.

174. Congress began to include such restrictions in 1998 and maintained them until 2007. *See, e.g.*, Omnibus Consolidated and Emergency Supplemental Appropriations Act, Pub. L. No. 105–277, 112 Stat. 2681–156 (1998).

175. Julio Jeldres, *Cambodia's Relations with France since the Paris Agreements of 1991*, *in* CAMBODIA: PROGRESS AND CHALLENGES SINCE 1991 134, 145–47 (Pou Sothirok et al. eds., 2012).

176. *See* Wang Jianwei, *Great Power Relations and Their Impact on Japan-Southeast Asian Relations: A Chinese Perspective*, *in* JAPAN'S RELATIONS WITH SOUTHEAST ASIA 70–79 (Lam Peng Er ed., 2013); Kitti Prasirtsuk, *Japan and ASEAN in East Asian Community-building: Activating the Fukuda Doctrine*, *in id.* at 105–6.

177. SIM VIREAK, CAMBODIA-JAPAN RELATIONS 76 (2010). Instead, Japan followed China to become one of the first states to recognize the legitimacy of the new Hun Sen government. Mikio Oishi & Fumitaka Furuoka, *Can Japanese Aid Be an Effective Tool of Influence?* 43 ASIAN SURVEY 890, 893–94 (2003).

178. Estimate based on data from Ek Chanboreth & Sok Hach, *Aid Effectiveness in Cambodia* 15–16 (Wolfenshon Center for Development, Working Paper no. 7, Dec. 2008).

179. For example, Sok An announced in September 1999 that his team would soon complete a draft domestic law for a Khmer Rouge tribunal—an apparent means of pressuring the UN negotiators. The next day, Japan announced a new $40 million soft loan. George Chigas, *The Trial of the Khmer Rouge: The Role of the Tuol Sleng and Santebal Archives*, 4 HARV. ASIA Q. (Winter 2000).

180. Nicole Sayres & Thomas Lum, *Cambodia: Background and U.S. Relations*, CRS REPORT FOR CONGRESS 4 (Aug. 21, 2002).

181. *See generally* ROGER FISHER & WILLIAM URY, GETTING TO YES (rev. ed. 2011).

182. Corell, *supra* note 147, at 4.

183. Robert Petit, *Lawfare and International Tribunals: A Question of Definition? A Reflection on the Creation of the Khmer Rouge Tribunal*, 43 CASE W. RES. J. INT'L L. 189, 197 (2010–11) (calling it "no doubt a flawed model" but holding out hope for delivering "a measure of justice").

184. Interview with Craig Etcheson, former investigator in the ECCC Office of the Co-Prosecutors, via telephone (Oct. 22, 2012).

Chapter 2

1. *See* Agreement between the United Nations and the Royal Government of Cambodia Concerning the Prosecution under Cambodian Law of Crimes Committed During the Period of Democratic Kampuchea (June 6, 2003) [hereinafter Framework Agreement], art. 2(2) (providing that the agreement would be implemented through a domestic law).

2. Sok An, Closing Remarks for the International Conference, Dealing with a Past Holocaust and National Reconciliation: Learning from Experiences, Phnom Penh, Aug. 28–29, 2006, *available at* www.eccc.gov.kh/english/cabinet/ speeches/3/dealing_with_a_past_holocaust.pdf.

3. *See, e.g., Report of the Secretary-General on Possible Options to Further the Aim of Prosecution and Imprisoning Persons Responsible for Acts of Piracy,* ¶ 12, U.N. Doc. S/2010/394 (July 26, 2010) (identifying the ECCC as "a Cambodian national court, based on the French civil law system, with a special jurisdiction, and with United Nations participation").

4. Decision on Appeal Against Provisional Detention Order of Kaing Guek Eav alias "Duch," Case No. 001/18-7-2007-ECCC/OCIJ (PTC01), ¶ 19 (Dec. 3, 2007) [hereinafter Decision on Duch's Detention Appeal].

5. Decision on Request for Release, Case 001/1/-07/2007/ECCC/TC, ¶ 10 (June 15, 2009).

6. *See* Statute of the Special Court of Sierra Leone, Jan. 16, 2002, art. 8(1),(2) [hereinafter SCSL Statute]; Statute of the Special Tribunal for Lebanon, § 1, art. 4(1), Annex, U.N. Doc. S/RES/1757 (May 30, 2007). The Kosovo and East Timor panels also had jurisdiction over offenses that would normally have fallen to ordinary domestic criminal courts.

7. Decision on Request for Release, *supra* note 5, ¶ 10–12 (also noting that "[a]s a court of special ('extraordinary') and independent character within the Cambodian legal system, the ECCC was designed to stand apart from existing Cambodian courts" and that ECCC officers have "no competence to appear before or sit in judgment over a decision by a domestic Cambodian court"). *See also* Decision on Duch's Detention Appeal, *supra* note 4, ¶ 19.

8. *See, e.g.,* Michael P. Scharf, *The Special Court for Sierra Leone,* ASIL INSIGHTS (Oct. 2000), *available at* http://www.asil.org/insights/insigh53.htm. *See also Report of the Secretary-General on the Establishment of a Special Court for Sierra Leone,* ¶ 6, U.N. Doc. S/2000/915 (Oct. 4, 2000) (citation omitted) [hereinafter SCSL Report of the S-G] (calling the SCSL "a treaty-based sui generis court of mixed jurisdiction and composition").

9. *See* Prosecutor v. Charles Ghankay Taylor, Case No. SCSL-2003-1-I, Decision on Immunity from Jurisdiction, ¶ 41(c) (Appeals Chamber, May 31, 2004); Prosecutor v. Agustine Gbao, Case No. SCSL-2004–15-AR72(E), Decision on Preliminary Motion

on the Invalidity of the Agreement Between the United Nations and the Government of Sierra Leone on the Establishment of the Special Court, ¶ 6 (Appeals Chamber, May 25, 2004).

10. *See Report of the Secretary-General on the Establishment of a Special Tribunal for Lebanon,* ¶ 7, U.N. Doc. S/2006/893 (Nov. 15, 2006) [hereinafter STL Report of S-G] (highlighting the STL's establishment via an international agreement as evidence of its international character despite many hybrid features).

11. *Report of the Secretary-General on Khmer Rouge Trials,* ¶ 15, U.N. Doc. A/57/769 (Mar. 31, 2003). *See also id.* ¶ 16(b),(c) (proposing to remedy these defects by a majority of international judges, a single prosecutor and single investigating judge, and a simpler two-tier structure with a trial chamber and appeals chamber).

12. Interview with Michael G. Karnavas, former Co-Lawyer for Ieng Sary, Phnom Penh (May 19, 2012).

13. The Special Panels in East Timor included an investigating judge, but the judge's role was limited to ensuring the rights of accused under investigation. *See* UNTAET Regulation 2000/11, § 12 (entered into force Mar. 6, 2000) *as amended by* Regulation 2000/14, § 4 (entered into force May 10, 2000).

14. Internal Rules of the ECCC, rev'd Aug. 3, 2011, r. 50(1) [hereinafter ECCC Internal Rules (rev. 8)].

15. *Id.* r. 53(3). The submission must contain, *inter alia,* a summary of the facts, the alleged offenses, the identity of the persons to be investigated, if applicable, and the signature of both Co-Prosecutors.

16. *Id.* r. 55(2)-(3).

17. *Id.* r. 55(4).

18. *Id.* r. 67(1),(4).

19. Framework Agreement, *supra* note 1, arts. 5(4), 6(4).

20. *Quoted in* Alex Bates, *Transitional Justice in Cambodia: Analytical Report,* Atlas Project (Oct. 2010), ¶ 135.

21. *Quoted in id.* ¶ 133.

22. *See* Interview with William Smith, ECCC deputy international Co-Prosecutor, Phnom Penh (June 5, 2012) (arguing that "it is inefficient to have two heads, though there are benefits for the Cambodian judicial system by injecting Cambodians into a proper system").

23. *See* Closing Order Against Kaing Guek Eav *alias* Duch, Case No. 001/18-7-2007-ECCC-OCIJ ¶ 4 (Aug. 8, 2008) [hereinafter *Duch* Closing Order] (noting that the Co-Prosecutors began their preliminary investigation in July 2006 and filed their introductory submission in July 2007).

24. *See* Bates, *supra* note 20, ¶ 134.

25. *Id.* ¶ 131 (quoting Judge Lemonde). *See also Quelles leçons tirer du procès des Khmers rouges?* REVUE DE SCIENCE CRIMINELLE 597 (2011) (featuring an interview with Lem-

onde, translated from French by the authors, noting that the procedure governing disputes between the Co-Investigating Judges could not be used daily because if a question was transmitted to the Pre-Trial Chamber it would result in weeks or months of delay).

26. Separation Order, Case No. 002/14-8-2006, at 1 (OCIJ, Sept. 19, 2007).

27. *See Duch* Closing Order, *supra* note 23, ¶ 7 (noting that the CIJs considered the investigation concluded in May 2008, three months prior to the Closing Order's issuance).

28. *See* Closing Order, Case No. 002/19-9-2007-ECCC-OCIJ ¶ 13 (Sept. 15, 2010) [hereinafter Case 002 Closing Order] (noting that the CIJs had completed the investigation eight months before the closing order's issuance).

29. *See generally* ANTONIO CASSESE, INTERNATIONAL CRIMINAL LAW 356–58 (2d ed. 2008).

30. ECCC Internal Rules (rev. 8), *supra* note 14, r. 55(5),(6).

31. Bates, *supra* note 20, ¶ 133; Göran Sluiter, *Due Process and Criminal Procedure in the Cambodian Extraordinary Chambers*, 4 J. INT'L CRIM. JUST. 314, 324 (2006).

32. Interview with Clint Williamson, former UN Special Expert to advise on the UN Assistance to the Khmer Rouge Trials and former U.S. Ambassador-at-Large for War Crimes Issues, via telephone (June 27, 2012). *See also* Interview with Anta Guissé, Co-Lawyer for Khieu Samphan, Phnom Penh (Nov. 15, 2012) (noting that because civil law trials are so short, the common law system may be more applicable to mass crimes proceedings); Interview with Panhavuth Long, Program Officer, Cambodian Justice Initiative, Phnom Penh (July 6, 2012) (noting that if the investigation was more public the trial could be shorter "instead of revisiting the same issues and prolonging everything").

33. *See, e.g.*, Charles C. Jackson, *Process and Problems: Defense Counsel at the Extraordinary Chambers in the Courts of Cambodia*, at 24 (updated Nov. 2010), available at http://www.cambodiatribunal.org/sites/default/files/resources/ctm_eccc_defense_charles_jackson.pdf. *But see Quelles leçons*, *supra* note 25 (arguing that for complex mass crimes trials, an investigative judge is more efficient than party-driven investigations because one party seeks to confuse the Tribunal and prevent it from working). *Cf.* Judge Marcel Lemonde, remarks at the conference "The Contribution of Criminal Proceedings before the ECCC to Cambodian Law," Royal University of Law and Economics, Phnom Penh, Dec. 4, 2012 [hereinafter Judge Lemonde Remarks] (saying that investigative judges should be employed at future mass crimes courts because "one of the main objectives of defense is to not go to the point right away").

34. *See, e.g.*, CASSESE, *supra* note 29, at 357 (noting that in domestic systems proceedings before investigating judges are often "excessively lengthy").

35. *See, e.g.*, Judge Lemonde Remarks, *supra* note 33 (noting that he expected the ECCC to follow the "new European model" being generated by decisions of the European Court of Human Rights, which brings together the best of both the adversarial and inquisitorial systems: a pretrial phase "more open but more efficient and richer" and a trial that is "shorter but respect[s] the rights of the parties"). The expectation of a short trial is implicit

in the Internal Rules, which provide extraordinarily limited opportunity for immediate appeal and—unique among mass crimes courts—include no provision for periodic review of defendants' detention during trial. *See* ECCC Internal Rules (rev. 8), *supra* note 14, r. 82(1), r. 104(4).

36. Interview with Michiel Pestman, former Co-Lawyer for Nuon Chea, Phnom Penh (June 9, 2012). One of the authors also heard this from the international CIJ upon her arrival in Phnom Penh.

37. Internal Rule 60(2) provides in part: "Except where a confrontation is organized, the [CIJs] or their delegates shall interview witnesses in the absence of Charged Persons . . . or their lawyers[.]" Judge Lemonde was reportedly the principal drafter of the Internal Rules. The exclusion of defense from witness questioning derives from Cambodian procedures based on obsolete French law. *See* Cambodian Criminal Procedure Code (*as adopted* Aug. 10, 2007) [hereinafter CPC], art. 153 (providing in part: "The investigating judge questions witnesses separately, without any presence of the charged person and any civil party. The investigating judge may also arrange a confrontation between the charged person, civil parties and witnesses").

38. Judge Lemonde Remarks, *supra* note 33. *Cf.* Michael Karnavas, Op-Ed., *It's Time to Salvage the Khmer Rouge Tribunal's Legacy*, CAMBODIA DAILY, Dec. 12, 2012 (responding to Judge Lemonde's remark by noting that the Court's mishmash of procedures derive from the Internal Rules, which the ECCC judges drafted and "to this day continue to be amended and unevenly interpreted and applied").

39. Karnavas interview, *supra* note 12 (arguing that "the judges should have read the entire dossier. They should decide which documents they want, which witnesses should come in. . . . But here we have judges abdicating their role—I wonder why? Big hint: They haven't read the file").

40. *See, e.g.*, Kathia Martin-Chenut, *Proces International et Modeles de Justice Penale*, *in* DROIT INTERNATIONAL PENAL 847, 854–56 (Hervé Ascensio et al., 2d ed. 2012) (discussing how reforms to the ICTY and ICTR rules, particularly in response to efficiency problems evident in the *Milosevic* trial, led to the "hybridization" of international criminal procedures, including allowing more written submissions and decisions in lieu of oral hearings).

41. Decision on Co-Prosecutors' Rule 92 Submission Regarding the Admission of Witness Statements and Other Documents Before the Trial Chamber, Case No. 002/19-9-2007-ECCC/TC, ¶ 26 (Trial Chamber, June 20, 2012).

42. *Id.* ¶ 27. *See* Anne Heindel, *Admissibility of Witness Statements In Lieu of Oral Testimony*, CAMBODIA TRIBUNAL MONITOR (July 31, 2012), http://www.cambodiatribunal.org/sites/default/files/CTM Heindel 12-07-31.pdf.

43. *See* Bates, *supra* note 20, ¶ 132 (reporting that the one-year *Duch* investigation included interviews of more than 60 witnesses, two days of *in camera* confrontation hearings between Duch and 12 key witnesses, and a repetition of the same questions at trial). *See*

also Anette Marcher, *Investigating Judge Seen as Obstacle to Justice for KR*, PHNOM PENH POST, Feb. 4–7, 2010 (noting that participants in a workshop on due process before the ECCC was established recommended abolishing investigative judges in the Cambodian national system because their role "makes no positive contribution to the administration of justice . . . [but] results in continuing dysfunction and unnecessary dual work.").

44. Smith interview, *supra* note 22.

45. You Bunleng, Cambodian Co-Investigating Judge at the ECCC, response to questionnaire from the authors, June 25, 2012 (translated from Khmer by Kimsroy Sokvisal).

46. *See, e.g.*, Interview with Rupert Skilbeck, former head of the ECCC Defence Support Section, via telephone (June 7, 2012).

47. *See* Bates, *supra* note 20, ¶ 132 (citing interviews with judicial staff); authors' interviews with parties.

48. *Id.* ¶ 133.

49. ECCC Internal Rules (rev. 8), *supra* note 14, r. 73(a); Interview with Hans Corell, former UN Legal Counsel, via telephone (Nov. 15, 2012) (Saying that he and his delegation invented the PTC to solve only one problem: disagreements between the Co-Investigating Judges and the Co-Prosecutors: "Ironically, there would be a positive effect of the super-majority rule here. In order to stop a prosecution before the ECCC at least one international judge on the Pre-Trial Chamber would have to support such a decision. I saw no other way of protecting all the work put into this. I saw this as an element that could bring some dignity in the proceedings that, irrespective of the final outcome, at least there would be a public hearing of the case in question before the ECCC.").

50. Decision on the Urgent Applications for Immediate Release of Nuon Chea, Khieu Samphan, and Ieng Thirith, Case No. 002/19-9-2007/ECCC/TC, ¶ 21 (Feb. 16, 2011).

51. *See* Michael Karnavas & Ang Udom, *The Diligent Defense of Ieng Sary Is Not a Delaying Tactic*, CAMBODIA DAILY, July 11, 2011.

52. A supermajority of the Supreme Court found the appeal inadmissible under its narrow interlocutory jurisdiction. Decision on Ieng Sary's Appeal Against the Trial Chamber's Decision on Ieng Sary's Rule 89 Preliminary Objections (*Ne Bis in Idem* and Amnesty and Pardon), Case No. 002/19-9-2007-ECCC-TC/SC(11) (Mar. 20, 2012). Two international judges dissented, arguing the SCC had an obligation "to give the Appeal full consideration at the earliest possible juncture." *Id.* Dissenting Opinion of Judges Klonowiecka-Milart and Jayasinghe ¶ 4. *See also* Anne Heindel, *Interpreting the Right of Appeal in the Interest of Fair Proceedings*, CAMBODIA TRIBUNAL MONITOR (July 12, 2012), http://www.cambodiatribunal.org/sites/default/files/CTM Heindel 12-07-12.pdf. Due to Ieng Sary's death, the issue will not be subject to further adjudication.

53. Karnavas interview, *supra* note 12.

54. Decision on Appeal against Provisional Detention Order of Ieng Sary, Case No. 002/19-9-2007-ECCC/OCIJ (PTC03), ¶ 23 (Oct. 17, 2008) [hereinafter Decision on Ieng Sary's Detention Appeal].

55. Decision on Duch's Detention Appeal, *supra* note 4, ¶ 63.

56. *See* Cable 08PHNOMPENH 947, U.S. Embassy Phnom Penh, *Khmer Rouge Tribunal: Rocky Road for New Cases, Steady Path for Trial of Five KR Leaders* ¶ 6 (Nov. 28, 2008), *available at* http://www.wikileaks.org/cable/2008/11/08PHNOMPENH947.html.

57. Decision on Ieng Sary's Detention Appeal, *supra* note 54, ¶¶ 57–63.

58. Decision on Ieng Sary's Appeal Against the Closing Order, Case No. 002/19-9-2007-ECCC/OCIJ (PTC75), ¶¶ 58–67 (Apr. 11, 2011).

59. Ieng Sary's Appeal Against the Closing Order, Case No. 002/19-9-2007-ECCC/OCIJ (PTC 75), ¶ 22 (Oct. 25, 2010).

60. In the Closing Order, the CIJs had ducked the question, finding that it should be decided in a public adversarial hearing before the Trial Chamber. *See* Case 002 Closing Order, *supra* note 28, ¶ 1333.

61. Decision on Ieng Sary's Appeal Against the Closing Order, *supra* note 58, ¶ 67.

62. *See, e.g.*, Interview with Craig Etcheson, former investigator at the ECCC Office of the Co-Prosecutors, via telephone (Oct. 22, 2012) (emphasizing that "[t]he amount of staff and lawyer time required [to address these repeated challenges] is quite remarkable").

63. Law on the Establishment of Extraordinary Chambers in the Courts of Cambodia for the Prosecution of Crimes Committed During the Period of Democratic Kampuchea, as amended and promulgated on Oct. 27, 2004, NS/RKM/1004/006, arts. 3 new, 4–6 [hereinafter ECCC Law].

64. *Id.* arts. 7–8. The ECCC may hear cases involving the destruction of cultural property under the 1954 Hague Convention for the Protection of Cultural Property in the Event of Armed Conflict, but that convention neither defines the elements of a crime nor establishes individual criminal responsibility. The ECCC Law also grants the Court jurisdiction to adjudicate crimes against internationally protected persons, citing the Vienna Convention of 1961 on Diplomatic Relations, but that convention also does not establish individual criminal responsibility.

65. Case 002 Closing Order, *supra* note 28, ¶ 1301.

66. Ieng Sary's Appeal Against the Closing Order, *supra* note 59, ¶ 8 (citations omitted).

67. Co-Prosecutors v. Kaing Guek Eav *alias* Duch, Case No. 001/18-7-2007/ECCC/SC, Appeal Judgment, ¶¶ 89–91 (Feb. 3, 2012) [hereinafter *Duch* Appeal Judgment]. *See also* Co-Prosecutors v. Kaing Guek Eav *alias* Duch, Case No. 001/18-7-2007/ECCC/TC, Judgment, ¶¶ 26–34 (July 26, 2010) [hereinafter *Duch* Trial Chamber Judgment].

68. *Duch* Appeal Judgment, *supra* note 67, ¶ 96, *citing* Prosecutor v. Hadzihasanovic et al., Case No. IT-01–47-AR72, Decision on Interlocutory Appeal Challenging Jurisdiction in Relation to Command Responsibility, ¶ 34 (Appeals Chamber, July 16, 2003).

69. *See, e.g.*, Prosecutor v. Hadzihasanovic et al., *supra* note 68, ¶ 62.

70. *See, e.g.*, Prosecutor v. Milutinović et al., Decision on Dragoljub Ojdanić's Motion

Challenging Jurisdiction—Joint Criminal Enterprise, Case No. IT-99-37-AR72, ¶ 42 (Appeals Chamber, May 21, 2003).

71. *See Duch* Appeal Judgment, *supra* note 67, ¶ 97.

72. Article 6 of the Penal Code of 1956 states in part, "[c]riminal law has no retroactive effect. No crime can be punished by the application of penalties which were not pronounced by the law before it was committed."

73. *See* Decision on Appeals by Nuon Chea and Ieng Thirith Against the Closing Order, Case No. 002/19-9-2007-ECCC/OCIJ (PTC 145 & 146), ¶ 88 (Feb. 15, 2011); Decision on Ieng Sary's Appeal Against the Closing Order, *supra* note 58, ¶ 204.

74. *See* Decision on Appeals by Nuon Chea and Ieng Thirith, *supra* note 73, ¶¶ 89–90; Decision on Ieng Sary's Appeal Against the Closing Order, *supra* note 58, ¶ 205.

75. *Duch* Appeal Judgment, *supra* note 67, ¶¶ 91, 96.

76. Prosecutor v. Hadzihasanovic et al., *supra* note 68, ¶ 34.

77. Decision on Appeals by Nuon Chea and Ieng Thirith, *supra* note 73, ¶ 97.

78. Decision on Ieng Sary's Appeal Against the Closing Order, *supra* note 58, ¶ 212.

79. Decision on Appeals by Nuon Chea and Ieng Thirith, *supra* note 73, ¶¶ 98, 100. *See also* Decision on Ieng Sary's Appeal Against the Closing Order, *supra* note 58, ¶ 213.

80. Decision on Appeals by Nuon Chea and Ieng Thirith, *supra* note 73, ¶ 99.

81. *Duch* Trial Chamber Judgment, *supra* note 67, ¶ 292. Duch did not challenge this on appeal.

82. Decisions on Appeals by Nuon Chea and Ieng Thirith, *supra* note 73, ¶¶ 134–48; Decision on Ieng Sary's Appeal Against the Closing Order, *supra* note 58, ¶¶ 304–13.

83. Decision on Co-Prosecutors' Request to Exclude Armed Conflict Nexus Requirement from the Definition of Crimes Against Humanity, Case No. 002/19-9-2007/ECCC/TC, ¶ 33 (Oct. 26, 2011).

84. Decision on Ieng Sary's Appeal Against Trial Chamber's Decision on Co-Prosecutors' Request to Exclude Armed Conflict Nexus Requirement from the Definition of Crimes Against Humanity, Case No. 002/19-9-2007/ECCC/TC/SC(10), ¶ 8 (Mar. 19, 2012) (finding the appeal inadmissible).

85. *Duch* Trial Chamber Judgment, *supra* note 67, ¶¶ 293–96.

86. *Duch* Appeal Judgment, *supra* note 67, ¶¶ 176, 179.

87. *Id.* ¶ 213.

88. *See* Decision on Appeals by Nuon Chea and Ieng Thirith, *supra* note 73, ¶ 154.

89. *See generally* Prosecutor v. Dusko Tadic, Case No. IT-94-1-A, Judgment, ¶¶ 226–28 (Appeals Chamber, July 15, 1999).

90. Ieng Sary's Expedited Request to Make Submissions on the Application of Joint Criminal Enterprise Liability in the Co-Prosecutors' Appeal of the Closing Order Against Kaing Guek Eav "Duch," Case No. 001/18-7-2007-ECCC/OCIJ (PTC02), at I.1 (Sept. 15, 2008).

91. Decision on Ieng Sary's Request to Make Submissions on the Application of the

Theory of Joint Criminal Enterprise in the Co-Prosecutors' Appeal of the Closing Order Against Kaing Guek Eav "Duch," Case No. 001/18/-07-2007-ECCC/OCIJ (PTC 2), ¶ 12 (Oct. 6, 2008).

92. Decision on Urgent Joint Defence Request to Intervene on the Issue of Joint Criminal Enterprise in the OCP Appeal Against the Duch Closing Order, Case No. 001/18/-07-2007-ECCC/OCIJ (PTC 2), ¶ 8 (Nov. 5, 2008).

93. Decision on Ieng Sary's Request to Make Submissions in Response to the Co-Prosecutors' Request for the Application of Joint Criminal Enterprise, Case No. 001/18-7-2007-ECCC/OCIJ (PTC 02), ¶ 4 (July 3, 2009).

94. *Duch* Trial Chamber Judgment, *supra* note 67, ¶¶ 511–12.

95. Decision on the Applicability of Joint Criminal Enterprise, Case No. 002/19/09-2007/ECCC/TC, ¶ 22 (Sept. 12, 2011) (noting the previous finding in the *Duch* judgment).

96. *Id.* ¶¶ 30–37.

97. *Id.* ¶ 16. For an argument applauding the PTC's ruling, *see* Luke Marsh & Michael Ramsden, *Joint Criminal Enterprise: Cambodia's Reply to Tadić*, 11 INT'L CRIM. L. REV. 137 (2011).

98. *Duch* Trial Chamber Judgment, *supra* note 67, ¶ 549.

99. Decision on Appeals by Nuon Chea and Ieng Thirith, *supra* note 73, ¶ 230. *See also* Rehan Abeyratne, *Superior Responsibility and the Principle of Legality at the ECCC*, 44 GEO. WASH. INT'L L. REV. 39 (2012) (arguing that although the PTC decided the matter correctly, the 1977 Additional Protocol I to the Geneva Conventions of 1949 would have provided a stronger basis for the ruling than post–World War II jurisprudence).

100. Decision on Ieng Sary's Appeal Against the Closing Order, *supra* note 58, ¶ 459.

101. SCSL Report of the S-G, *supra* note 8, ¶ 19.

102. *See, e.g.*, Report of the Group of Experts for Cambodia Established Pursuant to General Assembly Resolution 52/135, U.N. Doc. A/53/850, S/1999/231, ¶ 84 (Mar. 16, 1999) (noting that "Crimes under domestic law will generally lack the specific elements of many international crimes and thus generally be easier to prove").

103. Notably, international crimes were entirely excluded from the STL's jurisdiction, apparently because some Security Council members doubted the events at issue would satisfy the "widespread or systematic" threshold required for crimes against humanity. *See* STL Report of S-G, *supra* note 10, ¶¶ 23–25.

104. Co-Prosecutors' Appeal of the Closing Order Against Kaing Guek Eav "Duch" Dated 8 August 2008, Case No. 001/18-7-2007-ECCC/OCIJ (PTC 02), ¶ 30 (Sept. 8, 2008). *See also* Charles Chernor Jalloh, *The Contribution of the Special Court for Sierra Leone to the Development of International Law*, 15 AFR. J. INT'L & COMP. L. 165, 173 (2007) (noting that national charges "could have enhanced Sierra Leoneans' sense of identification with and ownership of the Court's processes").

105. According to trial monitors, the decision not to file national charges was both a

legal and a tactical decision by the prosecutor, who described national law as "'a legal mine field' that could complicate the court's response to jurisdictional challenges." Sarah Kendall & Michelle Staggs, *From Mandate to Legacy: The Special Court for Sierra Leone as a Model for "Hybrid Justice,"* UC Berkeley War Crimes Study Center (Apr. 2005) at 7. *But see* Jalloh, *supra* note 104, at 173 (finding it "regrettable" that national law was not invoked, "as its use in indictments would have at least played a symbolic role by signaling the restoration of the rule of law in the country thereby enhancing the legitimacy of its troubled system").

106. *See* ECCC Law, *supra* note 63, art. 3 new.

107. Decision on the Defence Preliminary Objection Concerning the Statute of Limitations of Domestic Crimes, Case No. 001/18-7-2007-ECCC/TC, ¶¶ 14, 20, 31 (July 26, 2010).

108. *Id.* ¶ 38. *See also* Constitutional Council Decision No. 040/002/2001, Feb. 12, 2001, at 2 (unofficial translation).

109. Decision on the Defence Preliminary Objection, *supra* note 107, ¶¶ 39–49.

110. *Id.* ¶¶ 52–54.

111. *Id.* ¶ 56.

112. Case 002 Closing Order, *supra* note 28, ¶ 1574.

113. Decision on Defence Preliminary Objections (Statute of Limitations on Domestic Crimes), Case No. 002/19-9-2007-ECCC/TC, ¶ 15 (Sept. 22, 2011).

114. *Id.* ¶ 22.

115. *See* Decision on Appeals Against Co-Investigating Judges' Combined Order D250/3/3 Dated 13 January 2010 and Order D250/3/2 Dated 13 January 2010 on Admissibility of Civil Party Applications, Case No. 002/19-9-2007-ECCCC/OCIJ (PTC47 & 48) (Apr. 27, 2010) (Judge Prak Kimsan dissenting with Judge Rowan Downing on one point of the decision).

116. Framework Agreement, *supra* note 1, art. 12(1). *See also* ECCC Law, *supra* note 63, arts. 20 new, 23 new, and 33 new. Comparatively, the SCSL Statute provides that in amending that court's rules the judges "may be guided, as appropriate, by the Criminal Procedure Act, 1965, of Sierra Leone." SCSL Statute, *supra* note 6, art. 14(2). The SCSL Trial Chamber found that this reference "is only a means of guidance for the Judges . . . and certainly not legally binding upon them." Prosecutor v. Allieu Kondewa, SCSL-2003-12-PD, Decision on the Urgent Defense Application for Release from Provisional Detention, ¶ 27 (Nov. 21, 2003).

117. *See* Framework Agreement, *supra* note 1, art. 12(1). *See also* ECCC Law, *supra* note 63, arts. 20 new, 23 new, and 33 new.

118. *See* SCSL Statute, *supra* note 6, art. 14.

119. *See, e.g.,* You Bunleng, *supra* note 45 (highlighting the challenge of applying Cambodian procedures in a court comprising staff and judges from diverse legal traditions); Judge Lemonde Remarks, *supra* note 33 (saying the ECCC's civil law system was applied by actors who are not familiar with it and do not want to discover or understand it); Inter-

view with Elisabeth Simonneau Fort, ECCC Civil Party Lead Co-Lawyer, Phnom Penh (June 1, 2012) (noting that although the Court should apply civil law, common law lawyers tend to advance the system they know, and most mass crimes jurisprudence is rooted in common law); Etcheson interview, *supra* note 62 (noting that learning the rules, and innovation, is part of working in any *sui generis* institution, and OCP staff often felt that they were "making [it] up as [they] went along").

120. Karnavas interview, *supra* note 12. *See also* Ieng Sary's Response to the "Co-Prosecutors' Request to Put Before the Chamber Two Letters by Amnesty International Addressed to KHIEU Samphan and IENG Sary," Case No. 002/29-09-2007-ECCC/TC, ¶¶ 6-21, 29 (Mar. 3, 2013) (including a description of inconsistencies in the Trial Chamber's application of document admission rules and a request that the Chamber "[e]stablish clear and fair rules regarding the admission of new documents that would apply to all parties in a uniform manner"). *Cf.* Confidential interview, Phnom Penh (May 14, 2012) (noting that, as at other hybrid courts including the Kosovo panels, Bosnian War Crimes Chamber, and Special Panels in East Timor, at the ECCC "rules are violated based on momentary convenience").

121. Interview with Diana Ellis, Co-Lawyer for Ieng Thirith, Phnom Penh (Nov. 11, 2012). *See also* Martin-Chenut, *supra* note 40, at 861 (raising the question of whether mixing the accusatorial and inquisitorial systems "destabilizes their coherence" or "represents a solution").

122. Karnavas interview, *supra* note 12.

123. Simonneau Fort interview, *supra* note 119.

124. *But see* Smith interview, *supra* note 22 ("It's better to have a process based on [domestic] civil law because Cambodia has a lot to gain from following the ECCC model, even with modifications"). *Cf.* Martin-Chenut, *supra* note 40, at 862 (arguing, citing Rupert Skilbeck, that international trials present special challenges making it impossible to simply transpose domestic models; hybridization is needed "despite the risk of creating monsters").

125. *See* Letter from Sok An, Senior Minister in Charge of the Office of the Council of Ministers to Hans Corell, UN Undersecretary for Legal Affairs (Jan. 22, 2002) (noting the Government's intent to establish "a hierarchy in which Cambodian law and procedure are relied upon before resorting to other international procedure where necessary to fill any gaps").

126. Yoshi Kodama, Japanese Ministry of Foreign Affairs, *For Judicial Justice and Reconciliation in Cambodia: Reflections upon the Establishment of the Khmer Rouge Trials and the Trials' Procedural Rules 2007*, 9 LAW & PRACTICE OF INT'L TRIBS. 37, 83 (2010). *See also* You Bunleng, *supra* note 45 (stating that the Internal Rules are a revision of Cambodia's procedures based on the challenges of prosecuting mass crimes cases in accordance with international standards).

127. *See, e.g.*, Preliminary Objection Concerning the Legality of the Internal Rules and

Effect of the Trial Chamber's Order of 17 January 2011, Case No. 002/19-9-2007-ECCC/TC, ¶ 16 (Feb. 11, 2011); Civil Party Co-Lawyer's Joint Request for Reconsideration of the Pre-Trial Chamber's Assessment of the Legal Status of the Internal Rules in the Decision on Nuon Chea's Appeal Against Order Refusing Request for Annulment, Case No. 002/19-9-2007-ECCC/OCIJ (PTC 06), ¶¶ 21–23 (Oct. 13, 2008); Douglas Gillison, *Nuon Chea, Parties: KRT Rules Unconstitutional,* CAMBODIA DAILY, Nov. 1–2, 2008; Sluiter, *supra* note 31, at 320.

128. Preliminary Objection Concerning the Legality of the Internal Rules, *supra* note 127, ¶ 12.

129. *Id.* ¶ 20 (arguing that "any departure from 'existing procedures in force' must . . . be justified by reference to one of the[] specific statutory exceptions . . . [and] creation of new rules for the sake of convenience or mere efficiency [. . .] is in direct violation of the terms of Article 12(1) of the ECCC agreement.").

130. *See, e.g.,* Decision on Request for Release, *supra* note 5, ¶ 11.

131. Decision on Nuon Chea's Preliminary Objections Alleging the Unconstitutional Character of the ECCC Internal Rules, Case No. 002/19-9-2007/ECCC/TC, ¶ 7 (Aug. 8, 2011).

132. *Id.*

133. ECCC Defence Support Section, *Press Statement on the Plenary Session of Judges of the ECCC 1–5 September 2008,* Sept. 5, 2008.

134. *Id.*

135. *Id.*

136. Previously two competing codes were in force, the Transitional Law adopted by the UN Transitional Authority in Cambodia in 1992 and the State of Cambodia (SOC) Law on Criminal Procedure (1993). The SOC arguably lacked legal authority to adopt it at the time, but the SOC Law remained the primary source of reference for Cambodian courts until the 2007 adoption of the CPC. Sluiter, *supra* note 31, at 319.

137. *See, e.g.,* Khuon Narim & Khy Sovuthy, *Municipal Court Sentences 13 Boeng Kak Protesters to Jail,* CAMBODIA DAILY, May 25, 2012 (reporting that 13 women arrested for protesting the confiscation of their land by a private company were "charged and then immediately sentenced" to two-and-a-half years in prison after their lawyers walked out "in order to protest the court's decision to deny their request for witnesses and to have the case delayed").

138. *See, e.g.,* Decision on Civil Party Co-Lawyers' Joint Request for a Ruling on the Standing of Civil Party Lawyers to Make Submissions on Sentencing and Directions Concerning the Questioning of Accused, Experts and Witnesses Testifying on Character, Case No. 001/18-7-2007/ECCC/TC (Oct. 9, 2009) (Judge Lavergne dissenting).

139. *See* Preliminary Objection Concerning the Legality of the Internal Rules, *supra* note 127, ¶ 20.

140. *See, e.g.,* Interview with Jeanne Sulzer, former Legal Officer in the ECCC Civil

Party Lead Co-Lawyer Section, Phnom Penh (June 1, 2012). Judge Lemonde Remarks, *supra* note 33 (saying the CPC is "a copy and paste" of the French Code before 2000 and is "not adapted to the 21st century" as the old French Code has gaps and fairness issues that have been sanctioned by the European Court of Human Rights).

141. Judge Lemonde Remarks, *supra* note 33.

142. *See, e.g.*, Transcript of Trial Proceedings—Case 002, Case No. 002/19-9-2007-ECCC/TC, at 70 (Aug. 27, 2009) (in which a French defense lawyer argued against following the civil law approach on civil parties' rights to question witnesses, highlighting debates on that issue in France).

143. Marcher, *supra* note 43.

144. Cable 06PHNOMPENH2095, U.S. Embassy Phnom Penh, *Cambodia's ECCC Stumbles and Stalls* (Nov. 28, 2006), *available at* http://www.wikileaks.org/cable/2006/11/06PHNOMPENH2095.html.

145. Joint Statement by National and International Judicial Officers of the ECCC, Nov. 25, 2006; Thet Sambath & Erika Kinetz, *KR Affiliates Not Surprised by Tribunal Holdup*, Cambodia Daily, Nov. 28, 2006.

146. *See* Cable 06PHNOMPENH2095, *supra* note 144, ¶ 2.

147. *See id.* ¶ 4.

148. Ian MacKinnon, *Cambodia: Khmer Rouge Genocide Trial Close to Collapse as Judges Dispute Rules*, The Guardian, Feb. 27, 2007, at 19.

149. *Id.* (quoting assistant prosecutor Alex Bates).

150. Thet & Kinetz, *supra* note 145.

151. MacKinnon, *supra* note 148, at 19 (quoting an unnamed senior Western diplomat in Phnom Penh as saying, "It's not that Hun Sen will be indicted, but one or two top generals could be.").

152. *See* Cable 07PHNOMPENH77, U.S. Embassy Phnom Penh, *Update on the ECCC; David Scheffer Coming to Cambodia* ¶ 4 (Jan. 17, 2007), *available at* http://dazzlepod.com/cable/07PHNOMPENH77/.

153. *Id.* (quoting Open Society Justice Initiative [OSJI] trial monitor Heather Ryan).

154. *See, e.g.*, OSJI, *Progress and Challenges and the Extraordinary Chambers in the Courts of Cambodia*, at 11 (June 2007).

155. MacKinnon, *supra* note 148, at 19.

156. *Bar Association Demands More ECCC Control*, Cambodia Daily, Nov. 17, 2006; Erika Kinetz & Prak Chan Thul, *Bar Threatens Lawyers over ECCC Training*, Cambodia Daily, Nov. 23, 2006.

157. *Bar Association*, *supra* note 156.

158. Cable 07PHNOMPENH77, *supra* note 152, ¶ 4.

159. Erika Kinetz, *Sok An Calls for UN "Dialogue" on KR Defense*, Cambodia Daily, Dec. 18, 2006 (quoting from his letter to the UN).

160. Cable 07PHNOMPENH103, U.S. Embassy Phnom Penh, *RGC Worried ECCC*

Prosecutions Could Affect Peace and Security ¶ 4 (Jan. 22, 2007), *available at* http://cables.mrkva.eu/cable.php?id=93358.

161. Former Ambassador-at-Large David Scheffer visited Phnom Penh and spoke with Sok An at the request of OSJI "at the behest of some ECCC staff members." *See id.* ¶ 7.

162. *See* ECCC Internal Rules (rev. 8), *supra* note 14, r. 11.

163. *See* Statement from the Review Committee of the Extraordinary Chambers in the Courts of Cambodia, Mar. 16, 2007; Press Statement, UNAKRT, International Judges of ECCC Say April Plenary Not Possible, Apr. 3, 2007.

164. *Cambodian Bar Association Accuses Foreign Judges of Hindering Khmer Rouge Tribunal*, CHINA POST, Mar. 26, 2007. *See also* Erika Kinetz & Pin Sisovann, *Bar Accuses Judges of Using Fees to Stall Tribunal*, CAMBODIA DAILY, Mar. 19, 2007.

165. Prak Chan Thul & Douglas Gillison, *Local ECCC Judges: If Bar Goes, We Go*, CAMBODIA DAILY, Apr. 6, 2007.

166. Douglas Gillison & Prak Chan Thul, *Bar Could be Kept Out of KR Trial: Int'l Judges*, CAMBODIA DAILY, Apr. 4, 2007.

167. *See* Erika Kinetz & Prak Chan Thul, *Int'l Lawyers Join in Condemnation of High Bar Association Fees*, CAMBODIA DAILY, Apr. 16, 2007; Cable O6PHNOMPENH2095, *supra* note 144, ¶ 6 (repeating speculation that the defense office's USD $4.8 million dollar budget was the primary reason for the BAKC's interest in the ECCC); Cable 07PHNOMPENH438, U.S. Embassy Phnom Penh, *Cambodian Bar Association Says to ECCC: Show Me the Money* ¶ 5 (Mar. 20, 2007), *available at* http://www.wikileaks.org/cable/2007/03/07PHNOMPENH438.html (reporting that most sources believed the BAKC was seeking money after losing international funds due to irregularities in the election for Bar president).

168. *See* Statement from the International Judges of the Extraordinary Chambers in the Courts of Cambodia, Apr. 30, 2007.

169. Cable 07PHNOMPENH826, U.S. Embassy Phnom Penh, *ECCC Passes Internal Rules* ¶ 2 (June 15, 2007), *available at* http://www.wikileaks.org/cable/2007/06/07PHNOMPENH826.html.

170. Decision on Nuon Chea's Preliminary Objection Alleging the Unconstitutional Character of the ECCC Internal Rules, Case No. 002/19-9-2007/ECCC/TC, ¶ 7 (Aug. 8, 2011) (citing Decision on Nuon Chea's Appeal Against Order Refusing Request for Annulment, Case No. 002/19-9-2007-ECCC/OCIJ (PTCO6), ¶ 14 (Aug. 26, 2008)).

171. Simonneau Fort interview, *supra* note 119. *But see* interview with former ECCC official, via telephone (June 10, 2012) (saying that as a separately constituted court, the ECCC is neither a civil nor a common law court, and the relative influence of each varies across issues).

172. Decision on Immediate Appeal by Khieu Samphan on Application for Release, Case No. 002/19-9-2007-ECCC-TC/SC(04), ¶ 31 (June 6, 2011).

173. *See* Amnesty International, *Sierra Leone: Recommendations on the Draft Statute of*

the Special Court (Nov. 14, 2000), at 17 (arguing similarly in anticipation of the SCSL "that the mixture of two different sets of rules of evidence may cause confusion.").

174. Decision on Immediate Appeal, *supra* note 172, ¶ 28.

175. *Id.* ¶ 28.

176. *Id.*

177. *Id.* ¶ 46.

178. *Id.* ¶ 47.

179. *Id.* Partially Dissenting Opinion of Judge Noguchi ¶ 6. Similarly, the CIJs have said that merely because some CPC provisions were not incorporated into the Internal Rules "does not constitute a 'lacuna'[.]" Rather "[t]hey were deliberately left out because they were manifestly ill-adapted to the unique circumstances of the ECCC." The Strategy of the Co-Investigative Judges in Regard to the Judicial Investigations, Case No. 002/19-9-2007-ECCC-OCIJ, ¶ 11 (Dec. 11, 2009).

180. *See, e.g.*, Civil Party Co-Lawyer Silke Studzinsky's response to Judge Klonowiecka-Milart regarding the interplay of the Internal Rules and CPC regarding civil party admission, Transcript of Appeal Proceedings—Kaing Guek Eav "Duch," Case File No. 001/18-7-2007-ECCC/SC at 67–68 (Mar. 30, 2011) (arguing that in view of a difference between CPC article 355 and Internal Rule 100, "the rules are clear in this regard . . . and therefore we see [the Internal Rules] as a specific and as a first-ranking source where we have to look, except where there is a gap.")

181. *Duch* Appeal Judgment, *supra* note 67, ¶ 409. *Cf. id.* ¶ 466 (noting that in considering Duch's appeal, "the Supreme Court Chamber begins with an examination of the relevant provisions of the 2007 Code of Criminal Procedure of Cambodia. The Chamber will then determine whether the Internal Rules deviate from this regime and, if so, to what extent."). *Cf.* Decision on Immediate Appeal Against the Trial Chamber's Order to Unconditionally Release the Accused Ieng Thirith, Case No. 002/19-9-2007 ECCC-C/SC, ¶ 33 (Dec. 14, 2012) (noting the "methodological uncertainty as to whether the Trial Chamber opted to innovate pursuant to Article 12 of the ECCC Agreement by incorporating [international procedural standards], or whether it remained grounded in Cambodian law and was interpreting existing provisions in light of international standards").

182. *See, e.g.*, Long interview, *supra* note 32 (arguing that enactment of the CPC during the life of the Court benefits the domestic system, because ECCC practice will influence how nationals apply the law in national courts).

Chapter 3

1. We set aside administrative functions related to outreach and victim support, which are discussed at length in subsequent chapters.

2. Interview with David Tolbert, former UN Special Expert to advise on the UN Assistance to the Khmer Rouge Trials, via telephone (June 19, 2012).

3. Law on the Establishment of Extraordinary Chambers in the Courts of Cambodia for the Prosecution of Crimes Committed During the Period of Democratic Kampuchea, as amended and promulgated on Oct. 27, 2004, NS/RKM/1004/006, arts. 30, 31 new [hereinafter ECCC Law]; Agreement between the United Nations and the Royal Government of Cambodia Concerning the Prosecution under Cambodian Law of Crimes Committed During the Period of Democratic Kampuchea (June 6, 2003), art. 8(2)-(3) [hereinafter Framework Agreement].

4. ECCC Law, *supra* note 3, art. 31 new.

5. Yoshi Kodama, *For Judicial Justice and Reconciliation in Cambodia: Reflections upon the Establishment of the Khmer Rouge Trials and the Trials' Procedural Rules 2007*, 9 L. & Prac. Of Int'l Cts. & Tribunals 37, 49 (2010).

6. Framework Agreement, *supra* note 3, art. 8(4).

7. John A. Hall, *Court Administration at the ECCC*, *in* On Trial: The Khmer Rouge Accountability Process 172, 181 (John D. Ciorciari & Anne Heindel eds., 2009).

8. Kodama, *supra* note 5, at 49.

9. *See* ECCC, *Office of Administration*, http://www.eccc.gov.kh/en/office-of-administration/ (visited July 6, 2012).

10. S.C. Res. 1757, U.N. Doc. S/RES/1757 (May 30, 2007), Annex, Agreement between the United Nations and the Lebanese Republic on the establishment of a Special Tribunal for Lebanon, art. 12 [hereinafter STL Agreement]; Statute of the Special Court of Sierra Leone, U.N. Doc. S/RES/1315, art. 16 (Jan. 16, 2002) [hereinafter SCSL Statute].

11. Cable 06PHNOMPENH1983, U.S. Embassy Phnom Penh, *Recent ECCC Developments* ¶ 8 (Nov. 2, 2006), *available at* http://dazzlepod.com/cable/06PHNOMPENH1983.

12. Anne Heindel, *Why the ECCC Office of Administration Would Benefit from Being Structured More Like a "Registry,"* Searching for the Truth (Oct. 2007).

13. Interview with Hans Corell, former UN Legal Counsel, via telephone (Nov. 15, 2012).

14. Erika Kinetz, *Another Delay for Justice?* Newsweek, Oct. 5, 2007 (citing a confidential report by UN experts Robin Vincent and Kevin St. Louis).

15. *See* Open Society Justice Initiative (OSJI), *Recent Developments at the Extraordinary Chambers in the Courts of Cambodia* 13 n.30 (May 2009).

16. *U.S. Urges Credible Khmer Rouge Genocide Tribunal*, Reuters, May 19, 2005.

17. Confidential interview responses (on file with the authors).

18. Interview with Clint Williamson, former UN Special Expert to advise on the UN Assistance to the Khmer Rouge Trials and former U.S. Ambassador-at-Large for War Crimes Issues and UN Special Expert, via telephone (June 27, 2012) (noting that "there was lots of skepticism about the ability of the Court to operate effectively in light of how

things were playing out initially" and that more effective administration was "important before the U.S. got behind the Court publicly").

19. *Michelle Lee Resigns*, DEV. WEEKLY, Oct. 1, 2007.

20. Williamson interview, *supra* note 18.

21. Confidential interview responses (on file with the authors).

22. Confidential interview with a senior ECCC staff member, Phnom Penh (Nov. 2012).

23. ECCC Law, *supra* note 3, art. 44(1) new.

24. *Id.* art. 44(4) new.

25. ECCC Law, *supra* note 3, art. 44(2) new; Framework Agreement, *supra* note 3, art. 17(a).

26. Framework Agreement, *supra* note 3, art. 17(c).

27. *Id.* art. 17(b), (d).

28. To date, approximately 35 UN member states have contributed to the ECCC. The United Nations also applied $5 million left in the UN's account from the UN Transitional Authority in Cambodia. Extraordinary Chambers in the Courts of Cambodia, *How Is the Court Financed?* http://www.eccc.gov.kh/en/faq/how-court-financed (last visited Apr. 24, 2012).

29. Statute of the International Tribunal for the Prosecution of Persons Responsible for Serious Violations of International Humanitarian Law Committed in the Territory of the Former Yugoslavia since 1991, *amended July 7, 2009*, art. 32; Statute of the International Tribunal for Rwanda, Annex, U.N. Doc. S/RES/955, art. 30 (Nov. 8, 1994).

30. Rome Statute of the International Criminal Court arts. 114–16, July 17, 1998, 2187 U.N.T.S. 90 (entered into force on July 1, 2002).

31. Agreement between the United Nations and the Lebanese Republic on the establishment of a Special Tribunal for Lebanon, S.C. Res. 1757, Annex, U.N. Doc. S/RES/1757, art. 5 (May 30, 2007).

32. S.C. Res 1315 (2000), ¶ 8(c); *Report of the Secretary-General on the Establishment of a Special Court for Sierra Leone*, U.N. Doc. S/2000/915 ¶¶ 68–72 (Oct. 4, 2000).

33. *Report of the Secretary-General on Khmer Rouge Trials*, ¶¶ 74–78, U.N. Doc. A/57/769 (Mar. 31, 2003) (citing difficulties in financing the SCSL as evidence of the need to use assessed contributions).

34. G.A. Res. 57/228B, ¶ 3, U.N. Doc. A/RES/57/228B (May 13, 2003).

35. Corell interview, *supra* note 13. *See also* Hans Corell, *Foreword*, *in* INTERNATIONAL PROSECUTORS v, vii (Luc Reydams et al. eds., 2012) (asking: "What credibility would national courts have if they were funded by different donors and not from taxes or other official revenues? It is obvious that the same reasoning should be applied at the international level.").

36. Confidential senior staff interview, *supra* note 22.

37. SCSL Statute, *supra* note 10, art. 25.

38. Internal Rules of the ECCC (rev. 8), *rev'd* Aug. 3, 2011, r. 19(2).

39. *Id.* r. 19(1) (noting that the Co-Prosecutors also participate in a consultative capacity).

40. Heindel, *supra* note 12.

41. Confidential senior staff interview, *supra* note 22.

42. Interview with Larry Johnson, former UN Assistant Secretary-General for Legal Affairs, via telephone (June 21, 2012).

43. *Id.*

44. Tolbert interview, *supra* note 2.

45. *Id.*

46. United Nations Assistance to the Khmer Rouge Trials, *UNAKRT Mission and Scope*, http://www.unakrt-online.org/01_home.htm (last visited Apr. 24, 2012).

47. A 2007 audit by UNDP, discussed in detail *infra*, found the oversight of the Cambodian side of the court to be sorely lacking. United Nations Development Program, *Audit of Human Resources Management at the Extraordinary Chambers in the Courts of Cambodia (ECCC)*, Report No. RCM0172 (June 4, 2007), at 20–21.

48. Erika Kinetz, *Officials Stand by Structure of KR Tribunal*, CAMBODIA DAILY, Oct. 3, 2007.

49. Cable 08TOKYO217_a, U.S. Embassy Tokyo, *DAS Marciel Engages Japan Interlocutors on SE Asia* ¶ 10 (Jan. 28, 2008), *available at* http://www.wikileaks.org/plusd/cables/08TOKYO217_a.html (paraphrasing comments made by Ihara Junichi, Ministry of Foreign Affairs of Japan). *See also* Cable 08USUNNEWYORK872, U.S. Mission to the United Nations, *Corruption Allegations Dominate Khmer Rouge Trials (UNKRT) Steering Committee Meeting in New York at UK Mission* ¶ 15 (Sept. 29, 2008), *available at* http://www.wikileaks.org/cable/2008/09/08USUNNEWYORK872.html (paraphrasing a statement by Peter Taksoe-Jensen, Assistant-Secretary for Legal Affairs, that the UN Office of Legal Affairs "does not presently have the resources to devote the necessary time and attention to the Tribunal").

50. Anne Heindel with John Ciorciari, *Possible Roles for a Special Advisor or Oversight Committee for the ECCC*, SEARCHING FOR THE TRUTH (Jan.–Mar. 2008); OSJI, *Recent Developments at the Extraordinary Chambers in the Courts of Cambodia* 10 (Dec. 7, 2007).

51. Susan Postlewaite, *Cambodia: The High Cost of Closure*, BLOOMBERG BUSINESSWEEK, Apr. 1, 2008.

52. Williamson interview, *supra* note 18.

53. *Id.*

54. Postlewaite, *supra* note 51.

55. Interview with Craig Etcheson, former investigator in the ECCC Office of the Co-Prosecutors, via telephone (Oct. 22, 2012).

56. Williamson interview, *supra* note 18.

57. Although the Special Expert post was not initially associated with the United States, subsequent U.S. funding and the appointment of former U.S. officials have created

a nexus since 2010. *See* Cable 09STATE15565, U.S. Secretary of State, *Demarche Request: U.S. Candidate for UN Special Expert for the Khmer Rouge Tribunal* ¶ 6 (Feb. 10, 2010), *available at* http://www.cablegatesearch.net/cable.php?id=10STATE15565 (noting that U.S. officials had offered to fund the position); *Cambodia: Ban Designates New Adviser for Khmer Rouge Trials*, UN NEWS CENTRE, Jan. 18, 2012.

58. *See* Letter from Nuon Chea Defense Team, Request for Information Related to Ex-Parte Meetings Between Judge Cartwright, Andrew Cayley, and/or Knut Rosandhaug (Nov. 4, 2011).

59. Email from Knut Rosandhaug to Michiel Pestman (Nov. 1, 2011), *available at* http://www.eccc.gov.kh/en/document/court.

60. Julia Wallace, *KRT Defense Alleges Ex Parte Meetings*, CAMBODIA DAILY, Nov. 7, 2011.

61. The *Nuon Chea* team demanded the dates and minutes of meetings to see if Judge Cartwright and Cayley had discussed issues pertaining to Case 002. Request for Information Regarding Ex-Parte Meetings Among Judge Silvia Cartwright, the International Co-Prosecutor, and the Deputy Director of Administration, Case no. 002/19-9-2007-ECCC-TC, ¶ 6 (Nov. 15, 2011). Defense lawyers sought to participate but were rebuffed on the grounds that the meetings are "informal" and "ad hoc" and defense teams could raise administrative or operational matters with the OA Deputy Director. Letter from Knut Rosandhaug to Mr. Udom and Mr. Karnavas (Nov. 7, 2011), *available at* http://www.eccc.gov.kh/en/document/court.

62. *See* Urgent Application for Disqualification of Judge Cartwright, Case No. 002/19-9-2007-ECCC-TC, ¶ 12 (Nov. 21, 2011) (arguing that that while the secret meetings may have been undertaken with good intentions, they violated the Cambodian Code of Judicial Ethics and raised concerns about Judge Cartwright's impartiality).

63. Ieng Sary's Request for Investigation Concerning *Ex Parte* Communications Between the International Co-Prosecutor, Judge Cartwright, and Others, Case No. 002/19-9-2007-ECCC-TC, ¶ 5 (Nov. 24, 2011).

64. Decision on Motions for Disqualification of Judge Silvia Cartwright, Case No. 002/19-9-2007-ECCC-TC, ¶¶ 19–21 (Dec. 2, 2011) (with reserve Judge Fenz filling in for Judge Cartwright).

65. Decision on Ieng Sary's Appeal Against the Trial Chamber's Decision on Motions for Disqualification of Judge Silvia Cartwright, Case No. 002/19-9-2007-ECCC-TC, ¶ 24 (Apr. 17, 2012).

66. Cable 05CANBERRA1215, U.S. Embassy Canberra, *Australia Does Not Support Management Committee for Khmer Rouge Tribunal* ¶ 2 (July 18, 2005), *available at* http://www.wikileaks.org/cable/2005/07/05CANBERRA1215.html.

67. SCSL Statute, *supra* note 10, art. 7.

68. *Second Report of the Secretary-General Submitted Pursuant to the Security Council Resolution 1757 (2007)*, U.N. Doc. S/2008/173 (Mar. 12, 2008).

69. Cable 05CANBERRA1215, *supra* note 66, ¶ 3.

70. Cable 07PHNOMPENH429, U.S. Embassy Phnom Penh, *Friends of the ECCC or RGC?* (Mar. 16, 2007), *available at* http://dazzlepod.com/cable/07PHNOMPENH429/.

71. Cable 06PHNOMPENH1118, U.S. Embassy Phnom Penh, *Inaugural Meeting of the Friends of the ECCC* ¶¶ 1–2 (June 15, 2006), *available at* http://dazzlepod.com/cable/06PHNOMPENH1118/.

72. Kodama, *supra* note 5, at 107–8.

73. Cable 06PHNOMPENH1118, *supra* note 71, ¶ 9.

74. Cable 07PHNOMPENH429, *supra* note 70, ¶ 1.

75. *Id.* ¶ 7. The U.S. Embassy supported that approach, but with exceptions in "rare circumstances" on "issues that could threaten the ECCC's existence [or] credibility." The Australians also did "not support joint diplomatic engagement." *Id.* ¶¶ 5–6.

76. *Id.* ¶¶ 8–9.

77. *Id.* ¶ 6.

78. Kodama asserts that the Friends Group "never uses bilateral assistance to force issues on the Office of Administration." Kodama, *supra* note 5, at 108.

79. Williamson interview, *supra* note 18.

80. *Id.* (describing some "natural" differences in view between the New York–based group, which tended to take a "more legal or administrative view," and ambassadors in Phnom Penh, who tended to put things in the "broader political context" of their relations with Cambodia, leading to "a bit of a disconnect" at times).

81. John Hall, *Donors Should Adopt a Balanced Approach to Funding ECCC*, Cambodia Daily, July 21, 2008 (suggesting that the shift may have been partly an effort to avoid exposure to another UN audit amid an ongoing corruption scandal).

82. Stuart Ford, *How Leadership in International Criminal Law Is Shifting from the United States to Europe and Asia*, 55 St. Louis U. L. J. 955, 979 (2011). By the end of 2011, Japan accounted for 47%, and the United States had risen to 6%. ECCC, *ECCC Financial Outlook* (July 31, 2013).

83. Ford, *supra* note 82, at 977.

84. *See, e.g., In Cambodia, UN Legal Chief Warns on Interference in Work of Genocide Tribunal*, UN News Centre (Oct. 20, 2011); *UN Defends Judge in Khmer Rouge Trial Row*, Agence France Presse, Jan. 25, 2012 (reporting on meetings between Sok An and senior UN officials regarding the Case 003 and 004 disputes).

85. Erika Kinetz, *Report Finds Flaws in ECCC Administration*, Cambodia Daily, Sept. 25, 2007; Kinetz, *supra* note 14.

86. Tolbert interview, *supra* note 2.

87. United Nations Development Program, Office of Audit and Performance Review, *Audit of Human Resources Management at the Extraordinary Chambers in the Courts of Cambodia (ECCC)*, Report No. RCM0172, at 12 (June 4, 2007), edited to include Cambodian responses in the text and to remove individual names, *available at* http://old.eccc.gov.kh/english/cabinet/OAPR.pdf [hereinafter UNDP Audit].

88. Cable 06PHNOMPENH1362, U.S. Embassy Phnom Penh, *Khmer Rouge Tribunal Building Momentum* ¶ 10 (July 27, 2006), *available at* http://dazzlepod.com/cable/06PHNOMPENH1362/.

89. OSJI, *Memorandum to the Group of Interested States: Priority Issues for the Extraordinary Chambers in the Courts of Cambodia (ECCC)* 14 (Oct. 2006), *available at* http://www.soros.org/sites/default/files/cambodia_20061004.pdf. OA Director Sean Visoth rejected this claim in a meeting with the Friends Group shortly afterward. Cable 06PHNOMPENH1983, *supra* note 11, ¶ 4.

90. The UNDP's Office of Audit and Performance Review and a Malaysia-based firm performed the audit in early 2007, and the ECCC later released it publicly. UNDP Audit, *supra* note 87, at 9.

91. The 2007 ECCC personnel handbook specifically asserts that only national section chiefs can perform those roles. *Id.* at 18–19.

92. *Id.* at 1–5, 15–16 (adding that the performance evaluation system was inadequate).

93. *Id.* at 9–11.

94. *Id.*

95. *Id.* at 5.

96. Kodama, *supra* note 5, at 57. Kodama was the Japanese Co-Chair of the Friends of the ECCC donor group in 2006–7 and supports the Cambodian Government's position on sovereignty over domestic staff management and hiring, subject to reasonable outside critiques. *Id.* at 77.

97. UNDP Audit, *supra* note 87, at 6.

98. Hall, *supra* note 7, at 186.

99. Rory Byrne, *UN Reports Call for Changes in Structure of Khmer Rouge Tribunal*, Voice of America, Oct. 5, 2007.

100. *Id.*

101. Erika Kinetz & Prak Chan Thul, *Bar Demands Same Pay for Cambodian, Int'l Lawyers*, Cambodia Daily, Apr. 10, 2007.

102. *Id.*

103. These arguments were not unique to Cambodia. National staffers made very similar arguments at the Special Panels in East Timor. Suzannah Linton, *Rising from the Ashes: The Creation of a Viable Criminal Justice System in East Timor*, 25 Melb. U. L. Rev. 122, 150 (2001).

104. UNDP Audit, *supra* note 87, at 11, 20–21 (adding that the Project Board's process did not "provide sufficient assurance that the implementation of the project will be properly directed and controlled").

105. *Id.* at 6, 20–21.

106. *Id.*

107. Cable 07PHNOMPENH429, *supra* note 70, ¶ 4.

108. Extraordinary Chambers in the Courts of Cambodia, Personnel Handbook (Na-

tional) (2d ed., Aug. 2, 2007), *available at* http://www.cambodiatribunal.org/sites/default/files/resources/Personnel_Handbook_English.pdf.

109. United Nations Development Program, *UNDP Statement—Cambodia* (Sept. 25, 2007), http://content.undp.org/go/newsroom/2007/september/undp-statement-cambodia-20070926.en.

110. Deloitte Touche Tohmatsu India Pvt. Limited, *Report on the Special HRM Review* 3–4 (Apr. 25, 2008), *available at* http://www.cambodiatribunal.org/sites/default/files/reports/full_report.pdf.

111. *Id.* at 2.

112. Jo Scheuer, UNDP Country Director, *UNDP Statement on the ECCC Human Resources Management Review* (Apr. 25, 2008).

113. *Audit Says Management of Cambodian Tribunal Has Improved After Calls for Reform*, Int'l Herald Tribune, Apr. 25, 2008.

114. Douglas Gillison, *KR Victims Unit Officers Dismiss Questions on Appointments*, Cambodia Daily, Aug. 6, 2009; Julia Wallace, *Khmer Rouge Tribunal Victims Unit Gets New Chief*, Cambodia Daily, Sept. 2, 2010 (noting that Helen Jarvis and her successor, Rong Chhorn, were both appointed head of the Victims Unit without such a competition).

115. Cable 09PHNOMPENH316, U.S. Embassy Phnom Penh, *Khmer Rouge Tribunal "Friends Group" Meets for First Time in a Year: Solid Judicial Performance Meets External Shocks* ¶ 4 (May 14, 2009), *available at* http://dazzlepod.com/cable/09PHNOMPENH316/.

116. Cat Barton, *Kickback Claims Stain the KRT*, Phnom Penh Post, Feb. 23–Mar. 8, 2007; Hall, *supra* note 7, at 187–88.

117. Press Release, OSJI, *Corruption Allegations at Khmer Rouge Court Must Be Investigated* (Feb. 24, 2007).

118. Erika Kinetz & Pin Sisovann, *ECCC Cools to NGO After Kickback Charge*, Cambodia Daily, Feb. 19, 2007.

119. Mean Veasna, *ECCC Denies Allegations of Pay Kickbacks*, VOA Khmer (Feb. 16, 2007).

120. Cable 07PHNOMPENH422, U.S. Embassy Phnom Penh, *The ECCC and OSJI* ¶¶ 2–5 (Mar. 15, 2007), *available at* http://dazzlepod.com/cable/07PHNOMPENH422/.

121. *Id.* ¶ 10 (noting that Cambodian staffers feared making accusations openly given the lack of a "whistleblower culture" but were glad international staffers revealed information to OSJI, hoping media attention would end the practice).

122. *Id.* ¶ 6, 8 (noting that Scheffer also thought OSJI had erred by "going public too quickly").

123. *Id.* ¶¶ 8–9.

124. United Nations Development Program, *supra* note 109. *See also* Kinetz, *supra* note 14.

125. Cable 07PHNOMPENH826, U.S. Embassy Phnom Penh, *ECCC*

Passes Internal Rules ¶ 10 (June 15, 2007), *available at* http://dazzlepod.com/cable/07PHNOMPENH826/.

126. *See, e.g.*, Kinetz, *supra* note 85 (including a staffer's confidential allegation that he had to "hand over 25 percent of his salary for his job"); Douglas Gillison, *ECCC Reviews New Graft Allegations on Eve of Funds Drive*, Cambodia Daily, July 29, 2008 (noting that Sean Visoth circulated a memo within the ECCC concerning new allegations of corruption).

127. John Hall, *New Corruption Allegations Pose Test for Future of KR Tribunal*, Cambodia Daily, Aug. 15, 2008.

128. Douglas Gillison, *ECCC Funding Delayed Over Graft Claims*, Cambodia Daily, Aug. 6, 2008.

129. Tolbert interview, *supra* note 2; Hall, *supra* note 7, at 191.

130. Georgia Wilkins, *KR Court Graft Review Unfairly Names and Shames Gov't Says*, Phnom Penh Post, Sept. 22, 2008.

131. Sopheng Cheang, *Cambodian Genocide Lawyer Hits at Corruption Issue*, Associated Press, Apr. 3, 2009.

132. *Tribunal Staff Sets Up Anti-Corruption Team*, VOA (Khmer), Aug. 15, 2008.

133. Cable 08PHNOMPENH841, U.S. Embassy Phnom Penh, *Core Donors Updated on Khmer Rouge Tribunal Are United in Addressing the Corruption Issue* ¶ 1 (Oct. 10, 2008), *available at* http://dazzlepod.com/cable/08PHNOMPENH841/. Key donors approached the Cambodian Government bilaterally about the need to address the corruption issue but did not issue a joint demarche. *Id.* ¶ 6 (noting that the Japanese embassy saw a joint demarche as too confrontational and one-sided, and France and Australia agreed).

134. Tolbert interview, *supra* note 2 (noting that donors had helped arrange the meeting after Sok An initially resisted meeting with him, because the RGC objected to the creation of the Special Expert post).

135. *Id.* (paraphrasing Sok An and noting that Sok An had asked Tolbert to provide a copy of the OIOS report and to remove OA Deputy Director Knut Rosandhaug, both of which Tolbert refused to do). *See also* Cable 08PHNOMPENH883, U.S. Embassy Phnom Penh, *Sok An on the Khmer Rouge Tribunal* ¶¶ 6, 7, 9, 13 (Nov. 3, 2008), *available at* http://dazzlepod.com/cable/08PHNOMPENH883/.

136. *The Court on Trial*, Economist, Apr. 2, 2009. After his departure as OA Director, Sean reportedly took a job working for Sok An in the Council of Ministers. Kong Sothanarith, *Absence of Tribunal Administrator Raises Concerns*, VOA Khmer (June 23, 2010), http://www.voacambodia.com/content/absence-of-tribunal-administrator-raises-concerns-96980264/1360061.html.

137. Royal Government of Cambodia and United Nations, *Joint Statement* (Feb. 23, 2009), *available at* http://old.eccc.gov.kh/english/cabinet/fileUpload/108/Joint_Statement_EN.pdf.

138. Seth Mydans, *Corruption Allegations Affect Khmer Rouge Trials*, N.Y. Times, Apr.

9, 2009; Cable 09PHNOMPENH168, U.S. Embassy Phnom Penh, *Donors Urge Resumed Funding, More Negotiation on Khmer Rouge Tribunal Anti-Corruption Mechanism* ¶ 3 (Mar. 17, 2009), *available at* http://dazzlepod.com/cable/09PHNOMPENH168/.

139. Cable 09PHNOMPENH168, *supra* note 138, ¶ 6.

140. *Id.* ¶¶ 10–12.

141. *Long-Delayed Khmer Rouge Genocide Trial to Begin*, Wash. Times, Mar. 29, 2009. Japan notably made no mention of the corruption issue in a January 2009 meeting with Hun Sen on funding the tribunal. *Japan Pledges More Money for Khmer Rouge Tribunal*, Int'l Herald Tribune, Jan. 11, 2009 (discussing contributions to the UN side of the court).

142. Cable 09PHNOMPENH264, U.S. Embassy Phnom Penh, *Khmer Rouge Tribunal: Donors Chart a More Unified Course* ¶ 3 (Apr. 24, 2009), http://www.wikileaks.nl/cable/2009/04/09PHNOMPENH264.html.

143. Cable 09PHNOMPENH243, U.S. Embassy Phnom Penh, *Khmer Rouge Tribunal: UN Formalizes Own Anti-Corruption Mechanism as Sok An Mulls Over UN Proposal* ¶¶ 1, 11 (Apr. 10, 2009), *available at* http://dazzlepod.com/cable/09PHNOMPENH243.

144. The ambassadors present represented Japan, France, Australia, Germany, the United Kingdom, and the United States, as well as the European Union chargé. Cable 09PHNOMPENH264, *supra* note 142, ¶¶ 5–6, 11. She added, "The donors have rallied around a position that will encourage both sides to re-think their positions. We have been frank in stating that we believe it is time for the Cambodians to make some concessions, but also believe the UN must be seen as engaged."

145. *Id.* ¶ 6.

146. Cable 09TOKYO1434, U.S. Embassy Tokyo, *Ending the Cambodian War Crimes Tribunal Deadlock: Anti-Corruption Mechanism Proposed to Japan* (June 25, 2009), *available at* http://leaks.hohesc.us/?view=09TOKYO1434.

147. Cable 09PHNOMPENH333, U.S. Embassy Phnom Penh, *Khmer Rouge Tribunal: S/WCI Ambassador Williamson Begins Talks on Anti-Corruption Mechanism,* ¶ 4 (May 22, 2009), *available at* http://dazzlepod.com/cable/09PHNOMPENH333/.

148. Cable 09PHNOMPENH333, *supra* note 147, ¶ 6.

149. Cable 09PHNOMPENH343, U.S. Embassy Phnom Penh, *Khmer Rouge Tribunal: Sok An Enthusiastic About Proposed Anti-Corruption Mechanism,* ¶¶ 3–14 (May 28, 2009), *available at* http://dazzlepod.com/cable/09PHNOMPENH343/; Cable 09PHNOMPENH564, U.S. Embassy Phnom Penh, *Khmer Rouge Tribunal: Sok An Signs Agreement on Anti-Corruption Mechanism,* ¶ 4 (Aug. 7, 2009), *available at* http://dazzlepod.com/cable/09PHNOMPENH564/.

150. Joint Statement on Establishment of Independent Counsellor at Extraordinary Chambers in Courts of Cambodia, United Nations Press Release L/3146 (Aug. 12, 2009).

151. *Id.*

152. Sophal Ear, *Cambodian 'Justice,'* Wall St. J. Asia, Sept. 1, 2009 (noting that Uth's

National Audit Authority had not made a single audit public since it began work in 2002); Douglas Gillison & Neou Vannarin, *Government Auditor Named New ECCC Graft Monitor*, Cambodia Daily, Aug. 13, 2009.

153. Cable 09PHNOMPENH564, *supra* note 149, ¶ 9 (noting that ECCC drivers had told embassy drivers that they had not been asked to pay kickbacks for some time—another indication of how widely known the kickback scheme was among diplomatic missions in Phnom Penh).

154. Cable 09STATE15565, *supra* note 57, ¶ 4.

155. OSJI, *Recent Developments at the Extraordinary Chambers in the Courts of Cambodia* 16 (Dec. 2010) [hereinafter OSJI Dec. 2010 Report]. Some Court personnel interviewed for this book asserted confidentially that they believe some corrupt activity is still occurring but that the Government has been more successful in keeping staffers from going public.

156. OSJI, *Recent Developments at the Extraordinary Chambers in the Courts of Cambodia: May 2009 Update* 11 (2009) [hereinafter OSJI May 2009 Report].

157. Cable 09PHNOMPENH316, *supra* note 115, ¶ 1.

158. Sok An even noted the similar role that U.S. officials played in the impasses of the 1999–2003 period and 2009. Cable 09PHNOMPENH333, *supra* note 147, ¶ 5.

159. James O'Toole, *UN Keeps Corruption Probe Confidential*, Phnom Penh Post, Oct. 18, 2010.

160. *Independent Counsellor Holds Townhall Meeting*, ECCC Court Report (Oct. 2012), at 2.

161. Sebastian Strangio & Cheang Sokha, *New Report Criticizes Cambodia Court Funding*, Phnom Penh Post, Mar. 21, 2008.

162. Cable 06PHNOMPENH1983, *supra* note 11, ¶ 5 (noting that head of the Defense Support Unit Rupert Skilbeck warned the Friends group in 2006 that fees paid to Cambodian prosecutors and defense lawyers at the ECCC—which far exceed normal pay in Cambodia—would raise public relations questions).

163. Luke Hunt, *The Price Scale of Justice*, Phnom Penh Post, Feb. 15, 2012.

164. *Id.*

165. David Cohen, *Seeking Justice on the Cheap: Is the East Timor Tribunal Really a Model for the Future?* 61 Asia Pacific Issues 5 (E.-W. Ctr., Aug. 2002). *See also* Steven R. Ratner et al., Accountability for Human Rights Atrocities in International Law 253 (3d ed. 2009) (emphasizing that the Panels and SCU "could not adequately protect at-risk witnesses; public defenders were underpaid and poorly trained; and investigators lacked basic tools").

166. Cohen, *supra* note 165, at 3.

167. Caitlin Reiger & Marieke Wierda, *The Serious Crimes Process in Timor Leste: In Retrospect* 30 (International Center for Transitional Justice, Prosecutions Case Studies Series, Mar. 2006).

168. *Id.* at 14–16, 22–24; David Cohen, *Indifference and Accountability: The United Nations and the Politics of International Justice in East Timor*, E.-W. Ctr. Spec. Reps., June 2006, at 1–4, 44–46, 89–90.

169. Mark Dodd, *Massacres Go Unpunished as UN Crimes Unit Heads for Collapse*, Sydney Morning Herald, May 25, 2001.

170. *See Report of the Secretary-General on the United Nations Transitional Administration in East Timor (for the period 27 July 2000 to 16 January 2001)*, ¶ 23, U.N. Doc. S/2001/42 (Jan. 16, 2001); *Report of the Secretary-General on the United Nations Transitional Administration in East Timor: For the period from 25 July to 15 October 2001*, ¶ 20, U.N. Doc. S/2001/983 (Oct. 18, 2001).

171. S.C. Res. 1543, ¶ 1, U.N. Doc. S/RES/1543 (May 14, 2004).

172. Rupert Skilbeck, *Finding Justice: The Price of War Crimes Trials*, Human Rights Brief (2008), at 8.

173. Confidential senior staff interview, *supra* note 22.

174. Framework Agreement, *supra* note 3, art. 14.

175. *Id.* art. 17(b).

176. Kodama, *supra* note 5, at 56.

177. Heindel, *supra* note 12. *See also* Phillip Rapoza, *Hybrid Criminal Tribunals and the Concept of Ownership: Who Owns the Process?* 21 Am. U. Int'l L. Rev. 525, 531–32 (2005) (noting that similar lack of ownership contributed to the East Timor Special Panels' inadequate facilities and woeful security for the courthouse, victims, and witnesses).

178. *Report of the Secretary-General on the United Nations Transitional Administration in East Timor*, ¶ 17, U.N. Doc. S/2002/432 (Apr. 17, 2002).

179. Cable 06PHNOMPENH1362, *supra* note 88, ¶ 6.

180. OSJI, *Recent Developments at the Extraordinary Chambers in the Courts of Cambodia* 4 (Oct. 2008) [hereinafter OSJI Oct. 2008 Report]. This limitation remains true today.

181. Cable 09PHNOMPENH316, *supra* note 115, ¶ 3.

182. Respondent no. 2, confidential questionnaire to Cambodian ECCC staffers (June 2012) (on file with the authors) [hereinafter ECCC respondent no. 2].

183. Etcheson interview, *supra* note 55.

184. *See, e.g.*, Request by Mr. KHIEU Samphan's Defence for Review of the French Transcripts of the Proceedings, Case No. 002/19-9-2007-ECCC/TC (May 16, 2012); Anne Heindel, *Playing "Telephone": Relay Interpretation in Case 002*, Cambodia Tribunal Monitor (Aug. 15, 2012), http://www.cambodiatribunal.org/sites/default/files/CTM Heindel 12-08-15.pdf.

185. *See* Decision on Khieu Samphan's Appeal against the Order on Translations Rights and Obligations of the Parties, Case No. 002/19-7-2007/OCIJ (PTC 11) (Feb. 20, 2009).

186. Interview with Anta Guissé, Co-Lawyer for Khieu Samphan, Phnom Penh (Nov. 15, 2012).

187. Etcheson interview, *supra* note 55.

188. Confidential senior staff interview, *supra* note 22.

189. Tolbert interview, *supra* note 2 (calling the budget preparation and adjustment process "very inefficient").

190. Kodama, *supra* note 5, at 81–82.

191. *Id.* at 63–64.

192. The original budget for the tribunal was set at $30 million, but when Japan announced its $21 million contribution, both international and Cambodian participants in the talks reportedly feared Japanese dominance and raised the figure to $56 million. Youk Chhang, *The Thief of History—Cambodia and the Special Court,* 1 INT'L J. OF TRANS. JUST. 157, 165 (2007).

193. The United States was conspicuously absent, barred by law from providing financial support directly to the Cambodian Government.

194. Kodama, *supra* note 5, at 45–46.

195. As early as September 2006, ECCC officials reported to U.S. officials that "the ECCC's budget office has concluded that the original USD 56.3 million three-year budget for the ECCC is now widely believed among Cambodian and UN staff to be inadequate." Cable 06PHNOMPENH1691, U.S. Embassy Phnom Penh, *Ambassador Meets with ECCC Co-Prosecutor; Funding Shortfalls Highlighted* ¶ 6 (Sept. 6, 2006).

196. Interview with Rupert Skilbeck, former head of the ECCC Defence Support Section, via telephone (June 7, 2012) (noting as an example that initial budgets planned for a three-month investigation—an unrealistic time frame that any civil law investigating judge could have corrected).

197. Ek Madra, *Khmer Rouge Trial Taps Donors for Another $114 Mln,* REUTERS, Feb. 7, 2008; *Donors Turning Up Heat on KR Tribunal,* WALL ST. J. ASIA, Apr. 3, 2008; OSJI, *Recent Developments at the Extraordinary Chambers in the Courts of Cambodia: May 2008 Update* 20–21 (2008).

198. OSJI Oct. 2008 Report, *supra* note 180, at 3–4.

199. *Id.* at 4.

200. OSJI Dec. 2010 Report, *supra* note 155, at 18.

201. *Tribunal Officials Take Funding Case to UN,* PHNOM PENH POST, Feb. 17, 2012; *Khmer Rouge Tribunal Faces Staff Resignations,* CAMBODIA HERALD, Jan. 22, 2013.

202. Kofi Annan did request that the SCSL be funded through assessed contributions, but when that request was denied, it had to rely on voluntary contributions instead. The SCSL also scaled back its initial request of $114.6 million for its first three years to $57 million. Celina Schocken, *The Special Court for Sierra Leone: Overview and Recommendations,* 20 BERKELEY J. INT'L L. 436, 453–54 (2002).

203. *The Rule of Law and Transitional Justice in Conflict and Post-conflict Societies: Report of the Secretary-General,* ¶ 43 and n.9, U.N. Doc. S/2004/616 (Aug. 23, 2004).

204. Marlise Simons, *Test for a Court as Prosecutors Face Liberia's Ex-Ruler,* N.Y. TIMES,

Dec. 20, 2009; *The SCSL and the* Taylor *Judgment*, IntLawGrrls (Apr. 25, 2012), http://www.intlawgrrls.com/2012/04/scsl-and-taylor-judgment.html.

205. You Bunleng, Cambodian Co-Investigating Judge at the ECCC, response to questionnaire from the authors, June 25, 2012 (translated from Khmer by Kimsroy Sokvisal).

206. Etcheson interview, *supra* note 55.

207. ECCC Respondent no. 2, *supra* note 182.

208. Respondent no. 3, confidential questionnaire to Cambodian ECCC staffers (June 2012) (on file with the authors).

209. Respondents nos. 5 and 6, confidential questionnaires to Cambodian ECCC staffers (June 2012) (on file with the authors).

210. Respondent no. 4, confidential questionnaire to Cambodian ECCC staffers (June 2012) (on file with the authors).

211. ECCC, *ECCC Revised Budget Requirements—2012–2013*, Annex B.1 (Jan. 29, 2013); ECCC, *ECCC Financial Outlook* (May 31, 2013).

212. *Id.* at Annex A. Shortfalls in funding for victims' participation and outreach are discussed further in chapters 7 and 8.

213. ECCC, *Trial Chamber Reduces Number of Weekly Hearing Days in Case 002/1*, http://www.eccc.gov.kh/en/articles/trial-chamber-reduces-number-weekly-hearing-days-case-0021 (visited Nov. 29, 2012).

214. Abby Seiff, *KRT Could Face Major Layoffs, Scheffer Tells Staffers*, Phnom Penh Post, Oct. 26, 2012.

215. Maya Wolfe-Robinson, *Cambodia Court Hearing Khmer Rouge Trials Close to Bankruptcy*, The Guardian, Dec. 4, 2012.

216. *Strike Suspends Khmer Rouge Trial*, Bangkok Post, Mar. 4, 2013.

217. Lauren Crothers, *National Staff Let Go at War Crimes Tribunal*, Cambodia Daily, July 4, 2013.

218. Stuart White, *KRT Strike Threats Resurface*, Phnom Penh Post, Aug. 1, 2013.

219. Kong Sothanarith, *Tribunal Staff Walkout Could Shutter Whole Operation, Cambodia Says*, VOA Khmer (Feb. 15, 2013).

220. Prak Chan Thul, *Salaries as Elusive as Justice at Cambodia's Khmer Rouge Trial*, Reuters, Feb. 1, 2013.

221. OSJI Dec. 2010 Report, *supra* note 155. Administrative austerity has continued to impact defense rights in these cases. In June 2013, a UN Administrative Judge lambasted the international head of the Defence Support Section (DSS) for arbitrarily disregarding established defense counsel reimbursement guidelines in an effort to save money. *See* Decision on Application Requesting Funding for Legal Consultant's Flight to the Office of the Co-Lawyer, Case No. 001/21-05-2013-UNAJ (June 25, 2013), *available at* http://www.eccc.gov.kh/en/dss/defence-support-section/claims-decisions.

222. Confidential discussion (on file with the authors).

223. *See* International Federation for Human Rights, *States Should Not Hinder ICC's*

Independence and Victims' Rights through Budget Cuts (Nov. 13, 2012), http://www.fidh.org/States-should-not-hinder-ICC-s-12423.html.

224. ECCC, *ECCC Revised Budget Requirements, supra* note 211, at 9–10, 15, Annex B.1.

225. Rapoza, *supra* note 177, at 539.

226. Clancy McGilligan, *KRT Administrator Talks War Crimes Courts at Royal School,* CAMBODIA DAILY, Sept. 15, 2010, at 28.

227. Confidential senior staff interview, *supra* note 22.

228. *See, e.g.,* Cable 06PHNOMPENH1845, U.S. Embassy Phnom Penh, *Cambodia's ECCC Making Good Progress* ¶ 9 (Oct. 10, 2006), *available at* http://www.wikileaks.org/cable/2006/10/06PHNOMPENH1845.html (paraphrasing the view of UN Office of Human Rights director Margo Picken that "there may be aspects of the ECCC that are flawed but . . . donor engagement remains the best option to see that the ECCC accomplishes its objectives and meets the expectations of the Cambodian people").

229. *See* Erika Kinetz, *Officials Stand by Structure of KR Tribunal,* CAMBODIA DAILY, Oct. 3, 2007 (quoting OSJI court monitor Heather Ryan as saying the Framework Agreement and ECCC Law actually allow for "great flexibility in establishing an effective administration system and making modifications to deal with problems that are identified"). *But see* Erika Kinetz, *ECCC Hopes to Be New Model for Tribunals,* CAMBODIA DAILY, Oct. 19, 2009, quoting Chief of Court Management (and current acting OA Director) Tony Kranh as arguing that increased international oversight would be "just for control").

Chapter 4

1. Transcript of Trial Proceedings—Kaing Guek Eav "Duch," Case No. 001/18-7-2007-ECCC/TC, at 111 (Nov. 25, 2009) [hereinafter 11/25/2009 Trial Transcript].

2. *See* Prosecutors v. Kaing Guek Eav *alias* Duch, Case No. 001/18-7-2007/ECCC/TC, Judgment ¶ 141–42 (July 26, 2010) [hereinafter *Duch* Trial Chamber Judgment]. *See also id.* ¶ 143 (noting that the number of S-21 victims "are likely to be considerably greater than indicated").

3. Except where otherwise noted, the information in this introduction comes from the *Duch* Trial Chamber Judgment, *supra* note 2, ¶¶ 111–224; Anne Heindel, *The Duch Verdict: Khmer Rouge Tribunal Case 001* (Documentation Center of Cambodia, 2010), *available at* http://www.d.dccam.org/Tribunal/Documents/pdf/Case_001_The_Duch_Verdict.pdf.

4. Cable 07PHNOMPENH826, U.S. Embassy Phnom Penh, *ECCC Passes Internal Rules* ¶ 11 (June 15, 2007), *available at* http://www.wikileaks.org/cable/2007/06/07PHNOMPENH826.html (quoting the Japanese Embassy).

5. *See, e.g.,* "3rd Division Units: Short Biographies of those Associated with the Ten-

dency," Documentation Center of Cambodia File No. D21311 (a list of S-21 prisoners beside which Duch wrote "kill them all"); Nate Thayer, *Death in Detail*, FAR EAST. ECON. REV., May 13, 1999 (in which Duch recalls a 1978 episode in which Nuon Chea ordered him to kill 300 CPK prisoners without interrogation and "I [Duch] just did" and describes that to kill victims without wasting bullets, he and comrades usually slit their throats and "killed them like chickens").

6. *Duch* Trial Chamber Judgment, *supra* note 2, at 69.

7. For a detailed history of S-21, *see generally* DAVID P. CHANDLER, VOICES FROM S-21 (2000).

8. Nic Dunlop & Nate Thayer, *Duch Confesses*, FAR EAST. ECON. REV., May 6, 1999.

9. The civil party scheme and outreach efforts are discussed in detail in chapters 7 and 8.

10. *See generally Duch* Trial Chamber Judgment, *supra* note 2. For the leading journalistic account of the *Duch* trial, *see generally* THIERRY CRUVELLIER, LE MAÎTRE DES AVEUX (2011).

11. The international Co-Prosecutor reported that 238 of 351 facts were not being contested by the defense during trial. Transcript of Trial Proceedings—Kaing Guek Eav "Duch," Case No. 001/18-7-2007-ECCC/TC, at 95 (Mar. 31, 2009) [hereinafter 3/31/2009 Trial Transcript] ("Regarding the remaining 112 of the 351, they have either not been agreed to or alternatively they have been agreed, partly agreed or not disputed with some comments").

12. *See, e.g.*, Douglas Gillison, *Duch Seeks Release and a Sentence Reduction*, CAMBODIA DAILY, Apr. 2, 2009.

13. *Duch* Trial Chamber Judgment, *supra* note 2, ¶ 38 (emphasis added; referencing rule 87(2) of the Court's Internal Rules).

14. Internal Rules of the ECCC, *rev'd* Aug. 3, 2011, r. 87(3) [hereinafter ECCC Internal Rules (rev. 8)].

15. *See, e.g.*, Transcript of Trial Proceedings—Kaing Guek Eav "Duch," Case No. 001/18-7-2007-ECCC/TC, at 17–18 (Nov. 26, 2009) [hereinafter 11/26/2009 Trial Transcript] ("[I]t is true that before this Court we have a civil law system. The guilty plea does not exist as such, but I should like to know what could have prevented any attempts to promote such a plea because it is stated in our Internal Rules that what is not provided for in national law can be sourced from international law.").

16. *See* 11/25/2009 Trial Transcript, *supra* note 1, at 22 (including an assertion by the prosecution that "he has mostly admitted crimes that are undoubtedly established by the documentary evidence and not more").

17. *See, e.g.*, Douglas Gillison, *Duch Denies Teaching to Kill; Also Denies Personally Killing*, CAMBODIA DAILY, June 18, 2009.

18. ECCC, Compilation of Statements of Apology Made by Kaing Guek Eav alias Duch During the Proceedings, at 2 (Feb. 16, 2012) [hereinafter Compilation of Duch

Apologies]; 3/31/2009 Trial Transcript, *supra* note 11, at 68 (providing slightly different translated text). *See generally* Terith Chy, A Microsocial Analysis of a War Crimes Trial in Cambodia: Rituals of Apology, Justice and Condemnation (Sept. 2012) (unpublished Master of Arts dissertation, University of Hull (on file with authors).

19. *See, e.g.*, Prak Chan Thul & Isabelle Roughol, *Duch Apology Is Heard, But Not All Accept*, CAMBODIA DAILY, Apr. 2, 2009 (quoting a student saying, "If he was not honest, he would not have dared to confess").

20. *Id.*

21. Transcript of Trial Proceedings—Kaing Guek Eav "Duch," Case File No. 001/18-7-2007-ECCC/TC, at 72 (Aug. 27, 2009) [hereinafter 8/27/2009 Trial Transcript]. *See also* Michelle Staggs Kelsall et al., *Lessons Learned from the 'Duch' Trial: A Comprehensive Review of the First Case Before the Extraordinary Chambers in the Courts of Cambodia*, Asian International Justice Initiative, KRT Trial Monitoring Group, at 22 (Dec. 2009) (paraphrasing Roux in an interview explaining "that while Civil Parties are allowed to intervene in the proceedings to further their interest in obtaining reparations, this is only relevant when an accused denies responsibility, which was not the case with his client").

22. *See, e.g.*, Alex Bates, *Transitional Justice in Cambodia: Analytical Report*, Atlas Project, ¶ 109 (Oct. 2010) (noting "the often repetitious and irrelevant questioning from Civil Party lawyers" in the *Duch* case); Erika Kinetz, *Civil Party Ruling Goes to the Heart of the ECCC's Role*, CAMBODIA DAILY, Mar. 19, 2008 (quoting Nuon Chea's lawyers with regard to the participation of civil parties: "[T]he record will reflect that nearly two hours was spent simply repeating previously articulated arguments").

23. *See* Staggs Kelsall et al., *supra* note 21, at 33.

24. Judge Silvia Cartwright, Speech to the ECCC Plenary Session (Sept. 7, 2009).

25. Staggs Kelsall et al., *supra* note 21, at 28. *See also* Sarah Thomas & Terith Chy, *Including the Survivors in the Tribunal Process*, *in* ON TRIAL: THE KHMER ROUGE ACCOUNTABILITY PROCESS 214, 261 (John D. Ciorciari & Anne Heindel eds., 2009) (highlighting the judges' "hands-off approach" and disinclination "to attempt meaningful management of civil party participation" and arguing that many of the identified problems with the original civil party scheme could have been easily avoided "through timely and robust judicial intervention").

26. Michael Saliba, *Interview with Alain Werner*, CAMBODIA TRIBUNAL MONITOR (Sept. 21, 2009), http://www.cambodiatribunal.org/sites/default/files/ctm_blog_9-21-2009_.pdf. *See also* Staggs Kelsall et al., *supra* note 21, at 34 (noting that "[t]he occurrence of repetitious questions significantly decreased after the Civil Party Lawyers finally followed the Chamber's suggestion from Week 15 and appointed one or two Counsels to ask questions on behalf of all the Groups").

27. *Quoted in* Bates, *supra* note 22, ¶ 212.

28. 8/27/2009 Trial Transcript, *supra* note 21, at 70.

29. *See* Decision on Civil Party Co-Lawyers' Joint Request for a Ruling on the Standing of the Civil Party Lawyers to Make Submissions on Sentencing and Directions Concerning the Questioning of the Accused, Experts and Witnesses Testifying on Character, Case No. 001/18-7-2007/ECCC/TC, ¶ 4 (Oct. 9, 2009) [hereinafter Decision on Civil Party Submissions].

30. *See* Groups 1 and 2—Civil Parties' Co-Lawyers' Joint Request for a Ruling on the Standing of Civil Party Lawyers to Make Submissions on Sentencing, Case No. 001/18-7-2007/ECCC/TC, ¶¶ 9–11, 20, 32 (June 9, 2009) [hereinafter Civil Parties' Joint Request] (citing Internal Rule r. 91(1), which provides: "The Chamber shall hear the Civil Parties, witness and experts in the order it considers useful"); Cambodian Code of Criminal Procedure (*as adopted* Aug. 10, 2007), art. 335, which allows civil parties *and* their lawyers to make brief closing statements, which in practice sometimes addresses sentencing).

31. *See* Civil Parties' Joint Request, *supra* note 30, ¶ 6.

32. Decision on Civil Party Submissions, *supra* note 29, ¶¶ 12–13.

33. *Id.* ¶ 26.

34. *Id.* ¶¶ 28–35.

35. *Id.* ¶¶ 44–46.

36. 8/27/2009 Trial Transcript, *supra* note 21, at 68–69.

37. Staggs Kelsall et al., *supra* note 21, at 18.

38. *Quelles leçons tirer du procès des Khmers rouges?* Revue de Science Criminelle 597 (2011) (featuring an interview with Lemonde, translated from French by the authors).

39. *Id.*

40. *Id.* Indeed, Judge Lemonde allowed a documentary team following his investigative work to film the encounter. The tribunal's national spokesperson and Duch's national lawyer reported that while visiting Choeung Ek, Duch had cried—an allegation both the national Co-Investigating Judge and the international Co-Prosecutor denied. Prak Chan Thul, *Duch Sheds Tears at Choeung Ek Killing Fields,* Cambodia Daily, Feb. 27, 2008. The episode drew positive media reaction internationally; however many in Cambodia felt that the incident had been manufactured for public consumption. Documentation Center of Cambodia Director Youk Chhang commented, "For PR purposes, it has been effective[] reaching out across the world[.]" Erika Kinetz & Prak Chan Thul, *Duch Returns to S-21, Discusses Role As Chief,* Cambodia Daily, Feb. 28, 2008.

41. *Quoted in* Bates, *supra* note 22, ¶ 133.

42. Staggs Kelsall et al., *supra* note 21, at 18.

43. 8/27/2009 Trial Transcript, *supra* note 21, at 71–72.

44. Staggs Kelsall et al., *supra* note 21, at 18. Indeed, in a subsequent interview Roux said, "Ultimately we should strive to find some common rules for victim participation in international tribunals. We should begin with the civil law system and adapt it accordingly as we confront the unique challenges of trials in international criminal tribunals." Michael

Saliba, *Interview with Defense Counsel François Roux*, CAMBODIA TRIBUNAL MONITOR (Sept. 21, 2009) (on file with the authors).

45. 3/31/2009 Trial Transcript, *supra* note 11, at 87.

46. *See* Transcript of Trial Proceedings—Kaing Guek Eav "Duch," Case No. 001/18-7-2007-ECCC/TC, at 117–18 (Nov. 23, 2009) (closing statement by civil party team 4 arguing that Duch was not a pawn because he in fact had saved the lives of a few select people).

47. *Duch* Trial Chamber Judgment, *supra* note 2, ¶ 122.

48. Compilation of Duch Apologies, *supra* note 18, at 14; Transcript of Trial Proceedings—Kaing Guek Eav "Duch," Case No. 001/18-7-2007-ECCC/TC, at 85 (Sept. 2, 2009) (providing slightly different translated text).

49. Compilation of Duch Apologies, *supra* note 18, at 14; 11/25/2009 Trial Transcript, *supra* note 1, at 68 (providing slightly different translated text).

50. *See, e.g.*, Compilation of Duch Apologies, *supra* note 18, at 2; 3/31/2009 Trial Transcript, *supra* note 11, at 68 (providing slightly different translated text).

51. Prosecutor v. Erdemovic, Sentencing Judgment, Case No. IT-96-22-Tbis (Trial Chamber, Mar. 5, 1998).

52. Rome Statute of the International Criminal Court, July 17, 1998, 2187 U.N.T.S. 90 (entered into force on July 1, 2002), art. 31(1)(d).

53. *Duch* Trial Chamber Judgment, *supra* note 2, ¶ 557.

54. *Id.* ¶ 558.

55. *Id.* ¶ 609.

56. Bethany Lindsay, *Defense Lawyers Unveil a More Remorseful Duch*, CAMBODIA DAILY, June 24, 2009.

57. *See* Law on the Establishment of Extraordinary Chambers in the Courts of Cambodia for the Prosecution of Crimes Committed During the Period of Democratic Kampuchea, as amended and promulgated on Oct. 27, 2004, NS/RKM/1004/006, art. 29 [hereinafter ECCC Law] (stating that the fact that a suspect acted pursuant to superior orders does not relieve his or her criminal responsibility).

58. *See, e.g.*, Transcript of Trial Proceedings—Kaing Guek Eav "Duch," Case No. 001/18-7-2007-ECCC/TC, at 32–33 (Mar. 28, 2011) [hereinafter 3/28/2011 Trial Transcript].

59. 11/25/2009 Trial Transcript, *supra* note 1, at 83.

60. *Duch* Trial Chamber Judgment, *supra* note 2, ¶ 552.

61. *Id.* ¶ 607.

62. Kheang Un & Judy Ledgerwood, *Is the Trial of 'Duch' a Catalyst for Change in Cambodia's Courts?* 95 ASIA PACIFIC ISSUES 5 (E.-W. Ctr., June 2010).

63. 11/26/2009 Trial Transcript, *supra* note 15, at 20.

64. *See, e.g.*, 3/31/2009 Trial Transcript, *supra* note 11, at 80–81. *See id.* at 81 ("Why Duch was imprisoned? Was it because he killed less people? This is the lesson").

65. *See, e.g., id.* at 78. In his view, this was a breach of the Cambodian Constitution's protection of equal rights. *See, e.g.*, Transcript of Trial Proceedings—Kaing Guek Eav "Duch," Case No. 001/18-7-2007-ECCC/TC, at 77–79 (Mar. 21, 2009). However, as noted by Case 001 ECCC Civil Party Co-Lawyer Karim Khan, "Counsel obviously misunderstands this article which grants equality in having and getting rights. It does not guarantee a right to 'equality in injustice.'" 11/26/2009 Trial Transcript, *supra* note 15, at 98. *Cf.* Rachel Irwin, *Defense Says Lubanga a Scapegoat*, THE LUBANGA TRIAL DAILY REPORT (Jan. 27, 2009), http://www.lubangatrial.org/2009/01/27/defense-says-lubanga-a-scapegoat/.

66. The ICTR noted that it has "finite financial and human resources and cannot realistically be expected to prosecute every offender which may fall within the strict terms of its jurisdiction. It must of necessity make decisions as to the nature of the crimes and the offenders to be prosecuted." Prosecutor v. Jean-Paul Akayesu, ICTR-96-4-A, Judgment, ¶ 94 (Appeals Chamber, June 1, 2001) (citing Prosecutor v. Delalic et al. (Celebici), Case No. IT-96-21-A, Judgment, ¶ 602 (Appeals Chamber, Feb. 20, 2001)). Nevertheless, prosecutors must not discriminate on impermissible bases, such as race, color, religion, opinion, national or ethnic origin. *Celebici* Appeals Judgment, *supra*, ¶¶ 605, 614.

67. *See* Transcript of Trial Proceedings—Kaing Guek Eav "Duch," Case No. 001/18-7-2007-ECCC/TC, at 11–12 (Nov. 24, 2009) (arguing that S-21 "was at the apex" of the network of prisons and uniquely received prisoners from all parts of the country, including high-ranking officials from whom Duch forced confessions that contributed to mass purges). Duch disputed the idea that "S21 was unique in the network of security centres given its direct link to the Central Committee and its role in the detention and execution of CPK cadre." *Duch* Trial Chamber Judgment, *supra* note 2, ¶¶ 119–20.

68. Isabelle Roughol & Prak Chan Thul, *For Tribunal Attendees, an Emotional First Day of Duch Trial*, CAMBODIA DAILY, Mar. 31, 2009.

69. *See, e.g.*, 11/25/2009 Trial Transcript, *supra* note 1, at 107.

70. *See, e.g.*, 3/31/2009 Trial Transcript, *supra* note 11, at 80–81.

71. *Id.* at 75–76. *See also id.* at 82 ("Duch is not a senior leader or the most responsible for the crimes"); Douglas Gillison, *Duch to Victims: 'I Regret Every Murder,'* CAMBODIA DAILY, Apr. 1, 2009 (quoting Kar Savuth as saying Duch was one of nearly 200 prison chiefs, some of whom were responsible for more deaths, and that Duch fell outside the court's personal jurisdiction).

72. 3/31/2009 Trial Transcript, *supra* note 11, at 77–79.

73. *Id.* at 77. He compared this uncertainty to the fear cadre suffered during the DK that they might be arbitrarily arrested and killed. 11/25/2009 Trial Transcript, *supra* note 1, at 108.

74. Transcript of Trial Proceedings—Kaing Guek Eav "Duch," Case No. 001/18-7-2007-ECCC/TC, at 18 (Apr. 1, 2009).

75. *See* 11/25/2009 Trial Transcript, *supra* note 1, at 99.

76. *See id.* at 103, 110, 112.

77. *Id.* at 117.

78. 11/26/2009 Trial Transcript, *supra* note 15, at 2.

79. *See id.* at 8.

80. *See id.* at 16 (referencing the *Obrenovic* plea agreement at the ICTY).

81. *See* 8/27/2009 Trial Transcript, *supra* note 21, at 40.

82. *Id.* at 52.

83. *Id.* at 59.

84. *Id.* at 62.

85. Letter from Richard Rogers, Chief, Defence Support Section, to Judge Nil Nonn, Trial Chamber President, re Request by Mr Kaing to Withdraw Co-Lawyer François Roux (July 5, 2010) (stating, "In his request, Mr. Kaing states that he has lost confidence in Maitre Roux and provides three underlying reasons[,]" which were not made public); Notification of Withdrawal of Designation of Co-Lawyer, Case No. 001/18-7-2007/ECCC/TC (July 9, 2010).

86. Douglas Gillison & Phorn Bopha, *In Duch Sentence, How Many Days for His Victims*, CAMBODIA DAILY, July 26, 2010.

87. Tribunal UN spokesperson Lars Olsen reportedly explained, "Duch has chosen a second local attorney . . . to represent him because 'we cannot find international lawyers that met his criteria'[.]"

88. Phorn Bopha & Douglas Gillison, *Duch Seeking Chinese Lawyer, Kar Savuth Says*, CAMBODIA DAILY, July 12, 2010.

89. *See generally* Appeal Brief by the Co-Lawyers for Kaing Guek Eav Alias "Duch" Against the Trial Chamber Judgment of 26 July 2010 (Nov. 18, 2010); Reply by the Co-Lawyers for Kaing Guek Eav Alias "Duch" to the Co-Prosecutors' Response of 20 December 2010 (Jan. 14, 2011).

90. Erika Kinetz & Prak Chan Thul, *Duch's Lawyer Becomes First Foreign Bar Member in Cambodia*, CAMBODIA DAILY, Aug. 9, 2007.

91. *Quoted in* Bates, *supra* note 22, ¶ 112.

92. Thierry Cruvellier, *Duch Trial Ends with a Twist*, 95 INT'L JUSTICE TRIBUNE (Dec. 9, 2009).

93. Interview with Michael G. Karnavas, former Co-Lawyer for Ieng Sary, Phnom Penh (May 19, 2012).

94. Douglas Gillison, *Duch Fires French Lawyer As Verdict Looms*, CAMBODIA DAILY, July 10–11, 2010.

95. *See, e.g.*, Reply by the Co-Lawyers, *supra* note 89, ¶¶ 14(b), 23.

96. Phorn & Gillison, *supra* note 88. Later before the Supreme Court Chamber, he argued, "Because this is a national court, it is not an international court. Therefore it has to use the domestic law. And . . . as I said, there are a number of existing laws . . . [.] There is no need to refer to the international law." 3/28/2011 Trial Transcript, *supra* note 58, at 35.

97. Phorn & Gillison, *supra* note 88.

98. *Id.*

99. Karnavas interview, *supra* note 93; Interview with Richard Rogers, former Head of the ECCC Defence Support Section, Phnom Penh (May 29, 2012).

100. Interview with Michiel Pestman, former Co-Lawyer for Nuon Chea, Phnom Penh (June 9, 2012). *Cf.* Interview with Diana Ellis, Co-Lawyer for Ieng Thirith, Phnom Penh (Nov. 11, 2012) ("It can be difficult where co-lawyers come from different legal systems; the extent to which this causes problems will depend in part on the personalities involved [but] the difficulties need not be insuperable"); Julia Wallace, *Duch Defense Victim of Teamwork's Complications*, CAMBODIA DAILY, Nov. 30, 2009 (paraphrasing David Scheffer's speculation that the divergence may have resulted "because they come from very different educational and cultural backgrounds").

101. Karnavas interview, *supra* note 93.

102. *Duch* Trial Chamber Judgment, *supra* note 2, ¶ 486.

103. *FM Hor Namhong Not Happy with Duch's Sentence*, RADIO FREE ASIA (July 27, 2007), http://www.rfa.org/khmer/indepth/hor_nam_hong_reacted_2duch_verdict-07272010062809.html.

104. Cheang Sokha, *Government Respects Duch Verdict*, PHNOM PENH POST, Aug. 5, 2010.

105. *See, e.g.*, Transcript of Trial Proceedings—Kaing Guek Eav "Duch," Case No. 001/18-7-2007-ECCC/TC, at 46 (Aug. 17, 2009); Transcript of Trial Proceedings—Kaing Guek Eav "Duch," Case No. 001/18-7-2007-ECCC/TC, at 42 (Aug. 20, 2009); 11/25/2009 Trial Transcript, *supra* note 1, at 63.

106. *See* Staggs Kelsall et al., *supra* note 21, at 10.

107. Phorn Bopha & Douglas Gillison, *Even Before Verdict, Duch Defense Vows to Appeal*, CAMBODIA DAILY, July 26, 2010.

108. 3/28/2001 Trial Transcript, *supra* note 58, at 35.

109. *See* 11/25/2009 Trial Transcript, *supra* note 1, at 9–10.

110. Notably, François Roux first raised this during trial closing arguments. 8/27/2009 Trial Transcript, *supra* note 21, at 48.

111. *Duch* Trial Chamber Judgment, *supra* note 2, ¶ 574.

112. *See* Separate and Dissenting Opinion of Judge Jean-Marc Lavergne on Sentence, Case No. 001/18-7-2007-ECCC/TC (July 26, 2010).

113. *See id.*

114. *Id.* ¶ 5. Comparatively, "It is well recognised within the jurisprudence of the [ICTY] Tribunal that although it must consider sentencing practices in the former Yugoslavia, the Tribunal is not bound by such practice," and indeed the ICTY's maximum sentence of life imprisonment shows that it is not bound by the national legal system. Prosecutor v. Obrenovic, Case No. IT-02-60/2-S, Sentencing Judgment, ¶ 56 (Trial Chamber, Dec. 10, 2003) (citations omitted).

115. Co-Prosecutors' Appeal Against the Judgment of the Trial Chamber in the

Case of Kaing Guek Eav Alias Duch, ¶ 127 (Oct. 13, 2010). *See also* Transcript of Trial Proceedings—Kaing Guek Eav "Duch," Case No. 001/18-7-2007-ECCC/TC, at 43 (Mar. 29, 2011) [hereinafter 3/29/2011 Trial Transcript].

116. ECCC Internal Rules (rev. 8), *supra* note 14, r. 98(5).

117. *See* 3/29/2011 Trial Transcript, *supra* note 115, at 42.

118. *See id.* at 71–72.

119. *Id.* at 70–71.

120. *See* Prosecutors v. Kaing Guek Eav *alias* Duch, Case No. 001/18-7-2007/ECCC/SC, Appeal Judgment ¶ 348 (Feb. 3, 2012) [hereinafter *Duch* Appeal Judgment].

121. *Id.* ¶ 351.

122. *See id.*, Partially Dissenting Joint Opinion of Judges Agnieszka Klonowiecka-Milart & Chandra Nihal Jayasinghe ¶ 23 [hereinafter Partial Dissent from the Appeal Judgment].

123. *Id.* ¶¶ 24–26.

124. *Id.* ¶ 27.

125. *See, e.g.*, Prosecutor v. Dragon Nikolic, Case No IT-94-2-S, Sentencing Judgment (Trial Chamber, Dec. 18, 2003) (considering as aggravating factors the gravity of the crimes, vulnerability of the victims, and the convicted person's abuse of his position of authority, and as mitigating factors the convicted person's guilty plea, remorse, contribution to reconciliation, the substantiality of his cooperation, and his character.)

126. *Duch* Trial Chamber Judgment, *supra* note 2, ¶ 606. *Cf.* Prosecutor v. Obrenovic, Case No. IT-02-60/2-S, Sentencing Judgment, ¶ 121 (Trial Chamber, Dec. 10, 2003) (finding remorse to be a substantial mitigating factor where the convicted person was "genuinely remorseful for his role in the crimes for which he has been convicted, and seeks to atone for his criminal conduct").

127. *Duch* Trial Chamber Judgment, *supra* note 2, ¶¶ 629, 631.

128. On sentencing practices at other tribunals, *see* Mark Drumbl, Atrocity, Punishment, and International Law ch. 3 (2007); Mark B. Harmon & Fergal Gaynor, *The Sentencing Practices of International Tribunals: Ordinary Sentences for Extraordinary Crimes*, 5 J. Int'l Crim. Just. 683, 684–85 (2007).

129. *Duch* Appeal Judgment, *supra* note 120, ¶ 379.

130. *Id.* ¶ 363.

131. *Id.* ¶ 368.

132. *Id.* ¶ 369.

133. *Id.* ¶ 376.

134. *See id.* ¶ 372, n.794 (citing international jurisprudence). *See, e.g.*, Prosecutor v. Semanza, Case No. ICTR-96-13-A, Judgment, ¶ 396 (Appeals Chamber, Nov. 17, 2001) ("If a Trial Chamber finds that mitigating circumstances exist, it is not precluded from imposing a sentence of life imprisonment, where the gravity of the offence requires the imposition of the maximum sentence provided for.").

135. As of 2007, at the ICTY only one accused (1.8% of persons convicted) had received a life sentence, while at the ICTR, 37% had received life sentences. *See* Harmon & Gaynor, *supra* note 128, at 684 (noting the discrepancy in the length of sentences between the ICTY and the ICTR). The SCSL has not sentenced any of its nine convicted persons to life imprisonment.

136. *See* Decision on Request for Release, Case 001/1/-07/2007/ECCC/TC, ¶ 14 (June 15, 2009); Decision on Appeal Against Provisional Detention Order of Kaing Guek Eav alias "Duch," Case No. 001/18-7-2007-ECCC/OCIJ (PTC01), ¶ 21 (Dec. 3, 2007).

137. Decision on Request for Release, *supra* note 136, ¶ 15. *See also* Anne Heindel, Amicus Brief In the Matter of the appeal by Kang Guek Eav (Duch) against the order of provisional detention by the Office of the Co-Investigating Judges dated 31 July 2007, ¶ 24 (PTC, Oct. 4, 2007), *available at* http://www.eccc.gov.kh/en/document/court/amicus-curiae-brief-anne-heindel-dc-cam.

138. Decision on Request for Release, *supra* note 136, ¶ 16. *See also* Heindel, *supra* note 137, ¶ 2.

139. Decision on Request for Release, *supra* note 136, ¶¶ 35, 36.

140. *Duch* Trial Chamber Judgment, *supra* note 2, ¶ 627.

141. *Quoted in* Bates, *supra* note 22, ¶ 232.

142. *Duch* Appeal Judgment, *supra* note 120, ¶ 399.

143. *See, e.g., Shock for Khmer Rouge Leader Duch As His Sentence Is Increased to Life*, TELEGRAPH, Feb. 3, 2012.

144. Press Release, Amnesty International, *Cambodia. Khmer Rouge Judgment Welcome, But Raises Human Rights Concerns* (Feb. 8, 2012).

145. Rogers interview, *supra* note 99 (calling Judge Noguchi's support for the majority a "mistake" and noting that political pressure could also be brought to bear to try to "turn" a single international judge to achieve a supermajority).

146. *See* Jean-Bosco Barayagwiza v. Prosecutor, Case No. ICTR-97-19, Decision, ¶¶ 61–62 (Appeals Chamber, Nov. 3, 1999).

147. *See id.* ¶ 54. Likewise, in the *Kajelijeli* case, the Appeals Chamber considered the link between the detaining state and the tribunal in determining the responsibility of the ICTR for violations of the accused's rights while in state custody. *See* Juvénal Kajelijeli v. Prosecutor, Case No. ICTR-98-44A-A, Judgment, ¶ 232 (Appeals Chamber, May 23, 2005).

148. Defense Appeal Brief Challenging the Order of Provisional Detention of 31 July 2007, Case No. 002/14-8-2006, ¶ 3 (Sept. 5, 2007). *See also id.* ¶¶ 68–73; Detention Order, Military Court No. 16DK/2002 (Feb. 22, 2002) (holding Duch for crimes against humanity pursuant to the ECCC Law); Gillison, *supra* note 12 (noting that when renewing the charges against Duch in 2007, the Military Court "said it was merely holding him until the Khmer Rouge tribunal began operations").

149. *Duch* Appeal Judgment, *supra* note 120, ¶¶ 392–99.

150. Partial Dissent from the Appeal Judgment, *supra* note 122, ¶ 7.

151. *Id.* ¶¶ 9–14.

152. *Id.* ¶ 15.

153. ECCC Law, *supra* note 57, art. 33 new.

154. Cambodia acceded to the ICCPR in 1992. *See* Office of the High Commissioner for Human Rights Information on the Status of Ratifications and Reservations of the ICCPR, *available at* http://www.ohchr.org/english/countries/ratification/4.htm.

155. International Covenant on Civil and Political Rights, *adopted* 16 Dec. 1966, *entered into force* 23 Mar. 1976, 999 U.N.T.S. 171, art. 2(1) [hereinafter ICCPR]. *See also* General Comment No. 31, The Nature of the General Legal Obligation Imposed on States Parties to the Covenant, ¶ 4 (Mar. 29, 2004) (noting that "[a]ll branches of government (executive, legislative and judicial) . . . at whatever level—national, regional or local—are in a position to engage the responsibility of the State Party").

156. ICCPR, *supra* note 155, arts. 14(2), (3)(a),(c).

157. Partial Dissent from the Appeal Judgment, *supra* note 122, ¶ 17.

158. *Id.* ¶¶ 20, 28.

159. *Id.* ¶ 30.

160. Cambodian Center for Human Rights, *Third Bi-Annual Report: Fair Trial Rights—One Year Progress* (Jan. 2012), at 44.

161. *Quoted in* Bates, *supra* note 22, ¶ 146.

162. *See* Internal Rules of the ECCC (Rev. 3), *rev'd* Mar. 6, 2009, r. 23(11).

163. *Id.* r. 23(12).

164. All teams requested "at a minimum," the compilation and dissemination of Duch's statements of apology with civil party comments, access to free medical care for their clients, the funding of educational programs about the Khmer Rouge and S-21 in particular, the erection of memorials and pagoda fences, and the inclusion of civil party names in the final judgment. *See* Civil Parties' Co-Lawyers' Joint Submission on Reparations, Case No. 001/18-7-2007-ECCC/TC, ¶¶ 12–30 (Sept. 14, 2009) [hereinafter Civil Parties' Reparations Submission].

165. *Duch* Trial Chamber Judgment, *supra* note 2, ¶¶ 664–75. The Court announced on August 5, 2010, that it had begun producing 5,000 hard copies of the judgment and 17,000 of the judgment summary to be distributed around the country. Press Release, *ECCC to Distribute the "Duch" Verdict Nationwide* (Aug. 6, 2010). The compilation was not put on the website until February 2012. The Press Office claimed that it could not be done until the Supreme Court Chamber verdict was issued. The statements were also published in some local newspapers in serial form.

166. *See* Civil Parties' Reparations Submission, *supra* note 164, ¶¶ 31–32.

167. *Id.* ¶¶ 33–39.

168. *See generally* Appeal Against Judgment on Reparations by Co-Lawyers for Civil Parties-Group 2 (SCC, Nov. 2, 2010). *See also* Appeal of the Co-Lawyers for the Group 3 Civil Parties against the Judgment of 26 July 2010, ¶¶ 97–102 (Oct. 5, 2010).

169. *See Duch* Trial Chamber Judgment, *supra* note 2, ¶¶ 663–65.

170. *Id.* ¶ 662.

171. *See, e.g.*, Patrick Kroker, *Transitional Justice Policy in Practice: Victim Participation in the* Khmer Rouge *Tribunal*, 53 Ger. YB Int'l L. 754, 783 (2010) (noting that "[i]n light of the strong dependence of the civil party mechanism on the reparations claim, which the Trial Chamber itself had pointed at on several occasions, it could have been more creative and courageous concerning the awarded measures").

172. Karnavas interview, *supra* note 93.

173. *Duch* Appeal Judgment, *supra* note 120, ¶ 641.

174. *Id.* ¶ 644.

175. *Id.* ¶ 654.

176. *Id.*

177. *Id.* ¶ 653.

178. *Id.* ¶ 654.

179. *See, e.g.*, Press Release, Open Society Justice Initiative (OSJI), *Duch Verdict Marks Milestone for Khmer Rouge Tribunal: Closure of First Case Brings Millions of Cambodians Closer to Justice* (July 26, 2010), *at* http://www.soros.org/initiatives/justice/news/cambodia-duch-20100726; Thierry Cruvellier, *Duch: Down with Subtleties*, 145 Int'l Justice Tribune (Feb. 15, 2012) (finding the judgment to be "a serious and faithful account of the 9-month long proceedings in 2009 and a delicate effort to find an impossible balance between the status of the accused [as the only senior KR official to admit his guilt] and the gravity of the crimes").

180. *See, e.g.*, Press Release, Cambodian Center for Human Rights, *The Duch Trial: A Good Example for the Cambodian Courts* (July 26, 2010), *at* http://www.soros.org/press-releases/duch-trial-good-example-cambodian-courts; John D. Ciorciari, *The Duch Verdict*, Cambodia Tribunal Monitor (July 28, 2010), http://www.cambodiatribunal.org/sites/default/files/resources/the_duch_verdict.pdf.

181. *See generally* Documentation Center of Cambodia, *The Duch Verdict: A DC-Cam Report from the Villages: Witnessing Justice, Village Screenings of the First Khmer Rouge Verdict of the Extraordinary Chambers in the Court of Cambodia* (July 26, 2010), http://www.d.dccam.org/Projects/Living_Doc/ECCC_Tour_and_Field_Trip_Reports.htm (including reaction and interviews from verdict screenings in seven provinces and Phnom Penh). Media reports immediately following the verdict also emphasized the dismay of many civil parties at the sentence. *See, e.g.*, Seth Mydans, *Anger in Cambodia over Khmer Rouge Sentence*, N.Y. Times, July 26, 2010; Guy De Launey, *Tears and Disbelief at Duch Verdict*, BBC, July 26, 2010.

182. Norng Sarath, Siem Reap Province, unpublished interview by staff of the Documentation Center of Cambodia (2009).

183. *Cf.* Sophal Ear, Letter, *Khmer Rouge Tribunal vs. Karmic Justice*, N.Y. Times, Mar. 17, 2010 (relaying how his mother "always said that no matter what happened to the Khmer Rouge leadership in their current lifetime, Karmic justice would prevail in the next: They would be reborn as cockroaches").

184. Documentation Center of Cambodia, *supra* note 181, at 21.

185. *See generally* Anne Heindel, *The Duch Verdict: Forum on Forgiveness and Genocide Education in the Former Khmer Rouge Stronghold of Malai* & *The Duch Verdict: A DC-Cam Report from Former Khmer Rouge Strongholds of Samlot and Pailin* (Documentation Center of Cambodia, 2010), at http://www.d.dccam.org/Projects/Living_Doc/ECCC_Tour_and_Field_Trip_Reports.htm.

186. *See* Savina Sirik, *Duch Final Judgment: Justice and Humanity* (Documentation Center of Cambodia, Feb. 2–3, 2012), at 5–6, 10–11, http://www.d.dccam.org/Projects/Living_Doc/ECCC_Tour_and_Field_Trip_Reports.htm.

187. *See, e.g.*, OSJI, *Recent Developments at the Extraordinary Chambers in the Courts of Cambodia* 12 (Feb. 2012) (stating that due to the failure to remedy Duch's illegal detention, "[T]he outcome casts a shadow on the achievements made in Duch's trial"); Press Release, Amnesty International, *Cambodia: Khmer Rouge Judgment Welcome, But Raises Human Rights Concerns* (Feb. 8, 2012).

188. Bridget Di Certo, *Duch Verdict Worries*, PHNOM PENH POST, Feb. 6, 2012.

189. *See* Statement of the Co-Chairs of the Friends of the ECCC (Feb. 3, 2012) ("On this very special occasion, [the Embassies of France and Japan] reaffirm the expectations that judges and lawyers as well as the national and international staff of the ECCC will uphold the highest standards of law and due process.")

190. Nget Uy, Kampong Thom Province, unpublished interview by staff of the Documentation Center of Cambodia (2011).

191. Him Mom, Takeo Province, unpublished interview by staff of the Documentation Center of Cambodia (2011).

192. Ly Hor, Banteay Meanchey Province, unpublished interview by staff of the Documentation Center of Cambodia (2011).

Chapter 5

1. *See, e.g.*, Michelle Fitzpatrick, *Biggest Trial Since Nazi Era*, AGENCE FRANCE PRESSE, June 26, 2011.

2. Robert Petit & Anees Ahmed, *A Review of the Jurisprudence of the Khmer Rouge Tribunal*, 8 N'WESTERN J. INT'L HUM. RTS. 165, 184–85 (2010).

3. Closing Order, Case No. 002/19-09-2007-ECCC-OCIJ, ¶ 156 (Sept. 15, 2010).

4. *Id.* ¶ 157.

5. *Id.* ¶¶ 33–47. *See also* STEPHEN HEDER WITH BRIAN D. TITTEMORE, SEVEN CANDIDATES FOR PROSECUTION 46–55 (2d ed. 2004).

6. *See* Bohler Avocaten, The Cambodia Tribunal, *available at* http://www.bohler.eu/en/cases/.

7. Transcript of Trial Proceedings—Case 002, Case No. 002/19-09-2007-ECCC/TC, at 3–5 (Nov. 23, 2011).

8. Transcript of Ieng Thirith Appeal Hearing, Case No. 002/19-09-2007-ECCC/OCIJ (PTC 16), at 47–51 (Feb. 24, 2009).

9. Unlike the Genocide Convention and ECCC Law, the 1979 tribunal decree defined

genocide as "planned massacres of groups of innocent people; expulsion of inhabitants of cities and villages in order to concentrate them and force them to do hard labor in conditions leading to their physical and mental destruction; wiping out religion; destroying political, cultural and social structures and family and social relations." *See* Decree Law No. 1: Establishment of People's Revolutionary Tribunal at Phnom Penh to Try the Pol Pot-Ieng Sary Clique for the Crime of Genocide (July 15, 1979).

10. *See generally* Ronald C. Slye, *The Cambodian Amnesties: Beneficiaries and the Temporal Reach of Amnesties for Gross Violation of Human Rights*, 22 Wis. Int'l L.J. 99 (2004).

11. Agreement between the United Nations and the Royal Government of Cambodia Concerning the Prosecution Under Cambodian Law of Crimes Committed During the Period of Democratic Kampuchea (June 6, 2003) [hereinafter Framework Agreement], art. 11(2); Law on the Establishment of Extraordinary Chambers in the Courts of Cambodia for the Prosecution of Crimes Committed During the Period of Democratic Kampuchea, as amended and promulgated on Oct. 27, 2004, NS/RKM/1004/006 [hereinafter ECCC Law], art. 40.

12. *See* Decision on Ieng Sary's Rule 89 Preliminary Objections (*Ne bis In Idem* and Amnesty and Pardon), Case No. 002/19-09-2007-ECCC/TC, ¶¶ 12–14 (Nov. 3, 2011) [hereinafter Decision on Ieng Sary].

13. *See id.* ¶¶ 16–17.

14. Prosecutor v. Morris Kallon, Case No. SCSL-04-15-AR72(E) & Prosecutor v. Ibrahim Bazzy Kamara, Case No. SCSL-04-16-AR72(E), Decision on Challenge to Jurisdiction: Lomé Accord Amnesty, ¶ 73 (Appeals Chamber, Mar. 13, 2004).

15. *See* Convention for the Amelioration of the Condition of the Wounded and Sick in Armed Forces in the Field (Geneva Convention No. I), Aug. 12, 1949, art. 49, 75 UNTS 31; Convention for the Amelioration of the Condition of the Wounded, Sick, and Shipwrecked Members of Armed Forces at Sea (Geneva Convention No. II), Aug. 12, 1949, art. 50, 75 UNTS 85; Geneva Convention Relative to the Treatment of Prisoners of War (Geneva Convention No. III), Aug. 12, 1949, art. 129, 75 UNTS 135; Convention Relative to the Protection of Civilian Persons in Time of War (Geneva Convention No. IV), Aug. 12, 1949, art. 146, 75 UNTS 287; 1948 Convention on the Prevention and Punishment of the Crime of Genocide, arts. I, IV, 78 U.N.T.S. 277, entered into force Jan. 12, 1951.

16. Decision on Ieng Sary, *supra* note 12, ¶ 39.

17. *Report of the Secretary-General on the Establishment of a Special Court for Sierra Leone*, ¶ 22, U.N. Doc. S/2000/915 (Oct. 4, 2000) (footnote omitted).

18. Decision on Challenge to Jurisdiction, *supra* note 14, ¶ 82.

19. Decision on Ieng Sary, *supra* note 12, ¶ 47.

20. *Id.* ¶ 53.

21. *But see* David Scheffer, *The Extraordinary Chambers in the Courts of Cambodia*, *in* International Criminal Law 219, 232 (M. Cherif Bassiouni ed., 3d ed. 2008) (re-

counting how he was told in 2000 that Hun Sen claimed to have "personally drafted the pardon and amnesty for Ieng Sary in 1996 and purposely made it so that Ieng Sary would be subject to prosecution for the Pol Pot era crimes").

22. *See* Decision on Ieng Sary, *supra* note 12, ¶ 55. Moreover, it ruled that because the 1979 tribunal was not independent and impartial, its judgment against Ieng "can not be characterized as a genuine judicial decision" and "is therefore incapable of producing valid legal effects" subject either to a pardon or to the principle of *res judicata* in the Cambodian Code of Criminal Procedure. *Id.* ¶¶ 30–31.

23. Youk Chhang, *Arrest of Ieng Sary and Wife Is an Important Victory for Victims,* CAMBODIA DAILY, Nov. 15, 2007.

24. *See* Ieng Sary's Appeal Against the Trial Chamber's Decision on Ieng Sary's Rule 89 Preliminary Objections (*Ne Bis In Idem* and Amnesty and Pardon), Case No. 002/19-09-2007-ECCC/SC, ¶¶ 3, 16–17 (Dec. 5, 2011).

25. Decision on Ieng Sary's Appeal Against the Trial Chamber's Decision on Ieng Sary's Rule 89 Preliminary Objections (*Ne Bis in Idem* and Amnesty and Pardon), Case No. 002/19-09-2007-ECCC-TC/SC(11) (Mar. 20, 2012).

26. *Quelles leçons tirer du procès des Khmers rouges?* REVUE DE SCIENCE CRIMINELLE 597 (2011) (featuring an interview with Lemonde, translated from French by the authors).

27. Interview with Anta Guissé, Co-Lawyer for Khieu Samphan, Phnom Penh (Nov. 15, 2012).

28. Interview with Jeanne Sulzer, former Legal Officer at the ECCC Civil Party Lead Co-Lawyers Section, Phnom Penh (June 1, 2012) (stating that France is phasing out investigative judges due to concerns that excessive power and pressure have led to errors and abuse).

29. *See also id.* (noting that investigating judges from national systems are unaccustomed to leading teams on mass crimes cases).

30. *See* Internal Rules of the ECCC, *rev'd* Aug. 3, 2011 [hereinafter ECCC Internal Rules (rev. 8)], r. 55(5).

31. Order on the Request for Investigative Action to Seek Exculpatory Evidence in the SMD, Case No. 002/19-09-2007-ECCC-OCIJ, ¶ 14 (June 19, 2009) [hereinafter SMD Order].

32. ECCC Internal Rules (rev. 8), *supra* note 30, r. 55(10).

33. Response to your letter dated 20 December 2007 concerning the conduct of the judicial investigation (Jan. 10, 2008), *cited in* Urgent Joint Defense Request for Investigative Action to Seek Exculpatory Evidence in the Shared Materials Drive, Case No. 002/19-09-2007-ECCC-OCIJ, ¶ 8 (Apr. 20, 2009).

34. Decision on the Appeal from the Order on the Request to Seek Exculpatory Evidence in the Shared Materials Drive, Case No. 002/19-09-2007-ECCC/OCIJ (PTC 24), ¶ 22 (Nov. 18, 2009) [hereinafter SMD Decision].

35. Decision on the Ieng Thirith Defense Appeal Against "Order on Requests for Investigative Action by the Defence for Ieng Thirith" of 15 March 2010, Case No. 002/19-09-2007-ECCC/OCIJ (PTC 62), ¶¶ 17–20 (June 14, 2010).

36. *See, e.g.*, Decision on Reconsideration of Co-Prosecutors' Appeal Against the Co-Investigating Judges Order on Request to Place Additional Evidentiary Material on the Case File Which Assists in Proving the Charged Persons' Knowledge of the Crimes, Case No. 002/19-09-2007-ECCC/OCIJ (PTC 67), ¶ 68 (Sept. 27, 2010) (in which the PTC reviews the request due to the CIJs' "failure to meet their obligation to provide reasoned orders"); Decision on Ieng Sary's Appeal Regarding the Appointment of a Psychiatric Expert, Case No. 002/19-09-2007-ECCC/OCIJ (PTC 10), ¶ 24 (Oct. 21, 2008) (admitting an appeal due to the "failure of the Co-Investigating Judges to rule on the Request as soon as possible").

37. One defense lawyer argues that by shutting parties out of the process, Judge Lemonde created the defense "monster" that continually challenged his work. Interview with Andrew Ianuzzi, former Legal Consultant to Nuon Chea, Phnom Penh (May 29, 2012).

38. Interview with Michael G. Karnavas, former Co-Lawyer for Ieng Sary, Phnom Penh (May 19, 2012).

39. *See* SMD Decision, *supra* note 34, ¶ 22 (affirming its prior finding that the CIJs "are independent in the way they conduct their investigation").

40. *See* Guissé interview, *supra* note 27 ("Investigative judges are so powerful, if they are good it is perfect; if they are bad it is very bad.").

41. Statement of Wayne Bastin (Oct. 8, 2009). *See also* Douglas Gillison, *Claim of Bias Made Against ECCC Judge*, CAMBODIA DAILY, Oct. 9, 2009.

42. Consolidated Response by Co-Investigating Judge Marcel Lemonde to Applications to Disqualify Field on Behalf of Ieng Sary and Khieu Samphan, Case No. 002/19-09-2007-ECCC/OCIJ (PTC24), ¶ 8 (Nov. 5, 2009).

43. Ieng Sary's Application to Disqualify Co-Investigating Judge Marcel Lemonde & Request for a Public Hearing, Case No. 002/19-09-2007-ECCC/OCIJ(PTC01), ¶ 29 (Oct. 9, 2009).

44. Decision on Ieng Sary's Application to Disqualify Co-Investigative Judge Marcel Lemonde, Case No. 002/19-09-2007-ECCC/OCIJ(PTC01), ¶¶ 22–25 (Dec. 9, 2009) (emphasizing the event's informality and the fact the discussion was not in Lemonde's native language).

45. The Ieng Sary defense team has consistently argued prejudice arising from the fact that Stephen Heder "worked for the Co-Prosecutor in drafting the introductory submissions, and later for the Co-Investigating Judges in confirming the introductory submission by his involvement in the preparation of the Closing Order." *See, e.g.*, Decision on Objections to Documents Proposed to be Put Before the Chamber on the Co-Prosecutors' Annexes A1-A5 and to Documents Cited in Paragraphs of the Closing Order Relevant to the First Two Trial Segments of Case 002/01, Case No. 002/09-07-2009-ECCC-TC, ¶ 10

(Apr. 9, 2012). The prosecution says that Heder "left their office before the introductory submission was written in the second quarter of 2007." *Id.* ¶ 13.

46. Decision on the Charged Person's Application for Disqualification of Drs. Steven Heder and David Boyle, Case No. 002/08-07-2009-ECCC-PTC, ¶ 20 (Sept. 22, 2009).

47. Decision on Appeal Against the Co-Investigating Judges' Order on the Charged Person's Eleventh Request for Investigative Action, Case No. 002/19-09-2007-ECCC/OCIJ (PTC 21), ¶ 50 (Aug. 18, 2009).

48. SMD Order, *supra* note 31, ¶ 6.

49. Guissé interview *supra* note 27. *But see* Interview with Craig Etcheson, former investigator in the ECCC Office of the Co-Prosecutors, via telephone (Oct. 22, 2012) (saying that the investigating judges "largely ignored the final submission" when writing the closing order, which is problematic because the prosecution is responsible for carrying the closing order into court and may not agree with the form of the charges).

50. SMD Order, *supra* note 31, ¶ 6.

51. SMD Decision, *supra* note 34, ¶¶ 36–37.

52. Interview with Richard Rogers, former head of the Defence Support Section, Phnom Penh (May 29, 2012) (arguing further that formal investigatory requests cannot compensate for the absence of client instructions regarding potential lines of inquiry).

53. Karnavas interview, *supra* note 38.

54. *Id. See also* Guissé interview, *supra* note 27 ("Investigators from different judicial backgrounds don't have the same habits, don't consider the consequences of what they are doing as they don't know how the evidence will be used.").

55. Guissé interview, *supra* note 27.

56. Interview with Michiel Pestman, former Co-Lawyer for Nuon Chea, Phnom Penh (June 9, 2012). *See also* Sulzer interview, *supra* note 28 (arguing that the judges could have taken a middle ground on confidentiality and disclosed the scope of the investigation earlier to facilitate civil party admissibility).

57. *See, e.g.*, Letter from the Ieng Sary defense team to Deputy Director Rosandhaug and the Co-Investigative Judges (Dec. 18, 2008), *quoted in* Order on Breach of Confidentiality of the Judicial Investigation, Case No. 002/14-08-2006, ¶ 2 (Mar. 3, 2009) (stating that the defense team created a public website because the CIJs were suppressing defense filings that "may be embarrassing or which call into question the legitimacy and judiciousness of acts and decisions of the judges").

58. *See generally* Memorandum from the CIJs regarding Your "Request for Investigative Action" Concerning *inter alia* the Strategy of the Co-Investigating Judges in Regard to the Judicial Investigation, Case No. 002/19-09-2007-ECCC-OCIJ-D171, D130/7 & D130/7/2 (Dec. 11, 2009).

59. Ieng Sary's Third Request for Investigative Action, Case No. 002/19-09-2007-ECCC/OCIJ, ¶ 3 (May 21, 2009) (citations omitted).

60. Karnavas interview, *supra* note 38. The conduct of OCIJ interviews was a major

issue of contention at trial. *See, e.g,* Anne Heindel, *Decision on Defense Allegations of Irregularities during the Judicial Investigation,* Cambodia Tribunal Monitor (Dec. 13, 2012), http://www.cambodiatribunal.org/sites/default/files/CTM Heindel 12-12-13.pdf.

61. Karnavas interview, *supra* note 38.

62. ECCC Internal Rules (rev. 8), *supra* note 30, r. 60(1) (emphasis added), r. 55(5)(a),(d).

63. *Id.* r. 87(4), r. 104*bis*.

64. *See, e.g.*, Letter from CIJ Marcel Lemonde to H.E. Hor Namhong (Sept. 25, 2009); Decision on NUON Chea's and IENG Sary's Appeal Against OCIJ Order on Requests to Summons Witnesses, Case No. 002/19-09-2007-ECCC-TC, ¶ 3 (June 8, 2010) [hereinafter Decision on Summons Appeal].

65. ECCC Internal Rules (rev. 8), *supra* note 30, r. 41(1).

66. *Id.* r. 60(3). The Cambodian Criminal Procedure Code also states that appearance is mandatory once summoned. Cambodian Criminal Procedure Code (*as adopted* Aug. 10, 2007), art. 153. *See also id.* art. 179.

67. Prosecutor v. Radoslav Brdjanin *et al.*, Case No. IT-99-36-AR73.9, Decision on Interlocutory Appeal, ¶ 31 (Appeals Chamber, Dec. 11, 2002).

68. Prosecutor v. Sefer Halilovic, Case No. IT-01-48-AR73, Decision on the Issuance of Subpoenas, ¶ 10 (Appeals Chamber, June 21, 2004).

69. Prosecutor v. Sam Hinga Norman et al., Case No. SCSL-2004-14-T, Decision on Interlocutory Appeals Against Trial Chamber Decision Refusing to Subpoena the President of Sierra Leone, ¶ 29 (Appeals Chamber, Sept. 11, 2006) [hereinafter *Norman* Appeal Decision on Kabbah Motion].

70. Prosecutor v. Issa Hassan Sesay *et al.*, Case No. SCSL-04-15-T, Written Reasoned Decision on Motion for Issuance of a Subpoena to H.E. Dr. Ahmad Tejan Kabbah, Former President of the Republic of Sierra Leone, ¶ 20 (Trial Chamber, June 30, 2008) [hereinafter *Sesay* Decision on Kabbah Motion] (footnotes omitted). *See also* Prosecutor v. Théoneste Bagosora *et al.*, Case No. ICTR-98-41-T, Decision on Request for a Subpoena for Major Jacques Biot, ¶ 2 (Trial Chamber, July 14, 2006) [hereinafter ICTR Decision on Biot]; Prosecutor v. Slobodan Milosevic, Case No. IT-02-54-T, Decision on Assigned Counsel Application for Interview and Testimony of Tony Blair and Gerhard Schröder, ¶ 41 (Trial Chamber, Dec. 9, 2005) [hereinafter ICTY Decision on Blair & Schröder].

71. Prosecutor v. Sam Hinga Norman et al., Case No. SCSL-04-14-T, Decision on Motions by Moinina Fofana and Sam Hinga Norman for the Issuance of a Subpoena *Ad Testificandum* to H.E. Alhaji Dr. Ahmad Tejan Kabbah, President of the Republic of Sierra Leone, ¶¶ 40, 45 (Trial Chamber, June 13, 2006) [hereinafter *Norman* Decision on Kabbah Motion].

72. *Id.* ¶ 41. The Trial Chamber decided with little analysis that this information was obtainable through other means, and on appeal the SCSL Appeals Chamber agreed. *Norman* Appeal Decision on Kabbah Motion, *supra* note 69, ¶ 32.

73. *Sesay* Decision on Kabbah Motion, *supra* note 70, ¶ 19 (finding that Kabbah could provide evidence on Sesay's relations with UN peacekeepers).

74. *Id.*, Concurring opinion of Hon. Justice Itoe ¶¶ 35–37.

75. *Id.*, Concurring opinion of Hon. Justice Itoe ¶¶ 30–31.

76. *Norman* Decision on Kabbah Motion, *supra* note 71, Dissenting opinion of Hon. Justice Thompson ¶¶ 2–3.

77. *Id.*, Dissenting opinion of Hon. Justice Thompson ¶ 27.

78. *Id.*, Dissenting opinion of Hon. Justice Thompson ¶ 29.

79. *See* Summary of IENG Sary's Reply to the International Co-Prosecutor's Observations on Ieng Sary and Nuon Chea's Appeals on the Summoning of Additional Witnesses, at 1 (Apr. 13, 2010), *available at* https://sites.google.com/site/iengsarydefence/.

80. *See* Decision on Summons Appeal, *supra* note 64, ¶¶ 25, 30–31.

81. Prosecutor v. Charles Ghankay Taylor, Case No. SCSL-2003-01-I, Decision on Immunity of Jurisdiction, ¶ 17(c) (Appeals Chamber, May 31, 2004) (citing Sands' amicus brief to the Court).

82. *See, e.g., Cambodia's King Ready to Face Genocide Tribunal*, BBC NEWS, Jan. 4, 1999; Kim Chhan, Thet Sambath, & Porter Barron, *King Wants to Testify at KR Tribunal*, CAMBODIA DAILY, Apr. 29, 2004.

83. *Sihanouk Refuses to Testify at Cambodian Trials*, ABC RADIO AUSTRALIA, Sept. 10, 2009.

84. CONSTITUTION OF THE KINGDOM OF CAMBODIA, art. 7 (adopted 1993, *as amended through* 2008) [hereinafter CAMBODIAN CONSTITUTION].

85. Law on the Titles and Privileges of the Former King and Queen of Cambodia (Oct. 29, 2004).

86. Douglas Gillison & Yun Samean, *Nuon Chea's Lawyers Seek Hun Sen, Retired King Testimony*, CAMBODIA DAILY, Mar. 2, 2009, at 28 (quoting Prince Sisowath Thomico); Yun Samean & Emily Lodish, *Gov't Rejects Call to Investigate King Father*, CAMBODIA DAILY, Aug. 27, 2007; email from Ambassador Julio A. Jeldres, Official Biographer to King Father Sihanouk (Aug. 13, 2009).

87. Sok Khemara, *Court Mulls Bringing 'King Father' to Court*, VOA KHMER (May 4, 2009), http://www.voacambodia.com/content/a-40-2009-05-04-voa3-90174962/1354885.html (quoting Ke Kim Se, Sihanouk's former cabinet chief).

88. Erika Kinetz & Yun Samean, *Retired King Invites Staff to Palace*, CAMBODIA DAILY, Aug. 31, 2007.

89. Asian Human Rights Commission, *Cambodia: Immunity from Prosecution for Former King Sihanouk is Illegitimate, Unconstitutional and Indefensible*, Sept. 3, 2007, *available at* http://www.ahrchk.net/statements/mainfile.php/2007statements/1174/. *See also* Sok, *supra* note 87 (citing legal monitors who assert that calling Sihanouk would not be "against the Constitution" but would be "a sensitive risk").

90. *See* CAMBODIAN CONSTITUTION, *supra* note 84, art. 136 (providing that "The

Constitutional Council shall . . . interpret the Constitution and laws adopted by the National Assembly and reviewed completely by the Senate").

91. Decision on Summons Appeal, *supra* note 64, ¶ 24. *Cf.* Decision on Ieng Sary, *supra* note 12, ¶ 29 (finding that it is "not in a position to determine the respective powers of the King and National Assembly" and thus the constitutional validity of Ieng Sary's 1996 pardon and amnesty).

92. *See* Cambodian Constitution, *supra* note 84, arts. 80, 104, 126.

93. *See Norman* Decision on Kabbah Motion, *supra* note 71, Separate concurring opinion of Hon. Justice Benjamin Mutanga Itoe ¶ 130.

94. *Id.*, Dissenting opinion of Hon. Justice Thompson ¶ 14 (quoting the decision with approval).

95. *See* ICTR Decision on Biot, *supra* note 70, ¶ 4; ICTY Decision on Blair & Schröder, *supra* note 70, ¶ 28; Prosecutor v. Radislav Krstic, Case No. IT-98-33-A, Decision on Application for Subpoenas, ¶ 27 (Appeals Chamber, July 1, 2003).

96. ICTY Decision on Blair & Schröder, *supra* note 70, ¶ 28.

97. *See* Summary of IENG Sary's Appeal Against the OCIJ's Order on Nuon Chea and IENG Sary's Request to Summon Witnesses referred to in his Letter dated 16 December 2009 and in Paragraph 21(D) of his 11th Investigative Request, at 2 (Mar. 15, 2010), *available at* https://sites.google.com/site/iengsarydefence/ [hereinafter Summary of Ieng Sary Appeal on Request to Summon Witnesses]. As the PTC recognized, this objection is inconsistent with the SMD Decision discussed above, which rejected the "principle of sufficiency" of evidence. Decision on Summons Appeal, *supra* note 64, ¶ 24.

98. Phann Ana & Douglas Gillison, *Hun Sen Criticizes Summoning of CPP Officials*, Cambodia Daily, Oct. 9, 2009.

99. *See* Summary of Ieng Sary Appeal on Request to Summon Witnesses, *supra* note 97, at 3; Note of International Investigating Judge Marcel Lemonde, at 3 (Jan. 11, 2010).

100. Note of International Investigating Judge Marcel Lemonde, *supra* note 99, at 3.

101. ECCC Law, *supra* note 11, art. 33 new; ECCC Internal Rules (rev. 8), *supra* note 30, r. 14(5), r. 15.

102. Decision on Summons Appeal, *supra* note 64, ¶¶ 69–71.

103. *Id.* ¶ 68.

104. *See* Julia Wallace & Neou Vannarin, *Nuon Chea Lawyers Sue Hun Sen, 10 Others*, Cambodia Daily, Oct. 25, 2011.

105. Sebastian Strangio & Cheang Sokha, *Govt Testimony Could Bias KRT: PM*, Phnom Penh Post, Oct. 9, 2009.

106. The scope of authority for one CIJ or Co-Prosecutor to act alone is discussed in chapter 6.

107. Order in Response to the Appeals Chamber's Decision on Nuon Chea and Ieng Sary's Requests to Summon Witnesses, Case No. 002/19-09-2007-ECCC-OCIJ, ¶ 5 (June 11, 2010).

108. Second Decision on NUON Chea's and IENG Sary's Appeal Against OCIJ Order on Request to Summon Witnesses, Case No. 002/19-09-2007-ECCC-PTC (Sept. 9, 2010), Opinion of Judges Prak, Ney, and Huot ¶ 9.

109. *Id.*, Opinion of Downing & Marchi-Uhel ¶ 6.

110. *See, e.g.*, Decision on Nuon Chea Motions Regarding Fairness of Judicial Investigation (E/51/3, E82, E88 and E92), Case No. 002/19-09-2007-ECCC-TC (Sept. 9, 2011); Decision on Immediate Appeal by Nuon Chea Against the Trial Chamber's Decision on Fairness of Judicial Investigation, 002/19-09-2007-ECCC-TC/SC(08) (Apr. 27, 2012).

111. Pestman interview, *supra* note 56 (noting that the list remained tentative, providing the defense no opportunity to object to their exclusion).

112. *Id.* (contending that Heng was the highest-level Khmer Rouge commander in Phnom Penh during the evacuation who is still alive and was Nuon Chea's bodyguard before the DK period). *See also* Sixth and Final Request to Summons TCW-223, Case No. 002/19-09-2007-ECCC-TC (July 22, 2013). Karnavas does not view the witnesses as crucial to Ieng Sary's case and believes the Government's refusal to cooperate is not about political interference but instead about maintaining control. Karnavas interview, *supra* note 38.

113. *Quelles leçons, supra* note 26 (authors' translation from the original French).

114. Transcript of Trial Proceedings—Case 002, Case File No. 002/19-09-2007-ECCC/TC, at 88–93 (June 11, 2012). The witness denied making the statements. *See also* Joseph Freeman, *Defence Grills Witness About PM Statements*, PHNOM PENH POST, June 12, 2012.

115. *See* Anne Heindel, *Decision on Nuon Chea Defence Counsel Misconduct*, CAMBODIA TRIBUNAL MONITOR (July 1, 2012), http://www.cambodiatribunal.org/sites/default/files/CTM Heindel 12-07-01 AH.pdf.

116. *See, e.g.*, Lauren Crothers, *Courts Failing to Grant Bail, Provide Free Lawyers*, CAMBODIA DAILY, June 30–July 1, 2012 (reporting the view of Yeng Virak, executive director of the Community Legal Education Center, that "detention ahead of trial is used excessively, and the presumption of guilt is widespread in the court system," as well as a report by local human rights group Licado stating that "'noncustodial sentencing remains unheard of, bail is underutilized' and pretrial detainees still make up over one-third of the prison population").

117. ECCC Internals Rules (rev. 8), *supra* note 30, r. 63(b).

118. *Id.* r. 63(6)(a), (7).

119. *See, e.g.*, Ilijkov v. Bulgaria, App. No. 33977/96, Eur. Ct. H.R., ¶ 84 (July 26, 2001); Jorge A. Giménez v. Arg., Case No. 11.245, Report 12/96, Inter-Am.C.H.R., OEA/Ser.L/V/II.91, Doc. 7 at 33, ¶ 84 (1996); W.B.E. v. Neth., HRC Comm. No. 432/1990, ¶ 6.3 (1992).

120. *See, e.g.*, Prosecutor v. Issa Hassan Sesay et al., Case No. SCSL-04-15-AR65, Sesay—Decision on Appeal Against Refusal of Bail, ¶ 36 (Appeals Chamber, Dec. 14, 2004); Prosecutor v. Radoslav Brdanin et al., Case No. IT-99-36, Decision on Application

for Leave to Appeal (Appeals Chamber Bench, Sept. 7, 2000). *See generally* Andrew Trotter, *Pre-Conviction Detention in International Criminal Trials,* 11 J. Int'l Crim. Just. 351 (2013).

121. *See, e.g.,* Judie Kaberia, *Kenyan Suspects to Remain Free During ICC Trials,* Institute for War & Peace Reporting (July 13, 2012).

122. *See* Decision on Appeal Against Provisional Detention Order of Ieng Sary, Case No. 002/19-09-2007-ECCC/OCIJ (PTC03), ¶¶ 101–6 (Oct. 17, 2008) [hereinafter Ieng Sary Detention Decision] (highlighting their past travels and contacts and the gravity of their alleged crimes).

123. *Id.* ¶¶ 111–17.

124. *See id.* ¶¶ 118–23.

125. *See, e.g.,* Prosecutor v. Jovica Stansic, Case No. IT-03-68-PT, Decision on Provisional Release, ¶ 39 (Trial Chamber, July 28, 2004)] (need for treatment); Prosecutor v. Simo Drljaca et al., Case No. IT-97-24-T, Decision on Defense Motion for Provisional Release, ¶ 12 (Trial Chamber, Jan. 20, 1998) (humanitarian grounds); Prosecutor v. Pavle Strugar, Case No. IT-01, Decision re the Defence Motion to Terminate Proceedings, ¶ 35 (Trial Chamber, May 26, 2004) (fitness); Prosecutor v. Pavle Strugar, Case No. I-01-42-A, Decision on Defense Request for Provisional Release for Providing Medical Aid in the Republic of Montenegro, ¶ 5(d) (Appeals Chamber, Dec. 16, 2005) (requiring return to detention as soon as treatment was complete).

126. *See, e.g.,* Prosecutor v. Radolav Brdanin et al., Case No. IT-99-36-T, Decision on the Motion for Provisional Release of the Accused Momir Talic, ¶ 35 (Trial Chamber, Sept. 20, 2002).

127. Ieng Sary Detention Decision, *supra* note 122, ¶ 123.

128. With regard to one accused, the Supreme Court Chamber found the Trial Chamber "could have investigated in a deeper fashion alternative measures other than detention which could have equally ensured the presence of the accused at trial," but did not consider the issue itself because the accused's submissions "did not provide any details as to the means of securing such presence." Decision on Immediate Appeal by Khieu Samphan on Application for Release, Case No. 002/19-09-2007-ECCC-TC/SC(04), ¶ 58 (June 6, 2011).

129. *See Former Khmer Rouge Minister Argues to Go Free,* Agence France Presse, May 21, 2008 (reporting that when asked how many children she has, Ieng Thirith said, "Three or four. I forget . . . I have four children. I almost forgot."); *Khmer Rouge 'First Lady' in Cambodia Court Tirade,* Agence France Presse, Feb. 24, 2009 (reporting an infamous 15-minute tirade during which she rejected the charges against her and said, "Don't accuse me of being a murderer, otherwise you will [be] cursed to the seventh circle of hell").

130. *See* Report Prepared in Response to the Trial Chamber's Order Assigning Expert—E62/3, Case No. 002/19-09-2007-ECCC/TC, ¶ 32 (June 23, 2011) (including

findings by a geriatrician that Alzheimer's disease is the primary cause of her condition, but "personal stress, exposure to trauma and restricted environment and stimulation" have affected her).

131. Prosecutor v. Pavle Strugar, Case No. IT-01, Decision re the Defence Motion to Terminate Proceedings, ¶¶ 35, 38, 47 (Trial Chamber, May 26, 2004).

132. *See* Indication of Documents Relevant to the Early Segments from the Defence of Madame Ieng Thirith, Case No. 002/19-09-2007-ECCC/TC, ¶ 4 (July 22, 2011).

133. Decision on Ieng Thirith's Fitness to Stand Trial, Case No. 002/19-09-2007-ECCC-TC, ¶¶ 79–80 (Nov. 17, 2011).

134. *Id.*

135. *See generally* Decision on Immediate Appeal Against the Trial Chamber's Order to Release the Accused Ieng Thirith, Case No. 002/19-09-2007-ECCC-TC/SC(09) (Dec. 13, 2011).

136. *See, e.g.*, Sreinith S. Ten, *Too Painful to Accept*, SEARCHING FOR THE TRUTH (Khmer edition, Sept. 2011).

137. *See, e.g.*, OSJI, *Recent Developments at the Extraordinary Chambers in the Courts of Cambodia*, at 18 (Feb. 2012).

138. *See* Decision on Co-Prosecutors' Request for Stay of Release Order of Ieng Thirith, Case No. 002/19-09-2007-ECCC-TC/SC(16) (Sept. 16, 2012).

139. Cable 09PHNOMPENH765, U.S. Embassy Phnom Penh, *Friends of the ECCC Discuss Staffing Challenges, Budget, and the Way Forward* ¶ 4 (Oct. 16, 2009), *available at* http://www.wikileaks.org/cable/2009/10/09PHNOMPENH765.html.

140. Ieng Sary, Ieng Thirith, and Khieu Samphan's third year would have expired in November 2010.

141. *See* Press Release, *Pre-Trial Chamber Dismissed Appeals from Ieng Sary, Khieu Samphan and Ieng Thirith Against Extension of Provisional Detention* (Apr. 30, 2010).

142. *See* ECCC Internal Rules (rev. 8), *supra* note 30, r. 81(2), r. 82(1).

143. *Id.* r. 68(1).

144. *Id.* r. 68(2).

145. Decision on the Urgent Applications for Immediate Release of Nuon Chea, Khieu Samphan and Ieng Thirith, Case No. 002/19-09-2007/ECCC/TC, ¶ 35 (Feb. 16, 2011).

146. Decision on Immediate Appeal by Khieu Samphan on Application for Release, *supra* note 128, ¶ 37.

147. *See* Prosecutor v. Vujadin Popovic et al., Case No. IT-05-88-AR65.1, Decision on Interlocutory Appeal of Trial Chamber Decision Denying Drago Nikolic's Motion for Provisional Release, at 5 (Appeals Chamber, Jan. 24, 2006) (noting that the Trial Chamber has "considerable discretion" when determining how to weigh factors relevant to determining the necessity of pretrial detention).

148. Karnavas interview, *supra* note 38.

149. Interview with Panhavuth Long, Program Officer, Cambodian Justice Initiative,

Phnom Penh (July 6, 2012) (emphasizing that judges and prosecutors at in-country tribunals are sometimes concerned about "public outcry instead of considering [the] best interests of justice").

150. Internal Rule 89*ter* allows the Trial Chamber to separate the proceedings at any stage and try them in the order it deems appropriate "[w]hen the interests of justice so requires."

151. Ieng Sary's Motion to Conduct the Trial Through Half-Day Sessions, Case no. 02/19-09-2007-ECCC/TC (Jan. 19, 2011).

152. *See, e.g.*, Kong Sothanarith, *Health Failing Nuon Chea and Ieng Sary: Lawyers*, VOA Khmer (Jan. 11, 2013), http://www.voacambodia.com/content/health-failing-nuon-chea-and-ieng-sary-say-lawyers/1581376.html; Assoc. Press, *Second of 3 Aging Defendants at Cambodia's Khmer Rouge Tribunal Sent to Hospital*, Jan. 16, 2013 (reporting that both Nuon Chea and Khieu Samphan were sent to the hospital in the same week).

153. ECCC Internal Rules (rev. 8), *supra* note 30, r. 81(1). Although the Special Tribunal for Lebanon also upholds the right to presence, it uniquely makes provision for *in absentia* proceedings in specific circumstances. *See* Statute of the Special Tribunal for Lebanon, arts. 16(4)(d), 22, Annex, U.N. Doc. S/RES/1757 (May 30, 2007).

154. *See, e.g.*, Zigiranyirazo v. Prosecutor, Case No. ICTR-2001-73-AR73, Decision on Interlocutory Appeal, ¶ 14 (Appeals Chamber, Oct. 30, 2006); Prosecutor v. Stanisic & Simatovic, Case No. IT-03-69-AR73.2, Decision on Defence Appeal of the Decision on Future Course of Proceedings, ¶¶ 11, 18–20 (Appeals Chamber, May 16, 2008).

155. ECCC, Behind the Scenes: Holding Cells, http://www.eccc.gov.kh/en/articles/behind-scenes-holding-cells (last visited May 23, 2012).

156. Ieng Sary's Motion, *supra* note 151, ¶ 13.

157. Bridget Di Certo, *Ieng Sary Health Woes Prompt Adjournment*, Phnom Penh Post, May 22, 2012 (quoting Michael Karnavas).

158. Decision on Accused Ieng Sary's Fitness to Stand Trial, Case No. 002/19-09-2007-ECCC/TC (Nov. 26, 2012). *See* Anne Heindel, *Trial Chamber Decides that Accused Ieng Sary Is Fit and May Be Ordered to Participate by Video-Link*, Cambodia Tribunal Monitor (Nov. 30, 2012), http://www.cambodiatribunal.org/sites/default/files/CTM Heindel 12-11-30.pdf.

159. "Considering that the Accused [Ieng Sary and Nuon Chea] both suffer several chronic physical ailments and regularly participate in proceedings from the holding cell" the Trial Chamber scheduled a hearing to review their fitness for trial in March 2013. Memorandum from Trial Chamber President Nil Nonn, Re-Appointment of Experts to Review the Health and Fitness of IENG Sary and NUON Chea during the week of 11 March 2013 (Dec. 18, 2012). Nuon Chea was found fit for trial. *See* Second Decision on Accused NUON Chea's Fitness to Stand Trial, Case No. 002/19-09-2007/ECCC/TC (Apr. 2, 2013).

160. *See, e.g.*, Prosecutor v. Milosevic, Order Terminating the Proceedings, Case No. IT-

02-54-T (Trial Chamber, Mar. 14, 2006); Prosecutor v. Norman et al., Decision on Registrar's Submission of Evidence of Death of Accused Samuel Hinga Norman and Consequential Issues, Case No. SCSL-04-14-T, ¶¶ 14–18 (Trial Chamber, May 21, 2007); Prosecutor v. Kony et al., Decision to Terminate the Proceedings Against Raska Lukwiya, Case No ICC-02/04-01/05, at 4 (July 11, 2007).

161. Confidential interview, Phnom Penh (May 14, 2012).

162. Press Release, *Severance of Proceedings Ordered in Case 002* (Sept. 22, 2011).

163. Severance Order Pursuant to Internal Rule 89*ter*, Case No. 002/19-09-2007-ECCC/TC, ¶ 8 (Sept. 22, 2011) [hereinafter Severance Order].

164. Decision on Co-Prosecutors' Request for Reconsideration of the Terms of the Trial Chamber's Severance Order (E124/2) and Related Motions and Annexes, Case No. 002/19-09-2007/ECCC/TC, ¶ 4 (Oct. 18, 2011) [hereinafter Severance Order Reconsideration] (finding also that this was unnecessary in a purely inquisitorial legal system where indictments are judicially controlled). Importantly, the Supreme Court Chamber has since ruled that the Trial Chamber committed an error of law by failing to consult with the parties on the terms of severance, noting in part:

> [The Trial Chamber] fails to appreciate the *sui generis* mixed jurisdictional nature of the ECCC and ignores provisions explicitly referring to the adversarial nature of the ECCC proceedings and to the Co-Prosecutors' crucial role and responsibility in creating ECCC indictments and proving the charges therein.

Decision on the Co-Prosecutors' Immediate Appeal of the Trial Chamber's Decision Concerning the Scope of Case 002/01, Case No. 002/19-09-2007-ECCC-TC/SC(18), ¶ 42 (Feb. 8, 2013) [hereinafter SCC Severance Decision].

165. Severance Order, *supra* note 163, ¶ 7.

166. Press Release, *supra* note 162.

167. Co-Prosecutors' Request for Reconsideration of "Severance Order Pursuant to Internal Rule 89*ter*," Case No. 002/19-09-2007-ECCC/TC, ¶ 3 (Oct. 3, 2011).

168. *Id.* ¶ 36.

169. Ieng Sary's Response to the Co-Prosecutors' Request for Reconsideration of "Severance Order Pursuant to Internal Rule 89*ter*," Case No. 001/19-09-2007-ECCC/TC, ¶ 6 (Oct. 13, 2001).

170. *See, e.g.*, Decision on Immediate Appeal Against the Trial Chamber's Order to Unconditionally Release the Accused Ieng Thirith, Case No. 002/19/09-2007 ECCC-TC/SC(16), ¶ 37 (Dec. 14, 2012) ("Traditionally, most civil law jurisdictions have adopted the principle of legalism . . . pursuant to which the prosecution has no discretion to discontinue or ask for the discontinuation of a criminal action once it has been initiated and the court, which has sole authority to terminate proceedings, can only do it for a reason specifically expressed in the law." (citations omitted)).

171. Karnavas interview, *supra* note 38.

172. *See, e.g.*, Interview with Diana Ellis, Co-Lawyer for Ieng Thirith, Phnom Penh (Nov. 11, 2012) (saying the prosecution's initial submission should have focused only on good crime evidence).

173. Confidential interview, Phnom Penh (May 14, 2012).

174. Sulzer interview, *supra* note 28. The Supreme Court Chamber appears to agree, as it suggested that the Trial Chamber may wish to "state clearly" that due to the declining health of the accused "justice is better served by concluding with a judgment" on a smaller number of representative charges. SCC Severance Decision, *supra* note 164, ¶ 50.

175. Interview with Elisabeth Simonneau Fort, international Lead Co-Lawyer for Case 002 ECCC Civil Parties, Phnom Penh (June 1, 2012). *See, e.g.*, Co-Prosecutors' Request to Admit Witness Statements Relevant to Phase 2 of the Population Movement . . . , Case No. 002/19-09-2007-ECCC/TC, ¶ 15 (July 5, 2012) (noting witness statements "suggest[ing] the existence of a CPK policy to conduct a large scale relocation of Cham People in order to disperse them throughout Khmer villages with only a minority of Cham people allowed in each village").

176. Karnavas interview, *supra* note 38.

177. Long interview, *supra* note 149.

178. *See* OSJI, *Recent Developments at the Extraordinary Chambers in the Courts of Cambodia*, at 19 (Feb. 2012).

179. SCC Severance Decision, *supra* note 164, ¶ 43.

180. *See* Decision on Severance of Case 002 Following Supreme Court Chamber Decision of 8 February 2013, Case No. Case No. 002/19-09-2007-ECCC/TC, ¶ 4 (Apr. 26, 2013) [hereinafter Second Decision on Severance] (affirming the appropriateness of the status quo, finding it most likely to promote legal certainty and "to represent a proportionate balance between the factors identified by the SCC Decision and necessary in order to safeguard [the Chamber's] ability to reach any timely verdict in Case 002" due to the advanced age and fragile health of the accused and many victims). *See also* Decision on Immediate Appeals Against Trial Chamber's Second Decision on Severance of Case 002, Summary of Reasons, Case No. 002/19-09-2007-ECCC/TC/SC(28), ¶ 11 (July 23, 2013) (determining that "to order an expansion of Case 002/01 . . . would inevitably result in unnecessary delays").

181. Memorandum from Trial Chamber President Nil Nonn, Scheduling of Trial Management Meeting to Enable Planning of the Remaining Trial Phases in Case 002/01 and Implementation of Further Measures Designed to Promote Efficiency, ¶ 1 (Aug. 3, 2012).

182. ECCC Press Release, *supra* note 162.

183. A year and a half into proceedings, the Trial Chamber estimated that over the course of the Case 002/01 trial it had heard testimony "on an approximate average of 7.3 courtroom days per month." Second Decision on Severance, *supra* note 180, ¶ 14 (attributing the slow pace to "the health of the Accused, witness availability, and the appeal pro-

cess"). During 21 months of hearings, the Trial Chamber heard only 52 fact witnesses, 3 experts, 5 character witnesses, and 32 civil parties—nearly half of whom provided victim impact statements during a special four-day hearing. Statistics for Case 002/01 are available at http://www.eccc.gov.kh/en/articles/statistics-case-0021.

184. Two months before the end of hearings, the Co-Prosecutors noted that due to the unsettled status of the severance decision, the Trial Chamber had been "managing and planning the trial on a week to week basis[.]" Co-Prosecutors' Immediate Appeal of Second Decision on Severance of Case 002, Case No. 002/19-09-2007-ECCC/SC, ¶ 75 (May 10, 2013). *But see id.* ¶ 70 (nevertheless arguing that "the most significant impediment [to expeditious proceedings] had been the four-day trial schedule . . . and the frequent judicial recesses scheduled by the Trial Chamber").

185. *See generally* Letter from Co-Lawyers for Ieng Sary to Susan Lamb, Trial Chamber Senior Legal Officer, Re: Scheduling of the Substantive Trial (Oct. 17, 2011) (listing myriad unresolved procedural topics and seeking clarification in advance of trial).

186. *See* Objections, Observations, and Notifications Regarding Various Documents to be Put Before the Trial Chamber, Case No. 002/19-09-2007-ECCC-TC, ¶¶ 22–23 (Nov. 14, 2011) (describing efforts by all parties for a pretrial conference and arguing that "the principal obstacle to an efficient trial in Case 002 is undoubtedly the Chamber's consistent failure to engage the parties in anything resembling a meaningful discussion."). *Cf.* Radosa Mulitunovic, *Mladic: Just Another "False Start,"* 152 INT'L JUSTICE TRIB. at 1 (May 23, 2012) (noting that "a shrinking staff, limited resources and smaller budget, combined with its congenital bureaucratic nature, have made the ICTY prone to succumb to pressure to 'start the trial now and solve problems as we go'").

187. Additional procedural debates are discussed at http://www.cambodiatribunal.org/category/commentary/expert-commentary/.

188. *See* ECCC Internal Rules (rev. 8), *supra* note 30, r. 90(2) (noting that in addition to the judges, the parties and their lawyers "shall also be allowed to ask questions with the permission of the President").

189. *See* Memorandum from Trial Chamber President Nil Nonn to Co Prosecutors, Advance Notice of Assignment of Four Witnesses During First Trial Segment (5–16 December 2011) (Nov. 28, 2011).

190. Karnavas interview, *supra* note 38; Sulzer interview, *supra* note 28 (arguing that the judges' material inability to lead most witnesses and civil party interviews at trial has led to confusion).

191. *See generally* Prosecutor v. Karemera et al., ICTR-98-44-AR73.8, Decision on Interlocutory Appeal Regarding Witness Proofing (Appeals Chamber, May 11, 2007).

192. This bar to "proofing" witnesses, followed by the ICC, intends to prevent "a rehearsal of in-court testimony." *See* Prosecutor v. Lubanga, Case No. ICC-01/04-01/06, Decision Regarding the Practices Used to Prepare and Familiarize Witnesses for Giving Testimony at Trial, ¶ 51 (Trial Chamber, Nov. 30, 2007).

193. Pestman interview, *supra* note 56.

194. Karnavas interview, *supra* note 38 ("They are the captain of the ship but without access to the navigational gear, be it the compass or the ship's wheel."); Sulzer interview, *supra* note 28 (arguing that "the court selects witnesses but doesn't question them, so questioning is not focused").

195. Ianuzzi interview, *supra* note 37.

196. Co-Prosecutors' Request, *supra* note 167, ¶ 35.

197. Memorandum from President Nil Nonn to Co Prosecutors, Re: Advance Notice of Assignment of Four Witnesses During First Trial Segment (5–16 December 2011) (Nov. 28, 2011).

198. Ianuzzi interview, *supra* note 37.

199. *See* Memorandum from Trial Chamber President Nil Nonn to all Parties, Re: Order of Witnesses for Current Segment of Case 002/02 (May 11, 2012).

200. *See* Memorandum from Trial Chamber President Nil Nonn to all Parties, Re: Updated Information Regarding Scheduling of Proposed Experts (May 25, 2012).

201. Karnavas interview, *supra* note 38. *Cf.* Prosecutor v. Ratko Mladic, Case No. IT-09-92-PT, Decision on Consolidated Prosecution Motion to Sever the Indictment, to Conduct Separate Trials, and to Amend the Indictment, ¶ 34 (Oct. 13, 2011) (rejecting a prosecution request to sever an indictment into two trials due to potential inefficiencies, including the likelihood of parties presenting evidence in the first trial "on events to be taken up in the second trial").

202. Second Decision on Severance, *supra* note 180, ¶ 117.

203. *See* Letter to the Editor by Anta Guisse, Kong Sam Onn & Arthur Vercken, *Khieu Samphan Is Forced to Remain Silent*, PHNOM PENH POST (July 19, 2013), *available at* http://www.phnompenhpost.com/analysis-and-op-ed/khieu-samphan-forced-remain-silent.

204. Severance Order, *supra* note 163, ¶ 8.

205. Co-Prosecutors' Request, *supra* note 167, ¶ 26. Judicial notice "establishes a well-founded presumption for the accuracy of [a] fact" and shifts the burden to the disputing party to disprove it. Prosecutor v. Krajisnik, Case No. IT-00-39-PT, Decision on Prosecution Motions for Judicial Notice of Adjudicated Facts and for Admission of Written Statements of Witnesses Pursuant to Rule 92*bis*, ¶ 16 (Trial Chamber, Feb. 28, 2003). *See also* Prosecutor v. Delalic, Case No. IT-96-21-T, Judgment, ¶ 228 (Trial Chamber, Nov. 16, 1998) (holding that *res judicata* only applies *inter partes* to matters already fully determined in a case or to an individual if a prior criminal case had fully litigated the issue).

206. Decision on IENG Sary's Motions Regarding Judicial Notice of Adjudicated Facts from Case 001 and Facts of Common Knowledge Being Applied in Case 002, Case No. 002/19-09-2007-ECCC/TC, at 3 (Apr. 4, 2011). By contrast, both the ICTY and ICTR may take judicial notice of adjudicated facts or documentary evidence. ICTY Rules of Procedure and Evidence (rev. 49), *rev'd* May 22, 2013, r. 94(B) (allowing only for the *authenticity* of documentary evidence to be recognized); ICTR Rules of Procedure and Evidence, *as amended* Oct. 1, 2009, r. 94(B).

207. Severance Order Reconsideration, *supra* note 164, ¶¶ 8, 10.

208. The Supreme Court Chamber has ordered the Office of Administration "to immediately explore" the creation of a second trial chamber if consecutive trials are intended, both to eliminate appearance of bias and to allow a second trial to begin while the Trial Chamber is drafting the Case 002/01 judgment. Order Regarding the Establishment of a Second Trial Panel, Case No. 002/19-09-2007-ECCCC-TC/SC (28) (July 23, 2013); SCC Severance Decision, *supra* note 164, ¶ 51. *Cf. Mladic* decision, *supra* note 202, ¶ 35 (rejecting a prosecution request to sever an indictment into two trials in part due to concern that "if the writing of the judgment in the first case were taking place during the pre-trial period or start of the second case, this could negatively affect the pace of the second case"; moreover, "partiality and appearance of partiality of the Chamber could be raised if the Chamber were to hear both cases").

209. Pestman interview, *supra* note 56.

210. Simonneau Fort interview, *supra* note 175.

211. Guissé interview, *supra* note 27 (noting that at the ICTR there was one system and people knew the rules, while at the ECCC rules are constantly changing and "it's one document rule one day, another the next").

212. Karnavas interview, *supra* note 38; Ianuzzi interview, *supra* note 37 (stating that the trial judges appear to be making up rules as they go).

213. Opening Statement of Son Arun, Case No. 002/19-09-2997-ECCC/TC, ¶ 12 (Nov. 23, 2011). *See also* Ieng Sary's Motion to Add New Trial Topics to the Trial Schedule, Case No. 002/19-09-2007-ECCC/TC, ¶¶ 3–6 (May 23, 2011); Motion in Support of "Ieng Sary's Motion to Add New Trial Topics to the Trial Schedule" and Request to Add Additional Topics, Case No. 001/19-09-2007-ECCC/TC, ¶ 9 (May 25, 2011).

214. Pestman interview, *supra* note 56.

215. Memorandum from Trial Chamber President Nil Nonn to all Parties, Directive in Advance of Initial Hearing Concerning Proposed Witnesses at 2 (June 3, 2011). The prosecution noted that relevant pre-1975 issues can be raised during scheduled witness and expert testimony. *See* Co-Prosecutors' Joint Response, Case No. 002/10-09-2007-ECCC/TC, ¶ 6 (June 6, 2011). Defense teams attempted to do so whenever possible.

216. *See, e.g.*, Julie Flint & Alex de Waal, *Case Closed: A Prosecutor Without Borders*, World Affairs J. (Spring 2009) (noting that human rights groups and women's groups warned that the limited charges brought "risk offending the victims and strengthening the growing mistrust of the work of the [ICC] in the DRC").

Chapter 6

1. *See, e.g.*, Confidential interview with former national staff, Phnom Penh (June 18, 2012) (stating that joint operations work well unless politics are involved because national authority is not based inside the Court, but on the outside).

2. The *Nuon Chea* team has argued that, as a corollary to vocal government opposition and efforts to shut down Cases 003 and 004, vocal government support of Case 002 shows that the accused will be convicted no matter what the evidence shows. *See* Application for Immediate Action Pursuant to Rule 35, Case No. 002/19-9-2007-ECCC/TC, ¶ 3 (Apr. 25, 2012). *See also* Julia Wallace & Kuch Naren, *UN 'Concerned' About Judge's Resignation*, CAMBODIA DAILY, Mar. 21, 2012 (quoting Ou Virak, CCHR president, "If the government is willing to go to such lengths to block cases it doesn't want to go ahead, how confident can we really be that it hasn't already determined the outcome in the cases that have been allowed to go ahead—Cases 001 and 002?").

3. Report of the Special Representative of the Secretary-General for Human Rights in Cambodia, Yash Ghai, U.N. General Assembly, U.N. Doc. A/HRC/7/42 (Feb. 29, 2008) [hereinafter Yash Ghai Report].

4. OSJI, *Recent Developments at the Extraordinary Chambers in the Courts of Cambodia*, at 24 (May 2008).

5. OSJI, *Recent Developments at the Extraordinary Chambers in the Courts of Cambodia*, at 6 (Feb. 2009). *See also* Erika Kinetz, *ECCC to Name More Defendants: Prosecutor*, CAMBODIA DAILY, June 13, 2008 (saying expanded prosecution "has become, for some, a test of the political independence of the ECCC.").

6. Statement of Cambodian Human Rights Action Committee (CHRAC), *Civil Society Calls for Investigation of Further Suspects by the ECCC* (Jan.14, 2009).

7. Decision on Preliminary Motion Based on Lack of Jurisdiction (Judicial Independence), Case No. SCSL-2004-14-AR72(E), Separate Opinion of Justice Robertson ¶ 1 (Appeals Chamber, Mar. 13, 2004) [hereinafter SCSL Judicial Independence Opinion].

8. *See, e.g.*, Interview with Michael G. Karnavas, former Co-Lawyer for Ieng Sary, Phnom Penh (May 19, 2012) (asking: "Do you want to push 003 and 004 to the point that it damages 002 and then you have nothing?").

9. MARK OSIEL, MAKING SENSE OF MASS ATROCITY 3–4 (2009) (arguing that "coping with mass atrocity reduces, in a sense, to [this] single dilemma").

10. ANTONIO CASSESE, INTERNATIONAL CRIMINAL LAW 332 (2d ed. 2008) (noting that this was partly to reduce the costs associated with the ad hoc tribunals, with their longer lists of suspects).

11. Agreement Between the United Nations and the Royal Government of Cambodia Concerning the Prosecution Under Cambodian Law of Crimes Committed During the Period of Democratic Kampuchea (June 6, 2003) [hereinafter Framework Agreement], art. 1; Law on the Establishment of Extraordinary Chambers in the Courts of Cambodia for the Prosecution of Crimes Committed During the Period of Democratic Kampuchea, as amended and promulgated on Oct. 27, 2004, NS/RKM/1004/006 [hereinafter ECCC Law]. *See also* Prosecutors v. Kaing Guek Eav *alias* Duch, Case No. 001/18-7-2007/ECCC/SC, Appeal Judgment ¶ 52 (Feb. 3, 2012) [hereinafter *Duch* Appeal Judgment] (holding that only former Khmer Rouge officials may be tried).

12. Prosecutor v. Brima *et al.*, SCSL-2004-16-A, Judgment on Appeal, ¶ 282 (Appeals Chamber, Feb. 22, 2008); *Report of the Secretary-General on the Establishment of a Special Court for Sierra Leone*, ¶ 30, U.N. Doc. S/2000/915 (Oct. 4, 2000).

13. *Duch* Appeal Judgment, *supra* note 11, ¶¶ 57, 61, 63, 79.

14. Valérie Dervieux, *The French System*, *in* EUROPEAN CRIMINAL PROCEDURES 218, 232 (Mireille Delmas-Marty & J. R. Spencer eds., 2002).

15. *Id.* at 236.

16. *See, e.g.*, Internal Rules of the ECCC, *rev'd* Aug. 3, 2011, r. 13(6), r. 49(1) [hereinafter ECCC Internal Rules (rev. 8)] (giving the Co-Prosecutors exclusive authority to initiate prosecution at their discretion or on the basis of a complaint). *See also* Updated Statute of the ICTY, *rev'd* July 7, 2009, art. 18(1) [hereinafter ICTY Statute]; Statute of the ICTR, *amended* Dec. 16, 2009, art. 17(1).

17. *See* ECCC Internal Rules (rev. 8), *supra* note 16, r. 19. *Cf.* ICTY Statute, *supra* note 16, art. 16(2); Prosecutor v. Delalic et al. (Celebici), Case No. IT-96-21-A, Judgment, ¶¶ 602–3, 606 (Appeals Chamber, Feb. 20, 2001) (stating that prosecutorial discretion is broad, but prosecutors must not seek or receive instructions "from any government or other source").

18. *See* ECCC Internal Rules (rev. 8), *supra* note 16, r. 55(2), r. 55(3).

19. *See, e.g.*, Note of the International Reserve Co-Investigating Judge to the Parties on the Egregious Dysfunctions within the ECCC Impeding the Proper Conduct of Investigations in Cases 003 and 004, Case No. 003/07-9-2009-ECCC-OCIJ and 004/07-9-2009-ECCC-OCIJ, ¶ 8 (Mar. 21, 2012).

20. Considerations of the Pre-Trial Chamber Regarding the International Co-Prosecutor's Appeal Against the Decision on the Re-Filing of Three Investigative Requests, Case No. 003/07-9-ECCC/OCIJ (PTC06), Opinion of Judges Lahuis and Downing on the Co-Prosecutor's Appeal ¶ 18 (Nov. 15, 2011) [hereinafter Lahuis and Downing Opinion on the Co-Prosecutor's Appeal] (citations omitted).

21. *See* ECCC Internal Rules (rev. 8), *supra* note 16, r. 55(4).

22. *See id.* r. 55(4).

23. *See id.* r. 67(1).

24. *Id.* r. 67(3).

25. Decision on Appeal Against Closing Order Indicting Kaing Guek Eav Alias "Duch," Case No. 001/18-7-2007-ECCC/OCJ (PTC2), ¶ 37 (Dec. 5, 2008). Similarly, with regard to prosecutorial discretion, the international PTC judges found that, because the Internal Rules provide that the Co-Prosecutors "shall" open a judicial investigation if they "have reason to believe that crimes within the jurisdiction of the ECCC have been committed," once they have made that determination they are obliged to do so by forwarding an introductory submission. *See* Considerations of the Pre-Trial Chamber Regarding the Disagreement Between the Co-Prosecutors Pursuant to Internal Rule 71, Case No. 001/18-11-2008-ECCC/PTC, Opinion of Judges Lahuis and Downing ¶ 23 (Aug. 18, 2009) [hereinafter PTC Considerations on Co-Prosecutors' Dispute].

26. *See* Dervieux, *supra* note 14, at 239.

27. *See* Decision on International Co-Prosecutor's Re-Filing of Three Investigative Requests in Case 003, Case No. 003/07-9-2009-ECCC/OCIJ, ¶ 6(c) (July 27, 2011); Press Release by the Co-Investigating Judges Regarding Civil Parties in Case 004 (Aug. 8, 2011); PTC Considerations on Co-Prosecutors' Dispute, *supra* note 25, ¶ 32 (noting Chea Leang's argument).

28. *See generally* Decision on Personal Jurisdiction and Investigative Policy Regarding Suspect, Case No. 003/07-9-2009-ECCC/OCIJ (May 2, 2012).

29. *See, e.g., Report of the Secretary-General, supra* note 12, ¶ 30; ICTY Rules of Procedure and Evidence (rev. 49), *rev'd* May 22, 2013, r. 11 *bis* [hereinafter ICTY Rules] (stating that those most responsible and thus suitable for ICTY prosecution are determined by "the gravity of the crimes charged and the level of responsibility of the accused").

30. Prosecutor v. Stankovic, Decision on Referral of Case Under Rule 11*Bis*, Case No. IT-96-23/2-PT, ¶ 19 (Referral Bench, May 17, 2005).

31. *See Duch* Appeal Judgment, *supra* note 11, ¶ 76.

32. Prosecutor v. D. Milosevic, Case No. IT-98-29/1-PT, ¶ 22 (Referral Bench, July 8, 2005).

33. Report of the Group of Experts for Cambodia Established Pursuant to General Assembly Resolution 52/135, U.N. Doc. A/53/850, S/1999/231, ¶ 109 (Mar. 16, 1999) [hereinafter Group of Experts Report] (emphasis added).

34. *Report of the Secretary-General, supra* note 12, ¶ 30.

35. Situation in the Democratic Republic of Congo, Judgment on the Prosecutor's Appeal Against the Decision of Pre-Trial Chamber I Entitled "Decision on the Prosecutor's Application for Warrants of Arrest, Article 58," Situation No. ICC-01/04, ¶ 77 (Appeals Chamber, July 13, 2006).

36. Carla del Ponte, *Prosecuting the Individuals Bearing the Highest Level of Responsibility*, 2 J. INT'L CRIM. JUST. 516 (2004) (emphasis in original).

37. *See* Rome Statute of the International Criminal Court, July 17, 1998, 2187 U.N.T.S. 90 (entered into force on July 1, 2002) [hereinafter Rome Statute], art. 53(1). *See also* James A. Goldston, *More Candor About Criteria: The Exercise of Discretion by the Prosecutor of the International Criminal Court*, 8 J. INT'L CRIM. JUST. 383, 386 (2010) (describing the ICC prosecutor's discretionary authority as "grounded in law and evidence, but, of necessity taking into account broader considerations of policy, even while refraining from 'politics' in the sense of partisanship and/or bias . . .").

38. Group of Experts Report, *supra* note 33, ¶ 219(2). For one legal scholar's argument on how prosecutors at the ECCC, ICC, and elsewhere can balance between the aims of prosecution and reconciliation, *see generally* Neha Jain, *Between the Scylla and Charybdis of Prosecution and Reconciliation: The Khmer Rouge Trials and the Promise of International Criminal Justice*, 20 DUKE J. COMP. & INT'L L. 247 (2009–10).

39. *See* Rome Statute, *supra* note 37, art. 53(3)(b).

40. Only the Security Council has the authority to prevent an ICC investigation or prosecution, and then only to delay it for a 12-month period. *See* Rome Statute, *supra* note 37, art. 16.

41. *See, e.g.*, Yun Samean, *No More KR Prosecutions, Hun Sen Says*, CAMBODIA DAILY, Apr. 1, 2009; Neou Vannarin & Douglas Gillison, *Hun Sen Again Warns ECCC of Civil War*, CAMBODIA DAILY, Sept. 8, 2009.

42. PTC Considerations on Co-Prosecutors' Dispute, *supra* note 25, ¶ 32.

43. *Id.* ¶ 34.

44. *See* Vannarin & Gillison, *supra* note 41 (quoting former international Co-Prosecutor Robert Petit saying that "fears of civil war in Cambodia were 'hogwash'"). *Cf.* Human Rights Watch, *Selling Justice Short: Why Accountability Matters for Peace*, at 3 (July 2009) (noting that in practice "the anticipated negative consequences of pressing for accountability often do not come to pass").

45. As far back as 1999, the UN Group of Experts reached a similar conclusion. *See* Group of Experts Report, *supra* note 33, ¶ 109.

46. *See* Terith Chy, *A Thousand Voices*, Documentation Center of Cambodia (Mar. 5, 2009), *available at* www.d.dccam.org/Tribunal/Analysis/pdf/A_Thousand_Voices.pdf.

47. PTC Considerations on Co-Prosecutors' Dispute, *supra* note 25, ¶ 34.

48. *See* Decision on Ieng Sary's Rule 89 Preliminary Objections (*Ne bis In Idem* and Amnesty and Pardon), Case No. 002/19-9-2007-ECCC/TC, ¶¶ 54, 55 (Nov. 3, 2011) [hereinafter Decision on Ieng Sary].

49. *Quelles leçons tirer du procès des Khmers rouges?* REVUE DE SCIENCE CRIMINELLE 597 (2011) (featuring an interview with Lemonde, translated from French by the authors).

50. Interview with Panhavuth Long, Program Officer, Cambodian Justice Initiative, Phnom Penh (July 6, 2012).

51. *Cf.* Human Rights Watch, *Unfinished Business: Closing Gaps in the Selection of ICC Cases*, at 4 (2011).

52. Margaret deGuzman, *Choosing to Prosecute: Expressive Selection at the International Criminal Court*, 33 MICH. J. INT'L L. 265, 312–15 (2012).

53. Robert Petit, *Lawfare and International Tribunals: A Question of Definition? A Reflection on the Creation of the Khmer Rouge Tribunal*, 43 CASE W. RES. J. INT'L L. 189, 199 (2010–11).

54. Comparably, the ICC operates on the principle of complementarity, meaning that it does not investigate or prosecute when a national jurisdiction is able and willing to genuinely do so. *See* Rome Statute, *supra* note 37, art. 17. The ICTY and ICTR have the capacity to refer lower-level offenders to national jurisdictions. *See* ICTY Rules, *supra* note 29, r.11*bis*; ICTR Rules of Procedure and Evidence, *amended* Oct. 1, 2009, r. 11*bis*. In Sierra Leone there was a truth commission process acting parallel to the SCSL.

55. *See* Jaya Ramji-Nogales, *Designing Bespoke Transitional Justice: A Pluralist Process Approach*, 32 MICH. J. INT'L L. 1, 39–41 (2010–11).

56. The first international Co-Prosecutor Robert Petit had the phrase "too many names" embossed in Khmer on baseball hats as his parting gift for international OCP staff, who used the expression when discussing the national side's unwillingness to proceed. Confidential email from former OCP staff (June 13, 2012).

57. Cable 09PHNOMPENH648, U.S. Embassy Phnom Penh, *Khmer Rouge Tribunal: Five More for Prosecution* ¶ 5 (Sept. 1, 2009), *available at* http://www.wikileaks.org/cable/2009/09/09PHNOMPENH648.html. *See also id.* ¶ 9 (noting that they "took direct orders from the likes of DK Security Minister and Pol Pot himself to carry out purges and 'smashing' on a mass scale").

58. *See* Stephen Heder with Brian D. Tittemore, Seven Candidates for Prosecution 115–33 (2d ed. 2004); Second Introductory Submission (redacted), *available at* http://www.theinvestigativefund.org/files/managed/Cambodia2nd_Intro_Submission.pdf.

59. *See* Jared Ferrie, *Khmer Rouge Crimes in Legal Limbo*, The National (Thailand), July 24, 2011; Third Introductory Submission (redacted), *available at* http://www.theinvestigativefund.org/files/managed/Cambodia3rd_Intro_Submission.pdf.

60. Press Release, *ECCC International Co-Prosecutor Robert Petit* (Apr. 24, 2009).

61. ECCC Law, *supra* note 11, art. 20 new. *See also* ECCC Internal Rules (rev. 8), *supra* note 16, r. 71(4)(c) (providing that where there is no supermajority "the action or decision done by one Co-Prosecutor shall stand or . . . the action or decision proposed to be done by one Co-Prosecutor shall be executed").

62. *See* PTC Considerations on Co-Prosecutors' Dispute, *supra* note 25.

63. Interview with Craig Etcheson, former investigator in the ECCC Office of the Co-Prosecutors, via telephone (Oct. 22, 2012) (calling the dispute between the Co-Prosecutors the "seed of paralysis in Cases 003 and 004").

64. Press Release, *Statement of the Acting International Co-Prosecutor: Submission of Two New Introductory Submissions* (Sept. 8, 2009). Deputy international Co-Prosecutor Bill Smith filed the submissions as Robert Petit had recently resigned.

65. *See, e.g.*, Seth Mydans, *Efforts to Limit Khmer Rouge Trials Decried*, N.Y. Times, Jan. 31, 2009; Ek Madra, *Cambodian PM Rejects Wider Khmer Rouge Trials*, Reuters, Mar. 31, 2009.

66. *See* Suy Se, *Cambodian PM Says No Third Khmer Rouge Trial*, Agence France-Presse, Oct. 27, 2010.

67. James O'Toole, *Wrangling Ahead in Case 003*, Phnom Penh Post, May 17, 2011.

68. Alice Foster & Phorn Bopha, *Judge Resigns KR Court Over Gov't Pressure*, Cambodia Daily, Oct. 11, 2011.

69. Julia Wallace & Neou Vannarin, *Additional KR Arrests in Cambodia's Hands, Hor Namhong Says*, Cambodia Daily, Oct. 5, 2011.

70. *See* PTC Considerations on Co-Prosecutors' Dispute, *supra* note 25, Opinion of Judges Prak, Ney & Hout ¶ 8; Confidential email from former OCP staff (June 13, 2012).

71. Confidential email from former OCP staff (June 13, 2012). *See also* Cable 08PH-

NOMPENH947, U.S. Embassy Phnom Penh, *Khmer Rouge Tribunal: Rocky Road for New Cases, Steady Path for Trial of Five KR Leaders* ¶ 5 (Nov. 28, 2008), *available at* http://www.wikileaks.org/cable/2008/11/08PHNOMPENH947.html (stating the views of the OSJI monitor that Chea Leang was "explicitly told not to agree to the new cases so as to protect Cambodia's peace and stability").

72. *See, e.g.*, David Scheffer, *Opinion: How Many Are Too Many Defendants at the KRT?* Phnom Penh Post, Jan. 8, 2009 (stating that the prosecutorial dispute "was anticipated in the negotiations and strikes [him] as demonstrating that the ECCC is working its will as it was designed to do").

73. Etcheson interview, *supra* note 63 (noting that the OCP has "been able to isolate [the Co-Prosecutor's dispute over Cases 003 and 004] and keep it from contaminating [their joint work on] Case 002 to a significant extent."

74. *See* Press Release, *Statement of the Co-Prosecutors* (Dec. 8, 2008); Press Release, *Statement of the Co-Prosecutors* (Jan. 5, 2009). *But see* Press Release, *supra* note 60.

75. Robert Petit's successor Andrew Cayley has said, "[S]he has never stopped me from doing what is right. . . . We are working together, and even where there are moments she can't join, I make sure things are done." Julia Wallace, *KR Prosecutors Say Conscience Dictates Work*, Cambodia Daily, Oct. 10, 2011.

76. *See* Press Release, *Statement from the Co-Investigating Judges* (June 9, 2010) (including letter as an annex); Decision and Referral to the Supreme Council of Magistracy on the Judicial Misconduct of National Co-Investigating Judge You Bunleng, Case No. 003/07-9-2009-ECCC-OCIJ, ¶ 5 (May 4, 2012) [hereinafter Decision on You Bunleng] (quoting the letter and providing an unofficial translation from the French).

77. *See* Letter to Marcel Lemonde, *Lettre du co-juge d'instruction international en date du 02 juin 2010 re Dossiers 003 et 004* (June 8, 2010).

78. Douglas Gillison, *KRT Begins Investigation of Five New Regime Suspects*, Cambodia Daily, June 8, 2010.

79. Decision on You Bunleng, *supra* note 76, ¶ 9.

80. Press Release, *Statement from the Co-Investigating Judges* (Feb. 2, 2011).

81. *See Press Release from the Co-Investigating Judges* (Apr. 29, 2011).

82. Press Release, *Statement by the International Co-Prosecutor Regarding Case File 003* (May 9, 2011).

83. *See* Decision on International Co-Prosecutor's Re-Filing of the Request for an Extension of Time for the Filing of Civil Party Applications in Case 003, Case No. 003/07-9-ECCC/OCIJ, ¶¶ 7, 8 (Aug. 9, 2011); Press Release, *Statement from the Co-Investigating Judges Related to Case 003 Request from the International Co-Prosecutor* (June 7, 2011). Andrew Cayley said, "[T]his amounts to a deliberate gross violation of the Victim's rights." International Co-Prosecutor's Appeal Against the "Decision on Time Extension Request and Investigative Requests by the International Co-Prosecutor Regarding Case 003," Case No. 003/07-9-ECCC/OCIJ, ¶ 66 (July 7, 2011).

84. Rob Carmichael, *Tribunal's Credibility Under Threat as Controversial Cases Head for*

Closure (May 11, 2011), at http://www.robertcarmichael.net/Robert_Carmichael/Cambodia_Radio_News/Archive.html.

85. Considerations of the Pre-Trial Chamber Regarding the Appeal Against Order on the Admissibility of Civil Party Applicant Robert Hamill, Case No 003/07-9-ECCC/OCIJ (PTC02), Opinion of Judges Lahuis and Downing ¶ 5 (Oct. 24, 2011) [hereinafter Lahuis and Downing Opinion on Hamill].

86. Press Release, *Statement by the International Co-Prosecutor Regarding Case File 003* (May 9, 2011).

87. *See* Decision on You Bunleng, *supra* note 76, ¶ 12.

88. Press Release, *Statement by the International Co-Prosecutor Regarding Case File 003* (May 9, 2011). *See also* Douglas Gillison, *Justice Denied*, Foreign Policy (Nov. 23, 2011) (reporting that on Blunk's arrival, "he told his office that his inquiries would be 'suspect-based,' seeking first to determine the guilt or innocence of defendants before examining the facts and allegations, a backwards approach his staff said appeared designed either for a frame-up or a cover-up").

89. *See* Press Release, *Statement from the Co-Investigating Judges* (Apr. 29, 2011); OSJI, *Recent Developments at the Extraordinary Chambers in the Courts of Cambodia*, at 11 (June 2011). *See also* Lahuis and Downing Opinion on the Co-Prosecutor's Appeal, *supra* note 20, ¶ 12 (noting that the Case 002 documents and other evidence collected during the entire investigation were not placed into the case file until very late in the process).

90. *See, e.g.*, Lahuis and Downing Opinion on Hamill, *supra* note 85, ¶¶ 9–15 (in which the CIJs replaced a defective civil party rejection order while challenges to the defects were on appeal).

91. *Id.* ¶ 9.

92. Gillison, *Justice Denied*, *supra* note 88.

93. Decision on You Bunleng, *supra* note 76, ¶ 13.

94. *See, e.g.*, Douglas Gillison, *UN Legal Team Walks Out on Stymied KR Cases*, Cambodia Daily, June 13, 2011; Gillison, *Justice Denied*, *supra* note 88 (quoting from their letter to the Secretary-General: "It is our duty to notify you that we consider, as a matter of law and procedure, that the co-investigating judges did not conduct a genuine, impartial or effective investigation and as such did not discharge their legal obligation to ascertain the truth." . . . "In our view, the decision to close the investigation at this stage breaches international standards of justice, fairness and due process of law.").

95. *See* Gillison, *UN Legal Team*, *supra* note 94; Decision on You Bunleng, *supra* note 76, ¶ 14. *See also* Press Release, *Public Statement by Co-Investigating Judges* (June 12, 2011) (saying that they "welcome the departure of all staff members who ignore the sole responsibility of the CIJs" to decide whether or not to close the Case 003 investigation).

96. *See* Gillison, *UN Legal Team*, *supra* note 94.

97. *See* Press Release, *Statement by the International Co-Prosecutor Regarding Case File 004* (June 16, 2011).

98. *See Press Release by the International Co-Investigative Judge* (Oct. 10, 2011). It is not clear why Blunk resigned. The only consensus was that he was "a bizarre man." Gillison, *Justice Denied*, *supra* note 88. Nevertheless, his departure was precipitated by an internal investigation he initiated after the Documentation Center of Cambodia published an interview with a witness he had previously questioned. Some claim the investigation revealed his role in "the falsification of evidence, including witness tampering, and the back-dating of orders." *Id.* However, it was more likely a confluence of events. There have been suggestions that the internal investigation revealed to him that, despite his friendship and shared agenda with Judge You Bunleng, the national side had been acting behind his back to stage-manage his contact with the few witnesses he interviewed. Finally, there were unconfirmed rumors that state donors confronted him with his aberrant judicial orders and asked him to resign.

99. Foster & Phorn, *supra* note 68. *But see* Julia Wallace, *No Pressure on Tribunal, Gov't Insists*, CAMBODIA DAILY, Oct. 13, 2011 (backtracking to say, the Government "understands very well that it is at the exclusive discretion of the ECCC to decide who to indict").

100. *Press Statement by National Co-Investigating Judge* (Mar. 26, 2012).

101. *See also* Framework Agreement, *supra* note 11, art. 5(6) ("In case there is a vacancy or a need to fill the post of the international co-investigating judge, the person appointed to fill this post must be the reserve international co-investigating judge").

102. Compare Statute of the Special Court of Sierra Leone, Jan. 16, 2002, art. 12(1) [hereinafter SCSL Statute] *with* Framework Agreement, *supra* note 11, art. 3(6) and ECCC Law, *supra* note 11, art. 11 new. *See also* Constitutional Council Decision No. 040/002/2001, Feb. 12, 2001, at 3 (unofficial translation) (finding that the United Nations "only provides a list of candidates, and has no decision-making rights" in appointments).

103. *See* Douglas Gillison, *Cambodia Rejects UN Genocide Judge*, THE INVESTIGATIVE FUND (Jan. 15, 2012); Bridget Di Certo & Cheang Sokha, *Judge OK Not a "Must,"* PHNOM PENH POST, Jan. 17, 2012.

104. Julia Wallace, *Gov't Claims No Obligation to Appoint Judge*, CAMBODIA DAILY, Jan. 17, 2012 (quoting Keo Remy, vice chairman of the Press and Quick Reaction Unit at the Council of Ministers). *But see* Bridget Di Certo & Mary Kozlovski, *Judge's OK an "Obligation," UN Says*, PHNOM PENH POST, Jan. 19, 2012.

105. *Press Release by the International Reserve Co-Investigating Judge* (Dec. 6, 2011).

106. *See* ECCC Law, *supra* note 11, art. 11 new (providing that the President of each Chamber may designate reserve judges already appointed by the SCM "to replace a foreign judge if that judge is unable to continue sitting"). *See also* Opinion of Pre-Trial Chamber Judges Downing and Chung on the Disagreement Between the Co-Investigating Judges Pursuant to Internal Rule 72, Case No. 003/16-12-2011-ECCC/PTC, ¶ 37 [hereinafter Downing and Chung Opinion] (Feb. 10, 2012) (arguing: "If a reserve judge is not able to temporarily replace an absent judge pending his permanent replacement then one must logically inquire as to the purpose of having a Reserve Investigating Judge"). Notably, a

reserve international Trial Chamber judge has repeatedly replaced an absent judge without any challenge to her authority to do so. *See, e.g.*, Transcript of Trial Proceedings—Case 002, Case No. 002/19-9-2007-ECCC/TC, at 104 (Jan. 18, 2012).

107. Summary Report of the Meeting of the Supreme Council of the Magistracy on the Proposed Appointment of Mr. Laurent Kasper-Ansermet as International Co-Investigating Judge in the ECCC (Jan. 13, 2012). *See also* Press Statement, The Office of the Council of Ministers, Royal Government of Cambodia (Jan. 12, 2012); L. Kasper-Ansermet at http://twitter.com/lkasperansermet.

108. Martin Nesirky, U.N. Secretary-General Spokesman, *U.N. Calls on Cambodia to Take Immediate Steps to Appoint Reserve International Co-Investigations Judge* (Jan. 20, 2012).

109. Statement Attributable to the Spokesperson for the Secretary-General on Cambodia, *International Co-Investigating Judge of the Extraordinary Chambers in the Courts of Cambodia* (Jan. 20, 2012). *See also* Downing and Chung Opinion, *supra* note 106, ¶ 33 (stating that the appointment of a new international CIJ was ongoing and is unrelated to the reserve international CIJs' ability to temporarily replace the absent judge "in order to ensure that court proceedings go on timely and smoothly").

110. *See generally* Decision on You Bunleng, *supra* note 76. *But see* Bridget Di Certo, *Judge's Exit Shakes KRT*, PHNOM PENH POST, Mar. 21, 2012 (quoting Judge You Bunleng saying, "I didn't obstruct him, I just did not recognize his work").

111. *See Press Statement of the National Co-Investigating Judge* (Jan. 9, 2012). *See also* Press Statement of the National Co-Investigating Judge (Dec. 6, 2011); *Press Statement by the National Co-Investigating Judge* (Feb. 10, 2012).

112. *See, e.g., Press Release by the International Reserve Co-Investigating Judge* (Feb. 9, 2012); *Press Statement by the National Co-Investigating Judge* (Feb. 10, 2012); Public Letter from National Co-Investigating Judge, *Abrupt Stop of Unlawful Acts and the Use of My Name to Link to These Acts* (Feb. 27, 2012); Public Letter from Reserve International Co-Investigating Judge, *Your Letter of 27 Feb. 2012* (Mar. 3, 2012).

113. *See generally* Decision on You Bunleng, *supra* note 76.

114. *See* Note of the International Reserve Co-Investigating Judge, *supra* note 19, ¶¶ 33–54; Decision on You Bunleng, *supra* note 76, ¶¶ 40–66. *See also Press Statement by National Co-Investigating Judge* (Mar. 26, 2012) (acknowledging that he had told national staff not to follow the directions of Judge Kasper-Ansermet).

115. *See Press Release of the Reserve International Co-Investigating Judge* (May 4, 2012) ("For reasons which are manifestly more political and financial than strictly legal, the Reserve International Judge . . . found himself in a highly hostile environment and was severely impeded in the day-to-day performance of his duties, as a result of which he tendered his resignation to the United Nations Secretary General."); Julia Wallace, *From Phnom Penh with Love*, INT'L JUST. TRIB. (Mar. 28, 2012).

116. *See generally* OSJI, *The Future of Cases 003/004 at the Extraordinary Chambers in the Courts of Cambodia* (Oct. 2012).

117. *See Statement by the Co-Investigating Judges* (Feb. 28, 2013); Decision on Motion and Supplemental Brief on Suspect's Right to Counsel, Case No. 004/07/-09-2009-ECCC-OCIJ (May 17, 2013); Press Release, *Statement by the International Co-Investigating Judge Regarding Additional Crime Sites in Case 004* (Dec. 19, 2012); Lawyers Recognition Decision Concerning All Civil Party Applications on Case File No. 003, Case No. 003/07-09-2009-ECCC-OCIJ (Feb. 26, 2013); Lawyers Recognition Decision Concerning All Civil Party Applications on Case File No. 004, Case No. 004/07-09-2009-ECCC-OCIJ (Apr. 1, 2013).

118. *See, e.g.*, ECCC Court Report (Oct. 2013), at 5 (reporting that "the International side of the [OCIJ] continued the investigation of Case Files 003 and 004"). *See also* Abby Seiff, *Wanted: Lawyers for Hot Cases*, Phnom Penh Post, May 15, 2013 (discussing Judge Harmon's unsuccessful efforts to recruit Cambodian lawyers to assist the international side of the office); Considerations of the Pre-Trial Chamber Regarding the Appeal Against Order on the Admissibility of Civil Party Applicant [REDACTED], Case No. 003/07-09-2009-ECCC/OCIJ (PTC 05) (Feb. 13, 2013) (describing additional irregularities in the administration of Case 003, which the national judges remain unwilling to acknowledge and remedy).

119. *See, e.g.*, Sok Khemara, *Suspect Questions "Most Responsible" Tribunal Mandate*, VOA Khmer (Aug. 16, 2011), http://www.voacambodia.com/content/suspect-questions-most-responsible-tribunal-mandate-127880513/1356676.html (quoting Case 003 suspect Meas Muth expressing no concerns about being prosecuted, saying, "Now the senior-most leaders and the most responsible persons are at the court already"); Kuch Naren & Julia Wallace, *KRT Suspect Im Chaem Informed of Her Rights*, Cambodia Daily, Mar. 6, 2012 (quoting Case 004 suspect Im Chaem saying, "I don't need a court to judge me, and Prime Minister Hun Sen has already told the public that the tribunal is just for hearing cases 001 and 002").

120. *UN Prosecutor: "The Law Ties Me to Do This,"* VOA Khmer (Nov. 4, 2011), http://www.voacambodia.com/content/un-prosecutor-the-law-ties-me-to-do-this-133245133/1353743.html.

121. Karnavas interview, *supra* note 8.

122. The Trial Chamber did not reach a supermajority once regarding the applicability of a national statute of limitations to domestic crimes in the ECCC Law, but no allegations of political interference were raised on that occasion.

123. *See* David Scheffer, *The Value of Steve Heder's Research on the ECCC's Personal Jurisdiction, and an Afterword on the Purpose of the Dispute Settlement Mechanisms*, Cambodia Tribunal Monitor (Aug. 8, 2011) (on file with the authors) ("It was precisely because negotiators foresaw a possible rift between the Co-Prosecutors, in particular, over additional individuals to bring to trial that the dispute mechanism was developed.").

124. *See, e.g.*, ECCC Law, *supra* note 11, arts. 16, 23 new. During negotiations, the United Nations sought to give the international Co-Prosecutor independent authority to indict suspects on his own authority; however, the Cambodian Government insisted that the two

Co-Prosecutors must make decisions by consensus. *See Hun Sen Proposes Judges to Aid Prosecutors in K. Rouge Trial*, JAPAN ECON. NEWSWIRE, Apr. 6, 2000.

125. ECCC Internal Rules (rev. 8), *supra* note 16, r. 13(3), r. 14(4) (addressing the Co-Prosecutors and CIJs, respectively).

126. *Id.* r. 54, r. 56.

127. *Id.* r. 71(3), r. 72(3) (noting that during the dispute settlement period, the disputed action "shall be executed").

128. *See Statement from the Co-Investigating Judges* (June 9, 2010).

129. *See id.*

130. Co-Prosecutors may not act unilaterally if the dispute relates to an introductory submission, supplemental submission relating to new crimes, final submission, or a decision relating to an appeal. CIJs may not act unilaterally if the dispute features a decision that would be open to appeal by the charged person or a civil party, a notification of charges, or an arrest and detention order. ECCC Internal Rules (rev. 8), *supra* note 16, r. 71(3), r. 72(3). *See also* PTC Considerations on Co-Prosecutors' Dispute, *supra* note 25, ¶ 16 ("[O]nly cases of major concern specifically identified in the Internal Rules would a disagreement prevent one ["co"] from proceeding with a given action pending a decision by the Pre-Trial Chamber.").

131. ECCC Internal Rules (rev. 8), *supra* note 16, r. 71(1), r. 72(1).

132. PTC Considerations on Co-Prosecutors' Dispute, *supra* note 25, ¶ 27.

133. Decision on IENG Sary's Appeal Against the Closing Order, Case No. 002/19-09-2007-ECCC/OCIJ (PTC75), ¶ 274 (Apr. 11, 2011).

134. *See* Decision on Time Extension Request and Investigative Requests by the International Co-Prosecutor Regarding Case 003, Case No. 003/07-9-2009-ECCC/OCIJ (June 6, 2011).

135. ECCC Press Release, Office of the Co-Investigating Judges, *Statement from the Co-Investigating Judges Related to Case 003 Requests from International Co-Prosecutor* (June 7, 2011).

136. Considerations of the Pre-Trial Chamber Regarding the International Prosecutor's Appeal Against the Decision on Time Extension Request and Investigative Requests Regarding Case 003, Case No. 003/07-9-2009-ECCC/OCIJ (PTC 04), ¶ 3 Separate opinion of Judges Downing & Lahuis (Nov. 2, 2011).

137. *Id.* ¶ 12 Separate opinion of Judges Prak, Ney & Huot.

138. *See, e.g.*, Note of the International Reserve Co-Investigating Judge, *supra* note 19, ¶ 34.

139. *See* Public Letter from Reserve International Co-Investigating Judge, *Your Letter of 27 February 2012* (Mar. 5, 2012); Downing and Chung Opinion, *supra* note 106, ¶ 50.

140. *See* Alex Bates, *Transitional Justice in Cambodia: Analytical Report*, Atlas Project, ¶ 79 (Oct. 2010).

141. Interview with Hans Corell, former UN Legal Counsel, via telephone (Nov. 15,

2012). *Cf. Quelles leçons, supra* note 49 (arguing that the "co" system is inefficient and that the dispute settlement procedure is unworkable on a day-to-day basis).

142. Cable 09PHNOMPENH648, *supra* note 57, ¶ 1.

143. Open Society Justice Initiative (OSJI), *Political Interference at the Extraordinary Chambers in the Courts of Cambodia*, at 11 (July 2010).

144. Corell interview, *supra* note 141.

145. Framework Agreement, *supra* note 11, art. 7; ECCC Law, *supra* note 11, arts. 20 new, 23 new.

146. Cable 09PHNOMPENH264, U.S. Embassy Phnom Penh, *Khmer Rouge Tribunal: Donors Chart a More Unified Course* ¶¶ 3–4 (Apr. 24, 2009), *available at* http://www.wikileaks.org/cable/2009/04/09PHNOMPENH264.html (reporting that the national judges convinced the international judges not to release the decision until "the time was right").

147. *See* Lahuis and Downing Opinion on the Co-Prosecutor's Appeal, *supra* note 20; Lahuis and Downing Opinion on Hamill, *supra* note 85. *See also* Considerations of the Pre-Trial Chamber Regarding the International Co-Prosecutor's Appeal Against the Co-Investigating Judges' Order on International Co-Prosecutor's Public Statement Regarding Case 003, Case No 003/07-9-ECCC/OCIJ (PTC03) (Oct. 24, 2011).

148. David Scheffer, *The Extraordinary Chambers in the Court of Cambodia*, *in* 3 INTERNATIONAL CRIMINAL LAW 219, 246 (M. Cherif Bassiouni ed., 2008). *See also* Scheffer, *supra* note 123; Douglas Gillison, *Genocide Judges Duel It Out in Phnom Penh*, THE INVESTIGATIVE FUND (Dec. 7, 2011) (reporting that David Tolbert believes this shows the tribunal "did not have sufficient procedural or legal safeguards to respond effectively to a Blunk scenario and that this experience should not be repeated elsewhere").

149. *See* discussion of this issue in chapter 5.

150. Gillison, *Genocide Judges*, *supra* note 148.

151. Interview with Richard Rogers, former head of the ECCC Defence Support Section, Phnom Penh (May 29, 2012).

152. *See* Memorandum to Tony KRANH from Judge PRAK, Returning the Document Communicated to Pre-Trial Chamber by the Office of Administration (Feb. 3, 2012); Press Release, *International Reserve Co-Investigating Judge* (Feb. 9, 2012) (quoting from the President's memorandum).

153. Downing and Chung Opinion, *supra* note 106, ¶¶ 14–15.

154. Press Release, *Clarification of the National Judges of the Pre-Trial Chamber on the Note of Mr. Laurent Kasper-Ansermet, D38, dated 21 March 2012* (March 26, 2012).

155. *Id.*

156. Downing and Chung Opinion, *supra* note 106, ¶¶ 15, 28–39, 50.

157. *See* Press Release, *Statement by Judges Downing and Chung* (Mar. 20, 2012); Wallace & Kuch, *supra* note 2.

158. Framework Agreement, *supra* note 11, art. 4; ECCC Law *supra* note 11, art. 14 new(1); ECCC Internal Rules (rev. 8), *supra* note 16, r. 98(4).

159. Scheffer, *supra* note 148, at 246.

160. Karnavas interview, *supra* note 8. *See also* Michael Karnavas, Op-Ed, *It's Time to Salvage the Khmer Rouge Tribunal's Legacy*, CAMBODIA DAILY, Dec. 12, 2012 (saying "[t]he ECCC is failing as a model court because the international judges have not been robust in insisting on the uncompromising application of international standards and best practices").

161. Karnavas Op-Ed, *supra* note 160.

162. Long interview, *supra* note 50.

163. Interview with Michiel Pestman, former Co-Lawyer for Nuon Chea, Phnom Penh (June 9, 2012).

164. *Cf. Quelles leçons*, *supra* note 49 (authors' translation from the French).

165. Rogers interview, *supra* note 151. *Cf.* Interview with Diana Ellis, Co-Lawyer for Ieng Thirith, Phnom Penh (Nov. 11, 2012) (emphasizing that the moment you have political interference, the process cannot be fair because "judicial independence lies at the heart of a fair judicial system and interference compromises the whole system. You don't know if a decision is being taken based on a level of proof, or if a judge has been directed to take a specific decision.").

166. *See, e.g.*, Kuch & Wallace, *supra* note 119 (noting that the PTC international judges and Kasper-Ansermet "have expressed concern that the rights of the suspects have already been violated" by the years-long presumptive investigation being undertaken without their participation or official awareness).

167. Di Certo, *supra* note 110.

168. Corell interview, *supra* note 141.

169. *See* ECCC Law, *supra* note 11, art. 11 new.

170. *See* Constitution of the Kingdom of Cambodia, art. 132 (adopted 1993, *as amended through* 2008) ("The King is the guarantor of the independence of the Judiciary. The Supreme Council of the Magistracy shall assist the King in this matter").

171. *See, e.g.*, Surya P. Subedi, Report of the Special Rapporteur on the Situation of Human Rights in Cambodia, ¶ 24, U.N. Doc. A/HRC/15/46 (Sept. 16, 2010). *But see* Julia Wallace, *UN Concerned Over Dilatory Appointment of KRT Judge*, CAMBODIA DAILY, Jan. 12, 2012 (quoting a government spokesperson saying that the SCM "is very independent. Our government has nothing to do with that one, even though a number of the government people sit on that one").

172. *See* Joint Public Statement, *The United Nations Special Representative of the Secretary General for Human Rights in Cambodia and the Special Rapporteur on the Independence of Judges and Lawyers Express Concern Over Judicial Independence in Cambodia in Light of Recent Judicial Appointments* (Aug. 23, 2007) (noting that the decision sidelines the SCM and raises concerns about the independence of the judicial appointment process).

173. *See* Samantha Melamed, *Criteria for KR Judge Selection Still Unreleased*, CAMBODIA DAILY, Nov. 28, 2005 (quoting the executive director of the Cambodia Defenders Project: "Before the government appoints any judges, there must be time for the public to comment[.] . . . At the least we want [judges] with integrity, competence, [who are] clean and independent.").

174. OSJI, *Progress and Challenges at the Extraordinary Chambers in the Courts of Cambodia*, 8 (June 2007).

175. *See* Douglas Gillison, *Officials Mum on KR Tribunal Judicial Appointments Memo*, CAMBODIA DAILY, June 20–21, 2009 (reporting that government officials and Cambodian ECCC officials could not explain a discovered 2006 memorandum from Deputy Prime Minister Sok An to Hun Sen asking him to approve the exact list of 29 Cambodian judges and prosecutors who were appointed to the Court by the King six weeks later on the nomination of the SCM).

176. *See* Mark Ellis, *Safeguarding Judicial Independence in Mixed Tribunals: Lessons from the ECCC and Best Practices for the Future*, INT'L BAR ASS'N, at 36 (Sept. 2011).

177. Cherie Booth & Philippe Sands, *International Judges Must Be Independent and Representative*, GUARDIAN, July 13, 2001. *See also* Ruth Mackenzie & Philippe Sands, *International Courts and Tribunals and the Independence of the International Judge*, 44 HARV. INT'L L. J. 271, 278 (2003) (noting that many candidates are former ministers, legal advisors, or diplomats who lack courtroom experience).

178. *See* Ellis, *supra* note 176, at 25. *See also* International Center for Transitional Justice, *Handbook on the Special Tribunal for Lebanon*, at 21 (Apr. 10, 2008).

179. *See* International Center for Transitional Justice, *supra* note 178, at 19.

180. *Id.* (stating that for the STL the panel comprised an ICTY judge, an ICTR judge, and the UN Legal Counsel).

181. Thomas Miller, *KRT Judge Talks Court Controversies*, PHNOM PENH POST, Aug. 18, 2011.

182. David Cohen, *Indifference and Accountability: The United Nations and the Politics of International Justice in East Timor*, at 3, E.-W. CTR. SPEC. REPS. (June 2006) (highlighting "serious flaws in the UN recruitment process" in Timor).

183. *See, e.g.*, Group of Experts Report, *supra* note 33, ¶¶ 133, 136.

184. Bates, *supra* note 140, ¶ 145. *See also* Kelly McEvers & Phann Ana, *Disorder in the Courts*, CAMBODIA DAILY, Mar. 4–5, 2000 (reporting that a "handful" of judges queried said that "no matter how far away from Phnom Penh they were, they felt the pressure of the Prime Minister"); Statement of Lao Mong Hay, *Institutions for the Rule of Law and Human Rights in Cambodia*, at 8 (Mar. 21, 2006), *cited in* Request for Investigation Pursuant to Rule 35, Case No. 002/19-9-2007-ECCC/TC, n.14 (Apr. 28, 2011):

> Apart from some 40 judges and prosecutors appointed after the new constitution, the rest, some 120, did not have any legal training, let alone a law degree, when

> they were appointed during the communist era. Their appointment was then based on their membership of—and loyalty to—the communist party. [. . .] All were instructed to serve the party. Those who were subsequently appointed were also compelled one way or another to join the current power, the Cambodian People's Party (the 'CPP'). [. . .] Even reformist judges and prosecutors feel pressure from people at the top [. . .].

185. ECCC Law, *supra* note 11, art. 10 new. *See generally* ECCC Code of Judicial Ethics (Sept. 5, 2008).

186. *See, e.g.*, Cambodian League for the Promotion and Defense of Human Rights (LICADHO), *Human Rights in Cambodia: The Charade of Justice*, at 25 (Dec. 2007).

187. *See* Mackenzie & Sands, *supra* note 177, at 282 (noting that outside activities may give rise to an appearance of bias or "simply compete for the time of judges and thus interfere with the work of the court or tribunal").

188. ECCC Internal Rules (rev. 8), *supra* note 16, r .34(2) (emphasis added).

189. Rogers interview, *supra* note 151.

190. Public Decision on the Co-Lawyers' Urgent Application for Disqualification of Judge Ney Thol Pending the Appeal Against the Provisional Detention Order in the Case of Nuon Chea, Case No. 002/19-9-2007-ECCC/OCIJ (PTC 01), ¶ 20 (Feb. 4, 2008), *citing* Prosecutor v Furundzija, Case No. IT-95–17/1-A, Judgment, ¶ 189 (Appeals Chamber, July 21, 2000).

191. *Id.* ¶¶ 28–33.

192. *See* James Welsh & Prak Chan Thul, *Filmmaker: KR Judge Says He Accepted Cash*, CAMBODIA DAILY, June 10–11, 2006; LICADHO, *supra* note 186, at 25. Judges who admit taking money often say it was only a "gift" or "fee" from a grateful litigant after the decision was rendered, and deny that it was a bribe. *See, e.g.*, McEvers & Phann, *supra* note 184; Kheang Un & Judy Ledgerwood, *Is the Trial of 'Duch' a Catalyst for Change in Cambodian Courts?* 95 ASIA PACIFIC ISSUES 6 (E.-W. Ctr., June 2010).

193. Decision on Ieng Sary's Application to Disqualify Judge Nil Nonn and Related Requests, Case No. 002/19-9-2007/ECCC/TC, ¶ 8 (Jan. 28, 2011).

194. *See id.* ¶¶ 9, 11–14.

195. *See id.* ¶¶ 14–15.

196. *See, e.g.*, Public Decision on the Co-Lawyers' Urgent Application for Disqualification of Judge Ney Thol Pending the Appeal Against the Provisional Detention Order in the Case of Nuon Chea, Case No. 002/19-9-2007-ECCC/OCIJ (PTC 01), ¶ 30 (Feb. 4, 2008).

197. SCSL Judicial Independence Opinion, *supra* note 7, Separate Opionion of Justice Robertson ¶ 18.

198. *Id.*

199. *Statement by Judges Downing and Chung, International Judges of the Pre-Trial Chamber* (Mar. 20, 2012).

200. *See* Di Certo, *supra* note 110. *See also* Memorandum from Judge Kong Srim, President JAC to Judge Prak Kimsan, President PTC, *Decision of the JAC Regarding the Request to Appoint Two International Judges to Hear the Application for Disqualification of the President of the Pre-Trial Chamber* (Mar. 23, 2012) (including the forceful dissent of Judge Lavergne, stating that neither the PTC nor the JAC has the authority to review the validity of a judge's decision to recuse him- or herself on any matter).

201. *See also* Olga Martin-Ortega & Johanna Herman, *Hybrid Tribunals & the Rule of Law: Notes from Bosnia & Herzegovina & Cambodia*, JAD-PbP Working Paper Series No. 7, 18 (May 2010) (noting that of the internationals, "only one judge and two reserve judges had experience at other international criminal tribunals").

202. *See, e.g.*, Marlise Simons, *An American with Opinions Steps Down Vocally at War Crimes Court*, N.Y. TIMES, Jan. 24, 2002 (reporting the views of former ICTY Judge Patricia Wald: "You need people who know how a court room works—what the basic elements of a crime and of evidence are[.] . . . Running a criminal trial is complex."); Hans Corell, *Foreword, in* INTERNATIONAL PROSECUTORS v, at ix (Luc Reydams et al. eds., 2012) (stating his "firm opinion" that the requirement for experience in international law "is overstated in comparison for the need for courtroom experience"); Michael Bohlander, *The International Criminal Judiciary—Problems of Judicial Selection, Independence and Ethics* (2007), *available at* http://papers.ssrn.com/sol3/papers.cfm?abstract_id=1592840.

203. Corell interview, *supra* note 141; Corell, *supra* note 202, at ix–xi.

204. *Cf.* Framework Agreement, *supra* note 11, art. 3(3) (providing in part that judges shall "possess the qualifications required in their respective countries for appointment to judicial offices").

205. *See, e.g.* ICTY Statute, *supra* note 16, art. 13; ICTR Statute, *supra* note 16, art. 12; SCSL Statute, *supra* note 102, art. 13 (requiring "qualifications required in their respective countries for appointment to the highest judicial offices" and taking into account experience in criminal and international law); Rome Statute, *supra* note 37, art. 36(3)(b) (requiring "qualifications required in their respective States for appointment to the highest judicial offices," competence and relevant experience in criminal or international law).

206. *Cited in* Bohlander, *supra* note 202, at 21.

207. Yash Ghai Report, *supra* note 3, ¶ 18.

208. *Id.* ¶ 43 (noting the removal and appointment of judges on executive instructions, contrary to the law in force).

209. *Id.* ¶ 54.

210. Luis Moreno-Ocampo, Address at the International Conference "Building a Future on Peace *and* Justice," Nuremberg (June 25, 2007), *available at* www.peace-justice-conference.info/download/speech%20moreno.pdf.

211. *Quoted in* Bates, *supra* note 140, ¶ 277.

212. *See, e.g.*, Group of Experts Report, *supra* note 33, ¶ 98.

213. Steve Heder, *The Personal Jurisdiction of the Extraordinary Chambers in the Courts of Cambodia As Regards Khmer Rouge "Senior Leaders" and Others "Most Responsible" for Khmer Rouge Crimes: A History and Recent Developments*, at 40 (April 26, 2012). *See also* Cable 07PHNOMPENH103, U.S. Embassy Phnom Penh, *RGC Worried ECCC Prosecutions Could Affect Peace and Security* ¶ 9 (Jan. 22, 2007), *available at* http://www.wikileaks.org/cable/2007/01/07PHNOMPENH103.html (noting, "In a country whose judiciary does nothing with respect to any politically related case without instructions, it is little surprise that the RGC is reticent about a legal process that they might not be able to control").

214. Reach Sambath, *Khmer Rouge Leaders Will Not Escape the Law: Hun Sen*, AGENCE FRANCE-PRESSE, Sept. 11, 2000. *See also* Un & Ledgerwood, *supra* note 192, at 4 (noting that the PRK government collapsed all stories of the DK period into a standard "national narrative" exemplified by the Tuol Sleng Genocide Museum). *Cf.* THIERRY CRUVELLIER, COURT OF REMORSE: INSIDE THE INTERNATIONAL CRIMINAL TRIBUNAL FOR RWANDA 166 (2006) (noting that when meeting with Rwanda officials to discuss the events of 1994, "one question must first be answered: who stopped the genocide? There is only one right answer—the RPF").

215. Situation in Uganda, Decision Assigning the Situation in Uganda to Pre-Trial Chamber II, Situation No. ICC-02/04 (July 5, 2004) (containing the Letter from Prosecutor Moreno Ocampo to President Kirsch [June 17, 2004]).

216. *See, e.g.*, International Refugee Rights Initiative, Discussion Paper 1: *A Poisoned Chalice?*, at 9 (Oct. 2011) ("[I]t was assumed that the government of Uganda's co-operation was contingent on the ICC *not* investigating it [i.e., government forces], and therefore it appeared that the ICC had made this decision for political reasons rather than on the basis of any proper analysis of the crimes committed"); William A. Schabas, *First Prosecutions at the International Criminal Court*, 27 HUM. RTS. L. J. 24, 31 (2006) ("The suspicion is inescapable that the Prosecutor has a tacit, if not an explicit, understanding with the Ugandan authorities that he will prosecute the rebel leaders only").

217. *See, e.g.*, Human Rights Watch, *supra* note 51, at 25, 27 (2011).

218. *See, e.g.*, Dina Temple, *Carla del Ponte's Days in Rwanda Look Numbered*, N.Y. SUN, Aug. 7, 2003 (noting that the United States and United Kingdom supported Rwanda on this issue). *See also* CRUVELLIER, *supra* note 214, at 132 (highlighting that "Rwandan authorities have managed to use, shake up, manipulate, and intimidate the ICTR . . . [, having] no qualms about subjecting the tribunal to their interests[.]"); Ellis interview, *supra* note 165 (noting that because no RPF officers were prosecuted, the ICTR provided victors' justice, which was inevitable as the tribunal could not function without the cooperation of the 'victors' now running the Rwandan government).

219. *But see* CRUVELLIER, *supra* note 214, at 105–13 (recounting the story of how, when the Appeal Chamber dismissed all charges in the *Barayagwiza* Case, Rwanda formally withdrew cooperation and the prosecutor was forced to ask the Chamber to reconsider). *Compare* Barayagwiza v. Prosecutor, Case No. ICTR-97-19, Decision (Appeals Chamber,

Nov. 3, 1999) (ordering the release of the accused for abuse of process for fundamental violations of his rights), *with* Barayagwiza v. Prosecutor, Case No. ICTR-97-19-AR72, Decision on the Prosecutor's Request for Review or Reconsideration, ¶¶ 54–55 (Appeals Chamber, Mar. 31, 2000) (finding dismissal of the charges to be "disproportionate" upon the presentation of new evidence).

220. International Co-Prosecutor Andrew Cayley has noted, "I think that in a number of international courts in which I have worked, states might deny trying to exercise influence, but they still do, to varying degrees, behind the scenes. Such political influence is not always motivated by bad faith. Sometimes intervention takes place for well-founded reasons." Interview with Andrew Cayley, Global Brief (Sept. 9, 2011), *available at* http://globalbrief.ca/blog/2011/09/09/on-international-criminal-justice/.

221. Cable 07PHNOMPENH429, U.S. Embassy Phnom Penh, *Friends of the ECCC or RGC?* ¶ 8 (Mar. 16, 2007), *available at* http://dazzlepod.com/cable/07PHNOMPENH429 (stating former Director of Administration Sean Visoth's view that the Chinese were placing pressure on the Government with regard to the tribunal).

222. *See, e.g.*, Press Release, *Australia Announces New Pledge of AUD 1.61 Million* (Mar. 27, 2012) (reporting that the Australian Foreign Minister announced the donation in Phnom Penh, including 0.61 million for the national side). Three days earlier, in the midst of Kasper-Ansermet's allegations of massive dysfunction, the Government called the ECCC a "model court" that "is running smoothly and normally." Bridget Di Certo, *KRT Is a Model Court Says State*, PHNOM PENH POST, Mar. 23, 2012.

223. Cable 07PHNOMPENH429, *supra* note 221, ¶ 8 (finding it of concern "that the two countries are focusing exclusively on the preservation of their bilateral relationships with the RGC in their discussions about the ECCC, and are not taking a more nuanced approach as co-chairs of the Friends").

224. *See, e.g.*, Letter from HRW, FIDH, Amnesty International and OSJI to Stephen Mathias, UN Assistant Secretary General for Legal Affairs, *Extraordinary Chambers in the Courts of Cambodia* (Mar. 29, 2011) (on file with author); OSJI, *Recent Developments at the Extraordinary Chambers in the Courts of Cambodia*, at 33 (June 2011); *But see* Press Release, *United Nations Rejects "Media Speculation that Judges Received Instructions to Dismiss Case Before Extraordinary Chambers in the Courts of Cambodia*, SG/SM/13642 (June 14, 2011).

225. Cambodian Center for Human Rights, *Open Letter to United Nations Special Expert on the Khmer Rouge Tribunal Clint Williamson* (May 25, 2011).

226. Mike Eckel, *Cambodia's Kangaroo Court*, FOREIGN POLICY (July 20, 2011).

227. *Id.*

228. Nathan J. Miller, Independence of the International Judiciary: General Overview of the Issues, Project on International Courts and Tribunals (Working Draft), 16 (Jan. 24, 2002).

229. Corell, *supra* note 202, at vi. *See, e.g.*, RICHARD GOLDSTONE, FOR HUMANITY:

REFLECTIONS OF A WAR CRIMES INVESTIGATOR 105 (2000) (recounting how as the first ICTY prosecutor he was told "at least one indictment had to be issued before the November [budget] meeting in order to demonstrate that the system was working and that the tribunal was worthy of financial support[,]" which led to the indictment of an available low-level offender).

230. Cable 09PHNOMPENH648, *supra* note 57, ¶ 4. *But see New KRT Judge: "I Will Assume This Mission,"* CAMBODIA DAILY, Feb. 15, 2012 (quoting Judge Kasper-Ansermet: "I don't have to consider political or financial issues because we speak now as there are budget problems, and we have, of course, the political side of cases, but I have to not care about it"). Nevertheless, there have been rumors that donors have sought to target their funding to Case 002 and away from Case 003 and 004. If this is true, it appears that—to its credit—the UN has not agreed to this kind of direct donor influence over the Court's docket.

231. *See also* Confidential Cable, U.S. Embassy Phnom Penh, *Friends of the ECCC Discuss Budget and Judicial Calendar* ¶ 1 (Jan. 14, 2010), *available at* http://www.wikileaks.org/cablegate.html. *Cf. id.* ¶ 7 (reporting that Deputy Director Knut Rosandhaug "suggested that the law could be changed to transfer [Case 003] entirely to the domestic court[.]").

232. *See, e.g.*, Jared Ferrie, *Wikileaks: UN Discussed Dropping #003*, CHRISTIAN SCIENCE MONITOR, Aug. 3, 2011 (noting that "[s]uch a move would . . . undoubtedly kill the problematic case"). *See also* Julia Wallace, *Chaos Now Bites KR Defence*, 153 INT'L JUST. TRIB. (June 6, 2012) (noting that Rosandhaug asked You Bunleng to clarify Judge Kasper-Ansermet's order recognizing Richard Rogers as Case 004 accused Ta An's international counsel, knowing You would "respond[], as could have been expected, in the negative" and adding that "Rosandhaug, a UN career bureaucrat, is widely perceived to be uninterested in pursuing new cases.") *See also* Interview with Richard Rogers, former head of the ECCC Defence Support Section, Phnom Penh, via telephone (June 12, 2012) ("I don't have any evidence that OLA instructed Knut, but at least he must be pretty confident of some support to take steps like this"). This is particularly concerning as the Case 003 and 004 accused were not informed of their rights before Judge Kasper-Ansermet arrived and the Court had consistently maintained the legal fiction that they are not entitled to counsel because they are not charged and the investigation is secret, even though their names had been public for over a year and multiple media outlets had since interviewed them about their alleged crimes. In October 2012, Göran Sluiter was assigned international Co-Counsel for Ta An (Case 004) (joining national Co-Counsel Mom Luch); however, in June 2013, it was revealed that the international head of the Defence Support Section (DSS), a formally autonomous arm of OA, had been arbitrarily disregarding existing funding guidelines in an effort to save money in violation of Ta An's defense rights. *See* Decision on Application Requesting Funding for Legal Consultant's Flight to the Office of the Co-Lawyer, Case No. 001/21-05-2013-UNAJ (June 25, 2013), *available at* http://

www.eccc.gov.kh/en/dss/defence-support-section/claims-decisions (noting that the DSS head had placed Sluiter and Ta An "in a disadvantageous situation in comparison with the other Defence teams and their clients in Cases 001 and 002 ... in breach of the principle of equality before the law").

233. SCSL Judicial Independence Opinion, *supra* note 7, ¶ 24.

234. *Id.* ¶¶ 25, 37. In contrast, at the ECCC, as discussed in chapter 3, the salaries of national staff—including judges—were not paid by the Cambodian Government on more than one occasion despite its obligation to do so under the ECCC Agreement, due to a lapse in international donations. *See, e.g., Cash Crunch Threatens Cambodia's War Crimes Court*, AGENCE FRANCE-PRESSE, Feb. 10, 2013.

235. SCSL Judicial Independence Decision, *supra* note 7, Separate Opinion of Justice Robertson ¶ 3.

236. *See* Miller, *supra* note 228 (stating that Basic Principle 7 on the Independence of the Judiciary ["It is the duty of each Member State to provide adequate resources to enable the judiciary to properly perform its functions"] "reflects the understanding that the budget of the court cannot be used as a means to limit the scope of its operation").

237. Luc Côté, *Reflections on the Exercise of Prosecutorial Discretion in International Criminal Law*, 3 J. INT'L CRIM. JUST. 162, 184 (2005).

238. Bates, *supra* note 140, ¶ 275. *See also* Kong Sothanarith, *Major Donors Support Tribunal, But Want Some Haste*, VOA KHMER (Sept. 2, 2011), http://www.voacambodia.com/content/major-donors-support-tribunal-but-want-some-haste-129074913/1357878.html.

239. Prosecutor v. S. Milosevic, Case No. IT-02–54-AR73.4, ¶ 20 Dissenting Opinion of Judge David Hunt on Admissibility of Evidence in Chief in the Form of Written Statement (Appeals Chamber, Oct. 21, 2003). *See also* Radosa Mulitunovic, *Mladic: Just Another "False Start,"* INT'L JUST. TRIB. (May 23, 2012) (noting "for seasoned court observers, the 'false start' to the Mladic trial indicates pressure from the UN Security Council" to finish all trials before the Residual Mechanism takes effect in July 2013); *Cf.* Cohen, *supra* note 182 (noting that in a judgment drafted in East Timor Judge Blunk wrote: "Mitigation is ... that before the Court he pled guilty on the second day of the trial, *so that* the Court whose lifespan ends on 20 May 2005, can turn its resources to the remaining trials, which according to [the Security Council resolution] should be concluded '*as soon as possible*.'" [emphasis in original]).

240. *See, e.g.*, James O'Toole, *Ban Hits Back at Tribunal Critics*, PHNOM PENH POST, June 16, 2011; UN Press Release, *supra* note 224 (calling the closure of Case 003 "'an interim procedural step' subject to an independent judicial process" and saying that the CIJs "are under no obligation to provide reasons for their actions at this stage of the investigation").

241. Cambodian Center for Human Rights, *supra* note 225 (stating, "Unless the United

Nations takes immediate steps to ensure that investigations take place in Cases 003 and 004 in earnest, the international community will have to take its measure of the blame—along with the RGC—for [failing victims]").

242. *See* Ellis interview, *supra* note 165 ("[The UN] has real [cultural] problems dealing with internal issues. If people are accused of wrongdoing the tendency is to move them sideways or upwards, but not out of the organization.").

243. Statement by the Spokesperson for the UN Secretary-General (Mar. 30, 2012); Wallace & Kuch, *supra* note 2.

244. Di Certo, *supra* note 110 (quoting country representative Rupert Abbot). *See also* James A. Goldston, *Justice Delayed Is Justice Denied*, N.Y. TIMES, Oct. 13, 2011; *Cambodian Law Body Reportedly Blocking Swiss Judge*, RADIO AUSTRALIA (Jan. 17, 2012) (quoting OSJI monitor Clair Duffy noting that "as [attempts to shut down Case 003] continue to unfold and the UN hasn't taken any strong action in relation to this, its credibility even more come (*sic*) under fire, particularly for future engagements by the UN in these kind (*sic*) of institutions").

245. Julia Wallace, *UN Lawyer to Visit Cambodia to Address Alleged Interference*, CAMBODIA DAILY, Oct. 17, 2011.

246. Press Statement by Patricia O'Brien, UN Under Secretary-General for Legal Affairs (Oct. 20, 2011); Julia Wallace, *Don't Interfere in Khmer Rouge Tribunal, UN Tells Government*, CAMBODIA DAILY, Oct. 21, 2011.

247. Robert Carmichael, *Cambodia: UN Visit Ends Without Decision*, INT'L JUST. TRIB., Oct. 22, 2011.

248. *See* Julia Wallace, *Nuon Chea Takes Meddling Charge to Court*, CAMBODIA DAILY, Oct. 24, 2011.

249. Email from attendee of "Legal Issues Facing the United Nations—Reflections from Three Years as Legal Counsel," American Bar Association, Oct. 28, 2011, on file with author (Nov. 26, 2011) (recounting O'Brien's statement that while it would be incredibly easy to begin an investigation tomorrow, the UN knows what it will find, and is afraid that those findings will affect Case 002. As the results of Cases 003 and 004 are "inevitable," it is just trying to keep things on track to get through Case 002.).

250. *See UN Prosecutor*, *supra* note 120. *Cf.* OSJI, *Recent Developments at the Extraordinary Chambers in the Courts of Cambodia*, at 4 (June 2011) (reporting that "[a] number of donors have underscored the importance of the court's second case . . . seeming to imply that preserving the case may require ceding the ability to proceed with Cases 003 and 004"). *Cf.* Rogers telephone interview, *supra* note 232 (stating that donors generally share the UN's view that Cases 003 and 004 should go away, and some donors were staying with them only to save Case 002); Long interview, *supra* note 50 (saying, "Donors don't care if their funding is properly managed and justice is being properly done. They want to feel they are contributing something to Cambodia instead of considering if Cambodia is establishing real criminal accountability.").

251. *See* Neou Vannarin & Julia Wallace, *Council of Ministers' Press Unit Puts Own Spin on O'Brien Visit*, Cambodia Daily, Oct. 25, 2011.

252. Scheffer, *supra* note 148, at 246.

253. *Report of the Secretary-General on Khmer Rouge Trials*, ¶ 30, U.N. Doc. A/57/769 (Mar. 31, 2003).

254. Theary Seng, Khmer Rouge Victims in Cambodia, *Time is Prime for UN to withdraw from KRT* (Jan. 23, 2012), *available at* http://anonymouse.org/cgi-bin/anon-www.cgi/http://ki-media.blogspot.com/2012/01/commentary-by-theary-c-seng-time-is.html; Men Kimseng, *UN Faces Tough Decision in Appointing New Judge: Analyst*, VOA Khmer (Mar. 27, 2012), http://www.voacambodia.com/content/un-faces-tough-decision-in-appointing-new-judge-analyst-144452965/1358586.html (in which Cambodian rights activist Ou Virak says that the United Nations should withdraw if a new CIJ faces obstruction); Peter Maguire, *ECCC's Tarnished Legacy and the UN*, Cambodia Tribunal Monitor (Mar. 27, 2012), http://www.cambodiatribunal.org/sites/default/files/03-27-12-Maguire Commentary.pdf.

255. *See, e.g.*, Un & Ledgerwood, *supra* note 192, at 7.

256. *See, e.g.*, Rogers telephone interview, *supra* note 232 ("The combination of two-faced donors and a weak UN have allowed this whole process to drift"). *Cf.* David Cohen, *Seeking Justice on the Cheap: Is the East Timor Tribunal Really a Model for the Future*, 61 Asia Pacific Issues 6 (E.-W. Ctr., Aug. 2002) (stating that the Timorese case did not "bode well for future hybrid tribunals if the United Nations uses [the tribunal's] unique status as an excuse for not meeting the very standards it as an institution is supposed to embody"); Michael E. Hartmann, *International Judges and Prosecutors in Kosovo: A New Model for Post-Conflict Peacekeeping*, U.S. Institute for Peace, at 14 (Oct. 2003) (finding that the Kosovo example proves that future international missions "should condition their initial deployment in the judiciary upon a worst-case scenario" and "[l]ocal or national jurists should not be expected to be impartial and impervious to coercion and threats").

257. Confidential interview with a senior ECCC staff member, Phnom Penh (June 2012). *See also* Men Kimseng, *UN Not Fulfilling Tribunal Role As Partner: Monitor*, VOA Khmer (Nov. 9, 2011), http://www.voacambodia.com/content/un-not-fulfilling-tribunal-role-as-partner-monitor-133527368/1359597.html (quoting Panhavuth Long: "Some UN officials see their role as just coming in to assist, which requires that they give only advice" but in performing their official duties, they should see themselves as a "partner" not an "adviser").

258. Phillip Rapoza, *Hybrid Criminal Tribunals and the Concept of Ownership: Who Owns the Process?*, 21 Am. U. Int'l L. Rev. 525, 530 (2006). Judge Rapoza is now a reserve ECCC Supreme Court Chamber judge. *See also* Cohen, *supra* note 182, at 3 (noting that "the root of all the problems of the Serious Crimes process was the failure by the UN to ensure proper leadership, a clear mandate, political will, and clear 'ownership' of the process from the beginning").

Chapter 7

1. ECCC, *Germany Pledges More Financial Support to Maximise Victims' Participation in KR Trials* (June 17, 2010).

2. *See, e.g.*, Yael Danieli, *Reappraising the Nuremberg Trials and Their Legacy: The Role of Victims in International Law*, 27 Cardozo L. Rev. 1633, 1641–43 (2005–6). *But cf.* Interview with Diana Ellis, Co-Lawyer for Ieng Thirith, Phnom Penh (Nov. 11, 2012) (agreeing that victims have been forgotten, but emphasizing that they "should obtain redress through a different mechanism" because the point of a criminal trial is to determine if an accused is guilty of crimes and not the proper forum to discuss wrongs unrelated to the specific charges); Response to "Demande des co-avocats principaux pour les parties civiles afin de définir l'étendue de la declaration sur la souffrance des parties civiles déposantes," Case No. 002/19-9-2007-ECCC/TC (Nov. 12, 2012) (raising the "delicate" situation of some civil parties providing personal statements of suffering at the Case 002/01 trial referencing facts outside the scope of the now significantly reduced charges, potentially harming the rights of accused Khieu Samphan).

3. Press Release by the Office of the Prosecutor, *Address to the Security Council by Carla Del Ponte, Prosecutor of the International Criminal Tribunals for the Former Yugoslavia And Rwanda, to the UN Security Council* (Nov. 24, 2000).

4. David Donat-Cattin, *Article 68 Protection of the Victims and Witnesses and Their Participation in the Proceedings*, *in* Commentary on the Rome Statute of the International Court 869, 871 (Otto Triffterer ed., 1999).

5. U.N. Declaration of Basic Principles of Justice for Victims of Crime and Abuse of Power, G.A. Res. 40/34, annex, 40 U.N. GAOR Supp. (No. 53) at 214, U.N. Doc. A/40/53 (1985) [hereinafter UN Declaration].

6. For discussion of the evolution of victims' rights at the international level, *see* Sarah Thomas & Terith Chy, *Including the Survivors in the Tribunal Process*, *in* On Trial: The Khmer Rouge Accountability Process 214, 217–30 (John D. Ciorciari & Anne Heindel eds., 2009).

7. UN Declaration, *supra* note 5, §§ 4, 6(a)–(c) (through, *inter alia*, being kept informed about proceedings, having the opportunity to present views and concerns, and receiving assistance throughout the process); *id.* § 7 (including restitution, compensation, services, and assistance).

8. *See Report of the Secretary-General on the Establishment of a Special Tribunal for Lebanon*, ¶ 31, U.N. Doc. S/2006/893 (Nov. 5, 2006) (noting that although the statute does not recognize victims as civil parties, "it permits their views and concerns to be presented and considered at all stages of the proceedings"); Statut des Chambres Africaines Extraordinaires, art. 14 (Jan. 30, 2013), *available at* http://www.hrw.org/node/113271 (providing that the terms of civil party participation will be governed by domestic Senegalese criminal procedure).

9. Law on the Establishment of Extraordinary Chambers in the Courts of Cambodia

for the Prosecution of Crimes Committed During the Period of Democratic Kampuchea, as amended and promulgated on Oct. 27, 2004, NS/RKM/1004/006 [hereinafter ECCC Law], art. 36*new*.

10. David Scheffer, *The Extraordinary Chambers in the Courts of Cambodia, in* 3 International Criminal Law 219, 253 (M. Cherif Bassiouni ed., 2008).

11. Confidential interview, Phnom Penh (May 14, 2012).

12. Civil party participation was included in the draft Internal Rules in November 2006, which Lemonde largely drafted. *See* ECCC Draft Internal Rules (Nov. 3, 2006), *available at* http://www.unakrt-online.org/Docs/Court%20Documents/Eng_Draft-IRs-For_Plenary.pdf.

13. *See, e.g.*, Cable 06PHNOMPENH2046, U.S. Embassy Phnom Penh, *ECCC Issues Draft Internal Rules* ¶ 3 (Nov. 16, 2006), *available at* http://www.wikileaks.org/cable/2006/11/06PHNOMPENH2046.html.

14. Confidential interview, *supra* note 11.

15. Anyone who witnessed, was a victim of, or has knowledge of an alleged crime within the jurisdiction of the ECCC can lodge a complaint. *See* Internal Rules of the ECCC, *rev'd* Aug. 3, 2011, r. 49 [hereinafter ECCC Internal Rules (rev. 8)]. However, unlike under domestic law, a victim cannot initiate a criminal action at the ECCC. *Compare* Cambodian Criminal Procedure Code (*as adopted* Aug. 10, 2007), art. 5 [hereinafter CPC], *with* ECCC Internal Rules (rev. 8), *supra*.

16. Internal Rules of the ECCC, *adopted* June 12, 2007, r. 23(6)(a) [hereinafter ECCC Internal Rules (original)] (providing that, "When joined as a Civil Party, the Victim becomes a party to the criminal proceedings"). This provision has since been removed from the Rules.

17. Cable 08USUNNEWYORK872, U.S. Mission to the United Nations, *Corruption Allegations Dominate Khmer Rouge (UNAKRT) Steering Committee Meeting In New York at UK Mission* ¶ 5 (Sept. 29, 2008), *available at* http://www.wikileaks.org/cable/2008/09/08USUNNEWYORK872.html (also asserting that this was "an area . . . where the Tribunal is weakest" and that the VU lacked an adequate procedure for processing its nearly 2,000 victim complaints).

18. *See, e.g.*, Interview with Jeanne Sulzer, former Legal Officer in the ECCC Civil Party Lead Co-Lawyers Section, Phnom Penh (June 1, 2012).

19. Interview with Rupert Skilbeck, former Head of the ECCC Defence Support Section, via telephone (June 7, 2012).

20. ECCC Internal Rules (original), *supra* note 16, r.12; Internal Rules of the ECCC (rev. 5), *rev'd* Feb. 9, 2010, r. 12*bis* [hereinafter ECCC Internal Rules (rev. 5)] (mandating these responsibilities to the newly established Victim Support Section).

21. *See* ECCC, Practice Direction on Victim Participation, 02/2007/Rev. 1, *amended* Oct. 27, 2008 [hereinafter Practice Direction], *attaching* Victim Information Form, Appendix A/Rev. 1.

22. *See* Alex Bates, *Transitional Justice in Cambodia: Analytical Report*, Atlas Project, ¶ 189 (Oct. 2010); Youk Chhang, Comment, *Sad Situation for Civil Parties*, PHNOM PENH POST, Oct. 1, 2009; Open Society Justice Initiative (OSJI), *Recent Developments at the Extraordinary Chambers in the Courts of Cambodia* (Oct. 2008). Similar problems have faced the ICC in Kenya. *See, e.g.*, Press Release, Redress, *Concern over VPRS's Potential Inability to Process in Time the Sheer Number of Victim's Applications for Participation in the 2 Kenya Cases* (June 29, 2011) (noting that the ICC victims unit had received 2,350 applications for participation but would only be in a position to process 400 by the deadline). *See also* You Bunleng, Response to questionnaire from the authors, June 25, 2012 (translated from Khmer by Kimsroy Sokvisal) (noting that the OCIJ's assessment of the large number of civil party applications was extremely time consuming).

23. OSJI, *Recent Developments at the Extraordinary Chambers in the Courts of Cambodia* (Feb. 2008) (noting that the draft 2008 budget lacked funds for outreach trips or legal representation for victims).

24. *See, e.g.*, Erika Kinetz, *ECCC Confronts Difficulty of Involving Victims*, CAMBODIA DAILY, Aug. 15, 2007 (noting the dismay of a local court monitor that "the administration of the ECCC considers the Victims Unit just an administrative unit").

25. *See, e.g.*, Patrick Kroker, *Transitional Justice Policy in Practice: Victim Participation in the* Khmer Rouge *Tribunal*, 53 GER. Y.B. INT'L L. 754, 767 (2010).

26. Bates, *supra* note 22, ¶ 189 n. 340.

27. Eric Stover et al., *Confronting Duch: Civil Party Participation in Case 001 at the Extraordinary Chambers in the Courts of Cambodia*, 93 INT'L REV. OF THE RED CROSS 14 (June 2011); Phuong N. Pham et al., *Victim Participation and the Trial of Duch at the Extraordinary Chambers in the Courts of Cambodia*, 3 J. HUM. RTS. PRAC. 264, 273 (2011).

28. ECCC, *Proposed Budget for 2012–2013*, at 36, 43 (Feb. 17, 2012).

29. *Id.* at 16.

30. OSJI, *Recent Developments at the Extraordinary Chambers in the Courts of Cambodia* 18 (Dec. 2010).

31. OSJI, *Recent Developments at the Extraordinary Chambers in the Courts of Cambodia* 13 n.31 (Sept. 2010) [hereinafter OSJI Sept. 2010 Report].

32. In its revised 2012–13 budget, the UN side of the Court did allocate one slot for an Associate Information Systems Officer to support the national side of the VSS. ECCC, *Revised Budget Requirements—2012–13* (Jan. 29, 2013), at 21.

33. Press Release, *Khmer Rouge Victims in Cambodia* (May 12, 2011), *available at* www.thearyseng.com (suggesting that Rosandhaug's lack of support for the VU was responsible).

34. Cable 07PHNOMPENH77, U.S. Embassy Phnom Penh, *Update on the ECCC; David Scheffer Coming to Cambodia* ¶ 5 (Jan. 17, 2007), *available at* http://dazzlepod.com/cable/07PHNOMPENH77.html. *Cf.* Confidential interview with former VSS staff member, Phnom Penh (June 11, 2012) (stating that Keat had no power because she was

not connected within the Cambodian Government, but came from the UN/NGO community).

35. ECCC, *Revised Budget Requirements—2010–2011* (Jan. 24, 2011), at 9.

36. *See, e.g.*, OSJI, *Recent Developments at the Extraordinary Chambers in the Courts of Cambodia* 33 (Feb. 2012).

37. Cable 09PHNOMPENH343, U.S. Embassy Phnom Penh, *Khmer Rouge Tribunal: Sok An Enthusiastic About Proposed Anti-Corruption Mechanism* ¶ 7 (Apr. 28, 2009), *available at* http://www.wikileaks.org/cable/2009/05/09PHNOMPENH343.html (asserting that Jarvis would not qualify as a "neutral, independent, and impartial" candidate for an anticorruption counselor position because she reports "directly" to Sok An).

38. *See* Douglas Gillison, *Public Affairs Chief Named to KR Victims Office*, CAMBODIA DAILY, May 19, 2009.

39. *See, e.g.*, Robbie Corey-Boulet, *Attacks on Jarvis Multiply*, PHNOM PENH POST, June 8, 2009; Douglas Gillison & Phann Ana, *KR Victims Say Troubled by Jarvis' Marxist-Leninist Ties*, CAMBODIA DAILY, June 18, 2009 (noting a letter from 40 victims asking how a Leninist could lead the victims of Leninist ideology); Sophal Ear, Letter, *Khmer Rouge Tribunal vs. Karmic Justice*, N.Y. TIMES, Mar. 17, 2010 (arguing that "appointment of a devout Marxist-Leninist as head of the Victims Unit . . . fully endorsed by the U.N. head of the tribunal, sealed the tribunal's fate as an international and domestic farce").

40. Robbie Corey-Boulet, *Nationality and the Jarvis Debate*, PHNOM PENH POST, June 12, 2009 (quoting Youk Chhang).

41. Confidential interview with former VSS staff member, *supra* note 34.

42. *See* Douglas Gillison, *KRT Personnel Chief Temporarily Named to Victims Unit*, CAMBODIA DAILY, June 28, 2010 (noting that he would "take care of both sections" temporarily).

43. OSJI Sept. 2010 Report, *supra* note 31, at 13. At the ECCC, Rong has reportedly served as Special Program Manager for the OA Director—essentially the number two position on the national side of the OA—and more recently as head of the Court's incipient Legacy Office. In October 2012, reportedly due to quiet pressure from the U.S. Government in response to allegations of financial misappropriation, Rong stepped down from formal, if not *de facto* leadership of VSS.

44. Sulzer interview, *supra* note 18.

45. Internal Rules of the ECCC (rev. 6), *rev'd* Sept. 17, 2010, r. 12 [hereinafter ECCC Internal Rules (rev. 6)] (stating that the OA shall provide the Civil Party Lead Co-Lawyers Section "necessary administrative support"). Half of the Lead Co-Lawyers' funding is also channeled through the VSS, creating, at least in perception, a mechanism for control by the national side of the Court.

46. *See, e.g.*, Theary C. Seng et al., Complaint Alleging Obstruction of Justice . . . (Oct. 24, 2010), http://www.cambodiapolitics.info/samrainsyparty/archives/achieve_2010/

October/Cambodia%20REVISED%20ECCC%20COMPLAINT%20ECCC%20COPY.htm.

47. Cable 07PHNOMPENH77, *supra* note 34, ¶ 5.

48. Wendy Leung, *Individual Cases Could Expand Scope of KR Trial*, CAMBODIA DAILY, Mar. 11, 2005.

49. *Id.*

50. *Id.*

51. Interview with Panhavuth Long, Program Officer, Cambodian Justice Initiative, Phnom Penh (July 6, 2012).

52. *See, e.g.*, Sulzer interview, *supra* note 18.

53. OSJI Sept. 2010 Report, *supra* note 31, at 13.

54. Michelle Staggs Kelsall et al., *Lessons Learned from the 'Duch' Trial: A Comprehensive Review of the First Case Before the Extraordinary Chambers in the Courts of Cambodia*, Asian International Justice Initiative's KRT Trial Monitoring Group (Dec. 2009), at 33 (reporting the view of civil party lawyers in Case 001 that the VU "did not appear to have sufficient funds to facilitate adequate lawyer-client interaction and case preparation"). *Cf.* ICC Rules of Procedure and Evidence, *adopted* Sept. 9, 2002, r. 90(5) [hereinafter ICC Rules] (ensuring financial assistance for victim participant representation by common legal representatives); Prosecutor v. Katanga et al., Case No. ICC-01/04-1/07, Order on the Organisation of Common Legal Representatives of Victims, ¶ 17 (Trial Chamber, July 22, 2009) [hereinafter *Katanga* Order] (tasking the ICC Registry to "propose a suitable support structure . . . to provide the common legal representative with the necessary legal and administrative support, both at the seat of the Court and in the field" to keep their clients informed, receive their instructions, maintain files, and obtain legal support).

55. *See* Kroker, *supra* note 25, at 767 (stating that civil society organizations helped organize civil party representation in Case 001 "due to passivity on the part of the Court").

56. Bates, *supra* note 22, ¶ 208.

57. Interview with Karim A.A. Khan QC, ECCC Civil Party Co-Lawyer in Case 001, via telephone (June 5, 2012).

58. *See* ECCC Internal Rules (rev. 5), *supra* note 20, r. 12.

59. *Id.* r. 12*ter*(4).

60. *Id.* r. 12*ter*(5)(b).

61. *Id.* r. 12*ter*(3).

62. *See* ECCC Internal Rules (original), *supra* note 16, r. 23(7) (generally), r. 82 (regarding right to representation at trial), r. 105 (regarding appeals from the Trial Chamber judgment).

63. *See* ECCC Internal Rules (rev. 5), *supra* note 20, r. 23(3).

64. *See, e.g.*, Silvia Cartwright, Opening Speech to the ECCC 7th Plenary Session (Feb. 2, 2010) (noting that with over 4,000 civil party applicants, "[i]t is clear . . . that this greatly exceeds the capacity of the Trial Chamber to involve them individually").

65. Youk Chhang, *Conducting a Legal Experiment at Victims' Expense*, Cambodia Trial Monitor (Sept. 29, 2009), http://www.cambodiatribunal.org/blog/2009/09/conducting-legal-experiment-victims-expense (noting that in Case 001 "no attempt was ever made by the Co-Investigating or Trial Judges in the Duch/S-21 case to limit the number of civil parties by applying the qualifying criteria or otherwise vetting the applications" in advance).

66. ECCC Internal Rules (original), *supra* note 16, r. 23(2).

67. Practice Direction, *supra* note 21, art. 3.1 (emphasis added).

68. Similarly, at the ICC, victims include "natural persons who have suffered harm as a result of the commission of any crime within the jurisdiction of the Court." ICC Rules, *supra* note 54, r. 85(a).

69. ECCC Internal Rules (rev. 5), *supra* note 20, r. 23*bis*(2) (emphasis added). *Cf.* Prosecutor v. Lubanga Dyilo, Case No. ICC-01/04-1/06 OA9 OA10, Judgement on the Appeals of the Prosecutor and the Defence Against Trial Chamber I's Decision on Victims' Participation of 18 January 2008, ¶ 58 (July 11, 2008) (finding that "the participation of victims in the trial proceedings, [. . .] is limited to those victims who are linked to the charges).

70. Co-Prosecutors v. Kaing Guek Eav *alias* Duch, Case No. 001/18-7-2007/ECCC/SC, Appeal Judgment, n.866 (Feb. 3, 2012) [hereinafter *Duch* Appeal Judgment].

71. *Id.* ¶¶ 409–14.

72. Decisions on victim status will no longer be made in the judgment. The revised rules require the Co-Investigating Judge to make a decision—appealable to the Pre-Trial Chamber—on applications prior to the issuance of the Closing Order. *See* ECCC Internal Rules (rev. 5), *supra* note 20, r. 23*bis*.

73. *See* Prosecutors v. Kaing Guek Eav *alias* Duch, Case No. 001/18-7-2007/ECCC/TC, Judgment, ¶¶ 645–49 (July 26, 2010) [hereinafter *Duch* Trial Chamber Judgment]. *See also* You Bunleng, *supra* note 22 (noting that civil party applications did not always provide sufficient information, and the credibility of their stories could not always be verified).

74. Transcultural Psychosocial Organization [TPO], *Report on TPO's After-Verdict Intervention with Case 001 Civil Parties* (July 27, 2010), § 2.

75. *See, e.g., Duch* Appeal Judgment, *supra* note 70, ¶¶ 445–50, 558–63 (regarding special bonds of affection).

76. ECCC, *Pre-Trial Chamber Overturns Previous Rejection of 98% of Appealing Civil Party Applicants in Case 002* (June 24, 2011), *at* http://www.eccc.gov.kh/en/articles/pre-trial-chamber-overturns-previous-rejection-98-appealing-civil-party-applicants-case-002.

77. Decision on Appeals Against Orders of the Co-Investigating Judges on the Admissibility of Civil Party Applications, Case No. 002/19-9-2007-ECCC/OCIJ, ¶ 29 (June 24, 2011) [hereinafter PTC Decision on Case 002 Civil Party Applications].

78. *Id.* ¶ 42 (emphasis in original).

79. *Id.* ¶ 75. *See also id.* ¶ 72.

80. *Id.* ¶ 77.

81. *Id.*, Separate and Partially Dissenting Opinion of Judge Marchi-Uhel ¶ 4.

82. *Id.* ¶ 29.

83. *Id.* ¶¶ 83–89.

84. *Id.* ¶ 93. *See also id.* Separate and Partially Dissenting Opinion of Judge Marchi-Uhel ¶¶ 67–68.

85. *Id.* ¶ 97.

86. Interview with Elisabeth Simonneau Fort, International Lead Co-Lawyer for Case 002 ECCC Civil Parties, Phnom Penh (June 1, 2012) (arguing that "It is a judicial process, not reconciliation" and that PTC judges were loath to deal with the issue of selecting among prospective civil parties). *Cf.* Anushka Sehmi, *New Victim Participation Regime in Kenya,* VRWG Bulletin, Issue 22 (Spring 2013), *available at* http://www.redress.org/newsletters/vrwg-bulletin (noting with concern that the novel collective approach for registering victim participants in the ICC's Kenya cases could reduce the integrity of the victim participation regime by undercutting the causal link between individual victims' harms and the alleged crime). *See generally* Prosecutor v. Ruto & Sang, Case No. ICC-01/09-01/11, Decision on Victims' Representation and Participation (Oct. 3, 2012) [hereinafter *Ruto & Sang* Decision].

87. Sulzer interview, *supra* note 18.

88. Severance Order Pursuant to Internal Rule 89*ter*, Case No. 002/19-9-2007-ECCC/TC, ¶ 8 (Sept. 22, 2011).

89. Lead Co Lawyers and Civil Party Lawyers Request for Reconsideration of the Terms of the Severance Order E124, Case No. 002/19-9-2007-ECCC/TC (Oct. 18, 2011); Urgent Request on the Scope of Trial One and the Need for a Reasoned Decision Following the Civil Parties Request for Reconsideration of the Severance Order, Case No. 002/19-9-2007-ECCC/TC, ¶ 8 (Nov. 17, 2011) [hereinafter Urgent Request on the Scope of Trial One]. *See also id.* ¶ 9 (requesting that the Trial Chamber "clarify the legal criteria and threshold that must be met in order for Civil Parties to participate in the first trial of Case 002").

90. *See* Lead Co-Lawyers Urgent Request on the 19 October 2011 Hearing Following the Chambers' Memorandum E125, ¶¶ 12–13 (Trial Chamber, Oct. 7, 2011).

91. Decision on Severance of Case 002 following Supreme Court Chamber Decision of 8 February 2013, Case No. 002/19-09-2007/ECCC/TC, ¶ 157 (Apr. 26, 2013) [hereinafter 2013 Severance Decision] ("[T]he Trial Chamber has not sought to re-open admissibility decisions taken during the pre-trial phase and . . . membership of the consolidated group also remains unchanged following renewed severance of Case 002.").

92. *See, e.g.,* Sulzer interview, *supra* note 18 (noting with concern that because of the PTC decision admitting everyone in Case 002 and the severance decision, many victims will never have their claims discussed in court). Former Civil Party Lawyer Silke Studzinsky said, "The severance order has a huge impact on more than 70 percent of our clients . . .

Their participation rights are moot. They cannot address the crimes and the suffering for which they are admitted [as civil parties]." Julia Wallace, *'Mini-Trials' a Mixed Blessing for KR Victims*, CAMBODIA DAILY, July 11, 2012.

93. Simonneau Fort interview, *supra* note 86. Interview with Nushin Sarkarati, ECCC civil party lawyer, Phnom Penh (Nov. 15, 2012) (noting that her U.S.-based clients say their main reason for participating is the opportunity to contribute to a judgment, followed secondarily by their wish to be recognized as victims).

94. Order on Admissibility of the Civil Party Application of Rob Hamill, Case No. 003/07-9-2009-ECCC-OCIJ, ¶ 6 (Apr. 29, 2011).

95. *Id.* ¶ 8.

96. Order on the Admissibility of the Civil Party Application of [REDACTED], Case No. 003/07-9-2009-ECCC-OCIJ, ¶ 5 (July 27, 2011).

97. *Id.* ¶ 9.

98. *Id.* ¶ 10.

99. *See, e.g.*, UN Declaration, *supra* note 5, §A.2 ("The term 'victim' also includes, where appropriate, the immediate family or dependants of the direct victim and persons who have suffered harm in intervening to assist victims in distress or to prevent victimization"). In supreme understatement, the international PTC judges noted on appeal that "the approach and procedures in the judicial investigation for Case 003 are significantly different from those taken in Case 001 and 002"). Considerations of the Pre-Trial Chamber Regarding the Appeal Against Order on the Admissibility of Civil Party Applicant Rob Hamill, Case No 003/07-9-ECCC/OCIJ (PTC02), Opinion of Judges Lahuis and Downing ¶ 2 (Oct. 24, 2011).

100. *See* PTC Decision on Case 002 Civil Party Applications, *supra* note 77, ¶ 29.

101. Considerations of the Pre-Trial Chamber Regarding the Appeal Against Order on the Admissibility of Civil Party Applicant [REDACTED], Separate opinion of Downing & Chung ¶¶ 27–37 (Feb. 13, 2013) (finding that the decision violated "legal certainty and equality before the law," contravened the intention of the Internal Rules as well as national and international practice, lacked reasoning, and violated the fundamental rights of victims). When reserve international CIJ Kasper-Ansermet took office, he admitted both rejected civil parties on reconsideration, a decision adopted by his successor Judge Harmon. *See* Lawyers Recognition Decision Concerning All Civil Party Applications on Case File No. 003, Case No. 003/07-09-2009-ECCC-OCIJ, ¶ 8 (Feb. 26, 2013).

102. *See, e.g.*, War Crimes Research Office, *Efficient Representation of Victims at the International Criminal Court* (Dec. 2011), at 16–18 (noting that the ICC Victims Participation and Reparations Section has been unable to process victim participation applications in time to ensure all applicants are able to participate in confirmation hearings). Due to the large number of victims seeking to participate, the ICC Assembly of State Parties is currently reevaluating the practicality of the ICC's individualized approach to victim participation. *See generally* Report of the Court on the Review of the System for Victims

to Apply to Participate in Proceedings, ICC-ASP/11/22 (Nov. 5, 2012); REDRESS, The Participation of Victims in International Criminal Court Proceedings: A Review of the Practice and Considerations of Options for the Future (Oct. 2012).

103. *See* Douglas Gillison, *KR Judges Discuss Future Role of Civil Parties*, CAMBODIA DAILY, Sept. 4, 2009.

104. *See, e.g.*, Interview with Craig Etcheson, former investigator in the ECCC Office of the Co-Prosecutors, via telephone (Oct. 22, 2012).

105. ECCC Internal Rules (rev. 8), *supra* note 15, r. 23(1).

106. *See id.* r. 55(1), 74(4), 80(2), 86, 88(1), 89(2), 90(2), 91(1), 92, 94(1)(a).

107. *See generally* Co-Lawyers for the Civil Parties' Fourth Investigative Request Concerning Forced Marriages and Sexually Related Crimes, Case No. 002/19-9-2007-ECCC/OCIJ (Dec. 4, 2009); Order on Request for Investigative Action Concerning Forced Marriages and Forced Sexual Relations, Case No. 002/19-9-2007-ECCC/OCIJ (Dec. 18, 2009).

108. *See* Press Release, *Statement by the International Co-Prosecutor Regarding Case File 004* (June 16, 2011).

109. ECCC Law, *supra* note 9, art. 35 new(c).

110. Jerome de Hemptinne, *The Creation of Investigating Chambers at the International Criminal Court*, 5 J. INT'L CRIM. JUST. 402, 412 (2007).

111. Case of Berger v. Fr., ECHR App. No. 48221/99, ¶ 38 (Dec. 3, 2002).

112. *Id.* ¶ 30.

113. *Id.*

114. *See* Decision on Civil Party Participation in Provisional Detention Appeals, Case No 002/19-9-2007-ECCC/OCIJ (PTC01), ¶ 5 (Mar. 20, 2008).

115. Rome Statute of the International Criminal Court, art. 68(3), July 17, 1998, 2187 U.N.T.S. 90 (entered into force on July 1, 2002). *See also* Statute of the Special Tribunal for Lebanon, art. 17, Annex, U.N. Doc S/RES/1957 (May 30, 2007) ("Where the personal interests of the victims are affected, the Special Tribunal shall permit their views and concerns to be presented and considered at stages of the proceedings determined to be appropriate by the Pre-Trial Judge or the Chamber and in a manner that is not prejudicial to or inconsistent with the rights of the accused and a fair and impartial trial.").

116. Prosecutor v. Lubanga Dyilo, Case No. 01/04-1/06, Decision on Victims' Participation, ¶ 101(Trial Chamber, Jan. 18, 2008). *But see generally Ruto & Sang* Decision, *supra* note 86 (establishing a new simplified mode of "collective" participation for Kenyan victims participating only through a common legal representative).

117. *See, e.g.*, ECCC Internal Rules (rev. 8), *supra* note 15, r. 55(10),(11) (authorizing civil parties to request the CIJs to make orders and undertake investigative actions and to consult the case file); r. 59(5) (authorizing civil parties to request the CIJs to "interview him or her, question witnesses, go to a site, order expertise or collect other evidence on his or her behalf"); r. 74(4) (authorizing civil parties to appeal against certain orders of Co-

Investigating Judges, including primarily those relating to investigative actions and civil party applications). *See also* CPC, *supra* note 15, art. 134.

118. Prosecutor v. Lubanga Dyilo, Case No. 01/04-1/06(OA 8), Decision of the Appeals Chamber on the Joint Application of Victims a/0001/06 to a/0003/06 and a/0105/06 concerning the "Directions and Decision of the Appeals Chamber of 2 February 2007, Separate Opinion of Judge Georghios M. Pikis ¶ 11 (Appeals Chamber, June 13, 2007). *See also* Situation in the Democratic Republic of the Congo, ICC-01/04–556, Judgment on Victim Participation in the Investigation Stage of the Proceedings in the Appeal of the OPCD . . . , ¶ 55 (Appeals Chamber, Dec. 19, 2008) (noting that "participation pursuant to article 68(3) . . . does not equate victims[. . .] to parties to the proceedings before a Chamber[.]").

119. Decision on Civil Party Participation in Provisional Detention Appeals, Case No. 002/19-9-2007-ECCC/OCIJ (PTC01), ¶ 36 (Mar. 20, 2008). *See also id.* ¶ 38.

120. *See* ECCC Internal Rules (original) *supra* note 16, r. 94(a) (providing the opportunity for the "lawyers" of civil parties to make a closing statement).

121. Written Version of Oral Decision of 1 July 8 on the Civil Party's Request to Address the Court in Person, Case No. 002/19-9-2007-ECCC/OCIJ (PTC03), ¶ 3 (July 3, 2008) [hereinafter Decision on Request to Address the Court] (finding that Rule 77(10) clearly prescribes "that the Civil Party is not permitted to address the Court in person"). *See* Internal Rules of the ECCC (rev. 1), *rev'd* Feb. 1, 2008, r. 77(10) (providing in part with regard to the procedure for pretrial appeals: "the Co-Prosecutors and the lawyers for the parties may present brief observations").

122. Decision on Application for Reconsideration of Civil Party's Right to Address Pre-Trial Chamber in Person, Case No. 002/19-9-2007-ECCC/OCIJ (PTC03), ¶ 6 (Aug. 28, 2008). *See also* Mahdev Mohan, *The Paradox of Victim-Centrism: Victim Participation at the Khmer Rouge Tribunal*, 9 Int'l Crim. L. Rev. 733, 752–54 (2010) (noting the perception that by promoting her individual interests in the proceedings, the civil party had precipitated restrictions on civil parties' active involvement).

123. Decision on Request to Address the Court, *supra* note 121, Dissenting Opinion of Judge Downing ¶ 3. *See also* Decision on Application for Reconsideration of Civil Party's Right to Address Pre-Trial Chamber in Person, Case No. 002/19-9-2007-ECCC/OCIJ (PTC03), ¶ 20 (Aug. 28, 2008) [hereinafter PTC Decision on Application for Reconsideration] (citing arguments by civil party lawyers that the obligation to have a lawyer "would be unjust in the absence of funds for legal representation being provided by the ECCC").

124. PTC Decision on Application for Reconsideration, *supra* note 123, ¶ 22.

125. Directions on Unrepresented Civil Parties' Right to Address the Pre-Trial Chamber in Person, Case No. 002/19-9-2007-ECCC/OCIJ (PTC03), ¶¶ 9–10 (Aug. 29, 2008). *See also id.* at 4 (requiring notice in writing explaining the content and relevance of the proposed submission at least 10 days prior to a hearing).

126. CPC, *supra* note 15, art. 326 (providing in part, "The presiding judge shall listen to

the statements of civil parties, civil defendants, victims, witnesses and experts in the order which he deems useful").

127. ECCC Internal Rules (rev. 6), *supra* note 45, r. 23*ter*(2). *Cf.* Special Tribunal for Lebanon Rules of Procedure and Evidence, *as amended* Feb. 20, 2013, r. 86(C)(ii) [hereinafter STL Rules] (providing, "A victim participating in the proceedings may only do so through a legal representative unless the Pre-Trial Judge authorises otherwise"). Although not explicit, it appears that at the ICC victims are also mandated to participate through their legal representative. *See* ICC Rules, *supra* note 54, r. 90.

128. Bates, *supra* note 22, ¶ 110.

129. Transcript of Trial Proceedings—Kaing Guek Eav "Duch," Case No. 001/18-7-2007-ECCC/TC, at 64 (Aug. 20, 2009).

130. Michael Saliba, *Interview with Alain Werner*, CAMBODIA TRIBUNAL MONITOR (Sept. 21, 2009), *at* http://www.cambodiatribunal.org/sites/default/files/ctm_blog_9-21-2009_.pdf. *See generally* Stover et al., *supra* note 27 (analyzing the experience of the 22 civil parties who testified).

131. Decision on the Request of the Co-Lawyers for Civil Parties Group 2 to Make an Opening Statement During the Substantive Hearing, Case No. 001/18-7-2007-ECCC/TC (Mar. 27, 2009) [hereinafter Decision on the Request of Group 2]; Trial Chamber response to Lead Co-lawyers and Civil Party lawyers' request to make a brief preliminary remarks on behalf of Civil Parties (E131/4), Case No. 002/19-9-2007-ECCC/TC (Nov. 15, 2011) [hereinafter Response to Request to Make Preliminary Remarks].

132. ECCC Internal Rules (rev. 8), *supra* note 15, r. 89*bis*

133. Decision on the Request of Group 2, *supra* note 131, ¶ 7.

134. Lead Co-lawyers and Civil Party Lawyers' Request to Make Brief Preliminary Remarks on Behalf of Civil Parties After Co-Prosecutors' Opening Statement, Case No. 002/19-9-2007-ECCC/TC, ¶¶ 6–7 (Nov. 2, 2011).

135. *Id.* ¶ 22.

136. Response to Request to Make a Preliminary Remarks, *supra* note 131, at 1.

137. *See, e.g.*, Interview with Andrew Ianuzzi, former Legal Consultant to Nuon Chea, Phnom Penh (May 29, 2012).

138. ICC Rules, *supra* note 54, r. 89(1) ("[T]he Chamber shall . . . specify the proceedings and manner in which participation is considered appropriate, which may include making opening and closing statements").

139. Decision on Civil Party Co-Lawyers' Joint Request for a Ruling on the Standing of the Civil Party Lawyers to Make Submissions on Sentencing and Directions Concerning the Questioning of the Accused, Experts and Witnesses Testifying on Character, Case No. 001/18-7-2007/ECCC/TC, Dissenting Opinion of Judge Lavergne ¶ 8 (Trial Chamber, Oct. 9, 2009).

140. *Id.*, Dissenting Opinion of Judge Lavergne ¶ 4.

141. *Id.*, Dissenting Opinion of Judge Lavergne ¶ 13 (stating that "[a]ny other interpretation can only be contrary to the law").

142. *Id.*, Dissenting Opinion of Judge Lavergne ¶¶ 16, 35.

143. Prosecutor v. Lubanga Dyilo, Case No. ICC-01/04-1/06, Scheduling Order Concerning Timetable for Sentencing and Reparations, ¶ 3 (Trial Chamber, Mar. 14, 2012).

144. STL Rules, *supra* note 127, r. 87(C) (providing, "[a]t the sentencing stage, subject to the authorisation by the Trial Chamber, a victim participating in the proceedings may be heard by the Trial Chamber or file written submissions relating to the personal impact of the crimes on them").

145. Julia Wallace, *Losing Civil Parties in Cambodia*, 143 INT'L JUSTICE TRIB. (Jan. 18, 2012). *See also* Sarkarati interview, *supra* note 93 (noting that with the 11 civil party legal teams in Case 002 often disagreeing among themselves, the lead co-lawyer system promotes coherence and efficiency).

146. Sulzer interview, *supra* note 18. *See, e.g., Ruto & Sang* Decision, *supra* note 86, ¶¶ 36, 43; *Report of the Court on the Review of the System for Victims to Apply to Participate in Proceedings*, ICC-ASP/11/22 (Nov. 5, 2012) (considering a range of options for dealing with victims' applications, including a "fully collective application process leading to collective participation in proceedings"); ICC Assembly of States Parties, Victims and Reparations, ICC-ICC-ASP-11/Res.7 (Nov. 21, 2012) ("*request[ing]* the Bureau to prepare, in consultation with the Court, any amendments to the legal framework for the implementation of a predominantly collective approach in the system for victims to apply to participate in the proceedings").

147. *See* ECCC Internal Rules (original), *supra* note 16, r. 23(8)(c),(d). *Cf.* ICC Rules, *supra* note 54, r. 90(4) (providing that the court shall take "all reasonable steps to ensure that in the selection of common legal representatives, the distinct interests of the victims, . . . are represented and that any conflict of interest is avoided"). At the ICC, before assigning common representation the court considers "tensions between them in terms of ethnicity, age, gender or the type of crimes they were allegedly the victim of." *Katanga* Order, *supra* note 54, ¶ 12(b). Thus in the *Katanga* case, the Trial Court found it appropriate to assign common representation to two different groups: one general group of victims, and one group of victims who had been child soldiers. *See id.* ¶¶ 6, 12(c), 13.

148. ECCC Internal Rules (rev. 8), *supra* note 15, r. 12*ter*(3).

149. Instead, the Lead Co-Lawyers are tasked with developing their own internal procedures "in consultation" with the civil party lawyers. *See id.* Comparatively, an ICC Trial Chamber has said that if a conflict of interest arises, it may split the consolidated group. *See Katanga* Order, *supra* note 54, ¶ 16 ("In case the conflicting instructions are irreconcilable with representation by one common legal representative, and thus amount to a conflict of interest, the common legal representative shall inform the Chamber immediately, who will take appropriate measures and may, for example, appoint the Office of Public Counsel for the Victims to represent one group of victims with regard to the specific issue which gives rise to the conflict of interest.").

150. ECCC Internal Rules (rev. 8), *supra* note 15, r. 12*ter*(6).

151. *See* Request for Admission of Belated Filing According to Article 10.2 and 9 of the Practice Direction, Case No. 002/19-9-2007-ECCC/TC, ¶¶ 7–9 (Mar. 21, 2011).

152. *See id.* ¶ 14.

153. ECCC Internal Rules (rev. 5), *supra* note 20, r. 12 *ter.*

154. *Id.*, r. 12*ter*(5)(b).

155. Comparatively, an ICC Trial Chamber has emphasized, "The common legal representative shall be responsible for both representing the common interests of the victims during the proceedings and for acting on behalf of specific victims when their individual interests are at stake." *Katanga* Order, *supra* note 54, ¶ 13.

156. Christine Van den Wyngaert, *Victims Before International Courts, Some Views and Concerns of an ICC Trial Judge*, Case West Res. Univ. (Nov. 21, 2011) [hereinafter Van den Wyngaert] at 12.

157. Wallace, *supra* note 145 (paraphrasing her comments).

158. *Id.*

159. Indeed, some say the Lead Co-Lawyers are too deferential to the civil party teams and fail to exercise their authority to select a course of action when consensus cannot be reached, reducing the effectiveness of the group.

160. *See* Urgent Request for the Trial Chamber to Amend Memorandum E62/3/10 (formerly E106), Case No. 002/19-9-2007-ECCC/TC, ¶¶ 5–6 (July 15, 2011).

161. *Id.* ¶ 17.

162. *Id.* ¶ 14.

163. *Id.* ¶ 20.

164. Decision on Lead Co-Lawyer's "Urgent Request for the Trial Chamber to Amend Memorandum E62/3/10 (formerly E106)" (E62/3/10/1), Case No. 002/19-9-2007-ECCC/TC, at 2 (July 29, 2011).

165. Dissenting Opinion of Judge Jean-Marc Lavergne Concerning the Trial Chamber Decision in Memorandum E62/3/10/4, Case No. 002/19-9-2007-ECCC/TC, ¶¶ 1, 7–10 (Aug. 23, 2011).

166. *Id.* ¶ 11.

167. *Id.* ¶¶ 12–15.

168. *See, e.g.,* Transcript of Trial Proceedings—Case 002, Case No. 002/19-9-2007-ECCC/TC, at 69–70 (June 29, 2011) (in which the Trial Chamber cautioned that "where a number of the lawyers, like in the civil parties groups, need to make their presentations, they have to make sure that there is no repetition," asking them to "allocate amongst yourselves to stand and make the presentations," and limiting presentations to two.

169. *See, e.g.,* Transcript of Trial Proceedings—Case 002, Case No. 002/19-9-2007-ECCC/TC, at 33 (June 30, 2011).

170. Indeed, it is conceivable that civil party questioning could unknowingly undermine the prosecution case. *See, e.g.,* Van den Wyngaert, *supra* note 156, at 10 (noting that

"[t]here is even a risk that a 'victim case' may, unwittingly, undermine the case of the prosecution"); Khan interview, *supra* note 57 (stating that the *Bashir* case at the ICC is showing that "civil parties can sometimes be used as a Trojan Horse to undermine the prosecution").

171. Transcript of Trial Proceedings—Case 002, Case No. 002/19-9-2007-ECCC/TC, at 30 (Feb. 2, 2012).

172. Wallace, *supra* note 145. *See also* Sarkarati interview, *supra* note 93 (noting that the judges "opened this amazing opportunity, and expectations skyrocketed" but "[n]ow they treat civil parties like an ineffective part of the process"); Urgent Request on the Scope of Trial One, *supra* note 89, ¶ 4 (discussing the fact that although the Trial Chamber had notice that civil parties were filing a request for reconsideration of the severance order, it did not wait to read their submission before issuing its decision and never ruled on the specific civil party concerns raised); Notice of Trial Chamber's Disposition of Remaining Pre-Trial Motions . . . and Further Guidance to the Civil Party Lead Co-Lawyers, 1–2 (Nov. 29, 2011) (saying it wouldn't respond to the civil party severance arguments because they were "repetitive").

173. Etcheson interview, *supra* note 104. *See also* Susana SáCouto, *Victim Participation at the International Criminal Court and the Extraordinary Chambers in the Courts of Cambodia: A Feminist Project?* 18 MICH. J. GENDER & L. 297, 324–27, 335–50 (2011–12) (emphasizing both the limitations in Case 001 and the further restrictions on civil party participation in Case 002).

174. *Cf. Ruto & Sang* Decision, *supra* note 86, ¶¶ 56–58 (limiting the right of individual participation in the Kenya situation to a few victims who are selected to express their views and concerns directly to the ICC).

175. *But see* Prosecutor v. Lubanga Dyilo, Case No. ICC-01/04-1/06, Decision Establishing the Principles and Procedures to Be Applied to Reparations, ¶ 178 (Trial Chamber, Aug. 7, 2012) [hereinafter *Lubanga* Reparations Decision] (agreeing with the Pre-Trial Chamber that "[t]he [ICC] reparation scheme . . . is not only one of the Statute's unique features. It is also a key feature. In the Chamber's opinion, the success of the Court is, to some extent, linked to the success of its reparation system.").

176. ECCC Internal Rules (rev. 8), *supra* note 15, r. 23 *quinquies*(1). The Rules define "collective and moral" as measures that: (a) acknowledge the harm suffered by civil parties as a result of the commission of the crimes for which an Accused is convicted and (b) provide benefits to the civil parties which address this harm. *Id.*

177. *Duch* Trial Chamber Judgment, *supra* note 73, ¶ 661 n. 1144.

178. ECCC Internal Rules (original), *supra* note 16, r. 23 (11).

179. *See Duch* Trial Chamber Judgment, *supra* note 73, ¶¶ 663–64; Press Release, *ECCC to Distribute the "Duch" Verdict Nationwide* (Aug. 6, 2010).

180. *See Duch* Trial Chamber Judgment, *supra* note 73, ¶¶ 667–75.

181. ECCC Internal Rules (rev. 6), *supra* note 45, r. 23*quinquies*(3)(b) (giving the judges

the power to "recognise that a specific project appropriately gives effect to the award sought by the [Civil Party] Lead Co-Lawyers and may be implemented. Such project shall have been designed or identified in cooperation with the Victims Support Section and have secured sufficient external funding").

182. Nevertheless, as of November 2012, the VSS is seeking 5 million dollars to establish a "Reconciliation Foundation of the Kingdom of Cambodia for the Victims of the Khmer Rouge Regime 1975–1979" "to implement, manage and maintain the requested reparation projects as well as nonjudicial measures and to secure their long-term funding." Draft Concept Paper of the Victims Foundation of Cambodia (on file with authors). Although the VSS is seeking international participation for the foundation's governing organs, in light of ongoing reports of rampant financial corruption in Cambodian institutions, including at the ECCC, the 2009 admonition of Youk Chhang should be taken seriously:

> In the current political and cultural climate of Cambodia, it would be impossible to establish a fund of money involving the Government or local NGOs that would be transparently administered and reach its intended beneficiaries: the victims.

Letter from Youk Chhang, Director, Documentation Center of Cambodia, to Judge Cartwright, Trial Chamber Judge, ECCC (Aug. 20, 2009) (on file with authors).

183. Trial Chamber Memorandum, *Trial Chamber's Response to the Lead Co-Lawyers' Initial Specifications of Civil Party Priority Projects as Reparations Pursuant to Rule 80 bis(4) (E218/7/1)*, ¶¶ 3, 6–7 (Aug. 1, 2013) [hereinafter TC 2013 Reparations Response]. *See generally* Lead Co-Lawyers' Indication to the Trial Chamber of the Priority Projects for Implementation As Reparations (Internal Rule 80*bis*(4) with Confidential Annexes, Case No. 002/19-09-2007-ECCC/TC (Feb. 12, 2013).

184. *See* TC 2013 Reparations Response, *supra* note 183, ¶¶ 3–5. *See also* Trial Chamber Memorandum, *Initial Specification of the Substance of Reparations Awards Sought by the Civil Party Lead Co-Lawyers Pursuant to Internal Rule 23quinquies(3)*, at 3 (Sept. 23, 2011).

185. Stuart White, *Little Time for Reparations at KRT*, PHNOM PENH POST, Aug. 7, 2013. As of July 2013, the German Federal Ministry for Economic Cooperation and Development (BMZ) had committed up to a total of EUR 400,000 for a variety of NGO reparations projects. *Judicial Updates: Reparations and Non-Judicial Measures*, ECCC COURT REPORT (Aug. 2013), at 8.

186. Sarkarati interview, *supra* note 93.

187. ECCC Internal Rules (rev. 8), *supra* note 15, r. 23 *quinquies* (1).

188. 2013 Severance Decision, *supra* note 91, ¶ 158.

189. *See, e.g.*, Cartwright, *supra* note 64 (highlighting the importance of this "enhancement," which will allow the newly named VSS "to develop and implement programmes and measures that will benefit all victims whether they are civil parties or not").

190. ECCC Internal Rules (rev. 5), *supra* note 20, r. 12*bis*(3).

191. Cartwright, *supra* note 64.

192. OSJI, *Recent Initiatives at the Extraordinary Chambers in the Courts of Cambodia* 26 (Mar. 2010).

193. Julia Wallace, *New Report Questions KRT Administration*, CAMBODIA DAILY, Feb. 24, 2012. *See also* OSJI, *Recent Developments at the Extraordinary Chambers in the Courts of Cambodia* 33 (Feb. 2012) (highlighting that victims, civil parties, and NGOs have looked to the VSS for leadership on the court's nonjudicial measures mandate but that "these initiatives are stagnating"). The VSS reports that it had developed "an action plan for a number of projects under the schemes of Reparation and Non-Judicial measures in close collaboration with all stakeholders involved." Rong Chhorng, Letter, *KRT Victims Support Section Doing What It's Supposed To*, CAMBODIA DAILY, Feb. 27, 2012. The VSS also reports that it has held meetings and conducted field visits to plan for memorials and other projects. *See, e.g.*, updates from the Victims Support Section *in* ECCC COURT REPORT (Mar. 2012), at 9; ECCC COURT REPORT (Dec. 2011), at 9; ECCC COURT REPORT (Aug. 2011), at 9. *See also* Press Release, *Victims Support Section Convenes Roundtable Discussion on Broader Support to Victims* (Sept. 8, 2010).

194. Wallace, *supra* note 193.

195. According to the partner Transcultural Psychosocial Organization Cambodia (TPO) website, it is a three-year project in partnership with VSS and the Cambodian Defenders Project (CDP) "to promote gender equality and improve access to justice" for female victims of gender-based violence under the Khmer Rouge. UN Trust Fund to End Violence Against Women has given the project $600,000 to encourage participation of female civil parties and the creation of gender-based violence self-help groups.

196. Rong, *supra* note 193.

197. Interviewees confirm that the Cambodian Defenders Project and the Transcultural Psychosocial Organization implement the majority of activities.

198. Memorandum from President of the Trial Chamber, Initial Specification of the Substance of Reparations Awards Sought by the Civil Party Lead Co-Lawyers Pursuant to Internal Rule 23*quinquies*(3), at 2 (Sept. 23, 2011) (noting that provision of expanded reparations "presupposes the development of awards . . . in parallel with the ongoing trial" and that a VSS program manager had been tasked with this responsibility).

199. *See, e.g.*, Staggs Kelsall et al., *supra* note 54, at 45–46 (calling for VSS to "adopt a greater role in ensuring non-legal measures that facilitate greater access to information about the ECCC and a greater sense of engagement with the justice process underway").

200. *See, e.g.*, Stover et al., *supra* note 27, at 43 (noting that "[d]uring the *Duch* trial, civil party participation often appeared as if it were a work-in-progress rather than a process guided by well-honed rules and procedures"); Pham et al., *supra* note 27, at 274, 284 (noting that civil parties rejected from the proceedings at judgment reacted most commonly with "anger, helplessness, shame, and feelings of worthlessness").

201. *See* John D. Ciorciari & Anne Heindel, *Trauma in the Courtroom*, *in* CAMBODIA'S INVISIBLE SCARS 121 (Daryn Reicherter & Beth Van Schaack eds., 2011).

202. *See generally* Victims Participation Before the Extraordinary Chambers in the Courts of Cambodia: Baseline Study of the Cambodian Human Rights and Development Association's Civil Party Scheme for Case 002 (Jan. 2013), *available at* http://giz-cambodia.com/?p=747 (evaluating also the broader process of civil party participation at the ECCC).

203. *But cf.* Confidential interview with senior court staff, Phnom Penh (Nov. 1, 2012) (judging civil party participation "ill-advised" on the grounds that a formalized victim participation procedure embedded in a mass crimes trial process adds length but not depth to proceedings, and has a number of other adverse spin-offs, such as high costs, heavy administrative burdens, and a tendency to promote unrealistic expectations among victims as to the likely outcomes of participation).

204. Sulzer interview, *supra* note 18.

205. Interview with Michael G. Karnavas, former Co-Lawyer for Ieng Sary, Phnom Penh (May 19, 2012) (arguing that although they are called a party and sometimes expect the "bells and whistles" of a party, civil parties' role is limited to supporting the prosecution). *See also* Ianuzzi interview, *supra* note 137 (calling civil parties "second-class citizens").

Chapter 8

1. *But see generally* Oskar N.T. Thoms et al., *State-Level Effects of Transitional Justice: What Do We Know?*, INT'L J. TRANS. JUST. 1–26 (2010) (finding the empirical evidence insufficient to support claims that transitional justice mechanisms contribute to larger policy goals such as reconciliation, psychological healing, respect for human rights or the rule of law, or increased democratic governance).

2. Elena Baylis, *Reassessing the Role of International Criminal Law: Rebuilding National Courts through Transnational Networks*, 50 B.C. L. REV. 1, 1–2 (2009) (noting that the ad hoc tribunals have had limited "on-the-ground domestic impact").

3. Report of the Secretary-General, *The Rule of Law and Transitional Justice in Conflict and Post-conflict Societies*, ¶ 44, U.N. Doc. S/2004/616 (Aug. 23, 2004).

4. *Id. See also* Laura A. Dickinson, *The Promise of Hybrid Courts*, 97 AM. J. INT'L L. 295, 307–8 (2003) (noting potential for "on-the-job training" of local judicial personnel and potential for "cross-fertilization of international and domestic norms"); Helen Horsington, *The Cambodian Khmer Rouge Tribunal: The Promise of a Hybrid Tribunal*, 5 MELBOURNE J. INT'L L. 462, 479 (2004).

5. ECCC, *Why Was This Model Chosen for the ECCC?* http://www.eccc.gov.kh/en/faq/why-was-model-chosen-eccc (visited Aug. 17, 2013).

6. ECCC, *Legacy*, http://www.eccc.gov.kh/en/dss/legacy (visited Aug. 13, 2013).

7. Clara Ramírez, *Making an Impact* 9–10, Int'l Ctr. for Trans. Just. (Jan. 2011); Victor Peskin, *Courting Rwanda: The Promises and Pitfalls of the ICTR Outreach Programme*, 3 J. INT'L CRIM. JUST. 950, 953–54 (2005) (discussing both the "transparency" and "engagement" outreach models). *See generally* Mychelle Balthazard, Cambodians' Knowledge and Attitudes Towards the Cambodian Post-Conflict Justice Process (2012) (unpublished Ph.D. dissertation, Tulane University) (comparing the outreach models adopted by internationalized courts including the ECCC).

8. International Criminal Court, *Integrated Strategy for External Relations, Public Information and Outreach*, §IV(2), *at* http://www.icc-cpi.int/NR/rdonlyres/425E80BA-1EBC-4423-85C6-D4F2B93C7506/185049/ICCPIDSWBOR0307070402_IS_En.pdf (visited Aug. 13, 2013). *See also* RAMÍREZ, *supra* note 7, at 7 (defining outreach as a "combination of materials and activities . . . to build *direct* channels of communication with affected communities").

9. Ou Virak, *Letter to the Editor: KRT Has Potential to Strengthen Cambodia's Justice System*, CAMBODIA DAILY, Sept. 14, 2010.

10. OFF. OF THE U.N. HIGH COMM'R FOR HUM. RTS., RULE-OF-LAW TOOLS FOR POST-CONFLICT STATES 4–5 (2008) [hereinafter OHCHR Report].

11. *See id.* at 18 (asserting that "a hybrid court may be seen as largely irrelevant unless there is a robust outreach program that informs the public about its activities").

12. Human Rights Watch, *Courting History* 116 (2008).

13. David Cohen, *"Hybrid" Justice in East Timor, Sierra Leone, and Cambodia: "Lessons Learned" and Prospects for the Future*, 43 STAN. J. INT'L L. 1, 36 (2007) (calling outreach and legacy "among the most seriously under funded [areas] at all the tribunals" and arguing that "[w]ithout effective outreach, many of the courts' stated goals cannot be achieved").

14. Varda Hussain, *Sustaining Judicial Rescues: The Role of Outreach and Capacity-Building Efforts in War Crimes Tribunals*, 45 VA. J. INT'L L. 547, 581 (2005).

15. Peskin, *supra* note 7, at 955.

16. *See* Sara Darehshori, *Lessons for Outreach from the Ad Hoc Tribunals, the Special Court for Sierra Leone, and the International Criminal Court*, 14 NEW ENG. J. OF INT'L & COMP. L. 299, 302–6 (2008); Human Rights Watch, *supra* note 12, at 118–21.

17. CHANDRA LEKHA SRIRAM, A REVOLUTION IN ACCOUNTABILITY 104 (2005) (arguing that the SCSL's "outreach effort has been impressive . . . extensive, and in comparison to other tribunals, quite timely").

18. David Crane, *Dancing with the Devil: Prosecuting West Africa's Warlords—Current Lessons Learned and Challenges*, *in* ATROCITIES AND INTERNATIONAL ACCOUNTABILITY 133, 139 (Edel Hughes et al. eds., 2007).

19. *Id.* at 136.

20. Ramírez, *supra* note 7, at 10.

21. SRIRAM, *supra* note 17, at 104–5.

22. Thierry Cruvellier, *From the Taylor Trial to a Lasting Legacy: Putting the Special*

Court Model to the Text, Int'l Ctr. for Trans. Just. and Sierra Leone Court Monitoring Programme, at 29 (2009).

23. *See generally* Rachel Kerr & Jessica Lincoln, *The Special Court for Sierra Leone—Outreach, Legacy and Impact: Final Report,* War Crimes Research Group Department of War Studies Kings College London (Feb. 2008); *id.* at 14 (finding that Sierra Leoneans' "general knowledge [of the court] was high but depth of understanding was poor").

24. Sriram, *supra* note 17, at 104–5. The European Union funded most of the SCSL's outreach efforts. Ramírez, *supra* note 7, at 12.

25. Nehal Bhuta, *Great Expectations—East Timor and the Vicissitudes of Externalised Justice,* 12 Finnish Y.B. Int'l L. 179, 197–98 (2001); Mark Dodd, *Massacres Go Unpunished as UN Crimes Unit Heads for Collapse,* Sydney Morning Herald, May 25, 2001.

26. Cohen, *supra* note 13, at 18.

27. *Id.*

28. *Id.*

29. Correspondence with Peter Foster, former UNAKRT Public Affairs Officer, June 13, 2012 (adding that during his interview for his position, he was asked how he would deal with "a colleague or supervisor who was actively working against [him]").

30. Tracey Gurd, *Outreach in Cambodia: An Opportunity Too Good to Miss, in* Justice Initiatives: The Extraordinary Chambers, Open Society Justice Initiative (Spring 2006), at 123–24.

31. Interview with Craig Etcheson, former investigator in the ECCC Office of the Co-Prosecutors, via telephone (Oct. 22, 2012).

32. Extraordinary Chambers in the Courts of Cambodia, Internal Rules, June 12, 2007 [hereinafter ECCC Internal Rules (original), r. 9(4).

33. *Id.* r. 12 (h).

34. In February 2010, the ECCC judges updated the Internal Rules and expanded the mandate of the renamed Victim Support Section to include working with NGOs and government agencies to develop and implement "programs and measures other than those of a legal nature addressing the broader interests of victims." Extraordinary Chambers in the Courts of Cambodia, Internal Rules [rev. 5], *rev'd* Feb. 5, 2010, r. 12 *bis* (2).

35. International Center for Transitional Justice, *Outreach Strategies in International and Hybrid Courts,* Report of the ICTJ-ECCC Workshop (Apr. 2010), at 5 [hereinafter ICTJ Report]; Foster correspondence, *supra* note 29.

36. *Id.*

37. *See* a list of ECCC events *at* http://www.eccc.gov.kh/en/media-center/activities-outreach.

38. Foster correspondence, *supra* note 29.

39. *Id.*

40. ICTJ Report, *supra* note 35, at 5.

41. Cable 06PHNOMPENH1983, U.S. Embassy Phnom Penh, *Recent ECCC Developments* ¶ 3 (Nov. 2, 2006), http://dazzlepod.com/06PHNOMPENH1983. *See also*

Cable 06PHNOMPENH1845, U.S. Embassy Phnom Penh, *Cambodia's ECCC Making Good Progress* ¶ 6 (Oct. 10, 2006), http://dazzlepod.com/06PHNOMPENH1845.

42. Cable 06PHNOMPENH1983, *supra* note 41, ¶ 8 (paraphrasing Tolbert).

43. Open Society Justice Initiative (OSJI), *Recent Developments at the Extraordinary Chambers in the Courts of Cambodia* 11 (Dec. 2007) [hereinafter OSJI Dec. 2007 Update].

44. *See, e.g.*, ECCC, *Revised Budget Estimates from 2005 to 2009* 36–37 (July 2008).

45. ECCC, *Proposed Budget for 2012–2013* 37–38, 44 (Feb. 17, 2012).

46. ECCC, *Revised Budget Requirements, 2010–2011* 16, 19 (Jan. 24, 2011); ECCC, *ECCC Revised Budget Requirements—2012–2013*, at 12, 16 (Jan. 29, 2013).

47. *See* Norman Henry Pentelovitch, Note, *Seeing Justice Done: The Importance of Prioritizing Outreach Efforts at International Criminal Tribunals*, 39 GEO. J. INT'L L. 446, 465–80 (2007–8).

48. Cable 06PHNOMPENH1983, *supra* note 41, ¶ 3 (quoting OA Director Sean Visoth).

49. Christoph Sperfeldt, *Cambodian Civil Society and the Khmer Rouge Tribunal*, INT'L J. TRANS. JUST. 1, 10 (2012).

50. *Id.* at 4–5. *See also* Pentelovitch, *supra* note 47, at 490–91 (arguing that overreliance on NGOs can result in "garbled, politicized, and confusing messages").

51. Sperfeldt, *supra* note 49, at 5. *See also* OHCHR Report, *supra* note 10, at 20 (recommending that hybrid courts employ such an officer). *Cf.* Pentelovitch, *supra* note 47, at 469–70, 489–90 (asserting that as of early 2008 the ECCC kept civil society "at arm[']s length with regard to planning and feedback of outreach activities" and contending that in this regard, the ECCC had an "institutional under-reliance on civil society").

52. Email from Mychelle Balthazard, Ph.D. (focus on ECCC outreach) (Nov. 4, 2012) (on file with author, citing EVERETT M. RODGERS, DIFFUSION OF INNOVATION 205 (5th ed. 2003)).

53. Interview with Panhavuth Long, Program Officer, Cambodian Justice Initiative, Phnom Penh (July 6, 2012).

54. For online copies, *see* ECCC COURT REPORT, http://www.eccc.gov.kh/en/articles/new-issue-eccc-court-report.

55. ECCC, *Trial Chamber Verdict: Case 001 Kaing Guek Eav alias Duch*, *available at* http://www.eccc.gov.kh/sites/default/files/publications/verdict_leaflet_english.pdf; ECCC, *How Can You Apply to Become a Civil Party in Cases 003 and 004?*, *available at* www.eccc.gov.kh/sites/default/files/publications/01-CPleafletEnglish.pdf.

56. *See generally* www.eccc.gov.kh and www.cambodiatribunal.org.

57. Pentelovitch, *supra* note 47, at 466 (arguing that the printed materials "missed the mark" of educating ordinary survivors).

58. ECCC posters have featured drawings relevant to the Court and messages such as "Every decision must have the support of both Cambodian and International Judges" and "Everyone can be involved in the process." *See* ECCC, *Posters*, http://www.eccc.gov.kh/en/public-affair/publication/poster (visited Aug. 13, 2013). Stickers say "I support the KR

Trials: Moving forward through justice." *See* ECCC, *Stickers*, http://www.eccc.gov.kh/en/public-affair/publication/sticker (visited Aug. 13, 2013).

59. Information and MP3s are *available at* http://www.eccc.gov.kh/en/media-center/weekly-radio.

60. *See* ECCC COURT REPORT (Jan. 2013), at 6; ECCC COURT REPORT (Sept. 2013), at 10.

61. Douglas Gillison & Pin Sisovan, *ECCC Judges to Hold Public Forum in Pailin*, CAMBODIA DAILY, Jan. 15, 2008.

62. Peter Manning, *Governing Memory: Justice, Reconciliation and Outreach at the Extraordinary Chambers in the Courts of Cambodia*, MEMORY STUDIES 1, 3 (2011).

63. *Id.* at 4–5.

64. *See, e.g.*, Savina Sirik, *Village Forum: Reactions to the Senior Khmer Rouge Leaders' Remarks* (Mar. 2010), http://www.d.dccam.org/Projects/Living_Doc/pdf/Pursat_Field_Report.pdf (visited Aug. 13, 2013); *DC-Cam Village Forum in Phnom Voar Commune* (Sept. 29, 2010), http://vimeo.com/16070457 (visited Aug. 13, 2013).

65. Funding for ADHOC's program expired in 2010. Thet Sambath, *Adhoc Halts ECCC Outreach as Programme's Funding Dwindles*, PHNOM PENH POST, Apr. 5, 2010.

66. Agreement between the United Nations and the Royal Government of Cambodia Concerning the Prosecution under Cambodian Law of Crimes Committed During the Period of Democratic Kampuchea art. 12 (June 6, 2003) (citing article 14 of the International Covenant on Civil and Political Rights and indicating that any deviation must be "strictly necessary").

67. Law on the Establishment of Extraordinary Chambers in the Courts of Cambodia for the Prosecution of Crimes Committed During the Period of Democratic Kampuchea, as amended and promulgated on Oct. 27, 2004, NS/RKM/1004/006, art. 34 new. Under the Internal Rules, the Pre-Trial Chamber proceedings are *in camera* unless the Chamber decides otherwise at the request of one of the judges or parties. Internal Rules of the ECCC [rev. 8], *rev'd* Aug. 3, 2011, r. 77(6) [hereinafter ECCC Internal Rules (rev. 8)].

68. ECCC Internal Rules (rev. 8), *supra* note 67, r. 79(6)(a). Exceptions are made when the Chamber believes that a public hearing "would be prejudicial to public order" or would violate necessary protective measures. *Id.* r. 79(6)(b).

69. Yoshi Kodama, *For Judicial Justice and Reconciliation in Cambodia: Reflections upon the Establishment of the Khmer Rouge Trials and the Trials' Procedural Rules 2007*, 9 L. & PRAC. OF INT'L CTS. & TRIBUNALS 37, 104–5 (2010).

70. Heather Ryan, *Learning from the East: Lessons for Africa from Cambodia's Genocide Trials*, Open Society Initiative for Southern Africa (Mar. 7, 2012), *available at* http://www.osisa.org/sites/default/files/lessons_for_africa_from_cambodia_genocide_trials__heather_ryan.pdf, at 73; ICTJ Report, *supra* note 35, at 10 n. 10 (estimating that an average of 360 people per day attended the trials in addition to media).

71. Human Rights Watch, *Justice in Motion* 32 (Nov. 2005).

72. Kheang Un & Judy Ledgerwood, *Is the Trial of 'Duch' a Catalyst for Change in Cambodia's Courts?* 95 ASIA PACIFIC ISSUES 5 (E.-W. Ctr., June 2010).

73. ECCC, *ECCC Surpasses 100,000 Visitors Milestone*, http://www.eccc.gov.kh/en/articles/eccc-surpasses-100000-visitors-milestone (visited Aug. 17, 2013).

74. *See Evidentiary Hearings End, Final Statements Set*, ECCC Court Report (Aug. 2013), at 2.

75. *See id.*

76. Interview with Huy Vannak, former ECCC Public Affairs Officer, Phnom Penh (June 11, 2012).

77. Confidential questionnaire to Cambodian ECCC Personnel, Respondent No. 2, June 2012 [hereinafter ECCC Respondent No. 2] (on file with the authors).

78. Huy interview, *supra* note 76.

79. *See, e.g.*, Cable 09PHNOMPENH626, U.S. Embassy Phnom Penh, *Khmer Rouge Tribunal: The Trial of S-21 Interrogation Center Head Kaing Guek Eav, Week 17* ¶ 3 (Aug. 25, 2009), *available at* http://www.wikileaks.org/cablegate.html (noting that some "farmers said they had left their villages at about 2 AM to take the ECCC buses to the court" and that others "complained that they had not been prepared for the trip to Phnom Penh and the length of the proceedings"); Cable 09PHNOMPENH645, U.S. Embassy Phnom Penh, *Khmer Rouge Tribunal: The Trial of S-21 Interrogation Center Head Kaing Guek Eav, Week 18* ¶ 3 (Sept. 1, 2009), *available at* http://www.wikileaks.org/cablegate.html (noting that most of the villagers attending "had to leave before the trial ended").

80. Huy interview, *supra* note 76. *Cf.* Cable 09PHNOMPENH58, U.S. Embassy Phnom Penh, *Khmer Rouge Tribunal: Results of Public Perception Survey* ¶ 8 (Jan. 23, 2009), *available at* http://www.wikileaks.org/cablegate.html ("What media cannot provide for Cambodians is a sense of participation or greater buy-in of the process through opportunities to ask questions and discuss personal accounts.").

81. Phuong Pham et al., *So We Will Never Forget: A Population-Based Survey on Knowledge and Perception of Justice and the Extraordinary Chambers in the Courts of Cambodia* (Jan. 2009), at 36.

82. Phuong Pham et al., *After the First Trial: A Population-Based Survey on Knowledge and Perception of Justice and the Extraordinary Chambers in the Courts of Cambodia* (June 2011), at 21.

83. *Id.* at 23.

84. *Id.* at 22. For Case 002, Asian International Justice Initiative is again collaborating with Mekong Films, with sponsorship by the U.S. Department of State, to broadcast a half-hour TV show about weekly court developments called "Facing Justice." They have a companion show on radio, where listeners can call in and ask questions about the proceedings from Cambodian experts. Interview with Kris Baleva, Asian International Justice Initiative, Phnom Penh (July 5, 2012).

85. Confidential interview with national staff. *See also* Kaing Menghun & Colin Meyn, *Study Shows Newspapers' Penchant for Violence*, Cambodia Daily, Sept. 28, 2012 (noting scant ECCC coverage by Khmer-language newspapers due to "a lack of reader interest in the day-to-day happenings at the court," which Pen Samithy, presi-

dent of the Cambodian Club of Journalists, attributes to the fact that "[t]he process is boring").

86. *See* Julia Wallace, *'Mini-Trials' a Mixed Blessing for KR Victims*, CAMBODIA DAILY, July 11, 2012.

87. Long interview, *supra* note 53.

88. Foster correspondence, *supra* note 29 (adding that due to the office's hybrid structure under Cambodian leadership, he "could easily have ended up in a corner office completely shut out of any national outreach activities").

89. *Id.*

90. *Id.*

91. *Id.* (calling this "the biggest difference" in national and international approaches to outreach and noting that Cambodian appointees in the public affairs office were committed to two-way exchange).

92. Confidential interview with national staff.

93. OSJI, *Progress and Challenges at the Extraordinary Chambers in the Courts of Cambodia* 14 (2007).

94. Foster correspondence, *supra* note 29.

95. ICTJ Report, *supra* note 35 (noting that the two-sided nature of the Court had "created some confusion" in relation to outreach).

96. Douglas Gillison, *KRT Begins Investigation of Five New Regime Suspects*, CAMBODIA DAILY, June 8, 2010 (emphasis added).

97. *Id.*

98. Request for Investigation pursuant to Rule 35, Case No. 002/19-9-2007-ECCC/TC (Apr. 28, 2011), ¶ 8 (citing an OCIJ Internal Memorandum dated June 8, 2010).

99. Douglas Gillison, *Khmer Rouge Tribunal Judge Backs Out of New Inquiries*, CAMBODIA DAILY, June 10, 2010; Douglas Gillison, *KR Judge Does Not Sign on to New Investigations*, CAMBODIA DAILY, June 9, 2010.

100. Reach Sambath, Letter, *KRT's UN Side Wasn't Warned of Media Alert*, CAMBODIA DAILY, June 11, 2010. *See also* Gillison, *Judge Backs Out of New Inquiries*, *supra* note 99 (quoting the UN spokesperson saying that the Cambodian statement was "sent without the prior knowledge of the UN side and was not approved and endorsed by the UN side").

101. Confidential questionnaire to Cambodian ECCC Personnel, Respondent No. 4, June 2012 [hereinafter ECCC Respondent No. 4] (on file with the authors).

102. ECCC Internal Rules (rev. 8), *supra* note 67, r. 56.

103. Long interview, *supra* note 53.

104. *See* Press Release, *Statement from the Co-Investigating Judges* (May 18, 2011); Order on International Co-Prosecutor's Public Statement Regarding Case File 003, Case No. 003/07-9-2009-ECCC-OCIJ (May 18, 2011); Considerations of the Pre-Trial Chamber Regarding the International Co-Prosecutor's Appeal Against the Co-Investigating Judges' Order on International Co-Prosecutor's Public Statement Regarding Case 003, Case No. 003/07-9-2009-ECCC/OCIJ (PTC03) (Oct. 24, 2011). *But cf.* Decision on Appeals

Against Orders of the Co-Investigating Judges on the Admissibility of Civil Party Applications, Case No. 002/19-9-2007-ECCC/OCIJ, ¶¶ 51–55 (June 24, 2011) (finding in Case 002 that the CIJs are obligated by Internal Rule 21(1)(c) to ensure that "victims are kept informed . . . *throughout* the proceedings" and not merely before the end of the investigation so that they are able to fully exercise their right to file civil party applications). Justice Harmon invoked this rule in unilaterally informing the public about additional crime sites under investigation in Case 004. Press Release, *Statement by the International Co-Investigating Judge Regarding Additional Crime Sites in Case 004* (Dec. 19, 2012).

105. *Id.* r. 35(1)(a) (allowing sanctions for anyone who "discloses confidential information in violation of an order of the Co-Investigating Judges or the Chambers").

106. *See* Order on Breach of Confidentiality, Case No. 002/14-8-2006 (Mar. 3, 2009). The Nuon Chea defense was similarly warned in 2012. *See* Decision on Nuon Chea Defence Counsel Misconduct, Case No. 002/14-8-2006 (Trial Chamber, June 29, 2012).

107. Letter from Ieng Sary Defense to Deputy Director Knut Rosenhaug (Dec. 18, 2008), *available at* https://sites.google.com/site/iengsarydefence/.

108. *Cf.* Alejandro Chehtman & Ruth Mackenzie, *Capacity Development in International Criminal Justice: A Mapping Exercise of Existing Practice*, DOMAC/2 at 31–32 (Sept. 2009) (noting that decisions from the Kosovo panels will not be useful to the local courts because they are generally not published).

109. *See* Krista L. Nelson, Comment, *Protecting Confidential Investigations or Gagging the Press? Freedom of Expression and Interference with the Administration of Justice at the Extraordinary Chambers in the Courts of Cambodia*, 35 SEATTLE U. L. REV. 265, 277–87 (2011).

110. Warning for Unauthorized Disclosure of Confidential Information, Case No. 002/19-9-2007-ECCC/OCIJ (PTC), ¶ 1 (July 9, 2010); Directive on Classification of Pre-Trial Chamber Documents, Case No. 002/07-7-2010-ECCC/PTC10, ¶ 5 (Sept. 9, 2010).

111. Press Release, ECCC Co-Investigating Judges, *Public Statement by the Co-Investigating Judges* (June 9, 2011), *available at* http://www.eccc.gov.kh/en/articles/public-statement-co-investigating-judges; Press Release from the Co-Investigating Judges Regarding Contempt of Court Proceedings (Aug. 31, 2009) (threatening VOA Khmer with contempt for releasing confidential information about Case 004).

112. *See* Douglas Gillison, *File on Sou Met, Meas Muth Leaks from Court*, CAMBODIA DAILY, June 10, 2011.

113. *See* Human Rights Watch, *supra* note 12, at 117 (warning the ICC and other courts to resist the temptation to produce "propaganda" or "one-sided information").

114. *See* ECCC COURT REPORT (May 2011), at 1.

115. Kong Sothanarith, *Few Take Part in Two Tribunal Cases: Monitors*, VOA KHMER (Jan. 9, 2013), http://www.voacambodia.com/content/few-take-part-in-two-tribunal-cases-monitors/1579892.html (noting a steep reduction in complaints for Cases 003 and 004 relative to Case 002 and quoting Latt Ky of the human rights group ADHOC as saying, "The fewer number of people interested is due to a lack of outreach"). As of October

2013, 1,700 persons had applied to be civil parties in Cases 003 and 004 combined, primarily due to recent outreach efforts by Judge Harmon. *See* ECCC COURT REPORT (Oct. 2013), at 5. As discussed in chapter 7, in Case 002 there were nearly 4,000 applicants.

116. *See, e.g.*, Interview with Youk Chhang, Director of the Documentation Center of Cambodia, Phnom Penh (July 10, 2012) (saying the Court created PAS to hide its mistakes, but public respect is undermined when PAS information is inconsistent with what they hear from sources outside of the Court).

117. Huy interview, *supra* note 76.

118. *See, e.g.*, Foster correspondence, *supra* note 29; Huy interview, *supra* note 76; Confidential Questionnaire to Cambodian ECCC Personnel, Respondent No. 3, June 2012 (on file with the authors); Confidential Questionnaire to Cambodian ECCC Personnel, Respondent No. 5, June 2012 (on file with the authors); Confidential Questionnaire to Cambodian ECCC Personnel, Respondent No. 6, June 2012 (on file with the authors).

119. SRIRAM, *supra* note 17, at 105.

120. *Report of the Secretary-General on Possible Options to Further the Aim of Prosecuting and Imprisoning Persons Responsible for Acts of Piracy and Armed Robbery at Sea off the Coast of Somalia . . .*, 39–40, U.N. Doc. S/2010/394 (July 26, 2010).

121. *Report of the Secretary-General on Khmer Rouge Trials*, ¶ 27, U.N. Doc. A/59/432 (Oct. 12, 2004).

122. OHCHR Report, *supra* note 10, at 15; Chandra Lekha Sriram, *Wrong-Sizing International Justice? The Hybrid Tribunal in Sierra Leone*, 29 FORDHAM INT'L L. J. 472, 502–3 (2005) (noting brain drain concerns in Sierra Leone).

123. SRIRAM, *supra* note 17, at 105.

124. *Id.* at 106–8.

125. Mohamad Suma, *The Charles Taylor Trial and Legacy of the Special Court of Sierra Leone*, Int'l Ctr. for Trans. Just. (Sept. 2009), at 2.

126. Laura A. Dickinson, *The Relationship Between Hybrid Courts and International Courts: The Case of Kosovo*, 37 NEW ENG. L. REV. 1059, 1068–70 (2002–3).

127. *See* Jane E. Stromseth, *Justice on the Ground?: International Criminal Courts and Domestic Rule of Law Building in Conflict-Affected Societies, in* GETTING TO THE RULE OF LAW 169, 199–201 (James E. Fleming ed., 2011).

128. Baylis, *supra* note 2, at 18.

129. ECCC Internal Rules (rev. 8), *supra* note 67, r. 11(2)(k).

130. Tessa Bialek, *Legacy at the Extraordinary Chambers in the Courts of Cambodia: Research Overview*, Documentation Center of Cambodia, at §II(3) (2011).

131. *Id.* (citing deputy international Co-Prosecutor William Smith).

132. *Id.* at §III(1).

133. OSJI, *Recent Developments at the Extraordinary Chambers in the Courts of Cambodia* (Aug. 2009), at 10–11.

134. *See* Administrative Circular on Establishment of ECCC's Legacy Advisory Group and Legacy Secretariat (Mar. 26, 2010).

135. Confidential interview with a senior ECCC staff member, Phnom Penh (Nov. 1, 2012).

136. Long interview, *supra* note 53.

137. *See generally* OHCHR Report, *supra* note 10.

138. A more complete list is available in Bialek, *supra* note 130.

139. *See* ECCC, *Proposed Budget for 2012–2013* (Feb. 17, 2012), http://www.eccc.gov.kh/sites/default/files/ECCC%20Budget%202012-2013.pdf, at 65.

140. By late 2012, the fruitful completion of the VT project appeared uncertain due to efforts by the head of legacy on the national side of the Court to assume control before the proprietary interactive features were incorporated. *See id.* at 66 (calling Hoover Institution of Stanford University and the War Crimes Studies Center of the University of California, Berkeley, "former partners").

141. *Id.* at 11, 16.

142. *Id.* at 13, 17.

143. ECCC, *ECCC Revised Budget Requirements—2012–2013*, *supra* note 46, at 5–6, 18.

144. *See, e.g.*, Long interview, *supra* note 53.

145. Interview with Rupert Skilbeck, former head of the ECCC Defence Support Section, via telephone (June 7, 2012).

146. Confidential interview with former national staff member, Phnom Penh (June 18, 2012) ("Cambodians can learn from international work habits: independence, timeliness, and preparation. Cambodians bring familiarity with local law, local culture, the general context and history, as well as an ability to help with fieldwork").

147. Interview with Karim A.A. Khan QC, ECCC Civil Party Co-Lawyer in Case 001, via telephone (June 5, 2012).

148. Etcheson interview, *supra* note 31.

149. *Id.*

150. Confidential interview with former staff member.

151. Etcheson interview, *supra* note 31.

152. Huy interview, *supra* note 76.

153. Jörg Menzel, *Justice Delayed or Too Late for Justice? The Khmer Rouge Tribunal and the Cambodian "Genocide" 1975–1979*, 9 J. GENOCIDE RES. 215, 227 (2008).

154. Alex Bates, *Transitional Justice in Cambodia: Analytical Report*, Atlas Project (Oct. 2010), at 50–51.

155. Ryan, *supra* note 70, at 73.

156. Bates, *supra* note 154, at 50.

157. Skilbeck interview, *supra* note 145.

158. ECCC, *Legacy*, http://www.eccc.gov.kh/en/dss/legacy (visited Aug. 13, 2013).

159. *See* ECCC COURT REPORT, *supra* note 114, at 7.

160. John Coughlan et al., *The Legacy of the Khmer Rouge Tribunal: Maintaining the Status Quo of Cambodia's Legal and Judicial System*, 4 AMSTERDAM L. FOR. 16, 26 (2012).

161. Bialek, *supra* note 130, at §III(1); Email response from national OCIJ staff (June 3, 2012) ("Some ECCC officials serve in the governmental judicial system. Therefore, the experiences they gained from the ECCC will have an impact on the Cambodian legal system.").

162. Duncan McCargo, *Politics by Other Means? The Virtual Trials of the Khmer Rouge Tribunal*, 87 Int'l Aff. 613, 615 (2011) (noting that "the ECCC was conceived partly as a showcase for international standards of justice," one that would have a "contagion effect" upon the wider Cambodian justice system by exemplifying best practice).

163. *See, e.g.*, Joint Press Statement, H.E. Deputy Prime Minister Sok An and UN Assistant Secretary-General Patricia O'Brien, Apr. 19, 2010, http://www.unakrt-online.org/articles/joint-statement-he-deputy-prime-minister-sok-and-ms-patricia-o'brien-under-secretary-general (asserting that the ECCC "is living up to the hope for it to be a model court"); Statement by Ministry of Foreign Affairs of Japan, June 13, 2007 ("The Khmer Rouge Trials are instrumental in realizing the rule of law and justice in Cambodia and the Trials will provide a good model for strengthening Cambodia's judicial system"); Decision on IENG Sary's Application to Disqualify Judge Nil Nonn and Related Requests, E5/3, ¶ 14 (Jan. 28, 2011) (noting that as a model court, the ECCC may "serve to encourage and underscore the significance of institutional safeguards of judicial independence and integrity"); Special Representative of the Secretary-General for Human Rights in Cambodia, *Situation of Human Rights in Cambodia*, at 19, U.N. Doc. E/CN.4/2005/116 (Dec. 20, 2004) ("It is hoped that the establishment of a transparent process that complies with international standards will have an educational effect on existing formal institutions and create . . . further demand for a well functioning judicial system.").

164. Sok An named the ECCC as an appropriate model for a 2007–9 Model Court Project to develop Cambodian courts. *See* Minute[s] of the meeting of the Council of Legal and Judicial Reform, Doc. No. 017/07 KN.ASS, Aug. 1, 2007, at 2, *at* http://www.cljr.gov.kh/eng/report/doc/2007/meeting-note-2007-6-6.pdf. *See also* H.E. Sok An, Remarks at the Swearing-In Ceremony of National and International Judicial Officers for the Extraordinary Chambers in the Courts of Cambodia, July 3, 2006, *at* http://www.eccc.gov.kh/sites/default/files/media/Sok_An_speech_for_reception_3_July_2006.pdf (noting the Government's hope and expectation that "the ECCC will be a model court for Cambodia").

165. *Compare* Bates, *supra* note 154, at 51 (citing Co-Prosecutor Chea Leang as saying that constraints on human and financial resources will make it challenging to transfer skills to the local judiciary), *with* Long interview, *supra* note 53 (emphasizing that legacy doesn't have to be expensive; instead, measures can be practical and realistic).

166. *See, e.g.*, Email response from national VSS staff (June 5, 2012); Coughlan et al., *supra* note 160, at 23–24 (saying the strong role of defense counsel and the Internal Rules' provision of a right to silence are welcome in a society in which too few accused have even minimal fair trial rights).

167. *See, e.g.*, David Boyle, *The Legacy of the ECCC Proceedings in Cambodian Law*, Draft Thematic Report Published by the Center of Applied Research in Law (Sept. 2012) (on

file with author) (presenting "a thematic selection of case law of the [ECCC] relevant to the interpretation of Cambodian criminal law and procedure, especially as regards respect for international fair trial standards").

168. *See* Michael G. Karanvas, *Bringing Domestic Cases into Compliance with International Standards: Applicability of ECCC Jurisprudence and Procedural Mechanisms at the Domestic Level* (Nov. 2012) (on file with author).

169. ECCC Respondent No. 4, *supra* note 101.

170. Long interview, *supra* note 53.

171. Huy interview, *supra* note 76.

172. Response to questionnaire from Co-Investigating Judge You Bunleng, Cambodian Co-Investigating Judge at the ECCC (June 25, 2012). *See also* Long interview, *supra* note 53; David Boyle & Buth Reaksmey Kongkea, *Court Extension, a First Step to Reform*, PHNOM PENH POST (Oct. 11, 2012) (reporting the Court of Appeal's incorporation of the ECCC case database management system).

173. Long interview, *supra* note 53.

174. You Bunleng, *supra* note 172.

175. *See, e.g.*, Judge Marcel Lemonde, remarks at the conference "The Contribution of Criminal Proceedings before the ECCC to Cambodian Law," Royal University of Law and Economics, Phnom Penh, Dec. 4, 2012 ("The rule of law cannot be built within a day. Cambodia cannot, from one day to another, become Sweden."); Kelly McEvers & Phann Ana, *Disorder in the Courts*, CAMBODIA DAILY, Mar. 4–5, 2000 (quoting Janet King, in-country director of the University of San Francisco's Community Legal Education Center: "They're not going to change their mental mindsets by sitting in on a lot of seminars and workshops. This change will take decades.").

176. ECCC Respondent No. 2, *supra* note 77. *See also* LICADHO, *Human Rights in Cambodia: The Charade of Justice* (Dec. 2007) at 1 (noting that "despite . . . millions of dollars invested by foreign donors in reform programs since 1992, there has been no progress whatsoever in the single most important issue affecting the courts: their lack of independence from political and financial influence. . . . [T]he donor community remains focused upon short-term, material indicators of progress. They consistently ignore what is actually happening in the Cambodian courts on a daily basis: where existing legislation is routinely ignored, and training courses are routinely forgotten, as soon as political or financial influences come into play").

177. Confidential interview with former national staff member, *supra* note 146.

178. Clancy McGillian & Van Roeun, *UN Office Starts Project to Transfer Court Skills*, CAMBODIA DAILY, Oct. 1, 2010.

179. Confidential interview with former national staff member, *supra* note 146 ("Cambodia doesn't need good laws, it already has most of the laws it needs; what is needed is judicial reform").

180. Phorn Bopha, *With Scant Debate, Glut of Laws Clears Assembly*, CAMBODIA DAILY, Dec. 2, 2011.

181. Coughlan et al., *supra* note 159, at 28–33. *See also* Jackie Mulryne, *Legacy of the Khmer Rouge Tribunal*, THE PLATFORM (Dec. 17, 2011); Zsombor Peter, *Sonando Verdict Tests KR Tribunal's Legacy*, CAMBODIA DAILY (Oct. 4, 2012).

182. Interview with Michael G. Karnavas, former Ieng Sary Co-Lawyer, Phnom Penh (May 19, 2012).

183. Confidential interview with former national staff member, *supra* note 146.

184. Say Mony, *With Trial Under Way, Tribunal Faces Questions of Legacy*, VOA KHMER (Dec. 5, 2011), http://www.voacambodia.com/content/with-trial-under-way-tribunal-faces-questions-of-legacy-135024278/1356258.html.

185. Interview with Jeanne Sulzer, Legal Officer in the ECCC Civil Party Lead Co-Lawyers Section, Phnom Penh (June 1, 2012).

186. *Cambodian Legislature Passes Anti-corruption Law*, ASIAN CORRESPONDENT, Mar. 11, 2010.

187. Transparency International, *Corruption Perceptions Index 2012*, http://www.transparency.org/cpi2012/results.

188. *Id.* at 30.

189. Pham et al., *supra* note 82, at 26.

190. *Id.*

191. *Id.* at 29.

192. Nadine Kirchenbauer et al., *Victims Participation before the Extraordinary Chambers in the Courts of Cambodia*, at 33 (Jan. 2013).

193. *Id.* at 34–38.

194. Interview with Hans Corell, former UN Legal Counsel, via telephone (Nov. 15, 2012).

195. Long interview, *supra* note 53.

196. Interview with Youk Chhang, Director of the Documentation Center of Cambodia, Phnom Penh (July 10, 2012).

197. Interview with Clint Williamson, former UN Special Expert for advising on UN Assistance to the Khmer Rouge Trials and former U.S. Ambassador-at-Large for War Crimes Issues, via telephone (June 27, 2012).

198. Youk Chhang, Letter, *History Weighs Heavily on Cambodia's Human Rights Struggle*, CAMBODIA DAILY, Dec. 12, 2012.

199. *See* Documentation Center of Cambodia, *Genocide Education, 2004–present*, http://www.d.dccam.org/Projects/Genocide/Genocide_Education.htm (visited Aug. 13, 2013). The textbook now used to teach the subject is KHAMBOLY DY, A HISTORY OF DEMOCRATIC KAMPUCHEA (1975–1979) (2007).

200. Sok-Kheang Ly, *Conveying Khmer Rouge History to Young People* 24–27 (Feb. 2008), *available at* http://www.d.dccam.org/Projects/Living_Doc/PIR_Road_trip_report_to_Svay_Rieng_Feb_24–26–8.pdf.

201. *See, e.g.*, Transcultural Psychosocial Organization, *Justice and Relief for Survivors*

of the Khmer Rouge, http://tpocambodia.org/uploads/media/Khmer_Rouge_Tribunal_Project_Information_English.pdf (visited Aug. 13, 2013).

202. Confidential senior staff interview, *supra* note 135.

203. Long interview, *supra* note 53. *But see* Interview with Diana Ellis, Co-Lawyer for Ieng Thirith, Phnom Penh (Nov. 11, 2012) (stating that a significant problem with all international courts is that they are mandated, *inter alia*, to create a historical record, whereas this should not be seen as the function of a court, which necessarily tells a partial story based on the available evidence).

Conclusion

1. *Former Khmer Rouge Chief Jailer Gets Life Imprisonment*, KYODO NEWS SERVICE, Feb. 3, 2012.

2. Mujib Mashal, *Tribunal Helps Cambodia Confront Its History*, AL-JAZEERA, Feb. 3, 2012.

3. Sophal Ear, *Cambodian 'Justice,'* WALL ST. J. ASIA, Sept. 1, 2009; Sophal Ear, Letter, *Khmer Rouge Tribunal vs. Karmic Justice*, INT'L HERALD TRIBUNE, Mar. 17, 2010. *See also 'History Cannot Be Hidden' as Khmer Rouge Leaders Tried*, USA TODAY, Sept. 15, 2010 (in which Ear asserts that "everyone, including the donors, know that [the ECCC is] a lemon").

4. Press Release, *Khmer Rouge Victims in Cambodia* (Nov. 15, 2011), *available at* http://ki-media.blogspot.com/2012/03/judges-remain-at-loggerheads-theary.html.

5. *Khmer Rouge Mixed Tribunal Is a 'Sham,'* DEUTSCHE PRESSE AGENTUR, Nov. 15, 2011.

6. Mark Ellis, *The ECCC—A Failure of Credibility*, INT'L BAR ASS'N (Feb. 2012), at 5.

7. Peter Maguire, *Cambodia and the Pitfalls of Political Justice*, INT'L HERALD TRIBUNE, June 20, 2011.

8. David Scheffer, *Why the Cambodia Tribunal Matters to the International Community*, CAMBODIA TRIBUNAL MONITOR (Sept. 2007) (on file with the authors).

9. Abby Seiff, *Imperfect Justice Worth Pursuing, Says War Crimes Expert*, CAMBODIA DAILY, June 18, 2012.

10. S.J. Williams, *The Cambodian Extraordinary Chambers—A Dangerous Precedent for International Justice?* 53 INT'L & COMP. L. Q. 227 (2004); conversation with a UN official, Oct. 2012.

11. Mike Eckel, *Cambodia's Kangaroo Court*, FOR. POL'Y, July 20, 2011.

12. Interview with Hans Corell, former UN Legal Counsel, via telephone (Nov. 15, 2012).

13. *Id.*

14. *Id.*

15. Interview with William Smith, ECCC deputy international Co-Prosecutor,

Phnom Penh (June 5, 2012); interview with Panhavuth Long, Program Officer, Cambodian Justice Initiative, Phnom Penh (July 6, 2012).

16. Corell interview, *supra* note 12.

17. Elena Baylis, *Reassessing the Role of International Criminal Law: Rebuilding National Courts Through Transnational Networks*, 50 B.C. L. REV. 1, 18 (2009) (noting that some mixed courts have found it difficult to recruit experienced judges).

18. *Id.* at 18–20.

19. Interview with Rupert Skilbeck, former head of the ECCC Defence Support Section, via telephone (June 7, 2012).

20. *Quelles leçons tirer du procès des Khmers rouges?* REVUE DE SCIENCE CRIMINELLE 597 (2011) (featuring an interview with Lemonde, translated from French by the authors). *See also* MARCEL LEMONDE WITH JEAN REYNAUD, UN JUGE FACE AUX KHMERS ROUGES (2013).

21. *Id.*

22. *See* Special Tribunal for Lebanon (STL) Rules of Procedure and Evidence, *as amended* Feb. 20, 2013, part 5; STL, *Pre-trial Judge*, http://www.stl-tsl.org/en/about-the-stl/structure-of-the-stl/chambers/pre-trial-chamber (visited Aug. 20, 2013).

23. *See generally* Rome Statute of the International Criminal Court arts. 12–15, 18–19, 39, 53–60, July 17, 1998, 2187 U.N.T.S. 90 (entered into force on July 1, 2002).

24. Gregory Townsend, *Structure and Management*, *in* INTERNATIONAL PROSECUTORS 171, 302–3 (Luc Reydams et al. eds., 2012) (quoting an interview with Petit).

25. Corell interview, *supra* note 12.

26. Rupert Abbott & Stephanie A. Barbour, *Khmer Rouge Tribunal: Last Chance to Salvage Justice?* ILAWYER (Dec. 17, 2012), http://ilawyerblog.com/khmer-rouge-tribunal-last-chance-to-salvage-justice/.

27. Human Rights Watch, *Cambodia: Judges Investigating Khmer Rouge Crimes Should Resign* (Oct. 3, 2011), http://www.hrw.org/news/2011/10/03/cambodia-judges-investigating-khmer-rouge-crimes-should-resign.

28. Phuong Pham et al., *After the First Trial: A Population-Based Survey on Knowledge and Perception of Justice and the Extraordinary Chambers in the Courts of Cambodia* 26–30 (June 2011) (noting, *inter alia*, that in late 2012, 75% of respondents believed the ECCC was "neutral," 81% believed the ECCC would help promote reconciliation, and 76% believed the ECCC will have a positive impact on Khmer Rouge victims and their families).

29. Mashal, *supra* note 2 (in which Chak Sopheap of the Cambodian Center for Human Rights argues that "[t]his court has brought about public participation and debate" and has catalyzed "a public argument about the right of fair trial for the accused").

SELECTED REFERENCES

Rupert Abbott & Stephanie A. Barbour. *Khmer Rouge Tribunal: Last Chance to Salvage Justice?* iLAWYER (Dec. 17, 2012).

Rehan Abeyratne. *Superior Responsibility and the Principle of Legality at the ECCC.* 44 GEO. WASH. INT'L L. REV. 39 (2012).

DENISE AFFONÇO. TO THE END OF HELL (2005).

Amnesty International. *Kingdom of Cambodia: Amnesty International's Position and Concerns Regarding the Proposed "Khmer Rouge" Tribunal.* Document ASA 23/005/2003 (Apr. 24, 2003).

M. CHERIF BASSIOUNI. INTRODUCTION TO INTERNATIONAL CRIMINAL LAW (2003).

M. Cherif Bassiouni. *Mixed Models of International Criminal Justice. In* INTERNATIONAL CRIMINAL LAW: VOL. III: INTERNATIONAL ENFORCEMENT (M. Cherif Bassiouni ed., 3d ed. 2008).

Alex Bates. *Transitional Justice in Cambodia: Analytical Report.* Atlas Project (Oct. 2010).

Elena Baylis. *Reassessing the Role of International Criminal Law: Rebuilding National Courts through Transnational Networks.* 50 B.C. L. REV. 1 (2009).

ELIZABETH BECKER. WHEN THE WAR WAS OVER: CAMBODIA UNDER THE KHMER ROUGE REVOLUTION (1986).

Mats Berdal & Michael Leifer. *Cambodia. In* THE NEW INTERVENTIONISM, 1991–1994 (James Mayall ed., 1996).

Nehal Bhuta. *Great Expectations—East Timor and the Vicissitudes of Externalised Justice.* 12 FINNISH Y.B. INT'L L. 179 (2001).

Tessa Bialek. Documentation Center of Cambodia. *Legacy at the Extraordinary Chambers in the Courts of Cambodia: Research Overview* (2011).

Michael Bohlander. *The International Criminal Judiciary—Problems of Judicial Selection, Independence and Ethics* (2007) (unpublished manuscript).

Cherie Booth & Philippe Sands. *International Judges Must Be Independent and Representative.* GUARDIAN, July 13, 2001.

Cambodian Center for Human Rights. *Open Letter to United Nations Special Expert on the Khmer Rouge Tribunal Clint Williamson* (May 25, 2011).

Cambodian Center for Human Rights. *Third Bi-Annual Report: Fair Trial Rights—One Year Progress* (Jan. 2012).

Cambodian League for the Promotion and Defense of Human Rights (LICADHO). *Human Rights in Cambodia: The Charade of Justice* (Dec. 2007).
Antonio Cassese. International Criminal Law 332–33 (2d ed. 2008).
Nayan Chanda. Brother Enemy: The War After the War (1988).
Nayan Chanda. *China and Cambodia: In the Mirror of History*. 9 Asia-Pac. Rev. 1 (2002).
David P. Chandler. The Tragedy of Cambodian History: Politics, War, and Revolution since 1945 (1993).
David P. Chandler. Voices from S-21: Terror and History in Pol Pot's Secret Prison (1999).
Alejandro Chehtman & Ruth Mackenzie. *Capacity Development in International Criminal Justice: A Mapping Exercise of Existing Practice*. DOMAC/2 (Sept. 2009).
King C. Chen. China's War with Vietnam. 1979: Issues, Decisions, and Implications (1987).
Youk Chhang. *The Thief of History—Cambodia and the Special Court*. 1 Int'l J. of Trans. Just. 157 (2007).
Youk Chhang. *Arrest of Ieng Sary and Wife Is an Important Victory for Victims*. Cambodia Daily, Nov. 15, 2007.
Youk Chhang. *Conducting a Legal Experiment at Victims' Expense*. Cambodia Trial Monitor (Sept. 29, 2009).
Youk Chhang. Comment. *Sad Situation for Civil Parties*. Phnom Penh Post, Oct. 1, 2009.
George Chigas. *The Trial of the Khmer Rouge*. 4 Harv. Asia Q. (Winter 2000).
Children of Cambodia's Killing Fields (Dith Pran ed., 1997).
Noam Chomsky & Edward Herman. *Distortions at Fourth Hand*. The Nation, June 25, 1977.
Terith Chy. *A Thousand Voices*. Documentation Center of Cambodia (Mar. 5, 2009).
John D. Ciorciari. *Great-Power Posturing and the Khmer Rouge Tribunal*. Searching for the Truth (Fall 2002).
John D. Ciorciari. *History and Politics Behind the Khmer Rouge Trials*. *In* On Trial: The Khmer Rouge Accountability Process (John D. Ciorciari & Anne Heindel eds., 2009).
John D. Ciorciari. *The Duch Verdict*. Cambodia Tribunal Monitor (July 28, 2010).
John D. Ciorciari. *Cambodia's Trek Toward Reconciliation*. 23 Peace Rev. 438 (2011).
John D. Ciorciari. *China and the Pol Pot Regime*. 13 Cold War History 1 (2013).
John D. Ciorciari & Anne Heindel. *Trauma in the Courtroom*. *In* Cambodia's Invisible Scars (Daryn Reicherter & Beth Van Schaack eds., 2011).
John D. Ciorciari & Sok-Kheang Ly. *The ECCC's Role in Reconciliation*. *In* On Trial: The Khmer Rouge Accountability Process (John D. Ciorciari & Anne Heindel eds., 2009).
John D. Ciorciari & Jaya Ramji-Nogales. *Lessons from the Cambodian Experience with Truth and Reconciliation*. 19 Buff. Hum. Rts. L. Rev. (forthcoming 2013).

John D. Ciorciari with Youk Chhang. *Documenting the Crimes of Democratic Kampuchea. In* BRINGING THE KHMER ROUGE TO JUSTICE (Jaya Ramji & Beth Van Schaack eds., 2005).

David Cohen. *Seeking Justice on the Cheap: Is the East Timor Tribunal Really a Model for the Future?* 61 ASIA PACIFIC ISSUES (E.-W. Ctr., Aug. 2002).

David Cohen. *Indifference and Accountability: The United Nations and the Politics of International Justice in East Timor.* E.-W. CTR. SPEC. REPS. (June 2006).

David Cohen. *"Hybrid" Justice in East Timor, Sierra Leone, and Cambodia: "Lessons Learned" and Prospects for the Future,* 43 STAN. J. INT'L L. 1 (2007).

Hans Corell. *Why the UN Backed Off: No Justice for Victims of the Khmer Rouge.* INT'L HERALD TRIB., June 19, 2002.

Hans Corell. *Foreword. In* INTERNATIONAL PROSECUTORS (Luc Reydams et al. eds., 2012).

Luc Côté. *Reflections on the Exercise of Prosecutorial Discretion in International Criminal Law.* 3 J. INT'L CRIM JUST. 162 (2005).

John Coughlan et al. *The Legacy of the Khmer Rouge Tribunal: Maintaining the Status Quo of Cambodia's Legal and Judicial System.* 4 AMSTERDAM L. FOR. 16 (2012).

David Crane. *Dancing with the Devil: Prosecuting West Africa's Warlords—Current Lessons Learned and Challenges. In* ATROCITIES AND INTERNATIONAL ACCOUNTABILITY (Edel Hughes et al. eds., 2007).

Thierry Cruvellier. *From the Taylor Trial to a Lasting Legacy: Putting the Special Court Model to the Test.* International Center for Transitional Justice and Sierra Leone Court Monitoring Program (2009).

Thierry Cruvellier. *Duch Trial Ends with a Twist.* 95 INT'L JUST. TRIB. (Dec. 9, 2009).

THIERRY CRUVELLIER. COURT OF REMORSE: INSIDE THE INTERNATIONAL CRIMINAL TRIBUNAL FOR RWANDA (2010).

THIERRY CRUVELLIER. LE MAÎTRE DES AVEUX (2011).

Thierry Cruvellier. *Duch: Down with Subtleties.* 145 INT'L JUST. TRIB. (Feb. 15, 2012).

Nicholas J. Cummins. *The 1997 Coup in Cambodia* (Monash Asia Institute, 2007).

Mirjan Damaska. *Problematic Features of International Criminal Procedure. In* THE OXFORD COMPANION TO INTERNATIONAL CRIMINAL JUSTICE (Antonio Cassese et al. eds., 2009).

Yael Danieli. *Reappraising the Nuremberg Trials and Their Legacy: The Role of Victims in International Law.* 27 CARDOZO L. REV. 1633 (2005–6).

Sara Darehshori. *Lessons for Outreach from the Ad Hoc Tribunals, the Special Court for Sierra Leone, and the International Criminal Court.* 14 NEW ENG. J. OF INT'L & COMP. L. 299 (2008).

Sylvia de Bertodano. *Current Developments in Internationalized Courts.* 1 J. INT'L CRIM. JUST. 226 (2003).

Margaret deGuzman. *Choosing to Prosecute: Expressive Selection at the International Criminal Court.* 33 MICH. J. INT'L L. 265 (2012).

Jerome de Hemptinne. *The Creation of Investigating Chambers at the International Criminal Court.* 5 J. Int'l Crim. Just. 402 (2007).

Carla del Ponte. *Prosecuting the Individuals Bearing the Highest Level of Responsibility.* 2 J. Int'l Crim. Just. 516 (2004).

Howard J. De Nike. *East Germany's Legal Advisor to the 1979 Tribunal in Cambodia.* Searching for the Truth (July 2008).

Valérie Dervieux. *The French System. In* European Criminal Procedures (Mireille Delmas-Marty & J.R. Spencer eds., 2002).

Laura A. Dickinson. *The Relationship Between Hybrid Courts and International Courts: The Case of Kosovo.* 37 New Eng. L. Rev. 1059 (2002–3).

Laura A. Dickinson. *The Promise of Hybrid Courts.* 97 Am. J. Int'l L. 295 (2003).

David Donat-Cattin. *Article 68 Protection of the Victims and Witnesses and Their Participation in the Proceedings. In* Commentary on the Rome Statute of the International Court (Otto Triffterer ed., 1999).

Fidelma Donlon. *Hybrid Tribunals. In* Routledge Handbook of International Criminal Law (William Schabas & Nadia Bernaz eds., 2011).

Mark Drumbl. Atrocity, Punishment, and International Law (2008).

The Duch Verdict: A DC-Cam Report from the Villages: Witnessing Justice. Village Screenings of the First Khmer Rouge Verdict of the Extraordinary Chambers in the Court of Cambodia (Documentation Center of Cambodia, July 26, 2010).

Khamboly Dy. A History of Democratic Kampuchea (1975–1979) (2007).

Sophal Ear. *Cambodian 'Justice.'* Wall St. J. Asia, Sept. 1, 2009.

Sophal Ear. Letter. *Khmer Rouge Tribunal vs. Karmic Justice.* N.Y. Times, Mar. 17, 2010.

Mike Eckel. *Cambodia's Kangaroo Court.* Foreign Policy (July 20, 2011).

Ek Chanboreth & Sok Hach. *Aid Effectiveness in Cambodia* (Wolfenshon Center for Development. Working Paper no. 7, Dec. 2008).

Mark Ellis. *Safeguarding Judicial Independence in Mixed Tribunals: Lessons from the ECCC and Best Practices for the Future.* Int'l Bar Ass'n (Sept. 2011).

Mark Ellis. *The ECCC—A Failure of Credibility.* Int'l Bar Ass'n (Feb. 2012).

Craig Etcheson. The Rise and Demise of Democratic Kampuchea (1984).

Craig Etcheson. Reconciliation in Cambodia (2004).

Craig Etcheson. After the Killing Fields: Lessons from the Cambodian Genocide (2005).

Tom Fawthrop & Helen Jarvis. Getting Away with Genocide? Elusive Justice and the Khmer Rouge Tribunal (2004).

Roger Fisher & William Ury. Getting to Yes (rev. ed. 2011).

Julie Flint & Alex de Waal. *Case Closed: A Prosecutor Without Borders.* World Affairs J. (Spring 2009).

Stuart Ford. *How Leadership in International Criminal Law Is Shifting from the United States to Europe and Asia.* 55 St. Louis U. L. J. 955 (2011).

Genocide in Cambodia: Documents from the Trial of Pol Pot and Ieng Sary (Howard J. DeNike et al. eds., 2000).

James Goldston. *An Extraordinary Experiment in Transitional Justice.* Just. Initiatives (Spring 2006).

James A. Goldston. *More Candor About Criteria: The Exercise of Discretion by the Prosecutor of the International Criminal Court.* 8 J. Int'l Crim. Just. 383 (2010).

James A. Goldston. *Justice Delayed Is Justice Denied.* N.Y. Times, Oct. 13, 2011.

Richard Goldstone. For Humanity: Reflections of a War Crimes Investigator (2000).

Evan Gottesman. Cambodia After the Khmer Rouge: Inside the Politics of Nation-Building (2002).

John Hall. *Donors Should Adopt a Balanced Approach to Funding ECCC.* Cambodia Daily, July 21, 2008.

John A. Hall. *Court Administration at the ECCC. In* On Trial: The Khmer Rouge Accountability Process (John D. Ciorciari & Anne Heindel eds., 2009).

Gret Haller. *The Human Rights Regime in Bosnia and Herzegovina in the European Context. In* Human Rights in Bosnia and Herzegovina After Dayton (Wolfbang Benedek et al. eds., 1999).

Bernard Hamel. De Sang et De Larmes: La Grande Déportation du Cambodge (1977).

Thomas Hammarberg. *How the Khmer Rouge Tribunal Was Agreed: Discussions Between the Cambodian Government and the UN.* Searching for the Truth (July–Nov. 2001).

Hurst Hannum & David Hawk. *The Case Against the Standing Committee of the Communist Party of Kampuchea.* Draft ICJ Memorial (1986).

Mark B. Harmon & Fergal Gaynor. *The Sentencing Practices of International Tribunals: Ordinary Sentences for Extraordinary Crimes.* 5 J. Int'l Crim Just. 683 (2007).

Michael E. Hartmann. *International Judges and Prosecutors in Kosovo: A New Model for Post-Conflict Peacekeeping.* U.S. Institute for Peace (Oct. 2003).

Stephen P. Heder. *The Kampuchean-Vietnamese Conflict. In* The Third Indochina Conflict (David W.P. Elliott ed., 1981).

Stephen R. Heder. Reflections on Cambodian Politicial History (1991).

Stephen R. Heder. *Dealing with Crimes Against Humanity: Progress or Illusion? In* Southeast Asian Affairs 2001 (2001).

Steve Heder. Cambodian Communism and the Vietnamese Model: Imitation and Independence, 1930–1975 (2004).

Steve Heder. *The Personal Jurisdiction of the Extraordinary Chambers in the Courts of Cambodia . . .* (Apr. 26, 2012).

Stephen Heder with Brian D. Tittemore. Seven Candidates for Prosecution (2d ed. 2004).

Anne Heindel. *Why the ECCC Office of Administration Would Benefit from Being Structured More Like a "Registry."* Searching for the Truth (Oct. 2007).

Anne Heindel. Amicus Brief In the Matter of the Appeal by Kang Guek Eav (Duch) Against the Order of Provisional Detention by the Office of the Co-Investigating Judges dated 31 July 2007 (ECCC Pre-Trial Chamber, Oct. 4, 2007).

Anne Heindel. *The Duch Verdict: Khmer Rouge Tribunal Case 001* (Documentation Center of Cambodia, 2010).

Anne Heindel. *The Duch Verdict: Forum on Forgiveness and Genocide Education in the Former Khmer Rouge Stronghold of Malai & The Duch Verdict: A DC-Cam Report from Former Khmer Rouge Strongholds of Samlot and Pailin* (Documentation Center of Cambodia, 2010).

Anne Heindel. *Expert Commentary on Legal Filings: Decision on Nuon Chea Defence Counsel Misconduct.* Cambodia Tribunal Monitor (July 3, 2012).

Anne Heindel with John Ciorciari. *Possible Roles for a Special Advisor or Oversight Committee for the ECCC.* Searching for the Truth (Jan.–Mar. 2008).

Ethel Higonnet. *Restructuring Hybrid Courts: Local Empowerment and National Criminal Justice.* Yale Law School Legal Student Scholarship Papers 6 (2005).

George Hildebrand & Gareth Porter. Cambodia: Starvation and Revolution (1976).

Chanrithy Him. When Broken Glass Floats (2001).

Alexander Laban Hinton. Why Did They Kill? Cambodia in the Shadow of Genocide (2005).

Helen Horsington. *The Cambodian Khmer Rouge Tribunal: The Promise of a Hybrid Tribunal.* 5 Melbourne J. Int'l L. 462 (2004).

Human Rights Watch. *Serious Flaws: Why the U.N. General Assembly Should Require Changes to the Draft Khmer Rouge Tribunal Agreement* (Apr. 30, 2003).

Human Rights Watch. *Courting History* (2008).

Human Rights Watch. *Unfinished Business: Closing Gaps in the Selection of ICC Cases* (2011).

Human Rights Watch. *Cambodia: Judges Investigating Khmer Rouge Crimes Should Resign* (Oct. 3, 2011).

Varda Hussain. *Sustaining Judicial Rescues: The Role of Outreach and Capacity-Building Efforts in War Crimes Tribunals.* 45 Va. J. Int'l L. 547 (2005).

Charles C. Jackson. *Process and Problems: Defense Counsel at the Extraordinary Chambers in the Courts of Cambodia* (updated Nov. 2010) (on file with the authors).

Karl D. Jackson. *The Ideology of Total Revolution. In* Cambodia 1975–1978: Rendezvous with Death (Karl D. Jackson ed., 1989).

Neha Jain. *Between the Scylla and Charybdis of Prosecution and Reconciliation: The Khmer Rouge Trials and the Promise of International Criminal Justice.* 20 Duke J. Comp. & Int'l L. 247 (2009–10).

Charles Chernor Jalloh. *The Contribution of the Special Court for Sierra Leone to the Development of International Law.* 15 AFR. J. INT'L & COMP. L. 165 (2007).

Julio Jeldres. *Cambodia's Relations with France Since the Paris Agreements of 1991. In* CAMBODIA: PROGRESS AND CHALLENGES SINCE 1991 (Pou Sothirok et al. eds., 2012).

Suzanne Katzenstein. *Hybrid Tribunals: Searching for Justice in East Timor.* 16 HARV. HUM. RTS. J. 245 (2003).

Michelle Staggs Kelsall et al. *Lessons Learned from the 'Duch' Trial: A Comprehensive Review of the First Case Before the Extraordinary Chambers in the Courts of Cambodia.* Asian International Justice Initiative, KRT Trial Monitoring Group (Dec. 2009).

Sarah Kendall & Michelle Staggs. *From Mandate to Legacy: The Special Court for Sierra Leone as a Model for "Hybrid Justice."* UC Berkeley War Crimes Study Center (Apr. 2005).

BEN KIERNAN. *The Samlaut Rebellion, 1967–70: The Origins of Cambodia's Liberation Movement* (Monash University Centre of Southeast Asian Studies Working Papers No. 4 and 5, ca. 1975).

BEN KIERNAN. THE POL POT REGIME: RACE, POWER, AND GENOCIDE IN CAMBODIA UNDER THE KHMER ROUGE, 1975–79 (1996).

BEN KIERNAN. THE POL POT REGIME: RACE, POWER, AND GENOCIDE IN CAMBODIA UNDER THE KHMER ROUGE, 1975–79 (2d ed. 2002).

Ben Kiernan. *The Demography of Genocide in Southeast Asia: The Death Tolls in Cambodia, 1975–1979, and East Timor, 1975–1980.* 35 CRIT. ASIAN STUD. 585 (2003).

BEN KIERNAN. HOW POL POT CAME TO POWER: COLONIALISM, NATIONALISM, AND COMMUNISM IN CAMBODIA, 1930–1975 (2d ed. 2004).

Ben Kiernan. *The Cambodian Genocide and Imperial Culture. In* 90 YEARS OF DENIAL (Apr. 2005).

Yoshi Kodama. *For Judicial Justice and Reconciliation in Cambodia: Reflections upon the Establishment of the Khmer Rouge Trials and the Trials' Procedural Rules 2007.* 9 L. & PRAC. OF INT'L CTS. & TRIBUNALS 37 (2010).

Patrick Kroker. *Transitional Justice Policy in Practice: Victim Participation in the* Khmer Rouge *Tribunal,* 53 GER. YB INT'L L. 754 (2010).

Wendy Lambourne. *The Khmer Rouge Tribunal: Justice for Genocide in Cambodia?* Paper for the Law and Society Association of Australia and New Zealand (Dec. 10–12, 2008).

MARCEL LEMONDE WITH JEAN REYNAUD. UN JUGE FACE AUX KHMERS ROUGES (2013).

Suzannah Linton. *Cambodia, East Timor, and Sierra Leone: Experiments in International Justice.* 12 CRIM. L. FORUM 185 (2001).

Suzannah Linton. *Rising from the Ashes: The Creation of a Viable Criminal Justice System in East Timor.* 25 MELBOURNE U. L. R. 122 (2001).

Suzannah Linton. *Putting Cambodia's Extraordinary Chambers into Context.* 11 SINGAPORE Y.B. INT'L L. 195 (2007).

HENRI LOCARD. POL POT'S LITTLE RED BOOK (2004).

Ly Sok-Kheang. *Conveying Khmer Rouge History to Young People*. SEARCHING FOR THE TRUTH (Feb. 2008).

Ruth Mackenzie & Philippe Sands. *International Courts and Tribunals and the Independence of the International Judge*. 44 HARV. INT'L L. J. 271 (2003).

PETER H. MAGUIRE. FACING DEATH IN CAMBODIA (2005).

Peter Maguire. *Cambodia and the Pitfalls of Political Justice*. INT'L HERALD TRIB., June 20, 2011.

Peter Maguire. *ECCC's Tarnished Legacy and the UN*. CAMBODIA TRIBUNAL MONITOR (Mar. 27, 2012).

Kalyanee Mam. *An Oral History of Family Life under the Khmer Rouge*. Yale Genocide Studies Working Paper No. 10 (1999).

Peter Manning. *Governing Memory: Justice, Reconciliation and Outreach at the Extraordinary Chambers in the Courts of Cambodia*. MEMORY STUDIES 1 (2011).

ROSS MARLAY & CLARK D. NEHER. PATRIOTS AND TYRANTS (1999).

Luke Marsh & Michael Ramsden. *Joint Criminal Enterprise: Cambodia's Reply to Tadić*. 11 INT'L CRIM. L. REV. 137 (2011).

Kathia Martin-Chenut. *Proces International et Modeles de Justice Penale*. *In* DROIT INTERNATIONAL PENAL (Hervé Ascensio et al. eds., 2d ed. 2012).

Olga Martin-Ortega & Johanna Herman. *Hybrid Tribunals & the Rule of Law: Notes from Bosnia & Herzegovina & Cambodia*. JAD-PbP Working Paper Series No. 7 (May 2010).

Duncan McCargo. *Cambodia: Getting Away with Authoritarianism?* 16 J. OF DEMOCRACY 98 (2005).

Duncan McCargo. *Politics by Other Means? The Virtual Trials of the Khmer Rouge Tribunal*. 87 INT'L AFF. 613 (2011).

Jörg Menzel. *Justice Delayed or Too Late for Justice? The Khmer Rouge Tribunal and the Cambodian "Genocide" 1975–1979*. 9 J. GENOCIDE RES. 215 (2008).

JAMIE FREDERIC METZL. WESTERN RESPONSES TO HUMAN RIGHTS ABUSES IN CAMBODIA, 1975–80 (1996).

Nathan J. Miller. Independence of the International Judiciary: General Overview of the Issues, Project on International Courts and Tribunals (Jan. 24, 2002) (unpublished manuscript).

Mahdev Mohan. *The Paradox of Victim-Centrism: Victim Participation at the Khmer Rouge Tribunal*. 9 INT'L CRIM. L. REV. 733 (2010).

STEPHEN P. MORRIS. WHY VIETNAM INVADED CAMBODIA (1999).

Krista L. Nelson. Comment, *Protecting Confidential Investigations or Gagging the Press? Freedom of Expression and Interference with the Administration of Justice at the Extraordinary Chambers in the Courts of Cambodia*. 35 SEATTLE U. L. REV. 265 (2011).

OFF. OF THE U.N. HIGH COMM'R FOR HUM. RTS. RULE-OF-LAW TOOLS FOR POST-CONFLICT STATES (2008).

Mikio Oishi & Fumitaka Furuoka. *Can Japanese Aid Be an Effective Tool of Influence?* 43 Asian Survey 890 (2003).

Open Society Justice Initiative (OSJI). *Memorandum to the Group of Interested States: Priority Issues for the Extraordinary Chambers in the Courts of Cambodia (ECCC)* (Oct. 2006).

Mark Osiel. Making Sense of Mass Atrocity (2009).

OSJI. *Progress and Challenges and the Extraordinary Chambers in the Courts of Cambodia* (June 2007).

OSJI. *Recent Developments at the Extraordinary Chambers in the Courts of Cambodia* (May 2008).

OSJI. *Recent Developments at the Extraordinary Chambers in the Courts of Cambodia* (Oct. 2008).

OSJI. *Recent Developments at the Extraordinary Chambers in the Courts of Cambodia* (Feb. 2009).

OSJI. *Recent Developments at the Extraordinary Chambers in the Courts of Cambodia* (May 2009).

OSJI. *Political Interference at the Extraordinary Chambers in the Courts of Cambodia* (July 2010).

OSJI. *Recent Developments at the Extraordinary Chambers in the Courts of Cambodia* (Sept. 2010).

OSJI. *Recent Developments at the Extraordinary Chambers in the Courts of Cambodia* (Dec. 2010).

OSJI. *Recent Developments at the Extraordinary Chambers in the Courts of Cambodia* (Feb. 2012).

Ou Virak. *Letter to the Editor: KRT Has Potential to Strengthen Cambodia's Justice System.* Cambodia Daily, Sept. 14, 2010.

Taylor Owen & Ben Kiernan. *Bombs Over Cambodia.* The Walrus (Oct. 2006).

Norman Henry Pentelovitch. Note, *Seeing Justice Done: The Importance of Prioritizing Outreach Efforts at International Criminal Tribunals.* 39 Geo. J. Int'l L. 446 (2007–8).

Sorpong Peou. *Diplomatic Pragmatism: ASEAN's Response to the July 1997 Coup.* Accord (1998).

Sorpong Peou. *Cambodia in 1998: From Despair to Hope?* 39 Asian Survey 20 (1999).

Sorpong Peou. Intervention & Change in Cambodia: Towards Democracy? (2000).

Sorpong Peou. *The Challenge for Human Rights in Cambodia. In* Human Rights in Asia (Thomas W.D. Davis & Brian Galligan eds., 2011).

Victor Peskin. *Courting Rwanda: The Promises and Pitfalls of the ICTR Outreach Programme.* 3 J. Int'l Crim. Just. 950 (2005).

Robert Petit. *Lawfare and International Tribunals: A Question of Definition? A Reflection on the Creation of the Khmer Rouge Tribunal.* 43 Case W. Res. J. Int'l L. 189 (2010–11).

Robert Petit & Anees Ahmed. *A Review of the Jurisprudence of the Khmer Rouge Tribunal.* 8 N'western J. Int'l Hum. Rts. 165 (2010).

Phuong N. Pham et al. *Victim Participation and the Trial of Duch at the Extraordinary Chambers in the Courts of Cambodia.* 3 J. Hum. Rts. Prac. 264 (2011).

Phuong Pham et al. *After the First Trial: A Population-Based Survey on Knowledge and Perception of Justice and the Extraordinary Chambers in the Courts of Cambodia* (June 2011).

Pol Pot Plans the Future: Confidential Leadership Documents from Democratic Kampuchea. 1976–1977 (David Chandler, Ben Kiernan, & Chantou Boua eds. and trans., 1988).

François Ponchaud. Cambodia Year Zero (1978).

Samantha Power. A Problem from Hell: America and the Age of Genocide (2002).

Kitti Prasirtsuk. *Japan and ASEAN in East Asian Community-building: Activating the Fukuda Doctrine. In* Japan's Relations with Southeast Asia (Lam Peng Er ed., 2013).

PRK Research and Publication Office. Tribunal for the Prosecution of the Genocidal Pol Pot-Ieng Sary Clique (1979).

Public Papers of the Presidents of the United States: Gerald Ford 1975 (1976).

Quelles leçons tirer du procès des Khmers rouges? Revue de Science Criminelle 597 (2011).

Clara Ramírez. Making an Impact (Int'l Ctr. for Trans. Just., Jan. 2011).

Jaya Ramji. *Reclaiming Cambodian History: The Case for a Truth Commission.* 24 Fletcher F. World Aff. 127 (2000).

Jaya Ramji-Nogales. *Designing Bespoke Transitional Justice: A Pluralist Process Approach.* 32 Mich. J. Int'l L. 1 (2010–11).

Phillip Rapoza. *Hybrid Criminal Tribunals and the Concept of Ownership: Who Owns the Process?* 21 Am. U. Int'l L. Rev. 525 (2005).

Steven R. Ratner. The New UN Peacekeeping (1996).

Steven R. Ratner et al. Accountability for Human Rights Atrocities in International Law (3d ed. 2009).

Reach Sambath. Letter, *KRT's UN Side Wasn't Warned of Media Alert.* Cambodia Daily, June 11, 2010.

Caitlin Reiger & Marieke Wierda. *The Serious Crimes Process in Timor Leste: In Retrospect.* (International Center for Transitional Justice, Prosecutions Case Studies Series, Mar. 2006).

Sophie Richardson. China, Cambodia, and the Five Principles of Peaceful Co-existence (2010).

David W. Roberts. Political Transition in Cambodia 1991–99: Power, Elitism and Democracy (2001).

Rong Chhorng. Letter, *KRT Victims Support Section Doing What It's Supposed To*. CAMBODIA DAILY, Feb. 27, 2012.

ROBERT S. ROSS. THE INDOCHINA TANGLE: CHINA'S VIETNAM POLICY, 1975–1979 (1988).

Heather Ryan. *Learning from the East: Lessons for Africa from Cambodia's Genocide Trials*. Open Society Initiative for Southern Africa (Mar. 7, 2012).

Susana SáCouto. *Victim Participation at the International Criminal Court and the Extraordinary Chambers in the Courts of Cambodia: A Feminist Project?* 18 MICH. J. GENDER & L. 297 (2011–12).

Nicole Sayres & Thomas Lum. *Cambodia: Background and U.S. Relations*. CRS REPORT FOR CONGRESS (Aug. 21, 2002).

David Scheffer. *Why the Cambodia Tribunal Matters to the International Community*. CAMBODIA TRIBUNAL MONITOR (Sept. 2007).

David Scheffer. *The Extraordinary Chambers in the Courts of Cambodia*. *In* INTERNATIONAL CRIMINAL LAW (M. Cherif Bassiouni ed., 3d ed. 2008).

David Scheffer. *Opinion: How Many Are Too Many Defendants at the KRT?* PHNOM PENH POST, Jan. 8, 2009.

David Scheffer. *The Negotiating History of the ECCC's Personal Jurisdiction*. CAMBODIA TRIBUNAL MONITOR (May 22, 2011).

David Scheffer. *The Value of Steve Heder's Research on the ECCC's Personal Jurisdiction, and an Afterword on the Purpose of the Dispute Settlement Mechanisms*. CAMBODIA TRIBUNAL MONITOR (Aug. 8, 2011).

DAVID SCHEFFER. ALL THE MISSING SOULS (2012).

Celina Schocken. *The Special Court for Sierra Leone: Overview and Recommendations*. 20 BERKELEY J. INT'L L. 436 (2002).

William J. Schulte. *The History of the* Renakse *Petitions and Their Significance to the ECCC Proceedings*. SEARCHING FOR THE TRUTH (Dec. 2007).

The SCSL and the Taylor *Judgment*. INTLAWGRRLS (Apr. 25, 2012).

WILLIAM SHAWCROSS. SIDESHOW: KISSINGER, NIXON, AND THE DESTRUCTION OF CAMBODIA (1979).

SIM VIREAK. CAMBODIA-JAPAN RELATIONS (2010).

Savina Sirik. *Duch Final Judgment: Justice and Humanity* (Documentation Center of Cambodia, Feb. 2–3, 2012).

Rupert Skilbeck. *Finding Justice: The Price of War Crimes Trials*. HUMAN RIGHTS BRIEF (2008).

Göran Sluiter. *Due Process and Criminal Procedure in the Cambodian Extraordinary Chambers*. 4 J. INT'L CRIM. JUST. 314 (2006).

Ronald C. Slye. *The Cambodian Amnesties: Beneficiaries and the Temporal Reach of Amnesties for Gross Violation of Human Rights*. 22 WIS. INT'L L. J. 99 (2004).

Christoph Sperfeldt. *Cambodian Civil Society and the Khmer Rouge Tribunal*. INT'L J. TRANS. JUST. 1 (2012).

Chandra Lekha Sriram. A Revolution in Accountability (2005).

Chandra Lekha Sriram. *Wrong-Sizing International Justice? The Hybrid Tribunal in Sierra Leone*. 29 Fordham Int'l L. J. 472 (2005).

Gregory L. Stanton. *The Cambodian Genocide and International Law*. *In* Genocide and Democracy in Cambodia (Ben Kiernan ed., 1993).

Gregory Stanton. *The Call*. *In* Pioneers of Genocide Studies (Samuel Totten & Steven L. Jacobs eds., 2002).

Gregory H. Stanton. *Perfection Is the Enemy of Justice: A Response to Amnesty International and Human Rights Watch's Criticisms of the Agreement Between the Cambodian Government and the U.N. to Establish the Khmer Rouge Tribunal*. Genocide Watch (May 19, 2003).

Eric Stover et al. *Confronting Duch: Civil Party Participation in Case 001 at the Extraordinary Chambers in the Courts of Cambodia*. 93 Int'l Rev. of the Red Cross (June 2011).

Jane E. Stromseth. *Justice on the Ground?: International Criminal Courts and Domestic Rule of Law Building in Conflict-Affected Societies*. *In* Getting to the Rule of Law (James E. Fleming ed., 2011).

Mohamad Suma. *The Charles Taylor Trial and Legacy of the Special Court of Sierra Leone*. Int'l Ctr. for Trans. Just. (Sept. 2009).

Nate Thayer. *Pol Pot: The End*. Far East. Econ. Rev., Aug. 7, 1997.

Nate Thayer. *Dying Breath*. Far East. Econ. Rev., Apr. 30, 1998.

Nate Thayer. *End of Story? Last Khmer Rouge Defections Don't Bring Closure—Yet*. Far East. Econ. Rev., Dec. 17, 1998.

Sarah Thomas & Terith Chy. *Including the Survivors in the Tribunal Process*. *In* On Trial: The Khmer Rouge Accountability Process (John D. Ciorciari & Anne Heindel eds., 2009).

Gregory Townsend. *Structure and Management*. *In* International Prosecutors (Luc Reydams et al. eds., 2012).

Kheang Un & Judy Legerwood. *Is the Trial of 'Duch' a Catalyst for Change in Cambodia's Courts?* 95 Asia Pacific Issues (E.-W. Ctr., June 2010).

Luong Ung. First They Killed My Father: A Daughter of Cambodia Remembers (2006).

United Nations Development Program. *Audit of Human Resources Management at the Extraordinary Chambers in the Courts of Cambodia (ECCC)*. Report No. RCM0172 (June 4, 2007).

Christine Van den Wyngaert. *Victims Before International Courts, Some Views and Concerns of an ICC Trial Judge*. Case West Res. Univ. (Nov. 21, 2011).

Michael Vickery. Cambodia, 1975–1982 (1984).

Julia Wallace. *Losing Civil Parties in Cambodia*. 143 Int'l Just. Trib. (Jan. 18, 2012).

Julia Wallace. *From Phnom Penh with Love*. 148 Int'l Just. Trib. (Mar. 28, 2012).

Julia Wallace. *Chaos Now Bites KR Defence*. 153 Int'l Just. Trib. (June 6, 2012).

Wang Jianwei. *Great Power Relations and Their Impact on Japan-Southeast Asian Relations:*

A Chinese Perspective. *In* JAPAN'S RELATIONS WITH SOUTHEAST ASIA (Lam Peng Er ed., 2013).

War Crimes Research Office. *Efficient Representation of Victims at the International Criminal Court* (Dec. 2011).

Kelly Whitley. *History of the Khmer Rouge Tribunal: Origins, Negotiations, and Establishment*. *In* THE KHMER ROUGE TRIBUNAL (John D. Ciorciari ed., 2006).

S.J. Williams. *The Cambodian Extraordinary Chambers—A Dangerous Precedent for International Justice?* 53 INT'L & COMP. L. Q. 227 (2004).

Interviews & Correspondence Cited

1. Kris Baleva, Asian Int'l Justice Initiative, Phnom Penh (July 5, 2012).
2. Youk Chhang, Director of the Documentation Center of Cambodia, Phnom Penh (July 10, 2012).
3. Hans Corell, former UN Legal Counsel, via telephone (Nov. 15, 2012).
4. Craig Etcheson, former investigator in the ECCC Office of the Co-Prosecutors—via telephone (Oct. 22, 2012).
5. Diana Ellis, Co-Lawyer for Ieng Thirith, Phnom Penh (Nov. 11, 2012).
6. Elisabeth Simonneau Fort, international Lead Co-Lawyer for Case 002 ECCC Civil Parties, Phnom Penh (June 1, 2012).
7. Peter Foster, former UNAKRT Public Affairs Officer at the ECCC, via email (June 13, 2012).
8. Anta Guissé, Co-Lawyer for Khieu Samphan, Phnom Penh (Nov. 15, 2012).
9. Huy Vannak, former ECCC Public Affairs Officer, Phnom Penh (June 11, 2012).
10. Andrew Iannuzzi, former lawyer for the Nuon Chea defense team, Phnom Penh (May 29, 2012).
11. Larry Johnson, former UN Assistant Secretary-General for Legal Affairs, via telephone (June 21, 2012).
12. Michael G. Karnavas, former Co-Lawyer for Ieng Sary, Phnom Penh (May 19, 2012).
13. Karim A.A. Khan QC, ECCC Civil Party Co-Lawyer in Case 001, via telephone (June 5, 2012).
14. Panhavuth Long, Program Officer, Cambodian Justice Initiative, Phnom Penh (July 6, 2012).
15. Michiel Pestman, former Co-Lawyer for Nuon Chea, Phnom Penh (June 9, 2012).
16. Richard Rogers, former head of the ECCC Defence Support Section, Phnom Penh, (May 29, 2012) and via telephone (June 12, 2012).
17. Nushin Sarkarati, ECCC civil party lawyer, Phnom Penh (Nov. 15, 2012).
18. David Scheffer, UN Special Expert to advise on UN Assistance to the Khmer Rouge Trials and former U.S. Ambassador-at-Large for War Crimes Issues, Phnom Penh (June 16, 2012).

19. Rupert Skilbeck, former head of the ECCC Defence Support Section, via telephone (June 7, 2012).

20. William Smith, ECCC deputy international Co-Prosecutor, Phnom Penh (June 5, 2012).

21. Jeanne Sulzer, former Legal Officer in the ECCC Civil Party Lead Co-Lawyers Section, Phnom Penh (June 1, 2012).

22. David Tolbert, former Special Expert to advise on UN Assistance to the Khmer Rouge Trials, via telephone (June 19, 2012).

23. Clint Williamson, former UN Special Expert to advise on UN Assistance to the Khmer Rouge Trials and former U.S. Ambassador-at-Large for War Crimes Issues, via telephone (June 27, 2012).

24. You Bunleng, Cambodian Co-Investigating Judge at the ECCC, via email in response to a questionnaire from the authors (June 25, 2012).

The authors also conducted several confidential interviews with Cambodian and international ECCC personnel and received confidential responses from several Cambodian staff members to a questionnaire.

INDEX

ADHOC (Cambodian Human Rights and Development Association), 240, 257–58, 392*n*65
Administration, ECCC. *See* Office of Administration, ECCC
Albright, Madeleine, 25
Amnesties
  ECCC Law agreement on effect of Cambodian amnesties, 34
  Ieng Sary's domestic amnesty (1996), 21, 30, 31–32, 48–49, 135, 138–41, 174
  peace and security concerns, 174
Amnesty International, 36, 126, 200, 270
Annan, Kofi
  Framework Agreement, concerns about, 34–35, 200–201
  legacy potential, views on, 248
  "most responsible," definition of, 172
  negotiations to create the ECCC, role in, 22, 25, 27–33, 291*n*148
  UN Group of Experts, creation of, 286*n*60
  victim participation, views on hybrid court benefits for, 231–32
  voluntary donor financing of hybrid courts, arguments against, 74–75, 319*n*202
Anticorruption mechanism, ECCC, 89–92
Association of Southeast Asian Nations (ASEAN), 19, 33
Australia
  corruption allegations, role in addressing, 77–78, 80, 90–92, 315*n*144
  diplomatic approach to the ECCC, 312*n*75, 315*n*133
  funding for the ECCC, 82, 98–99, 197, 367*n*222
  key ECCC personnel, 112, 208, 235
  negotiations to create the ECCC, role in, 14, 33, 291*n*148

Ban Ki-moon, 9, 42, 100, 177, 248
Bar Association of the Kingdom of Cambodia, 65–66, 249, 306*n*167
Bias allegations, ECCC judicial, 78–79, 143–45, 193–94, 336*n*45, 337*n*49, 349*n*208
Blunk, Siegfried
  appointment and qualifications, 179, 191–92
  Case 003/004 dispute, role in, 171, 179–82, 186–88, 197–99, 215, 357*n*98
Bosnia and Herzegovina
  Human Rights Chamber, 7
  War Crimes Chamber (*see* War Crimes Chamber (Bosnia and Herzegovina))
Bou Meng, 220, 261
Brazil, 5

Cambodian Government
  Case 002 defendants, past dealings with, 21, 23, 134, 138
  Case 003/004 dispute, views on, 174–75, 265
  controlling role in the ECCC, 35–37, 266
  corruption allegations at the ECCC, role in addressing, 87–92, 255
  funding to the ECCC, 74–75, 95–96, 97–98, 101, 237
  human resources problems at the ECCC, role in, 85–87
  legacy initiatives at the ECCC, role in, 251
  negotiations to create the ECCC, role in, 14–15, 21–34, 37–40, 262
  oversight of the ECCC, role in, 81–83
  political interference in the ECCC, alleged, 135, 145–51, 168–69, 182–84, 196–97, 201
  reparations at the ECCC, role in, 130
  rules of evidence and procedure, views on, 61–62
  United Nations Special Expert, views on, 77–78
  victim participation at the ECCC, views on, 205
Cambodian Human Rights Action Committee, 168, 238

Cambodian People's Party (CPP)
control over the ECCC process, efforts to exert, 38, 40, 196, 201, 209, 363–64*n*184
Khmer Rouge organization, links to, 30, 284*n*20
negotiations to create the ECCC, role in, 24, 26–27, 31
1990s emergence and reconciliation policy toward the Khmers Rouges, 20–23
Capacity building
hybrid courts, potential advantages of, 231–33, 273
potential of the ECCC for, 248, 251–53, 273
Cartwright, Silvia
administrative meetings, participation in informal ECCC, 78–79, 311*n*61
institutional structure of the ECCC and blending of civil and common law traditions, views on, 48, 113
leadership on ECCC procedural matters, 63
victim participation at the ECCC, views on, 110, 228
Case 001 (against Duch)
apology, accused's public, 108–9
background, 105–7
Choeung Ek "killing fields," 105–6, 112, 115–16, 129, 131–32
civil party participation, 109–12, 128–30, 212, 219–21, 272, 324*n*44
defense lawyer split, national/international, 117–21, 328*n*100
duress, defense of, 114–15
guilty plea, defense efforts to secure, 107–8, 322*n*15
mitigation, recognition of, 124–25
mixture of civil law and common law rules, critique of, 107–13
pretrial detention, illegality of accused's domestic, 106, 125–28
reparations, 128–30, 331*n*164
selective memory of accused, 108
selective prosecution, defense of, 115–17, 326*n*66
sentencing, impact of national law on, 122–24, 328*n*114
superior orders, defense of, 114–15
verdict, reaction to, 121–22, 130–32
Case 002 (against former senior leaders)
amnesty and pardon (1996), effect of Ieng Sary's domestic, 138–41, 335*n*22
background, 135–38
bias allegations, 78–79, 143–45, 193–94, 336*n*45, 337*n*49
Case 003/004 dispute, interaction with, 200, 350*n*2, 370*nn*249–50
civil party participation, 212–15, 220, 272–73, 378*n*92
management problems in, 161–63, 346*n*183, 347*n*184, 347*n*186
political interference allegations in, 150–51, 254, 341*n*112, 350*n*2
presence of accused at trial, 157–58
pretrial detention of accused, 152–56, 342*n*128, 342*n*130
severance of indictment against accused (*see* Severance of Case 002 indictment)
summon testimony of government officials, failed efforts to, 145–51, 341*n*112, 350*n*2
Case 003 (against former military cadre), dismissal of, 179–81, 183, 186, 197–98, 369*n*240
Case 003/004 dispute
acting alone, impact on understanding of scope of authority of "co"s, 186–87
Blunk, Siegfried, role of, 171, 179–82, 186–88, 197–99, 215, 357*n*98
Case 002, interaction with, 200, 350*n*2, 370*nn*249–50
Cayley, Andrew, role of, 179–81, 183, 186, 198, 355*n*83
Chea Leang, role of, 171, 174, 177–78
civil parties, impact on, 179–80, 183, 215–16, 379*n*101, 395*n*115
disagreement procedure, application of, 176–79, 182–83, 186–87
fair trial rights of suspects, impact on, 101, 320*n*221, 362*n*166, 368*n*232
funding decisions related to, 101–2, 197–98, 320*n*221, 368*n*230, 368*n*232
investigatory irregularities related to, judicial, 177–84, 356*nn*88–90, 356*n*94, 357*n*98
Harmon, Mark, role of, 102, 186, 189, 379*n*101
Hor Namhong, views of, 177
Hun Sen, views of, 177, 245
Kasper-Ansermet, Laurent, role of, 171, 183, 186, 188–89, 194, 199–200, 368*n*232, 379*n*101
legacy impact on domestic judicial system, potential, 256
Lemonde, Marcel, role of, 178–79, 185, 189–90, 245
personal jurisdiction's role in, 167–69, 171

Petit, Robert, role of, 176–77
reserve judges, dispute over power of appointment of, 181–83
Rosandhaug, Knut, role of, 198, 368*n*232
Smith, William, role of, 177, 354*n*64
supermajority voting rule, application of, 177, 188–89
Supreme Council of Magistracy, role of, 181–83
United Nations, role of, 182, 199–201, 270
Case file, role in proceedings of, 46
Cassese, Antonio, 6
Cayley, Andrew
administrative meetings, participation in informal ECCC, 78–79, 311*n*61
Case 001 (*Duch*) appeals verdict, comments on, 126
Case 003/004 dispute, role in, 179–81, 183, 186, 198, 355*n*83
fundraising efforts, 100
national counterpart, working relationship with, 178, 355*n*75
political interference, views on, 367*n*220
Center for Social Development, 239
Cham Muslims, alleged crimes against, 16, 176, 346*n*175
Chea Leang
Cambodian Government, links to, 191, 293*n*173
Case 003/004 dispute, role in, 171, 174, 177–78
international counterparts, working relationship with, 178, 252, 355*n*75
Chea Sim, 17, 146
Chhang, Youk, 140, 211, 258–59
China, People's Republic of
Democratic Kampuchea (DK) regime, relations with, 15–16
Duch's experience with and attitude toward, 106, 120
Khmer Rouge forces before and after the DK era, support for, 15, 18–20
International Criminal Tribunals for the former Yugoslavia and Rwanda, views on, 5
Japanese policy toward Cambodia, relevance to, 81, 293*n*177
negotiations to create the ECCC and opposition to an international criminal tribunal for Cambodia, role in, 22–23, 26, 37–39, 197
relations with Cambodia, contemporary, 27
Choeung Ek "killing fields"
Case 001 (against Duch), relevance to, 105–6, 112, 115–16, 129, 131–32
outreach efforts by the ECCC, role in, 241
Chum Mey, 220
Civil law system
civil parties (*see* Civil party participation)
difficulties merging with common law, 47, 112–13, 141, 144–45, 268
investigating judges (*see* Investigating judges)
Civil party legal representation
civil party lawyers, role of, 109–11, 210, 221–24
funding of, 210, 375*n*45, 376*n*54
International Criminal Court compared, 221, 383*n*149, 384*n*155
Lead Co-Lawyers, role of, 208, 210, 221–24, 383*n*149, 384*n*159
Civil party participation
administrative reluctance to support, 205–9
admission standards for victims, 211–16, 377*n*72, 378*n*86
Case 001, participation in, 109–12, 212, 219–21, 272, 324*n*44
Case 002, participation in, 212–15, 220, 243, 272–73, 378*n*92
Cases 003 & 004, participation in, 179–80, 183, 215–16, 356*n*90, 379*n*101, 395*n*115
consolidated group participation, 210, 213–14, 221–24
expectations of victims, failure to manage, 216, 229, 243, 385*n*172, 388*n*203
funding of, 206–7, 210
genesis of ECCC role for, 204–5
individual participation, elimination of, 210–11, 214, 216, 218, 222, 225, 227, 229
International Criminal Court compared, 204, 218, 220–21, 379*n*102
judicial reluctance to support, 110, 204–5, 209, 216, 224–25
negotiators views on, 204
scope of civil party rights, 111–12, 216–21
Civil party reparations
Case 001, 128–30, 225, 331*n*164, 331*n*165
Case 002, 226–27
funding of, 225–26, 386*n*182
International Criminal Court compared, 225, 385*n*175
Non-judicial measures, overlap with, 228–29
scope under Internal Rules, expansion of, 225–26
Civil society. *See* Non-governmental organizations

Clinton, Hillary, 91
Closing order
civil law restrictions on amendment of, 159, 345*n*170
"mini-judgment," potential function as, 158
Coalition Government of Democratic Kampuchea, 19
Cohen, David, 94
Co-Investigating Judges, ECCC. *See* Investigating judges
Cold War, impact on Cambodian conflict of, 15–21
Common law system
merging with civil law, difficulties in, 47, 112–13, 141, 144–45, 268
UN staff orientation toward, 45, 141, 268, 302*n*119
Communist Party of Kampuchea (CPK)
Case 002 charged persons, roles of, 11, 136–37
Case 003/004 suspects, roles of, 176
Democratic Kampuchea (DK), rule over, 2–4, 16–17, 23
Duch, role of, 9, 27, 113–14, 116, 117–18, 326*n*67
Hun Sen and King Sihanouk, links to, 147
structure and functions, importance to the ECCC trials, 46–47, 172, 175, 213
Constitutional Council (Cambodia), 58, 148–49
Co-Prosecutors, ECCC
acting alone, scope of authority of one "co" for, 44–45, 182–87, 360*n*130
Case 003/004 dispute, role in, 176–78, 187
discretion to charge suspects, scope of, 170–71, 173, 326*n*66, 351*n*25
investigative role at ECCC, 44, 45
Corell, Hans
critiques of the ECCC's institutional structure and funding mechanisms, 9–10, 72–73, 75, 186–87, 196, 198, 263
negotiations to create the ECCC, role in, 29–32, 34, 39, 291*n*148
public impact of ECCC, views on, 258
selecting qualified and impartial personnel, views on importance of, 191, 194, 266, 269
Corruption at the ECCC
anti-corruption mechanism, creation of, 89–92
Australia, role in addressing allegations, 77–78, 80, 90–92
France, role in addressing allegations, 77–78, 80–81, 88, 90, 92, 197
human resource irregularities, 84–87
Japan, role in addressing allegations, 315*n*133
kickback allegations, 87–92, 143, 317*n*155
UN Group of Experts, concerns during negotiations of, 24
Council of Ministers, Cambodia, 181, 208
Coup of July 1997, Cambodian, 22, 39
Crane, David, 234
Crimes against humanity, defense challenges to ECCC jurisdiction over, 53–54
Criminal Procedure Code of Cambodia
generally, 61, 63, 304*n*136
Internal Rules, divergence from ECCC, 62, 66–69, 307*n*179
obsolescence of, 63, 141, 297*n*37
Cultural property, crime of destruction of, 50

Defence Support Section, ECCC
Bar Association of the Kingdom of Cambodia, relationship with, 65
capacity building, role in, 249, 253
criticism of the limited right of appeal, 62–63
funding challenges and controversies, 101, 320*n*221, 368–69*n*232
leadership by a UN appointee, 36, 72
Defense counsel, ECCC
Case 001 split between "co" national and international, 117–21, 328*n*100
dispute over the eligibility of foreign defense counsel, 65–66
funding of generally, 74
Defense rights
administrative austerity impacting, 101, 320*n*221
Case 003/004 dispute, impact on suspects' fair trial rights of, 101, 320*n*221, 362*n*166, 368*n*232
rule drafting controversy regarding scope of, 65–66
vigorous exercise in Case 002, novelty for Cambodians of, 151, 254
Democratic Kampuchea (DK), historical overview of, 15–17
Diplomatic personnel, crime of attacks against, 50
Disagreement procedure for "co" heads of prosecution and judicial investigation
generally, 31, 44, 48
acting alone, scope of authority for one "co", 44, 45, 182–87, 360*n*130
Case 003/004 dispute, application in, 176–79, 182–83, 186–87

presumption to investigate and prosecute, 31, 64–65, 173, 177, 185–87, 351*n*25
Documentation Center of Cambodia
establishment, 20
outreach activities, 239–40
public education activities, 258–59
source of potential evidence, 143
views of director, 140, 211
Domestic criminal laws and procedures
Cambodian crimes under the ECCC's jurisdiction, 50, 57
Cambodian criminal procedures (*see* Criminal Procedure Code of Cambodia)
inapplicability of domestic procedures to mass crimes cases, 60–61, 113, 264–65, 303*n*124
international courts' ability to try domestic crimes, 57–59, 301*n*105
Donors, bilateral
"Friends of the ECCC" donor group, 80–81, 86, 132, 312*n*78, 367*n*223
kickback allegations, muted donor reaction to, 88, 90, 315*n*133
leverage on Cambodian Government, 38
oversight of ECCC, weak 72–82, 86, 88, 92, 102–3, 270–71
political interests, 38, 197, 367*n*223
Downing, Rowan, 45, 219
"Duch" (Kaing Guek Eav)
arrest of, 27
biography, 105–6
Case 001 proceedings and (*see* Case 001)
Case 003 testimony, 180
China, experience and attitude toward, 106, 120
Communist Party of Kampuchea, role in, 9, 27, 113–14, 116, 117–18, 326*n*67

Ear, Sophal, 256, 261
Earmarking of funds, political concerns regarding, 101–2
East Timor
Serious Crimes Unit, 95, 235
Special Panels for Serious Crimes (SPSC) (*see* Special Panels for Serious Crimes, East Timor (SPSC))
Ek Tha, 101
Ellis, Diana, 60
Equality of arms and civil party participation, 110–12, 217, 220–21
Etcheson, Craig
cooperation and capacity-building at the ECCC, views on, 252
funding challenges at the ECCC, views on, 100
institutional structure of the ECCC, views on, 10, 40
need for the ECCC, views on, 35
outreach efforts by the ECCC, views on, 236
translation challenges at the ECCC, views on, 96–97
UN Special Expert, views on need for, 78
victim participation at the ECCC, views on, 216, 224–25
European Court of Human Rights, 58, 63, 153, 217
European Union
negotiations to create the ECCC, role in, 33, 316*n*144
1998 Cambodian elections, support for, 23
Special Court for Sierra Leone outreach, funds for, 390*n*24
Extraordinary African Chambers (Senegal and the African Union), 8–9, 204

Fairness concerns, defense
judicial investigation, 47–48, 141–45
suspects' rights in Cases 003 & 004, 101, 320*n*221, 362*n*166, 368*n*232
Fitness of Case 002 accused, concerns regarding, 153–54, 157
Forced evacuation of Phnom Penh, 1, 158–59, 165
Forced marriage under the Khmer Rouge, allegations/charges of, 16, 136, 175, 214, 217
Ford, Gerald, 15
Foster, Peter
institutional structure of the ECCC, views on, 85
outreach efforts by the ECCC, role in, 235, 237, 244
Framework Agreement (United Nations and Cambodia, 2003)
ambiguity in characterizing the legal status of the ECCC, 41–42
appointments, provisions on, 181–82
breach of, UN assertion that failure to appoint Judge Kasper-Ansermet amounted to, 182, 199–200
cooperation between national and international personnel, provisions on, 44, 71–72
early criticisms of, 34–37
funding and donor oversight, provisions on, 75, 79–80, 95
legacy, absence of provision on, 249

Framework Agreement (*continued*)
negotiations to reach, 31–34
nullum crimen principle, absence of provision on, 51
personal jurisdiction, provisions on, 169
procedural rules, provisions on, 59–62, 113
transparency, provision on, 240
victim participation, absence of provision on, 204
vulnerability to political influence, structural, 36–37
withdrawal, provision for UN, 37
France
civil party scheme, support for ECCC, 205
corruption allegations, role in addressing ECCC, 77–78, 80–81, 88, 90, 92, 197, 316*n*143
funding for the ECCC, role in, 82, 98–99
influence on Cambodian law and criminal procedures, 63, 141, 204, 297*n*37
key ECCC personnel, origin of, 63, 107, 112, 214
negotiations to create the ECCC, role in, 14, 23, 33, 38, 291*n*148
place of study for key Khmer Rouge leaders, 136–37
source of civil law practices at the ECCC, 12, 30, 44, 46, 108
Funcinpec (Cambodian political party), 20–22
Funding, ECCC
Australia, role of, 82, 98–99, 197, 367*n*222
civil party scheme, 206–7, 375*n*45, 376*n*54
France, role of, 82, 98–99
inefficiency of model, 93–96, 267–68
Japan, role of, 98–99, 101, 312*n*82, 319*n*192
legacy efforts, 100, 251
outreach efforts, 95, 98, 100, 237–38
split structure of Court, impact of, 74–75, 97–98
strikes and other staff morale problems, 98–102
United Kingdom, role of, 82
United States, role of, 99, 312*n*82, 319*n*193
voluntary contribution model, problems with, 74–75, 98–102, 309*n*35

Genocide charges
People's Revolutionary Tribunal (1979) charges against Pol Pot and Ieng Sary, 18, 333*n*9
severance of case 002, impact of, 158–59
German Agency for International Cooperation (GIZ), 207
German Society for Technical Cooperation (GTZ), 207
Ghai, Yash, 167, 195
Guissé, Anta
judicial confusion, ECCC, views on, 164
merging civil and common law, views on challenges of, 141, 144–45
translation challenges, views on ECCC, 97

Habré, Hissène, 8
Hammarberg, Thomas
negotiations to create the ECCC, role in, 22, 25, 27–28, 30
truth commission in Cambodia, call for, 21
Harmon, Mark
appointment as international Co-Investigating Judge, 183
Case 003/004 dispute, role in, 102, 186, 189, 379*n*101
Health problems of elderly accused, ECCC
impact on trial, 156–58, 346–47*n*183
pretrial detention issues, 153–56, 342*n*130, 342*n*130
Heder, Stephen, 180, 336–37*n*45
Heng Samrin, 17, 146
Him Huy, 131
Hor Namhong
Case 003/004 dispute, views on, 177
Duch's sentence by the ECCC Trial Chamber, views on, 121
negotiations to create the ECCC, role in, 20–21, 25
summons by international investigative judge, 146, 150–51
Human resources
importance of selecting qualified and impartial personnel, 164, 191, 194, 266, 269
irregularities in the ECCC Office of Administration, 84–87
reforms of ECCC practices, 86–87
Human rights
Democratic Kampuchea, violations during, 1–2, 15–17
Duch's pretrial detention, violations during, 121–22, 125–26
International Covenant on Civil and Political Rights (ICCPR), 51–52, 127, 331*n*154
obligations of Cambodian Government, ECCC recognition of, 127–28, 130, 140, 154, 254
Human Rights Chamber (Bosnia and Herzegovina), 7
Human Rights Watch, 9, 32, 35, 93, 270

Hun Sen
  Case 001 (*Duch*) Trial Chamber verdict, reaction to, 121–22
  Cases 003 & 004, public opposition to, 177, 245
  Duch's defense counsel, relationship with, 119–20
  interests in the ECCC process, political and personal, 13, 35–36, 83, 196, 289*n*108
  negotiations to create the ECCC, role in, 22–30, 33, 38–39
  political emergence of, 17, 20, 293*n*177
  reconciliation policy toward the Khmers Rouges, 21, 137
  selection of ECCC personnel, role in 191
  summons by the ECCC in Case 002, possible, 145–51
Huy Vannak, 241, 247
Hybrid courts
  generally, 5–7, 8–9, 27, 32, 74–75, 263–64
  administrative and funding challenges, 71, 84, 86, 93, 96, 267–71
  advantages and challenges for outreach and victim participation, 202–3, 207, 209, 233–35, 259–60
  capacity building potential and challenges, 152, 231, 248–50
  difficulty applying novel crimes, 54
  importance of experienced international officials and judges, 73, 76–77, 99, 135, 164, 192, 194–95, 208, 253, 266, 269–70, 275, 365*n*202
  in-country location, impact of, 27, 143, 156, 231–32, 234–36, 248, 259–60
  "ownership" problems, 270
  potential cost savings, 6, 12, 70, 92–93, 267
  problems associated with procedural rules, 47–48, 60, 113, 160–64, 303*n*120
  unique features of the ECCC, 7–8, 14, 34, 42–44, 50, 72, 83, 89
  vulnerability to political interference, 156, 164–65, 168, 190, 194–95, 201, 266–67

Ianuzzi, Andrew, 162
Ieng Sary
  amnesty and pardon (1996), domestic, 21, 30, 31–32, 48–49, 135, 138–41, 174, 335*n*22
  Case 002 defendant, status as former, 11, 134, 262
  death of, 11–12, 137
  defection to the Cambodian Government, 21, 27
  Democratic Kampuchea, role in, 136–37
  illness during trial and fitness concerns, 153–54, 157
  People's Revolutionary Tribunal (1979), conviction by, 18, 58
Ieng Thirith
  Case 002 defendant, status as former, 11–12, 134, 262
  dementia and severance from Case 002/01, 154, 157, 189, 223
  Democratic Kampuchea, role in, 137–38
  detention of, 153
Im Chaem, 177, 359*n*119
India, 33
Institutional structure of the ECCC
  adversarial trial after long judicial investigation, 48, 141, 268
  appellate jurisdiction, two bodies with, 44–45, 269
  "co" heads of offices, 30, 44–45, 269
  investigatory powers, two bodies with, 44, 45, 268
  Office of Administration, split (*see* Office of Administration, ECCC)
  UN Special Expert, addition of, 77–78
Internal Rules
  Cambodian procedures, relationship to, 59–60, 66–69, 113, 303*n*125, 307*n*179, 307*n*181
  drafting controversies, 64–66, 297*n*37, 373*n*12
  legitimacy and legality, 61–64
  new roles created by judges, 48, 205–6
International Covenant on Civil and Political Rights (ICCPR), 51–52, 127, 331*n*154
International crimes, ECCC jurisdiction over, 50–57
International Criminal Court (ICC)
  generally, 5, 276, 277, 353*n*40, 353*n*54
  appointment of judges, 194
  cost to date, estimated, 94
  establishment of, 23
  funding structure, 74, 101
  lessons from the ECCC, possible, 8, 13, 272, 273–74
  model for future courts, possible, 264–65, 269, 273
  outreach efforts, 232, 234
  personal jurisdiction jurisprudence, 172–73
  political pressure at, 196–97
  pretrial detention jurisprudence, 153
  proofing witnesses, bar to, 347*n*192
  registry, role of, 72
  single-charge approach in the *Lubanga* case, 165–66
  translation issues, 96

International Criminal Court (*continued*)
victim participation, 203–4, 211, 216, 218, 220–21, 223, 225, 374*n*22, 377*n*68, 382*n*127, 383*n*147, 383*n*149, 384*n*155
International Criminal Tribunal for Cambodia, rejection of, 24–26
International Criminal Tribunal for the former Yugoslavia (ICTY)
bias, jurisprudence on judicial, 193
Bosnian War Crimes Chamber, relationship to, 8
criticisms pertaining to costs and connection the post–conflict state, 5–6, 27, 37–38, 92–93
duress, jurisprudence on the defense of, 114–15
establishment, 5, 20
estimated costs to date, 94, 267
fitness jurisprudence, 154
funding through assessed contributions, 74
Joint Criminal Enterprise jurisprudence, 54–55
jurisdiction and referrals, 171–72, 199, 353*n*54
model for Cambodia, possible, 22–23
nullum crimen principle jurisprudence, 51–52
pretrial detention jurisprudence, 153
registry, role of, 72
role as a precedent-setting body, 50
rules of procedure and evidence, 60–61, 123, 161, 348*n*206
sentencing practices, 123, 125, 328*n*114, 330*n*135
subpoena rules, 146–47, 149–50
translation issues, 96
victim participation, limited, 110, 203, 232–34
International Criminal Tribunal for Rwanda (ICTR)
costs to date, estimated, 94, 267
criticisms pertaining to costs and connection the post–conflict state, 5–6, 27, 37–38, 92–93
establishment of, 5, 20
funding through assessed contributions, 74
personal jurisdiction and prosecution decisions, 326*n*66, 353*n*54
possible model for Cambodia, 22–23
precedent-setting body, role as, 50
pretrial detention jurisprudence, 126–27, 153, 330*n*147
registry, 72
rules of procedure and evidence, 60–61, 161
Rwandan government, tensions with, 26, 197
sentencing practices, 123, 125, 330*n*135
subpoenas of government officials, jurisprudence on, 149
translation issues, 96
victim participation, limited, 203, 233–34
"Internationalized" court, ambiguous legal identity of ECCC as an, 42–43
Introductory submissions, role of prosecutorial, 44
Investigating judges
acting alone, scope of authority at ECCC for one "co", 44, 45, 182–87, 360*n*130
bias allegations at ECCC regarding, 142–45, 336*n*45, 337*n*49
discretion to charge suspects, scope of, 170–71, 173
efficiency in mass crimes cases, 46–47, 141, 145, 268
elimination of role in domestic systems, 63, 142
impartiality, importance of, 142–45, 268
negotiations establishing, ECCC, 30
role at ECCC, 44
transparency in mass crimes cases, need for, 46–47, 145
Investigations
Case 003/004 irregularities, 178–84, 356*nn*88–90, 356*n*94
Co-investigating judges (*see* Investigating judges)
confidentiality of at ECCC, 45, 145
confrontation during investigation, right of, 47–48, 141, 297*n*37
Co-Prosecutors' role in, 44, 45

Japan
aid to Cambodia in the 1990s, 23, 27, 293*n*177, 293*n*179
civil party scheme, concerns about, 205
corruption allegations, role in addressing ECCC, 88, 90–92, 197, 316*n*141, 316*n*144
donor oversight, approach to, 77–81
funding for the ECCC, 82, 98–99, 101, 312*n*82, 319*n*192
negotiations to create the ECCC, role in, 14, 33, 38, 291*n*148
support for legacy initiatives, 250
UN Transitional Authority in Cambodia, role in, 285*n*36
Jarvis, Helen
costs of ECCC, views on, 93

negotiations to create the ECCC, views on, 28, 288*n*96
public affairs and outreach, role in, 83, 235, 237, 240
Victims Unit, role in, 208
Joint Criminal Enterprise
Case 002 prosecution strategy, 135–36
civil party applications, relevance to, 213
jurisprudence, ECCC 49, 54–56, 59
Judicial Administration Committee, ECCC, 76, 78, 194
Judicial appointments, ECCC
Cambodian control of, 36–37, 181, 195
negotiations regarding, 29, 31
qualifications for, 192, 194–95, 266
selection process, 191–92, 363*n*175
Supreme Council of Magistracy (Cambodia), role of, 29, 37–37, 181–83, 191, 363*n*175
Judicial disqualification, efforts to seek, 78–79, 143, 192–94
Judicial independence and impartiality. *See* Judicial appointments, ECCC; Political influence/interference
Jurisdiction of the ECCC
overlap between chambers, 48–50
personal (*see* Personal jurisdiction, ECCC)
relationship with Cambodian courts, 42–43
substantive, 50–59
temporal, 29, 50–51, 165

Kabbah, Ahmad Tejan, 147
Kaing Guek Eav. *See* "Duch"
Kar Savuth
defense strategy as co-lawyer for Duch, 104, 114–17, 122, 133
split with Duch's international co-lawyer, 117–20
Karnavas, Michael
amnesty and pardon of Ieng Sary, views on, 49
civil party scheme, views on, 130, 230
cooperation between national and international lawyers at the ECCC, views on, 119, 121
detention of Ieng Sary, views on, 155–56
institutional structure of ECCC, views on, 44
Internal Rules application, criticisms of, 60–61, 162–64, 183
legacy of ECCC, views on, 254, 256
Office of the Co-Investigating Judges, views on, 142, 144–45
political pressure faced by the ECCC judges, views on, 159–60, 189
Kasper-Ansermet, Laurent
appointment of, 181–82
Case 003/004 dispute, role in, 171, 183, 186, 188–89, 194, 199–200, 368*n*232, 379*n*101
Keat Bophal, 208
Keat Chhon, 146
Khan, Karim, 210, 251–52
Khieu Kanharith, 150, 177
Khieu Samphan
Case 002 defendant, status as, 11–12, 134, 262
defection to the Cambodian Government, 24, 27, 289*n*108
Democratic Kampuchea, role in, 19, 137
illness during trial, 157
Joint Criminal Enterprise, challenges to, 55
pretrial detention, 343*n*140
translation practices, challenges to ECCC, 97
Khieu Sopheak, 245
Khmers Rouges
atrocities by, 2, 15–17
defections from, 20–22, 30
former cadre in Cambodian Government, political implications of, 24, 26, 30, 196, 284*n*20
ideology, 2, 16
origins, 15
outlawing of by Peoples Republic of Kampuchea (PRK) government, 15
Kickbacks at ECCC, allegations of mandatory staff, 87–92, 143
Kissinger, Henry, 15
Klonowiecka-Milart, Agnieszka, 123
Kosovo Regulation 64 hybrid panels
generally, 7, 32, 38, 43, 195, 294*n*6
capacity building at, 248
funding structure, 74
Kranh, Tony, 73, 202, 252
Ky Tech, 65–66

Lath Nhoung, 64
Lavergne, Jean-Marc, 63, 122, 221
Law of the Extraordinary Chambers of the Courts of Cambodia (ECCC Law)
2001 draft, 30–31, 34
2004 ECCC law, adoption of, 36, 39
ambiguity in characterizing the ECCC, 41–42
appointments, provisions on, 181, 192
Case 003/004 dispute, provisions relevant to, 173, 184–85

Law of the Extraordinary Chambers of the Courts of Cambodia (ECCC Law) (*continued*)
cooperation between national and international personnel, provisions on, 72
due process, provision on, 127
enforcement, provision on, 150
funding, provisions on, 74
jurisdiction, provisions on, 52, 169, 299*n*64, 333–34*n*9
national crimes, provisions on, 57
nullum crimen principle, absence of provision on, 51
Pre-Trial Chamber, provisions on, 48
removal of judges, absence of provisions on, 193
rules of evidence and procedure, provisions on, 61–63, 68, 113, 126
sentencing, provisions on, 123–24
statutes of limitations, provision on, 57, 359*n*122
superior responsibility, provision on, 56
transparency, provision on, 240
victim participation, absence of provisions on, 204, 209
Lee, Michelle, 73, 81
Legacy potential of the ECCC
capacity building, 248, 251–53, 273
defense rights, exercise of vigorous, 151, 254
domestic legal system, potential impact on, 127–28, 130, 140, 154, 254–56, 274, 398*n*164
educational initiatives by non-governmental organizations, 259
funding limitations, 100, 251
in-country location, impact of, 248, 259–60
informational, 247, 250–51
institutional ECCC mechanisms, 249–50
mandate at the ECCC, lack of, 249
mass crimes courts future design, 262–63, 275–77
mass crimes courts past experiences, 248–49
negative legacy, potential for, 255–56
non-governmental organization involvement in building, 253
outreach distinguished, 232–33
pretrial detention decisions of ECCC as, 128, 156
public discussion, ECCC as a catalyst for, 258–59
public perceptions of the ECCC, 256–58, 272
Lemonde, Marcel
bias, defense challenge of, 143
Case 003/004 dispute, role in, 178–79, 185, 189–90, 245
civil party scheme, support for, 205
criticism of Cambodian Government objection to additional prosecutions, 174–75
difficulties of applying sound civil law practices at the ECCC, views on, 47, 63, 112–13, 141, 268
filmed encounter with Duch at Choeung Ek, 324*n*40
institutional structure of the ECCC, views on, 44, 269
Internal Rules, role in drafting, 297*n*37, 373*n*12
opacity, defense criticism of, 336*n*37
summons of Cambodian officials, 146, 149–51
Leuprecht, Peter, 33, 35
Lomé Peace Agreement (Sierra Leone), 139
Lon Nol, 1, 15, 105–6
Long, Panhavuth
additional ECCC prosecutions, views on, 175
legacy of the ECCC, views on, 254, 258, 260
political interference at the ECCC, views on, 189
severance of Case 002, views on, 160
victim participation at the ECCC, views on, 209, 243, 245
Ly Tayseng, 86

Marchi-Uhel, Catherine, 213–14
Meas Muth, 120, 176, 359*n*119
Milosevic, Slobodan, 165
"Mini" trials. *See* Severance of Case 002 indictment
Modes of liability, challenges of applying international, 51–52, 54–57
Mok, 23, 25, 27, 160, 176
"Most responsible," definition of persons, 171–73
Mussomeli, Joseph, 81

National Assembly (Cambodia)
creating the ECCC, passage of laws, 30–31, 36, 39
key officials, 17, 35, 146
outlawing of the Khmer Rouge organization, 20
privileges to King Sihanouk, law granting, 148

National laws and procedures. *See* domestic laws and procedures
Negotiations to create the ECCC, role in
  Annan, Kofi, 22, 25, 27–33, 291*n*148
  ASEAN Foreign Ministers, 33
  Australia, 14, 33, 291*n*148
  Cambodian People's Party, 24, 26–27, 31
  China, 22–23, 26, 37–39, 197
  Corell, Hans, 29–32, 34, 39, 291*n*148
  distrust between Cambodian and UN negotiators, 14–21, 25–26, 29, 40
  European Union, 33, 316*n*144
  France, 14, 23, 33, 38, 291*n*148
  Hammarberg, Thomas, 21, 22, 25, 27–28, 30
  Hor Namhong, 20–21, 25
  Hun Sen, 22–30, 33, 38–39
  India, 33
  Japan, 33, 38–39
  Kerry, John, 27
  Norodom Ranariddh, 21–22
  Russia, 23, 26
  Scheffer, David, 23–24, 28–29
  United Nations Group of Experts, 24, 29
  United Nations Human Rights Commission, 33
  United Nations Office of Legal Affairs, 27
  United Nations pullout during negotiations, 32–34
  United States, 22–25, 27–29, 33, 38
Ney Thol, 126, 193
Nguon Nhel, 148
Nil Nonn
  bias, allegations of, 193
  capacity building, role in, 252–54
  directive limiting evidence outside of the 1975–79 period, 165
  Duch's pretrial detention, views on, 128
  judicial independence, views on, 192
Noguchi, Motoo, 68, 123, 330*n*145
Non-governmental organizations
  advocacy for due process and justice at the ECCC, 132
  educational programs, 259
  non-judicial measures, role in, 228
  outreach efforts by the ECCC, role in, 206–7, 237–40, 247, 260, 271–72, 393*n*84
  victim participation at the ECCC, role in, 204, 206–7, 210, 226–27
Non-judicial measures, ECCC, 227–29, 386*n*189, 387*n*193, 387*n*195, 387*n*199
Norodom Ranariddh, 20–22
Norodom Sihanouk
  Democratic Kampuchea, role in, 147–48
  interview request by the ECCC, 145–49, 176
  negotiations to create the ECCC, role in, 24, 31, 288*n*100
  pardon and amnesty for Ieng Sary, role in, 21, 137–38
  political roles after the DK era, 19, 20, 285*n*41
  political roles before the DK era, 15, 105, 137
Nullum crimen principle, application of, 51–54, 58
Nuon Chea
  Case 002 defendant, role as, 12, 134
  defection to the Cambodian Government, 24, 27, 289*n*108
  Democratic Kampuchea, role in, 11, 136, 165
  Hun Sen, alleged 1970s meeting with, 151
  illness during trial, 157, 223
  Internal Rules, challenges to the legitimacy of the, 62
  Joint Criminal Enterprise, challenge to, 55
  pretrial detention, extended, 155, 217–19
Nuremberg trials, 50, 53, 115, 134

O'Brien, Patricia, 78, 190, 200
Office of Administration, ECCC
  Cambodian control of, 36
  Case 003/004 dispute, role in, 198
  civil party participation, reluctance to support, 205–9
  defense rights, austerity impacting exercise of, 101, 320*n*221, 368*n*232
  deference by international side, 73, 102–3
  human resource problems, 84–87
  kickback allegations, 87–92
  Public Affairs Section (*see* Public Affairs Section, ECCC)
  registries compared, 72–73
  role at ECCC, 71–72
  split leadership and reporting, 71–72, 83, 84
Office of the Co-Investigating Judges, ECCC. *See* Investigating judges
Office of the Co-Prosecutors, ECCC. *See* Co-Prosecutors, ECCC
Office of the UN High Commissioner for Human Rights, 233, 250, 253
Olsen, Lars, 149–50, 245, 327*n*87
Open Society Justice Initiative
  appointments, role in, 191–92
  Case 003/004 dispute, views on, 168, 200
  corruption allegations at the ECCC, role in addressing, 84, 88, 197, 306*n*161

Open Society Justice Initiative (*continued*)
  legacy initiatives at the ECCC, views on, 249
  non-judicial measures, views on, 228
  outreach efforts by the ECCC, role in, 237–38
  victim participation at the ECCC, views on, 207, 229
Ou Kamela, 219
Ou Virak, 200, 232–33, 255
Ouk Bunchhoeun, 146
Outreach efforts, ECCC
  funding challenges, 95, 98, 100, 237–38, 273
  in-country location, advantages of, hybrid courts', 231–32, 234–36
  internet resources on ECCC, 238–39
  legacy potential distinguished, 232–33
  mass crimes courts, experience of, 233–35
  non-governmental organizations, roles of, 206–7, 237–40, 247, 260, 271–72, 393*n*84
  public communications (*see* Public Affairs Section, ECCC)
  public forums, 239–40
  public knowledge, impact on, 242–43
  victim population, targeted to (*see* Victim Support Section, ECCC)
Oversight of ECCC by UN, donor states, and Cambodia, 76–83
"Ownership," failure of United Nations to take, 10, 102–3, 199–201, 270, 371*nn*257–58

Pardons
  ECCC Law agreement regarding, 34
  Ieng Sary's domestic pardon (1996), 21, 30, 31–32, 48–49, 135, 138–41, 174, 335*n*22
  peace and security concerns regarding scope of prosecutions, Cambodian, 25, 174–75, 179
Paris Peace Agreement (1991), 20
People's Republic of Kampuchea, 17–20, 24
People's Revolutionary Tribunal (1979)
  charges against Pol Pot and Ieng Sary, 18, 137–38, 333*n*9
Personal jurisdiction, ECCC
  Case 001 arguments, 117–20
  Case 003/004 dispute, 167–69
  discretion to charge, relationship to, 170
  "most responsible," definition of, 171–73
  negotiations, ECCC, 29–30, 266–67
  "senior leaders," definition of, 171–73
Pestman, Michiel
  Case 002, challenges to the ECCC's handling of, 151, 161–62, 164–65
  confidentiality by the Co-Investigating Judges, criticism of, 145
  distinct approaches of national and international lawyers, views on, 121
  political interference at the ECCC, views on, 189
Petit, Robert
  Case 003/004 dispute, role in 176–77, 354*n*56, 354*n*64
  institutional structure of the ECCC, views on, 39, 269
  working relationship with the national counterpart, 178, 252
Phay Siphan, 89, 177, 181
Pol Pot
  death of, 23
  Democratic Kampuchea, leadership of, 16, 136–37
  international trial of, efforts toward, 22–23
  People's Revolutionary Tribunal (1979), conviction by, 18, 58, 137–38
  "People's Tribunal" (1997), conviction by, 21
Political influence/interference
  Cambodian government officials, failed efforts in Case 002 to summon, 145–51, 341*n*112
  Case 003/004 dispute, 177–79, 181–82, 187–89, 245, 350*n*2, 358*n*115, 368*n*230
  completion strategies as a form of, 199, 369*n*239
  donor pressure/financial uncertainty as a form of, 75, 101–2, 198–99, 368*n*230
  Framework Agreement, structural vulnerabilities of, 36–37, 168
  independent/impartial judges, need for (*see* Judicial appointments)
  interests of states and UN, impact of, 195–200
  international courts, impact at, 26, 196–99, 366*n*216, 366*nn*218–19, 377*n*220, 367*n*229
  negotiations, concerns expressed during, 24, 35–36
  outreach efforts by the ECCC, impact on, 246–47, 271
  rules designed to address (*see* Disagreement procedure for "co" heads of prosecution and judicial investigation; Supermajority voting rule)
  Victim Support Section, concerns regarding, 208
Prak Kimsan, 188–89, 194
Presence at trial, Case 002 suspects, 157–58
Pre-Trial Chamber
  appellate jurisdiction, 44–45, 48–50

disagreements between "co" heads of an office, jurisdiction to resolve, 31, 44 298*n*49
jurisdictional overlap with Trial Chamber, exercise of, 49
Pretrial detention
Case 002 accused, ECCC propensity to detain, 152–56, 342*n*128
Duch, illegal detention by the Cambodian Military Court of, 106, 125–28
Prey Sar prison (S-24), 105, 129
Public Affairs Section, ECCC
approaches, challenges in coordinating national and international, 243–47
bifurcated structure, impact of, 235–36, 243–45
Cambodian Government influence on, 36
funding, 237
key personnel, 83
outreach, role in, 236–43, 391*n*58
public access to proceedings, facilitation of, 240–42
public forums, involvement in, 239
role at ECCC, 235, 237, 243
transparency concerns regarding, 245–47, 271–72
VSS role compared, 236
Public opinion
influence on the work of ECCC, perceptions of, 126, 154–56
reactions to the Duch verdict, 130–32
surveys on Cambodian views of the ECCC, 242–43, 256–58

Rape as a crime against humanity, ECCC jurisdiction over, 53–54
Rapp, Stephen, 198, 219*n*153
Ratner, Steven, 24, 286*n*60
Reach Sambath, 235, 237, 240, 245
Reconciliation
efforts prior to the ECCC, 3, 17–19, 20–23, 137, 285*n*41
possible effects of the ECCC on, 257–58, 260
Registry, role of, 36, 72–73, 75–76, 79, 268–70
Religious persecution, allegations/charges of, 2, 16, 57, 136, 158–59
Renakse (Salvation Front), 19
Reparations. *See* Civil party reparations
Robertson, Geoffrey, 168, 194, 199
Rodley, Carol, 90
Rogers, Richard
Case 004 defense counsel, controversy over appointment as, 368*n*232
defense split in the *Duch* case, views on, 120–21
institutional structure of ECCC, views on, 126, 144
supermajority voting rule, criticisms of, 188, 190, 193
Rohrabacher, Dana, 24
Rong Chhorn, 83, 208, 293*n*173
Rosandhaug, Knut, 73, 78, 102, 155, 205–6, 208, 253, 368*n*232
Roux, François, 107–9, 111–14, 116–21
Royal Government of Cambodia. *See* Cambodian Government
Rules of procedure and evidence, ECCC. *See* Internal Rules
Russia, 23, 26
Rwanda, efforts to control ICTR process by, 26, 197, 366*nn*218–19

Sam Rainsy, 26, 31, 289*n*108
Sam Rainsy Party, 33
Sanctions threatened for public release of confidential information, 246
Sarkarati, Nushin, 227
Scheffer, David
corruption allegations, role in addressing, 88, 197, 306*n*161
fundraising efforts, ECCC, 100–101
institutional structure of the ECCC, views on, 189, 200, 204, 262
negotiations to create the ECCC, role in, 23–24, 28–29
UN Special Expert, appointment as, 78
Sean Visoth
corruption at the ECCC, alleged involvement in, 81, 83–84, 89, 91, 255, 313*n*89
outreach by the ECCC, concerns about funding, 237
Seng, Theary, 208, 261
"Senior leaders," definition of, 171–73
Sentencing
Case 001, impact of national law on, 122–24, 328*n*114
ECCC Law, provisions on, 123–24
International Criminal Tribunal for the former Yugoslavia (ICTY), practices of, 123, 125, 328*n*114, 330*n*135
International Criminal Tribunal for Rwanda (ICTR), practices of, 123, 125, 330*n*135
Special Court of Sierra Leone (SCSL), practices of, 123, 330*n*135
Serious Crimes Unit (East Timor), 95, 235

Severance of Case 002 indictment
  additional Case 002 trials, barriers to, 163–64, 349*n*208
  amendment of closing order in civil law system, restrictions on, 159, 355*n*170
  civil party participation and reparations, effect on, 214–15, 227, 243, 378*n*92
  consultation with parties prior to, lack of, 158, 345*n*164
  outreach regarding, lack of, 243
  procedural novelties/confusion related to, 156, 160, 162–64
  rationale for, 156, 158, 346*n*180
  representativeness of charges and, 159–60, 165–66
  scope of Case 002/01 charges, uncertainty regarding, 163, 347*n*184
Sim Ka, 146
Simmoneau Fort, Elisabeth
  civil law rules at the ECCC, views on difficulty of applying, 61, 66–67, 164
  civil party scheme, views on, 214, 221, 224, 226
Sisowath Thomico, 209
Skilbeck, Rupert, 251, 253
Smith, William
  blending civil and common law at the ECCC, views on, 112
  Case 003/004 dispute, role in, 177, 354*n*64
  institutional structure of the ECCC, views on, 13, 48
  national counterpart, working relationship with, 252
Soam Met, 131
Sok An
  corruption allegations, role in addressing, 88–90, 306*n*161, 317*n*157
  defense counsel at the ECCC, role in dispute over foreign, 65
  "Friends of the ECCC" donor group, request to establish, 80–81
  human resources shortcomings, role in addressing, 84–85
  key ECCC staff, links to, 208, 235
  legal characterization of the ECCC, views on, 42
  model court, argument that ECCC is, 9, 35, 254, 398*n*164
  negotiations to create the ECCC, role in, 31, 33, 293*n*79
  oversight role for the ECCC's national side, 83
Son Arun, 165
Son Sann, 19
Sou Met, 120, 176
South African Truth and Reconciliation Commission, 25
Sovereignty concerns, Cambodian, 5, 23–28, 73
Special Court for Sierra Leone (SCSL)
  amnesties, treatment of, 139–40
  cost, estimated, 94, 95, 267
  establishment, 7, 32–33
  funding, 74–75, 82, 99, 319*n*202, 390*n*24
  Joint Criminal Enterprise, application of, 54
  jurisdiction, 42, 57–58, 169, 172
  legacy, 248
  legal status, 43, 60
  outreach, 234, 240–41
  oversight, 75–76, 77–80, 82, 98
  political independence, concerns about, 198–99, 291*n*153
  pretrial detention jurisprudence, 153
  registry, 72
  rules of evidence and procedure, 61, 302*n*116
  sentencing practices, 123, 330*n*135
  summons of government officials, jurisprudence on, 146–49, 332*n*72
  translation issues, lack of, 96
  truth commission, parallel running of, 353*n*54
  victim participation, 203
Special Panels for Serious Crimes, East Timor (SPSC)
  capacity building, 248, 267–68, 271
  civil society development, impact of lack of, 237
  creation of, 7, 32, 294*n*6, 295*n*13
  dependence on UN and donor support, 38
  funding challenges, 74, 94–95, 281*n*30, 313*n*103
  international judges, concerns about, 192
  judicial capacity, lack of, 5–6
  outreach problems, 234–35, 271
  ownership problems, 102, 201
  translation challenges, 96
Special Tribunal for Lebanon (STL)
  establishment, 8, 289*n*28
  funding, 74
  jurisdiction, 42, 301*n*103
  legal status, 43
  oversight, 80
  presence at trial, jurisprudence on right to, 344*n*143
  pretrial chamber, 269
  registry, 72

translation issues, 96
victim participation, 204, 221, 273
Statute of limitations for national crimes, effect of, 58–59
Strikes by national staff due to nonpayment of salaries, 101
Structural problems, ECCC. *See* Institutional features of the ECCC
Successes, ECCC, 9, 106–7, 132, 240–41, 260
Sulzer, Jeanne
civil party scheme, views on, 214, 229
legacy of ECCC, views on, 256
Summoning witness testimony, obstruction in
Case 002, government officials in, 145–51, 341*n*112
Cases 003 & 004, internal investigation by Judge Kasper-Ansermet in, 182
Superior responsibility, 56–57, 121, 124
Supermajority voting rule
Case 003/004, application in, 177, 187–90
ineffectiveness as substitute for independent judges, 188–90, 265, 361*n*148, 362*n*165
negotiations establishing, 28–29, 31
Trial Chamber application of, 154, 189
Supplementary submissions, role of prosecutorial, 44
Supreme Council of Magistracy (Cambodia)
controversy over Judge Laurent Kasper-Ansermet, role in, 192–93
judicial appointments, role in, 29, 181–82, 363*n*175
political independence of, 191
Supreme Court Chamber
interpretive process for rule application, 67–69, 307*n*181
remedy for illegal pretrial detention in Case 001, overturning, 126–28, 188

Ta An, 176, 368–69*n*232
Ta Tith, 176
Taksoe-Jensen, Peter, 89
Taylor trial, Charles, 99, 234
Temporal jurisdiction, ECCC, 29, 50–51, 165
Tolbert, David
corruption allegations, role in addressing, 89
institutional structure, views on ECCC, 71, 83
outreach efforts, concern about underfunding of ECCC, 237
registry, recommendation to establish an ECCC, 72
UN Special Expert, appointment as, 78
Torture
domestic crime under the ECCC's jurisdiction, 50, 57
Duch's selective confessions, 108
general incidence in Democratic Kampuchea, 2
Tuol Sleng prison, occurrence at, 9, 104–6, 116
Transcultural Psychosocial Organization, 259, 387*n*195
Transitional justice mechanisms
alternative, 3, 14
criminal courts, 5–6
truth commissions (*see* Truth commissions)
Translation challenges, 96–97
Transparency, ECCC
achievements, 91, 191–92, 244, 247, 254, 271–72, 274
concerns, 46, 91–92, 145, 191–92, 240, 244–47, 277
Trial Chamber
inconsistent rule application, 160–64, 303*n*120
interpretive process for rule application, 66
management problems, 110, 161–63, 346*n*183, 347*n*184, 347*n*186, 387*n*200
supermajority voting rule, application of, 154, 189
Truth commissions
generally, 3, 14, 353*n*54
Cambodia, possibility of creation in, 21, 25, 287*n*77
international or hybrid criminal trials, distinction from, 46, 165, 175–76
Truth-telling at the ECCC
advantages and disadvantages of an inquisitorial system, 46–48, 180
importance of supplementing the historical record, 3–4, 16, 21, 175–76, 202
limits imposed by the ECCC's narrow jurisdiction and small caseload, 11–12, 165
representativeness of suspects and charges in ECCC indictments, 159–60, 165–66, 175–76
tension with the requirements of a fair and expeditious trial, 217, 272–73
Tuol Po Chrey execution site, 158, 162, 214
Tuol Sleng Genocide Museum, 115–16, 241, 279*n*8

Tuol Sleng prison (S-21)
Duch's role, 9, 105, 115–16
Khmer Rouge accountability process, centrality in, 172, 175, 215, 220

Uganda, efforts to limit scope of International Criminal Court investigation by, 196–97
UN Assistance to the Khmer Rouge Trials (UNAKRT), 77–78, 85
UN Controller, 76–77, 270
UN Department of Economic and Social Affairs (DESA), 76–77, 102, 270
UN Development Program (UNDP)
corruption allegations at the ECCC, role in addressing, 88–90
human resources shortcoming at the ECCC, role in addressing, 84–87, 310*n*47, 313*n*90
oversight role at the ECCC, 77, 82, 97–98, 270
UN General Assembly
funding international criminal tribunals, role in, 74–75, 99
negotiations to create the ECCC, role during, 22–23, 33–34
People's Republic of Kampuchea period, role during, 19
UN Group of Experts (1998–99)
composition of, 286*n*60
negotiations to establish the ECCC, role in, 24, 29
political interference by the Cambodian Government, concerns about, 196
recommendations on the jurisdiction of a tribunal to try the Khmers Rouges, 172–73
UN Office of Legal Affairs
corruption allegations at ECCC, role in addressing, 89
negotiations to create the ECCC, role in, 27
oversight of the ECCC, role in, 76–77, 102, 270
selecting ECCC personnel, role in, 192
UN Security Council
creation of international criminal tribunals, 5–6, 26
International Criminal Court investigation or prosecution, power to delay, 353*n*40
International Criminal Tribunal for Cambodia, possible role in creating, 22–24, 37
Paris Peace talks to resolve the Cambodian conflict, role in, 20
reports on international and hybrid courts, receipt of, 203, 231, 248
Special Court for Serious Crimes in East Timor, cessation of funds for, 95
Special Court for Sierra Leone, imposition of voluntary funding on, 74–75
Special Tribunal for Lebanon, creation of, 281*n*28, 301*n*103
UN Transitional Authority in Cambodia (UNTAC), 20, 131, 285*n*36
Union of Soviet Socialist Republics (USSR), 16, 18
United Kingdom
civil parties, support for ECCC, 210
funding for the ECCC, 82
negotiations to create the ECCC, role in, 290*n*131
United Nations
generally (*see* UN headings above)
possible withdrawal from the ECCC, 35, 37, 201
reputational risk arising from the ECCC, 10, 40, 201, 263, 270, 275, 370*n*244
United States
Case 003/004 dispute, role in, 187, 198
Cold War, role in Cambodia during, 15, 19, 165
corruption allegations at ECCC, role in resolving, 88, 90–92, 316*n*144, 375*n*43
donor oversight at the ECCC, proposals for stronger, 79–81
funding for the ECCC, 73, 82, 99, 312*n*82, 319*n*193
negotiations to create the ECCC, role in, 14, 20, 22–25, 27, 28–29, 31, 33, 38–39, 290*n*131, 291*n*148
outreach by the ECCC, support for non-governmental organization activities related to, 393*n*84
UN Special Expert position at the ECCC, connection to, 77–78, 310–11*n*57
Uth Chhorn, 90–92

Vajpayee, Atal Bihari, 33
Van Rith, 176, 178
Victim participation
advantages of hybrid courts for, 231–32
civil party participation (*see* Civil party participation)
complaints with Co-Prosecutors, right to file, 205, 373*n*15

institutional ECCC support for (*see* Victim Support Section, ECCC (VSS))
management of victim expectations at the ECCC, 216, 229, 238, 243, 245, 258, 272–73, 385*n*172, 388*n*203, 387*n*200
mass crimes courts and, 203–4
Victims Support Section, ECCC (VSS)
nationalization of, 207–10, 229
non-governmental organization support for, 206
non-judicial measures mandate, implementation of 227–29, 386*n*189, 387*n*193, 387*n*195, 387*n*199
outreach by, 206, 227–29
political independence of, 208
Public Affairs Section role compared, 236
reparations awards, role in developing, 226–27, 228–29
Victims Unit, ECCC. *See* Victims Support Section, ECCC
Vietnam
Hun Sen's links to, 30
Ieng Sary, birthplace of, 136
invasion and occupation of Cambodia (1979–91), 3, 17–20, 105, 112, 165
People's Revolutionary Tribunal (1979), role in, 18, 137–38
Second Indochina War and embroilment of Cambodia, 1, 15–17
Vietnamese, alleged Khmer Rouge crimes against, 106, 136, 284n20
Vincent, Robin, 83, 234, 248

War crimes
Case 001 consideration of, 107, 109, 114, 121, 136
crime under the ECCC's jurisdiction, 50, 53, 56
War Crimes Chamber (Bosnia and Herzegovina)
cost savings relative to other hybrid courts, 95, 267
description, 8
legacy efforts, 248
Werner, Alain, 110, 219
Wiedemann, Kent, 28
Williamson, Clint
corruption allegations at ECCC, role in addressing, 90
donor oversight of the ECCC, views on, 77–78, 82
institutional structure of ECCC, views on, 46
public impact in Cambodia, views on ECCC's, 259
UN Special Expert, appointment as, 78
Witness testimony
government officials, summons of, 145–51, 341*n*112
mixed-rule approach to, ECCC Trial Chamber, 47–48, 113, 161–63

Yeth Chakrya, 252
You Bunleng
appointment and ties to the Cambodian Government, 191
bias, allegations of, 143
Case 003/004 dispute, role in, 171, 178–83, 186–87, 215, 245
defense counsel at the ECCC, role in the dispute over foreign, 66
funding problems at the ECCC, views on, 100
legacy for domestic courts, role in the ECCC's, 254–55
Office of the Co-Investigating Judges, views on, 48
summons of witnesses in Case 002, role in dispute over, 149–50